ADVANCES in
PSYCHODYNAMIC
PSYCHIATRY

EDITORS
César A. Alfonso
Richard C. Friedman
Jennifer I. Downey

THE GUILFORD PRESS
New York London

WORLD
PSYCHIATRIC
ASSOCIATION

AAPDPP
The American Academy of Psychodynamic Psychiatry and Psychoanalysis

One Regency Drive
P. O. Box 30
Bloomfield, CT 06002

Published by The Guilford Press
A Division of Guilford Publications, Inc.
370 Seventh Avenue, Suite 1200
New York, NY 10001

www.guilford.com

Compiled from articles in the journal *Psychodynamic Psychiatry*.

Printed in the United States of America

This book is printed on acid-free paper.

Last digit is print number: 9 8 7 6 5 4 3 2

Library of Congress Cataloging-in-Publication Data is available from the publisher.

ISBN 978-1-4625-3863-8

About the Editors

César A. Alfonso, MD, Deputy Editor of *Psychodynamic Psychiatry*, is Clinical Associate Professor of Psychiatry at Columbia University in New York and Visiting Professor at Universiti Kebangsaan Malaysia in Kuala Lumpur. He also teaches at New York Medical College and Northwell Health. His recent work includes the study of the psychodynamic determinants of treatment adherence, the clinical care of persons with low vision and medical multi-morbidities, and the design and implementation of psychotherapy training programs.

Richard C. Friedman, MD, Editor-in-Chief of *Psychodynamic Psychiatry*, is Clinical Professor of Psychiatry at Weill Cornell Medical College, Lecturer in Psychiatry at Columbia University College of Physicians and Surgeons, and Faculty Member at the Columbia Center for Psychoanalytic Training and Research. His book on male homosexuality was the first to integrate neuroscience, sexology, developmental psychology, and psychoanalytic theory and practice. He began a collaboration with Jennifer I. Downey in 1991 that led to many publications and a book on sexual orientation and psychoanalysis. Drs. Friedman and Downey served as Co-Chairs of the Human Sexuality Committee of the Group for the Advancement of Psychiatry. Dr. Friedman is a recipient of the Mary S. Sigourney Award from the Sigourney Trust. He practices in New York City.

Jennifer I. Downey, MD, Deputy Editor of *Psychodynamic Psychiatry*, is Clinical Professor of Psychiatry at Columbia University College of Physicians and Surgeons and Faculty Member at the Columbia Center for Psychoanalytic Training and Research. Dr. Downey has conducted research on sexual orientation in women, Turner Syndrome, and mental health effects of infertility in women, and was the first investigator to demonstrate that sex hormones in homosexual and heterosexual women do not differ. Past president of the American Academy of Psychoanalysis and Dynamic Psychiatry, Dr. Downey was the first recipient of the Academy's Victor J. Teichner Award. She was Visiting Professor at the University of Kentucky from 2009 to 2011. She practices in New York City.

Contributors

Stewart Adelson, MD, is Assistant Clinical Professor, Divisions of Child and Adolescent Psychiatry and of Gender, Sexuality and Health, Columbia University College of Physicians and Surgeons, and Adjunct Clinical Assistant Professor, Weill Cornell Medical College.

César A. Alfonso, MD, is Clinical Associate Professor of Psychiatry at Columbia University, Visiting Professor of Psychiatry at Universiti Kebangsaan Malaysia Medical Center, WPA Chair of the Psychotherapy Section and Secretary of the Psychoanalysis in Psychiatry Section, and Deputy Editor of *Psychodynamic Psychiatry*.

Scott E. Anderson, PhD, is Chief Clinical Officer/Clinical Director at Cornerstone of Recovery in Louisville, Tennessee.

Louise Balfour, PhD, is Associate Professor in the Department of Medicine, University of Ottawa and The Ottawa Hospital, Ottawa, Ontario, Canada.

Robinette Bell, MD, was Associate Professor of Psychiatry at Columbia University and a member of the Group for the Advancement of Psychiatry, Committee on Human Sexuality.

Michael Brus, MD, is Clinical Instructor of Psychiatry at the Icahn School of Medicine at Mount Sinai in New York.

Fredric N. Busch, MD, is Clinical Professor of Psychiatry, Weill Cornell Medical College and Faculty, Columbia University Center for Psychoanalytic Training and Research.

Nicole M. Cain, PhD, is Assistant Professor in the Department of Psychology at Long Island University, Brooklyn.

Erika R. Carr, PhD, is Assistant Professor of Psychiatry at Yale University School of Medicine.

C. Sue Carter, PhD, is Director of the Kinsey Institute and Rudy Professor of Biology, Indiana University, Bloomington.

Joanna Chambers, MD, is Associate Professor of Clinical Psychiatry, Indiana University School of Medicine, and President-Elect of the American Academy of Psychodynamic Psychiatry and Psychoanalysis.

Thomas Cheuk Wing Li, MBBS, FRANZCP MMed, is a psychiatrist in private practice in Hong Kong.

Lindsey Colman McKernan, PhD, is Assistant Clinical Professor, Vanderbilt University School of Medicine, and works at the Osher Center of Integrative Medicine at Vanderbilt University.

Contributors

Circe Cooke, MD, is a staff psychiatrist with New River Valley Community Services in Blacksburg, Virginia.

Jennifer I. Downey, MD, is Clinical Professor of Psychiatry at Columbia University College of Physicians and Surgeons in New York and Faculty Member at the Columbia Center for Psychoanalytic Training and Research. She is Deputy Editor of *Psychodynamic Psychiatry*.

Ahron Friedberg, MD, is Clinical Professor of Psychiatry at the Icahn School of Medicine at Mount Sinai in New York and Book Review Editor of *Psychodynamic Psychiatry*.

Richard C. Friedman, MD, is Clinical Professor of Psychiatry at Weill Cornell Medical College in New York, Lecturer in Psychiatry at Columbia University, and Faculty Member at the Columbia Center for Psychoanalytic Training and Research. He is Editor-in-Chief of *Psychodynamic Psychiatry*.

Myron L. Glucksman, MD, is Clinical Professor of Psychiatry at New York Medical College and Supervising and Training Analyst at the Psychoanalytic Institute of New York Medical College in Valhalla, New York.

David Goldenberg, MD, is Clinical Assistant Professor of Psychiatry at Weill Cornell Medical College and a member of the Group for the Advancement of Psychiatry Committee on Human Sexuality.

William H. Gottdiener, PhD, is a tenured full professor of psychology at John Jay College of Criminal Justice of the City University of New York (CUNY) and Director of Training of the college's clinical psychology doctoral program and the addiction studies program.

Adam Graff, MD, is Chairman of the Department of Psychiatry at Northern Arizona Healthcare Flagstaff Medical Center and was a fellow of the Group for the Advancement of Psychiatry Committee on Human Sexuality.

Elizabeth Haase, MD, is Assistant Clinical Professor of Psychiatry at Columbia Presbyterian Hospital and a member of the Group for the Advancement of Psychiatry Committee on Human Sexuality.

Herbert Hendin, MD, is CEO and Medical Director of Suicide Prevention Initiatives and Professor of Psychiatry at New York Medical College.

Mardi Horowitz, MD, is Distinguished Professor of Psychiatry at the UCSF School of Medicine in San Francisco.

Douglas H. Ingram, MD, is Fellow of the American Academy of Psychodynamic Psychiatry and Psychoanalysis and Clinical Professor of Psychiatry at New York Medical College.

Horst Kächele, MD, PhD, is Professor at the International Psychoanalytic University in Berlin, Germany.

Contributors

Anita Kanapathy, MBBS, is a Resident in the Department of Psychiatry at Universiti Kebangsaan Malaysia Medical Center in Kuala Lumpur, Malaysia.

Marcia J. Kaplan, MD, is Training and Supervising Analyst at the Cincinnati Psychoanalytic Institute and Volunteer Professor of Clinical Psychiatry, Department of Psychiatry, University of Cincinnati College of Medicine.

Debra A. Katz, MD, is Professor of Psychiatry and Neurology at the Department of Psychiatry at the University of Kentucky College of Medicine.

David Kealy, MSW, is Clinical Assistant Professor in the Psychotherapy Program in the Department of Psychiatry at the University of British Columbia in Vancouver.

Elspeth Kelly, MA, is a PhD candidate at the Program in Clinical Psychology, Long Island University, Brooklyn and Mount Sinai Services/Elmhurst Hospital, Elmhurst, New York, Adult Psychology Track.

Clarice J. Kestenbaum, MD, is Professor of Clinical Psychiatry at Columbia University College of Physicians and Surgeons.

Warren E. Lambert, PhD, was at the Vanderbilt Kennedy Center, Vanderbilt University School of Medicine.

Brittany Lannert, PhD, is Assistant Professor/Clinical Psychologist, Department of Psychiatry and Behavioral Sciences, Emory University, Atlanta.

Alytia A. Levendosky, PhD, is Professor and Director of Clinical Training, Department of Psychology, Michigan State University.

W. John Livesley, MD, is Professor Emeritus in the Department of Psychiatry at the University of British Columbia, Canada, and Past Editor of the *Journal of Personality Disorders*.

Odhran McCarthy, MPsychSc, AFPsSI, Reg Psychol PsSI, is Principal Clinical Psychologist–Specialist and Adjunct Professor, School of Psychology, Trinity College Dublin.

Beth McEvoy, DClinPsych, is at the School of Psychology, Trinity College Dublin.

Abby L. Mulay, MA, is a doctoral candidate in Clinical Psychology at Long Island University, Brooklyn.

Michael R. Nash, PhD, is Professor of Psychology Emeritus at The University of Tennessee.

Vladan Novakovic, MD, is Assistant Clinical Professor of Psychiatry at the Icahn School of Medicine at Mount Sinai in New York.

John O'Connor, DClinPsych, is Assistant Professor, School of Psychology, at Trinity College Dublin and Course Director MPhil in Psychoanalytic Studies and MSc in Psychoanalytic Psychotherapy at Trinity College Dublin.

Contributors

John S. Ogrodniczuk, PhD, is Professor and Director of the Psychotherapy Program in the Department of Psychiatry at the University of British Columbia.

Björn Salomonsson, MD, PhD, is Associate Professor and Psychoanalyst, Department of Women's and Children's Health, Karolinska Institute, Stockholm, Sweden.

Larry S. Sandberg, MD, is Associate Clinical Professor of Psychiatry at Weill Cornell Medical College, and a Faculty Member at the Columbia University Center for Psychoanalytic Training and Research.

Joseph Schachter, MD, PhD, is a Faculty Member at the Columbia University Center for Psychoanalytic Training and Research.

Judith S. Schachter, MD, is Past President of the American Psychoanalytic Association.

Ginny Sprang, PhD, is Professor in the College of Medicine at the University of Kentucky and Executive Director of the Center on Trauma and Children.

Michael H. Stone, MD, is Professor of Clinical Psychiatry at Columbia University College of Physicians and Surgeons.

Luke Sy-Cherng Woon, MD, is a Resident at the Department of Psychiatry, Universiti Kebangsaan Malaysia Medical Center in Kuala Lumpur, Malaysia.

Giorgio A. Tasca, PhD, is Associate Professor in the School of Psychology in the Clinical Program, University of Ottawa Brain and Mind Research Institute, Ottawa, Ontario, Canada.

Valerie H. Taylor, MD, PhD, FRCPC, is Psychiatrist-in-Chief, Women's College Hospital; Scientist, Women's College Research Institute; and Associate Professor in the Department of Psychiatry, University of Toronto, Ontario, Canada.

Simone N. Vigod, MD, MSc, FRCPC, is Staff Psychiatrist, Women's College Hospital; Scientist, Women's College Research Institute; and Associate Professor, Department of Psychiatry, University of Toronto, Ontario, Canada.

Matthew Yalch, PhD, is Assistant Professor in the Clinical Psychology Program, Palo Alto University, Palo Alto, California.

Hazli Zakaria, MBBS, DrPsych, is Lecturer and Head of Clinical Services in the Department of Psychiatry, Universiti Kebangsaan Malaysia Medical Center, Kuala Lumpur, Malaysia, and Vice President of the Malaysian Psychiatric Association.

Foreword

Jennifer I. Downey, MD

Advances in Psychodynamic Psychiatry was developed by the editors Friedman, Alfonso, and Downey to bring together into a single volume some of the most important papers published in *Psychodynamic Psychiatry* since its inception in 2012. Although the American Academy of Psychoanalysis and Dynamic Psychiatry had always published a journal, in 2012, *Psychodynamic Psychiatry* was conceived to address the most current clinical and science-based writing about psychodynamic psychiatry—its foundations, its applications, and the studies that have been done to understand how it works.

For many years, writings about psychoanalysis—one of the bases of psychodynamic psychiatry but only one of the four, the others being psychiatry, academic psychology, and neuroscience—had focused on the history of the ideas of the different theorists in psychoanalysis beginning with Freud but including many followers and intellectual adversaries. There was extensive argument about which aspects of psychoanalytic thinking were most useful, most true. While key ideas of psychoanalysis such as the importance of childhood experiences for life-long development, the importance of the unconscious mind, and the value of transference and counter-transference to understand patients in the clinical situation retained their key utility, the field spent little time investigating the scientific basis of psychodynamic thinking. To this day, many books about psychoanalytic theory confuse the reader because of the unacknowledged controversies between practitioners of the different psychoanalytic schools.

Psychodynamic Psychiatry was intended to address this problem. The articles come from thinkers of a variety of psychoanalytic and academic psychiatry backgrounds. The topics are up to date, as are the references. Our goal in publishing the journal, with the support of The American Academy of Psychodynamic Psychiatry and Psychoanalysis, was to bring attention to current ideas about psychodynamic psychiatry—what it is as a discipline, what its intellectual foundations are, how it can be used to help suffering individuals everywhere and, most importantly, how to help our colleagues stay current with what is going on right now in psychodynamic psychiatry.

Over several years, it became evident to us that articles in *Psychodynamic Psychiatry*—because of their relevance and because of their modernity—offered an educational opportunity for psychiatrists all over the world to learn about psychodynamic psychiatry and its use in clinical settings. Further, the research articles published in *Psychodynamic Psychiatry* demonstrate how psychodynamic research can be done currently, using the technologies we now have as mental health professionals and academics. The journal editors discovered that articles in *Psychodynamic Psychiatry* could constitute a course of study: a number of these articles are already being used in diverse countries where psychiatrists are undertaking the study of psychodynamic principles for their own clinical settings.

It turns out, however, that an anthology such as *Advances in Psychodynamic Psychiatry* also offers a quick way to stay up to date for those of us already practicing psychodynamic psychiatry but trained in days when issues such as clinical trials comparing different psychotherapy techniques, or cross-cultural applications about trauma were not considered part of psychodynamic training.

Another way to use an anthology like *Advances* is to employ it as a reference book.

Foreword

Imagine, for instance, that a new patient comes to your clinic. You think the symptom constellation, intensity of symptoms, and distress of the patient's family suggest that he or she may suffer from borderline personality disorder. As you evaluate this individual and consider the different modalities of treatment, you could also consult *Advances* and read one of its articles on borderline personality disorder. There, you will be quickly reminded of what current controversies exist about which treatments have been found most helpful for borderline personality disorder as well as what the history of long-term follow-up demonstrates, that is, that many people with severe symptoms of borderline personality disorder in youth became dramatically improved over several decades. Thus, when presented with a new patient in your clinic, you can rapidly access new ideas and up-to-date data that may apply to your case.

Recently, some psychoanalysts have sought to integrate varying psychoanalytic theories in comprehensive textbooks. *Advances in Psychodynamic Psychiatry* has taken a different approach. Choosing from recent issues of *Psychodynamic Psychiatry*, we have selected the most cutting-edge articles, ones we consider "state of the art." These articles are written by scholars of various disciplines and trainings. They represent no single school of thought. But these chapters represent the newest, freshest work we have been able to find. We hope you find that *Advances in Psychodynamic Psychiatry* furthers your understanding of your patients and your field and, most of all, that this volume opens windows for you in your work.

The editors of *Advances in Psychodynamic Psychiatry* acknowledge the steadfast support of our publisher, The Guilford Press; our administrative staff, Marie Westlake and Sara Elsden; and our parent organization, The American Academy of Psychodynamic Psychiatry and Psychoanalysis. Without their help, this book could never have been published.

Preface

César A. Alfonso, MD

The idea for *Advances in Psychodynamic Psychiatry* originated from pedagogical efforts by the editors teaching psychodynamic psychiatry to psychiatric residents, medical students, and early career psychiatrists in academic medical centers in Asia, Europe, Africa and the Americas. This volume is a collection of review articles and selected research articles published over the last six years in the journal *Psychodynamic Psychiatry* under the editorship of Richard C. Friedman. *Psychodynamic Psychiatry*, the journal, is clinically focused and from its inception has emphasized the need for psychodynamically informed assessment in formulating treatment plans for psychiatric patients. The journal is committed to the implementation of such treatment planning via a number of potentially therapeutic routes—including individual intensive psychotherapy.

Advances in Psychodynamic Psychiatry provides a structured overview to guide clinicians through the vicissitudes of psychiatric care in everyday practice and in a variety of treatment settings. Fifty-five distinguished international authors contribute to the 27 chapters of the book. It is organized in four sections: Psychodynamic Psychiatry—An Emerging Field, A Psychodynamic Approach to Complex Psychiatric Disorders, Psychodynamic Psychiatry in Special Populations, and Psychodynamic Psychiatry and Neuroscience. Each section is preceded by editorial annotations as a helpful reference to trainees and students of psychodynamics.

Part 1 describes the evolution of the field and defines contemporary psychodynamic psychiatry. Part 2 examines in detail the psychodynamics of anxiety disorders, eating disorders, grief, internet and social networking excessive use, mood disorders, obsessive-compulsive disorder, eating disorders, personality disorders, schizophrenia, somatic symptom disorders, addictive disorders, and trauma-related disorders.

Part 3 describes the practice of psychodynamic psychiatry in special populations including parent-infant dyads, children at risk, spouses of the medically ill, survivors of intimate partner violence, criminal offenders in forensic settings, and the elderly. Part 4 reviews how advances in neuroscience inform clinical practice, with particular attention to the importance of epigenetics and the neurobiology of attachment.

The editors propose a contemporary approach to constructing clinically relevant psychodynamic formulations. They identify transtheoretical common factors that should be incorporated to expand biopsychosocial formulations when designing psychotherapeutic strategies. The core psychodynamic factors of clinical relevance in the assessment and treatment of complex psychiatric disorders include: affective dysregulation, attachment insecurities, deficits in mentalization and reflective functioning, inadequate defensive functioning and adaptation, unconscious conflicts, disruptions in development, early childhood trauma with subsequent retraumatization, and

Preface

neurophysiologic instability caused by allostatic overload.

The editors would like to acknowledge the support of the Executive Council of The American Academy of Psychodynamic Psychiatry and Psychoanalysis and the officers and committee members of the World Psychiatric Association Sections of Psychotherapy, Psychoanalysis in Psychiatry, and Education in Psychiatry. We are also grateful for the sophisticated editorial work of Jody Falco and Stefanie Bendik from The Guilford Press and efficient editorial coordination and assistance of Sara Elsden and Marie Westlake from S&S Management.

We would like to dedicate this book to our patients, who heroically and creatively find ways to adapt to overwhelming life stressors, distress, stigma, and discrimination, and to our medical students and psychiatric trainees, who enthusiastically embrace the challenges of psychiatric care.

Contents

Contents

Contents

Part 3

Contents

Part 4

Advances in Psychodynamic Psychiatry
Introduction
Richard C. Friedman, MD

The chapters in this book were composed of articles originally published in the journal, *Psychodynamic Psychiatry*, the only one of its kind in the English language and the official journal of The American Academy of Psychodynamic Psychiatry and Psychoanalysis.

Psychiatric disorders often have their onset in childhood or adolescence. During their early years, patients with clinically meaningful disorders tend to have been exposed to adverse events (Green, McLaughlin, Berglund et al., 2010). In addition, psychiatric disorders are common among members of their families. For example, a well known prospective study of psychopathology in New Zealand revealed that 55% of 1,037 patients experienced the onset of their disorder prior to age 15. This is but one of many relevant research findings indicating the necessity for clinicians who treat adults to ascertain the age of onset of their patients' difficulties in order to construct an adequate treatment plan (Kim-Cohen, Caspi, Moffitt et al., 2003). Given the importance of early childhood events for the development of adult psychiatric disorders, the relevance of a biopsychosocial developmental model of the mind is even more compelling. Time has shown that Freud's insights about the way that childhood events and fantasy have enduring influences on adult psychological functioning were remarkably prescient. Although he over-emphasized sexuality in his psychology of the mind, his more general appreciation of the relationship between child and adult psychology was a critical insight. Responses to childhood experience may be warded off from consciousness, yet have powerful influences on the motivation and experience of adults. As a result of diverse childhood traumata, adults may engage in repetitive maladaptive behaviors and experience the diverse psychological symptoms and syndromes that require treatment by mental health professionals. (Of course, later-occurring traumas may produce enduring psychological damage that also requires appropriate treatment.)

Studies have shown that about 14% of the population suffers from chronic severe mental disorders. Co-morbidities occur in the vast majority of cases (Friedman, Garrison, Bucci, Gorman, 2005). The number of people with severe psychiatric disorders and resultant disability is enormous and approaches 50 million Americans. Approximately 25% of American women have been victims of intimate partner abuse (compared to approximately 8% of men) (Levendosky, Lannert, & Yalch, 2012); 20% of women and 1.4% of men have been victims of attempted or completed rape. Approximately 45 thousand Americans commit suicide each year, and suicide is the tenth leading cause of death in the United States. At least 8 million Americans are alcoholic and additional millions are problem drinkers. The United States is in the midst of a major opioid epidemic resulting in widespread distress and disability.

The severity of the mental health problem is such that a vast additional number of mental health professionals is needed to assist the afflicted population. Looking at mental illness issues from a public health perspective, social workers, psychologists, psychiatrists, counselors, and case-managers are all in short supply and are all greatly needed.

No matter the clinical specialty, however, psychodynamic reasoning and psychodynamically oriented case formulations provide the anchoring perspective of a model of psychological functioning.

The psychosocial context within which psychiatric disorders are experienced and treatment occurs is of substantial importance. In many areas of the world, including the United States, mental illness tends to be stigmatized.

Stigma often influences people to deny symptoms and the need for appropriate treatment. This has been reported and emphasized somewhat unevenly across types of disorder, more for some than for others. For example, women who have been raped and/or sexually abused as children often fail to report it to anyone for months, years, or sometimes not for their entire lives. They may live with the symptoms of Post Traumatic Stress Disorder (PTSD) because they are ashamed to reveal their history to anyone.

This bears on other points. Throughout the world, in every geographical area males are more aggressive and violent than females. In addition, women are more likely to be patients in mental health systems than are males, who are more likely to be incarcerated. Differential rates of trauma lead to different experiences with stigma. Much of the reason that depression and attempted suicide is more common among women is because of violence committed by males against females. Although political gender equality exists in some nations, this is by no means the norm.

These combined effects of gender inequality influence the way stigma is experienced and expressed within families and communities. They also influence the experience and expression of psychiatric disorders. An important reason that a reductionistic medical model of psychiatric disorders is inadequate is that many of these disorders are caused or exacerbated by political-vocational-social interactions between the genders.

Of course the reasons for stigma around mental illness are greater than those caused by gender inequality. Attitudes toward psychiatric disorder can be influenced by politicians, for example, since financial resources are necessary for adequate patient treatment.

The values of kindness, altruism and compassion in keeping with the historically influenced myths and narratives are more endorsed in some nations and cultures than others.

Patients with severe, complex psychopathology often need several different kinds of treatment. For example, patients treated in hospitals with medication and group therapies may be discharged and need long term follow-up in individual or family work in order to remain stable in the community. The majority of patients will benefit from a combination of therapies, rather than a single one.

Of the total number of patients requiring treatment for mental disorders, only some will be candidates for individual psychotherapy, with or without concurrent pharmacotherapy. Yet, all patients should receive detailed and psychodynamically informed diagnostic assessment. Following such assessment, the recommended therapeutic approach might be individual psychodynamic psychotherapy, but not necessarily. It might also consist of a manualized psychotherapeutic technique such as Cognitive Behavioral Therapy (CBT), Dialectical Behavioral Therapy (DBT), Transference Focused Psychotherapy (TFP), Interpersonal Psychotherapy (IPT), psychopharmacology, couple or family therapy, group therapy, Alcoholics Anonymous, some other type of specialized therapeutic approach such as sex therapy, or some combination of these. Therapy may be recommended on an outpatient basis or in a hospital or an intermediate facility such as a day hospital program. In any case, a flexible approach must be used, especially to treat the more chronically and severely mentally ill.

Psychiatrists, like other physicians, must often make judgments about therapeutic decisions that are inferential and even speculative, since in many instances controlled research studies have not yet been carried out to provide therapeutic direction. Physicians across all subspecialties must often make therapeutic decisions that are based on clinical judgment and are not the result of algorithms stemming from evidence-based studies. This Inferential approach frequently leads to practical and ethical problems. Insurance companies may use the absence of "hard" scientific evidence as grounds to withhold reimbursement for treatment. Intrusion on clinical practice by profit-driven insurance administrators is an important source of controversy in contemporary mental health care. The conflict between competing models and competing philosophies for treatment reimbursement is a major unsolved problem in American society today.

Modern psychodynamic psychiatry rests on the ideas of such luminaries as William Osler, Adolph Meyer and George Engel, not just Sigmund Freud. In its emphasis on understanding and treating the whole person, not simply the person's illness, psychodynamic psychiatry is part of the Hippocratic tradition of medical care. The papers selected to be part of *Advances in Psychodynamic Psychiatry* are but some that illustrate this central principle. Hopefully as future volumes appear, the maladaptive political-social conflicts that provide an obstacle to optimal care today will have been ameliorated.

REFERENCES

Friedman, R.C., Garrison, W.B. 3rd, Bucci, W., & Gorman, B.S. (2005). Factors affecting change in private psychotherapy patients of senior psychoanalysts: An effectiveness study. *Journal of the American Academy of Psychoanalysis and Dynamic Psychiatry, 33*, 583-610.

Green, J., McLaughlin, K.A., Berglund, P.A., et al. (2010). Childhood adversities and adult psychiatric disorders in the national comorbidity survey replication I: Associations with first onset of DSM-IV disorders. *Archives of General Psychiatry, 67*, 113-123.

Kim-Cohen, J., Caspi, A., Moffitt, T.E., et al. (2003). Prior juvenile diagnoses in adults with mental disorder: Developmental follow-back of a prospective-longitudinal cohort. *Archives of General Psychiatry, 60*, 709-717.

Levendosky, A. A., Lannert, B., & Yalch, M. (2012). The effects of intimate partner violence on women and child survivors: An attachment perspective. *Psychodynamic Psychiatry, 40*(3), 397-433.

ABOUT THE AMERICAN ACADEMY AND *PSYCHODYNAMIC PSYCHIATRY*

Initially named the American Academy of Psychoanalysis, the Academy was founded in 1956 in order to provide a forum for psychiatrists to discuss diverse psychoanalytic ideas. It arose because of doctrinaire rigidities of major psychoanalytic associations at that time.

The Academy has published a journal since its inception. The current name and format of the journal were created in 2012, when Richard C. Friedman, MD, assumed the position of Editor-in-Chief and César A. Alfonso, MD and Jennifer I. Downey, MD, became Deputy Editors.

Friedman, Alfonso and Downey had become alarmed at the fragile state of psychodynamic thought in American Psychiatry. Naming the journal *Psychodynamic Psychiatry* reflected our conviction that this important area of psychiatry was newly emerging and needed an appropriate home. Modern psychodynamic psychiatry is only partially anchored in psychoanalytic psychology. It is equally rooted in neuroscience, academic psychology and psychiatry. It is best considered a branch of psychiatry, not an extension or application of psychoanalysis. The journal accepts articles that have a clinical and/or scientific focus and welcomes research. It does not publish psychoanalytically oriented articles in the arts or humanities. *Psychodynamic Psychiatry* considers psychoanalytic treatment as one of a number of diverse therapeutic modalities. More importantly, it emphasizes the importance of psychodynamically oriented diagnoses and formulations in constructing a treatment plan for all psychiatric patients.

Part 1
Psychodynamic Psychiatry: An Emerging Field

Psychodynamic Psychiatry and Psychoanalysis: Two Different Models

Richard C. Friedman, MD, César A. Alfonso, MD, and Jennifer I. Downey, MD

MODERN PSYCHIATRY AVOIDS PSYCHOANALYTIC CONCEPTS

Psychoanalytic ideas, while useful in the treatment of the mentally ill, have largely been eliminated from modern psychiatry. The articles published in major psychiatric journals (excepting *Psychodynamic Psychiatry*) and the qualifications and interests of academic psychiatrists indicate that American psychiatry in 2015 is firmly bio-descriptive. The attempt to merge psychoanalytic and neurobiological thought in American medical schools during the three decades following World War II failed. Psychiatry seems to be reverting back to the state it was in prior to the discovery of the principles of psychoanalytic psychology by Freud.

This is unfortunate since many ideas that come from psychoanalytic psychology are useful in the treatment of mental illness. Perhaps the quietly anti-psychoanalytic tone of American psychiatry is at least in part a reaction to past rigidities of organized psychoanalysis. Ill will between psychoanalytic practitioners and bio-descriptive psychiatrists probably has been influential as

well. We have attended meetings of psychiatric organizations, for example, in which a plenary speaker openly stated that she would "never" stand on the same podium as a psychoanalyst. Academic psychiatrists judged psychoanalysts to be arrogant, grandiose, insular, and anti-scientific.

On the other side of the spectrum, a speaker who declared psychoanalytic process to be inherently indescribable and who derided efforts to study it recently addressed a plenary meeting of the American Psychoanalytic Association. The audience, like-minded and enthusiastic, gave him a standing ovation (Hoffman, 2009). The notion that a putative therapeutic modality is unresearchable is profoundly anti-scientific. How do we know whether an intervention is helpful without studying outcome? How can we protect patients from being harmed without assessing behavioral change over time? How can we charge patients a fee for therapeutic services when no therapeutic progress or process can be objectively verified? Therapists who believe that their interventions are inherently beyond objective assessment should be viewed with caution by patients, clients, and their families.

PSYCHOANALYSIS, A DEPTH PSYCHOLOGY THAT APPLIES TO EVERYONE VS. PSYCHODYNAMIC PSYCHIATRY, A BRANCH OF MEDICINE

Freud believed that psychoanalysis was a depth psychology that included vast mental territory and that only a small segment of psychoanalysis was or should be devoted to its therapeutic application (S. Freud, 1927).

In "The Problem of Lay Analysis" he writes,

> For we do not consider it at all desirable for psychoanalysis to be swallowed up by medicine and to find its last resting place in a text-book of psychiatry under the heading "Methods of Treatment"... It deserves a better fate and it may be hoped will meet with one. As a depth-psychology, a theory of the mental unconscious, it can become indispensable to all the sciences which are concerned with the evolution of human civilization and its major institutions such as art, religion and the social order. (S. Freud, 1927, p. 83)

The distinction Freud made between psychoanalytic psychology and the segment of it that is applied in treatment is crucially important for understanding the differences between psychoanalysis and psychodynamic psychiatry. The latter emerging discipline is concerned with only part of general psychoanalytic theory, namely that part that is directly relevant to empirical science and/or therapeutic practice.

POSTMODERNISM, ENDORSED BY PSYCHOANALYSIS, REJECTED BY PSYCHODYNAMIC PSYCHIATRY

Psychodynamic psychiatry embraces standards of assessment and scientific relevance used in academic psychiatry and psychology. Interestingly, this is also true of a group of innovative and insightful psychoanalytic researchers who have emerged from *within* organized psychoanalysis. These individuals, however, do not represent the voice of organized psychoanalysis as a whole.

Psychodynamic psychiatry seeks to identify incorrect beliefs about basic scientific and clinical issues and to avoid building theory upon them. Organized psychoanalysis has no way of doing the same. Formed from many local institutes, organized psychoanalysis and its practitioners espouse different and often conflicting ideas about psychoanalytic theory and practice. Most are deemed acceptable. Few are explicitly rejected. All find their way into the numerous psychoanalytic journals that define the field as a whole. No scientific method serves to validate or invalidate psychoanalytic theories. For this reason, psychoanalysis gravitates naturally toward a postmodern perspective.

Sokal and Briemonet (1998) have characterized postmodernism as follows:

> Vast sectors of the humanities and the social sciences seem to have adopted a philosophy that we call for want of a better term "postmodernism," an intellectual current characterised by the more or less explicit rejection of the rationalist tradition of the Enlightenment, by theoretical discourses disconnected from any empirical test and by a cognitive and cultural relativism that regards science as nothing more than a "narration," a myth," or "social construction among others." (p. 1)

Taking the position that it is impossible to identify as invalid any ideas if one accepts postmodernism as a guiding philosophy, modern psychodynamic psychiatry rejects it as a way of understanding therapeutic interventions. Psychodynamic psychiatry relies on standard criteria used by academic psychology and psychiatry to assess validity, reliability, and the usefulness (or its opposite) of beliefs about behavior. This leaves psychodynamic psychiatry more or less in the same position as clinical medicine.

Physicians make countless decisions on a day-to-day basis that cannot be completely supported by controlled studies. They form relationships with patients and try to maximize the likelihood of the patient following a sound, mutually agreed on treatment plan. They often operate in ambiguous therapeutic territory but use common sense and empiricism to whatever degree they can. They anchor their decisions in empirical knowledge to the degree that this is available. Psychodynamic psychiatry as a discipline adopts this approach. Organized psychoanalysis has not done so.

A qualification is necessary here. The fact that we compare psychodynamic psychiatry to medical practice does not suggest that we believe that only physicians should practice psychodynamic psychotherapy. We welcome the psychodynamically informed therapeutic practices of our nonmedical colleagues who must confront the same ambiguities and complexities.

The discipline of psychodynamic psychiatry is much more discrete and limited than psychoanalysis, the depth psychology. This bounded focus does come at a cost. In its largest sense psychoanalysis is best considered a branch of the humanities, and as such has greatly enriched modern thought.

THE IDENTITY OF PSYCHIATRISTS

Modern psychiatry has distanced itself from psychoanalysis—almost as if the latter had never existed. Unfortunately, a field that disavows its own past history is akin to an individual who disavows his or her family, cultural, and/or ethnic background. Amputation of the past comes at considerable cost. This is particularly salient since much psychodynamically oriented therapy, research, and theory is as empirically supported as psychopharmacological therapy, research, and theory (Lazar & Yeomans, 2014).

Organized psychiatry is indeed experiencing conflicts about what its appropriate social role and sense of identity should be. Should psychiatrists expect to spend their careers prescribing medications for patients whom they barely know, in an endless series of very brief interviews? The notion that they should, popular in certain quarters today, paints a professional role that is shrunken to Lilliputian proportions. Should psychiatrists be applied neurobiologists? If so, why is a psychiatric specialty needed at all? Perhaps, as some have suggested, psychiatry should simply be considered part of neurology. Should psychiatrists practice psychotherapy? If so, how should it be reimbursed?

Arguably, the most important schism in the field is between those who have a narrow view of psychiatry as medical specialty (i.e., physicians who use drugs to treat diseases) and those who have a broader biopsycho-social view (i.e., physicians who understand and treat the people who are their patients and who are ill). This schism is reflected in disagreement about the proper role of the *DSM-5* (American Psychiatric Association, 2013).

Some psychiatrists believe that this manual appropriately characterizes the intellectual territory of modern psychiatry. This should influence the identity of psychiatrists and the ideal identity presented by teachers to psychiatrists in training. Other psychiatrists take a broader view. They recognize the need to make reliable symptom-based diagnoses but emphasize the need to conceptualize mental illness in ways that are not captured by the *DSM-5* (American Psychiatric Association, 2013). This includes the idea that subjectively constructed narratives of personal history are important in understanding an individual's motivation across all psychiatric disorders and combinations of disorders. This latter view is also widely endorsed by non-medical mental health professionals. It is only by interviewing patients about their circumstances and past history that therapists can understand the *context within which their symptoms occur.*

DEFENSE MECHANISMS: USEFUL KNOWLEDGE FOR ALL PHYSICIANS

There is no question that psychiatrists must be conversant with psychopharmacology. They should be equally conversant with the psychological defenses, which probably influence psychopathology and therapeutics as much as drugs do (Cramer, 2006.)

As an example, consider the mental mechanism of *denial*, which operates in non-patients and patients alike—"I light up a Lucky Strike whenever I feel like it. Other people might get cancer, but I won't. I've always been lucky." Patients with diverse diagnoses and in fact millions of people who have never seen a psychiatrist and never even heard of psychoanalysis use denial in their daily lives.

During the decades when psychoanalytic ideas were freely expressed and applied in American psychiatry, many clinically useful concepts were put forth. These may have had less to do with the practice of psychoanalysis as a therapeutic technique than the application of depth psychology to routine psychopathological disorders seen in office practice and the general community. They made it easier to treat patients with mental disorders because psychiatrists were better able to understand their motivations. This was true despite the fact that the disorders were diverse and complex and their etiologies were usually obscure.

Military psychiatrists, for example, have been well aware of this. During WWII psychiatrists with a psychoanalytic perspective were able to be helpful to their patients in a way that those who relied entirely on bio-descriptive paradigms could not be (Bion,

1961). A "psychoanalytic perspective" as we use it here does not refer to the practice of treating patients with four or five weekly sessions on the couch, analyzing dreams and encouraging free associations. On the contrary, military psychiatrists saw patients wherever was convenient. The duration of treatment was dictated by practical necessities. The goal was restoration of function and diminution of suffering (Lewis & Engle, 1954). The therapists were flexible, interactive, and relational. Their "psychoanalytic perspective" usually consisted of an awareness of depth psychology and the importance of the personal narrative as discussed by Freud and his followers. Subsequent generations of military psychiatrists and others who specialized in understanding and treating psychic trauma have had similar experience.

Sophistication about denial is part of the effective practice of medicine according to the Hippocratic oath and certainly is not restricted to psychiatrists or psychoanalysts. At any given time physicians and psychotherapists of all disciplines can summon up dramatic examples of denial in their daily practices. Experienced physicians wisely understand that the beliefs expressed by a patient in denial are not entirely motivated by feelings and thoughts that are in the patient's conscious mind. The range of defenses that a patient uses may well influence the degree to which he or she cooperates in a treatment plan (Cramer, 2006; Vaillant, 1994).

Freud described a handful of basic defense mechanisms, all relevant to the treatment of psychiatrically disturbed patients (S. Freud, 1926). His daughter, Anna Freud, discussed these in more detail and spelled out their role in psychological functioning (A. Freud, 1936). The defenses are unconsciously motivated in response to an inner signal of anxiety. They function in diverse ways to keep the person's sense of self stabilized by diverting the attention of the conscious mind from psychological conflict. Sometimes these defensive processes are adaptive, sometimes maladaptive (Perry & Cooper, 1989). They may directly influence the therapist–patient relationship and the patient's willingness to participate in any form of treatment, including pharmacological treatment.

Another defense commonly seen in general psychiatric and medical practice is *identification*. Identification, an unconscious psychological process, does not necessarily connote psychopathology. Children routinely identify with caretakers, for example, and students, with teachers. Identification may, however, become part of psychological symptoms and syndromes. Internists and family physicians are aware that pain without known organic cause can occur as a result of identification with a caretaker or other loved person following the death of that individual. In such instances, identification becomes part of a complex grief reaction. This is but one of many examples of the relation between identification and psychopathology.

The entire subject area of conversion reactions and somatization is based on knowledge of awareness of maladaptive defenses expressed as a result of unconscious conflict. This issue also illustrates how complex modern psychiatry actually is. For example, there is no drug that adequately treats conversion reactions, whereas a psychodynamically informed approach is often effective (Kaplan, 2014).

Assessment of defensive style does not depend on whether a given patient is to be treated with psychodynamically oriented psychotherapy or not. Such assessment should be carried out as a *routine* part of the psychiatric diagnostic interview in similar fashion as discussion of the patient's history of past psychiatric illness.

CONCLUSION

The historical roots of the schism between psychiatry and psychoanalysis were present at the very beginning of the psychoanalytic movement. Eugin Bleuler, one of the most prominent psychiatrists of his time and director of the Eergholzi hospital in Switzerland was originally enthusiastic about Freud's discoveries. He studied with Freud and introduced psychoanalytic ideas in his discussion of schizophrenia (Bleuler, 1950). Bleuler rapidly became disenchanted with Freud's insistence on the role of infantile sexuality in the etiology of neurosis, however. Like Breuer, Freud's first collaborator, Bleuler found Freud's rigidity and inability to tolerate alternative ideas unacceptable. He distanced himself from psychoanalysis and in so doing brought to a halt an early effort to integrate psychiatric understanding and treatment of the psychoses with psychoanalytic psychology (Breger, 2000).

Decades later, psychiatrists again made energetic but ultimately unsuccessful efforts to integrate psychoanalytic and psychiatric thought. In the United States it is probably fair to say that a passionate romance developed between the two fields from about 1945 or so until the early 1980s. Sadly, the passionate romance between psychiatry and psychoanalysis ended in divorce. As matrimonial lawyers and mental health professionals know, however, not all divorces are alike. Some divorces are acrimonious and some are not. Sometimes divorced partners actually remain friends.

Psychiatry needs to move along its own path, heavily influenced by psychoanalytic ideas that have proven useful in the treatment of the mentally ill. The organizational inadequacies and painful feelings that have led to the wholesale rejection of psychoanalytic ideas should and must be dealt with more adaptively in the future than is presently the case.

Biological reductionism on the part of psychiatrists has been paralleled by anti-scientific dogmatism on the part of some psychoanalysts resulting in a schism that is not in the best interests of either discipline. More important, ongoing professional conflict like this is not in the best interests of the troubled and mentally ill individuals treated by mental health professionals of all disciplines, who are influenced by our professional disagreements.

The practical problems to insure that integration occurs are daunting. Departments of psychiatry often lack adequately informed faculty, for example. Telemedicine offers a partial but not entirely adequate solution to this problem. Hopefully, clinical and educational needs will inevitably lead to innovative approaches to re-integrate psychodynamic ideas into the mainstream of psychiatric thought. Were this to happen, the struggling new discipline of psychodynamic psychiatry would be recognized and given a home in academic departments of psychiatry and psychology. In order for this to occur, however, there would have to be widespread enthusiasm for paradigms that integrate biological, psychological, and social influences on behavior. Whether this happens or not remains to be seen.

REFERENCES

American Psychiatric Association. (2013). *Diagnostic and statistical manual of mental disorders* (5th ed.). Arlington, VA: Author.

Bion, W. R. (1961). *Experiences in groups.* London: Tavistock.

Bleuler, E. (1950). *Dementia Praecox or the group of schizophrenias.* J. Zinkin (Ed. & Trans.). New York: International Universities Press.

Breger, L. (2000). *Freud: Darkness in the midst of vision.* New York: Wiley.

Cramer, P. (2006). *Protecting the self: Defense mechanisms in action.* New York: Guilford.

Freud, A. (1936). *The ego and the mechanisms of defense.* London: Hogarth Press and Institute of Psycho-Analysis.

Freud, S. (1926). *Inhibitions symptoms and anxiety.* New York: Norton.

Freud, S. (1927). The question of lay analysis. In J. Strachey (Ed. & Trans.), *The standard edition of the complete psychological works of Sigmund Freud* (Vol. 20, pp. 251-258). London: Hogarth Press.

Hoffman, I. (2009). Double thinking our way to "scientific" legitimacy. The destruction of human experience. Plenary Address. *Journal of the American Psychoanalytic Association, 57,* 1043-1069.

Kaplan, M. J. (2014). A psychodynamic perspective on treatment of patients with conversion and other somatoform disorders. *Psychodynamic Psychiatry, 42*(4), 593-617.

Lazar, S. G., & Yeomans, F. E. (Eds.). (2014). Special issue: Psychotherapy, the Affordable Care Act and mental health parity: Obstacles to implementation. *Psychodynamic Psychiatry, 42*(3).

Lewis, N. D. C., & Engle, B. (1954). *Wartime psychiatry.* London: Oxford University Press.

Perry, J. C., & Cooper, S. H. (1989). An empirical study of defense mechanisms. *Archives of General Psychiatry, 46*(5), 444-452.

Sokkal, A., & Briemont, J. (1998). *Fashionable nonsense: Postmodern intellectuals' abuse of science.* New York: Picador.

Vaillant, G. E. (1994). Ego mechanisms of defense and personality psychopathology. *Journal of Abnormal Psychology, 103,* 44-50.

Contemporary Psychodynamic Psychiatry

Richard C. Friedman, MD, Jennifer I. Downey, MD,
and César A. Alfonso, MD

Some psychoanalysts refer to psychodynamic *psychotherapy* (and by implication, psychodynamic *psychiatry*) as the "child" of psychoanalysis. This may have been so years ago but no longer. Times have changed although the model of the mind that classical psychoanalysts advocate has not. Free association by the patient and evenly hovering attention by the analyst *initially* advanced knowledge of the mind and the treatment of patients. One would be hard put to argue that this method has led to progress in knowledge or in improved therapeutic results in the past four or five decades (Kandel, 1999). In fact, major theoretical advances have primarily come from reactions of psychoanalysts to extra-psychoanalytic research. In a previous editorial we listed a partial list of important topics and areas including: Harlow's studies of primates, Kinsey and colleagues' research on human sexual behavior, Masters and Johnson's research on the human sexual response cycle, epidemiological studies of the incidence, prevalence, and onset of mental illnesses in the general population, studies of childhood and adult trauma, behavioral genetics, the field of evolutionary psychology, the field of attachment psychology, the field of sexual differentiation of behavior, and research on mirror neurons (Friedman & Downey, 2012).

Modern psychodynamic psychiatry as a *new discipline* is emerging from a fusion of psychoanalytic and extra-analytic psychology, neuroscience, and academic psychiatry (Friedman, Downey, Alfonso, & Ingram, 2013). The new discipline "psychodynamic psychiatry" finds itself in a harsh intellectual environment. Neither academic psychiatry nor academic psychology advocates for the integration of biological-psychological and social influences on behavior, and certainly not from a developmental perspective. The internist and psychoanalyst George Engel proposed the need for an integrative model many years ago (Engel, 1977). His perspective provides the guiding paradigm of *Psychodynamic Psychiatry* (the journal).

Contemporary psychodynamic psychiatry as we conceptualize it differs from the paradigm that Chessick alludes to in a number of important respects.

1. Modern Psychodynamic Psychiatry Has a Positive Attitude Toward Neuroscience and Psychobiology

In fact we believe that the mind and personality cannot be understood without the awareness of developments in neuroscience. This has far-reaching consequences and sharpens the distinction between *psychodynamics* (motivational influences that are actively warded off from awareness) and *etiology* (causes of pathological behaviors). We will not list the numerous recent advances in neuroscience here but simply point out that models of the mind originating in psychoanalysis must recognize them since they have implications for psycho-analytic theory and practice (Kandel, 2012; Kandel, Schwartz, Jessell, Siegelbaum, & Hudspeth, 2012).

2. Psychodynamic Psychiatry Has a Positive Attitude Toward Research

In discussing this, a historical perspective is necessary. Today psychoanalytic organizations, including for example, the International Psychoanalytic Association (IPA) and American Psychoanalytic Association (APSA) have a positive attitude toward research although many analytic clinicians do not (Hoffman. 2009). During the years when psychoanalytic psychology had maximal influence in American Psychiatry, however, psychoanalytic attitudes toward research were predominately negative (Schachter & Luborsky, 1998). The psychoanalytic literature emphasized case reports, most of which illustrated (then) accepted psychoanalytic beliefs. This well-documented anti-research attitude led to an evidence vacuum regarding the effectiveness of psychoanalytic psychotherapy and psychoanalysis and a knowledge gap about psychopathology. This contributed to the sundered relationship between psychiatry and psychoanalytic psychology in the U.S. today. Freud and the group closest to him believed that psychoanalysis had discovered a new area of knowledge, indeed a new *type* of knowledge that did not lend itself to standard academic research (Breger, 2001, 2009). This attitude influenced subsequent leaders of organized psychoanalysis and was expressed in the way psychoanalytic associations were structured nationally and internationally. As organized psychiatry became more and more descriptive and invested in psychobiology, the rift between the two ways of looking at behavior became too great for both to coexist at the same academic medical institutions (at least in the U.S.). Psychoanalysts were ousted

from most academic medical centers but in fairness to the bio-descriptive psychiatrists that remained, *both* groups failed to build bridges. Instead they had "debates." These were entertaining but unproductive. We don't hold a decline in the quality of civilized society responsible for the loss of influence of psychoanalytic psychology in American psychiatry. Rather, we are reminded of Cassius's reflections about responsibility in Shakespeare's *Julius Caesar*.

"The fault, dear Brutus, is not in our stars but in ourselves."
—Shakespeare, *Julius Caesar*, 1.2,147-148

3. Psychodynamic Psychiatry Has a Positive Attitude Toward Academic Psychology and Psychiatry

It rejects the pluralistic, postmodern frame of reference commonly espoused by psychoanalysts today. In rejecting this postmodern perspective, we also take a somewhat critical attitude toward the diverse psychoanalytic institutes that together characterize the international psychoanalytic community. We accept these as sites of learning but not as arbiters of "truth," however this is defined. Thus, it is only of historical interest whether insights and speculates come from Jung, Kohut, or Lacan. These ideas are not privileged beyond the evidence base that supports them.

This has consequences for the way in which many psychoanalysts fashion their identities. When a psychoanalyst proclaims herself "A Kleinian," or "A Jungian," or "A Kohutian," she is endorsing a *belief system* about behavior. We see this as a manifestation of a primitive field with a sparse database. Contemporary psychodynamic psychiatry views itself as inherently empirical while acknowledging the often-daunting problems of applying empirical methods to the study of the mind and personality.

4. Psychodynamic Psychiatry Takes a Critical View of Freud's Contributions

We continue to study Freud's publications but do not endorse some of his ideas. We see Freud's work as a potpourri of outdated theories and uncannily brilliant insights and observations. Arguably the finest writer of clinical and scientific psychology who ever lived, Freud's contributions are paradoxically not those of a scientist. They are observational, insightful, speculative, philosophical, and as virtually all of his critics have pointed out embedded in the Victorian worldview of his time.

As clinicians we do not regard Freud's behavior toward his patients as a model for our own. Freud himself was less interested in the therapeutic aspects of psychoanalysis than its scientific importance. His therapeutic results were mixed and his behavior toward patients inconsistent to say the least (Breger, 2001; Gay, 1988). On the scientific side, we note that Freud's observations might be thought of as falling into different categories.

One category concerns childhood sexual behavior and its relationship to adult psychological functioning. Some of Freud's ideas about this were prescient but many were erroneous. The paradigm that Freud posited *in toto* including libido theory and the role of oedipal conflicts in the etiology of psychopathology is outdated. It is important to emphasize that in 1959 a whole new area of sexual development was discovered: "Sexual Differentiation Theory." This involved the "prenatal effects of sex steroids on brain embryogenesis and subsequent sexual and non-sexual behavior," an area that Freud was not aware of (Breedlove, 1994; Wallen, 2009). Reassessment of Freud's ideas about psychosexual development in light of modern knowledge remains an ongoing process.

5. Psychodynamic Psychiatry Has a Positive Attitude Toward Psychopharmacology

The abuses of psychiatry by drug corporations, so called "big pharma," have been exposed (Whitaker, 2011), and largely corrected. Also well documented is the fact that too much was hoped for and expected from the pharmacological revolution. There is no pill that cures mental illness. Optimal effects of many psychopharmacological interventions require simultaneous psychosocial treatments (Mallo & Mintz, 2013). It is also becoming increasingly apparent, however, that there is a population of patients in whom optimal effects of psychotherapeutic intervention require simultaneous psychopharmacological treatment. The patient population is diverse and "mental illness" is not a unitary entity. There is no single therapeutic modality that is effective in all cases. In fact, excessive enthusiasm for psychopharmacology followed upon earlier occurring enthusiasm for psychoanalysis. It is understandable that we longed for and continue to long for a simple solution to the suffering that so many members of our species are prone to. All in all, the salutary effects of psychopharmacological agents can hardly be overemphasized.

Whereas a past generation of psychoanalysts was opposed to the introduction of pharmacological agents, believing that their use contaminated the transference, the present generation of psychodynamic psychiatrists has more positive attitudes. Recognizing that concurrent psychoanalytic and pharmacological treatment can be salutary for many patients, modern psychodynamic psychiatry is openly appreciative of the therapeutic gains made possible by psychopharmacology.

6. Psychodynamic Psychiatry Has a Positive Attitude Toward Descriptive Psychiatry

Psychodynamic psychiatry owes a considerable dept to descriptive psychiatry. Epidemiological knowledge of the incidence and prevalence of major psychiatric disorders and their age of onset, for example, has emerged from meticulous descriptive research. While recognizing the usefulness of descriptive diagnosis, psychodynamic psychiatry also endorses the simultaneous assessment of a psycho-biographical history. Personal narratives remain a core part of patient assessment. Both parts of an assessment, present and past history of psychiatric diagnoses and psycho-biographical history as represented in narratives are necessary in order to form an adequate picture of an individual. These, of course, must also be supplemented by a family history.

7. Psychodynamic Psychiatry Emphasizes Diagnostic Assessment More than Any Specific Type of Treatment

Psychoanalysis derives insights about the mind and personality from application of the psychoanalytic method. Most patients that are assessed in a psychodynamically informed manner, however, are not candidates for long-term psychodynamically oriented psychotherapy (LTT) or psychoanalysis. We do not afford psychoanalysis a privileged position in the hierarchy of possible treatments. Clinical experience indicates that *some patients* who do not respond to supportive psychotherapy or manual-based treatments or even twice per week long-term psychotherapy may achieve therapeutic gains with psychoanalysis. It is not yet possible to guarantee success in advance, however, a common problem in medicine. Oncologists struggle with this difficult situation regularly as well.

As a treatment psychoanalysis may be transformative for some people but how it transforms remains mysterious and a topic for ongoing research (Bucci, 1997).

CONCLUSION

It is astonishing, even shocking, that American psychiatry is in serious danger of throwing out the "baby" (viable and useful ideas that originally came from psychoanalysis) with the "bathwater" (psychoanalytic dogmatism). Most ideas accepted by modern psychodynamic psychiatry and psychology rest on a sound empirically validated foundation. A rescue effort is needed lest psychiatry discard the notion of the dynamic unconscious itself. This core idea, crucial in understanding all mental illness (and psychological functioning), does not depend for its validity or its usefulness on application of the classical psychoanalytic method. The problems of restoring a developmental bio-psycho-social paradigm that includes the dynamic unconscious in its psychological component are formidable. Many and perhaps most departments of psychiatry no longer have faculty members that are knowledgeable in psychodynamically informed interviewing or reasoning. University-based programs for psychodynamically informed education are not generally available. We note that there are still a few exceptional programs in which psychiatric residents learn integrated paradigms from faculty who teach the developmental bio-psycho-social model.

These considerable obstacles notwithstanding, the principles of psychodynamic psychiatry are slowly emerging on a case-by-case basis. The reason for this is that the field of psychiatry itself, a whole greater than any of its parts, needs this new discipline in order to adequately understand and treat psychiatric patients.

REFERENCES

Breedlove, S. M. (1994). Sexual differentiation of the human nervous system. *Annual Review of Psychology, 45*, 389-418.

Breger, L. (2001). *Freud: Darkness in the midst of vision.* New York: Wiley.

Breger, L. (2009). *A dream of undying fame: How Freud betrayed his mentor and invented psychoanalysis.* New York: Basic Books.

Bucci, W. (1997). *Psychoanalysis and cognitive science: A multiple code theory.* New York: Guilford.

Engel, G. (1977). The need for a new medical model: A challenge for biomedicine. *Science, 196*, 129-136.

Friedman, R. C., & Downey, J. I. (2012). Psychodynamic psychiatry and psychoanalysis. *Psychodynamic Psychiatry, 40*(1), 5-22.

Friedman, R. C., Downey, J. I., Alfonso, C., & Ingram, D. (2013). What is "psychodynamic psychiatry?" *Psychodynamic Psychiatry, 41*(4), 511-512.

Gay, P. (1988). *Freud: A life for our time.* New York: Norton.

Hoffman, I. (2009). Double thinking our way to "scientific" legitimacy: The destruction of human experience. Plenary address. *Journal of the American Psychoanalytic Association, 57*, 1043-1069.

Kandel, E. R. (1999). Biology and the future of psychoanalysis: A new intellectual framework for psychiatry revisited. *American Journal of Psychiatry, 156*, 505-524.

Kandel, E. R. (2012). *The age of insight.* New York: Random House.

Kandel, E. R., Schwartz, J. H., Jessell, T. M., Siegelbaum, S. A., & Hudspeth, A. J. (2012). *Principles of neural science, 5th edition.* New York: McGraw-Hill.

Mallo, C. J., & Mintz, D. L. (2013). Teaching all the evidence bases: Reintegrating psychodynamic aspects of prescribing into psychopharmacology training. *Psychodynamic Psychiatry, 41*(1), 13-39.

Schachter, J., & Luborsky, L. (1998). Who's afraid of psychoanalytic research? Analysts' attitudes toward reading clinical versus empirical research papers. *International Journal of Psychoanalysis, 79*, 965-969.

Shakespeare, W. (1992). *Julius Caesar.* New York: Folger Shakespeare Library, Washington Square Press.

Wallen, K. (2009). Special issue on the 50th anniversary of the publication of Phoenix, Goy, Gerral, and Young, 1959. Organizational effects of hormones. *Hormones and Behavior, 55*(5), 561-666.

Whitaker, R. (2011). *Anatomy of an epidemic.* New York: Crown Publishers.

Part 2
A Psychodynamic Approach to Complex Psychiatric Disorders

César A. Alfonso, MD

Psychodynamic psychiatrists regularly treat persons with comorbid or multimorbid disorders. Posttraumatic stress disorder (PTSD), substance use disorders, mood disorders, complicated grief, anxiety disorders, obsessive-compulsive disorder (OCD), eating disorders, personality disorders, and somatic symptom disorders often coexist and it is quite common for patients to have multiple diagnoses in outpatient and inpatient clinical settings. Compounding this inherent complexity, comorbid chronic or acute non-psychiatric medical illnesses cause significant disability when concomitantly present, not only in consultation and liaison psychiatry settings but also in general psychiatric practice. Impairment in functioning is greater with medical comorbidity and psychiatrists as physicians are in a salient position to provide effective multidimensional biopsychosocial care that could improve quality of life and reduce morbidity and mortality. While we rarely come across patients who present with discrete rather than comorbid disorders, it is helpful to understand the pathogenesis of each clinical disorder from a psychodynamic perspective.

Psychodynamic formulations were traditionally constructed by framing clinical data using the language and theoretical concepts of diverse psychoanalytic schools of thought. Prominent theoretical frameworks include the *Freudian metapsychologies* (dynamic hypothesis or theory of intrapsychic conflict, libido or energy transfer theory, the structural hypothesis, the topographic hypothesis, and the genetic hypothesis or theory of psycho-

sexual development), revisions of Freudian theory such as *object relations theory* (with contributions of Fairbairn, Bion, Klein, Winnicott, Kernberg, Greenberg, and Mitchell), *ego psychology and developmental theories* (with contributions of Anna Freud, Hartmann, Mahler and Erikson), *Lacanian theory* (integrating concepts from philosophy and linguistics), *culturalist theories* (with contributions of Horney, Sullivan and Fromm), *analytical psychology* (developed by Jung), *attachment theory* (with contributions by Bowlby, Main, Ainsworth, and Fonagy), and *self-psychology* (as proposed by Kohut). Given the vast psychoanalytic literature and variety of viewpoints, constructing a formulation can be cumbersome and feel insufficient if one tries to be all encompassing. In our experience, a biopsychosocial formulation (as proposed by Engel) is often sufficient to guide adequate clinical care. Psychoanalytically informed psychodynamic explorations, moreover, can enrich biopsychosocial formulations. But because our ultimate goal is to tailor treatment to meet the clinical needs of patients, formulations should be concise and clinically relevant to effectively guide psychotherapeutic work. Rather than trying to describe case material from a particular school of thought focusing heavily on theory and using language that may be obtuse and not clinically relevant, it is often helpful to identify the transtheoretical psychodynamic common factors involved in the pathogenesis of psychiatric disorders.

In this section we will examine the psychodynamic underpinnings of psychopathology in complex psychiatric disorders. Although psychodynamic explorations and insights may seem transdiagnostic and non-specific at times, a transdiagnostic psychodynamic paradigm that considers relevant transtheoretical common factors may actually be clinically relevant considering that psychological disorders are usually multimorbid. *Affective dysregulation, attachment insecurities, deficits in mentalization and reflective functioning, inadequate defensive functioning and adaptation, unconscious conflicts, disruptions in development, early childhood trauma with subsequent retraumatization* and *neurophysiologic instability caused by allostatic overload* may be core psychodynamic factors in complex psychiatric disorders. A nuanced and case-specific understanding of the relevance of these factors is essential in order to successfully guide psychotherapeutic treatments. Psychodynamic formulations help clinicians gain a profound and textured understanding of pathogenesis, but this can only happen contextually by becoming aware of the interaction of the patient's life experiences, constitutional vulnerabilities and environmental stressors. Our retrospective explorations should not be formulaic since they are meant to guide prospective reparative psychotherapeutic treatments of individual patients.

ANXIETY DISORDERS

Busch and Sandberg and Cornell/Columbia associates are at the forefront of applying psychoanalytic concepts to effectively treat persons with *panic disorder*. Their model emphasizes linking conflicts surrounding loss and separation, dependency and anger as triggers of panic symptoms. Anxiety symptoms in this framework can be understood as avoidance or symbolic somatic displacements of unconscious conflicts. They propose that panic may constitute instinctual excitations that are not adequately modulated by mentalized affective states. Additionally, dissociation from trauma, where narrative

discourse and affect become unlinked, could also trigger panic states when repression fails its defensive function. The Freudian concept of accumulation of excitation leading to anxiety attacks is thus revised by understanding that excitation interferes with mentalization, and deficiencies in the process of mentalization lead to the somatic discharge of physiological manifestations of anxiety.

Bion described with relative clarity how panic serves the adaptive purpose of releasing affective tension that cannot be emotionally processed. At a neurophysiological level, subcortical activation is heightened in anxiety states relative to cortical activation. Reparative psychodynamic psychotherapeutic work occurs when clinicians help patients translate somatic symptoms into mentalized symbolic representations and verbal discourse. Validating, identifying, representing and verbally elaborating negative affects results in symptomatic improvement through affective regulation.

McEvoy, O'Connor and McCarthy, academic clinicians from Trinity College Dublin, give us an in-depth review of the psychodynamics of *social anxiety disorder (SAD)* based on a research study of audio taped semi-structured interviews. Their hermeneutical analyses of case material considered narrative content, non-verbal and extra-verbal responses and countertransferences. Psychodynamic themes identified in the pathogenesis of SAD include having experienced highly critical home environments resulting in a diminished sense of self-worth and fear of reprimand, having had at a passive and submissive caregiver who was often viciously silenced by others, experiencing difficulties with separation and individuation, and a propensity to depersonalization by adopting ego-dystonic facades in social situations. The work of these investigators validates the theoretical contributions of Erikson (contextual development in order to socially succeed), Winnicott (absence of good-enough caregiving) and Mahler (separation-individuation developmental arrest or regression) in understanding obstacles to the development of socially comfortable interdependence.

EATING DISORDERS

Tasca and Balfour, researchers at the University of Ottawa, contextualize the psychodynamics of eating disorders through the lens of attachment theory. The basic premise in attachment insecurity is that caregiving that is inconsistent or neglectful results in dysregulation of affect. Susceptible persons with complex comorbidity with unmet unconscious attachment needs may develop eating disorder symptoms as a means of coping. In binge eating disorder, anorexia nervosa and bulimia nervosa disruptions in attachment are common and reflective functioning is compromised.

Those who have an avoidant attachment style are prone to excessive self-reliance, are less emotionally reactive, present with constriction of affect, and experienced parenting and subsequent relationships as disappointing or dangerous. They are rigid and provide a paucity of information in their narratives with a tendency to over idealize, minimize and devalue. These individuals up regulate affect, may be alexithymic and are prone to restrict caloric intake, often wanting to become invisible in order to escape toxic family dynamics. Anorexia nervosa, with high morbidity and mortality, is complicated by the transcultural idealization of thinness and stigmatization of any deviation from very strict aesthetic social constructs of body weight, shape and beauty.

Those who are preoccupied about relationships, highly anxious, and worried about re-experiencing loss and abandonment have affective hyperactivity, are prone to use action defenses and may binge and purge as a means of coping. Their narratives are chaotic and colored with anger, projections and passivity. The unquenchable thirst for love and support seeks fulfillment through binge eating and excessive guilt and intolerable shame through purging, escaping the danger of expected abandonment by engaging in a desperate cycle of devouring and cleansing to alleviate unbearable tension.

GRIEF

Horowitz, from University of California San Francisco School of Medicine, describes the normal stages of grief in order to understand the psychodynamics of patients with pathological, complicated or prolonged grief. His observations build on the work by Freud, Kubler-Ross, Lindemann and Parkes. Horowitz links the impact of grieving on identity formation from a developmental perspective delineating phases of self-organization in the mourning process. The five phases are *initial outcry, denial and avoidance, intrusive feelings, working through,* and *completion.*

In the phase of outcry intense affects of fear, sadness and anger trigger the sympathetic, parasympathetic and hormonal systems creating hyperarousal and shock that may impair reality testing and ward off shame and guilt. The phase of denial is associated with states of depersonalization and derealization. The phase of intrusion allows for the experience of paroxysmal intense emotions and conscious recognition of the significance of the loss. In working through the person strikes a balance between defensive numbing and emotional flooding. Completion allows for remembering with joy and serenity while developing reparative relationships to restore self-constancy.

INTERNET AND SOCIAL NETWORKING EXCESSIVE USE

With over 4 billion daily Internet users (slightly over half of the world population) online social networking has become ubiquitous and culturally normative, providing opportunities for socialization and novel self-object experiences. Cheuk Wing Li, from Hong Kong, describes the psychodynamics of Internet excessive use, social networking addiction, the phenomenon of compulsively posting selfies on social media and the functional significance of interactive phone and digital device touch-activated surfaces.

Similar to other addictions, excessive online social networking can both induce and relieve anxiety. Online documenting and sharing on social networks, either in meticulously curated ways or via random postings, results in an endogenous opioid mediated sense of elation that modulates the reward neuronal circuits of the ventral tegmental area, nucleus accumbens and prefrontal cortex. Fulfillment may be augmented by the unlimited use of the "like" function on social media, which becomes a source of mirroring self-object gratification. Those with sensitive depleted narcissistic personality traits engage in passive voyeuristic browsing of what others post while gregarious and self-assured exhibitionists or those who simply cherish social contact enhancement may post detailed colorful accounts of life experiences. Online sharing on social networks, from the momentous to the mundane, may become compulsive and excessive. But as tempting as it may be for the cyber-phobic to demonize regular use the Internet as a vehicle for socialization, it is important to clarify that only those who lack capacity for boundary awareness and nuanced intersubjective interactions may be at risk for excessive use that interferes with functioning and is detrimental to quality of life. Although in some social network platforms mutuality may be difficult to achieve because of real time delays and limited exposure to sensory cues, as technology improves particularly through enhanced video functions and real-time message sharing virtual communication is becoming increasingly life-like bridging geographic and other time-space barriers.

If front facing cameras introduced in phones in 2003 gave rise to phenomenal access to the portraiture, revolutionary affirmations and social commentary of selfies, the development of the touch screen interphase provided a sensate "second skin" animating phones as effective transitional objects. Devices now have the potential for gratifying autistic engagement and multiple levels of dissociation, with or without fragmentation, depending on ego strength and need to self soothe. It is important to consider, extrapolating from Khantzian formulations on the psychodynamics of addiction, that excessive use of devices and social networking platforms could impair genuinely embodied and reciprocal social and self-regulatory skills through disuse and cause distortions in mentalization and reflective functioning.

MOOD DISORDERS

Vigod and Taylor, from the University of Toronto, studied the interaction between sex, genes and the environment to understand the pathogenesis and higher prevalence of depression in women. Sex differences in genetic makeup partially explain sensitivity to adverse life events as these relate to psychopathology and resilience. Furthermore, women are differentially disadvantaged experiencing higher levels of violence, caregiving burden and socioeconomic instability. A biopsychosocial perspective can be clinically informed by recent discoveries in gene environment interactions.

Relevant gene-environment interactions include polymorphism in the brain-derived neurotrophic factor gene (Val 66 Met), which appears to increase the risk of depression in the face of psychosocial adversity. Similarly, a gene involved in the function of corticotrophin releasing factor (CRCH1) seems to mediate the link between childhood adversity and development of major depression. Sex differences in the prevalence of depression could be explained in part by a particular distribution of genotypes of the serotonin transporter gene-linked polymorphic region (5HTTLPR). Other polymorphisms associated with depression include certain variants of the monoamine oxidase A- upstream variable number tandem repeat (MAOA-uVN-TR) allele configurations. It has been well established over the past decade that genetic differences are important in determining susceptibility to depression in the face of adversity.

Adelson and colleagues from the Group for the Advancement of Psychiatry (GAP) Committee on Human Sexuality examined how hypersexuality may relate to juvenile bipolar disorder (JBD). Hypersexuality is not pathognomonic of bipolarity and can present transdiagnostically in posttraumatic stress disorder, attention deficit hyperactivity disorder, conduct disorder and oppositional defiant disorder. Psychosocial stressors such as sexual abuse, excessive exposure to sexual stimuli, overcrowding and poverty may also correlate with increased sexual activity, with or without hormonal surges. If hypersexuality is accompanied by elation, grandiosity, flight of ideas, delusional thinking, and psychomotor activation with decreased need for sleep a diagnosis of JBD may be appropriate. Rating scales such as the Adolescent Clinical Sexual Behavior Inventory and the Childhood Sexual Behavior Inventory may be clinically helpful to elicit data on sexual activity. Further research is needed to clarify if hypersexuality is caused by JBD or is only an associated factor.

OBSESSIVE-COMPULSIVE DISORDER

Sy-Cherng Woon and associates from the National University of Malaysia discuss how integrated care improves clinical outcomes in the care of persons with treatment resistant obsessive-compulsive disorder (OCD) who benefit from combined supportive and psychodynamic psychotherapy, cognitive behavioral therapy exposure and response prevention (CBT/ERP), psychopharmacology and other somatic treatments. In OCD presenting symptomatically with obsessions in the absence of compulsions, psychodynamic psychotherapy is particularly efficacious. Cognitive schemas associated with OCD include overestimation of danger, inflated responsibility, perfectionism, strong need to control,

thought-action fusion, and intolerance of uncertainty. From a psychodynamic perspective, persons with OCD have contradictory representations of self and others as a result of attachment insecurities. An object relations viewpoint highlights the importance of ambivalence and repressed anger resulting from identification with critical caregivers. This in turn leads to self-criticism, hypermorality, rigidity, and an inordinate need for control and autonomy.

PERSONALITY DISORDERS

Livesley, from the University of British Columbia, proposes an integrated approach to the treatment of patients with borderline personality disorder (BPD) as an alternative to applying the manualized and carefully researched specialized therapies. There is no doubt that specialized therapies for BPD are more efficacious than providing routine care with supportive psychotherapy or even supportive psychotherapy in combination with pharmacotherapy. Dialectical behavior therapy, transference-focused therapy and mentalizing-based therapy have robust positive results when administered with rigorous expertise in research settings. The increased efficacy of manualized specialized treatments is more evident with respect to short or intermediate term symptom outcome, such as improvement in emotional dysregulation or reduction in self-harm but not necessarily with respect to long term outcome of the illness itself. Very lengthy treatment is often necessary to achieve personality integration and higher level of functioning. There is robust evidence for a psychotherapy dose effect in the treatment of patients with borderline personality disorder that correlates with improved outcomes, achievement of therapeutic objectives, clinical remission and recovery.

Given the level of associated comorbidity and difficulty establishing a therapeutic alliance with patients with BPD in early phases of treatment in clinical settings, a creative integration of diverse elements from the specialized therapies in an organized and treatment phase-specific fashion seems reasonable.

Persons with BPD have impairments in the following spheres: affective dysregulation with anxiousness and dysphoria, chaotic interpersonal relationships, a fragmented sense of self and others stemming from disorganized attachments and trauma, deficits in mentalization, and self-injurious behaviors. Livesley proposes a treatment framework in five steps – to *establish the frame* of therapy that ensures safety, *build and maintain the therapeutic alliance, maintain a consistent process, build motivation for change,* and *promote self-reflection.* This is attained via support, empathy, validation, collaboration, genuineness, enforcing a clearly defined and consistent therapeutic frame, promoting understanding that actions are motivated by emotions and have an impact and consequences in self and others, establishing goals and reviewing progress to augment motivation, and decentering to promote contemplation, self-reflection and reduce reactivity.

Stone presents a detailed account of case material of forty patients with borderline personality disorder (BPD) and associated comorbidities in institutional (New York State Psychiatric Institute/Columbia University) and office practice settings treated for up to five decades, the longest follow-up period recorded in the literature for this clinical disorder. He observed that with consistent psychodynamically informed treatment two-thirds of patients reached clinical remission or recovery. Positive prognostic factors include high levels of agreeableness and conscientiousness resulting in steadier relationships and workplace success. Comorbid mood disorder and having experienced incest constitute negative prognostic factors. He also observed that as persons with BPD age into their fourth decade of life and beyond dramatic and disagreeable behavior tends to dissipate. The reasons for this are probably diverse but in any case have not been well described.

Kealy and Ogrodniczuk, from the University of British Columbia, provide a descriptive overview of narcissistic personality disorder from a psychodynamic perspective. Normal or adaptive narcissism serves the purpose of attainment of personal goals and maintenance of love relations through self-investment and positive appraisal. Grandiosity, bullying, and callousness alternating with helpless vulnerability, needing constant affirmations, feelings of inadequacy, fear of rejection and excessive shame characterize pathological narcissism. In pathological narcissism from an attachment perspective one observes preoccupation and anxiety, and from a self-psychology viewpoint empathic ruptures lead to a particular fragility that overcompensates with pathological grandiosity and helpless rage.

Kealy and Ogrodniczuk review formulations by Akhtar, Bowlby, Cooper, Fairbairn, Fonagy, Freud, Fromm, Kernberg, Klein, Kohut, Stolorow, Sullivan and Winnicott contributing to the psychodynamic appreciation of how narcissism may obstruct fulfilling relationships. Highlighting the contributions of Erich Fromm broadens our understanding of pathological narcissism by integrating social dimensions, in particular cultural values associated with consumerism. Accumulating material goods and having a certain image or lifestyle dilutes one's capacity to establish reciprocal and responsible love relations and social bonds. Bowlby's attachment theory and subsequent research found an association between narcissistic grandiosity and insecure anxious attachments, where there is preoccupation with loss or relationships and fear of abandonment. Kohut concluded that one needs selfobjects to sustain ego strength and vitality. In the absence of adequate caregiving and with parental failure of empathy a pathological quest for affirmations develops later in life resulting in grandiosity as a way to compensate for vulnerability. Chapter authors make the important observation that narcissistic self-absorption is hardly a form of self-love, as pathological narcissism interferes not only with interpersonal success but also with the love of the self.

SCHIZOPHRENIA

Brus and colleagues from the Icahn School of Medicine at Mt. Sinai present a review of evidence base psychotherapies of benefit in the treatment of schizophrenia. Modern psychodynamic theory and practice can be useful in treating many patients with schizophrenia despite the fact that the etiology of the schizophrenic syndrome itself is clearly predominately bio-psychological. Psychoeducation and behavior therapy seem helpful when combined with milieu therapy or when administered to patients living in structured supportive environments. Adjunctive cognitive behavior therapy has been shown to improve symptoms and insight in patients receiving adequate pharmacotherapy. Cognitive enhancement therapy targeting initiative, spontaneity, flexibility, perspective taking and context appraisal helps patients improve socialization and reduce negative symptoms. Psychodynamic psychotherapy helps strengthen ego fragility, improve reality testing and synthesizing functions. Viewing psychotic symptoms as meaningful while maintaining composure and validating vulnerability to sensory overload can help promote a therapeutic alliance in patients with schizophrenia. Social disenfranchisement and trauma are recognized as triggers of psychosis in vulnerable persons. The notion of persons with schizophrenia having a biological vulnerability to decompensation when faced with intolerable affectivity is also a helpful psychodynamic construct to guide individual and family therapy interventions.

SOMATIC SYMPTOM DISORDERS

Kaplan, from the University of Cincinnati College of Medicine, reviews the psychodynamics of somatic symptom disorders, which include functional neurologic symptom disorder (conversion disorder), somatization disorder and illness anxiety disorder. In both conversion and somatization early life trauma is an important antecedent and predictor. Current life stressors that symbolically resonate with early trauma often present in conversion. Alexithymia is also linked with the development of somatic symptom disorders. Various genetic factors have been associated with vulnerability to conversion disorder. Functional imaging shows that although clinically conversion does not correspond with neurological deficits, there is an actual dynamic reorganization of the fronto-parietal neuronal circuits that link volition, movement and perception. Lack of fantasy and concrete thinking makes psychotherapy treatment challenging, and helping patients speak the language of emotions is a necessary precondition. While interpretations in conversion are often transformative and curative, with somatization the capacity for symbolization is so compromised that treatment is quite challenging. However, helping the patient shift focus away from tedious descriptions of complex and intractable physical symptoms and having them describe relationships with others may be beneficial for symptomatic reduction, even in the absence of insight.

SUBSTANCE RELATED AND ADDICTIVE DISORDERS

McKernan and colleagues, in a collaborative effort between Vanderbilt University School of Medicine, Yale University School of Medicine, University of Tennessee, John Jay College of Criminal Justice, and Cornerstone of Recovery Addiction Treatment Center, designed a study to test the specificity of Khantzian's self-medication psychodynamic hypothesis of addiction. Khantzian postulated that addiction to substances is a *defensive attempt to soothe distressing affects* and that there is *specificity* in a person's choice of drugs. Those who gravitate towards alcohol and benzodiazepines use defenses of repression and isolation of affect, in particular anger, and are emotionally inhibited. Alcohol and other depressants cause emotional disinhibition and at low doses have euphoriant properties. Opioid users have difficulty managing aggression, have history of early life traumatic experiences and use externalizing defenses. Heroin and prescription opioids have anesthetic effects that ease distress caused by terrifying traumatic memories. Those who use stimulants as their drug of choice are anhedonic, fearful and emotionally disinhibited. Cocaine provides excitation to counter listlessness, emptiness and anhedonia. Stimulants also have organizing effects that can be therapeutic if there is comorbid attention deficit.

Other important dynamics of addiction, besides affective dysregulation, include inability to draw logical cause/consequence relationships and avoidance of self-care. Insecure attachments from child abuse and neglect have also been associated with dysregulation of the ventral striatal reward pathways, with increased novelty seeking later in adult life. Although Mckernan's study sample (Southeastern USA demographics, primarily Caucasian and affluent) was not sufficiently diverse, when their findings are combined with those of other investigators, such as the results of the Suh and colleagues study in New York City (primarily disenfranchised African Americans and Latinos), most elements of Khantzian's self-medication hypothesis are proven correct.

TRAUMA AND STRESSOR RELATED DISORDERS

Hendin, from Suicide Prevention Initiatives and New York Medical College, describes the psychodynamics of suicide in combat veterans with posttraumatic stress disorder from the Vietnam War and soldiers with multiple deployments in Iraq and Afghanistan. He draws on the work of Durkheim who in the 19th century identified that suicide rates in soldiers was higher than in civilians, and Kardiner and Spiegel's description of treatments with patients with traumatic war neuroses. More recent clinical observations and research findings identify persistent severe guilt over combat experiences as increasing suicide risk. Suicidal veterans often recall dreams that reflect guilt and punishment. Affective states that correlate with suicide in PTSD include anxiety, rage, desperation, loneliness, hopelessness, shame and humiliation. Hendin states "guilt is an emotion that can be harmful when it is self-punitive, but it can be a powerful force for changing the direction of one's life", implying that in psychotherapeutic work with a veteran forgiving oneself is essential in order to effectively release negative affectivity. He piloted a 12-session brief psychodynamic therapy intervention training psychiatrists in the Bronx and Manhattan VA hospitals, with the aim of reducing PTSD symptoms and suicidality by exploring the meaning of combat to the veteran, processing traumatic memories to decrease hyperarousal, and relieving guilt and other overwhelming negative affective states.

Katz and colleagues, from the University of Kentucky and New River Valley Community Services in Virginia, propose that psychodynamic psychiatrists should incorporate the concept of allostatic load in their formulations, in particular to understand the relationship between traumatic life events and negative health outcomes. *Allostasis* is defined as maintaining homeostasis through changes in the environment over time. Dysregulation of allostasis, referred to as *allostatic load* or allostatic overload, represents the physiological erosion caused by stressors on the brain circuitry involved in the stress response, or the multisystem response to stress.

Chronic stressors result in detrimental physiological alterations. These include neuronal loss in the hippocampus, development of atherosclerotic plaques, left ventricular hypertrophy, increased oxidative stress, and a prolonged inflammatory response. Measurable parameters of allostatic overload include obtaining levels of biomarkers such as catecholamines, cortisol, dehydroepian-drosterone, aldosterone, interleukin-6, tumor necrosis factor-alpha, c-reactive protein, insulin-like growth factor-1, HDL, LDL, total cholesterol, glycosylated hemoglobin, creatinine, variations in blood pressure and heart rate measurements, waist to hip ratio and body mass index. Currently these biomarkers are being studied in different combinations to create reasonable algorithms and testing guidelines amounting to an allostatic load composite score that could be followed up over time. The allostatic load composite score may possibly provide an assessment of inflammatory, neuroendocrine and immune function when faced with adversity. Examining how the composite score changes over time, as stress could lead to physical dysregulation, morbidity from illness and premature death may help optimize psychosocial interventions that are health protective.

Anxiety Disorders

Unmentalized Aspects of Panic and Anxiety Disorders

Fredric N. Busch and Larry S. Sandberg

Abstract: Somatic or emotional experience that has not been symbolically represented, referred to as unmentalized experience, has been given an increasingly prominent role in understanding psychopathology. Panic and anxiety disorders provide a useful model for exploring these factors, as the affective and bodily symptoms can be understood in part as unmentalized experience. The authors explore models of Freud's actual neurosis, Marty and DeM'uzan's pensee operatoire, Klein's unconscious fantasy, Bion's alpha function, Bucci's multiple code system, and relational models to describe how somatic and affective experiences can be translated into symbolic representations, and what factors can interfere with these processes. Approaches to unmentalized aspects of panic and anxiety include symbolizing somatic symptoms, identifying emotional states, and identifying contextual and traumatic links to symptoms.

Increasingly, "unmentalized" experience, somatic or emotional experience that is not symbolically represented, is seen as playing an important role in psychopathology. This concept has been usefully linked to Freud's description of "actual neurosis" (1895), Klein's concept of primary unconscious fantasy (1932), and Bion's (1962) notion of unmetabolized beta elements. Bucci (1997a, 1997b) has provided a three-tier "multiple code" system for differentiating a nonverbal nonsymbolic level from verbal and nonverbal symbolic levels that suggests how somatic emotional states can be linked with representational systems. This concept has been suggested as a bridge between neurophysiology, somatic and affective states, and psychoanalytic concepts (Waller & Scheidt, 2006). Nevertheless, the basis for identifying and addressing these unmentalized components, and differentiating them from unconscious symbolized intrapsychic content, remains less clear.

Panic and anxiety disorders provide a useful model for exploring these links, as they have been conceptualized as deriving from physiologically based maladaptive alarm systems, unconscious intrapsychic conflicts, and more recently, unmentalized experience. Our group has proposed a model emphasizing unconscious fantasies and conflicts surrounding loss and separation, dependency and anger (Busch, Cooper, Klerman, Shapiro, & Shear, 1991; Busch, Milrod, Singer, & Aronson, 2012; Milrod, Busch, Cooper, & Shapiro, 1997; Shear, Cooper, Klerman, Busch, & Shapiro, 1993). In this model, patients attempt to cope unconsciously with these conflicts and associated affects via the defenses of somatization, denial, repression, undoing, and reaction formation (Busch et al., 2012; Busch, Shear, Cooper, Shapiro, & Leon, 1995). Panic symptoms, including somatic aspects of panic, can represent a defensive avoidance of these fantasies, symbolic representations of these conflicts in symptomatic or bodily form, or potential emergence of these fantasies and affects into consciousness, which are experienced as threatening significant attachments.

As opposed to the notion of repressed conflict as a primary cause of symptoms, several psychoanalytic theorists (Bion, 1962; Bucci, 1997a, 1997b; Freud, 1895; Verhaeghe, Vanheule, & De Rick, 2007) have developed the theory that symptoms in general, and severe anxiety, panic, and somatic symptoms in particular, can emerge from instinctual excitations or affects not effectively modulated by psychic representations. These models include Freud's concept of actual neurosis, including anxiety neurosis, as stemming from a psychic insufficiency (1895), further described as representational deficits by the French theorists de M'Uzan (1977) and Marty (Marty & de M'Uzan, 1978); Bion's (1962) model of symptoms deriving from a defective alpha function leading to an excess of unmetabolized beta elements, elaborated by Ferro (1996) and others in relation to panic disorder; Bucci's (1997a, 1997b) multiple code system that identifies potential disruptions between subsymbolic and symbolic systems as a source of panic or somatization, and relational models that describe the impact of mirroring deficits on the capacity to modulate and identify affective states (Fonagy, Gergely, Jurist, & Target, 2002). Several authors have implicated trauma as an important source of disruption in representation (Bucci, 1997a; Krystal, 1988; Ogden & Minton, 2000). These authors describe the value of the therapist linking meanings and representations to somatic states or affects, allowing the patient to transform, elaborate, and integrate these excitations into images, thoughts, or signal affects that can be employed psychologically and psychotherapeutically.

The relationship between the regulation and identification of affects and somatic and anxiety symptoms has been of interest to both psychodynamic theorists and investigators in other fields (Waller & Scheidt, 2006). Much of the focus has been on the concept of alexithymia (Nemiah, 1977; Nemiah & Sifneos, 1970), problems in the conscious experience and identification of affects, which is believed to heighten the potential for somatization and other symptoms. Other theorists identify trauma as the source of poorly represented sensorimotor states that disrupt cognitive and emotional processing (Ogden & Minton, 2000). Like the psychoanalysts discussed above, these theorists believe that deficits in the capacity to symbolically represent or cognitively understand affects can intensify emotional distress and lead to a focus on and misinterpretation of the bodily sensations accompanying emotional arousal, or an increased tendency for intense emotions to be expressed in action.

Employing these models, we suggest that there are two broad types of contributors to panic: an unmentalized form in which the contents have not become part of the tripartite structure of the mind, and intrapsychic conflict as classically understood within an ego psychological model. The unmentalized elements include internal somatic and affective states that have not been identified or represented, and dissociative states, often stemming from trauma, in which traumatic experiences are separated from the accompanying affects and somatic states, precluding more classical (i.e., structural) conflict. In these instances, the analyst works to elaborate an emotional state and fantasy or link together dissociated elements, rather than "uncover" the fantasy. In intrapsychic conflict, symbolic and language systems are involved: the ego "disguises" the impulse but it also emerges in the symptom; for example, panic can represent both a defensive avoidance of and punishment for aggression and an expression of disguised aggression through a coercive pressure on others to respond. Thus, panic symptoms may exist on a continuum from "non-metabolized" somatic and affective states to the higher level "symbolic" conflicted fantasies. These unmetabolized and conflicted forms can operate in the same patient, variously contributing to severe anxiety and panic depending on intrapsychic and environmental circumstances.

Useful interventions involve translating affective and somatic states into meaningful psychological elements, including symbolic and verbal representations, along with identification of emotional states. Delineation of the context of symptoms, including environmental and developmental contributors, can help to identify dissociated traumatic experiences that are emerging in somatic, severe anxiety, and panic states. These interventions are of value in building "mentally usable" representations that can be employed to reduce symptomatic states and elaborate unconscious fantasies. We propose that therapeutic interventions have been aimed at developing representations of bodily and emotional states as part of the treatment that we have described, panic-focused psychodynamic psychotherapy (PFPP; Busch et al., 2012; Milrod et al., 1997), but these interventions and their role have been minimized relative to the uncovering of unconscious fantasy and conflict interpretation. We will describe how representational deficits or disruptions can interdigitate in various ways with intrapsychic conflicts in symptom formation. We will identify sources of disruption of representation including affective dysregulation, trauma, inadequate mirroring, and, the models that posit transforming these inchoate internal states into conscious images and/or verbal understanding. We will discuss how unmentalized experience may contribute to somatization, severe anxiety, and panic disorder and describe approaches to symptoms that aid in building representations and linking dissociated elements, elaborat-

ing on the therapeutic value of these interventions.

THEORIES OF REPRESENTATION AND PSYCHOPATHOLOGY, INCLUDING PANIC DISORDER

Instinctual Energy and Psychic Representations

Psychoanalysts have proposed several theories regarding the representation of emotional, somatic, and inchoate states and how disruption of these capacities leads to psychopathology. Freud (1915) described a model for how thought and words might bind instinctual energy, allowing for control over primary process thinking, and the development of a "higher psychical organization."

> [T]he conscious presentation of the object can now be split up into the presentation of the word and the presentation of the thing . . . the unconscious presentation is the presentation of the thing alone. The system Ucs. contains the thing-cathexes of the objects, the first and true object-cathexes; the system Pcs. comes about by this thing-presentation's being hypercathected through being linked with the word-presentations corresponding to it. It is these hypercathexes, we may suppose, that bring about a higher psychical organization and make it possible for the primary process to be succeeded by the secondary process which is dominant in the Pcs. (pp. 201-202)

Freud's concept echoes that of subsequent theorists in providing a model of how instinctual energies or somatic states may be converted into symbolized and verbal forms.

In addition, Freud (1895) developed theories for how psychical insufficiencies might account for the development of neurosis. He contrasted hysteria, in which repressed fantasies account for the failure to bind instinctual energy, to actual neuroses, in which there is an absence of mental content:

> If one goes into the mechanism of the two neuroses, so far as it has been possible to discover it hitherto, aspects come to light which suggest that anxiety neurosis is actually the somatic counterpart to hysteria. In the latter just as in the former there is an accumulation of excitation (which is perhaps the basis for the similarity between their symptoms we have mentioned). In the latter just as in the former we find a *psychical insufficiency, as a consequence of which abnormal somatic processes arise.* In the latter just as in the former, too, instead of a psychical working-over of the excitation, a deflection of it occurs into the somatic field; the difference is merely that in anxiety neurosis the excitation, in whose displacement the neurosis expresses itself, is purely somatic (somatic sexual excitation), whereas in hysteria it is psychical (provoked by conflict). (p. 115)

Several authors have interpreted Freud's description of anxiety neurosis as involving a failure to symbolically represent affective and somatic states (Mitrani, 1995; Solano, 2010; Verhaeghe et al., 2007). Solano (2010), for example, refers to actual neurosis as

> an internal process devoid of symbolic meanings . . . which produces tension without the capacity to reach an understanding, a translation in symbolic terms. Thus, what is proposed is a genesis of symptoms that is substantially different from that seen in hysteria—the latter being a situation in which mental, symbolic representation previously existed and has been repressed. In the case of anxiety neurosis, *mental representation has never existed* and has never taken shape. (pp. 1454-1455)

As has been noted previously, the symptoms of anxiety neurosis overlap with those of panic disorder. Thus, panic-like symptoms were at first understood by Freud in what we now call unmentalized terms. No-

tably, Freud (1895) viewed these symptoms as stemming from sexual excitation, whereas subsequent data and models, included clinical data derived from PFPP studies (Busch et al., 2012) identify anger and separation fears as primary sources of tension.

The French theorists de M'Uzan (1977) and Marty (Marty & de M'Uzan, 1978) expanded on this concept of instinctual excitations and representation, taking into account trauma and developmental factors. They refer to a form of operational thinking (pensee opératoire) in psychosomatic patients, in which there is an inability to fantasize, overlapping with the description of alexithymia. According to these authors, the representational capacity of the mental apparatus to bind excitations from instinctual life can be disrupted by developmental factors (e.g., a depressed caretaker) or trauma, with an inability to prevent economic pressures from overriding issues of meaning (Bouchard & Lecours, 2008). The representational deficit creates a surplus of the quantitative energy, interfering with the capacity to integrate mental contents and transform them into wishes, causing an actual neurosis. Thus, accumulated excitations can disrupt the quality of the representation, or a dearth of meaningful representations can lead to an excess of excitations. The accumulation of instinctual and drive excitations that are devoid of meaning are, in their models, discharged somatically or in action.

Translational Systems

Theorists subsequent to Freud developed what may be called translational models that are involved in converting unmentalized content into words and symbols (Bion, 1962; Bucci, 1997a, 1997b; Verhaeghe et al., 2007). Kleinian theorists have emphasized the existence of unconscious *phanta*sies prior to the development of the capacity for symbolization and verbalization (Klein, 1932; Isaacs, 1948; Mitrani, 1995). Subsequent theorists have recognized that these fantasies can be understood as unmentalized (Mitrani, 1995). Isaacs (1948) states that "The primary phantasies, the representatives of the earliest impulses of desire and aggressiveness, are expressed in and dealt with by mental processes far removed from words and conscious relational thinking, and determined by the logic of emotion" (p. 84), and that "The earliest phantasies, then, spring from bodily impulses and are interwoven with bodily sensations and affects" (p. 86). These primitive phantasies need to be distinguished from the ego psychological model of fantasies which are symbolized and verbalized but repressed. The Kleinian model is of particular interest because of its compatibility with the PFPP model of panic disorder, as it involves core threats surrounding aggression and disruption of attachment.

Bion (1962) suggested a process by which somatic and affective experience could become symbolically represented. In his model, beta elements, including sensory impressions and emotions, are transformed into alpha elements, pictograms, or other sensory patterns which synthesize the relation of self with others. This process occurs through the alpha function. Alpha elements constitute the building blocks of thoughts. Once the thoughts are formed, an apparatus for thinking organizes them. Alpha elements are essential for memories to be formed, and are thus necessary for learning from experience. In addition, they are needed for conscious thinking and reasoning. In this formulation symptoms develop from a deficiency or disruption of the alpha function and/or the apparatus for thinking. Emotions that cannot be metabolized or symbolized via the alpha function emerge in the form of anxiety, bodily symptoms, or impulsive actions. Ferro (1996), employing Bion's (1962) model, describes how in treating panic it is important for the patient to metabolize ". . . the uncontainable emotions of hate, jealousy, and anger . . ." (p. 997), transform them, and make them thinkable. In his formulation panic patients have a de-

ficiency of the alpha function and/or the apparatus of thinking. Panic attacks evacuate emotions that cannot be metabolized or symbolized via the alpha function. He described treatment of a patient with panic in which an apparatus of thinking was gradually introjected, and she was able to convert protoemotions to something thinkable, relieving her panic. The analyst's containing function while in a state of reverie is seen as central in facilitating this process.

Bucci's multiple code system (Bucci, 1997a, 1997b) provides another approach for identifying how emotional and somatic states are translated into consciousness. She describes three levels of the mental apparatus: the subsymbolic (nonverbal nonsymbolic), nonverbal symbolic, and verbal symbolic systems. The subsymbolic system "includes functions we are used to calling *bodily functioning, procedural memory, implicit memory* and *physiological levels of emotion*" (Solano, 2010, p. 1451). The Nonverbal Symbolic System resembles Bion's (1962) alpha function, as it processes visual images that can emerge in dreams and become linked to the verbal system. The Verbal Symbolic System consists of verbal thought and language and involves secondary process functioning. It aids in self-reflection, as well as in identifying and regulating emotion experienced at subsymbolic and nonverbal symbolic levels. According to Multiple Code Theory (Bucci, 1997a, 1997b), referential links allow for the translation of subsymbolic emotion into images and verbal representations. Psychosomatic symptoms or acting out can result from a disconnection between the systems, either secondary to a deficit or through defensive functioning (e.g., somatization). Triggering of a traumatic memory that is not linked to the symbolic system can lead to subsymbolic somatic and arousal patterns that are not symbolically processed, giving rise to psychosomatic symptoms, panic disorder, or phobias (Solano, 2010). However, unlike the models of Klein and Bion (1962), where internal conflicts around aggression are central, Bucci's (1997a, 1997b) focus is primarily on the role of traumatic experience triggering a dissociative response and impaired referential activity.

Relational Models and Deficits in Symbolization

Self psychologists and other relational theorists describe another component of modulation and representation of affective and somatic states, examining the role of the caregiver in mirroring and the internalization of affect modulating capacities. In these models, the caregiver's capacity to accept, respond to, and identify the child's emotional states impacts the child's capacity to differentiate, represent, and regulate affects (Connors, 1994). Patients who have experienced insufficient mirroring have deficits in self-soothing and affect-regulating capacities, and are therefore unable to tolerate intense affects. In self-psychological terms, feelings of fragmentation consistent with panic attacks and aggressive reactions to narcissistic injury can develop from inadequate responsiveness of the selfobject.

Kleinian theorists have also developed models about the significance of deficits stemming from problematic relations with caregivers in the development of symptoms. Bion (1962) refers to the mother's alpha function as necessary for reverie, the mother's capacity to receive and transform the infant's beta elements (raw sensory data) into meaningful thoughts (alpha elements), an aspect of the container function. Mitrani (1995) expands on this notion, noting that a failure of the mother to perform this role can lead to a disruption in the child's development of symbolization and the alpha function. The lack of these capacities leads to the persistence of unmentalized states and the development of somatlization and acting out in response to intense affective states. In contrast to self psychology, for Kleinian theorists, such interactions

are important insofar as they help the infant to deal with her own aggressive drives.

Verhaeghe et al. (2007), view panic disorder as an actual neurosis, stemming from a failure to psychically process endogenous excitation via representations. As opposed to Freud's notion, the deficient representational system is caused by a failure in mirroring. Employing Fonagy and colleagues' mentalization model (Fonagy et al., 2002), Verhaeghe et al. (2007) describe how mirroring can be inadequate due to premature separation from the caregiver or contamination by the caregiver's preoccupations. The capacity to identify, differentiate, and regulate affects is disrupted. These deficits lead to a lack of transition of primary affect to secondary representations, an inability to master bodily arousal, and a failure to develop a second-order representational system of the primary somatic and affective experiences. The lack of recognition of the relationship between symptoms and emotionally significant stressors derives in this model from experiences which have not been symbolically processed. These limitations cause patients to be more prone to panic because they cannot regulate arousal, cannot identify their symptoms as meaningful, and have a limited range of affective states and representations available with which to identify and manage intrapsychic dangers. Panic attacks and agoraphobia include an appeal to significant others in this way.

The Role of Trauma

Many theorists discussed above include trauma as a factor in disrupting representations of somatic and affective states, giving rise to symptoms that include severe anxiety and panic attacks (Bouchard & Lecours, 2008; Bucci 1997a; Krystal, 1988). Traumatic experiences are typically experienced as intrusive, creating feelings of lack of control and intense physiological activation. Traumatic memories, including accompanying physiological activation, frequently become dissociated from painful affects caused by the trauma, and individuals often do not recognize the impact of trauma on their current fears. Memory research on trauma, which has found hippocampal damage and difficulty with explicit recall, is consistent with these other, primarily psychological, explanations for why trauma is poorly represented in verbal systems (Bremner et al., 1997). Trauma can intensify negative affect states and interfere with the identification of unmentalized and dissociated emotions that are experienced as dangerous, damaging, or "bad." Mentalization can be disrupted by trauma or abuse, as it can lead individuals to avoid thinking about their own mental states and the mental states of others (Fonagy et al., 2002). These various factors can preclude the development of symbolized intrapsychic fantasies and conflict. As Bromberg (2006) noted, "a consequence of trauma as it becomes embedded in structural dissociation is to limit and often foreclose the possibility of conflictual experience." We believe that patients with a history of trauma and abuse have a greater degree of dissociated unmentalized elements contributing to their panic attacks.

INTERSUBJECTIVE AND INTERPERSONAL FACTORS

Although theorists have elaborated on the role of relational events in modulating the drives, these will not be a focus of this article. As noted above, theorists of different orientations have emphasized the role played by the caregiver in identifying and regulating affective and somatic states and developing representational capacities. The therapist continues and expands this role via exploration, clarification, and identification of internal states. Effective therapeutic outcomes typically include better communication about affective states between self and others. For example, a reduction in panic pa-

tients' fears of anger and separation, as well as differentiation of present circumstances from the past, aids them in assertive behavior that relieves anger and helps others to be more responsive to them. These interpersonal shifts play a further role in diminishing the intensity of their anger and dependency, easing fears of loss and disruption.

UNMENTALIZED CONTENT AND INTRAPSYCHIC CONFLICTS

The mechanism of symptom development deriving from deficits in representational capacities does not rule out the significant contributions of conflict to symptoms. Repressed symbolized conflicts within a tripartite structure can exist alongside representational deficits. Representational capacities can be disrupted by conflict. In treatment, some conflicts may be accessed by traditional interpretive approaches, others may require the development of representational capacities to access the fantasy, or the formulation of elements and representations may be necessary in order for a fantasy to exist. For instance, in many panic patients anger is accessible and relatively well tolerated in certain situations or mental constellations, whereas in others, often related to painful developmental experiences or trauma, it is not. In the latter instances the path to further psychic representation may be blocked or not present, and the anger may emerge in bodily symptoms or dissociated from a traumatic memory. This anger must be identified before a conflict about potential damage or disruption of relationships can be formulated. Clinical examples of this identification and representation are presented below.

SUMMARIZING THE MODELS OF REPRESENTATIONAL DEFICITS

AND THEIR ROLE IN PANIC DISORDER

The energic and actual neurosis models of Freud (1895), the translational models of Bion (1962) and Bucci (1997a, 1997b), and self psychological and relational models provide an understanding of the vicissitudes that can lead to unmentalized somatic and affective states. Neurophysiological or traumatic vulnerabilities, ego deficits or disruptions, and inadequate mirroring can interfere with the modulation and maturation of these emotional states and their cognitive representations. Neurophysiological vulnerabilities can induce overwhelming affects or cognitive distortions, as found in anxiety disorders or depression. Coping with excessively intense affect states, particularly toward and from caretakers, can lead to dissociation, which make these emotions and their contexts more difficult to identify and manage. Traumatic developmental events further exacerbate emotional intensity and dissociation, leading emotional states to be misidentified as somatic and catastrophic, instead of symbolically represented. Ego deficits can include an absence of skills in identifying emotional states (alexithymia) and recognizing meaningful and contextual aspects of somatic and affective experiences. Other deficits can include a limited capacity to identify the context of emotions and to appropriately express feelings behaviorally.

In line with these models, we believe that panic patients suffer from a lack of an integrated representational system that links affective, somatic, and verbal realms, adding to the vulnerability to panic and severe anxiety onset and persistence. These bodily and emotional experiences are dissociated from meaningful conscious links and the verbal symbolic realm. The sensations and affects need to be psychically represented to provide the capacity to define and regulate them. Developing representational capacities aid in modulating and translating affective and somatic states. The therapist works to further the normal development of somatic and affective regulation and control, providing clarification and mirroring. Developmental and therapeutic goals include the identification, regulation or "taming" of affect intensity and an increasing capacity to use affects as signals of information for oneself and, through behavioral expression, effective interpersonal communication. Translating these elements into representations also aids in the identification and, possibly, development of unconscious fantasy, which can then be approached with defense and transference interpretations (Lafarge, 2000).

The difficulties arising from unmentalized states also provide further theoretical understanding of the role of anger and separation in panic disorder. From the standpoint of Kleinian theory primary unconscious phantasies involving destructive aggression or loss of the object could trigger anxiety in settings in which these phantasies are activated but are not symbolized or verbalized. The object's capacity for containment and reverie is important in reducing anxiety derived from universal and developmentally normal destructive urges. This is in contrast with the self psychological standpoint in which poor mirroring can lead to reactive aggression toward the caregiver (not accompanied by capacities to identify or modulate intense negative emotions that could disrupt the relationship with the caregiver). Dissociated affects from trauma experienced in body memories or unidentified threats arising from unmentalized states render sudden surges of anxiety or somatic states harder to identify and place in context, adding to feelings of loss of control and helplessness.

Consistent with these concepts, neuroimaging studies of patients with panic disorder, as well as other disorders of emotional regulation, indicate that subcortical activation is heightened relative to cortical activation (see Busch, Oquendo, Sullivan, & Sandberg, 2010). On a neurophysiological level somatic and affective elements can be thought of as being generated on a limbic level and becoming more predominantly cortical as they are represented verbally or symbolically. The increased awareness and identification of affects and body states allow the patient to better recruit control mechanisms in the prefrontal cortex to regulate limbic system and affective states. Effective psychotherapeutic treatments of panic have been associated with a reduction in subcortical relative to prefrontal and cortical activity (see Busch et al., 2010). Although these findings are consistent with symbolization of unmentalized content, these shifts might also occur with the interpretation of unconscious conflicted fantasies.

APPROACHES TO DEVELOPING REPRESENTATION IN PANIC DISORDER

Several authors have proposed interventions for helping patients to identify unmentalized somatic and affective states (Bucci, 1997a, 1997b; Jurist, 2005; Lane & Pollermann, 2002; Ogden & Minton, 2000). Lane and Pollermann (2002) suggested that patients need help in identifying the feeling of different emotions, the differences between emotions, contextual triggers of emotions, the factors that intensify and diminish them, mental experiences and actions that can modify the intensity of emotional states, and ways to manage emotions behaviorally (Lane & Pollermann, 2002). Other authors have recommended interventions that focus on educating patients about their emotions, along with fostering emotional experience and helping the patient to develop better emotional skills (Krystal, 1979; Levant, 1998). Ogden and Minton (2000) described a technique of "somatic experiencing," attending to somatic sensations to access warded off dissociated affects and meaningful intrapsychic states. Jurist (2005) focused on the development of mentalized affectivity,

the capacity to reflect on and identify affect states, including their complexity and ambiguity.

Bucci (1997b) suggested a process by which somatic symptoms can be translated from subsymbolic to symbolic representations. Psychoanalytic treatment activates emotion schema at subsymbolic levels, often as a mood or somatic state dissociated from the object (Bucci, 1997a). Memories and images emerge, representing a shift from subsymbolic to symbolic forms, which are then verbalized and linked to the somatic states. The process continues in a third phase of reflection and verbal elaboration, in which logical processes and the relationship with the therapist aid in the introduction of new elements into the emotional schemas, allowing for a revision of these schemas.

For Bion (1962), the analyst's reverie in the setting of containing the patient's primitive beta elements is seen as pivotal in the evolution of increased symbolic capacities. Cassorla (2013), a contemporary Bionian, observes how enactments—both chronic and acute—are part of this process. While coming from a different theoretical perspective, Bromberg (2006) and other relational analysts highlight how dissociated aspects of the patient's mental life become evident in the psychotherapeutic field through enactments.

In PFPP, the translation of unmentalized affective, bodily, and experiential data occurs via identifying emotional states, verbalizing meanings of panic and somatic symptoms, and providing context in the form of traumatic, developmental, and environmental links. Identification and representation of these states via symbolic thinking and language, processed by the therapist and patient, can aid patients in regulating emotions and formulating intrapsychic conflicts. Individuals vary in the particular types of sensations and affects for which they experience processing deficits. In addition, they will have repressed unconscious fantasies relevant to panic alongside deficits in representation. Although psychotherapeutic interventions aimed at developing representations tend to occur earlier in treatment than conflict interpretation, these approaches often occur contiguously.

How do we translate emotional states and somatic symptoms into something thinkable to help patients manage panic and somatic symptoms? The therapist works to shift bodily experiences, somatic sensations, and affective states into symbolic and verbal representations. Additionally, the therapist demonstrates how to translate emotions and somatic states, in a sense using the alpha function, and helps the patient to develop these skills. Interventions include identification of the meaning of somatic symptoms, the emotional states associated with panic attacks and somatic preoccupations, and the context (current and past) of anxiety symptoms. The delineation of context can help to identify and address traumatic experiences that lead to dissociation and "not thinking" (Rudden, Milrod, Aronson, & Target, 2008) as part of their sequelae. The therapist can help the patient elaborate self-object representations, along with fantasies, that are particularly frightening. These approaches aid in relieving panic by making symptoms and affects symbolized and representational. Although the various interventions will be discussed separately, it is clear that in many instances each of them is involved in the therapist's approach. Although comorbidity is common, if not typical, for patients with panic disorder, for the sake of clarity we will focus on panic symptoms in the following vignettes.

SYMBOLIZING SOMATIC STATES

Panic patients are typically unable to identify bodily experiences and symptoms as representations or symbols of affective states. The threat is experienced as if it is occurring in the body rather than the mind, and as if it is a catastrophic danger to the body.

This subjective experience indicates a deficit in symbolizing, a subsymbolic state that has not been represented. The therapist works to translate somatic symptoms into mentalized symbolic and verbal content. This can occur partly through working with associations to bodily states or through linking traumatic dissociated states that have been incorporated as somatic body memories. In PFPP the approach includes having the patient associate to particular body symptoms to identify specific meanings.

The following case provides an example of a somatic symptom related to dissociation from traumatic experiences. Ms. F, who developed panic attacks in the context of conflicts with her boss, described an experience of her heart pounding in her chest during her attacks. In one session the patient pounded her fist into her other hand to describe the sensation. The therapist asked her what came to mind about this behavior. Ms. F associated to her father's temper, which included hitting her. The palpitations were identified as the dissociated remnants of her experience of fear/terror of being abused; that is, autonomic arousal. Pounding her fist was a dissociated and embodied expression of having been punched by her father. The therapist and patient worked to elaborate a fantasy and a conflict: she felt endangered by her critical boss, as she felt with her father, and feared that her anger at the boss-abuser may be dangerous. Asking her to associate to her tachycardia brought to mind a "beating heart" which, in the context of the treatment relationship, she could think about contextually and elaborate the "beatings" she received as a child. The unthinkable was being transformed into something that could be thought about and reflected upon. Elaborating this link was critical to the resolution of her symptoms.

IDENTIFYING EMOTIONAL STATES

In terms of affective states, panic patients have a particular difficulty identifying, verbalizing, and representing certain affects, although this capacity can vary depending on the context. The experience of certain emotions, including anger, dependent feelings, and separation fears, as dangerous is relevant to this difficulty, but identification of these feelings is necessary to identify the danger. In fact, understanding that emotions can trigger anxiety can be seen as part of the process of representing affects. The capacity to identify emotions also impacts patients' abilities to appropriately express feelings to others, an important step in interpersonal changes that help to reduce panic vulnerability. The therapist aids in identification of these emotions, allowing patients to work on safety and tolerance of affects. Therapist and patient also work on development of the alpha function, the capacity to identify and translate feelings and fears into conscious experience, including unmetabolized psyche/soma/affective experience into thoughts that can be thought by the thinker. Interventions defining emotions can also be viewed as developing mentalized affectivity (Jurist, 2005), including the capacity to identify affective states. Panic can be understood as a core basic signal not clearly defined or mentalized. Elaboration of affect includes identification of meaning of panic, converting it to an anxiety signal that does not overwhelm the cognitive system.

For instance, Ms. G reported the sensation of panic symptoms in the context of a session. The therapist asked her to describe what was going on within her body. In addition to palpitations and tremor the patient described a feeling of being "hot," "on fire," "like a volcano." "I get tingling . . . I get numbness . . . I get short of breath. I can feel my heart beating very quickly. I start to get really hot. . . . It would get worse and feel like a volcano in my head was going to explode because she [her mother] never stopped."

As this was explored in therapy it was understood to reflect a poorly differentiated affective somatic state. Over time the therapist and patient explored the patient's difficulty identifying her own anger, which was experienced as either helpless or potentially dangerous and damaging like her mother's. Volcanic became a useful term for identifying her mother's anger that terrified her while volcanic anger of her own variably felt either "impotent" or "volcanic" and deadly. Ms. G described her new view as understanding that there were many types of anger, rather than in her own home, in which there was either explosive anger or no anger. Once the anger was recognized, therapist and patient could explore her identification with the aggressor as a way of understanding why she was so frightened of causing damage with her anger.

The following case demonstrates how somatic experiences can be used to refine the identification and representation of emotional states.

Ms. D noted the onset of panic symptoms when she became frustrated with regard to technology, for instance after the disruption of formatting that occurred after changing a file so her husband could read it. She reported being angry at her husband for not being able to work with her format, but angry at herself for not being able to fix the problem. When asked to describe what she was feeling she focused on a knot in her stomach and shaking. She then said it was like feeling tortured. She was frustrated that the computer technician that was supposed to help her was not doing so, as her old technician used to just fix the problem. This one would make suggestions for her to try, but this would add to her anxiety. She would have a brief thought "Why don't you just do it?" but was mostly anxious, fearful that she would not be helped.

When asked what came to mind about being tortured, Ms. D described a sense of constant criticism of herself as a child, that she was told she was stupid, no one liked her, and why couldn't she be more like her brother. These comments made no sense to her, as she was a good student, and in fact her brother had serious problems. He was impulsive, threatening, and a poor student. The patient felt tortured by him as well, and her parents were unable to control him. He had a charming side, which contributed to her mother asking her to be more like him. The experience of feeling tortured was related to her not being able to get the help that she needed, and feeling helpless to cope with the situation. Ms. D developed a sense of hypercompetence to manage these feelings, but the threat of being back in the passive tortured state re-emerged whenever she felt incompetent. At that point she also believed that she had to manage things on her own as she could not possibly get help, as no help was forthcoming when she was a child. Clarifying her sense of feeling overwhelmed, helpless, tortured, and angry allowed her to better avail herself of help at these points. Her anxious bodily symptoms significantly diminished.

IDENTIFICATION OF CONTEXT

The PFPP therapist works with the patient to identify circumstances surrounding panic onset and persistence, including contextual and meaningful cues. Context includes current stressors and emotions, as well as developmental and traumatic origins. These interventions aid in developing psychic representations by providing meaning and context to the panic attacks. Although we include amongst these interventions more traditional genetic interpretations, we are focusing on aspects of these interventions separate from interpretation of unconscious fantasies, although these interventions can aid in addressing intrapsychic conflict. For instance patients may become aware that they experience panic attacks when they are actually angry at someone, and then identify that anger

became frightening to them based on past, possibly traumatic, experiences. These steps allow them to begin to identify unconscious angry wishes and fantasies that are sources of conflict. Being able to identify a previously dissociated link to developmental or traumatic origins provides the opportunity to "unlearn" how the panic is connected to environmental cues, traumatic origins, and intrapsychic fantasies. That is, patients can learn that their fears are more appropriate to past than current contexts.

As the therapist explored Mr. E's "out of the blue" panic attacks, it emerged that they occurred in the context of talking with customers he experienced as "bullying." This contextual representation allowed for links of his panic symptoms to past experience, which included Mr. E's struggle with bullying by his father over the course of his development. He had generalized his experience of his father to others who behaved aggressively toward him. However, the link to these past experiences was dissociated from his current experience of panic. Identifying his frightening feelings and the link to past events in these contexts was part of the groundwork that opened up exploration of his anxiety in relation to his anger, and he later recognized angry feelings emerging in these bullying situations. This data aided in the development of representation of the bodily symptoms by providing meaning and context to the panic attacks. Following these representations, the therapist and Mr. E were able to identify intrapsychic conflicts, including his own wish to bully others to be in control like his father, at the same time fearing being responded to with rejection and withdrawal, based in part on his father's reaction to his assertiveness. His anger unconsciously needed to be dissociated, denied, or taken back to relieve this threat. He would become unassertive and accepting of others' problematic behavior to reduce this risk, repressing the frustration that it created. In addition to building representations of his panic and the identification of intrapsychic conflict, this work helped Mr. E to delink the dangers associated with his past experiences, frightening feelings, and somatic symptoms, diminishing his panic and allowing appropriately assertive behavior.

CONCLUSION

Although PFPP has emphasized the central role of intrapsychic conflict in psychodynamic treatment of panic disorder, the treatment approach has included exploring the context of panic onset, identifying emotional states surrounding panic, and looking at the meaning of panic symptoms. Although seen as preliminary to conflict interpretation, these interventions likely helped to provide verbal and somatic representations of somatic and affective experiences. This lack of capacity in representation likely contributes to vulnerability to panic disorder and these interventions in and of themselves likely aid in reduction of panic attacks. In addition, the therapist is helping patients to develop this capacity, or what can be seen as the alpha function, to translate internal data on their own.

With these interventions, the therapist aids in developing the building blocks to help fantasies to come into being. Alternatively, it can be argued that the unconscious fantasy is already present at some level unconsciously and these approaches help to better identify it (Isaacs, 1948). In either case both types of interventions are important in addressing panic persistence and vulnerability to recurrence. In a sense these mental building blocks work to "bind" energy or modulate affects in ways that work to reduce panic. While the focus in this article has been on panic attacks, these ideas are meant to apply to a broad range of mental states, especially when somatic symptoms are present.

REFERENCES

Bion, W. R. (1962). *Learning from experience.* New York: Aronson.

Bouchard, M. A., & Lecours, S. (2008). Contemporary approaches to mentalization in the light of Freud's Project. In F. N. Busch (Ed.), *Mentalization: Theoretical considerations, research findings, and clinical implications* (pp. 103-129). New York: Taylor & Francis.

Bremner, J. D., Randall, P., Vermetten, E., Staib, L., Bronen, R., Mazure, C., et al. (1997). Magnetic resonance imaging-based measurement of hippocampal volume in posttraumatic stress disorder related to childhood physical and sexual abuse—A preliminary report. *Biological Psychiatry, 41,* 23-32.

Bromberg, P. M. (2006). *Awakening the dreamer: Clinical journeys.* New York: Routledge.

Bucci, W. (1997a). Discourse patterns in "good" and troubled hours: A multiple code interpretation. *Journal of the American Psychoanalytic Association, 45*(1), 155-187.

Bucci, W. (1997b). Symptoms and symbols: A multiple code theory of somatization. *Psychoanalytic Inquiry, 17,* 151-172.

Busch, F. N., Cooper, A. M., Klerman, G. L., Shapiro, T., & Shear, M. K. (1991). Neurophysiological, cognitive-behavioral and psychoanalytic approaches to panic disorder: Toward an integration. *Psychoanalytic Inquiry, 11,* 316-332.

Busch, F. N., Milrod, B. L., Singer, M., & Aronson, A. (2012). *Panic-focused psychodynamic psychotherapy, extended range.* New York: Routledge.

Busch, F. N., Oquendo, M. A., Sullivan, G. M., & Sandberg, L. S. (2010). An integrative model of panic disorder. *Neuropsychoanalysis, 12,* 67-79.

Busch, F. N., Shear, M. K., Cooper, A. M., Shapiro, T., & Leon, A. (1995). An empirical study of defense mechanisms in panic disorder. *Journal of Nervous and Mental Disease, 183,* 299-303.

Cassorla, R. M. (2013). When the analyst becomes stupid: An attempt to understand enactment using Bion's theory of thinking. *Psychoanalytic Quarterly, 82*(2), 323-360.

Connors, M. E. (1994). Symptom formation: An integrative self psychological perspective. *Psychoanalytic Psychology, 11,* 509-523.

de M'Uzan, M. (1973). A case of masochistic perversion and an outline of a theory. *International Journal of Psychoanalysis, 54*(4), 455-467.

de M'Uzan, M. (1977). The psychology of psychosomatic patients. *Psyche-Z Psychoanalysis, 31*, 318-332.

Ferro, A. (1996). Carla's panic attacks: Insight and transformation. What comes out of the "cracks"—Monsters or nascent thoughts? *International Journal of Psychoanalysis, 77*, 997-1011.

Fonagy, P., Gergely, G., Jurist, E., & Target, M. (2002). *Affect regulation, mentalization, and the development of the self*. New York: Other Books.

Freud, S. (1895). On the grounds for detaching a particular syndrome from neurasthenia under the description "anxiety neurosis." In J. Strachey (Ed. & Trans.), *The standard edition of the complete psychological works of Sigmund Freud* (Vol. 3). London: Hogarth Press.

Freud, S. (1915). The unconscious: On the history of the psycho-analytic movement, papers on metapsychology and other works. In J. Strachey (Ed. & Trans.), *The standard edition of the complete psychological works of Sigmund Freud* (Vol. XIV, pp. 159-215). London: Hogarth Press.

Isaacs, S. (1948). The nature and function of phantasy. *International Journal of Psycho-Analysis, 29*, 73-97.

Jurist, E. L. (2005). Mentalized affectivity. *Psychoanalytic Psychology, 22*(3), 426-444.

Klein, M. (1932). *The psycho-analysis of children*. New York: Norton.

Krystal, H. (1979). Alexithymia and psychotherapy. *American Journal of Psychotherapy, 33*, 17-31

Krystal, H. (1988). *Integration and self-healing: Affect, trauma, alexithymia*. Hillsdale, NJ: Analytic.

Lafarge, L. (2000). Interpretation and containment. *International Journal of Psychoanalysis, 81*(1), 67-84.

Lane, R. D., & Pollermann, B. Z. (2002). Complexity of emotion representations. In L. F. Barrett & P. Salovey (Eds.), *The wisdom in feeling: Psychological processes in emotional intelligence* (pp. 271-293). New York: Guilford.

Lane, R. D., & Schwartz, G. E. (1987). Levels of emotional awareness: A cognitive-developmental theory and its application to psychopathology. *American Journal of Psychiatry, 144*(2), 133-143.

Levant, R. F. (1998). Desperately seeking language: Understanding, assessing, and treating normative male alexithymia. In W. S. Pollack & R. F. Levant (Eds.), *New psychotherapy for men* (pp. 35-56). New York: John Wiley & Sons.

Marty, P. (1968). A major process of somatization: The progressive disorganization. *International Journal of Psychoanalysis, 49*(2), 246-249.

Marty, P., & de M'Uzan, M. (1978). The operational thinking ("Pensee opératoire"). *Psyche-Z Psychoanalysis, 32*, 974-984.

Milrod, B. L., Busch, F. N., Cooper, A. M., & Shapiro, T. (1997). *Manual of panic-focused psychodynamic psychotherapy*. Washington, DC: American Psychiatric Press.

Mitrani, J. L. (1995). Toward an understanding of unmentalized experience. *Psychoanalytic Quarterly, 64*, 68-112.

Nemiah, J. C. (1977). Alexithymia: Theoretical considerations. *Psychotherapy and Psychosomatics, 28*, 199-206.

Nemiah, J. C., & Sifneos, P. E. (1970). Affect and fantasy in patients with psychosomatic disorders. In O. W. Hill (Ed.), *Modern trends in psychosomatic medicine*, Vol. 2 (pp. 26-35). London: Butterworth.

Ogden, P., & Minton, K. (2000). Sensorimotor psychotherapy: One method for processing traumatic memory. *Traumatology, 6*(3), Article 3.

Rudden, M. G., Milrod, B., Aronson, A., & Target, M. (2008). Reflective functioning in panic disorder patients: Clinical observation and research design. In F. N. Busch (Ed.), *Mentalization: Theoretical considerations, research findings, and clinical implications* (pp. 185-205). New York: Taylor & Francis.

Shear, M. K., Cooper, A. M., Klerman, G. L., Busch, F. N., & Shapiro, T. (1993). A psychodynamic model of panic disorder. *American Journal of Psychiatry, 150*, 859-866.

Solano, L. (2010). Some thoughts between body and mind in the light of Wilma Bucci's multiple code theory. *International Journal of Psychoanalysis, 91*, 1445-1464.

Taylor, G. J. (1984). Alexithymia: Concept, measurement, and implications for treatment. *American Journal of Psychiatry, 141*, 725-732.

Verhaeghe, P., Vanheule, S., & De Rick, A. (2007). Actual neurosis as the underlying psychic structure of panic disorder, somatization, and somatoform disorder: An integration of Freudian and attachment perspectives. *Psychoanalytic Quarterly, 76*, 1317-1350.

Waller, E., & Scheidt, C. E. (2006). Somatoform disorders as disorders of affect regulation: A development perspective. *International Review of Psychiatry, 18*(1), 13-24.

Behind the Mask: A Psychodynamic Exploration of the Experiences of Individuals Diagnosed with Social Anxiety Disorder

Beth McEvoy, John O'Connor, and Odhran McCarthy

Abstract: The diagnostic category of social anxiety disorder (SAD) is one that is widely drawn upon in mental health settings; SAD is primarily characterized by a marked fear of social performance situations and possible scrutiny by other people (American Psychiatric Association [APA], 1994, 2013). The current study aims to explore the experiences of people diagnosed with SAD. Psychoanalytically informed research interviews, drawing on psychoanalytic ideas around the parameters of engagement and levels of engagement and analysis, were carried out with 4 male and 2 female participants with diagnoses of SAD. Four themes emerged strongly, reflecting the content and process of interviews: "A Critical Voice," "A Passive Presence," "Failure to Launch," and "Behind the Mask." These emerging themes and the overall findings are conceptualized through a Winnicottian lens, emphasising the role of the good-enough mother and facilitating environment in the struggle of participants to achieve an experience of individuation as well as authenticity with others. Theoretical, clinical, and research implications are discussed, including the need for clinicians to consider the role of early parent–child dynamics and the overall home environment and what these have left in the here and now for people presenting in this way, particularly in the way services are used and the therapeutic relationship develops. Further research into underlying dynamic issues in the origins and maintenance of social anxiety is proposed.

Social anxiety disorder (SAD) is characterized by a marked and persistent fear of social situations, and affected individuals worry that they will be negatively appraised or that they will act in a shameful or humiliating way (American Psychiatric Association [APA], 2013). Accounts of symptoms similar to the current conceptualization of SAD date back to Hippocrates in 400 B.C. who described very insecure, fearful, and inhibited individuals (Osório, Crippa, & Loureiro, 2010). Once viewed as a "neglected disorder" (Liebowitz, Gorman, Fyer, & Klein, 1985), SAD is now understood to be a highly prevalent disorder (Kessler, 2003) associ-

ated with significant impairments in social, psychological, and occupational functioning (Smits, Powers, Buxkamper, & Telch, 2006). The criteria for social anxiety disorder (SAD) has evolved over the various editions of the *Diagnostic and Statistical Manual of Mental Disorders (DSM)*; the condition known as social phobia in *DSM-IV* (APA, 1994) has been renamed social anxiety disorder in the fifth edition of the *DSM* (APA, 2013). This change reflects a broader understanding of the condition in a variety of social situations. SAD is the third most common psychological disorder with a lifetime prevalence of between 3% and 13% in North America (Kessler et al., 2005). There is a significant degree of comorbidity between SAD and other mental health problems; epidemiological studies estimate about 80% of people with SAD also experience a comorbid psychiatric condition, most commonly other anxiety disorders and depression (Farmer, Gros, McCabe, & Antony, 2014).

Receiving a diagnosis of SAD remains a contentious issue, with some researchers proposing a dimensional approach to the classification of SAD within a continuum of symptom severity, the degree of avoidance and level of suffering and impairment, rather than as an arbitrary category (Hetem et al., 2010). The causes of SAD are not well understood (Rapee & Spence, 2004), however there are a number of different theoretical models that highlight possible mechanisms, commonly grouped into the following categories: (1) evolutionary and genetic theories (Baumeister & Tice, 1990; Gilbert & Trower, 2001), (2) behavioral (Bandura, 1977; Rachman, 1977) and cognitive theories (Beck, Emery, & Greenberg, 1985; Clark & Wells, 1995; Hofmann, 2007; Rapee & Heimberg, 1997), (3) interpersonal theories (Leary, 2001; Schlenker & Leary, 1982), and (4) the lesser studied psychodynamic theories (e.g., Leichsenring et al., 2009). Social anxiety as a distinct concept is rarely directly addressed in psychoanalytic literature, despite the fact that anxiety, in general, is pervasive in psychoanalytic writings and is seen as a central issue in all psychological life. There is no comprehensive psychoanalytic theory of SAD; the apparent vacuum of research from this perspective serves as a catalyst for the completion of a research study from a psychoanalytic viewpoint.

While the above represents an abstraction of the current conceptualization of an experience that is now diagnosed as SAD, there is value in wider thinking on the subject, away from a more diagnostic viewpoint and toward more fundamental perspectives. Representative of the universality of social anxiety is Sartre's (1946) famous line "hell is other people," which represents a reality of suffering that is ubiquitous in humankind and one that is social by its very nature. Our experience of the presence of other people, what they arouse in us, what they leave with and in us, has been one of the most enduring subjects of our human psychologies. Freud altered the mode of consultation from chair-to-chair to chair-to-couch due, in part, to the intensity that face-to-face interaction over an extended period brings (Grotstein, 1995). Our social consciousness is developed from early in our lives; in the idea—present in Kleinian, post-Kleinian, Winnicottian, and other object relations theories—that the ego is present from birth or, more likely given what we know of differential responsiveness in the womb, prenatally. There is a kind of underlying apprehension of otherness and thus a potential for other-as-threat from the earliest points in our psychological lives. While it has not engaged specifically with the idea of SAD in any real way, psychoanalysis in its various perspectives from the Freudian to the Kleinian, Winniccotian, British Independent, Relational, and Lacanian traditions, has provided a vivid account of the tension within our human experience between a process of connecting in with others and a tendency to pull back and into ourselves. This process has received the widest confirmation in the idea of early secure and insecure attachments concretizing, to an extent, in the second year of life and forming the basis for later relations (Ainsworth, 1979; Bowlby, 1977). There is room for a level of caution around the very existence of the diagnostic category of SAD as it suggests the presence of something particular and set apart, which in actuality may relate to a simple variant or set of points within a normal process of relating to others. At the same time, it might help to draw attention to the reality that, for some people the typical day-to-day struggle of social relationships is exceeded and a kind of paralysis in relations develops. The word anxiety can appear mild in this context when we are describing a terror relating to other people;

here the line between paranoia, obsessional thought, and social anxiety can seem very thin. It is important to consider such a diagnostic category (SAD) to acknowledge the level of interference that this anxiety can bring, particularly concerning the associated retreat from relating or handling of relations. Taken from one angle, the fear of scrutiny by others appears to be a legitimate concern in a socially complex and demanding society; yet, an extreme version of this has become classified as the increasingly prevalent diagnosis of SAD.

When viewed through a psychoanalytic lens, SAD may be seen to span a number of different themes and encompass intrinsic unconscious fears. From early on, the role of "seeing and being seen" has been emphasized in psychoanalytic writings, be it as an expression of infantile sexual curiosity (Freud, 1905) or as a derivative of the super-ego and its heritage of the Oedipus complex (Weiss, 2015). Erikson (1950) traces the ego's progressive integration of the social world and the psychosexual experience of the individual. He describes personality development as a hierarchically ordered sequence of stages which "progress from initial narcissistic involvement with oneself, through stages of identification and socialization, to increasing individuation and establishment of an individual identity" (Franz & White, 1985, p. 224). It has been argued that the early onset of social anxiety is implicated in the failure of individuals to successfully achieve Erikson's developmental milestones (Baker-Smith & Moore, 2001). In the object relations and relational traditions of post-Freudian psychoanalysis, an idea emerges that the self develops through the mirroring presence of others— in what we experience with others, what we take in from others and our relations to and with them; through our experiencing of the mirroring other, we, in turn, become aware of ourselves. The nature of what is mirrored back to us (partly a projection of the other's internal world) is very important here; most

pointedly, this provides a basis for feelings of pride and a sense of shame.

In a rare reference to psychodynamic processes in SAD, Leichsenring et al. (2009) argued that the symptoms of social anxiety arise from unconscious core relationship conflicts rooted in early childhood experiences. It has often been in an account of what takes place in the therapeutic relationship that psychoanalysis has contributed its most vivid accounts of the power of anxiety and related states. Bion, in his 1979 paper, "Making the Best of a Bad Lot," commented on the emotional storm that takes place when therapist and client meet; there is a sense too that, in all interactions, the potential for such a storm exists, charged by the various internal processes of the two parties, the paranoiac pieces of our personalities projected onto and into one another. As social anxiety concerns the apprehension of threat involved in interaction with others, it is likely that this anxiety may manifest during the interview process, with the interviewer representing the "other" and the social world; the unconscious dynamics can be interpreted by the researcher providing valuable information on inter- and intrapsychic processes. Participants do not provide a sufficiently accurate account, so to speak, due to underlying dynamics—fantasy, phantasy, and defence mechanisms (Holloway & Jefferson, 2000, p. 3). Consciousness constitutes the starting point for the investigation of the psychical apparatus, but these conscious processes do not form continuous sequences; there are gaps in them (Bucci, 2000). Research can be enriched by psychoanalytically informed interviews and analysis by developing an understanding of the research relationships aiding in the development and evaluation of current theory (Cartwright, 2004; Midgley, 2006). Uniquely, it is not only the content of the narrative that is of interest but the way the narrative takes form (Cartwright, 2004). The value placed on free association in psychoanalytic interviews provides access to intrapsychic processes, defences, and unconscious meanings and helps to highlight transferential processes that may be occurring, focusing on the "lived human relation...of the encounter" (Kvale, 2003, p. 38). No published studies of social anxiety have previously been conducted using a psychoanalytically informed approach.

Assumptions and ideas featured include, but are not limited to, unconscious and conscious processes, the role of defence mechanisms, the formative impact of early experiences on the development of the self and its relation to others, as well as the significance of transference and countertransference responses in reaching intrapsychic insights. In this instance, countertransference refers to the interviewer's emotional attitude toward the participant, including his or her response to specific items of behavior. Heimann (1950, p. 83) asserts that "he must use his emotional response as a key to the patient's unconscious" and it is this belief, characteristic of psychoanalysis, that is applied in the interview context. This study is informed by the methods outlined by a number of authors and researchers (e.g., Cartwright, 2004; Holloway & Jefferson, 2000; Holmes, 2013; Kvale, 2003; Strømme, Gullestad, Stänicke, & Killingmo, 2010). The study had two main aims: first, to explore the experiences and accounts of people with a diagnosis of social anxiety disorder; and second, to consider potential links between material gathered in relation to different aspects of the participants' lives, the process surrounding interviews, and the transference-countertransference material developing over the course of this process.

METHOD

Design

A qualitative research design was employed, taking a psychoanalytically informed approach to the research process, particularly interview methods and analyses (Cartwright, 2004; Holloway & Jefferson,

2000; Holmes, 2013; Kvale, 2003; Strømme, Gullestad, Stänicke, & Killingmo, 2010). Interviews were semi-structured to allow narratives to emerge through free association.

Ethics

Ethical approval was granted by the research ethics committee in Trinity College Dublin. The researcher adhered to all national ethical guidelines. For any individual, being encouraged to speak about life experiences which are not usually addressed is potentially distressing. This potential for distress is exacerbated by the presentation of the participants; the interview situation may indeed represent the very thing that these individuals fear, exposure to and scrutiny by others, in this instance the researcher. Therefore, it was vital that participants were made aware of the clinical support available should they become upset as a result of participation. The clinical supervisor was available to provide support for participants if required during the interview process. Participants were made aware that they could withdraw from the study, without consequence to their future involvement with services. Furthermore, the researcher, being a psychologist in clinical training, monitored the psychological well-being of participants throughout the interview process. All identifiable details were altered or removed to ensure participant confidentiality while attempting to depict an accurate description of the individual's characteristics and life circumstances. Participants' names were replaced by pseudonyms; recordings were saved to a computer using a code and were password protected.

Participants

Six people (2 women and 4 men), aged 26–55 years, participated in the study: Anabel (26), Sarah (47), Joe (55), Adam (44), Ian (36), and Sean (36). Participants came from varying socio-educational backgrounds. Joe and Sean were married with children; Adam and Ian were in long-term relationships, and Anabel and Sarah were single. Anabel continued to reside in her family home while the five other participants had moved away from their family of origin to varying degrees. Anabel was a postgraduate college student at the time of interviews; Ian worked part-time from home; and Sarah, Joe, Sean, and Adam worked in full-time positions primarily in office environments. Inclusion criteria were: (1) self-referred to the social anxiety cognitive behavioral therapy (CBT) group, (2) diagnosis of SAD, (3) completed screening for group suitability, (4) aged over 18, and (5) fluent English speaker. Exclusion criteria were: (1) refusal of informed consent and (2) individuals representing an active suicide risk.

Approximately 50 people who had participated in the social anxiety program were contacted and 12 expressed interest in taking part in the study, contacting the researcher through e-mail. The researcher then replied to participants, confirmed their willingness to participate, and arranged appropriate interview times. Of these 12, 4 failed to respond to the initial contact e-mail to arrange an interview time, 2 arranged to meet the researcher and then cancelled or did not attend the interview, and 6 responded to the e-mail and attended their initial scheduled session. All 6 participants who attended the first interview remained engaged with the project completing the allocated three interview sessions, resulting in over 18 hours of taped interviews.

Supportive Framework

Prior to commencing this study, a supportive network of researchers was created to facilitate the completion of this study; members of this group were all engaged in similar research. The principal researcher and lone interviewer was in the process of completing a doctorate in clinical psychology and had previously co-facilitated social anxiety groups. The researcher also had an interest in psychodynamic approaches prior to commencing the current study and had been attending weekly group supervision consisting of discussions on psychodynamic theory and psychoanalytically informed research methods. These groups were led by the project's academic supervisor, who is a clinical psychologist and psychoanalytic psychotherapist. The supervisor worked closely with the principal researcher throughout data collection and analysis to provide a facilitating environment in which themes could emerge, evolve, and be discussed in line with psychoanalytic theory. A clinical advisor was also selected who worked as a senior clinical psychologist and facilitator of the group CBT therapy programs for SAD. The advisor's contibution involved practical assistance such as arranging participants and providing access to a room for interviews, as well as being available to support participants if they experienced distress in response to the interview process.

Research Credibility

Throughout the interview and analysis process, the researcher aimed to emphasize researcher reflexivity (Cartwright, 2004; Holloway & Jefferson, 2000; Holmes, 2013; Kvale, 2003; Strømme et al., 2010); this involves constant consideration of one's own impact on the research as well as consideration of possible alternative explanations for interpretations. This reflexivity was supported through frequent 1:1 supervision with the clinical supervisor as well as peer supervision through a regular psychoanalytically informed research group which provided a forum for discussion on emerging themes and relevant theory. Feedback was also provided on the themes generated by an external researcher and mental health practitioner, to ensure the conclusions were reliable and valid in the context of the data collected.

Process of Data Collection

Before initial interview, participants met with the researcher. The participant was provided with an information sheet detailing the nature of the study and the consent forms. The participant was also given the opportunity to ask additional questions before the research began. Six participants were interviewed three times, with each session lasting approximately an hour, resulting in over 18 hours of audiotaped interviews. All interviews took place in the clinical rooms of the service. The interviews were digitally recorded and later transferred to an encrypted, password protected computer for transcription; the principal researcher transcribed all interviews. At the end of the interview process, each participant was given a debriefing sheet to remind them of their rights as a participant and to provide contact details for the researcher and supervisor.

A comprehensive literature review was not undertaken until the process of interviewing participants was complete, in order to ensure that the researcher was not informed by existing conceptual understanding in the area and to help facilitate relatively free exploration. The first two interviews were unstructured, following the introduction of the particular subject of the research: social anxiety. This provided a context around which the interviewee was allowed to associate freely. There was an attempt to achieve minimal possible researcher intervention (Holmes, 2013), outside of active listening and questions necessary to follow the participants' dialogues (Clarke, 2002). A more direct approach involving questions or reflective comments was used in the final interviews, to seek clarification or to address any apparent gaps in the narrative, as identified in supervision between interviews.

Three types of data were collected: (1) Content: reflecting the words, ideas, memories of and connections made by participant and researcher; (2) Non-verbal and extra-verbal responses of participants: emotional responses (e.g., crying, anger), physical responses (e.g., movements, facial expressions, other physical responses), and behavior (e.g., arriving late, cancelling appointments); and (3) Countertransferential responses: responses of researcher such as emotional (e.g., anxiety, guilt, boredom), cognitive (e.g., memories), behavioral (e.g., forgetting to write in the reflective research journal, arriving late or early), and physical (e.g., sweating, yawning, headache).

Data Analysis and Synthesis

The three types of data described above were analyzed. The analysis comprised of four stages: First, there was the stage of immersion, where recordings were listened to multiple times and an overall "feel" of what was taking place was developed, without the reaching of conclusions. Second, the stage of transcription involved recording content, as well as non-verbal and countertransference responses, with the primary emphasis on an accurate written version of the content of the verbal engagement of the interview. The third stage was that of reflection on the interview relationship, including a closer attention to countertransference responses of the researcher before and after initial contact, each interview, and when listening to recordings or reading transcripts and reflecting on these in supervision. The fourth stage was that of reaching tentative conclusions. Toward this end, summaries of individual participant's stories were created, allowing themes to emerge across participants. These themes were further discussed and refined in supervision until a concise account of significant patterns was created.

RESULTS

Owing to the scope of the category of social anxiety, there is variation in the early life events, current experiences, and feared situations amongst participants interviewed. The ideas outlined below represent threads of possible topics that are woven within descriptions, but by no means reflect an all-encompassing analysis of the content of the interviews. These emerging themes describe core narratives, defences, and interactions between the interviewer and interviewee. Both objective and subjective material is discussed, with credence given to countertransference material and feeling states of the researcher. The results presented represent key aspects of the interviews conducted with Anabel, Sarah, Joe, Adam, Ian, and Sean.

Theme 1: A Critical Voice

This theme describes the inclusion of a dominant other in the participants' description of their early experiences. This individual generally dominated the interview narrative as well as dominating many of the participant's early life experiences. "A Critical Voice" encapsulates a feeling of being criticized and of calling into question one's sense of self-worth as a result. It relates to a hostile home environment and a feeling of being weighed, measured, and found wanting. In interviews, there was a strong sense of an outside presence holding participants back from full disclosure of their feeling states. A need to please and a dread of saying the wrong thing for fear of reprimand were also present.

Adam vividly described his father "sitting on my shoulder" continuously nagging him, calling to mind a hungry "woodpecker" tapping on the same weak spot until his prey becomes exposed. The incessant nature of how Adam experienced this criticism was evident, viewing it as "never-ending...non-stop...just couldn't let it drop." For Sarah there was an ominous, foreboding presence in her home; she described her father as dogmatic and dominant suggesting he "ruled the roost." She also experienced a strong critical voice from early childhood,

detailing bringing home artwork from school and being given the message "it's not good enough." Group family discussions were markedly terrifying, as "saying the wrong thing could rock the boat"; her father was bullying and controlling of herself, her mother, and her sisters. She suggested that her home environment did not foster a sense of self-worth and value. She struggles when criticized by others, suggesting it goes "deep to my bone" and "if you disagree with me then you completely reject me." Her father continued to exert his control over her; Sarah was initially reluctant to name him, referring vaguely instead to one parent being dominant. She was conflicted about assigning blame to him, often apologizing to the interviewer and recanting negative statements made about her father, as she didn't want to "lay too much at that door," as though his influence was present in the interview room.

For Ian, this dominant presence was not experienced as coming directly from his caregivers, but from a strongly held religious belief. As a child, he felt he was being watched and judged at all times and described "a sense that I was being seen" which prevented him from being himself. He suggested that while his parents weren't disciplinarians, there was an "overbearing sense" that he should be well behaved and suggested this created a cold and distant way of relating amongst family members. He described a formality to relationships formed between his family members and a notable lack of "intimacy and honesty." Sean described an outspoken father with whom he struggled to relate and felt embarrassed by as a teenager; he described him as having "no shame" and not caring what others thought of him. He suggested he had a lot of opinions and would have been the disciplinarian in their household. Sean now has a close relationship with his father and in hindsight admires his "strong" parenting. Sean experienced being dominated and bullied by his peers in secondary school, "it was more the threat of physical attacks rather than actual." This experience was shared by Adam, who emotionally recounted a violent physical assault by his peers during adolescence that he believed had a lasting impact on his ability to trust others as well as finding the experience of powerlessness humiliating. This feeling of humiliation was repeated in subsequent relationships, as he described extreme embarrassment when a girlfriend left him "without warning." This incident was discussed at several points during the interview process; despite having occurred over a decade ago, the associated shame remained palpable.

Joe's experience was somewhat different, with his mother dominating much of his early memories and narrative. Her constant paranoia, as a result of her diagnosis of schizophrenia, was hostile and threating to Joe and created an unpredictable environment with her children "tiptoeing around her." Joe appeared to idolize his father as he offered a consistency that directly contrasted with his experience of his mother; his father was outgoing and "cool," a wonderful man who rarely showed emotion. With Anabel, the absence of any detailed description or mention of her father was a notable anomaly. Her parents divorced in late childhood and she appears to have removed him from her narrative entirely; she dedicated just a few sentences in the course of 3 hours of interviews to him, describing him as odd and "mean with money" and that she had never felt comfortable with him. Instead, her narrative was dominated by descriptions of critical grandparents who became the villains of the piece as she described them as judgemental bullies filled with rage.

One potential impact of this critical voice was evident as participants portrayed current difficulties with people in positions of authority, with such individuals arousing a greater sense of anxiety than those deemed to be at a similar social level as themselves. For Sarah, this was particularly frustrating as she felt that valuing some people's opinions more than others contradicted a strongly held value system of equality. Joe described being more anxious around people of his own age or older and people with rank, he felt as a child he had "to bow down" to people and carried this with him. Anabel reported that making a mistake in front of someone in authority, such as her college professors, was particularly anxiety provoking for her and could send her into a "spin" if she felt they were judging her unfavorably. Ian described more of an anger toward, than fear of, authority figures suggesting he resents people trying to tell him what to do and relates this to feeling like he was "conned" into following the rules as a child.

Theme 2: A Passive Presence

The second emerging theme has a strong connection to the first, with many participants reporting growing up in an environment that consisted of a more passive, dominated caregiver. This caregiver disappeared into the background of the narrative presented and was conspicuous by their absence from the participants' accounts. Consequently, it became difficult for the researcher to present a clear account of this caregiver and the lack of detail provided became a salient theme, as though "A Passive Presence" had been silenced by "A Critical Voice" and subsequently diminished in importance in the minds of both interviewee and interviewer.

Sean gave the description of his mother being "quiet to a certain extent" before changing the subject to other family members. Sarah described trying to protect her mother a lot during childhood. Anabel described her mother as struggling to express her emotions and stand up to Anabel's grandparents during her childhood. Participants appeared to identify strongly with this caregiver and adopted a more passive stance within their own relationships. Sarah described a pattern of attaching herself to another, being on their "tailwinds," feeling like "a hanger-on" and that she was not adding anything to her peer group. Anabel also identified attaching herself to others and felt she used her sister as "a social passport" allowing her to open conversations in group settings. Sean identified taking a passive style of relating; not initiating contact and waiting for the environment to facilitate the formation of relationships. He identified the majority of his personal relationships as stemming from the workplace, including his marriage, and feeling like such connections "just kind of happened." Both Joe and Sean described being dependent on their wives in social situations, with Sean suggesting it extended to "relying on her for an awful lot" such as making phone calls for appointments as well as not attending gatherings without her. Ian and Sarah described a somewhat anomalous experience to their usual passive way of relating when expressing opinions they felt strongly about. They did this in a way that could be experienced as aggressive by other people, as though they could only present themselves at either end of the spectrum; either dominant or dominated with "A Critical Voice" overshadowing "A Passive Presence" for a fleeting moment before they retreated to their usual way of being in relationship with a sense of shame for such an outburst. The interviewer frequently found herself adopting a passive approach in interview—rarely asking a definite question, finishing most statements with a trailing off "or…" for fear of saying the wrong thing or being experienced as hostile or demanding by the participants.

Theme 3: Failure to Launch

The theme of "Failure to Launch" describes the difficulties individuals face when transitioning into the next phase of development, a stage which involves greater independence and responsibility; principally here, this is about the move between a childhood/adolescent reality and an adult reality.

A number of participants reported struggling to transition from the structured school environment to the outside world. College was reported as a distressing time as participants struggled to fit in and find their place within this unchartered territory. Subsequently, participants described a current sense of not yet achieving their desired goals in life and of being held back by their social anxiety. This resulted in a sense of loss and anger regarding what might have been. Participants continued to be tethered to, and in some cases weighed down by, their families, continuing to return to seemingly unhealthy relationships out of a sense of loyalty. This also appeared to be related to a failure to launch and individuate.

Ian described late adolescence as the worst four years of his life, when talking about his experience of anxiety; he had let go of his religious beliefs entirely and began to question all of the "standard assumptions" about what one does after school and found them all wanting. Without a "platform for living," he was like a "zombie" and spent these years doing nothing as a result. He reported a sense of loss as a consequence of believing he missed out on many meaningful experiences by removing himself from his peer group at that time and described feeling like he is now ready for these "adventures" but his friends are at a different life stage. Despite having initially made alternative career choices, both Ian and Adam are now working in family businesses with siblings that they have a less than close relationship with and expressed resentment at having ended up in this situation. For Anabel education is her "safe space," but when she attempted to transition from college into the working world, she found this extremely challenging. She found her niche in college and was able to connect somewhat with people who had similar interests to her and took pride in her academic successes. Her unsuccessful attempt to start work served as a catalyst to seek help with her social anxiety. At the time of the interview, Anabel was back in college completing a third degree and claimed: "I'm not ready for the real world."

Sarah's difficulties emerged prominently in later adolescence, particularly from the age of 18 when she felt like a less than valuable member of her peer group. She compared her life to her friends and felt "it just doesn't come up to muster," something she continues to experience today. This feeling of inferiority resulted in Sarah taking roles in work below her ability and feeling like she's "dug a big hole," "blotted my copybook," and "let myself down" by staying in safer, less socially demanding roles. Joe described taking certain opportunities in work as a means of "running away" from social situations; he spends a large portion of the day driving alone between locations as a protective career choice. Sean's whole teenage experience was tough and especially difficult when he entered college and was out of his "comfort zone." He identified his depression as "kicking off" in his early 20s. While Sean has had an arguably successful career, he has been working with the same company for over a decade as he feels comfortable there and the thought of doing another interview would "strike fear" into him. He has had to confront his social anxiety symptoms the more senior he has become, as the expectations and social demands have increased. Before receiving treatment, "it was starting to feel like it was getting too much." Sean, Anabel, and Joe all described making at least weekly visits to see their family members, more out of a sense of duty than receiving any personal enjoyment from the interactions.

Theme 4: Behind the Mask

This theme describes a common experience of wearing a mask or adopting another persona in social situations, in order to hide a part of oneself. The removal or slight slippage of this mask appeared to be a source of terror for participants. Sean's emotive description encapsulated the fear shared by a number of participants:

"Eventually, I'm going to get found out… that you're hiding this thing and you're trying to pretend that there's nothing wrong with you…and after 10 years of doing that if people see something it's going to be quite catastrophic…you'll get to a point and suddenly the mask drops…"

Sarah described a discomfort around establishing intimate relationships as "the more they get to know me, then the more my inadequacies are exposed" and has an overriding sense that she's just getting away with it but is always close to being revealed "warts and all." She described a pressure to perform to a high standard on tasks, as though any mistakes in this forum would result in a revealing glimpse of what lies behind the mask. Many participants identified undertaking such a performance, for which they engage in lengthy rehearsal and preparation. Anabel is striving to be as perfect as she can be to lower her profile and minimize the likelihood that she will be "shunned from the social network." She used the words "shield," "hiding," "my best face," and "putting on a front" when detailing her perfectionism and how terrifying it is to let go of the idea that you can control other people's opinion of yourself. Anabel compared the removal of her mask to "cutting the safety ropes as you're climbing," as though without this she has nothing to catch her should she slip and fall. Ian described being "a slightly different version" of himself with each of his social groups, as though he has a variety of masks in his possession and selects the one which best fits the social demands of a particular group. He described disliking when his social worlds collide as he does not know "how to be" as if by juggling multiple masks simultaneously, they will all come crashing to the ground and the inauthenticity of his display will be revealed; he will be judged as "a fraud in both camps."

A shared experience involved a difficulty disclosing their diagnosis of SAD to their family and friends, as though acknowledging its existence would carve an irreparable hole in the mask of perfection they had worked so hard to present. Sean did not tell his wife he had applied for the group. Adam told his partner that he was attending his regular group therapy sessions as opposed to a new disorder-specific group for social anxiety. Joe described packing his laptop bag with his social anxiety handbook and informing his wife that he would be working away from home once a week. Sarah finally brought up the subject with her sister after they had a few drinks, and is uncertain if she remembers the disclosure.

The researcher experienced a strong image of a group of party guests, dressed in their finery, with one tightly gripping an ornate masquerade mask. As the conversation progressed, it began to slip slowly from her grasp and panic rose as she desperately tried to slot it back into place, while all around her party guests continued to laugh and talk, oblivious to her rising terror. She also felt at moments during the interview process participants began to lose a grip of their masks and expose glimpses of themselves, through unexpected emotional outbursts or proclamations. These experiences were swiftly retreated from, or statements were withdrawn, and the mask was firmly in place once again. When analyzing transcripts and attempting to commit thoughts to paper, the researcher was reluctant to do so. Her fear of participants later reading the completed document and feeling criticized or unfairly represented was discussed in supervision and highlighted as a possible parallel process. She felt as though she was colluding with participants to keep their masks in place while simultaneously being fearful that she would reveal herself as a harsh, critical voice who had masqueraded as a naive researcher; this fear of saying the wrong thing or causing offence was, at some points, paralyzing.

DISCUSSION

This study focused on highlighting the underlying emotional aspects and early experiences that may contribute to the development and maintenance of social anxiety. During early analyses, the researcher began to question the value of attempting to conceptualize the vast category of social anxiety through the equally broad lens of psychodynamic/psychoanalytic theory. As a consequence of this, and to allow for a meaningful approach to this material, the results of this study are considered here with a particular focus on the overall perspective developed by Winnicott (e.g., 1953, 1958, 1960a, 1960b, 1961, 1964). His ideas on the importance of the facilitating early environment and the ordinary devoted mother seem to fit well with the emerging themes in this study in so far as these reflect concerns around presence, relationship, responsiveness to the other, and a felt need to disguise one's true feelings and psychological reality. The works of Mahler (1971) and Erikson (1950) are also useful in providing a theoretical context for the ideas of the epigenetic principle, and the topography of personality as well as the potential causes and consequence of a struggle to individuate.

Central to the narratives of these participants was their relationships with their parents, with reflections on early aspects of this, its development over time, and the situation in relation to this at the time of the interviews. The themes of "A Critical Voice" and "A Passive Presence" illustrate the apparently lasting impact of the parental relationship on participants' development of a sense of self, and later on an ability to relate to others and the broader external world. In participants' accounts, the father was not experienced as a consistent source of security, but as an unpredictable purveyor of threat and criticism. Without him fulfilling his role of supporting the mother, a facilitating environment was not generated in which to allow the "good-enough" mother to emerge and provide for the child's needs within the framework of the facilitating environment—in a manner reminiscent of Winnicott's belief that the father is responsible for providing a secure environment for the mother. Within the confines of a more hostile environment, as detailed by those interviewed, the mother placed energy in placating the dominant father, at the expense of attunement to her child. As such, the opportunity for these participants to cultivate a healthy sense of self-worth and trustworthiness and develop into a healthy, autonomous individual may have been compromised.

Participants subsequently recounted an ongoing struggle to individuate; this "Failure to Launch" may be viewed as a direct consequence of experiencing "A Critical Voice" and "A Passive Presence." Individuation refers to a process "by which a person becomes increasingly differentiated from a past or present relational context" (Karpel, 1976, p. 66). This theme could equally be conceptualized as an ongoing Winnicottian "struggle through the doldrums," or as Mahler's process of separation-individuation. It is vital to look at the early environment to garner a sense of how an individual was "launched" into the wider community and how the concept of "the other" was brought to their awareness; this appears to have been a painful experience for the participants in this study. Examination of participants' narratives revealed a period of struggle and psychological turmoil between late childhood and early adulthood. Disturbances in separation-individuation have resulted in patterns of personal and relational dysfunction throughout the life course and are manifested in a range of clinically significant problems including social anxiety.

Because of a lack of parental attunement (resulting from the dominant father's inability to provide a secure setting which prevented the passive mother from creating an appropriate facilitating environment for the child), it is possible that the external world was presented to these individuals more rapidly than they had developed the capacity to cope with, resulting in later individuation difficulties at this juncture. For these participants, it was as though individuation stalled at a vital point and they remain developmentally stuck in a phase between late childhood and early adulthood, grappling with an ever-oscillating desire for independence, the familiarity of dependence, and fear of the other. It is as though unsuccessful completion of Erikson's earliest developmental stages of Trust versus Mistrust and Autonomy versus Shame have resulted in an unstable foundation for these individuals to adequately address issues of Ego Identification versus Role Confusion and Intimacy versus Isolation. This delicate balance of appropriate levels of dependency appears to be an ongoing struggle for participants in this study, and may be a direct result of their earliest experience of relationships and their "launch" into the external world, as they continue to fluctuate between the extremes of isolation and overdependence in interpersonal relationships.

"A Mask of Perfection" reflects Winnicott's account of the false-self compromise. Participants present a masked or "false" version of themselves in social settings in the hopes of appearing in a way that is desired and accepted by others, to escape judgement and rejection. This mask wearing may be the means by which participants are able to survive in a more adult world despite ongoing preoccupation with unresolved adolescent issues; this way of being in relationship may have both regressive and progressive properties, allowing the participants to gain some experience of moving into the world while simultaneously preventing them from experiencing the full reality of presenting their true self to a potentially hostile other. The origins of adopting a false-self persona can be traced back to experiencing two distinct, competing voices in childhood; the extreme dissonance between parenting styles meant the "good-enough mother" was not present and perhaps she herself wore a mask when interacting with her child. Her child in turn, in response to the unnatural and inauthentic relationship with the mother, develops his or her own false self. This connection was illustrated in participants' identification with, and mirroring of, their mother's passive stance in relationships, both with the interviewer and in other interpersonal dynamics, as though her mask had become their own. Participants' accounts of feelings of otherness and being on the periphery in social settings may be supported by Winnicott's notion that individuals operating from the false-self position experience issues connecting with others and forming meaningful relationships; relationships that appear intimate on the surface may, in fact, be a product of a false-self construction. It also gives a rationale as to why many participants struggle to initiate and maintain more intimate relationships and felt the need to adopt a policy of secrecy with family members regarding their diagnosis, in keeping with their perfect but ultimately false self. Participants engaged in mask wearing in order to protect their true selves from destruction at the hands of the other and consequently struggle to maintain genuine and intimate relationships with the feared other.

The findings of this study are consistent with much previous research; background themes including shame, perfectionism, occupational difficulties, and poor friendship quality emerged in the interviews, as well as the more subtle patterns of the crucial nature of the early environment and critical period between late childhood and early adulthood as outlined in the results. Identified patterns encourage both theorists and practitioners to examine the early conditions and parental relationships of individuals with social anxiety as these may serve as a template for experiencing the outside world which extends long into adulthood. The experiences described by participants may resonate with many, with some level of social anxiety forming a vital part of normal development and growth. Recognizing

the moment where this becomes problematic and can be labelled as SAD, an entity that stands out from ordinary experience, involves closer inspection of primitive relationships. As social anxiety is a widespread and variable presentation, attempting to provide a cohesive rationale as to why an individual may receive a diagnosis of SAD is challenging. It reflects intrinsic human fears shared amongst the collective; therefore narrowly construing it as a disorder may not always be the most useful approach to this fear of scrutiny by others. It is interesting that the subject of social anxiety has not been the focus of psychoanalytic inquiry in a more concerted way; however, this may result from the overall emphasis that exists in psychoanalysis on this very experience: anxiety is viewed as inevitable and as being, to a lesser or greater extent, present at all points in the life of the person. From a theoretical perspective, accurately describing the phenomenological components of the complex constructs which underpin social anxiety may facilitate the development of new theories or add weight to existing ones; this research serves to generate greater understanding of the experience of developing a socially driven anxiety.

A number of implications for our clinical work with clients coming with a diagnosis of SAD can be readily formulated. First, as clinicians, we need to explore the possible benefit of working with clients to recognize and validate intrinsic human fears and understand the development of engrained views of the self, the world, and others by exploring the origins of this painful reality of dread in social situations. Second, if striving to understand social anxiety from Winnicott's perspective, the importance of the therapeutic environment cannot be underestimated; this environment functions along the same lines as ordinary parenting, providing holding and containment for the re-experiencing of distressing events (Abram, 2007). Many psychoanalytic authors, influenced by the work of Klein, Bion, and the post-Kleinians (e.g., Ruszczynski, 2010) now frame the role of clinicians as providers of a container for their client's projected unbearable emotions, in turn, allowing the client to observe how the clinician processes these emotions. Third, when taking into consideration the aspects of countertransference that emerged for the researcher during the interview process, a further treatment concern is that the client can become caught into the viewpoint and desire of the therapist, and present false-self compromises that may be represented as what is really taking place (e.g., Winnicott, 1960a). Features of the setting may be experienced as the therapist exercising power and placing the patient in an inferior position, similar to the critical voice, referred to widely here as having been prominently experienced in childhood. As a result, narcissistic defences may be mobilized allowing the patient to reverse the situation of dominance or the client may react by becoming "A Passive Presence" complying with the perceived demands of the therapist. Overall these findings point toward a need to prioritize the influence of the early environment on the therapeutic relationship and suggest that practitioners should be aware of how such experience sets up the quality of clinical interactions, unwittingly influencing the actions of clinicians and services.

With a recognition that while some material which emerged here may have reflected a need to be experienced positively by the interviewer, this method provided a space in which material important to and/ or pressing for participants could emerge. As with all empirical studies, there are strengths and limitations associated with the current study. The results of this study are consistent with much of the existing literature regarding the risk factors related to the development of social anxiety; however this study also identified possible underlying, unconscious processes that may interact with these risk factors. The approach undertaken, a psychoanalytically informed research interview, allows for the consideration not only of the narrative presented,

but of the transference and countertransference observed, which enriches the data, resulting in an in-depth account of an individual's experience. In order to represent this experience in its complex and conflictual wholeness, words have to be used in such a way that they are not devoid of the emotional, sensuous, desiring, and embodied life that they represent (Hollway, 2009). Significantly, psychoanalytically informed research incorporates the researcher into the process of the interview, embracing as opposed to dismissing the influences of the relationship dynamics between interviewer and participant.

The strengths of this study may also be viewed as potential limitations. The researcher's interest in the topic of social anxiety arises from the researcher's history, clinical observations, and subsequent curiosity about this presentation; this in itself brings a possible bias. Using the self as an instrument to measure what is taking place, in conscious and unconscious processes, may also result in the creation of thematic blind spots as the researcher's own defences are activated; there is value in multiple researchers undertaking studies of this nature to overcome this potential prejudice. The small sample size facilitated in-depth exploration of narratives but research looking to generalize themes may require increased numbers of participants or perhaps an expansion of the number of interviews conducted with each participant. The gap in the literature regarding a psychoanalytic perspective on social anxiety cannot be addressed by one study in isolation; future research may adapt the methodology, for example using it to focus on total immersion in one case study or utilizing it for group observation to look more closely at interpersonal dynamics. It is also important to note that the participants interviewed represent a particular subset of individuals with social anxiety—those who identified their own difficulty, self-referred to a social anxiety program and subsequently volunteered to share their story; as identified in the literature, a sizeable portion of people with social anxiety never seek treatment (Wang et al., 2005) and as a result remain under-represented in research and clinical practice. These participants may characterize individuals with a desire to be part of a particular diagnostic category as a means of validating and contextualizing their struggles; larger scale studies may alleviate this issue and increase the generalizability of findings but perhaps to the detriment of documenting the nuances of individual experience.

CONCLUSION

This study, in looking at the experiences of people diagnosed with SAD, at the same time reflects what is a wider human experience—of anxiety that arises in thinking about, being in the presence of, and actively relating to and with others. As human beings, we are ultimately dependent on others for survival, while simultaneously trying to individuate and find our place in the world. Consequently, relating to others can be a source of torment and suffering, as well as the root of joy and fulfilment. This tension is not time limited, but a life-long struggle for belonging. A psychoanalytic method and analysis was used in this qualitative investigation of the experience of people diagnosed with SAD. Emerging themes include the experience of both critical and passive caregiving resulting in a struggle to individuate and a concealing of the self. These themes were examined through a Winnicottian lens with a focus on the good-enough mother and the facilitating environment. The study also called into question the value of separating social anxiety out from the universal fear of negative evaluation that is an intrinsic human anxiety. Overarching themes are presented tentatively with the aim of encouraging future exploration and research in this vast and complex area, as opposed to representing an all-encompassing viewpoint.

The themes highlight how early experiences and relationships form a template by which individuals experience others and the external world, but also raises questions for future research regarding the significance and implications of the triangular relationship between mother, father, and child and its lasting impact on the development of the self long into adulthood.

REFERENCES

Abram, J. (2007). *The language of Winnicott: A dictionary of Winnicott's use of words*. London: Karnac.

Ainsworth, M. S. (1979). Infant–mother attachment. *American Psychologist, 34*(10), 932. doi: 10.1037/0003-066X.34.10.932

American Psychiatric Association. (1994). *Diagnostic and statistical manual for mental disorders* (4th ed.). Washington, DC: American Psychiatric Association.

American Psychiatric Association. (2013). *Diagnostic and statistical manual of mental disorders* (5th ed.). Arlington, VA: American Psychiatric Association. doi: 10.1176/appi.books.9780890425596

Baker-Smith, K., & Moore, K. A. (2001). Early onset of social anxiety: Impact on Erikson's stages of psychosocial development. Paper presented at the *Proceedings 1st Australian Psychological Society's Psychology of Relationships Conference*, Melbourne.

Bandura, A. (1977). Self-efficacy: Toward a unifying theory of behavioral change. *Psychological Review, 84*(2), 191. doi: 10.1037/0033-295X.84.2.191

Baumeister, R. F., & Tice, D. M. (1990). Point-counterpoints: Anxiety and social exclusion. *Journal of Social and Clinical Psychology, 9*(2), 165. doi: 10.1521/jscp.1990.9.2.165

Beck, A. T., Emery, G., & Greenberg, R. L. (1985). *Anxiety disorders and phobias: A cognitive approach*. New York: Basic Books.

Bion, W. R. (1979). Making the best of a bad job. In F. Bion (Ed.), *W. R. Bion: Clinical seminars and other works* (pp. 321-331). London: Karnac.

Bowlby, J. (1977). The making and breaking of affectional bonds. II. Some principles of psychotherapy. The fiftieth Maudsley Lecture. *The British Journal of Psychiatry, 130*(5), 421-431. doi: 10.1192/bjp.130.5.421

Brunello, N., den Boer, J. A., Judd, L. L., Kasper, S., Kelsey, J. E., Lader, M., & Wittchen, H. U. (2000). Social phobia: Diagnosis and epidemiology, neurobiology and pharmacology, comorbidity and treatment. *Journal of Affective Disorders*, 60(1), 61-74. doi: 10.1016/S0165-0327(99)00140-8

Bucci, W. (2000). The need for a "psychoanalytic psychology" in the cognitive science field. *Psychoanalytic Psychology*, 17(2), 203-224. doi: 10.1037/0736-9735.17.2.203

Cartwright, D. (2004). The psychoanalytic research interview: Preliminary suggestions. *Journal of the American Psychoanalytic Association*, 52(1), 209-242. doi: 10.1177/00030651040520010501.

Clark, D. M., & Wells, A. (1995). A cognitive model of social phobia. *Social Phobia: Diagnosis, Assessment, and Treatment*, 41(68), 00022-00023.

Clarke, S. (2002). Learning from experience, psycho-social research methods in the social sciences. *Qualitative Research*, 2(2), 173-197. doi: 10.1177/146879410200200203

Dickinson, E. (1924). Part three: Love. In M. D. Bianchi & E. Dickinson (Eds.), *The life and letters of Emily Dickinson*. London: Cape.

Erikson, E. H. (1950). *Childhood and society*. New York: Norton.

Farmer, A. S., Gros, D. F., McCabe, R. E., & Antony, M. M. (2014). Clinical predictors of diagnostic status in individuals with social anxiety disorder. *Comprehensive Psychiatry*, 55(8), 1906-1913. doi: 10.1016/j.comppsych.2014.07.019

Filho, A. S., Hetem, L. A., Ferrari, M. C., Trzesniak, C., Martín-Santos, R., Borduqui, T., et al. (2010). Social anxiety disorder: What are we losing with the current diagnostic criteria? *Acta Psychiatrica Scandinavica*, 121(3), 216-226. doi: 10.1111/j.1600-0447.2009.01459

Franz, C. E., & White, K. M. (1985). Individuation and attachment in personality development: Extending Erikson's theory. *Journal of Personality*, 53(2), 224-256. doi: 0.1111/j.1467-6494.1985.tb00365

Freud, S. (1905). Three essays on the theory of sexuality. In J. Strachey (Ed. & Trans.), *The standard edition of the complete psychological works of Sigmund Freud* (Vol. 7). London: Hogarth Press.

Gilbert, P., & Trower, P. (2001). Evolution and process in social anxiety. In W. R. Crozier & L. E. Alden (Eds.), *International handbook of social anxiety: Concepts, research and interventions relating to the self and shyness* (pp. 259-279). New York: Wiley.

Grotstein, J. S. (1995). A reassessment of the couch in psychoanalysis. *Psychoanalytic Inquiry*, 15(3), 396-405. doi: 10.1080/07351699509534045

Heimann, P. (1950). On counter-transference. *International Journal of Psychoanalysis*, 3(1), 81-84.

Hetem, L. A. B., Ferrari, M. C. F., Trzesniak, C., Martín-Santos, R., Borduqui, T., de Lima Osório, F.,...Crippa, J. A. S. (2010). Social anxiety disorder: What are we losing with the current diagnostic criteria? *Acta Psychiatrica Scandinavica*, 121(3), 216-226.

Hofmann, S. G. (2007). Cognitive factors that maintain social anxiety disorder: A comprehensive model and its treatment implications. *Cognitive Behaviour Therapy*, 36(4), 193-209. doi: 10.1080/16506070701421313

Holloway, W., & Jefferson, T. (2000). Narrative, discourse and the unconscious: The case of Tommy. *The uses of narrative: Explorations in sociology, psychology, and cultural studies* (Vol. 136-49). New Brunswick, NJ: Transaction Publishers.

Hollway, W. (2009). Applying the "experience-near" principle to research: Psychoanalytically informed methods 1. *Journal of Social Work Practice*, 23(4), 461-473. doi: 10.1080/02650530903375025

Holmes, J. (2013). Using psychoanalysis in qualitative research: Countertransference-informed researcher reflexivity and defence mechanisms in two interviews about migration. *Qualitative Research in Psychology*, 10(2), 160-173. doi: 10.1080/14780887.2011.586451

Karpel, M. (1976). Individuation: From fusion to dialogue. *Family Process*, 15(1), 65-82. doi: 10.1111/j.1545-5300.1976.00065.x

Kessler, R. C. (2003). The impairments caused by social phobia in the general population: Implications for intervention. *Acta Psychiatrica Scandinavica*, 108, 19-27. doi: 10.1034/j.1600-0447.108.s417.2.x

Kessler, R. C., Berglund, P., Demler, O., Jin, R., Merikangas, K. R., & Walters, E. E. (2005). Lifetime prevalence and age-of-onset distributions of *DSM-IV* disorders in the National Comorbidity Survey Replication. *Archives of General Psychiatry*, 62(6), 593-602. doi: 10.1001/archpsyc.62.6.593.

Kvale, S. (2003). The psychoanalytical interview as inspiration for qualitative research. In P. M. Camic, J. E. Rhodes, & L. Yardley (Eds.), *Qualitative research in psychology expanding perspectives in methodology and design* (pp. 275-295). Washington, DC: American Psychological Association.

Leary, M. R. (2001). Social anxiety as an early warning system: A refinement and extension of the self-presentational theory. In G. Hofmann & P. M. DiBartolo (Eds.), *From social anxiety to social phobia: Multiple perspectives* (pp. 1-7). Needham Heights, MA: Allyn and Bacon.

Leichsenring, D. S., F., Salzer, S., Jaeger, U., Kächele, H., Kreische, R., Leweke, F., Rüger, U., & Leibing, D. S. E. (2009). Short-term psychodynamic psychotherapy and cognitive-behavioral therapy in generalized anxiety disorder: A randomized, controlled trial. *American Journal of Psychiatry, 166*(8), 875-881. doi: 10.1176/foc.8.1.foc66

Liebowitz, M. R., Gorman, J. M., Fyer, A. J., & Klein, D. F. (1985). Social phobia: Review of a neglected anxiety disorder. *Archives of General Psychiatry, 42*(7), 729-736. doi: 10.1001/archpsyc.1985.01790300097013

Mahler, M. S. (1971). A study of the separation-individuation process: And its possible application to borderline phenomena in the psychoanalytic situation. *The Psychoanalytic Study of the Child, 26*, 403-424.

Midgley, N. (2006). Psychoanalysis and qualitative psychology: Complementary or contradictory paradigms? *Qualitative Research in Psychology, 3*, 213-231. doi: 10.1191/1478088706qp065oa

Osório, F. L., Crippa, J. A. S., & Loureiro, S. R. (2010). Study of the psychometric qualities of the Brief Social Phobia Scale (BSPS) in Brazilian university students. *European Psychiatry, 25*(3), 178-188. doi: 10.1016/j.eurpsy.2009.08.002

Rachman, S. (1977). The conditioning theory of fear acquisition: A critical examination. *Behaviour Research and Therapy, 15*(5), 375-387. doi: 10.1016/0005-7967(77)90041-9

Rapee, R. M., & Heimberg, R. G. (1997). A cognitive-behavioral model of anxiety in social phobia. *Behaviour Research and Therapy, 35*(8), 741-756. doi: 10.1016/S0005-7967(97)00022-3

Rapee, R. M., & Spence, S. H. (2004). The etiology of social phobia: Empirical evidence and an initial model. *Clinical Psychology Review, 24*(7), 737-767. doi: 10.1016/j.cpr.2004.06.004

Ruszczynski, S. (2010). Becoming neglected: A perverse relationship to care. *British Journal of Psychotherapy, 26*(1), 22-32. doi: 10.1111/j.1752-0118.2009.01153.x

Sartre, J. P. (1946). *No exit and other plays.* New York: Vintage International.

Schlenker, B. R., & Leary, M. R. (1982). Social anxiety and self-presentation: A conceptualization model. *Psychological Bulletin, 92*(3), 641. doi: 10.1037/0033-2909.92.3.641

Smits, J. A., Powers, M. B., Buxkamper, R., & Telch, M. J. (2006). The efficacy of videotape feedback for enhancing the effects of exposure-based treatment for social anxiety disorder: A controlled investigation. *Behaviour Research and Therapy, 44*(12), 1773-1785. doi: 10.1016/j.brat.2006.01.00

Strømme, H., Gullestad, S. E., Stänicke, E., & Killingmo, B. (2010). A widened scope on therapist development: Designing a research interview informed by psychoanalysis. *Qualitative Research in Psychology, 7*(3), 214-232. doi: 10.1080/14780880802659542

Wang, P. S., Berglund, P., Olfson, M., Pincus, H. A., Wells, K. B., & Kessler, R. C. (2005). Failure and delay in initial treatment contact after first onset of mental disorders in the National Comorbidity Survey Replication. *Archives of General Psychiatry, 62*(6), 603-613. doi: 10.1001/archpsyc.62.6.603.

Weiss, H. (2015). Introduction: The role of shame in psychoanalytic theory and practice. *The International Journal of Psychoanalysis, 96*(6), 1585-1588. doi: 10.1111/1745-8315.12418

Winnicott, D. W. (1953). Transitional objects and transitional phenomena. *The International Journal of Psychoanalysis, 34*, 89-97.

Winnicott, D. W. (1958). The capacity to be alone. *The International Journal of Psycho-Analysis, 39*, 416-420.

Winnicott, D. W. (1960a). Ego distortion in terms of true and false-self. In M. M. R. K. (Ed.), *The maturational processes and the facilitating environment: Studies in the theory of emotional development* (pp. 140-152). London: Hogarth Press.

Winnicott, D. W. (1960b). The theory of the parent-infant relationship. *The International Journal of Psycho-Analysis, 41*, 585-595.

Winnicott, D. W. (1961). Adolescence: Struggling through the doldrums. In D. W. Winnicott (Ed.), *The family and individual development* (pp. 79-87). London: Tavistock.

Winnicott, D. W. (1964). *The child, the family, and the outside world.* Middlesex, England: Penguin.

Eating Disorders

Eating Disorders and Attachment: A Contemporary Psychodynamic Perspective

Giorgio A. Tasca and Louise Balfour

Abstract: A contemporary psychodynamic framework can add much to our understanding of eating disorders. Eating disorders are associated with complex comorbidities, high levels of mortality, and therapist countertransferences that can complicate psychological treatments. Mainstream models currently focus on cognitive, biological, or cultural factors to the near exclusion of attachment functioning, and the individual's dynamics. As such, standard models appear to exclude person-centred and developmental considerations when providing treatments. In this article, we describe a contemporary psychodynamic model that understands eating disorder symptoms as a consequence of vulnerability to social pressures to be thin and biological predispositions to body weight. Individual vulnerabilities are rooted in unmet attachment needs causing negative affect, and subsequent maladaptive defenses and eating disorder symptoms as a means of coping. We describe how this model can inform transdiagnostic eating disorder treatment that focuses on symptoms as well as specific attachment functions including: interpersonal style, affect regulation, reflective functioning, and coherence of mind. Two clinical examples are presented to illustrate case formulations and psychological treatments informed by these conceptualizations.

Psychodynamic models have remained on the periphery of the mainstream of clinical thinking and research on eating disorders. Yet, contemporary psychodynamic approaches have much to add to current conceptualizations of eating disorders. Predominant models tend to be highly focused on cognitive and biological explanations in which developmental histories, and internal mental lives are not considered. Concurrently, standard treatments for eating disorders tend to take a highly symptom oriented, technical, or medical approach in which the person is often a passive recipient rather than an active co-creative participant in the therapy. In this article, we propose a contemporary psychodynamic model of eating disorders that is closer to a biopsychosocial framework (Engel, 1979) in which human development and the person's psychological dynamics are central elements that interact with social, cultural, and biological contexts. In describing this model, we rely on attachment theory and research to organize our understanding of eating disorders and their development. We will present two cases that illustrate attachment-based case formulations and individually tailored treatments based on these formulations.

EATING DISORDERS

Eating disorders are relatively prevalent in clinical practices and in the population. Anorexia nervosa (AN), characterized by a failure to maintain normal body weight, body image distortion, and drive for thinness, occurs in 0.9% of women (Smink, van Hoeken, & Hoek, 2012) and has the highest mortality rate of any psychiatric disorder (Arcelus, Mitchell, Wales, & Nielsen, 2011). Bulimia nervosa (BN), often characterized by binge eating and purging, has a point prevalence of 0.9% to 1.5% (Hudson, Hiripi, Pope, & Kessler, 2007; Preti, Girolamo, Vilagut, Alonso, de Graaf, et al., 2009). Binge eating disorder (BED), characterized by binge eating without purging is often comorbid with obesity, and has a prevalence of 3.5% in community samples (Hudson et al., 2007). The eating disorders are also associated with high levels of depression and anxiety (Mischoulon, Eddy, Keshaviah, Dinescu, Ross, et al., 2011), and eating disorders have a complex association with trauma (Tasca, Ritchie, Zachariadis, Proulx, Trinneer, et al., 2013), substance abuse (Harrop & Marlatt, 2010), and serious medical complications (Mitchell & Crow, 2006). Many of these comorbidities suggest that intolerance of negative affect and affect disregulation may play an important role in the expression and maintenance of eating disorder symptoms. Current evidence-based psychological treatments for eating disorders provide modest outcomes such that, at best, less than 50% of patients benefit from eating disorder symptom-focused treatments (Hubbard, 2013; Thompson-Brenner, Glass, & Westen, 2003). Outcomes are substantially poorer for AN so that only about 25% of patients recover (e.g., Zipfel et al., 2013).

One of the complicating factors in the psychological treatment of eating disorders is that therapists experience strong and difficult to manage countertransferences to patients (Satir, Thompson-Brenner, Boisseau, & Crisafulli, 2009; Thompson-Brenner, Satir, Franko, & Herzog, 2012). In a comprehensive study of clinician report of countertransference, 120 clinicians treating patients with eating disorders reported a variety of negative experiences including anger, incompetence, and boredom (Satir et al., 2009). Patient's emotional disregulation, constriction of affect, and lower level of functioning were particularly associated with therapist anger. Conversely, patient diagnosis did not explain much variance in countertransference experiences when other factors like patient personality, and therapist characteristics were controlled. Nevertheless, as Satir and colleagues (2009) indicated, current eating disorder treatment manuals do not commonly include specialized interventions or therapist considerations for patients with personality pathology.

To date the most prevalent psychological models of eating disorders rely on cognitive-behavioral therapy (CBT) conceptualizations. Briefly, in these models eating disorder symptoms are seen as maintained by cognitions related to weight and shape concerns, and dietary restriction that may in turn result in binge eating (Fairburn, 2008). These factors are seen by many writers as operating within a cultural context that idealizes a thin female body shape (Stice, 2001), and within biological contexts for some that include high or low set points for body weight (Bulik, Slof-Op't Landt, van Furth, & Sullivan, 2007; Williamson, Zucker, Martin, & Smeets, 2004). In an "enhanced" version of the basic CBT model, Fairburn discusses additional maintenance factors that may be at play for some, and these include: interpersonal problems, mood intolerance, clinical perfectionism, and low self-esteem (Fairburn, 2008). These additional maintenance factors, which are often at the heart of psychodynamic and interpersonal conceptualizations, were apparently added to help address issues that may contribute to non-response to CBT by more than half of patient with eating disorders. Most of these additional maintenance factors may operate transdiagnostically, that is, they likely maintain eating disorder symptoms regardless of eating disorder diagnosis (Tasca, Presniak, Demidenko, Balfour, Krysanski, et al., 2011).

As mentioned, psychodynamic models have remained on the periphery of research and clinical writings on eating disorders. However, psychodynamic interventions are often used by clinicians in real world practices to treat those with eating disorders (Tobin, 2007), and psychodynamic processes may predict outcomes in CBT interventions in general (Castonguay, Goldfried, Wiser, Raue, & Hayes, 1996). Psychodynamic treatments have rarely been tested in clinical trials of eating disorders, and in a few studies, psychodynamic therapies were not as effective as CBT (Garner, Rockert, Davis, Garner, Olmsted, & Eagle, 1993; Poulsen, Lunn, Daniel, Folke, Bork Mathiesen, Katznelson, & Fairburn, 2013). However, psychodynamic therapists in these trials were constrained and instructed not to directly discuss eating disorder symptoms thus very likely reducing the effectiveness, relevance, and generalizability of their interventions. In other words, these psychodynamic therapies likely were not representative of real world practice. However, a recent large-scale trial of focal psychodynamic therapy of AN that did directly address symptoms showed that it was as effective as CBT. There was also a trend toward greater effectiveness for the focal psychodynamic therapy compared to CBT at 1-year follow-up (Zipfel et al., 2013).

One can speculate on a number of historical, political, and cultural reasons for the marginalization of psychodynamic concepts in conceptualizing and treating eating disorders. Historically, psychoanalytic thinkers like Hilde Bruch (1978) were prominent in writing about AN as a disorder associated with difficulties with separation-individuation in which unempathic parents perceived their child as an extension of their selves. Concurrently, earlier drive theory models viewed unsublimated aggressive drives as displaced onto bulimic symptoms (e.g., Schwartz, 1988). Bulimic symptoms have also been described as symbolic expressions

of impulses (e.g., Lunn & Poulsen, 2012). Although some aspects of these psychodynamic concepts might remain useful (e.g., issues of separation-individuation), contemporary cultural shifts have resulted in negative reactions to many of these psychoanalytic conceptualizations. For example, some of Bruch's writings could be interpreted as blaming parents for their child's eating disorder, and ignoring cultural and biological contexts. Drive theory models eschew the importance of interpersonal and contextual factors in favor of concepts that appear to be distant from both patients' and therapists' experiences (i.e., sublimation and symbolization). More contemporary psychodynamic models place greater emphasis on social and cultural context and on the primacy of relational factors and attachments rather than drives (Fonagy, 2001). Nevertheless, there remains a dearth of writing and research on eating disorders from such contemporary psychodynamic perspectives. In this article, we outline a psychodynamic model of eating disorders that draws from attachment theory. Whenever possible, we will refer to empirical research evidence to support aspects of the model.

A contemporary psychodynamic framework for eating disorders using attachment theory will map developmental pathways for the disorders. Current non-psychodynamic models for eating disorders (e.g., CBT) are primarily concerned with pressures that impinge on the individual such as: maintenance factors that are primarily cognitive in nature, sociocultural factors related to the dieting and fashion industries, and biological factors such as set point for body weight. Although these certainly play a role, they do not speak to developmental issues that confer vulnerabilities within the individual to these pressures. Attachment theory provides an overarching model within which one can understand the complex interplay between developmentally based vulnerabilities such as interpersonal style, affect regulation, concurrent defensive functioning, and their impact on eating disorder symptoms. Such a developmental and person-centred approach is at the core of contemporary psychodynamic thinking (Luyten, Van Houdenhove, Lemma, Target, & Fonagy, 2013; Westen, 1998).

ATTACHMENT THEORY

Over the past several decades, attachment theory has emerged as one of the most important models of interpersonal relationships and affect regulation. The need to connect with a caregiver through attachment behaviors is biologically based and fundamental to the survival of our species (Fraley, Brumbaugh, & Marks, 2005). Repeated interactions based on attachment behaviors with caregiving others become encoded in the implicit memory system and result in internal working models of attachments (Amini, Lewis, Lannon, Louie, Baumbacher, et al., 1996), which are the basis for the organized attachment patterns and mental states (i.e., secure, preoccupied, dismissing) described below.

Attachment theory has its origins in the work of John Bowlby (1980), a British psychoanalyst, who worked with children separated from parents for reasons such as extended hospital stays in post-war England. In his early papers Bowlby argued that, contrary to psychoanalytic thinking at the time, attachment was primary to explain a child's libidinal ties to the parent. Attachment behaviors (e.g., sucking, clinging, crying, smiling, and following) help to tie the child to parent and parent to child. Bowlby suggested that children experienced separation anxiety when a situation (e.g., separations/loss, illness, stress) activated attachment behaviors and an attachment figure was not available or was not optimally responsive (Bretherton, 1994).

Mary Ainsworth drew from these concepts when she classified children as secure or insecure (i.e., with insecure further subclassified as ambivalent or avoidant) in relation to separations from and reunions with parents (Ainsworth, Blehar, Waters, & Wall, 1978). Based on observational studies of mothers and infants, Ainsworth developed a laboratory procedure called the Strange Situation for young children and their mothers. In the Strange Situation, mother and infant are placed in a room with toys, and typically the infant begins to explore the environment and play with the toys. A stranger enters the room and sits, at which point the infant may return to the mother's lap and, after a period of time, reinitiates tentative exploration of the toys. While the stranger plays with the baby, the mother leaves the room briefly at which point the child is distressed and cries. Then mother returns. The child's reunion behaviors were particularly telling. Secure infants were easily soothed by mother, and after a short time, the child resumed exploring the room and toys. That is, the child experienced the mother as a secure base from which the child's exploration was facilitated. Ambivalent infants swiped at or kicked at the mother, and could not be easily soothed. Avoidant babies had a very low keyed and withdrawn reaction to mother upon reunion even though they searched for mother when she was absent. Ambivalent and avoidant infants did not easily return to exploring the toys.

Mary Main developed the Adult Attachment Interview (AAI) to translate Ainsworth's infant–mother attachment patterns into corresponding adult patterns (Main, Goldwyn, & Hesse 2003). During the AAI, adult participants are asked to recall attachment relationships from childhood and the impact of these relationships on their adult development. In a key part of the interview, participants are asked to provide five adjectives to describe their childhood relationship to their mother and father and then to describe specific events from childhood memories to illustrate the adjectives. The quality and nature of their narratives are indicative of the participant's current mental state with regard to attachment. Main and colleagues used the linguistic philosopher Grice's (1989) nomenclature to define narrative coherence—which Main in turn used to define secure mental states. Narrative coherence requires four conditions or maxims: (1) *truth*: that attachment memories can be illustrated with credible and consistent examples; (2) *relation*: that the descriptors are specific and relevant; (3) *economy*: that the amount of information is adequate; and (4) *manner*, that the information is collaborative and contained. Three organized patterns of attachment emerged in adults that paralleled those that were seen in Ainsworth's work with infants: secure, preoccupied, and dismissing.

Individuals with *secure* attachments are capable of deep, meaningfully, and loving relationships (Mallinckrodt, 2000). Secure individuals can moderate their emotions without being overwhelmed or without dismissing them, and they are not overly self-critical (Fuendeling, 1998). They have coherent mental states characterized by a consistent, relevant, and contained narrative when discussing attachment relationships (Main et al., 2003). Their reflective functioning is adequate; that is, they are able to mentalize, appreciate their own internal states, and are able to empathize easily with others (Crittenden, 2006). Using Perry's (1990) model of hierarchical defensive functioning, one could speculate that the secure individual's defensive functioning tends to be more mature, such that they may use obsessional or high adaptive defenses (e.g., suppression, intellectualization).

Preoccupied individuals tend to be overly concerned with relationship loss or abandonment, they try to reduce anxiety by minimizing emotional distance and soliciting displays of love and support from others, and they may become angry if they perceive rejection (Bartholomew & Horowitz, 1991). These individuals easily and repeatedly access painful attachment-related memories and so they may become overwhelmed by anger or sadness. That is, preoccupied individuals upregulate their emotions, so their emotional system is hyperactivated (Mikulincer, 1995). Due to their anger, those with preoccupied

attachments have a difficult time making orderly sense of their past experiences. When conflicted childhood memories are recalled their coherence of mind is reduced due to overriding anger or passivity in their narratives (Foscha, 2000). Reflective functioning is impaired by these processes, and so preoccupied individuals have difficulty keeping in mind the needs and internal experiences of others and themselves. One could argue that preoccupied individuals might be prone to use action defenses (e.g., acting out) or major image distorting defenses (e.g., splitting; Perry, 1990).

Individuals with *dismissing* attachments are overly self-reliant and derogatory of the importance of attachment relationships, likely because they have learned that relationships can be disappointing or dangerous (Mikulincer, Shaver, Sapir-Lavid, & Avihou-Kanza, 2009). They tend to avoid affectively charged situations, and so they use emotional distancing strategies to deactivate or downregulate their emotions (Fonagy, 2001). Despite appearances, physiologically they can be quite activated and sensitive (Dozier & Kobak, 1992). As a result of deactivating their emotion system, these individuals have a difficult time remembering childhood attachment relationships. In the AAI, they have a tendency to idealize or be derogatory toward attachment figures, though they experience difficulty providing specific illustrative examples (Main et al., 2003). This indicates a mental state that is lacking in coherence. Because of their defensive memory structure, they have a difficult time considering their own or others' internal experiences, thus their reflective functioning is compromised (Wallin, 2007). Using Perry's (1990) scheme, one can speculate that their defense mechanisms might be characterized by disavowal (e.g., denial, rationalization) or minor image distorting (e.g., idealization, devaluation).

A fourth category, *disorganized* or unresolved mental states with regard to attachment was also identified in Strange Situation and AAI research. Disorganized mental states might occur *in addition to* organized attachments: secure, preoccupied, or dismissing. Disorganized attachments refers to mental states that become disorganized (i.e., mental states characterized by overriding guilt, absorption, or dissociation) in relation to the experience of trauma or loss of an attachment figure (Bakermans-Kranenburg & van IJzendoorn, 2009). Disorganized mental states are associated with childhood adversity, including abuse or neglect. In the AAI, adults with disorganized mental states with respect to attachment show disruptive lapses in reasoning when discussing the trauma or loss.

Attachment patterns are remarkably stable and consistent across the lifespan. Seventy percent of children classified as insecure or secure with the Strange Situation remain so when assessed with the AAI into adulthood (Waters, Merrick, Treboux, Crowell, & Albersheim, 2000). Recent large meta-analyses of over 10,000 AAIs drawn from community and clinical samples indicate that 58% of the population were securely attached, 19% were preoccupied, 23% were dismissing, and 18% were additionally classified as disorganized (Bakermans-Kranenburg & van IJzendoorn, 2009). Attachment insecurity is associated with adult psychopathology such as depression and personality disorders, and disorganized states of mind are associated with posttraumatic stress disorder. Despite the stability of attachments, they can change with negative (e.g., trauma, loss) or positive (e.g., romantic relationship, psychotherapy) experiences (Bakermans-Kranenburg & van IJzendoorn, 2009; Waters et al., 2000).

As indicated above, the nature of these adult attachment mental states have implications for attachment functioning especially in areas of interpersonal style, affect regulation, coherence of mind, reflective functioning or mentalizing, and maturity/adaptiveness of defense mechanisms. When the need for attachment security is not met or threatened, such as when there is mis-attunement, inconsistency, or neglect in childhood or by relational and other stressors in adulthood, individuals will experience negative affect and/or anxiety. The coherence of mental states with regard to attachment will affect individuals' ability to tolerate separations, losses, and other threats to a felt sense of security.

One indicator of adaptive coping is the ability to mentalize or to engage in reflective functioning (Fonagy, Target, Steele, & Steele, 1998). Reflective functioning refers to one's capacity to understand or appreciate one's own internal mental states, and the mental states of others. This is an important ability that allows one to maintain the soothing function of an internalized attachment figure in the absence of the attachment figure, and also allows one to empathize with others' experiences and so to provide adequate comfort and security to others. When intact, reflective functioning might reduce the experience of anxiety in the absence of an attachment figure and also reduce the use of maladaptive defense mechanisms. Recent treatment studies have shown an improvement in reflective functioning following transference-focused psychotherapy, which was an effective treatment for borderline personality disorder (Levy, Meehan, Kelly, Reynoso, Weber, et al., 2006). Defense mechanisms, in turn, are engaged particularly in the face of anxiety or negative affect. The adaptiveness of the defense mechanism is likely associated with the level of attachment security.

ATTACHMENT AND EATING DISORDERS: A PSYCHODYNAMIC MODEL

A transdiagnostic psychodynamic model for eating disorders that incorporates attachment concepts could help to organize a clinician's thinking and interventions regarding areas of functioning that lead to or maintain eating disorder symptoms. In a previous version of this model for BED, Tasca, Mikail, and Hewitt (2005) reinterpreted Malan's (1979) Triangle of Conflict into a contemporary relational model of adaptation (Figure 1). Malan

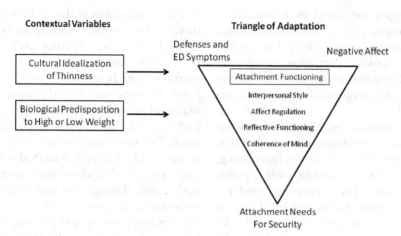

Contextual Variables

Cultural Idealization of Thinness

Biological Predisposition to High or Low Weight

Triangle of Adaptation

Defenses and ED Symptoms

Negative Affect

Attachment Functioning
Interpersonal Style
Affect Regulation
Reflective Functioning
Coherence of Mind

Attachment Needs For Security

FIGURE 1. A contemporary psychodynamic model of eating disorders (ED) based on attachment theory.

described a drive theory model of primitive impulses that gave rise to anxious affect that in turn required defense mechanisms in order to maintain some psychic equilibrium. Consistent with relational models, Tasca and colleagues (2005) suggested that attachment needs (i.e., needs for security which may be unconscious), and not primitive impulses, are primary for any individual.

Where do eating disorder symptoms fit in this model? The interpersonal model of binge eating (Ansell, Grilo, & White, 2012), for example, suggests that interpersonal stressors cause negative affect which in turn may lead to eating disordered symptoms as a means of coping. There is now substantial research on interpersonal sensitivities in those with BN, and how specific interpersonal stressors lead to negative affect and then binging and purging symptoms (e.g., Steiger, Gauvin, Jabalpurwala, Seguin, & Stotland, 1999). And so, a psychodynamic model of eating disorders starts with attachment needs for security that remain largely unmet and unconscious. These give rise to anxiety or negative affect, which in turn precipitate the use of defense mechanisms or eating disorder symptoms as a means of coping (Figure 1).

Concurrently, attachment functioning, especially if based on insecure states of mind, will define the nature and quality of affec-

tive states and defense mechanisms (Figure 1). Incoherence of mental states in those with attachment insecurity will exacerbate difficulties with affect regulation. Insecurely attached individuals, especially those with eating disorders (Fonagy, Leigh, Steele, Steele, Kennedy, et al., 1996) commonly have diminished reflective functioning, and so they have great difficulty in making use of internal resources for felt security or adequately reaching out for external resources for support. Because of fears of abandonment in those with preoccupied states, or unacknowledged fears of continued disappointments in those with attachment avoidance, their relationships do not provide a secure base from which they can manage their internal experiences and explore their environment. Their affect regulation strategies are consistent with their preoccupied (i.e., up-regulation of affect) or dismissing (i.e., down-regulation of affect) mental states, and these strategies further their anxiety and/or negative affect. As a result of difficult affective experiences and anxiety they may turn to binge eating or dietary restriction as a means of coping, which are likely consistent with maladaptive defensive functioning. Recent findings within a large clinical sample demonstrated that the relationship between preoccupied attachment styles and eating disorder symptoms could be largely explained by hyper-activation of emotions (Tasca, Szadkowski, Illing, Trinneer, Grenon, et al., 2009). Further, the relationship between dismissing attachment styles and depressive symptoms were largely explained by deactivation of emotions (Tasca et al., 2009).

Generally, insecure attachments characterized by limited coherence of mental states, and problems with reflective functioning, result in maladaptive coping with negative affect or anxiety. These processes confer a level of vulnerability to the biological (low or high set point for weight) and cultural (idealization of thin ideal) pressures, especially in young women, that could contribute to or maintain an eating disorder (Figure 1).

In the following, two clinical examples of patients with eating disorders will be discussed to illustrate difficulties related to attachment areas of functioning. Specific attachment areas of functioning (interpersonal style, affect regulation, coherence of mind, and reflective functioning) and the interplay among attachment needs, anxiety/negative affect, and defense mechanisms will be discussed in relation to eating disorder symptoms and treatment issues including countertransference.

CASE 1: BEATRICE*

Beatrice is a 27-year-old single woman with an undergraduate degree in psychology and who works as a server in a coffee shop. She was diagnosed with bulimia nervosa, purging type (APA, 2000). She described a difficult early family environment in which her mother was periodically depressed during which her mother spent days in her bedroom, leaving Beatrice and her siblings to fend for themselves at those times. Beatrice's father was often away at work, and he had significant problems with binge drinking. He was alternately playful with

her, or when he was drunk he was violent toward her mother and verbally abusive toward Beatrice. Beatrice often turned to teachers and coaches for security and warmth, but these relationships were short lived. Beatrice was sexually abused by her maternal grandfather between the ages of 10 and 12, and this stopped when she told an aunt. The abuse was never openly discussed in the family. Beatrice described a history of drug and alcohol abuse that started in her early teens. Though she had problems with restricted dieting for several years, she began regular binge eating and purging at 17. She has a very negative self-evaluation which includes her extreme dislike of her body. She had a few romantic relationships that did not last long. Her closest female friend no longer speaks to her after Beatrice had a sexual encounter with her friend's boyfriend. When asked about binging and purging, she said that her feelings get out of control and binging provides some comfort, but then she feels disgusted and then vomits.

Assessment of Beatrice's attachment functioning indicated that she was preoccupied with regard to attachments and that she also experienced disorganized mental states related to the abuse by her grandfather. Attachment figures during her childhood were inconsistent; her mother was periodically depressed, her father was absent or sometimes drunk and violent; and other positive adult figures (i.e., teaches, coaches, aunt) were only present occasionally. Hence, Beatrice developed a preoccupied mental state regarding potential loss and abandonment of attachment relationships that continued into her adult life. Beatrice's adult relationships are strained and tumultuous, and she might sabotage close relationships (e.g., by sleeping with a girlfriend's boyfriend) perhaps as a means of defending herself against the hurt of possible rejection. Her primary affective experience is characterized by anger that fluctuates with extreme self-loathing. Beatrice often replays past hurts and disap-

*All case material has been disguised to protect patient privacy.

pointments thus keeping these memories and feelings at the forefront of her mental life. As a result of her overwhelming anger and self-loathing she had a difficult time maintaining a coherent narrative. For example, when asked about her childhood relationship with her mother, Beatrice quickly became enraged because her mother did not show up for dinner just the week prior. This violated the AAI condition of relevance. That is, she was unable to maintain the current context of the conversation due to her present anger, and her response was not relevant to the question. As a result of these processes, Beatrice's reflective functioning suffered. She had a difficult time understanding her internal experiences and the role that eating disorder symptoms might play in regulating her emotions and mental states. Despite all of this, group therapy members in an eating disorders day treatment program in which Beatrice was receiving treatment found her to be quite likable, but her self-loathing made her struggle with appreciating the group's empathy toward her. Further, her mental state became easily disorganized when thoughts of her grandfather intruded. During these times her narrative was disrupted, she might lose awareness of the current context and showed problems in logic and reasoning. Her primary defenses where characterized as action-oriented. That is, she often acted out when she experienced heightened and unbearable anxiety—by substance use, binge eating, or sexually. At these times she was prone to binge and purge which provided her with temporary emotional respite, though this was often followed by self-loathing. Figure 2, top panel, briefly illustrates aspects of the attachment-based psychodynamic case formulation for Beatrice.

Treatment for Beatrice included a focus on the binge eating and purging. To that end she entered intensive time-limited, 12-week, group-based, 4-day-a-week day treatment for eating disorders that included nutritional rehabilitation and an agreement to refrain from symptoms (i.e., binge eating and purging). Psychotherapy groups were provided by a multidisciplinary team of therapists (psychiatrists, psychologists, social workers, nurses) from several theoretical perspectives including CBT and psychodynamic-interpersonal. The focus of psychotherapeutic interventions was to help her to regulate better her affect by addressing her fears of abandonment and by allowing herself to experience the group as a safe and secure base. Therapists were aware of their own countertransference hostility to Beatrice that was likely a projection of self-hatred, and therapists had to manage their feelings of hopelessness for her. Improving attachment security to the group was key to helping Beatrice experience others' empathy and liking. This in turn allowed her to be more empathic toward other group members and more compassionate toward herself. The group experience became a recapitulation of early family dynamics (Yalom & Leszcz, 2005) in which she initially expected abandonment (i.e., that the staff would discharge her, and that fellow group members would be angry at her), and so highlighting empathic responses from others was a corrective experience for Beatrice. Once she allowed for this empathic experience and appreciated the group as a secure base, it became easier for her to down-regulate her emotions. To facilitate this process therapists often encouraged Beatrice to step back from her intense emotions and learn ways to reflect on rather than impulsively act on what she was feeling. In this way her action defenses were undermined by a more adaptive reflective stance. Both her increasing reflective capacity and the empathic experience in the group improved Beatrice's ability to mentalize—that is, she had a better appreciation for others' caring and liking for her and she was able to provide genuine support to others who were suffering. By the end of the time-limited treatment, Beatrice still struggled with occasional eating disorder symptoms, but she seemed more confident and certainly more thoughtful and reflective. The disorganizing effect of the sexual abuse was still evident and Beatrice would clearly

Beatrice: Preoccupied Attachment and Bulimia Nervosa

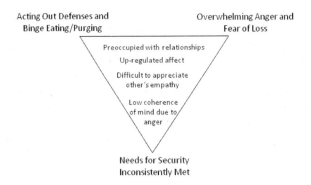

Acting Out Defenses and
Binge Eating/Purging

Overwhelming Anger and
Fear of Loss

Preoccupied with relationships

Up-regulated affect

Difficult to appreciate
other's empathy

Low coherence
of mind due to
anger

Needs for Security
Inconsistently Met

Anna: Dismissing Attachment and Anorexia Nervosa

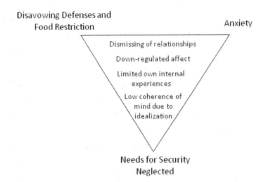

Disavowing Defenses and
Food Restriction

Anxiety

Dismissing of relationships

Down-regulated affect

Limited own internal
experiences

Low coherence of
mind due to
idealization

Needs for Security
Neglected

FIGURE 2. Illustration of aspects of two case formulations based on a
psychodynamic model of eating disorders.

require more psychotherapy to better manage its ongoing effects.

CASE 2: ANNA

Anna was an 18-year-old woman who was underweight and diagnosed with anorexia nervosa, restricting type (APA, 2000). She described an idealized early family history in which her parents were "loving, caring, and perfect," though specific details were scant. Both of her parents were competitive athletes, and Anna became a competitive long-distance runner. At 13, her mother died of cancer after a brief illness. Soon afterwards Anna began to restrict her food intake more seriously. She could not recall the specific feelings she had when her mother died, though she said she was "obviously sad" at the time but has "gotten over it." Anna claimed that she and her father discussed her mother's death, but she does not recall their last conversation about this. She did admit that she and her father argued frequently because of her slipping school grades. Her school achievement until recently was excellent and she plans to go to university to study human kinetics. Anna had sports-related acquaintances but no close friends from childhood or adolescence, and has never had a romantic relationship. She is concerned about her lack of friends, but also likes her independence. She came into the eating disorders treatment program partly because she became increasingly depressed and partly because she can no longer run due to a recurring injury and fatigue. Anna had a difficult time describing what function her eating disorder symptoms may have served in her life, though she did say that she felt better about herself and more in control when she restricted her diet.

As with many who have a dismissing attachment style, it was difficult to get a clear picture of Anna's childhood and current life experiences. She offered up idealized adjectives to describe early attachment relationships, but she could not provide any specific memories to illustrate these highly positive descriptors. This violated the AAI conditions of truth (i.e., by not providing adequate examples) and economy (i.e., by not providing enough information), thus her coherence of mind was limited. This style persisted even after her weight was restored to near normal. Anna described her parents as "high energy people" who were always on the go and busy with their own sports. Her father in particular, was driven and expected Anna to excel in sports and school. Recently, however, he was genuinely concerned for her health and wellbeing, which was met with derogatory comments from Anna. Anna was dismissive of any needs she might have for closeness, however, she was concerned that she had never dated, and on occasion she genuinely appeared to long for a romantic partner. Her emotional expressiveness was decidedly low key, and she often struggled with describing her emotions. Regarding reflective functioning, she had a profound lack of curiosity about herself, her family, and the nature of her eating disorder symptoms. Her defenses were characterized by disavowal, such as denial and rationalization. We suspected a disorganized mental state with regard the loss of her mother mainly because of Anna had few memories of her mother and her death, and when she did talk of her mother's death

she often lost track of the thread of the narrative. Figure 2, bottom panel, briefly illustrates aspects of the attachment-based psychodynamic case formulation for Anna.

Initially, Anna entered an inpatient treatment program for eating disorders that focused on medical stabilization. The early emphasis of inpatient treatment was on establishing a normalized diet and weight restoration. Weight restoration was a key first step in order for Anna to be cognitively sharp enough to make use of psychological interventions. When her weight stabilized to near normal she was transferred to a 12-week, time-limited, group-based intensive day treatment program for eating disorders (described above). Therapists who worked with Anna reported countertransference in which they felt bored or helpless, which likely paralleled her impoverished internal life and her dismissive attitude toward closeness. Therapists often described early therapy sessions as concrete, superficial, and food-oriented. Increased awareness of emotions and up-regulating of affect was an important goal for Anna's treatment. However, although those with dismissing mental states do not appear to be emotionally reactive, they often do experience a high level of anxiety especially in the face of conflict or when their preferred defensive stance is challenged (Dozier & Kobak, 1992). Those with dismissing attachments also tend to drop out of treatment at a higher rate (e.g., Tasca, Taylor, Bissada, Ritchie, & Balfour, 2004) possibly because of difficulty managing anxiety related to feeling vulnerable in close or challenging interpersonal situations. Hence therapists took a gradual and graded approach to helping Anna with her emotions. Initially, therapists simply encouraged Anna to describe her emotions or asked group members to imagine what Anna might be feeling given the circumstances. Once she was more comfortable within the group, therapists focused on empathizing with Anna's feelings. Group members were asked what they were feeling in relation to what Anna was talking about. Only after Anna became more comfortable and secure with the closeness implicitly required in the group did the therapists gently confront Anna's defenses against affect. For example, initially Anna smiled in group therapy sessions when talking about the loss of her mother. Therapists began to note how incongruent her smile was to the content and how the incongruence made it difficult for the group to connect with Anna's experience and feel close to her. This gradual exposure to her emotional life within a safe group environment allowed Anna eventually to admit to her vulnerabilities and imperfections, and to experience her emotions. Concurrently, her coherence of mind improved as she was able to admit to her parents' imperfections instead of idealizing them. This lead to a closer and more genuine relationship between Anna and her father. She developed a clearer understanding of her food restriction as a means of numbing and shutting down any affect. Anna took on a leadership role in the group during her later weeks in the program. She often took new members under her wing and she was particularly attuned to the needs of those who were highly dismissive. Feeling valued in her newly found leadership role helped Anna to feel more confident in her abilities to manage her own affective experiences.

CONCLUSIONS

Current conceptualizations for eating disorders tend to focus on cognitive factors and biological and social contexts, and underemphasize the role of the individual and their dynamics. That is, the person seems to be lost in mainstream models of eating disorders. Moreover, standard theories commonly do not include a developmental perspective to understanding attachment functioning and symptom development within a cultural and biological context. Psychodynamic concepts are well positioned to provide a truly biopsychosocial model of the person and their eating disorder symptoms. The framework presented in this article is relational and attachment based, while keeping in the forefront patients' symptoms and contexts. As such it can help clinicians to develop treatments that are tailored to the person and their particular dynamics.

REFERENCES

Ainsworth, M., Blehar, M., Waters, E., & Wall, S. (1978). *Patterns of attachment.* Hillsdale, NJ: Erlbaum.

American Psychiatric Association. (2000). *Diagnostic and statistical manual of mental disorders* (4th ed., text rev.). Washington, DC: Author.

Amini, F., Lewis, T., Lannon, R., Louie, A., Baumbacher, G., McGuinness, T., & Schiff, E. Z. (1996). Affect, attachment, memory: Contributions toward psychobiologic integration. *Psychiatry, 59,* 213-239.

Ansell, E. B., Grilo, C. M., & White, M. A. (2012). Examining the interpersonal model of binge eating and loss of control over eating in women. *International Journal of Eating Disorders, 45,* 43-50.

Arcelus, J., Mitchell, A. J., Wales, J., & Nielsen, S. (2011). Mortality rates in patients with anorexia nervosa and other eating disorders: A meta-analysis of 36 studies. *Archives of General Psychiatry, 68,* 724-731.

Bakermans-Kranenburg, M. J., & van IJzendoorn, M. H. (2009). The first 10,000 adult attachment interviews: Distributions of adult attachment representations in clinical and non-clinical groups. *Attachment and Human Development, 11,* 223-263.

Bartholomew, K., & Horowitz, L. M. (1991). Attachment styles among young-adults: A test of a 4-category model. *Journal of Personality and Social Psychology, 61,* 226-244.

Bowlby, J. (1980). *Attachment and loss.* New York: Basic Books.

Bretherton, I. (1994). The origins of attachment theory: John Bowlby and Mary Ainsworth. In R. D. Parke, P. A. Ornstein, J. J. Rieser, & C. Zahn-Waxler (Eds.), *A century of developmental psychology* (pp. 431-471). Washington, DC: APA.

Bruch, H. (1978). *The golden cage: The enigma of anorexia nervosa.* New York: Harvard University Press.

Bulik, C. M., Slof-Op't Landt, M. C., van Furth, E. F., & Sullivan, P. F. (2007). The genetics of anorexia nervosa. *Annual Review of Nutrition, 27,* 263-275.

Castonguay, L. G., Goldfried, M. R., Wiser, S. L., Raue, P. J., & Hayes, A. M. (1996). Predicting the effect of cognitive therapy for depression: A study of unique and common factors. *Journal of Consulting and Clinical Psychology, 64,* 497-504.

Crittenden, P. M. (2006). A dynamic-maturational model of attachment. *Australian and New Zealand Journal of Family Therapy, 27,* 105-116.

Dozier, M., & Kobak, R. R. (1992). Psychophysiology in attachment interviews: Converging evidence for deactivating strategies. *Child Development, 63,* 1473-1480.

Fairburn, C. G. (2008). *Cognitive-behavior therapy and eating disorders.* New York: Guilford.

Fonagy, P. (2001). *Attachment theory and psychoanalysis.* New York: Other Press.

Fonagy, P., Leigh, T., Steele, M., Steele, H., Kennedy, R., Mattoon, G., et al. (1996). The relation of attachment status, psychiatric classification, and response to psychotherapy. *Journal of Consulting and Clinical Psychology, 64,* 22-31.

Fonagy, P., Target, M., Steele, H., & Steele, M. (1998). *Reflective functioning manual: Version 5* (Unpublished manuscript). London: University College London.

Foscha, D. (2000). *The transforming power of affect: A model for accelerated change.* New York: Basic Books.

Fraley, R. C., Brumbaugh, C. C., & Marks, M. J. (2005). The evolution and function of adult attachment: A comparative and phylogenetic analysis. *Journal of Personality and Social Psychology, 89,* 808-822.

Fuendeling, J. M. (1998). Affect regulation as a stylistic process within adult attachment. *Journal of Social and Personal Relationships, 15,* 291-322.

Garner, D., Rockert, W., Davis, R., Garner, M., Olmsted, M., & Eagle, M. (1993). Comparison of cognitive-behavioral and supportive-expressive therapy for bulimia nervosa. *American Journal of Psychiatry, 150,* 37-46.

Grice, P. (1989). *Studies in the way of words.* Cambridge: Harvard University Press.

Harrop, E. N., & Marlatt, G. A. (2010). The comorbidity of substance use disorders and eating disorders in women: Prevalence, etiology, and treatment. *Addictive Behaviors, 35,* 392-398.

Hubbard, J. (2013). Psychotherapy outcome for eating disorders: A meta analysis. Unpublished manuscript. Brigham Young University, Utah.

Hudson, J. I., Hiripi, E., Pope, H. G., & Kessler, R. C. (2007). The prevalence and correlates of eating disorders in the national comorbidity survey replication. *Biological Psychiatry, 61,* 348-358.

Levy, K. N., Meehan, K. B., Kelly, K. M., Reynoso, J. S., Weber, M., Clarkin, J. F., & Kernberg, O. F. (2006). Change in attachment patterns and reflective function in a randomized control trial of transference-focused psychotherapy for borderline personality disorder. *Journal of Consulting and Clinical Psychology, 74,* 1027-1040.

Lunn, S., & Poulsen, S. (2012). Psychoanalytic psychotherapy for bulimia nervosa: A manualized approach. *Psychoanalytic Psychotherapy, 26,* 48-64.

Luyten, P., Van Houdenhove, B., Lemma, A., Target, M., & Fonagy, P. (2013). Vulnerability for functional somatic disorders: A contemporary psychodynamic approach. *Journal of Psychotherapy Integration, 23,* 250-262.

Main, M., Goldwyn, R., & Hesse, E. (2003). *Adult attachment classification system version 7.2* (Unpublished manuscript). Berkeley: University of California.

Mallinckrodt, B. (2000). Attachment, social competencies, social supports, and interpersonal process in psychotherapy. *Psychotherapy Research, 10,* 239-266.

Mikulincer, M. (1995). Appraisal and coping with a real-life stressful situation: The contribution of attachment styles. *Personality and Social Psychology Bulletin, 21,* 408-416.

Mikulincer, M., Shaver, P. R., Sapir-Lavid, Y., & Avihou-Kanza, N. (2009). What's inside the minds of securely and insecurely attached people? The secure-base script and its associations with attachment-style dimensions. *Journal of Personality and Social Psychology, 97,* 615-633.

Mischoulon, D., Eddy, K. T., Keshaviah, A., Dinescu, D., Ross, S. L., Kass, A. E., et al. (2011). Depression and eating disorders: Treatment and course. *Journal of Affective Disorders, 130,* 470-477.

Mitchell, J. E., & Crow, S. J. (2006). Medical complications of anorexia nervosa and bulimia nervosa. *Current Opinion in Psychiatry, 19,* 438-443.

Perry, J. C. (1990). *The Defense Mechanism Rating Scales* (DMRS; 5th ed.). Cambridge, MA: Cambridge Hospital.

Poulsen, S, Lunn, S., Daniel, S. I. F., Folke, S., Bork Mathiesen, B., Katznelson, H., & Fairburn, C. G. (2013). A randomized controlled trial of psychoanalytic psychotherapy or cognitive-behavioral therapy for bulimia nervosa. *American*

Journal of Psychiatry, AJP in Advance: doi: 10.1176/appi.ajp.2013.12121511

Preti, A., Girolamo, G., Vilagut, G., Alonso, J., de Graaf, R., Bruffaerts, R., & Investigators, ESEMeD-WMH. (2009). The epidemiology of eating disorders in six European countries: Results of the ESEMeD-WMH project. *Journal of Psychiatric Research, 43,* 1125-1132.

Satir, D. A., Thompson-Brenner, H., Boisseau, C. L., & Crisafulli, M. A. (2009). Countertransference reactions to adolescents with eating disorders: Relationships to clinician and patient factors. *International Journal of Eating Disorders, 42,* 511-521.

Schwartz, H. J. (1988). Bulimia: Psychoanalytic perspectives. In H. J. Schwartz (Ed.), *Bulimia: Psychoanalytic treatment and theory* (pp. 31-53). Madison, CT: International Universities Press.

Smink, F. R., van Hoeken, D., & Hoek, H. W. (2012). Epidemiology of eating disorders: Incidence, prevalence and mortality rates. *Current Psychiatry Reports, 14,* 406-414.

Steiger, H., Gauvin, L., Jabalpurwala, S., Seguin, J. R., & Stotland, S. (1999). Hypersensitivity to social interactions in bulimic syndromes: Relationship to binge eating. *Journal of Consulting and Clinical Psychology, 67,* 765-775.

Stice, E. (2001). A prospective test of the dual-pathway model of bulimic pathology: Mediating effects of dieting and negative affect. *Journal of Abnormal Psychology, 110,* 124-135.

Tasca, G. A., Mikail, S., & Hewitt, P. (2005). Group psychodynamic interpersonal psychotherapy: Summary of a treatment model and outcomes for depressive symptoms. In M. E. Abelian (Ed.), *Focus on psychotherapy research* (pp. 155-188). New York: Nova.

Tasca, G. A., Presniak, M. D., Demidenko, N., Balfour, L., Krysanski, V., Trinneer, A., & Bissada, H. (2011). Testing a maintenance model for eating disorders in a sample seeking treatment at a tertiary care center: A structural equation modeling approach. *Comprehensive Psychiatry, 52,* 678-687.

Tasca, G. A., Ritchie, K., Zachariades, F., Proulx, G., Trinneer, A., Balfour, L., et al. (2013). Attachment insecurity mediates the relationship between childhood trauma and eating disorder psychopathology in a clinical sample: A structural equation model. *Child Abuse and Neglect.* Advance online publication.

Tasca, G. A., Szadkowski, L., Illing, V., Trinneer, A., Grenon, R., Demidenko, N., et al. (2009). Adult attachment, depression, and eating disorder symptoms: The mediating role of affect regulation strategies. *Personality and Individual Differences, 47,* 662-667.

Tasca, G. A., Taylor, D., Bissada, H., Ritchie, K., & Balfour, L. (2004). Attachment predicts treatment completion in an eating disorders partial hospital program among women with anorexia nervosa. *Journal of Personality Assessment, 83,* 201-212.

Thompson-Brenner, H., Glass, S., & Westen, D. (2003). A multidimensional meta-analysis of psychotherapy for bulimia nervosa. *Clinical Psychology Science and Practice, 10,* 269-287.

Thompson-Brenner, H., Satir, D. A., Franko, D. L., & Herzog, D. (2012). Clinician reactions to patients with eating disorders: A review. *Psychiatric Services, 63,* 73-78.

Tobin, D. L., Banker, J. D., Weiseberg, L., & Bowers, W. (2007). I know what you did last summer (and it was not CBT): A factor analytic model of international psychotherapeutic practice in the eating disorders. *International Journal of Eating Disorders, 40,* 754-757.

Wallin, D. (2007). *Attachment in psychotherapy.* New York: Guilford.

Waters, E., Merrick, S., Treboux, D., Crowell, J., & Albersheim, L. (2000). Attachment security in infancy and early adulthood: A twenty-year longitudinal study. *Child Development, 71,* 684-689.

Westen, D. (1998). The scientific legacy of Sigmund Freud: Toward a psychodynamically informed psychological science. *Psychological Bulletin, 124,* 333-371.

Williamson, D. A., Zucker, N. L., Martin, C. K., & Smeets, M. A. (2004). Etiology and management of eating disorders. In H. E. Adams & P. B. Sutker (Eds.), Comprehensive psychopathology (3rd ed., pp. 641-670). New York: Springer.

Yalom, I. D., & Leszcz, M. (2005). The theory and practice of group psychotherapy (5th ed.). New York: Basic.

Zipfel, S., Wild, B., Groß, G., Friederich, H.-C., Teufel, M., et al. on behalf of the ANTOP study group. (2013). Focal psychodynamic therapy, cognitive behaviour therapy, and optimised treatment as usual in outpatients with anorexia nervosa (ANTOP study): Randomised controlled trial. *The Lancet.* Early Online Publication.

Grief

Grieving: The Role of Self-Reorganization

Mardi Horowitz

Abstract: Grieving is a well-known topic to psychodynamic clinicians. Nonetheless, the identity disturbance and identity growth issues that accompany the familiar problems are less well known. Phases of modification of self-organization during an adaptive mourning process can be facilitated by helping patients with pathological grief clarify the shifts they are experiencing in self-state and self-concepts.

As clinicians, we may see patients who develop stress response syndromes after bereavement even though most people go through mourning without psychiatric complications. We hear about pangs of severe longing for the lost relationship and listen to intrusive memories of what has been lost. Such patients may report anxious and depressive symptoms, but their grief-related task of self re-definition is less readily reported because diminishment or disturbance in a sense of identity is less expected and also hard to put into words. By clarifying how grieving can impact on identity, we may be able to augment our approach to our patients and assist them in forming new and adaptive attitudes. A brief vignette about Mary illustrates how such patients may present their experiences. Please note that all patient information has been disguised and that patients gave informed consent to the study of their cases for scholarly purposes.

MARY[1]

Mary's elderly mother died when Mary was middle-aged. Mary felt sorrowful, cried at the funeral, took a week away from her work, and went through her mother's belongings. Afterward, she resumed her life as usual, but two months later she was surprised to find herself preoccupied with unbidden images of hostile exchanges with her mother. She also found herself entering into an episodic state of being unusually remote or hostile to her friends and work associates. She observed herself entering such strange self-states and felt "like she was numbly just observing herself, as if from afar, and not knowing who she was anymore."

Mary said she wanted to feel grief for her loss, and she tried deliberately to recall her mother in the context of warm and empathic memories. In doing so, she found she could not conjure up any image of her mother's face. Instead, she intrusively pictured her own face, contorted with anger, as if seen in a ghastly mirror. She felt vulnerable and shaky because these episodes felt out of control.

In the course of therapy, Mary experienced a full restoration of her capacities to recall both positive and negative memories of herself in transactions with her mother. Mary encountered ambivalent attitudes as

---

1. All patients' information has been disguised and the patients had given informed consent to the study of their cases for scholarly purposes.

she forged a new narrative of the relationship history and gradually forgave herself for her past states of hot anger and cold withdrawal. She eventually felt an invigorated sense of self-confidence and self-esteem.

PHASES OF RESPONSE

Someone in the midst of grief can seldom accurately predict *when* he or she might enter a particular mood, *what* memories of self as relating with the deceased would be recalled, *when or if* strong emotions would be triggered by some reminder of the loss, or *why* a new attitude, perhaps of self-vulnerability, would emerge. In understanding these phenomena, it is helpful to have a general theory of phases of response. Freud (1917), Kubler-Ross (2005), Lindemann (1944), Parkes (1964, 1972), Parkes and Weiss (1983), Pollock (1978), Shear, Frank, Houck, and Reynolds (2005), and Zhang, El-Jawahri, and Prigerson (2006) described such stages of grief and I summarized them (Horowitz, 2011) as follows:

(1) Initial outcry phase: During a stage of initial impact of the bad news, some people experience an intense sense of urgency as well as an alarm reaction. This often includes an imperative impulse to search for and protect the deceased as if he or she were still alive and in mortal danger.

(2) Denial and avoidance phase: Next, a numbed and "business as usual" self-state may replace the acute alarm reactions, with the person then averting attention away from reminders of the loss.

(3) Intrusive feelings and ideas phase: The person in this phase may experience sudden entry into states of searing emotion. These intense pangs of feeling may be associated with so-matic components and altered identity experiences, including depersonalizations and dissociations.

(4) Working through phase: As intrusive pangs are less intense, and numbing is reduced, the oscillation of both extreme states is associated with progress as the person revises attitudes and expectations, forming new goals for his or her own future.

(5) Completion phase: When the work of grief has been mostly completed, attitudes have been modified and the person has accomplished changes in his or her sense of identity. This may include a readiness to engage in new attachments, a readiness that was absent in the previous phases.

People with frozen, pathological, complicated, or prolonged grief (as such syndromes have been called) have failed to reach the completion phase (Clayton, 1974; Deutsch, 1937; Freud, 1917; Glick, Weiss, & Parkes, 1974; Horowitz, Wilner, Marmar, & Krupnick, 1980; Lindemann, 1944; Osterweiss, Solomon, & Green, 1984; Pollock, 1978; Prigerson et al., 2009; Windholz, Marmar, & Horowitz, 1985). In recent years, psychotherapy has been empirically shown to be effective for these syndromes (Shear et al., 2005; Zhang et al., 2006). Understanding identity modification in each phase can aid in formulating how to do such therapies with individual cases.

The Phase of Outcry

Outcry contains a rapid assessment of the implications of the loss for the self. The sudden confrontation with bad news leads to a sharp rise in fear, sadness, and anger associated with physiological changes in sympathetic, parasympathetic, and hormonal systems. The result may range from hyperarousal to shock. In addition, a sense of failure to protect the deceased from death can lead to raw and warded-off potentials for shame and guilt.

A person may form a working model in which the deceased is viewed as seriously harmed and critically in need of help. Because the deceased is modeled as harmed, the self is aroused to act. As a result, the person may undertake frantic, but hopeless activity to repair the hazardous condition believed to be the state of the deceased. Some funeral rituals satisfy this motivation to "do something!"

The emotional expression of an outcry phase may come as actions and images, as well as words. There may be appeals for divine help ("Oh God!") or expressions of rage ("God damn it!") or remorse ("I'm so sorry!"). Rapid unconscious appraisals of the repercussions of the death may occur. The potential for intense negative emotional states may be resisted by automatic defenses. Some form of denial can occur ("Oh no! It can't be! Say it isn't so!").

A rapid appraisal of the self during the outcry phase can lead to conscious vows ("I'll survive this," or "I'm glad it's not me who died!"). Also, self-critical splits in identity organization may occur ("I'll never enjoy life again—ever!"). These attitudes may return to conscious representation in a later intrusive phase.

The Phase of Denial

A conscious self-state may feel frozen, insulated, de-realized, or de-personalized. Of course, some recognition of short-range consequences of the loss to the self are considered, but many other long-range effects have not been fully contemplated. A dissociative, "I am waiting here for return of the lost one" may be felt.

On the other hand, due to a numbing of feelings, the individual may feel self-criticism and anticipate social embarrassment because of his or her absence of expressed sorrow. Psychoeducation on what to expect during grief can be quite supportive in maintaining self-esteem during this phase. I have attempted to provide that in a self-help book called *Grieving As Well As Possible*" (Horowitz, 2010).

The denial phase may last for days, weeks, or even months. During this time, the mourner may have returned to many of the customary forms of his life. A sense of comparative safety returns. Then, intrusive experiences may increase in frequency and intensity.

The Phase of Intrusion

Conscious recognition of the significance of a loss to the self becomes prominent during this phase. There is less use of unconscious, defensive, and inhibitory operations. During this phase, one may become preoccupied with an aspect of identification of self with the deceased in which one views oneself as vulnerable to the same kind of death. One may experience the physical symptoms, like those of the disease that killed the other, or, in fantasy reveries, strike mental bargains with the gods that they might protect the self from the imminent threat. One may feel guilty for worrying about dying when it is the other who is actually dead.

Existing schemas still organize an expectation that the deceased will magically turn up as alive. But the other is not there to reflect the self. Situations that were experienced together seem particularly empty. Cooking a meal, going out with friends, or going to the movies painfully emphasize the absence of the habitual support of identity through reflectance in an expected companionship. Great joy at a seeming reunion during a dream is replaced by a pang of sorrow upon awakening.

Unanswered questions during the outcry phase of initial realization, such as, "Who is to blame?" and "Why did this happen to me?" often reemerge during an intrusive phase. These themes may be organized during this phase by usually dormant schemas, such as those wherein the self is viewed as bad and harmful to the other, or defective and abandoned by the other, assuming the other is gone because the self was unworthy. Survivor guilt, shame over feelings of anger at the deceased, and fear of future self-damage become preoccupations. These conflictual topics are examined repeatedly in psychotherapy, in a phase of work to modify identity and relationship attitudes.

The Phase of Working-Through

Avoidant and intrusive phenomena may recur during the working-through phase. These omissions and preoccupations oscillate, perhaps taking the edge off either extreme. Periods of equilibrium occur in which neither defensive numbness nor emotional flooding are prominent. This type of progress is postponed in complicated grief and then facilitated in psychotherapy.

During the grief process, one reviews the relationship with the deceased in terms of all the varied self-concepts that have participated in working models of the attachment (Bowlby, 1980). This may include examination of self-images as too strong and too weak, good and bad, clean and dirty, selfish and caring, and loving and hating. Reality is separated from fantasy, and a new narrative story evolves.

This process of self-understanding leads to plans for the self operating in the world in a realistic near future. Before this adaptive end of mourning is reached, the schemas and memories of the past self and of self in the relationship require review in order to decide what self-attributions are now true, which are now fantasy, and what new skills may now need development.

Completion

In this phase, the person may attempt a new relationship of the type that was lost. Another person is found to care for, relate to sexually, or to serve as a parental figure,

similar to the deceased loved one. Commonly the new relationship is then colored by efforts to restore within it some aspects of the lost relationship. The discrepancy between the preexisting role-relationship model with the deceased and the patterns occurring with the new person may lead to further emotional conflicts and personality growth, as in the following example.

CASE EXAMPLE

Before the murder of her young husband James, Patricia was content in her roles as wife, mother, and professional. The loss was traumatic and she was variously treated with supportive psychotherapy, anti-anxiety, and anti-depressant medications. She recovered control of her life, but two years into her passage through grief she sought a new kind of help because of a sense of conflicting identities. She was no longer on medication or seeing the supportive psychotherapist.

The precipitant of seeking a psychodynamic therapist was a new relationship with Sidney. Patricia desired to feel like a vibrant woman. Instead, as a moment of deepening intimacy occurred, she had intrusive images of herself, as if by attaching herself to Sidney she was cheating on James, her deceased husband. She experienced panic and withdrew.

She wavered between a desired self-schema as a vibrant woman and a dreaded self-concept of being a cheat by stabilizing herself in two alternative self-states. In one, she felt herself to be a vulnerable woman, pining for her lost husband, and feeling incompetent because she was bereft of his usual guidance of their activities. In the other, which was less problematic, she appeared cool and poised and spoke of herself as a competent caretaker who managed her home, children, and career activities. In this self-state, she planned to be aloof to men now and in the future. That would relieve her from the potential sense of guilty cheating if she gave in to loving Sidney.

In therapy, this aloof stance was challenged. The therapist told her she was avoiding some of the emotional pain of losing her husband and, therefore, did not yet fully realize that James was really dead. He said, supportively, "Your unconscious is the last to know such things."

As Patricia was able to tolerate intense negative affects, she could express new concepts about herself, in both memories of the relationship with James and new experiences and fantasies with Sidney. The therapist reflected back on what she said, repeating many statements while trying to clarify the difference between rational and irrational attitudes.

Understanding a dependent transference tendency helped her to resolve the dependence-autonomy conflict that had been latent, but held in check by her marriage. By comparing her expectations with the helpful expertise experienced in the therapist-patient relationship, she was able to see how and why her childhood past, her recent reality, and her near future could be different. She could be supported in her independence rather than losing her personal autonomy. If she experienced that autonomous identity with the therapist, she could experience it with Sidney; she would not be cheating on James, and she would not become as dependent on Sidney as she had been on James.

Excessive idealization of the therapist in a positive transference was also contrasted with realistic appraisals of what actually was happening. The therapist was not doing the work of grief; Patricia herself was engaged in revising her future self-definition. Helped by reflective conscious thinking, in the safe context of psychotherapy with a good therapeutic alliance, Patricia re-schematized her view of her relationship roles with her deceased husband and with the new man. She re-schematized James as beyond dying, as now safely dead, and no longer expecting her fidelity. She could then re-schematize the new intimacy as different from the prior marriage. She was wiser and more capable than when she accepted James's proposal with the urging of her parents to do so.

In comparing intimacies, Patricia modified her sense of current identity; she would be mutually, but not overly dependent on Sidney, as she had been on James. She was now a vibrant woman relating well to Sidney, and she could also remember being a loving wife in her memories of James. She had reduced contradictions between her roles and developed a stronger sense of identity in the course of grieving.

SUMMARY

During the outcry phase of mourning, alarming pangs of emotion may occur as the mind reacts to the serious mismatch between perception of the new situation and enduring schemas. The deceased may be modeled as harmed rather than dead. By the time of entry into a denial phase, the person has reconstituted defensive inhibitions. During this phase, depersonalization and dissociations may occur, with working models mentalizing the deceased both as dead and as alive.

With entry into an intrusive phase, the real finality of loss starts to be confronted. In a working-through phase, the mourning person contemplates and makes new decisions about what the loss means. This leads to new models in the mind as the new working models are repeated, and so they begin to be established as enduring schemas.

As the bereaved person slowly develops schemas that match the reality of permanent separation, the work of grief enters the completion phase. Equilibrium and self-constancy is restored.

REFERENCES

Bowlby, J. (1980). *Attachment and loss: Loss, sadness, and depression*. New York: Basic Books.

Clayton, P. J. (1974). Morality and morbidity in the first year of bereavement: A review. *Comprehensive Psychiatry, 14*, 151-157.

Deutsch, H. (1937). Absence of grief. *Psychoanalytic Quarterly, 6*, 12-22.

Freud, S. (1917). Transference. In Lecture XVII, introductory lectures on psychoanalysis. In J. Strachey (Ed.), *Standard edition, vol. 16* (pp. 431-447). London: Hogarth.

Glick, I., Weiss, R., & Parkes, C. M. (1974). *The first year of bereavement*. New York: Wiley.

Horowitz, M. J. (2011). *Stress response syndromes: PTSD, grief, adjustment, and dissociative disorders* (5th ed.). Northvale, NJ: Aronson.

Horowitz, M. J., Wilner, N., Marmar, C., & Krupnick, J. (1980). Pathological grief and the activation of latent self images. *American Journal of Psychiatry, 137*, 1157-1162.

Horowitz, M. J. (2010). *Grieving as well as possible*. Sausalito, CA: GreyHawk.

Kubler-Ross, E. (2005). *On grief and grieving: Finding the meaning of grief through five states of loss*. New York: Simon & Schuster.

Lindemann, E. (1944). Symptomatology and management of acute grief. American *Journal Psychiatry, 151*(6), 155-160.

Osterweiss, M., Solomon, F., & Green, M. (1984). *Bereavement: Reactions, consequences, and care.* Washington, DC: National Academy of Sciences Press.

Parkes, C. M. (1964). The effects of bereavement on physical and mental health: A study of the case records of widows. *British Medical Journal, 2*, 274.

Parkes, C. M. (1972). *Bereavement: Studies of grief in adult life*. Harmondsworth: Penguin.

Parkes, C. M., & Weiss, R. (1983). *Recovery from bereavement*. New York: Basic Books.

Pollock, C. (1978). Process and affect: Mourning and grief. *International Journal of Psycho-Analysis, 59*, 255-276.

Prigerson, H. G., Horowitz, M. J., Jacobs, S. C., Parkes, C. M., Aslan, M., Goodkin, K., et al. (2009). Prolonged grief disorder: Psychometric validation of criteria proposed for DSM-V and ICD-11. *PLoS Medicine, 6*(8).

Shear, K., Frank, E., Houck, P. R., & Reynolds, C. F., 3rd. (2005). Treatment of complicated grief: A randomized controlled trial. *Journal of the American Medical Association, 293*(21), 2601-2608.

Windholz, M., Marmar, C., & Horowitz, M. J. (1985). Review of research on conjugal bereavement. *Comprehensive Psychiatry, 26*, 433-447.

Zhang, B., El-Jawahri, A., Prigerson, H. G. (2006). Update on bereavement research: Evidence- based guidelines for the diagnosis and treatment of complicated bereavement. *Journal of Palliative Medicine, 9*, 1188-1203.

Psychodynamic Factors Behind Online Social Networking and Its Excessive Use

Thomas Cheuk Wing Li

"Any extension, whether of skin, hand, or foot, affects the whole psychic and social complex."
(McLuhan, 1964, p. 2)

Abstract: This article discusses the psychodynamic factors behind the popularity of one form of Internet activity, online social networking (SN). It views online SN as an extension of the social self, organized in a way that is more controllable than real life relating. The SN platforms reward its users with reassuring surfaces and novel self-object experiences while at the same time induces much anxiety. The addictive quality of online SN is understood in the context of collapse of dialectical space and the defensive use of this technology.

McLuhan, in his book *Understanding Media* (1964), asserted that electric technology represents the extension of our central nervous system. He further predicted an age when the extension of consciousness becomes possible, and the "creative process of knowing will be collectively and corporately extended to the whole of society" (McLuhan, 1964, p. 1). It appears that his prediction is now realized in the Internet. Since the advent of the so called Web 2.0, which enabled users to contribute content online, social networking (SN) sites have become highly popular. Some of the more popular ones include Facebook, Twitter, and LinkedIn. As of June 2015, there were 968 million daily active Facebook users, 87% of them accessing through mobile devices (Facebook, 2015).

Users between 15–19 years old spend at least 3 hours a day on social media, while those between 20–29 years old spend about 2 hours; 18% of users reported difficulties not checking FB for 3 hours (Go-globe, 2014). A longitudinal study by Kross and colleagues (2013) raised widespread media attention when they showed that Facebook use predicted declines in subjective well-being in young adults. Their result was supported by an experimental study (Sagioglou & Greitemeyer, 2014). In this context the term social networking addiction, considered as a subcategory of Internet addiction, has been proposed by some researchers as worthy of clinical and research attention (Kuss & Griffiths, 2011; Karaiskos, Tzavellas, & Balta, 2010).

Research in cyberpsychology is expanding, yet there are still debates over the concept of Internet addiction in regards to its validity and classification (Griffiths, 2013). Nevertheless, there is increasing consensus that addiction is not limited to substance use, and that behavioral addiction shares similar natural history, neurobiological mechanisms, and treatment response with substance addiction (Griffiths, 2013; Winkler et al., 2013).

In regards to the etiology of social networking addiction, Turel and Serenko (2012) reviewed recent literature and noted perspectives from cognitive-behavioral, social skill, and socio-cognitive models. Sherry Turkle has written extensively on her research findings on modern technology and the human psyche. In her book *Alone Together* (Turkle, 2013), she warned that we have come to expect more from technology and less from each other, and that puts us at risk of being diminished as human. Aron Balick published one of the first books specifically on social networking from a psychodynamic perspective (2013). This article narrows the focus on the psychodynamic factors behind the popularity of online SN and in some cases, its excessive use. Its scope covers both normal and pathological usage. In particular, it discusses how online SN has the potential to induce and relieve anxiety—an important feature common to other forms of addiction. It also highlights the role of surfaces in mobile computing. It shares Balick's (2013) belief that psychodynamic theories, being a study of the self in relation to others, has unique contribution to the understanding of this ubiquitous activity. In view of the ongoing contention in terminology, in this article the term "excessive use" is interchangeable with "addiction." The methodology used is one of selected literature review. The psychoanalytic writings of Heinz Kohut, Donald Winnicott, and Thomas Ogden form its theoretical base. Finally Khantzian's psychodynamic concept of substance addiction is applied to excessive online SN. As online SN itself is a nonclinical activity, everyday examples from the media are chosen as illustrations.

INTERSUBJECTIVE MOTIVATION BEHIND ONLINE SN

Human beings have an innate need for others in order to survive and feel secure. Stern (2004) used the term intersubjective motivation to describe this basic drive to be in contact with others in order to maintain intersubjective orientation and self-cohesion. The former refers to the need to read the intentions and feelings of others to know where we stand in the intersubjective field. When this is not achieved, anxiety arises and coping mechanisms are mobilized. The latter refers to our need for others to form and hold ourselves together, without which self-dissolution or fragmentation may occur. Sociologists Berger and Luckmann (1966) asserted that conversation is the most important vehicle of reality maintenance. It serves to maintain a measure of symmetry between objective and subjective reality. In the past this intersubjective motivation drove us to initiate contact with others through the telephone. Nowadays we have the convenience to go online. A quick login to check for new messages, a quick glance of our profile newsfeed, or a brief status update are all simple but significant acts that serve to keep our sense of self contained and grounded.

A higher-order need for others involves Kohut's (1984) concept of selfobject needs. These include mirroring, twinship, and idealization which are particular self-other dynamics that serve to maintain a stable, secure self. Selfobject needs continue throughout life but are especially prominent in persons with narcissistic personality structure. Given the nature of online SN it is hardly surprising that its use is associated with users' narcissistic traits (Mehdizadeh 2010; Paneka, Nardisa, & Konrath, 2013). The concept of others as selfobjects rather than subjects is based on the fact that the other is experienced as an extension of the self (Kohut, 1984). Turkle (2012) articulated this concept when she noted: "we can't get enough of one another if we can use technology to keep one another at distances we can control: not too close, not too far, just right...Lacking the capacity for solitude, we turn to other people but don't experience them as they are. It is as though we use them, need them as spare parts to support our increasingly fragile selves" (p. SR1). An important feature common to all online SN is the "like" button. This simple but extremely popular feature is ubiquitous in online SN sites and is widely endorsed as an indication of one's status. As of May 2013, there were approximately 4.5 billion unique "likes" generated daily on Facebook (Noyes, 2015). It means that one's post is being recognized, endorsed, and positively regarded—qualities of the mirroring selfobject function. This simple social gesture is often experienced as more gratifying than face-to-face recognition—the hyperpersonal effect described by Walther (1996). On the other end of the narcissistic spectrum, McWilliams (1994) noted the sensitive depleted type who seemed reserved but in fact is highly alert for potential criticisms and is intensely envious. Individuals with this trait may be more inclined to engage in passive browsing rather than content creation. This allows their grandiose selves to observe and devalue others without attracting direct criticisms. Gabbard (2001) remarked that the anonymity of the online world has a shame-reducing effect that boosts one's sense of omnipotence. This may be related to the absence of the interlocutor's gaze—"the stares that observes us" (Zangrilli, 2009, para. 14). Verduyn and colleagues (2015) found that passive Facebook usage is a determining factor for the negative effect of online SN use on mental health. Perhaps it reflects the other side of narcissism—the envy and bitterness that comes from a shamed and insecure self.

Ogden (1988a) described a form of pathological internal object relationship he called misrecognition. It refers to the defense against the anxiety that comes from not knowing how one feels and who one is. The individual has difficulty tolerating the agonies of the trial-and-error process of knowing the other and being known, therefore resorts to misnaming the experience through projection, omnipotent interpretation, and compulsions. These defenses create an illusion of knowing through "a range of substitute formations that fill the potential space (Winnicott, 1971) in which desire and fear, appetite and fullness, love and hate, might otherwise come into being" (Ogden, 1988a, p. 643).

For example, one may set up a stereotypic personality by imitating others as if this is how he or she actually feels. This is now easily achievable in online SN. Compared to the effort of being present to one's feelings and creating one's own self-representation, it is much easier to share other's representations or use the readily available "like" function and emoticons. In fact Facebook has inbuilt features that facilitate the naming of one's state of mind in its current version. Users who want to update their statuses are given a wide range of preset activities and feeling-states to choose from. These preset symbols and re-posted contents are the substitute formations of the online world, filling up the potential space, that is, the SN platforms as Ogden observed (1988a).

Balick (2013) preferred Benjamin's (1988) concept of mutual recognition as the motivating factor for online SN. It refers to the need to recognize others as subjects and have one's subjectivity recognized in turn. He asserted that by going into online SN, the individual is seeking to be in the mind of the other (Balick, 2013). On the other hand he noted that certain aspects of online SN facilitates "the functions of the false self and persona, transference and projection, that encourage relating as an object to objects rather than the fuller form of intersubjective relating" (p. 101). Indeed mutuality is difficult to achieve in online SN because of the asynchronic nature of electronic chat and the absence of real-time non-visual cues. It may be possible if it is used in the context of established close ties, in which online communications are used to compliment offline contacts.

The notions of intersubjective motivation and selfobject needs bring insights into the phenomenal proliferation of self-portraits, or "selfies" in the online SN context. Enabled by smart phone technology and popularized by celebrities worldwide, "selfie" was named the Word of the Year 2013 by Oxford Dictionaries (2013). There are more than one million selfies taken each day, which make up 30% of photos being taken by people between 18 to 24 years of age (Suk, 2014). The act of photographing oneself can be seen as intersubjectively driven—one seeks to see oneself from the position of the other. Not unlike the myth of Narcissus who became engrossed with his own reflection in the river, taking a selfie can be seen as an attempt to be one's own selfobject. The subsequent sharing of these images online with the expectation of getting "likes" reveals its narcissistic motivation. The powerful drive for attention means that selfies are becoming more extreme and quirky (Rosen, 2007). It was reported that more people have died while taking a selfie than from shark attacks in 2015 (Rizzo, 2015).

A recent news story in Hong Kong ("Woman Dies After," 2015) presents an extreme and tragic example of the intersubjective function of online SN. A 35-year-old woman was found dead after giving birth to a baby girl by herself in a subdivided flat. The father of the child was with his girlfriend during childbirth, but he fled the scene after he was shocked by the hemorrhage that followed. He claimed that he wasn't aware of the pregnancy until that day. It was reported that the woman posted a selfie of herself and her baby on Facebook before her death. The baby was sent to the hospital and survived. A small amount of illegal substances were found in the flat. It is telling that the woman chose to post a selfie online over other actions she could have taken, such as calling an ambulance. Perhaps out of the secluded environment she was seeking witnesses to confirm what had happened, that her experience was real. Taking the selfie of herself and her newborn could be understood as a concrete attempt to be her own witness. Perhaps she needed praise and acknowledgement in the form of "likes." Perhaps she felt so confused that she needed others to name her feelings for her. This story shows that intersubjective needs can sometimes take precedence over physical needs.

HOW ONLINE SN INDUCES ANXIETY—BOUNDARY AMBIGUITY AND THE PARANOID-SCHIZOID ORGANIZATION

Boundary separates two zones of social space-time that marks the differentiation between self and others (Diamond, Allcorn, & Stein, 2004). It is "the location of a relationship where the relationship both separates and connects" (Stapley, 1996, p. 69). Zhao (2006) suggested that the Internet necessitates a revision of the traditional view on social interaction that is based on face-to-face contact in the "here and now." The Internet, he pointed out, has created a new spatiotemporal zone—that of the "there and now." This vastly opens up the number and range of potential social connections, and markedly amplifies the selfobject experiences derivable from these sites. At the same time, activities in this new zone challenge our sense of boundary in regards to time, place, and relationships. As Stapley (1996, p. 69) stated, the "ambiguity that exists at the boundary is a source of anxiety, and it is the boundaries that matter."

Ogden (1988b) proposed a psychoanalytic framework on the processes involved in the generation of human experience. It involves the dialectical interplay between three modes of organization—the depressive mode, the paranoid-schizoid mode, and the autistic-contiguous mode. These modes are interdependent on each other in their existence, and the maintenance of dialectics between them constitutes psychological well-being. His concept corresponds to Winnicott's (1971) notion of potential space, which is an illusory space where creativity and aliveness transpire. In contrast, loss of dialectics within the framework—or collapse of its boundary—results in anxiety, boredom, and deadness. Ogden's notion of the paranoid-schizoid mode is characterized by splitting of experiences and concrete ideas. The self and others are experienced as objects with a single emotional valence at any given time.

Opposing emotional valences toward the same object are disconnected through rewriting of history such that time is experienced as an eternal present (Ogden, 1988b). These features also characterize online SN. The "like" and "share" functions require users to make quick dichotomous choices constantly. Individuals can set up multiple accounts with different profiles, delete posts, or block certain users on their page. These actions correspond to the paranoid-schizoid defenses of magical reparation, denial, and rewriting of history (Ogden, 1988b). Online chats are asynchronous and open ended, and users are often caught up in a perpetual now. Communications are disembodied—disconnected from nonverbal cues such as posture, facial expression, and tone of voice. Zangrilli (2009, para. 19) remarked that "the absence of the effigy makes the stasis moments between one interaction and the other more anxiety inducing." He likened Facebook to a virtual bar, where strangers meet and participate in conversations freely. The experience is best summed up by this quote from Ogden (1988b), when he was actually referring to the paranoid-schizoid mode of organization: "there is an almost continuous background of anxiety deriving from the fact that the individual unconsciously feels as if he is perpetually in uncharted territory in the presence of unpredictable strangers" (p. 25).

The phrase "fear of missing out" (FOMO) has appeared in the media for the last few years. It refers to a pervasive apprehension that others might be having rewarding experiences from which one is absent (Przybylski, Murayama, DeHaan, & Gladwell, 2013). In the context of online SN, it refers to the fear of missing out on the latest topics while offline so that one feels disconnected when returning online. FOMO is often implicated in Internet addiction. From the psychodynamic point of view it concerns the fear of losing one's intersubjective orientation in the community (Stern, 2004). In cyberspace this pressure to keep up-to-date is constant because not only is information endless, the paranoid-schizoid mode of organization

means that conversations and friends' statuses are ever-changing and unpredictable. A picture or video can "go viral" in an instant; conversations can take dramatic turns of direction in any moment. The FOMO phenomenon should therefore be appreciated in the intersubjective context.

THE SIGNIFICANCE OF SURFACES IN ONLINE SN

One novel aspect of online SN is that through technology, relational acts such as liking, befriending, and unfriending are now done by clicking or tapping on a surface. Fingers, not language, have become the points of discharge of impulse (Gabbard, 2001). The immediacy and sense of mastery that comes from these actions are rather appealing. More importantly, the role of the mobile phone as a physical object is often overlooked in studies on Internet addiction. Two common features of modern smart phones are the tablet form factor and the touch-based interface. The sensate experience of tapping, swiping, and scrolling constitutes a sensory ground that underlies our computing experience. Within Ogden's framework this aspect represents the autistic-contiguous dimension of the online SN experience. This mode of organization refers to the rhythmicity and sensory contiguity that made up the earliest pre-symbolic self-experience (Ogden, 1988b). It includes the sensate experience of a surface, the pattern, boundedness, shape, rhythm, texture, and so on. It serves a containing and going on being function (Winnicott, 1956). Against the anxiety that comes from ambiguous boundaries, online SN users may derive a sense of reassurance and containment from the surfaces of smart phones and the graphic interface. We fixed our eyes on virtual flat surfaces, referred to as "the wall," "page," or "dashboard". The rhythmicity of touching, tapping, and scrolling against smooth solid surfaces is both predictable and soothing. The sum of these sensations provides a safety-generating sense of edgedness that "defines, delineates, and protects one's otherwise exposed and vulnerable surface" (Ogden, 1989, p. 56). This defensive use of surfaces of objects has been termed "second skin formation" by Bick (1968) and "adhesive equation" by Tustin (1986).

Given that the mobile phone is primarily a communication device, one can see it as a transitional object—an object with symbolic meanings that has an illusory quality of being real and not-real (Winnicott, 1971). Drawing on ethnographic work among Israeli teenagers, Ribak (2009) concluded that for parents and their teenage children, the mobile phone is important more for the possibility of communication and less for the text and voice communication it actually carries. Therefore, just as a child attains security from holding a teddy bear, an individual is soothed by holding a mobile phone or swiping its screen for its transitional quality.

Another news story may help illustrate the significance of surfaces in mobile Internet use ("Man Arrested After," 2015). A 20-year-old man was arrested after injuring a woman with a knife on a busy street. The victim was walking with the girlfriend of the attacker one afternoon when he suddenly appeared and shouted at his girlfriend. He then pulled a knife out to attack her but instead injured her friend during the scuffle. After inflicting the injury the attacker stood still at the scene tinkering with his phone until the police arrived, all the while people were gathering around the scene and helping the injured. It is unlikely that the man would be making any purposeful messaging after such a bizarre event. Perhaps in a state of heightened emotion he was seeking to ground himself through autistic engagement with his phone. The touchscreen provided a surface for him both physically and psychologically, just enough to keep him in a dissociated state without fragmenting. Similar behavior can be seen in less dramatic situations such as the fearful patient tinkering with her phone at the beginning of a psychotherapy session.

TOWARD A PSYCHODYNAMIC VIEW OF EXCESSIVE ONLINE SN

Drawing on 30 years of clinical experience and research, Khantzian (2003) presented an evolving psychodynamic perspective on substance-use disorders. He described four stages wherein addiction is considered as (1) a special adaptation, (2) an attempt to self-medicate painful or confusing emotions, (3) an overarching problem in self-regulation, and (4) a reflection of disorder in personality organization. Khantzian asserted that addiction is a form of substituted suffering in that patients exchange their pre-existent world of overwhelming feelings for a life revolving around drugs, which is miserable but at least more predictable and controllable. He further remarked that substance addicted individuals almost always have deficits in regulating emotions and self-care, while disorder in self-esteem and relationships are contributing but not essential factors. It appears that Khantzian's framework can be meaningfully applied, albeit with several differences, to behavioral addiction such as excessive online SN. Online SN lacks the potent physiological effect of substances that directly sooth or numb emotions. Its use requires more organization skills and intelligence. However, it represents a convenient portal of selfobject experiences that can also sooth its users. As discussed earlier, online SN is less confronting and more controllable than that of the real world, which makes it ideal to be used defensively. We may speculate that compared to substance addicted individuals, those engaged in excessive online SN are not so much struggling with basic self-care as they are struggling with loneliness, low self-esteem, and relationships. At the same time the disembodied communications, the ambiguous boundaries, and the fatigue-inducing amount of information persistently induce anxiety in users. These alternating states of anxiety and relief form a pattern of excessive use. For some individuals this is more preferable than the pain and risks involved in genuine interpersonal relating. Finally, as is the case of substance dependence, persistent excessive behavior leads to further loss of self-regulatory skills through disuse, and completes the vicious cycle of addiction (Khantzian, 2003).

The following excerpt was taken from a discussion thread on an Internet forum titled "The Horror of a 'Read' Message but No Reply" (NotOnThisPlanet, 2014). It serves to illustrate the internal turmoil that underlies excessive checking of online messages:

> Messaged someone. They read it immediately and don't respond so I spend the next two days (yes two days) worrying about it trying to imagine what they're thinking, which basically boils down in my mind to: "I've seen this and I'm not responding to this person ever again."
>
> The dumb thing is what I wrote doesn't even require a response—it wasn't a question—but I am in need of completely irrational levels of reassurance that what I said wasn't stupid and I feel sick all the time. And then I read back through everything we've ever said to each other trying to read between the lines (that aren't even there!) to make sure that in fact I wasn't just crazy to reply in the first place. I always want the last word but I never want the last word.
>
> I have honestly never felt so out of control with this stuff before. I know why I feel like this at the moment and that this feeling crazy is a symptom of other things rather than the cause, but trying to combat something totally irrational with something completely rational isn't working.
>
> No questions, no answers, just feelings.

The user described clearly the anxiety that arises when a read message is not answered. The user felt that he had not been recognized or held in mind by the other. There is an element of obsessionality to his thinking. He was desperate for some kind of feedback that he didn't make a fool of himself on his last reply. The schizoid-paranoid

organization of cyberspace only allows messages to be either read or not read, replied or not replied. This lack of continuity is anxiety inducing. The user's projection of the other vacillated constantly in his mind. Perhaps the user has an underlying difficulty in dealing with silence from others, which may be perceived as rejection. The fact that text messages are stored in digital memory makes it harder to forget (Balick, 2013) and so easy to revisit over and over. If there was a reply from the other, it might be followed by a gust of relief, and then the user is faced with the dilemma of whether to reply or not ("to have the last word"), which perpetuates the cycle of checking.

Based on Ogden's (1988b) concept of the dialectical structure of experience, it is found that online SN is dominated by free-floating connections and splitting of experiences (paranoid-schizoid mode) complimented by physical and virtual surfaces (autistic-contiguous mode). The surface of the touchscreen is soothing but provides no actual restriction or delineation. The scrolling simply repeats itself without end—a sense of infinite going on being. The third element required to maintain dialectical tension and preserve aliveness is the depressive mode of organization. It is the most developmentally mature mode among the three, yet it can only exist in dialectical relations with them. Unlike the paranoid-schizoid mode, symbol formation is possible because the symbol and the symbolized can be experienced as similar but different. This enables individuals to experience each other as subjects, who are evolving yet remain more or less the same over time, each responsible for their own feelings and behavior (Ogden, 1988b). In the illustration above the depressive mode of organization will allow the user to contain his ambivalence of the other's non-reply, to be comfortable with not knowing. The user may come to a realization that ultimately he owns his actions and feelings and nothing more, that he is not responsible for the feelings and action of another subject. The user may take steps to regain his sense of boundary and embodiment by setting limits on his checking or practicing mindfulness exercises. Importantly, it appears that the depressive mode of organization is not inherent in the online SN platform. The media, that is, the information technology, does not necessarily come with the containing and reflective capacity of symbol formation. It is wise to be mindful that we are after all embodied beings, bounded in time and space, inbuilt for embodied experience, vulnerable to fatigue and fragmentation. Similarly it is best to conceive online SN as a transitional space for creative social interactions, not a platform that can replace embodied intersubjective meetings.

CONCLUSION

The extension of our social selves into cyberspace represents a significant and irreversible change in society's way of life. The popularity of online SN is underpinned by strong existential, intersubjective, and self-object needs. Engagement in these platforms is appealing for its controllability and ease of use. Its touch-based interface provides a sensate grounding experience and is highly reinforcing for its autistic quality. Turkle (as cited in Hanlon, 2001) states that through the Internet, people have an opportunity to rework old conflicts, seek new solutions, and play with unexplored or unexpected aspects of the self. This creative potential is primarily afforded by the schizoid-paranoid organization of the SN platforms and is contingent on the user's capacity to exert enough depressive mode of organization so that the dialectical space is maintained. In his review of Ogden's framework of organizing experience, LaMothe (2005) suggested that health or pathology is not determined merely by the presence of one mode or all modes, but that pathology results when one (or more) mode is used defensively and exclusively. This psychodynamic perspective helps explain the spectrum of users we encounter clinically and sheds light on the problem in defining addiction based on symptoms and behavior only. The anxiety-inducing aspect of online SN is crucial in the formation of excessive use and is discussed in the context of ambiguous boundary and unopposed paranoid-schizoid mode of organization. Consequently, individuals who lack capacities for boundary awareness and symbol formation are vulnerable to excessive use. Treatment programs for excessive use should encompass the need to restore one's sense of embodiment. These hypotheses warrant further studies. The impact of the modern connected-up lifestyle on our mental life is an important subject to explore, and the psychodynamic perspective is highly relevant to this endeavor. It is hoped that the insights in this article may be of use to clinicians not only in treating patients with problematic Internet use, but also other patients in general, for engagement in the cyber world is already a part of the modern life.

REFERENCES

Balick, A. (2013). *The psychodynamics of social networking: Connected-up instantaneous culture and the self.* London: Karnac.

Benjamin, J. (1988). *The bonds of love: Psychoanalysis, feminism, and the problem of domination.* New York: Pantheon.

Berger, P., & Luckman, T. (1966). *The social construction of reality: A treatise in the sociology of knowledge.* Garden City, NY: Doubleday.

Bick, E. (1968). The experience of the skin in early object relations. *International Journal of Psychoanalysis, 49,* 484-486.

Diamond, M., Allcorn, S., & Stein, H. (2004). The surface of organizational boundaries: A view from psychoanalytic object relations theory. *Human Relations, 57*(1), 31-53.

Facebook. (2015). *Company info* [Internet]. Palo Alto, CA: Facebook. Retrieved from: http://newsroom.fb.com/company-info/

Gabbard, G. (2001). Cyberpassion: E-rotic transference on the internet. *Psychoanalytic Quarterly, 70,* 719-737.

Go-globe. (2014). [Blog post]. *Social media addiction—Statistics and trends.* Retrieved from: http://www.go-globe.com/blog/social-media-addiction/.

Griffiths, M. D. (2013). Social networking addiction: Emerging themes and issues. *Journal of Addiction Research and Therapy*, 4, e118.

Hanlon, J. (2001). Disembodied intimacies: Identity and relationship on the Internet. *Psychoanalytic Psychology*, 18(3), 566-571.

Karaiskos, D., Tzavellas, E., Balta, G., & Paparrigopoulos, T. (2010). P02-232—Social network addiction: A new clinical disorder? *European Psychiatry*, 25(1), 855.

Khantzian, E. J. (2003). Understanding addictive vulnerability: An evolving psychodynamic perspective. *Neuro-Psychoanalysis*, 5(1), 5-21.

Kohut, H. (1984). *How does analysis cure?* (P. Goldberg & P. Stepansky, Eds.). Chicago: University of Chicago Press.

Kross, E., Verduyn, P., Demiralp, E., Park, J., Lee, D. S., Lin, N., et al. (2013). Facebook use predicts declines in subjective well-being in young adults. *PLoS ONE*, 8(8), e69841.

Kuss, D. J., & Griffiths, M. D. (2011). Excessive online social networking: Can adolescents become addicted to Facebook? *Education and Health*, 29, 63-66.

LaMothe, R. (2005). *Becoming alive: Psychoanalysis and vitality*. East Sussex, Great Britain: Routledge.

Man Arrested After Stabbing Mong Kok Clerk in Lovers' Spat. (2015, June 12). *Hong Kong Economic Journal*. Retrieved from: http://www.ejinsight.com/20150612-man-arrested-after-stabbing-mong-kok-clerk-in-lovers-spat/.

McLuhan, M. (1964). *Understanding media: the extensions of man*. London: Routledge.

McWilliams, N. (1994). *Psychoanalytic diagnosis: Understanding personality structure in the clinical process*. New York: Guilford.

Mehdizadeh, S. (2010). Self-presentation 2.0: Narcissism and self-esteem on Facebook. *Cyberpsychology, Behavior, and Social Networking*, 13(4), 357-364.

NotOnThisPlanet. (2014, Nov 20). *The horror of a read message and no reply* [Online forum post]. Retrieved from: https://www.reddit.com/r/Anxiety/comments/2mvcto/the_horror_of_a_read_message_and_no_reply_rant/.

Noyes, D. (2015, October 18). *The top 20 valuable Facebook statistics—Updated October 2015*. [Blog post]. Retrieved from: https://zephoria.com/top-15-valuable-facebook-statistics/.

Ogden, T. (1988a). Misrecognitions and the fear of not knowing. *The Psychoanalytic Quarterly*, 57, 643-666.

Ogden, T. (1988b). On the dialectical structure of experience: Some clinical and theoretical implications. *Contemporary Psychoanalysis*, 24, 17-45.

Ogden, T. (1989). *The primitive edge of experience*. Northvale, NJ: Jason Aronson.

Oxford Dictionaries. (2013, Nov 18). *The Oxford dictionaries word of the year 2013 is...*[Blog post]. Oxford university press. Retrieved from: http://blog.oxforddictionaries.com/2013/11/word-of-the-year-2013-winner/.

Paneka, E. T., Nardisa, Y., & Konrath, S. (2013). Defining social networking sites and measuring their use: How narcissists differ in their use of Facebook and Twitter. *Computers in Human Behavior*, 29(5), 2004-2012.

Przybylski, A. K., Murayama, K., DeHaan, C. R., & Gladwell, V. (2013). Motivational, emotional, and behavioral correlates of her of missing out. *Computers in Human Behavior*, 29(4), 1841-1848.

Ribak, R. (2009). Remote control, umbilical cord and beyond: The mobile phone as a transitional object. *The British Journal of Developmental Psychology*, 27(1), 183-196.

Rizzo, C. (2015). More people have died from selfies than shark attacks this year. [Blog post]. *MashableAsia*. Retrieved from: http://mashable.com/2015/09/21/selfie-deaths/#RUbELiKNSkq5.

Rosen, C. (2007). Virtual friendship and the new narcissism. *The New Atlantis*, 17(Summer), 15-31.

Sagioglou, C., & Greitemeyer, T. (2014). Facebook's emotional consequences: Why Facebook causes a decrease in mood and why people still use it. *Computers in Human Behavior*, 35, 359-363.

Stapley, L. (1996). *The personality of organization*. London: Free Association Books.

Stern, D. (2004). *The present moment in psychotherapy and everyday life*. New York: Norton.

Suk, T. (2014, March 16). *Selfie inforgraphic: "Selfiegraphic" facts and statistics* [Blog post]. Techinforgraphics. Retrieved from: http://techinfographics.com/selfie-infographic-selfiegraphic-facts-and-statistics/.

Turel, O., & Serenko, A. (2012). The benefits and dangers of enjoyment with social networking websites. *European Journal of Information Systems*, 21, 512-528.

Turkle, S. (2012, April 21). The flight from conversation. *The New York Times* (p. SR1). Retrieved from: http://www.nytimes.com/2012/04/22/opinion/sunday/the-flight-from-conversation.html?_r=2&ref=opinion#.

Turkle, S. (2013). *Alone together*. New York: Perseus.

Tustin, F. (1986). *Autistic barriers in neurotic patients*. London: Karnac.

Verduyn, P., Lee, D. S., Park, J. S., Shablack, H., Orwell, A., Bayer, J., et al. (2015). Passive Facebook usage undermines affective well-being: Experimental and longitudinal evidence. *Journal of Experimental Psychology, 144*(2), 480-488.

Walther, J. (1996). Computer mediated communication: Impersonal, interpersonal and hyperpersonal interaction. *Communication Research, 23*, 3-43.

Winkler, A., Dorsing, B., Rief, W., Shen, Y., & Glombiewski, J. (2013). Treatment of Internet addiction: A meta-analysis. *Clinical Psychology Review, 33*, 317-329.

Winnocott, D. W. (1956). Primary maternal preoccupation. In, *The maturational processes and the facilitating environment* (pp. 300-305). New York: International Universities Press.

Winnicott, D. W. (1971). *Playing and reality*. New York: Basic.

Woman Dies After Giving Birth by Herself and Taking Selfies. (2015, August 6). *Hong Kong Economic Journal*. Retrieved from http://www.ejinsight.com/20150806-woman-dies-after-giving-birth-by-herself-and-taking-selfies/.

Zangrilli, Q. (2009). The psychology of facebook. *Scienza e psicoanalisi* [Bog post]. Retrieved from: http://www.psicoanalisi.it/psicoanalisi/1434.

Zhao, S. (2006). The Internet and the transformation of the reality of everyday life: Toward a new analytic stance in sociology. *Sociological Inquiry, 76*(4), 458-474.

Mood Disorders

The Psychodynamic Psychotherapist's Guide to the Interaction among Sex, Genes, and Environmental Adversity in the Etiology of Depression for Women

Simone N. Vigod and Valerie H. Taylor

Abstract: From menarche to menopause, women are highly vulnerable to major depression. While biological and psychosocial differences between men and women have been established, the reason for the preponderance of depression in women has yet to be fully elucidated. Women may be predisposed to depressive illness because of biological factors related to brain structure, function, and the impact of reproductive life stages. They may also be at increased risk because they are differentially disadvantaged with respect to environmental stressors including interpersonal violence, socioeconomic instability, and care-giving burden, among others. However, not all women develop depression, nor do all individuals who suffer from adverse life events. This narrative review focuses on emerging research related to the interaction between sex, genetics, and environmental factors that may help offer clues about why some individuals suffer from depression, and why others may be resilient to this outcome. While many questions remain unanswered, the psychodynamic psychotherapist can use this information to help patients suffering from depression understand some of the complexities of the determinants of risk and resilience, with the goal of moving forward toward recovery.

While the question of why women are particularly vulnerable to depression at face value seems straightforward, the answer is anything but, and includes a variety of intersecting components of the nature versus nurture debate. As such, both biological and psychological theories have been investigated. Biological differences between men and women in terms of neuroanatomy, neurochemistry, and reactivity to hormones have been unequivocally established (Cosgrove, Mazure, & Staley, 2007), highlighting a hormonal milieu in women that is quite distinct from men. In addition, women are unique in that they experience rapid hormonal shifts secondary to reproductive life stages such as menstruation, childbirth, and perimenopause which again may predispose them to mood symptoms at such times (Payne, Palmer, & Joffe, 2009; Payne et al., 2007). Biology is not the only explanatory factor for the disproportionate number of women experiencing depression, however, and women are much more likely than men to be subject to significant psychosocial stressors that may increase the risk of developing depression

(Gulcur, 2000; Millaire, Bujold, Morency, & Gauthier, 2006; Stewart, 2006). Such stressors include high rates of physical, sexual, emotional, and financial abuse, as well as socioeconomic instability and relational burdens such as caring for young children and elderly parents in addition to work outside the home. Although stressful life events such as early childhood trauma or abuse, interpersonal violence, and financial loss or insecurity are risk factors for depressive disorders, not all individuals who experience negative life events and relational experiences develop these disorders. This interesting dichotomy between risk and resilience has become a focus of investigation for a number of high-risk populations and as a consequence, researchers are now placing emphasis on work examining how sex, genes, and the environment interact to investigate this conundrum. The risk-resilience spectrum is not only important for researchers, however, and it is important for the psychodynamic psychotherapist to understand how sex, genes, and the environment may interact to lead to the development of depressive disorders in women. This type of knowledge translation from research to clinical care will enable us to better understand the potential impacts of various early environmental events on the brain and on presenting symptomatology. To achieve this goal, this article provides a broad overview of the evolving literature related to the impact of sex-gene-environment interactions that may contribute to the etiology of depressive illness in women.

WHAT IS A GENE-ENVIRONMENT INTERACTION?

A gene-environment interaction can be broadly defined as a "stress-diathesis" model where the impact of an environmental event (or stress) is different depending on an individual's genetic composition (or diathesis). It is consistent with the classic "two-hit"

hypothesis where an individual may have a predisposition to a negative outcome, but will only develop it if there is a second "hit" from an environmental event or experience. In psychiatry, 1:1 relationships between genotype and phenotype are rarely, if ever seen. No psychiatric disorders are 100% heritable, and the phenomenology of illness is never exactly the same. As such, gene-environment interactions have been widely investigated in psychiatry in recent years to help explain illness and resilience in the context of major life stress.

WHAT GENE-ENVIRONMENT INTERACTIONS HAVE BEEN INVESTIGATED IN PSYCHIATRY?

The concept of the stress-diathesis model of behavioral outcomes, where an individual's sensitivity to adverse or stressful events depends upon their genetic makeup, is not a new concept in medicine but it is still relatively novel for psychiatry and it was only ten years ago that Caspi et al. (2003) became the first group to specifically study a gene-environment interaction as it relates to mental illness. They focused on the serotonin transporter gene-linked polymorphic region (5HTTLPR) because the serotonergic system has been implicated in the etiology and treatment of major depressive disorder, with specific 5HTTLPR polymorphisms resulting in either high or low expression of the serotonin transporter protein involved in the reuptake of serotonin at the neuron level in the brain (Moreno et al., 2002; Neumeister et al., 2006; Van der Does, 2001a, 2001b). Although their study did not differentiate between men and women, Caspi et al. (2003) found two important gene-environment interactions. They found that experience of early childhood abuse significantly increased the risk of adult-onset depression in those with two copies of the low expression gene— the short ("s") allele—but less so in individuals with only one copy of the short "s" allele and not in individuals with two copies of the high expression gene—the long ("l") allele. They also found that individuals with one or more short alleles were more likely to have psychiatric symptoms in the context of current environmental stressors such as finances, employment, medical illness, and relationship problems. Although not all studies have confirmed these links, over 50 studies have attempted to replicate these analyses and the findings have been confirmed in meta-analyses (Karg, Burmeister, Shedden, & Sen, 2011).

Subsequent to Caspi et al.'s seminal study, additional gene-environment interactions have been identified that involve other pathways relevant to depression. For example, the most consistent biological findings associated with a diagnosis of depression are irregularities in the hypothalamic pituitary adrenal (HPA) axis. As a direct consequence of this HPA dysregulation, elevated levels of corticotrophin releasing hormone (CRH) have been found in brain regions involved in depression, along with high levels of cortisol and enlarged pituitary and adrenal glands. Because of this, it has been hypothesized that abnormalities in an individual's cortisol response to stress can precipitate or perpetuate depression (Belmaker & Agam, 2008). In keeping with these findings, the common brain-derived neurotrophic factor (BDNF) polymorphism (Val 66 Met), a single nucleotide polymorphism (SNP) in the BDNF gene that codes for brain-derived neurotrophic factor, appears to increase risk of depression in the face of psychosocial adversity, likely through the impact of dysfunction in the HPA axis related to severe and chronic stress (Kim et al., 2007). Furthermore, CRCH1, a gene involved in the function of corticotrophin releasing factor appears to mediate the impact of childhood adversity on the development of major depressive disorder (Bradley et al., 2008) and a polymorphism in the stress-related gene FKBP5 appears to be associated with increased risk of posttraumatic stress dis-

order in individuals with a history of child abuse (Binder et al., 2008). The dopaminergic pathway is also involved in the development of depression, and a polymorphism of the dopamine type 2 receptor gene has been shown to influence the effect that previous stressful life events have on an individual's mood (Elovainio et al., 2007).

Interestingly, existing research in this area has been subject to great variability in terms of how early childhood adversity and current stressors are measured. For example, when self-report measures are used to measure environmental adversity, gene-environment interaction effects are often attenuated (Karg et al., 2011). Additionally, there is great variability in the populations in which these associations are studied. For example, many studies are only in women or only in Caucasians, whereas other studies have more heterogeneous populations. All of this speaks to the complex nature of the impact of life adversity on development of depression. As such, researchers in this area continue to look for reasons to explain inconsistencies in study findings. Sex differences in psychiatric epidemiology present a window of opportunity to investigate the mechanisms that underlie the development of specific disorders in more detail.

HOW MIGHT GENE-ENVIRONMENT INTERACTIONS EXPLAIN SEX DIFFERENCES IN THE PREVALENCE OF DEPRESSION?

An increased prevalence of depression in women could be explained in large part by the research regarding gene-environment interactions because, for example, while there are no sex differences in the frequency distribution of the 5HTLLPR genotypes, women with "s" alleles may be at higher risk because many psychosocial stressors differentially disadvantage women. There are, however, other sex differences in gene-environment interactions that may further explain the preponderance of these particular disorders in women.

Serotonin Gene-Linked Polymorphisms

At least four separate studies have found that the 5HTTLPR polymorphism may mediate the impact of stress on females and males differently. In a longitudinal study of male and female young adults (N = 200), Sjoberg et al. (2006) looked at different measures of psychosocial risk at the time of genotyping. First, they used a psychosocial risk index where psychosocial risk was defined as having two or more risk factors related to low parental education level, parental occupation, family economy, quality of family relationships, and traumatic conflicts. Additionally, they looked specifically at the risk factors of type of residence, separate families, and traumatic conflicts within the family. Three years later, they measured depressive symptoms in the sample using the Depression Symptom Rating Scale (DSRS) that corresponds to the *Diagnostic and Statistical Manual of Mental Disorders* (*DSM-IV-TR*) A-criteria for major depression (American Psychiatric Association, 2000). They found that for girls, both the psychosocial risk index and traumatic conflicts within the family interacted with 5HTTLPR genotype to increase risk of depression, where the "s" allele conferred increased risk with a gradient where girls homozygous for the "s" allele were at greatest risk. In contrast, for the boys, gene-environment interactions were revealed only for the individual variables of type of residence and separated families. Boys with the long "l" allele were at greatest risk of depression in this context. In another study, Brummett et al. (2008) investigated a sex-gene-environment interaction for the 5HTLLPR gene using two different chronic environmental stressors—past and current—using the Centre for Epidemiological Studies Depression Scale (CES-D) to measure de-

pressive symptomatology. To represent early childhood adversity, the environmental risk factor was low childhood socioeconomic status (N = 248, 74% female sample) while chronic stress was represented by the environmental risk factor of care-giving burden for a relative with Alzheimer's disease (N = 142, 42% female). For both of these environmental risk factors, the short "s" allele was associated with symptoms of depression *only* among women while the long "l" allele was associated with depressive symptomatology among men. These findings have not been limited to adult populations and important studies have focused specifically on the sex-gene-interaction in adolescents as well. Uddin et al. (2010) found that adolescent girls with one 5HTLLPR "s" allele were less likely to become depressed compared to adolescent girls homozygous for the "s" or "l" alleles independent of the socioeconomic status of their county of residence. In contrast, having one "s" allele protected boys from depression, but only in counties with substantial socioeconomic deprivation (Uddin et al., 2010). These findings converge with the idea that there are gender differences in gene-environment interactions. Another study examined the effects of 5-HTLPR, the monoamine oxidase A-upstream variable number tandem repeat (MAOA-uVNTR), and negative life events on the development of depression. The MAO-A gene encodes the MAO-A enzyme, which is important for degrading serotonin in the synaptic cleft. MAO-A inhibitors are antidepressant drugs whose mechanism for improving depression is likely related to reducing degradation of serotonin in the synaptic cleft and thus increasing serotonin levels. The MAOA-uVNTR polymorphism has been associated with depressive symptomatology and has multiple variants (Sabol, Hu, & Hamer, 1998). In a community sample of 309 adolescents, Priess-Groben and Hyde (2013) found that girls with both MAOA-uVNTR alleles associated with low expression of MAO-A *and* short 5-HTTLPR alleles exhibited elevated depressive symptoms (as measured by the

Child Depression Index) in the context of negative life events while boys were more likely to become depressed if they had low-expression MAOA-uVNTR alleles but long 5-HTTLPR alleles. This suggests that the low-expression MAOA allele may actually moderate the effect of the sex-gene-environment interaction of the 5-HTTLPR allele.

Other Sex-Gene-Environment Interactions

Kumsta et al. (2007) investigated sex-gene interactions in HPA axis responses to stress in 206 healthy subjects and they found that one glucocorticoid receptor (GR) gene variant had a protective effect as measured by dexamethasone suppression test in men, but not women. The BDNF Val66Met polymorphism has also been investigated for sex-gene-environment interactions because estrogen induces synthesis of BDNF in several brain regions. Monteggia et al. (2007) report that female, but not male, conditional *BDNF* knockout mice exhibit depressive-like behavior in the forced swim and sucrose preference test of anhedonia, replicating epidemiological findings of sexual dimorphism in depression vulnerability (Kendler, Kuhn, & Prescott, 2004). These outcomes were later replicated by Shalev et al. (2009) who found that the Val 66 Met polymorphism modulates the stress-response differently in men and women, and they posit that the findings may be related to gender differences in vulnerability to social stress. While not large in number, these studies further support women's differential vulnerability to depressive illness in the face of stress.

HOW CAN THE PSYCHODYNAMIC PSYCHOTHERAPIST USE THIS INFORMATION TO INFORM PRACTICE?

Psychotherapeutic treatments of depression, regardless of the modality, involve the reversal of maladaptive cognitive, affective, and behavioral processes. Often in psychodynamic psychotherapy, this involves insight into how early life events and relational experiences may have shaped these processes. Yet, not all individuals who suffer from adverse early life events develop depression. The above-mentioned studies support a consensus that there is a complex interplay between sex, genes, and environmental experiences that explains an individual's vulnerability to depression. Eventually research in this area will likely play a key role in the development of personalized interventions to prevent and treat psychiatric illness.

While knowledge that research is occurring that may one day lead to prevention and cure for mental illness creates hope, there are other reasons why it is important for the therapist to be aware of this work. In the course of psychodynamic psychotherapy, patients will often explore how their early childhood experiences may have influenced their present-day reactions, patterns of thinking, and behavior. Psychodynamic theories suggest that having a level of insight regarding the building blocks of these patterns can lead to reflective capacity where past events do not have to shape present day reactions. Through this reflective capacity, individuals begin to make choices to react differently and to behave differently, eventually undoing ineffective patterns of thought and behavior, and developing more functional responses. Ultimately, this leads to more functional capacity and satisfaction in love, work, and life. However, even after years of therapy, it is not uncommon for patients to ask: "Why, in the context of what I experienced as a child, did I end up with depression when my brother, sister, cousin, or friend did not?" The development of depression is associated with negative thinking and many times an inordinate amount of shame and self-blame around the development of the depression itself can occur, with individuals looking inward to find characterological weakness to explain their illness. The research discussed here on sex-gene-environment interactions enables the psychotherapist to address this issue and while many questions remain unanswered, it is important to be able to inform patients who are suffering from depression about these complexities to alleviate some of the shame and stigma associated with their illness, so that they can move forward, taking advantage of the plasticity of the brain to enable recovery.

CONCLUSIONS

Existing research suggests that there are genetic factors that predispose individuals to depressive illness. Certain genetic differences may make individuals more susceptible to depression in the face of specific early childhood adversities and/or specific chronic stressors in adulthood. In addition, certain genetic polymorphisms may be protective for individuals of one sex, but not another. All the pieces of the complex puzzle of the etiology of depressive illness have not been elucidated, but incorporation of knowledge related to sex-gene-environment interactions into the framework of the development of mental illness is useful for the psychodynamic psychotherapist.

REFERENCES

American Psychiatric Association. (2000). *Diagnostic and statistical manual of mental disorders, 4th edition, text revision (DSM-IV-TR)*. Washington, DC: American Psychiatric Association.

Belmaker, R. H., & Agam, G. (2008). Major depressive disorder. *New England Journal of Medicine, 358*(1), 55-68.

Binder, E. B., Bradley, R. G., Liu, W., Epstein, M. P., Deveau, T. C., Mercer, K. B., et al. (2008). Association of FKBP5 polymorphisms and childhood abuse with risk of posttraumatic stress disorder symptoms in adults. *Journal of the American Medical Association, 299*(11), 1291-1305.

Bradley, R. G., Binder, E. B., Epstein, M. P., Tang, Y., Nair, H. P., Liu, W., et al. (2008). Influence of child abuse on adult depression: Moderation by the corticotropin-releasing hormone receptor gene. *Archives of General Psychiatry, 65*(2), 190-200.

Brummett, B. H., Boyle, S. H., Siegler, I. C., Kuhn, C. M., Ashley-Koch, A., Jonassaint, C. R., et al. (2008). Effects of environmental stress and gender on associations among symptoms of depression and the serotonin transporter gene linked polymorphic region (5-HTTLPR). *Behavior Genetics, 38*(1), 34-43.

Burt, V. K., & Stein, K. (2002). Epidemiology of depression throughout the female life cycle. *Journal of Clinical Psychiatry, 63*(Suppl 7), 9-15.

Caspi, A., Sugden, K., Moffitt, T. E., Taylor, A., Craig, I. W., Harrington, H., et al. (2003). Influence of life stress on depression: Moderation by a polymorphism in the 5-HTT gene. *Science, 301*(5631), 386-389.

Cosgrove, K. P., Mazure, C. M., & Staley, J. K. (2007). Evolving knowledge of sex differences in brain structure, function, and chemistry. *Biological Psychiatry, 62*(8), 847-855.

Elovainio, M., Jokela, M., Kivimaki, M., Pulkki-Raback, L., Lehtimaki, T., Airla, N., et al. (2007). Genetic variants in the DRD2 gene moderate the relationship between stressful life events and depressive symptoms in adults: Cardiovascular risk in young Finns study. *Psychosomatic Medicine, 69*(5), 391-395.

Grant, B. F., Goldstein, R. B., Chou, S. P., Huang, B., Stinson, F. S., Dawson, D. A., et al. (2009). Sociodemographic and psychopathologic predictors of first incidence of *DSM-IV* substance use, mood and anxiety disorders: Results from the Wave 2 National Epidemiologic Survey on Alcohol and Related Conditions. *Molecular Psychiatry, 14*(11), 1051-1066.

Gulcur, L. (2000). Evaluating the role of gender inequalities and rights violations in women's mental health. *Health and Human Rights, 5*(1), 46-66.

Karg, K., Burmeister, M., Shedden, K., & Sen, S. (2011). The serotonin transporter promoter variant (5-HTTLPR), stress, and depression meta-analysis revisited: Evidence of genetic moderation. *Archives of General Psychiatry, 68*(5), 444-454.

Kendler, K. S., Kuhn, J., & Prescott, C. A. (2004). The interrelationship of neuroticism, sex, and stressful life events in the prediction of episodes of major depression. *American Journal of Psychiatry, 161*(4), 631-636.

Kessler, R. C., McGonagle, K. A., Swartz, M., Blazer, D. G., & Nelson, C. B. (1993). Sex and depression in the National Comorbidity Survey. I: Lifetime prevalence, chronicity and recurrence. *Journal of Affective Disorders, 29*(2-3), 85-96.

Kim, J. M., Stewart, R., Kim, S. W., Yang, S. J., Shin, I. S., Kim, Y. H., et al. (2007). Interactions between life stressors and susceptibility genes (5-HTTLPR and BDNF) on depression in Korean elders. *Biological Psychiatry, 62*(5), 423-428.

Kumsta, R., Entringer, S., Koper, J. W., van Rossum, E. F., Hellhammer, D. H., & Wust, S. (2007). Sex specific associations between common glucocorticoid receptor gene variants and hypothalamus-pituitary-adrenal axis responses to psychosocial stress. *Biological Psychiatry, 62*(8), 863-869.

Millaire, M., Bujold, E., Morency, A. M., & Gauthier, R. J. (2006). Mid-trimester genetic amniocentesis in twin pregnancy and the risk of fetal loss. *Journal of Obstetrics and Gynaecology Canada, 28*(6), 512-518.

Monteggia, L. M., Luikart, B., Barrot, M., Theobold, D., Malkovska, I., Nef, S., et al. (2007). Brain-derived neurotrophic factor conditional knockouts show gender differences in depression-related behaviors. *Biological Psychiatry, 61*(2), 187-197.

Moreno, F. A., Rowe, D. C., Kaiser, B., Chase, D., Michaels, T., Gelernter, J., et al. (2002). Association between a serotonin transporter promoter region polymorphism and mood response during tryptophan depletion. *Molecular Psychiatry, 7*(2), 213-216.

Neumeister, A., Hu, X. Z., Luckenbaugh, D. A., Schwarz, M., Nugent, A. C., Bonne, O., et al. (2006). Differential effects of 5-HTTLPR genotypes on the behavioral and neural responses to tryptophan depletion in patients with major depression and controls. *Archives of General Psychiatry, 63*(9), 978-986.

Payne, J. L., Palmer, J. T., & Joffe, H. (2009). A reproductive subtype of depression: Conceptualizing models and moving toward etiology. *Harvard Review of Psychiatry, 17*(2), 72-86.

Payne, J. L., Roy, P. S., Murphy-Eberenz, K., Weismann, M. M., Swartz, K. L., McInnis, M. G., et al. (2007). Reproductive cycle-associated mood symptoms in women with major depression and bipolar disorder. *Journal of Affective Disorders, 99*(1-3), 221-229.

Priess-Groben, H. A., & Hyde, J. S. (2013). 5-HTTLPR X stress in adolescent depression: Moderation by MAOA and gender. *Journal of Abnormal Child Psychology, 41*(2), 281-294.

Sabol, S. Z., Hu, S., & Hamer, D. (1998). A functional polymorphism in the monoamine oxidase A gene promoter. *Human Genetics, 103*(3), 273-279.

Shalev, I., Lerer, E., Israel, S., Uzefovsky, F., Gritsenko, I., Mankuta, D., et al. (2009). BDNF Val66Met polymorphism is associated with HPA axis reactivity to psychological stress characterized by genotype and gender interactions. *Psychoneuroendocrinology, 34*(3), 382-388.

Sjoberg, R. L., Nilsson, K. W., Nordquist, N., Ohrvik, J., Leppert, J., Lindstrom, L., et al. (2006). Development of depression: Sex and the interaction between environment and a promoter polymorphism of the serotonin transporter gene. *International Journal of Neuropsychopharmacology, 9*(4), 443-449.

Stewart, D. E. (2006). The international consensus statement on women's mental health and the WPA consensus statement on interpersonal violence against women. *World Psychiatry, 5*, 61-64.

Uddin, M., Koenen, K. C., de Los Santos, R., Bakshis, E., Aiello, A. E., & Galea, S. (2010). Gender differences in the genetic and environmental determinants of adolescent depression. *Depression and Anxiety, 27*(7), 658-666.

Van der Does, A. J. (2001a). The effects of tryptophan depletion on mood and psychiatric symptoms. *Journal of Affective Disorders, 64*(2-3), 107-119.

Van der Does, A. J. (2001b). The mood-lowering effect of tryptophan depletion: Possible explanation for discrepant findings. *Archives of General Psychiatry, 58*(2), 200-202.

Is Increased Sexual Behavior a Symptom of Bipolar Disorder in Children and Adolescents?

Stewart Adelson, Robinette Bell, Adam Graff, David Goldenberg, Elizabeth Haase, Jennifer I. Downey, and Richard C. Friedman

Abstract: While there is consensus that bipolar disorder exists in children and adolescents, its diagnostic criteria are debated. Excessive sexual behavior has been reported in youth who may have juvenile bipolar disorder (JBD), and has been termed "hypersexuality." Although there is no universal definition of this term, this observation has led to a hypothesis that increased sexual behavior characterizes the bipolar syndrome in children and adolescents, and differentiates it from attention deficit hyperactivity disorder. Although this hypothesis is plausible, evidence for it is incomplete, because testing it definitively would require both establishing a standard definition of hypersexuality in children and adolescents, and also reaching consensus about the other nonsexual criteria for pediatric bipolar disorder. In addition, studies to test it would need to control factors other than JBD that are known to increase sexual behavior in children and adolescents. These include sexual abuse and related posttraumatic stress disorder, excessive exposure to sexual stimuli, psychiatric illness in general, and social variables such as family chaos and social stress. Some of these factors might increase sexual behavior in youth with bipolar disorder through psychodynamic mechanisms rather than as a result of the illness itself. Therefore, further research is needed to determine whether increased sexual behavior can serve as a diagnostically valuable criterion for bipolar disorder in children and adolescents, and whether it differentiates the disorder from other conditions known to be associated with increased sexual behavior in youth.

There is consensus that bipolar disorder exists in children and adolescents. However, there is debate about how the adult symptoms of bipolar disorder should be adapted to be developmentally appropriate for the pediatric population (Juvenile Bipolar Disorder, or JBD; American Academy of Child and Adolescent Psychiatry, 2007; National Institutes of Mental Health, 2001). This debate mirrors general challenges of nosology in pediatric psychiatry (Costello et al., 1996).

One especially challenging question about JBD is how to adapt criteria involving increased sexual behavior to adolescents and children (Adelson, 2010). The Diagnostic and Statistical Manual of Mental Disorders, 4th edition, or *DSM-IV* (American Psychiatric Association, 1994) incorporated increased or disordered sexuality as a criterion for manic and mixed bipolar episodes under the symptom rubric "excessive involvement in pleasurable activities that have a high potential for painful consequences," examples of which include "sexual indiscretions." While sexual behavior and feelings are obviously different in children and adolescents than they are in adults, sexual development begins in childhood and continues to evolve through adolescence to adulthood.

Geller, Zimerman, Williams, DelBello, Bol-hofner, Craney, and colleagues (2002) have proposed that "hypersexuality" in children and adolescents is also a core feature of juvenile bipolar disorder and helps distinguish it from attention deficit hyperactivity disorder (ADHD), a condition that shares many features with bipolar disorder in youth. If hypersexuality is a feature of bipolar disorder in youth, then it may be appropriate to include it as a diagnostic criterion for the pediatric population as well as for adults, perhaps with examples of excessive juvenile sexual behavior as a guideline for clinicians in applying the criteria. The appropriateness of doing so would depend in part upon the reliability and validity with which increased juvenile sexual behavior can be distinguished from normally developing sexuality, and also from other abnormal behavior such as general patterns of disruptiveness or aggression. This article discusses hypersexuality as a possible symptom of JBD in the context of what is known about sexual development in children and adolescents.

EVIDENCE OF INCREASED SEXUAL BEHAVIOR IN JUVENILE BIPOLAR DISORDER

Geller and colleagues have conducted several studies of a cohort of youth with symptoms highly suggestive of bipolar disorder. One specifically studied the phenomenology of bipolar disorder in prepubertal children and young adolescents, including sexual symptoms (Geller, Zimmerman et al., 2000). This study explored symptoms of 93 consecutive 7- to 16-year-old male and female outpatients drawn from pediatric and psychiatric sites who met current *DSM-IV* criteria for mania for at least two weeks, or hypomania for at least two months. In an effort to reduce diagnostic confusion with ADHD and increase the sample's continuity with adult bipolar disorder, the researchers required that subjects display either elation

or grandiosity as a cardinal feature, and also a severity rating sufficient to be considered a definite case.

The subjects' symptoms were measured using a diagnostic instrument called the WASH-U-KSADS (Geller, Williams, Zimmerman, & Frazier, 1996; Geller et al., 2001). This instrument assesses symptoms of bipolar disorder, including increased sexual behavior, by means of separate maternal and child or adolescent semi-structured interviews that include clinically and developmentally appropriate questions. Interviewers' observations of any sexual behavior during the interview (such as propositioning the interviewer) are also incorporated. The interviewer writes a narrative description of a youth's hypersexual behavior, if any, and then codes the narrative description on a numerical scale.

The lead researcher supervised the research team on the use of the WASH-U-KSADS in the coding of sexual behavior derived from the interviews, and required team members to practice until they achieved consensus with one another. A statistical test of consensus documented their agreement in coding sexual behavior with high inter-rater reliability. Their coding of examples of increased sexual behavior was also confirmed by outside blind expert raters on a subset of subjects. High sexual behavior scores on the WASH-U-KSADS were referred to as "hypersexuality." In addition, puberty was assessed using the Duke Scale, a self-assessment of sexual maturation for adolescents (Duke, Litt, & Gross, 1980), and a history of sexual abuse was ascertained using the Psychosocial Schedule for School Age Children-Revised (PSS-R; Puig-Antich, Lukens, & Brent, 1986) and pediatric and medical records.

Hypersexuality was present in 43% ($n = 40$) of those who met the study's strict criteria for bipolar disorder. This included 42.1% of males ($n = 24$) and 44.4% of females ($n = 16$). The effects of gender, puberty, and comorbid attention deficit hyperactivity disorder on the rates of increased sexual behavior and various other symptoms were analyzed. When stratified by age, hypersexuality was present in 60.0% ($n = 24$) of the pubertal but only 30.2% ($n = 16$) of the prepubertal subjects, a significant difference. Data comparing the rates of hypersexuality between males and females in the pubertal sample were not reported.

The authors concluded that hypersexuality is a symptom of mania in children and adolescents and speculated that hypersexuality was greater in pubertal children due to normal developmental increases in sexuality with puberty. In a related paper (Geller, Bolhofner, Craney, Williams, et al., 2000) that examined the peer, parent-child, and family psychosocial functioning of these JBD subjects compared to samples with ADHD and community controls, sexual abuse was suspected in only one subject with bipolar disorder; this case was excluded from data analysis. Based on this, the authors concluded that sexual abuse was not the cause of the hypersexuality in these subjects. Presumably no sexually abused children were present among the subjects in the study because they were not a random population sample; rather, they were a clinical sample of youth with symptoms suggestive of early bipolar disorder. Apart from frank sexual abuse, measures of disturbance in other aspects of family sexual functioning, such as inappropriate sexual boundaries, family sexual beliefs, and sexual practices were not included in the study.

In another study, Geller and colleagues (Geller, Zimerman, Williams, DelBello, Bolhofner, Craney, et al., 2002) compared the degree to which hypersexuality was present among youth with symptoms of JBD in comparison with those with ADHD and normal controls. Hypersexuality was displayed by youth with symptoms of bipolar disorder, but not those with symptoms of ADHD or normal controls. They found that hypersexuality is one of five symptoms—along with elation, grandiosity, flight of ideas/racing thoughts, and decreased need for sleep—that characterize prepubertal children and young adolescents specifically displaying a JBD syndrome. They concluded that these five symptoms, including hypersexuality, constitute core discriminatory features that distinguish youth with JBD from those with ADHD or with no diagnosis.

CONTROVERSIES IN DEFINING JUVENILE BIPOLAR DISORDER

There are significant challenges in establishing diagnostic criteria for JBD. Affective dysregulation, a core feature of the illness, is also characteristic of other common psychiatric conditions affecting children and adolescents. For example, children and adolescents with attention deficit hyperactivity disorder (ADHD) often tolerate frustration poorly, and may be moody. JBD and ADHD additionally share overlapping features of inattentiveness, impulsive behavior, motoric overactivity, overtalkativeness, and disorganized thinking (Reich et al., 2005). This leads to debate about where to draw the boundary between JBD and other disorders (Biederman et al., 1998). In addition, the duration criteria for JBD present unique difficulties due to the preponderance of rapidly cycling and mixed states in youth with possible bipolar symptoms. Very rapidly cycling mood states lasting as little as four hours ("ultradian" cycling) has been found frequently; such brief cycles, which verge on the length of severe tantrums, may be clinically difficult to distinguish from maladaptive coping strategies in dysfunctional environments (Adelson, 2010; McClellan, Kowatch, Findling, & Work Group on Quality Issues, 2007).

The duration criterion for bipolar disorder was broadened concurrently with the publication of *DSM-IV* to reflect its conceptualization as a spectrum of illness that includes more chronic symptoms of dysregulated mood at one extreme. However, there is evidence suggesting that an overly broad application of the bipolar spectrum concept in children and adolescents may have led to over-diagnosis of the disorder in that age group. There was a 40-fold increase in diagnosis of bipolar disorder in youth between 1994-95 and 2002-3 (Moreno et al., 2007). If the broadly construed, very rapidly cycling, and mixed bipolar states are included in the conception of JBD, the incidence of juvenile bipolar disorder is out of proportion to epidemiological studies of the illness in the general population, and more closely resembles the epidemiology of oppositional defiant disorder (ODD; Leibenluft, Charney, Towbin, Bhangoo, &Pine, 2003). Conversely, if stricter episodic criteria are maintained, the epidemiology of JBD is more consistent with adult bipolar disorder.

In general, if a child displays symptoms that meet criteria for more than one diagnosis, the symptoms would be appropriately attributed to the diagnosis with the greatest prognostic value. For example, youth who display symptoms consistent with diagnoses of both bipolar disorder and ADHD would merit the diagnosis of bipolar disorder if it could be shown that the symptoms predict adult bipolar disorder in adulthood, and are characterized by biological markers such as genetic patterns shared with adult bipolar family members (Adelson, 2010). The predictive value of the current criteria of bipolar disorder in affectively dysregulated youth has not yet been definitively established (Leibenluft, 2011).

Over-diagnosis of bipolar disorder in children and adolescents may have several significant consequences. First, it may obscure the true diagnosis and impede appropriate treatment. Second, out of 154 office visits for treatment of youth diagnosed with bipolar disorder, 90.6% (n = 141) involved prescription of psychotropic medications including mood stabilizers, antipsychotics, and antidepressants (Moreno et al., 2007), pharmacological treatments with potentially serious side effects. Therefore, there is a pressing need to develop reliable and valid diagnostic criteria for JBD that have reasonable discriminative validity (Adelson, 2010).

Various studies have used different criteria for bipolar disorder in youth (Birmaher et al., 2009; Birmaher et al., 2006; DelBello, Hanseman, Adler, Fleck, & Strakowski, 2007), making cross-study comparison difficult. Some of these studies suggest that broadly defined *DSM-IV* bipolar spectrum criteria are valid in children and adolescents (Birmaher, 2007). However, other studies (Geller, Tillman, Bolhofner, & Zimmerman, 2008) suggest that a narrower definition of JBD limited to strict *DSM-IV* criteria for mixed or manic bipolar I episodes, and characterized by cardinal symptoms of either elation or grandiosity and unambiguously significant dysfunction, is more appropriate. The definition of JBD is critical in interpreting data about the association of the disorder with increased sexual behavior in youth, because studies purportedly of youth with bipolar disorder may actually be capturing a population of youth with affective dysregulation resulting from other causes that are known to be associated with increased sexuality.

Longitudinal studies (Birmaher, 2007; Birmaher et al., 2009; Birmaher et al., 2006; DelBello et al., 2007) of adolescents using various definitions of bipolar illness have found that psychosocial factors were correlated with the degree of psychopathology. For example, low socioeconomic status, poor adherence to pharmacological treatment, lack of psychotherapy, substance abuse, exposure to negative life events, low maternal warmth, and family psychopathology were found to worsen the course of illness. Since similar psychosocial factors are known to be associated with increased sexual behavior in youth (Friedrich, Lysne, Sim, & Shamos, 2004), these might be confounding variables that simultaneously worsen illness and increase sexual behavior. They may do so in ways that are developmentally specific to children and adolescents, such as exposure to family chaos among caregivers, and so might be fundamentally different from factors that cause increased sexual behavior in bipolar adults.

Table 1. Number of Items in Rating Scales Measuring Increased Sexuality in Children and Adolescents

Rating Scale	Number of Items
Child Sexual Behavior Inventory (CSBI)[1]	38
Adolescent Clinical Sexual Behavior Inventory (ACSBI)[2]	45
Sexual Problem Scale (SPS) of Child Behavior Checklist (CBCL)[3]	4
Lindblad, Gustafsson, Larsson, & Lundin scale[4]	17

Note. [1]Friedrich et al. (2001); [2]Friedrich et al. (2004); [3]Achenbach (1991); [4]Lindblad, Gustafsson, Larsson, and Lundin (1995).

LACK OF STANDARD DEFINITION OF "HYPERSEXUALITY" IN CHILDREN AND ADOLESCENTS

There is at present no consensus on how to define "hypersexuality" in children and adolescents (Adelson et al., 2012). Aspects of increased sexual behavior that are described in the literature include the frequency or variety of sexual behaviors, precocious emergence of normally mature sexual behaviors, sexual preoccupation, diminished impulse control, and socially inappropriate expression of sexuality such as aggression or coercion (Adelson, 2010).

In contrast with the WASH-U-KSADS used by Geller, Zimerman, Williams, DelBello, Bolhofner, Craney, and colleagues (2002) in which "hypersexuality" consisted in a statistically significant elevation of an item related to sexual behavior embedded within a measure of general bipolar symptoms, several rating scales have been developed that exclusively measure levels of sexual behavior in children and adolescents. Four such rating scales were summarized in a previous article on defining the term "hypersexuality" in children and adolescents (Adelson et al., 2012, Table 1). These rating scales were selected from the bibliographies of key reference works in child and adolescent sexual abuse and sexual development over the last decade (Bancroft, 2003; Friedrich, 2003; Friedrich, Lysne, Sim, & Shamos, 2004). These measures represent an illustrative selection rather than a comprehensive review (Adelson et al., 2012). They use a variety of strategies to obtain data on sexual activity, including caregiver report or a combination of parent- and self-report, and capture detailed data on various aspects of juvenile sexual behavior. Examples include the Childhood Sexual Behavior Inventory (CSBI; Friedrich et al., 2001) and the Adolescent Clinical Sexual Behavior Inventory (ACSBI; Friedrich, Lysne, Sim, & Shamos, 2004). The number of items related to sexual behavior on these scales is summarized in Table 1.

In addition to the WASH-U-KSADS, several other rating scales have been devised to measure bipolar symptoms in the pediatric population. Some of these have included items on sexual behavior, while others have not. An illustrative selection of those that do, and which have been used frequently in research studies, is presented in Table 2, including a description of their sexuality measures.

Table 3 contrasts the number of items related to sexual behavior that are included in measures of bipolar disorder in comparison with instruments dedicated entirely to measuring levels of pediatric sexual behavior. A marked difference is readily apparent between the number of items in these two categories of measures. Rating scales used in JBD include a much smaller number of items related to sexuality and capture less detailed information about abnormal qualities of child and adolescent sexuality in comparison with those that are used entirely to study children and adolescents' sexuality.

It is not surprising that bipolar rating scales capture less detailed information about sexual behavior than dedicated sexuality rating scales do, as the bipolar instruments must measure a variety of affective

Table 2. **Measures of Sexuality in Juvenile Bipolar Disorder Rating Scales**

Rating Scale	Age Range	Informant	Format	Measures of Sexuality
Young Mania Rating Scale for Parents, P-YMRS[1,2,3,4]	Scale first devised for use in adults, subsequently normed on youth from 5 through 17 years old	Informant is parent or clinician	Includes one item scored on 5-pt Likert scale related to inappropriate sexual behavior on an eleven-item inventory.	Sexual Interest rated as 0 = Normal; not increased 1 = Mildly or possibly increased 2 = Definite subjective increase on questioning 3 = Spontaneous sexual content; elaborates on sexual matters; hypersexual by self-report 4 = Overt sexual acts (toward patients, staff, or interviewer)
General Behavior Inventory, GBI[5]	youth 5 through 17 years old	guardian	Behavioral inventory screening non-clinical samples for bipolar traits on 4-point scale.	Item adapted for parent observation of Content and Scale Descriptor for "Sexual interest: I am electrified by sexual vitality; exhilarating sense of sexual potency; feel sexy constantly; Tremendously repulsed by sex," where 1 = never or hardly ever, 2 = sometimes, 3 = often, and 4 = very often or almost constantly
Child Mania Rating Scale – Parent version (CMRS-P)[6]	youth 5 through 17 years old	parent	One item scored on 4-pt Likert scale related to inappropriate sexual behavior on a 21-item inventory based on DSM-IV criteria.	"Does your child behave in a sexually inappropriate way (e.g., talks dirty, exposing, playing with private parts, masturbating, making sex phone calls, humping on dogs, playing sex games, touches others sexually)?"
Wash U K-SADS[7]	youth 6 through 17 years old	parent, youth and clinical interviewer	Items on hypersexuality rated as follows: 0 No information 1 Not at all 2 Doubtful - occasional sexual comment 3 Mild - makes inappropriate explicit sexual comments, drawings or gestures one time a week. 4 Moderate to severe - overt sexual behaviors or language occurs multiple times each week or at inappropriate times. Major episode one time a week, e.g. adolescent sleeps with 3 partners at the same time	**Parent of child 6–12:** Are there times when your child makes inappropriate sexual remarks to a teacher or adult? Does your child like to "talk dirty" (e.g., talk about private parts of the body inappropriately)? **Child 6-12:** What magazines do you like at the store? Observe child for sexually explicit language or behavior during the interview, e.g., trying to touch interviewer's body; propositioning the interviewer; talking about seeing sex. **Adolescents:** Are there times when you have to have sex no matter what time of day it is? Are there times when there are not enough sexual partners to meet your needs? Be sure to distinguish this behavior from provocation to sexual activity in the environment (e.g., see the Sexual Abuse Section of the Psychosocial Schedule for School-Age Children).

Note. [1]Gracious et al., 2002; [2]Youngstrom et al., 2003; [3]Fristad, Weller & Weller, 1992; [4]Fristad,1995; [5]Findling et al., 2002; [6]Pavuluri et al., 2006; [7]Geller et al., 2001

Table 3. Comparison of Number of Items Related to Sexuality in Pediatric Bipolar Rating Scales and Pediatric Sexuality Scales

Rating Scale	Type of Scale	Number of Items
Child Sexual Behavior Inventory (CSBI)[1]	Pediatric Sexuality Scale	38
Adolescent Clinical Sexual Behavior Inventory (A-CSBI)[2]	Pediatric Sexuality Scale	45
Sexual Problem Scale (SPS) of Child Behavior Checklist (CBCL)[3]	Pediatric Sexuality Scale	4
Lindblad, Gustafsson, Larsson, & Lundin scale[4]	Pediatric Sexuality Scale	17
Young Mania Rating Scale for Parents, P-YMRS[5, 6, 7, 8]	Juvenile Bipolar Disorder Scale	1
General Behavior Inventory, GBI[9]	Juvenile Bipolar Disorder Scale	1
Child Mania Rating Scale – Parent version (CMRS-P)[10]	Juvenile Bipolar Disorder Scale	1
Wash U K-SADS[11]	Juvenile Bipolar Disorder Scale	2[12]

Note. [1]Friedrich et al., 2001; [2]Friedrich et al., 2004; [3]Achenbach, 1991; [4]Lindblad, Gustafsson, Larsson, & Lundin, 1995; [5]Gracious et al., 2002; [6]Youngstrom et al., 2003; [7]Fristad, Weller, & Weller, 1992; [8]Fristad,1995; [9]Findling et al., 2002; [10]Pavuluri et al., 2006; [11]Geller et al., 2001; [12]Includes two questions for parent of 6–12-year-old and for adolescents; one question and one observation item for 6–12-year-old subjects.

symptoms, not just sexual behavior. However, abnormal sexual qualities such as aggression, compulsiveness, social boundary violations, and deviance have been described in association with sexual abuse and other trauma (Yates, 1991). Therefore, the dedicated sexuality measures described in Table 1 may better detect sexual signs of abuse and other trauma in youth than the bipolar rating scales in Table 2.

CAUSES OF INCREASED SEXUALITY IN YOUTH OTHER THAN BIPOLAR DISORDER

Sexual abuse is significantly related to increased sexual behavior in children. Among 2- to 12-year-olds, sexually abused children display significantly more sexuality than normal or psychiatrically ill children (Friedrich, 1993; Friedrich et al., 2001; Friedrich & Grambsch, 1992). In addition to frank sexual abuse, sexual overstimulation in chaotic, dysfunctional families also predicts increased sexual behavior children and adolescents (Friedrich, 2003; Friedrich, Fisher, Broughton, Houston, & Shafran, 1998; Friedrich et al., 2001; Friedrich & Grambsch, 1992;

Friedrich, Lysne, Sim, & Shamos, 2004). Given that children and adolescents with bipolar disorder are at increased genetic risk for having relatives with bipolar disorders (Smoller & Finn, 2003) and that adult bipolar disorder is associated with hypersexuality, youth living with bipolar adults may be exposed to adult hypersexual behavior more often than the general population of youth (Etain, Henry, Bellivier, Mathieu, & Leboyer, 2008). While these experiences may fall short of frank sexual abuse, they may be sexually overstimulating. Hypersexuality might thus be found more frequently in these youth due to the psychological influence of such environmental factors; sexual overstimulation that falls short of frank sexual abuse may also be an important confounding variable causing hypersexuality in bipolar youth, therefore (Adelson, 2010).

In addition to sexual abuse and overstimulation, increased sexuality in youth is associated with psychiatric illness in general and with a wide variety of internalizing and externalizing behaviors (Friedrich et al., 2004). In 6- to 10-year-old children, increased sexual behavior is associated with behavioral problems in general, especially in boys (Meyer-Bahlburg, Dolezal, & Sandberg, 2000).

High risk or increased sexual behavior has also been described in youth with depression and low self-esteem (Dolcini & Adler, 1994; Rotheram-Borus, Mahler, & Rosario, 1995; Whitbeck, Conger, & Kao, 1993). Given the fact that youth with bipolar disorder may have increased rates of depression—including in rapidly cycling patterns—it must be ruled out that depression rather than mania accounts partly or wholly for any association between hypersexuality and JBD. In addition, sexual risk-taking has been found in young adults who had childhood diagnoses of ADHD (Ball, Gilman, Fitzmaurice, Ganz, & Mick, 2007), a core feature of which is impulsiveness. Therefore, sexual risk-taking in ADHD might increase in adolescence along with the development of sexual impulses. While hypersexuality may help differentiate between JBD and ADHD in 7- to 16-year-olds (Geller, Zimerman, Williams, DelBello, Bolhofner, Craney, et al., 2002), it is not known whether it does so in older adolescents. This may be especially true among youth with ADHD who go on to develop comorbid disorders such as oppositional defiant disorder, conduct disorder, and substance abuse.

In addition to being associated with sexual abuse and psychiatric illnesses, an increase in sexual behavior has been reported in youth who experience stressors and life experiences such as "physical abuse, life stress, and impaired family relationships" (Friedrich et al., 1998). Sexual abuse, physical abuse, life stress, and impaired family relationships also predict increased sexual behavior in high-risk adolescents in inpatient, partial hospital, and outpatient psychiatric treatment (Friedrich et al., 2004). In these adolescents, there is a strong association between high-risk sexual behavior, emotional and behavioral problems, and sexual concerns, distress, and preoccupations. Increased sexual behavior in youth is also associated with lower maternal educational status, greater maternal

psychiatric problems, and with lower family integration (Paradise, Rose, Sleeper, & Nathanson, 1994). These predictors of increased sexual behavior might plausibly characterize families affected by bipolar disorder more frequently than the general population, and must also be considered as possible confounding causes of increased sexual behavior in JBD. Increased sexual behavior does not differentiate sexually abused from generally psychiatrically ill children well, because sexual behavior problems are so highly correlated with other behavior problems in children and adolescents (Sim et al., 2005). Therefore, increased sexual behavior may simply be a marker of psychiatric illness in youth, or of a general pattern of disregard for social norms in all youth with emotional dysregulation and disruptive behavior from any cause.

SUMMARY AND CONCLUSION

Preliminary evidence suggests that increased sexual drive or behavior may characterize bipolar disorder in some children and adolescents, as it does in some adults. Whether hypersexuality is consistently and uniquely associated with JBD and due to the disorder warrants further study, bearing in mind what is known about children and adolescents' sexuality both in normal development and in abnormal situations in which it is increased. Confirmatory studies would have to address the following issues:

Consensus must be established for the nonsexual criteria of bipolar disorder in youth before an unambiguous population with JBD can be delineated in which rates of sexual behavior can be measured.

Consensus must also be established about a definition of "hypersexuality" in children and adolescents that is both reliable and valid.

It must be demonstrated that increased sexual behavior is associated with JBD in comparison with relevant control groups characterized by variables that might commonly be associated with JBD and also cause an increase in sexual behavior. These include sexual abuse, inappropriate family sexual attitudes and boundaries, overstimulation and chaos, physical abuse, life stress, and impaired family relationships.

Future studies would have to include sexually abused youth in samples of bipolar subjects and non-bipolar controls to demonstrate that hypersexuality distinguishes bipolar disorder from sexual abuse in realistic clinical situations. Male-female differences in hypersexuality among bipolar adolescents should also be studied. Such differences, if any, might suggest causes of hypersexuality other than the bipolar illness. For example, hypersexuality in pubertal males with bipolar disorder might be related to developmental processes such as the higher testosterone surge associated with puberty in males. Conversely, hypersexuality in females with bipolar disorder might suggest significant risk among females for sexual abuse, harassment, or overstimulating experiences.

Since adolescents over age 16 may have particularly increased sexual drive and impulsiveness compared with younger adolescents, future studies would need to compare rates of hypersexuality in adolescents above age 16 with JBD and ADHD in order to determine that increased sexual behavior differentiates these conditions in older adolescents. It is also important to test whether hypersexuality differentiates bipolar disorder in older adolescents from those with Oppositional Defiant Disorder (ODD) and Conduct Disorder, which are characterized by patterns of defiant, aggressive, and impulsive behavior that may include sexual behavior.

By including measures of children and adolescents' sexual behavior, instruments such as the WASH-U-KSADS represent a significant advance in research on excessive sexuality in bipolar disorder. Other instruments for measuring sexuality in children and adolescents such as the Childhood Sexual Behavior Inventory (CSBI) and the Adolescent Clinical Sexual Behavior Inventory (ACSBI), described above, may provide further advantages. These measures have been empirically normed on diverse populations of youth. They have been employed successfully in studies of normal, sexually abused, and psychiatrically ill populations. Since these instruments include detailed measures of qualities of increased sexuality that are clinically important in detecting sexual abuse and overstimulation, measures such as these might provide important data if used in future studies of bipolar youth.

Further research is needed to confirm whether bipolar disorder causes increased sexual behavior in the pediatric age range and differentiates bipolar disorder from other conditions that are also known to increase sexual behavior in youth. Even if hypersexuality is associated with bipolar illness in youth, whether it is appropriate to include as a diagnostic criterion of the disorder in children and adolescents depends upon whether it is actually caused by the illness or by an associated factor like sexual abuse, family chaos, or life stress. Factors such as these might cause increased sexual behavior in youth with JBD through psychodynamic mechanisms, rather than as a result of the illness itself (Adelson, 2010). If so, the increased sexual behavior would be more appropriately attributed to these other variables, which may be the appropriate focus of therapeutic intervention. These would require conceptualization in a biopsychosocial model, rather than a reductionistic biological one, and may benefit from psychodynamic formulation and treatment integrated with any necessary somatic treatment for JBD.

REFERENCES

Achenbach, T. M. (1991). *Manual for the Child Behavior Checklist/4-18* (CBCL) *and 1991 profile*. Burlington, VT: University of Vermont Department of Psychiatry.

Adelson, S. L. (2010). Psychodynamics of hypersexuality in children and adolescents with bipolar disorder. *Journal of the American Academy of Psychoanalysis and Dynamic Psychiatry, 38*(1), 27-46.

Adelson, S. L., Bell, R., Haase, E., Goldenberg, D., Graff, A., Downey, J. I., & Friedman, R. C. (2012). Toward a definition of "hypersexuality" in children and adolescents. *Psychodynamic Psychiatry, 40*(3), 481-504.

American Academy of Child and Adolescent Psychiatry. (2007). Practice parameter for the assessment and treatment of children and adolescents with bipolar disorder. *Journal of the American Academy of Child and Adolescent Psychiatry, 46*(1), 107-125.

American Psychiatric Association. (1994). *Diagnostic and statistical manual of mental disorders* (4th ed.). Arlington, VA: American Psychiatric Publishing.

Ball, S. W., Gilman, S. E., Fitzmaurice, G. M., Ganz, M. L., & Mick, E. (2007). *Personal, economic and sexual outcomes associated with childhood ADHD in a representative sample of young adults*. Poster presentation at the Annual Meeting of the American Academy of Child and Adolescent Psychiatry.

Bancroft, J. (Ed.). (2003). *Sexual development in childhood*. Bloomington & Indianapolis: Indiana University Press.

Biederman, J., Klein, R. G., Pine, D. S., & Klein, D. F. (1998). Resolved: Mania is mistaken for ADHD in prepubertal children. *Journal of the American Academy of Child and Adolescent Psychiatry, 37*(10), 1091-1099.

Birmaher, B. (2007). Longitudinal course of pediatric bipolar disorder. *American Journal of Psychiatry, 164*(4), 537-539.

Birmaher, B., Axelson, D., Goldstein, B., Strober, M., Gill, M. K., Hunt, J., et al. (2009). Four-year longitudinal course of children and adolescents with bipolar spectrum disorders: The Course and Outcome of Bipolar Youth (COBY) study. *American Journal of Psychiatry, 166*, 795-804.

Birmaher, B., Axelson, D., Strober, M., Gill, M. K., Valeri, S., Chiappetta, L., et al. (2006). Clinical course of children and adolescents with bipolar spectrum disorders. *Archives of General Psychiatry, 63*, 175-183.

Browning, C. R., & Laumann, E. O. (2003). The social context of adaptation to childhood sexual maltreatment: A life course perspective. In J. Bancroft (Ed.), *Sexual development in childhood* (pp. 383-403). Bloomington & Indianapolis: Indiana University Press.

Costello, E. J., Angold, A., Burns, B. J., Stangl, D. K., Tweed, D. L., Erklani, A., & Worthman, C. M. (1996). The Great Smoky Mountains study of youth. Goals, design, methods, and the prevalence of *DSM-III-R* disorders. *Archives of General Psychiatry, 53*(12), 1129-1136.

DelBello, M. P., Hanseman, D., Adler, C. M., Fleck, D. E., & Strakowski, S. M. (2007). Twelve-month outcome of adolescents with bipolar disorder following first hospitalization for a manic or mixed episode. *American Journal of Psychiatry, 164*, 582-590.

Dolcini, M. M., & Adler, N. E. (1994). Perceived competencies, peer group affiliation, and risk behavior among early adolescents. *Health Psychology, 13*, 496-506.

Duke, P. M., Litt, I. F., & Gross, R. T. (1980). Adolescents' self-assessment of sexual maturation. *Pediatrics, 66*, 918-920.

Etain, B., Henry, C., Bellivier, F., Mathieu, F., & Leboyer, M. (2008). Beyond genetics: Childhood affective trauma in bipolar disorder. *Bipolar Disorders, 10*(8), 867-876.

Friedrich, W. N. (1993). Sexual behavior in sexually abused children. *Violence Update, 3*(1), 7-11.

Friedrich, W. N. (2003). Studies of sexuality of nonabused children. In J. Bancroft (Ed.), *Sexual development in childhood* (pp. 107-120). Bloomington & Indianapolis: Indiana University Press.

Friedrich, W. N., Fisher, J. L., Broughton, D., Houston, M., & Shafran, C. R. (1998). Normative sexual behavior in children: A contemporary sample. *Pediatrics, 101*(4), e9.

Friedrich, W. N., Fisher, J. L., Dittner, C. A., Acton, R., Berliner, L., Butler, J., et al. (2001). Child Sexual Behavior Inventory (CSBI): Normative, psychiatric and sexual abuse comparisons. *Child Maltreatment, 6*(1), 37-49.

Friedrich, W. N., & Grambsch, P. (1992). Child Sexual Behavior Inventory (CSBI): Normative, psychiatric and sexual abuse comparisons. *Psychological Assessment, 4*(3), 303-311.

Friedrich, W. N., Lysne, M., Sim, L., & Shamos, S. (2004). Assessing sexual behavior in high-risk adolescents with the Adolescent Clinical Sexual

Behavior Inventory (ACSBI). *Child Maltreatment,*
9(3), 239-250.

Fristad, M. A., Weller, E. B., & Weller, R. A.
(1992). The Mania Rating Scale (MRS): Can it
be used in children? A preliminary report. *Journal
of the American Academy of Child & Adolescent
Psychiatry,* 31(2), 252-257. [Erratum in *Journal
of the American Academy of Child & Adolescent
Psychiatry, 31,* 1001, 1992].

Fristad, M. A., Weller, R. A., & Weller, E. B.
(1995). The Mania Rating Scale (MRS): Further
reliability and validity studies with children. *Annals of Clinical Psychiatry,* 7(3), 127-132.

Geller, B., Bolhofner, K. E., Craney, J. L., Williams, M., DelBello, M. P., & Gundersen, K.
(2000). Psychosocial functioning in a prepubertal
and early adolescent bipolar disorder phenotype.
*Journal of the American Academy of Child and
Adolescent Psychiatry,* 39(12), 1543-1548.

Geller, B., Tillman, R., Bolhofner, K., & Zimerman, B. (2008). Child bipolar I disorder: Prospective continuity with adult bipolar I disorder;
characteristics of second and third episodes; predictors of 8-year outcome. *Archives of General
Psychiatry,* 65(10), 1125-1133.

Geller, B., Williams, M., Zimerman, B., & Frazier,
J. (1996). *Washington University in St. Louis Kiddie Schedule for Affective Disorders and Schizophrenia (WASH-U-KSADS).* St Louis: Washington University.

Geller, B., Zimerman, B., Williams, M., Bolhofner, K., Craney, J. L., DelBello, M. P., et al.
(2001). Reliability of the Washington University
in St. Louis Kiddie Schedule for Affective Disorders and Schizophrenia (WASH-U-KSADS) mania
and rapid cycling sections. *Journal of the American Academy of Child and Adolescent Psychiatry,*
40(4), 450-455.

Geller, B., Zimerman, B., Williams, M., Bolhofner, K., Craney, J. L., DelBello, M. P., & Soutullo,
C. A. (2000). Diagnostic characteristics of 93
cases of a prepubertal and early adolescent bipolar disorder phenotype by gender, puberty and
comorbid attention deficit hyperactivity disorder.
*Journal of Child and Adolescent Psychopharma-
cology,* 10(3), 157-164.

Geller, B., Zimerman, B., Williams, M., DelBello,
M. P., Bolhofner, K., Craney, J. L., et al. (2002).
DSM-IV mania symptoms in a prepubertal and
early adolescent bipolar disorder phenotype compared to attention-deficit hyperactive and normal
controls. *Journal of Child and Adolescent Psychopharmacology,* 12(1), 11-25.

Geller, B., Zimerman, B., Williams, M., DelBello,
M. P., Frazier, J., & Beringer, L. (2002). Phenomenology of prepubertal and early adolescent bipolar disorder: Examples of elated mood, grandiose behaviors, decreased need for sleep, racing

thoughts and hypersexuality. *Journal of Child and
Adolescent Psychopharmacology,* 12(1), 3-9.

Gracious, B. L., Youngstrom, E. A., Findling, R.
L., & Calabrese, J. R. (2002). Discriminative validity of a parent version of the Young Mania Rating Scale (YMRS). *Journal of the American Academy of Child and Adolescent Psychiatry,* 41(11),
1350-1359.

Larsson, I., & Svedin, C. G. (2002). Teachers' and
parents' reports on 3- to 6-year-old children's sexual behavior—A comparison. *Child Abuse and
Neglect,* 26, 247-266.

Leibenluft, E. (2011). Severe mood dysregulation,
irritability, and the diagnostic boundaries of bipolar disorder in youths. *American Journal of Psychiatry,* 168, 129-142.

Leibenluft, E., Charney, D. S., Towbin, K. E.,
Bhangoo, R. K., & Pine, D. S. (2003). Defining
clinical phenotypes of juvenile mania. *American
Journal of Psychiatry,* 160(3), 430-437.

Lindblad, F., Gustafsson, P. A., Larsson, I., &
Lundin, B. (1995). Pre-schoolers' sexual behav-
ior at day-care centers: An epidemiological study.
Child Abuse and Neglect, 19(5), 569-577.

McClellan, J., Kowatch, R., Findling, R.L., &
Work Group on Quality Issues. (2007). Practice
parameter for the assessment and treatment of
children and adolescents with bipolar disorder.
*Journal of American Academy of Child & Ado-
lescent Psychiatry,* 46(1), 107-125.

Meyer-Bahlburg, H. F. L., Dolezal, C., & Sandberg, D. E. (2000). The association of sexual behavior with externalizing behavior in a community sample of prepubertal children. *Journal of
Psychology and Human Sexuality,* 12(1-2), 61-79.

Moreno, C., Laje, G., Blanco, C., Jiang, H.,
Schmidt, A. B., & Olfson, M. (2007). National
trends in the outpatient diagnosis and treatment
of bipolar disorder in youth. *Archives of General
Psychiatry,* 64(9), 1032-1039.

National Institutes of Mental Health Research
Roundtable on Prepubertal Bipolar Disorder.
(2001). *Journal of the American Academy of
Child and Adolescent Psychiatry,* 40(8), 871-878.

Paradise, J. E., Rose, L., Sleeper, L. A., & Nathanson, M. (1994). Behavior, family function, school
performance, and predictors of persistent disturbance in sexually abused children. *Pediatrics,* 93,
452-459.

Puig-Antich, J., Lukens, E., & Brent, D. (1986).
*Psychosocial Schedule for School Age Children-
Revised (PSS-R) in 1986 and 1987.* Pittsburgh:
Western Psychiatric Institute and Clinic.

Reich, W., Neuman, R. J., Volk, H. E., Joyner, C.
A., & Todd, R. D. (2005). Comorbidity between
ADHD and symptoms of bipolar disorder in a

community sample of children and adolescents. *Twin Research and Human Genetics, 8*(5), 459-466.

Rotheram-Borus, M. J., Mahler, K. A., & Rosario, M. (1995). AIDS prevention with adolescents. *AIDS Education and Prevention, 7,* 320-336.

Sim, L., Friedrich, W. N., Davies, H., Trentham, B., Lengua, L., & Pithers, W. (2005). The child behavior checklist as an indicator of posttraumatic stress disorder and dissociation in normative, psychiatric and sexually abused children. *Journal of Traumatic Stress, 18*(6), 697-705.

Smoller, J. W., & Finn, C. T. (2003). Family, twin, and adoption studies of bipolar disorder. *American Journal of Medical Genetics. Part C, Seminars in Medical Genetics, 123,* 48-58.

Spitzer, R. L., Endicott, J., & Robins, E. (1978). Research diagnostic criteria: Rationale and reliability. *Archives of General Psychiatry, 35,* 773-782.

Whitbeck, L. B., Conger, R. D., & Kao, M. (1993). The influence of parental support, depressed affect, and peers on the sexual behaviors of adolescent girls. *Journal of Family Issues, 14,* 261-278.

Yates, A. (1991). Differentiating hypererotic states in the evaluation of sexual abuse. *Journal of the American Academy of Child and Adolescent Psychiatry, 30*(5), 791-795.

Youngstrom, E. A., Gracious, B. L., Danielson, C. K., Findling, R. L., & Calabrese, J. (2003). Toward an integration of parent and clinician report on the Young Mania Rating Scale (YMRS). *Journal of Affective Disorders, 77*(2), 179-190.

The authors are deeply grateful to Dr. Barbara Geller for her gracious help, and Dr. Gabrielle Carlson for her invaluable advice in preparation of this manuscript.

An Integrative Approach to Treatment-Resistant Obsessive-Compulsive Disorder

Luke Sy-Cherng Woon, Anita Kanapathy, Hazli Zakaria, and César A. Alfonso

Abstract: Obsessive-compulsive disorder (OCD) is a debilitating psychiatric disorder that often runs a chronic unremitting course. Treatment outcomes can be unsatisfactory despite the availability of various somatic and psychological therapies. Psychodynamic psychotherapy in combination with cognitive behavioral therapy (CBT) with exposure and response prevention (ERP) could help patients with treatment-resistant OCD achieve better outcomes. An integrative approach can help patients gain insight, strengthen the therapeutic alliance, improve treatment adherence, and provide symptomatic relief when other treatments seem insufficient or have failed. We describe the treatment process of a person with treatment-resistant OCD who received pharmacotherapy, concurrent CBT/ERP, and a brief course of psychodynamic psychotherapy. Case formulations from cognitive behavioral and psychodynamic perspectives are presented. The authors discuss the advantages of doing a psychodynamic assessment and formulation in treatment refractory cases and the wisdom of integrating psychotherapy interventions for OCD, as well as the unique clinical features of cases that warrant a multimodal treatment approach.

Obsessive-compulsive disorder (OCD) is a severe psychiatric disorder characterized by obsessions and/or compulsions that are time-consuming, clinically distressing, and cause significant functional impairment (*DSM-5*, American Psychiatric Association, 2013; *ICD-10*, World Health Organization, 2010). Persons with OCD usually become symptomatic in late adolescence or early adulthood. According to epidemiological studies, the lifetime prevalence of OCD ranges from 1.9 to 3.5% and the illness usually runs a chronic and deteriorating course (Angst et al., 2004; Karno, Golding, Sorenson, & Burnam, 1988; Subramaniam, Abdin, Vaingankar, & Chong, 2012). OCD results in considerable impairment in quality of life, especially in the domain of social functioning (Coluccia et al., 2016; Koran, Thienemann, & Davenport, 1996) and the extent of the impairment is closely associated with the severity of OCD symptomatology (Eisen et al., 2006).

Until the end of the 20th century OCD was considered to have a poor prognosis, with continuous symptoms, episodic exacerbations, and a remission rate of about 20% (Skoog & Skoog, 1999). Treatment advances have led to improved long-term prognosis for patients with OCD. A recent meta-analysis of studies on long-term outcome of OCD in adults shows a pooled remission rate of 53% (Sharma et al., 2014). However, subsets of patients who do not adequately respond to conventional treatments are still greatly burdened by this debilitating condition. OCD is associated with substantial comorbid psychiatric conditions, such as mood disorders, anxiety disorders, and substance use disorders. The British National Psychiatry Morbidity Survey found that comorbidity occurs in almost two-thirds of patients with OCD, with 37% of subjects with major depression (Torres et al., 2006). A quarter of the surveyed participants attempted suicide. Unmarried status and comorbid depression are factors associated with suicidal behavior in OCD (Alonso et al., 2010).

Combined pharmacotherapy and psychological interventions benefit patients with OCD. Serotonin reuptake inhibitors (SSRIs) have a robust evidence base (Fineberg, Reghunandanan, Brown, & Pampaloni, 2013). Equally effective alternatives include clomipramine and serotonin/norepinephrine reuptake inhibitors (Bokor & Anderson, 2014). Cases resistant to these first-line drugs may require augmentation with atypical antipsychotics, benzodiazepines, and other agents. More invasive therapies such as electroconvulsive therapy (Fontanelle et al., 2015), deep brain stimulation (Kohl et al., 2014), or psychosurgeries (Bear, Fitzgerald, Rosenfeld, & Bittar, 2010) are considered in treatment-refractory patients, after weighing in substantial risks and potential complications.

The psychological intervention most frequently offered to patients with OCD is cognitive behavioral therapy (CBT) in the form of exposure and response prevention (ERP), which is empirically well supported (Abramowitz, 2006). CBT/ERP emphasizes strategies of behavioral modification besides identification and correction of cognitive errors in the conscious mind (Meyer, 1966). Psychodynamic psychotherapy, a less favored treatment approach in countries that are underserved or in treatment settings with a high volume of patients, explores unconscious motivations behind the manifest OCD symptoms (Chlebowski & Gregory, 2009). These two therapy modalities seek to understand and treat the same clinical condition from different perspectives, at different levels, with different techniques and strategies. We believe that integration of CBT and psychodynamic psychotherapy has the potential of enhancing treatment effects, especially in complex refractory or resistant cases.

We report the case of a patient with chronic severe OCD and comorbid depression, who had marginal symptomatic improvement after sequentially administered pharmacologic, psychotherapy, and ECT treatments over several years. Treatment resistance lifted after he received parallel CBT and psychodynamic psychotherapies in combination with medication. Informed consent was obtained for this report and the manuscript draft was reviewed and approved by the patient.

CASE REPORT

Mr. B is a 32-year-old ethnic Chinese, single male working as a medical doctor who became progressively symptomatic with anxiety over the last 8 years. He was diagnosed with obsessive-compulsive disorder (fulfiulling *DSM-5* and *ICD-10* criteria) at the age of 24, with intrusive thoughts in the form of violent urges. The symptoms began with irrepressible urges to harm significant others, for example, thoughts of strangling his partner, and ideas that were harmful or ruinous to himself, such as scalding his skin with a hot iron while ironing clothes, or destructive urges like pouring water on his laptop. Often but not always, such thoughts increased when irritable or angered by circumstances. He was greatly distressed by obsessive thoughts, which resulted in prominent and constant anxiety. The intrusive thoughts consumed his thinking from 8 hours up to 12 hours a day each day.

Over time, Mr. B's obsessions generalized from acquaintances to random strangers. He developed intrusive violent thoughts to physically and sexually assault women. These obsessions were associated with a deep feeling of rage and contempt, feelings that he could not justify or comprehend. He had a strong urge to disclose the obsessive thoughts and a duty to warn. In order to distract himself from disclosing the obsessions, Mr. B spent increasing amounts of time ruminating over the potential calamitous consequences if the obsessions were to be acted out or disclosed, which invariably plunged him into feeling a profound sense of guilt and self-reproach for having such vile thoughts. He obsessively feared that his condition would eventually complicate with lawsuits, which would ruin his career as a physician. Throughout the course of his illness there were no compulsions, only obsessions, but he felt immense anxiety that at any time he could lose control. Although there was no objective evidence of being in situations where this could occur, he constantly ruminated stating he was "a ticking bomb," and "a disaster about to happen."

Mr. B isolated from friends and acquaintances to avoid chances of developing harmful thoughts against them. He minimized using social media because navigating the Internet triggered thoughts of sending random obscene messages. Mr. B's illness progressed and the thoughts grew more frequent and widespread. He changed his life routines and most of the time he was confined at home, only venturing out at odd hours. The overwhelming sense of loneliness that resulted from protective isolation compounded his misery and sadness. He denied suicidal thoughts but described that life would not be worth living if he were not to find symptomatic relief. There were no symptoms suggestive of mania or psychosis and he did not fulfil criteria for a comorbid personality disorder. The patient does not drink alcohol, use psychoactive substances, and denies experimenting with any drugs in the past.

Even before the appearance of OCD symptoms, it was quite apparent that Mr. B had difficulty forming relationships. He is a strongly opinionated person with unyielding and categorical views. When he feels he is right he craves recognition. He easily criticizes others and picks on their mistakes, with great rigidity. Following orders and being corrected by others is difficult for him. He perceives he comes across as unpleasant and unfriendly. These features that superficially appear to be narcissistic traits are in sharp contrast with his capacity for warmth, empathy, and genuine concern for others. The constant obsessions caused an intense sense of mental "static," angst, and sensory overload that lowered his frustration tolerance and capacity to attend to nuances of social interactions.

Mr. B grew up in a working class, ethnic Chinese family from a rural area in Peninsular Malaysia. The neighborhood was largely a Chinese community of low socioeconomic status. His parents were uneducated. His father had a blue-collar job and his mother was a homemaker. The family was financially constrained and could afford only enough to fulfill basic needs. Mr. B's father took on the typical traditional East Asian patriarchal role that emphasized unquestioned obedience, filial piety, and valuing collective interest over personal rights or indulgences. Mr. B's parents also expected him to excel academically, in line with the longstanding Malaysian Chinese ethnic-cultural belief that academic excellence is the key to success and prosperity. The patient felt that recognition from his parents was highly conditional depending on his academic performance with a "lack of genuine show of love from them."

Mr. B has conflicted relationships with family members, especially his father. As the middle child, he feels that his parents did not treat him equally as his two siblings, an elder sister and a younger brother. The patient's sister is two years older than him and presently lives with her husband in a neighbouring Asian country. As children, Mr. B and his sister did not spend much time playing or exploring, keeping distant and aloof. He describes feeling resentful because "she got more than what she deserved" and their father treated her as the preferred child. An early example he relates is that his sister was given the opportunity to go to kindergarten in an age appropriate way, but the patient was not allowed to do so until an aunt intervened on his behalf. To this day Mr. B only talks to his sister if it is absolutely necessary. The sister has a university degree and a stable professional job. The feeling of being overlooked and going about unnoticed became more pronounced after the birth of a younger brother when the patient was four years old. He states the brother was also favored over him, giving as an example that the brother was "a less choosy eater and grew up better," referring here to Mr. B's fragile physical appearance. He describes the relationship with his brother as cold and distant, and can hardly remember playing with him either. The brother is now married and lives in their hometown with nuclear and extended family, running a profitable small business. They are in contact occasionally, cordially, but in a superficial way.

Mr. B describes his father as absent because of work, but when at home behaved as an "unforgiving person" who "always appeared to be sullen," scolding the patient for trivial matters. He vividly remembers countless incidents describing uncaring harsh words from his father such as "I shouldn't have given birth to you!"; "I will kill you!"; "Why don't you just die!"; "Even ghosts are afraid of you!" These were clearly frightening traumatic experiences. He did not experience physical or sexual abuse during childhood. Although the father was viciously verbally abusive, he did not physically harm the patient, his siblings, or mother. Verbal violence toward the patient and his mother was pervasive and quite brutal. Mr. B has always had a diminutive figure and low weight, despite being healthy and without major medical illnesses. He was often criticized by his father and other relatives when compared to his other "normal looking" siblings. Hurt by such comparisons and the strong words used to make them, he came to view himself as weak and disliked his small size, which

he linked to feelings of powerlessness later in life when facing harsh criticism from authoritative figures that were in caregiving or supervisory roles. Mr. B is resentful that his father never appreciated his talents even though it was obvious that he was the brightest among the siblings. He was never praised for doing well with studies. The negativity, combined with lack of reassurance, minimal validation or recognition resulted in low self-esteem and a pessimistic outlook in life. The patient describes his mother as very caring toward him and his siblings. She would "attend to (them) when sick and always cooked (their) favorite dishes." As a child he remembers struggling with feelings of excessive guilt when gratified by his mother with food treats, fearing that the father would become punitive. It was around issues of dietary idiosyncrasies and dysfunctional eating behaviors that many arguments ensued, as the patient describes himself as a very "picky eater," and eating was ritualistic in ways that infuriated the father. While his mother certainly showed concern and leniency, he still felt that there was a lack of tenderness, not enough love, and she failed to create a sense of security at home. When he was in great fear of the father he felt he could not disclose these feelings to mother or get reassurance from her. Mr. B's mother was hardworking and took care of household chores effectively and without much grumble. Despite this, Mr. B's father constantly "ran her (his mother) down" with many insulting words, calling her "stupid" or "brainless" after minor mistakes, and their marriage was tense and unhappy. The patient remembers how persistent she was feeding him, ensuring that he would finish meals, taking up to 2 hours at times to complete a meal. When the patient was 11 years old, his mother suddenly fell ill and within two months died of complications of colon cancer. When she died he remembers "not crying" but rather describes feeling a sense of relief after witnessing the overwhelming suffering from physical pain during the last two weeks of her life. His father did not remarry. No other women were introduced into the household. As an adult, Mr. B remains quite critical of his parents stating that from a very young age he realized that "they were far worse than other children's parents." He is judgmental of their unrefined manners, poor grooming, and obesity, and is reluctant to consider a less polarized view of them.

Even though his cultural background is rich in Chinese traditions and religious beliefs (a mixture of Confucian, Buddhist, and Taoist influences), Mr. B does not participate in any expected religious practices such as making offerings to ancestors or worshipping in temples. He was exposed to Christianity through some Christian schoolmates in the past and came to believe in the idea of a God, but describes himself as agnostic. Sometimes he would pray to God when in distress, while doubting whether "a just, loving God really exists," given the vicissitudes he faced in life.

Academically, Mr. B was a stellar student and scored high enough in qualifying examinations that resulted in a scholarship-funded placement in a medical school abroad. He functioned adequately through medical school even though it was during this period that his OCD symptoms developed. He describes having had few affectionate peer relationships during his school years in Malaysia, remembering difficulty engaging socially with classmates since kindergarten and throughout his teenage years.

The patient became aware of being gay during puberty and began having same-sex relationships only when he was studying overseas in medical school. He described his initial attempts reaching out to same-sex companions as a "liberating" experience, which confirmed to him his sexual orientation. He now remembers having been attracted to males since he was in late elementary school. His first infatuation was with a teacher in junior high school, a neatly groomed middle-aged man with a rotund body shape. Mr. B associates that image concretely with that of "a successful fatherly figure." Even though he felt the urge to get physical with the teacher he did not obsess about it or act on these lustful feelings. He did not have best friends, boyfriends, or gay friends during secondary school. He was socially introverted and felt that it would be dangerous to express his sexuality, keeping it a secret until he went to study overseas. After trying online chatting, he became sexually active having few brief encounters. In medical school Mr. B established a long-term relationship with a middle-aged Caucasian academic. He found a partner who was mature, understanding, and loving, with whom he felt secure. He was 22 years old when he first had a sexual experience, with the man he dated for the duration of his medical school years. Even though the relationship broke off amicably mostly because of their age difference and logistical geographic reasons since he had to return to Malaysia, it significantly shaped Mr. B's view of "an ideal partner." It made him assume "that Westerners are more forthcoming in expressing their affection and better lovers than Asians."

Other than brief memories of affectionate bonding with mother before age 11, the patient describes "living a loveless life" until he was able to express his sexuality at age 22. Of note is that, although perhaps etiologically unrelated, soon after finding great comfort in a stable sexual and romantic relationship in early adulthood his OCD symptoms began. It is possible that unconsciously internalized homophobia and repressed unresolved grief triggered symptomatic onset. Despite the initial fear of family opposition, the patient was quite surprised yet relieved by his father's muted response and siblings' indifference to finding out he was gay, right before returning to Malaysia to practice medicine. Once back in Malaysia, while yearning very much for a stable loving relationship, Mr. B has had multiple brief romantic relationships that were tumultuous, punctuated by frequent petty verbal altercations and disagreements. Most of the time he chooses to exit relationships early as he feels "unworthy of love because of (his) violent thoughts." Over time, Mr. B developed a scripted set of specific conditions that a partner must fulfil: he should be older, Caucasian, well-groomed, and rotund. This fantasy discourse is accompanied by a wish for unconditional love and affection. He often lamented the "near impossible odds of finding someone interesting and interested in him," given his limited socialization in Malaysia and strict criteria for seeking partners. He continued to look for potential suitors, even considering the possibility of migrating to another country. When describing casual brief sexual encounters he admits feeling physically fulfilled when having sex but still craves deeper intimacy. His recurrent sexual fantasies are with men, primarily involving physical closeness in the form of cuddling and hugging. For him the warmth and sense of security from such proximity is more important than the sexual acts conventionally associated with desire, arousal, and orgasm.

There is no known family history of mental illnesses, suicide, or addiction. Although scrupulosity was not a characteristic of either parent, the father is described as having a subclinical obsessional cognitive style, being pedantic, rigid, perseverative, strict, demanding, and clearly rageful while not expressive of other affects.

Despite the emerging OCD symptoms, Mr. B managed to complete medical school and returned to Malaysia for a medical internship at a local hospital. The internship was extended twice due to unsatisfactory performance related to repeated fallouts with his superiors and colleagues and low performance. He took offence when supervised or criticized, becoming defensive and argumentative. At work, even though his OCD symptoms did not directly interfere with clinical care, he could not help having harmful thoughts toward patients from time to time. He is horrified by such thoughts and feels extremely guilty as these contradict the bioethical principles "of the noble profession of medicine." Frequent absenteeism and poor working relationships led to sanctions by the medical review board in Malaysia. When Mr. B presented to us for rehabilitative psychiatric treatment referred by the medical

licensing board, he had stopped working for two months due to his mental illness.

Treatment Course

Over a period of eight years Mr. B had tried a large number of medications given by different providers in other clinics including antidepressants (amitriptyline, clomipramine, maprotiline, fluoxetine, sertraline, and escitalopram) and atypical antipsychotics (risperidone, olanzapine, quetiapine) in various combinations. He often experienced prominent side effects at low doses with minimal therapeutic response. When beginning treatment in our clinic concurrent pharmacotherapy and CBT/ERP were initially recommended. Fluvoxamine, which he was taking when referred to us, was continued and further optimized to a total daily dose of 250 mg. Aripiprazole augmentation was added because of inadequate response to fluvoxamine, but Mr. B could only tolerate a dose of 10 mg per day. After three months without adequate symptomatic relief, bupropion up to 150 mg B.I.D. was given when both fluvoxamine and aripiprazole were tapered off. Bupropion then had to be stopped after two months as it caused significant tinnitus and inadequate symptomatic relief.

At that point in time the patient received a total of 12 sessions of CBT/ERP. The sessions included techniques of behavioral therapy, exposure and response prevention, and cognitive restructuring. He learned relaxation techniques during the course of treatment. Using the downward arrow technique, the schemata or core beliefs were identified. Mr. B would tell himself: "I am an unlucky person," "I am unlovable." Accompanying these core beliefs were automatic dysfunctional thoughts such as "I will not get what I deserve," "nobody genuinely likes me," and "everything is going wrong with my life," and information processing biases such as minimizing the goodness in himself and maximizing the failures that he faced, overgeneralizations, and catastrophic thinking. As CBT progressed beyond the initial sessions to ERP exercises and homework assignments, Mr. B started to resist and became only partially compliant. He was able to participate and complete the exposure exercises when these were done during the sessions but refused to try at home because of "fear of making mistakes." Although CBT therapists expect this type of resistance when working with people with OCD, the patient seemed to be deeply angered by the therapist's prescription for changes, instructions, directives, and assignments. Non-adherence generalized to an unwillingness to take medication, remembering side effects previously experienced and adamantly refusing to consider the possibility that medication could help alleviate symptoms. CBT came to a standstill for three weeks and the patient developed severe depressive symptoms (PHQ-9 score of 20). Given the critical impasse and emergence of severe depression electro-convulsive therapy was offered and accepted.

After eight ECT treatments the symptoms of depression stabilized (PHQ-9 score < 10) but the chronic OCD symptoms did not improve. CBT resumed at this point but Mr. B's resistance to practice the learned skills persisted. He began to research on his own other treatment modalities and demanded more invasive interventions such as deep brain stimulation and psychosurgery. At one point a consultation in another country to evaluate suitability for psychosurgery was considered. With the help of a supervisor, the CBT therapist noticed instances whereby Mr. B brought up anger-laden topics he wished to talk about instead of CBT scripted discussions, which hindered the progress of CBT sessions. The clinical picture of no overt compulsions, prominent interpersonal stressors, and much display of anger and resistance to assignments in CBT, all of which could be associated with unconscious motivations and conflicts, prompted the consideration of psychodynamic psychotherapy as a potentially helpful addition to treatment. A different therapist was assigned to conduct psychodynamic psychotherapy.

The initial goal of psychodynamic therapy was to establish a therapeutic alliance. The patient and therapist mutually agreed, primarily because of the therapist's limited availability, to plan the treatment as time limited, aiming to complete 14 to 16 weekly sessions. The therapy was not structured or manualized, but the therapist was well trained (having completed advanced training, and had experience supervising and co-teaching a psychodynamic psychotherapy course) and had over 10 years of clinical experience. Therapy was conducted within a supportive-expressive-uncovering continuum (Cabaniss, Cherry, Douglas, & Schwartz, 2010). The main treatment objective voiced by the patient was "to find closure" and understand if symptoms could be related to unresolved conflicts and unexpressed or misguided/displaced feelings. Therapist and patient agreed that exploration of certain themes could be helpful. These included why symptoms were characterized by specific recurrent obsessions with violent themes, understanding the urge to disclose and ruminate, understanding how guilt and self-loathing compound negative affective states, addressing repeated failures in love relationships, and understanding what motivates emotional distancing from surviving family members. Regulation of affect, in particular containing anxiety and irritability and neutralizing depressivity were desired. Exploration of the impact of traumatic childhood adverse events including violence and neglect, and allowing for expression of complex feelings associated with grief after the unexpected death of mother to catastrophic illness during the patient's young age were considered important as well.

Psychodynamic psychotherapy offered the patient an opportunity to speak beyond the symptoms, and as tempting as it was to spend most of the time in sessions focusing on how incapacitating his condition was the therapist encouraged with genuine curiosity getting to know the person beyond the symptoms. Distress was validated, and as the patient began to recount past events and developmental trajectory, a new narrative emerged and a number of issues became apparent. Mr. B harbored a great deal of anger toward his parents, consciously toward his father because of an authoritarian parenting style, exceedingly harsh words, judgmental attitude, and conditional attention. He realized he was traumatized by verbal abuse and neglect. His anger was coupled with an unconscious fear of being destroyed by a tyrannical, powerful figure that he had no means to oppose. His mother, while not harsh, provided no relief for his emotional suffering and was perceived as an accomplice. She was seen as inherently flawed, by introjecting the constant denigration by Mr. B's father. Her premature death when the patient was 11 years old was received with ambivalence and profound sadness, feelings that were repressed since her death and now for the first time addressed in psychotherapy.

Several defense mechanisms were recognized. Anger and aggressive impulses toward parents were separated from the ideational component and became unconscious in the form of isolation; direction of the urge was instead displaced from the true objects (parents) and manifested as violent thoughts toward acquaintances and strangers. The patient sought to reduce anxiety and control underlying impulses through the defense of undoing. The urge to disclose frightening obsessive thoughts becomes an attempt to undo or prevent the consequences irrationally anticipated from the obsessions. The intense fear caused by the obsessive thoughts is related to magical thinking or omnipotence of thought. Merely thinking about an unwanted event in the external world becomes equivalent in significance as its actual occurrence, especially in the moral sense (e.g., having bad thoughts is as bad or as sinful as actually committing the acts). As interpretations were made and the patient became aware of how the specific defenses were an attempt to cope with distress, some symptomatic relief accompanied the newly gained insights and more adaptive expressions of affect.

Unfulfilled wishes of gratification from caregivers were displaced into an idealized image of a near perfect partner, who symbolically represents a Buddha-like image of comfort, compassion, wisdom, and unconditional love. The patient's longing for unconditional love coexists in sharp contrast with his own highly conditional investment of affection; he expects others to love him, yet he could not even love himself. He internalized his father's critical attitude and came to believe that he was indeed a lousy person who did not deserve to be loved. Moreover, he developed idiosyncratic rules in a quest to find an idealized significant other. Such idiosyncrasies in expectations coupled with affective dysregulation and persistent obsessions, invariably led to repeated failures in establishing mature, mutually satisfying relationships. These failures compounded an anaclitic depression, which arose from the feelings of loss, loneliness, and ambivalent anger after parental neglect and object loss.

Through interpretations and reflections on transference enactments, part of the pathogenesis of Mr. B's illness was identified. Unresolved anger and fear associated with the unconscious loss of a loving parental figure resulted in a compulsive drive for child-like possession of love objects and obsessive hostility toward others. Ensuing guilt, the product of a harsh superego, in turn led to self-loathing, hopelessness, and depression.

The decision to commence psychodynamic therapy while CBT was still ongoing permitted the patient to redirect the disruptive therapeutic impasse from CBT sessions into another context where these issues could be safely explored. The supportive-expressive and uncovering psychodynamic approach provided timely support to allow the completion of CBT sessions. Moreover, the improved therapeutic relationship made it possible to reintroduce pharmacotherapy with the antidepressant escitalopram at 10 mg daily while tolerating combined psychotherapies, without a nocebo response, and the patient ceased to insist on invasive psychosurgery procedures. The concurrent psychodynamic sessions helped to overcome resistance in treatment and facilitated emotional expression. He became more capable of articulating feelings of anger, fear, and guilt, rather than merely describing incapacitating OCD symptoms. He gained insight into the origins of his anger and acquired better control over its expression, and became less irritable in general. While still being bothered by negative thoughts from time to time, Mr. B was more willing to entertain positive alternatives suggested to him. After an 11-month hiatus, he was able to return to work and is able to interact with others at the workplace without much conflict. He successfully passed his postgraduate medical examination. After the completion of 16 psychodynamic sessions, he transitioned to outpatient clinic supportive psychotherapy and CBT sessions fortnightly. He is beginning to reconnect with family and is comfortable visiting his hometown with relative frequency.

Of note is that after seeking supervisory consultation, the psychodynamic therapist was able to work through countertransference feelings that affected the team of healthcare workers involved in this treatment. Some of the providers were uncomfortable with the patient's sexual orientation. The discomfort was not in the form of overt negative judgmental attitudes but rather in the form of avoidance of the need to explore important psychological themes. Although Malaysian psychiatrists endorse the position statement of the World Psychiatric Association (Bhugra, Eckstrand, Levounis, Kar, & Bittar, 2016) that views homosexuality as a normal variant of sexual behavior, internalized homophobia (Friedman & Downey, 1994) is common in Southeast Asian countries among medical providers. In this case, it manifested by failing to see that the patient's interpersonal romantic difficulty needed to be reframed as a search for love and intimacy rather than focusing on aspects of sexual actions. The team was unconsciously colluding with the patient's categorical assumption and sense of hopelessness that he could not succeed in love because of being a gay person in a conservative society.

DISCUSSION

Psychodynamic psychotherapy seeks to uncover unconscious processes involving unresolved conflicts that arise from the past in order to gain awareness and understanding of their influence on current symptoms. Importance is given to develop awareness of developmental progress, obstacles, failures, and challenges when understanding the life narrative of patients. A common misconception is that psychodynamic psychotherapy needs to be prolonged in order to be effective (Bauer & Kobos, 1984). Another common misconception is that the main emphasis of psychodynamic psychotherapeutic technique is analyzing transferences. Empirical studies (Høglend et al., 2006) show that transference interpretations are quite important in the treatment of borderline and narcissistic personality disorders but less important or at times even superfluous in the absence of these conditions. The therapeutic alliance and curative factors such as goal consensus, empathy, positive regard, validation, affirmation, collaboratively developing mastery, earned attachments, and improving mentalization are transformative and of transdiagnostic importance in all psychodynamic treatments (Nahum, Tasman, Alfonso, & Sonmez, in press).

Various meta-analyses have shown that psychodynamic psychotherapy yields effect sizes as large as other evidence-based treatments (Abbass et al., 2014; Leichsenring, Abbass, Luyten, Hilsenroth, & Rabung, 2013; Leichsenring, Rabung, & Leibing, 2004; Shedler, 2010). The findings also show that there are substantial long-term psychological gains after therapy has ended. Recent reviews on the efficacy of psychodynamic psychotherapy in specific mental disorders suggest that it is efficacious for depressive disorders, some anxiety disorders, somatoform disorders, eating disorders, and personality disorders (Fonagy, 2015; Leichsenring & Klein, 2014). For OCD, psychodynamic psychotherapy has much weaker empirical support (Fonagy, 2015; Ponniah, Magiati, & Hollon, 2013). While psychoanalysis was seen as the treatment of choice for neuroses, including OCD, until the 1960s, psychodynamic psychotherapy is not emphasized in current clinical practice guidelines (The British Psychological Society & the Royal College of Psychiatrists, 2006; Koran, Hollander, Nestadt, & Simpson, 2007). In contrast, CBT/ERP is widely accepted as effective in treating OCD (Gava et al., 2007; Rosa-Alcázar, Sánchez-Meca, Gómez-Conesa, & Marín-Martínez, 2008). It has superior effect compared to medications alone, and it is associated with lower relapse rates (Simpson et al., 2004). However, effect sizes of CBT for adult OCD trials are significantly smaller than in child studies (Olatunji, Davis, Powers, & Smits, 2013). Moreover, CBT is less efficacious for patients with OCD when the disorder presents symptomatically with obsessions in the absence of compulsions (Christensen, Hadzi-Pavlovic, Andrews, & Mattick, 1987).

There are commonalities between psychodynamic and cognitive-behavioral formulations of OCD. Traditional psychoanalytic views conceptualize OCD in terms of ambivalence resulting from the disequilibrium between a harsh superego that results from identification with critical and demanding caregivers, and aggressive impulses emerging from repressed anger (Fenichel, 1945). When there is difficulty integrating these contradictory aspects within the self, the use of defense mechanisms such as reaction formation, isolation of affect, magical thinking, and undoing could lead to manifest OCD symptoms. From the point of view of object relations theory, early interactions with primary caregivers and other significant others result in ambivalent representations of the self and others in OCD (Blatt, Auerback, & Levy, 1997). Difficulty tolerating ambivalence produces internal representations based on negative attributes of the self, which is associated with self-criticism and hypermorality with the perception that others are punishing and critical. These dynamics are related to a pervasive tendency for rigidity and a strong need for control and autonomy.

Cognitive behavioral theory hypothesizes that a negative appraisal of intrusive thoughts, as the product of underlying maladaptive cognitive-affective schemas, is the key feature of OCD. Extensive research by The Obsessive Compulsive Cognitions Working Group (OCCWG; 1997) identified six important schemas in OCD: overestimation of danger, inflated responsibility, perfectionism, strong need to control, thought-action fusion, and intolerance of uncertainty. These cognitive-affective schemas bear remarkable similarities to psychodynamic formulations of OCD. Persons with OCD have contradictory representations of self and others rooted in failures of attachment. Parents who display love and acceptance as well as criticism and rejection create anxiety and insecurity (Bhar & Kyrios, 2007; Guidano & Liotti, 1983). Typical schemas in OCD are conceptualized as efforts to reduce ambivalent feelings.

There is considerable overlap between the cognitive behavioral ideas of cognitive schemas and the psychodynamic model of the role of defense mechanisms in OCD. Perfectionism, need for control, overemphasis of thinking, and responsibility are common features identified in OCD. Furthermore, there is a converging notion from both theoretical perspectives that self-ambivalence, the inner conflict between contradictory selves, forms the basis of the psychopathology of OCD (Kempke & Luyten, 2007). The pathogenesis of OCD symptomatology could be in part related to the types of attachments formed during critical periods early in life. In this case there are elements of disorganized and anxious attachments, with a secondary avoidant style with a tendency toward excessive self-reliance and resisting collaborative relationships.

There is increasing recognition that psychotherapy techniques can be combined with complementary or synergistic effects (Silva, Kim, Hofmann, & Loula, 2003; Wolfe, 2008). A changing attitude exists regarding the sharp demarcation between psychodynamic and cognitive behavioral theory and practice. A survey conducted by Alfonso and Olarte (2011) of experienced psychodynamic psychotherapists in the United States found that respondents substantially endorse and incorporate CBT theory and technique in their clinical practice. We feel it is reasonable to suggest that there is therapeutic potential in combining both CBT and psychodynamic psychotherapy when treating patients with OCD. This approach may be particularly useful for individuals who do not respond adequately to pharmacologic and other somatic treatments.

Concurrent CBT and psychodynamic therapy for OCD in our case was considered proper as it addressed the immediate problems of treatment resistance and impending rupture of the therapeutic alliance due to unexplored dynamic issues, characterized by excessive verbalizations of anger and worsening of depressive symptoms. There are other distinctive features that make the combined treatment approach in our case more reasonable. The patient had prominent violent-themed obsessions with little overt compulsions, which could have rendered CBT approach alone less effective. In OCD the distress caused by obsessions can be, at least partially and transiently, alleviated by compulsive rituals. These difficulties, and the ensuing sense of helplessness, contributed much to the challenge of engaging the patient in collaborative treatment.

Psychodynamic psychotherapy may help persons with OCD with prominent interpersonal issues associated with poor self-esteem and interpersonal stressors (Chlebowski & Gregory, 2009). In our case we sought to encourage expression of emotion within the context of a trusting therapeutic relationship and to understand the patient's needs through attentive listening and detailed inquiry. Unconditional support was given despite his repeated expressions of intense and often unpleasant emotions. We also strived to maintain a positive approach through measured, realistic reassurance to encourage

hope. In a sense, this can be seen as the application of the concept of container-contained as proposed by Wilfred Bion (1963), whereby the therapist acts as a safe recipient of the painful emotions expressed by patients.

In practice both CBT and psychodynamic psychotherapy seek to establish a positive therapeutic alliance. Instilling hope and expectations for positive outcomes are also crucial universal components for good outcomes in all forms of psychotherapy. In fact, even the mere goal of forming a therapeutic relationship in psychotherapy, which promises understanding and support, can bring about hope and lead to symptomatic improvement (Feinstein, Heiman, & Yager, 2015). This positive attitude and expectation is particularly essential for patients who lack a strong desire or confidence to change. Regardless of the type of therapy, certain positive characteristics in the therapist, such as capability for empathy, unconditional positive regard, and genuineness improve outcomes in treatment (Rogers, 1957).

One may question in hindsight if integrating both CBT and psychodynamic elements in a single therapy by the same therapist might be more efficient and cost effective. Integrated, multimodal treatment of OCD by a single therapist has been proposed to enhance therapeutic benefit (Leib, 2001). In complex cases such as this one, the presence of co-therapists may provide an additional support system to the therapists (the therapeutic effect of teamwork) in order to continue offering care when faced with strong countertransference reactions.

Cognitive behavioral therapy in our case was initially conducted over 12 sessions covering few important domains. There was no demonstrable marked clinical improvement observed. We postulate few possible reasons that could have led to this. First, OCD with comorbid depressive symptoms made it challenging for the therapist to focus on one single illness. CBT in our case targeted more on the depressive symptoms than the OCD symptoms as he resisted to the exposure and homework. Given risk for suicide, the therapist could not ignore the depressive symptoms and negative thoughts. It has been suggested that longer duration of cognitive behavioral therapy delivers better outcome in clinical improvement among patients, and in our case perhaps a longer course of CBT could have been effective (Fava et al., 2004). Despite the limitations, there is one aspect of the therapy that may have been advantageous. Since the patient had intrusive harmful thoughts against women and CBT was conducted by a female therapist, constant exposure was built inherently in the treatment framework.

At the completion of 16 psychodynamic sessions, although the symptoms diminished, Mr. B still had intrusive thoughts. He developed a more nuanced understanding of how life events related to his illnesses. The preoccupation to disclose thoughts and the sense of duty to warn were very much reduced. Depressive symptoms were in remission and he started to repair relationships with family members. He interacted better with colleagues at work, affective regulation resulted in less expressed anger and his outlook became more optimistic. The patient's insecure attachments and interpersonal conflicts were given attention during therapy. We started with exploring family dynamics, identifying anxious and avoidant attachment styles rooted in early life experiences, while encouraging expression of associated negative feelings. Subsequently, as the therapeutic alliance developed, the therapy focused on avoidance of intimacy by reparatively working through the transferences. Mr. B. realized, as he processed unresolved grief in sessions, that there are more adaptive ways to tolerate loss than to become avoidant, isolative, or rageful.

In conclusion, psychodynamic psychotherapy can be useful for patients with treatment-resistant OCD, and can be administered effectively in conjunction with CBT/ ERP. A psychodynamic assessment and psychodynamically informed treatment strategies improve insight, level of functioning, strengthen the therapeutic alliance, and pro-vide symptomatic relief, complementing other treatment modalities. Concurrent CBT/ psychodynamic psychotherapy may have a particular role in the treatment of persons with OCD with comorbidity and treatment resistance facing prominent interpersonal stressors. Integration of the psychodynamic approach in the multimodal care of patients with treatment-resistant OCD requires training, adequate supervision and experience, and well-conducted trials are needed to support it as an evidence-based practice.

REFERENCES

Abbass, A. A., Kisely, S. R., Town, J. M., Leichsenring, F., Driessen, E., De Maat, S., Gerber, A., Dekker, J., Rabung, S., Rusalovska, S., & Crowe, E. (2014). Short-term psychodynamic psychotherapies for common mental disorders. *The Cochrane Database of Systematic Reviews*, 7, CD004687.

Abramowitz, J. S. (2006). The psychological treatment of obsessive-compulsive disorder. *Canadian Journal of Psychiatry*, 51(7), 407-416.

Alfonso, C. A., & Olarte, S. W. (2011). Contemporary practice patterns of dynamic psychiatrists—Survey results. *Journal of the American Academy of Psychoanalysis and Dynamic Psychiatry*, 39(1), 7-26.

Alonso, P., Segalàs, C., Real, E., Pertusa, A., Labad, J., Jiménez-Murcia, S., Jaurrieta, N., Bueno, B., Vallejo, J., & Menchón, J. M. (2010). Suicide in patients treated for obsessive-compulsive disorder: A prospective follow-up study. *Journal of Affective Disorders*, 124(3), 300-308.

American Psychiatric Association. (2013). *Diagnostic and statistical manual of mental disorders* (5th ed.). Arlington, VA: Author.

Angst, J., Gamma, A., Endrass, J., Goodwin, R., Ajdacic, V., Eich, D., & Rössler, W. (2004). Obsessive-compulsive severity spectrum in the community: Prevalence, comorbidity, and course. *European Archives of Psychiatry and Clinical Neuroscience*, 254(3), 156-164.

Bauer, G., & Kobos, J. (1984). Short-term psychodynamic psychotherapy: Reflections on the past and current practice. *Psychotherapy: Theory, Research, Practice*, 21(2), 153-170.

Bear, R. E., Fitzgerald, P., Rosenfeld, J. V., & Bittar, R. G. (2010). Neurosurgery for obsessive-compulsive disorder: Contemporary approaches. *Journal of Clinical Neuroscience*, 17(1), 1-5.

Bhar, S., & Kyrios, M. (2007). An investigation of self-ambivalence in obsessive-compulsive disorder. Behaviour Research and Therapy, 45, 1845-1857.

Bhugra, D., Eckstrand, K., Levounis, P., Kar, A., & Javate, K. R. (2016). WPA position statement on gender identity and same-sex orientation, attraction and behaviours. World Psychiatry, 15(3), 299-300.

Bion, W. R. (1963). Elements of psycho-analysis. London: Heinemann.

Blatt, S. J., Auerbach, J. S., & Levy, K. N. (1997). Mental representations in personality development, psychopathology, and the therapeutic process. Review of General Psychology, 1, 351-374.

Bokor, G., & Anderson, P. D. (2014). Obsessive-compulsive disorder. Journal of Pharmacy Practice, 27(2), 116-130.

British Psychological Society & the Royal College of Psychiatrists, The. (2006). Obsessive-compulsive disorder: Core interventions in the treatment of obsessive-compulsive disorder and body dysmorphic disorder. NICE Clinical Guidelines (No. 31). Leicester: British Psychological Society.

Cabaniss, D. L., Cherry, S., Douglas, C. L., & Schwartz, A. R. (2010). Psychodynamic psychotherapy—A clinical manual. New York: Wiley-Blackwell.

Chlebowski, S., & Gregory, R. J. (2009). Is a psychodynamic perspective relevant to the clinical management of obsessive-compulsive disorder? American Journal of Psychotherapy, 63(3), 245-256.

Christensen, H., Hadzi-Pavlovic, D., Andrews, G., & Mattick, R. (1987). Behavior therapy and tricyclic medication in the treatment of obsessive-compulsive disorder: A quantitative review. Journal of Consulting and Clinical Psychology, 55(5), 701-711.

Coluccia, A., Fagiolini, A., Ferretti, F., Pozza, A., Costoloni, G., Bolognesi, S., & Goracci, A. (2016). Adult obsessive-compulsive disorder and quality of life outcomes: A systematic review and meta-analysis. Asian Journal of Psychiatry, 22, 41-52.

Eisen, J. L., Mancebo, M. A., Pinto, A., Coles, M. E., Pagano, M. E., Stout, R., & Rasmussen, S. A. (2006). Impact of obsessive-compulsive disorder on quality of life. Comprehensive Psychiatry, 47(4), 270-275.

Eisen, J. L., Pinto, A., Mancebo, M. C., Dyck, I. R., Orlando, M. E., & Rasmussen, S. A. (2010). A 2-year prospective follow-up study of the course of obsessive-compulsive disorder. Journal of Clinical Psychiatry, 71(8), 1033-1039.

Fava, G. A., Ruini, C., Rafanelli, C., Finos, L., Conti, S., & Grandi, S. (2004). Six-year outcome of cognitive behavior therapy for prevention of recurrent depression. American Journal of Psychiatry, 161(10), 1872-1876.

Feinstein, R., Heiman, N., & Yager, J. (2015). Common factors affecting psychotherapy outcomes: Some implications for teaching psychotherapy. Journal of Psychiatric Practice, 21(3), 180-189.

Fenichel, O. (1945). The psychoanalytic theory of neurosis. New York: Norton.

Fineberg, N. A., Reghunandanan, S., Brown, A., & Pampaloni, I. (2013). Pharmacotherapy of obsessive-compulsive disorder: Evidence-based treatment and beyond. Australian and New Zealand Journal of Psychiatry, 47(2), 121-141.

Fonagy, P. (2015). The effectiveness of psychodynamic psychotherapy: An update. World Psychiatry, 14, 137-150.

Fontenelle, L. F., Coutinho, E. S. F., Lins-Martins, N. M., Fitzgerald, P. B., Fujiwara, H., & Yücel, M. (2015). Electroconvulsive therapy for obsessive-compulsive disorder: A systematic review. Journal of Clinical Psychiatry, 767(July), 949-957.

Friedman, R. C., & Downey, J. I. (1994). Homosexuality. New England Journal of Medicine, 14, 923-930.

Frisell, T., Lichtenstein, P., Rahman, Q., & Långström, N. (2010). Psychiatric morbidity associated with same-sex sexual behaviour: Influence of minority stress and familial factors. Psychological Medicine, 40(JUNE), 315-324.

Gava, I., Barbui, C., Aguglia, E., Carlino, D., Churchill, R., De Vanna, M., & McGuire, H. F. (2007). Psychological treatments versus treatment as usual for obsessive compulsive disorder (OCD). Cochrane Database of Systematic Reviews, 1(2), CD005333.

Guidano, V. F., & Liotti, G. (1983). Cognitive processes and emotional disorders: A structural approach to psychotherapy. New York: Guilford.

Høglend, P., Amlo, S., Marble, A., Bøgwald, K., Sørbye, Ø., & Sjaastad, M. C. (2006). Analysis of patient-therapist relationship in dynamic psychotherapy: An experimental study of transference interpretations. American Journal of Psychiatry, 163(10), 1739-1746.

Karno, M., Golding, J. M., Sorenson, S. B., & Burnam, M. A. (1988). The epidemiology of obsessive-compulsive disorder in five U.S. communities. Archives of General Psychiatry, 45(12), 1094-1099.

Kempke, S., & Luyten, P. (2007). Psychodynamic and cognitive-behavioral approaches of obsessive-compulsive disorder: Is it time to work through our ambivalence? *Bulletin of the Menninger Clinic, 71*(4), 291-311.

Kohl, S., Schönherr, D. M., Luigjes, J., Denys, D., Mueller, U. J., Lenartz, D., Visser-Vandewalle, V., & Kuhn, J. (2014). Deep brain stimulation for treatment-refractory obsessive compulsive disorder: A systematic review. *BMC Psychiatry, 14*(1), 214.

Koran, L. M., Hollander, E., Nestadt, G., & Simpson, H. B. (2007). Practice guideline for the treatment of patients with obsessive-compulsive disorder. *American Journal of Psychiatry, 64*(7 suppl.), 5-53.

Koran, L. M., Thienemann, M. L., & Davenport, R. (1996). Quality of life for patients with obsessive-compulsive disorder. *American Journal of Psychiatry, 153*(6), 783-788.

Leib, P. T. (2001). Integrating behavior modification and pharmacotherapy with the psychoanalytic treatment of obsessive-compulsive disorder: A case study. *Psychoanalytic Inquiry, 21*(2), 222-241.

Leichsenring, F., Abbass, A., Luyten, P., Hilsenroth, M., & Rabung, S. (2013). The emerging evidence for long-term psychodynamic therapy. *Psychodynamic Psychiatry, 41*(3), 361-384.

Leichsenring, F., & Klein, S. (2014). Evidence for psychodynamic psychotherapy in specific mental disorders: A systematic review. *Psychoanalytic Psychotherapy, 28*(1), 4-32.

Leichsenring, F., Rabung, S., & Leibing, E. (2004). The efficacy of short-term psychodynamic psychotherapy in specific psychiatric disorders: A meta-analysis. *Archives of General Psychiatry, 61*(12), 1208-1216.

Meyer, V. (1966). Modification of expectations in cases with obsessional rituals. *Behaviour Research and Therapy, 4*(1-2), 273-280.

Nahum, D., Tasman, A., Alfonso, C. A., & Sonmez, E. (in press). Common factors in psychotherapy. In A. Javed (Ed.), *Advances in psychiatry.* New York: Springer.

Obsessive Compulsive Cognitions Working Group (OCCWG). (1997). Cognitive assessment of obsessive-compulsive disorder. *Behaviour Research and Therapy, 35,* 667-681.

Olatunji, B. O., Davis, M. L., Powers, M. B., & Smits, J. A. J. (2013). Cognitive-behavioral therapy for obsessive-compulsive disorder: A meta-analysis of treatment outcome and moderators. *Journal of Psychiatric Research, 47*(1), 33-41.

Ponniah, K., Magiati, I., & Hollon, S. D. (2013). An update on the efficacy of psychological therapies in the treatment of obsessive-compulsive dis-order in adults. *Journal of Obsessive-Compulsive and Related Disorders, 2*(2), 207-218.

Rogers, C. (1957). The necessary and sufficient conditions of therapeutic personality change. *Journal of Consulting Psychology, 21*(2), 95-103.

Rosa-Alcázar, A. I., Sánchez-Meca, J., Gómez-Conesa, A., & Marín-Martínez, F. (2008). Psychological treatment of obsessive-compulsive disorder: A meta-analysis. *Clinical Psychology Review, 28*(8), 1310-1325.

Sharma, E., Thennarasu, K., & Reddy, Y. C. (2014). Long-term outcome of obsessive-compulsive disorder in adults: A meta-analysis. *Journal of Clinical Psychiatry, 75*(9), 1019-1027.

Shedler, J. (2010). The efficacy of psychodynamic psychotherapy. *The American Psychologist, 65*(2), 98-109.

Silva, S. P., Kim, C. K., Hofmann, S. G., & Loula, E. C. (2003). To believe or not to believe: Cognitive and psychodynamic approaches to delusional disorder. *Harvard Review of Psychiatry, 11*(1), 20-29.

Simpson, H. B., Liebowitz, M. R., Foa, E. B., Kozak, M. J., Schmidt, A. B., Rowan, V.,...Campeas, R. (2004). Post-treatment effects of exposure therapy and clomipramine in obsessive-compulsive disorder. *Depression and Anxiety, 19*(4), 225-233.

Skoog, G., & Skoog, I. (1999). A 40-year follow-up of patients with obsessive-compulsive disorder. *Archives of General Psychiatry, 56*(2), 121-127.

Subramaniam, M., Abdin, E., Vaingankar, J. A., & Chong, S. A. (2012). Obsessive-compulsive disorder: Prevalence, correlates, help-seeking and quality of life in a multiracial Asian population. *Social Psychiatry and Psychiatric Epidemiology, 47*(12), 2035-2043.

Torres, A. R., Prince, M. J., Bebbington, P. E., Bhugra, D., Brugha, T. S., Farrell, M., Jenkins, R., Lewis, G., Meltzer, H., & Singleton, N.(2006). Obsessive-compulsive disorder: Prevalence, comorbidity, impact, and help-seeking in the British National Psychiatric Morbidity Survey of 2000. *American Journal of Psychiatry, 163*(11), 1978-1985.

Wolfe, B. E. (2008). Toward a unified conceptual framework of psychotherapy. *Journal of Psychotherapy Integration, 18*(3), 292-300.

World Health Organization. (2010). *International statistical classification of diseases and related health problems* (10th ed.). World Health Organization.

Personality Disorders

Moving Beyond Specialized Therapies for Borderline Personality Disorder: The Importance of Integrated Domain-Focused Treatment

W. John Livesley

Abstract: This article argues the recent emphasis on specializing treatments for borderline personality disorder needs to be replaced by a more integrated and evidence-based approach that combines effective methods from all therapies. This proposition is based on evidence that specialized treatments for borderline personality disorder do not differ significantly from each and that they are not more effective than good structured care designed to meet the needs of patients with the disorder. It is also argued that current therapies are limited because they do not recognize or accommodate the extensive heterogeneity of borderline personality disorder and its complex etiology. These factors make a one-approach-fits-all strategy inappropriate for treatment.

An integrated approach is proposed as an alternative to the specialized therapies that makes use of all effective interventions regardless of their conceptual origins and delivers them in a coordinated way. A two-component framework is proposed for organizing integrated treatment: 1. a system for conceptualizing borderline personality disorder based on current empirical knowledge about the structure, etiology, and stability of borderline pathology that serves as a guide when selecting and delivering interventions; and 2. a model of therapeutic change based on the general literature on psychotherapy outcome and specific studies of PD treatments. This framework proposes that integrated treatment be organized around principles of therapeutic change common to all effective therapies supplemented with more specific treatment methods taken from the different therapies as needed to tailor treatment to individual patients and treat specific problems and psychopathology.

Psychotherapy for borderline personality disorder (BPD) has evolved in two phases. The initial phase largely involved psychoanalytical therapies modified to treat borderline pathology. The second, more expansive phase, began in about 1990 and continues to the present, has involved the evaluation of manualized therapies designed specifically for the disorder. Randomly controlled trials indicate that seven specialized therapies are effective: transference-focused therapy (TFT; Clarkin, Yeomans, & Kernberg, 1999), dialectical behavior therapy (DBT; Linehan, 1993), schema-focused therapy (SFT; Young, Klosko, & Weishaar, 2003), systems therapy for emotional predictability and problems solving (STEPPS; Blum, St. John, Phofl, Stuart, McCormick, Allen, Arndt, & Black, 2008), mentalizing-based therapy (MBT; Bateman & Fonagy, 2004), and cognitive-analytic therapy (CAT; Ryle, 1975). These findings have prompted questions about which therapy is the most effective and studies pitting treatments against each other. They have also led to suggestions that treatment should invariably use one of these methods. There are, however, good reasons to question whether treatment will be advanced by further comparative studies and whether selecting a specialized therapy is the best treatment option because outcome does not differ significantly across treatments (Leichsenring & Leibing, 2003) and no one therapy includes methods needed for comprehensive treatment. Moreover, BPD is not the homogeneous condition that manualized therapies imply (Stone, 2010).

For these reasons, it may be better to base treatment on change mechanisms common to all effective treatments than to rely on a single approach and to tailor treatment to the personality and psychopathology of the individual than to use a one method fits all approach. Consequently, this article argues that the treatment of BPD needs to evolve to a third phase—the use of integrated therapy that combines interventions that work regardless of their conceptual origins that also accommodates the heterogeneity of borderline pathology. The article is divided into three parts. The first offers a rationale for integration based on the limitations of specialized treatments. The second part examines generic change mechanisms to identify change principles to guide integrated treatment. Finally, a conceptual framework is proposed for organizing treatment and coordinating the delivery of an eclectic array of interventions.

LIMITATIONS OF SPECIALIZED THERAPIES AND THE RATIONALE FOR INTEGRATION

Although the current zeitgeist emphasizes specialized therapy, the limitations of these therapies argues for integration: 1. Outcome is similar across treatment; 2. BPD is not a homogeneous condition: substantial cross-patient and intra-patient variability creates difficulty for fixed protocols; 3. BPD encompasses multiple problem domains and optimal interventions vary across domains; and 4. Theories of BPD guiding specialized treatments do not offer comprehensive explanations of the nature and origins of the disorder.

Implications of Outcome Studies

Outcome studies have generated robust findings that have radically changed ideas about treating BPD. The disorder responds to treatment. Improvement occurs in most domains of psychopathology leading to a better quality of life. All specialized treatments produce significant change, hence all include effective interventions. These observations also raise the critical question of whether outcome differs across treatments, a question addressed by both empirical studies and meta-analyses.

Giessen-Bloo and colleagues (2006) compared schema-focused and transference-focused therapy. SFT was associated with fewer drop-outs and better outcome. However, the small differences between treatments do not provide strong support for the greater efficacy of SFT, given questions about the comparability of psychotherapeutic expertise across treatments. A similar comparison of brief cognitive therapy and brief Rogerian supportive therapy (Cottraux, Note, Boutitie, Milliery, Genouihlac, Yao, et al., 2009) found few differences between treatments. Outcome for both treatments was poor, which questions the merit of short-term treatment for BPD. A meta-analysis also found that cognitive and psychodynamic treatments did not differ substantially in outcome (Leichsenring & Leibing, 2003). Despite claims that some treatments are more comprehensive, address more significant pathology, or have better empirical support, there is little evidence of differential efficacy (Bartak, Soeteman, Verheul, & Busschbach, 2007).

Nevertheless, specialized therapies are more efficacious than treatment as usual (TAU; Doering, Hörz, Rentrop, Fischer-Kern, Schuster, Benecke, Buchheim, Martius, & Buchheim, 2010; Linehan, Comtois, Murray, Brown, Gallop, Heard, Korslund, Tutek, Reynolds, & Lindenboim, 2006) which appears to suggest that advantages accrue from a specialized therapy. However, TAU is a rather modest standard because it is usually limited to whatever routine care is available. When specialized therapies are compared with well-specified general psychiatric care tailored to BPD, the results are different. For example, McMain and colleagues (2009) compared DBT with general psychiatric management that included a combination of psychodynamically informed therapy and symptom-targeted medication management based on APA guidelines for treating BPD (*DSM-IV-TR*; 2000). There were no significant differences in outcome between groups. Given that DBT is the most studied treatment for BPD, these findings have major implications for practice and the future of specialized treatments. A comparison of MBT and structured clinical management also reported that outcome was similar for the two groups, although problems decreased slightly faster with MBT (Bateman & Fonagy, 2009). Finally, Chanen and colleagues (2008) reported that CAT was not significantly better than manualized good clinical care.

Treatments for BPD quickly fall in and out of favor due more to fad and fashion and the charisma of their proponents than hard evidence of superior performance. The failure to demonstrate greater effectiveness than good clinical care largely negates arguments for using specialized treatments and the need for specialized training in them. It also casts doubt on the theories underlying these therapies and the need for further comparative trials. Overall, the results of outcome studies suggest that positive outcome is more a function of a structured approach tailored to the disorder and change mechanisms common to all effective treatments than to therapy-specific methods. This is not surprising given extensive evidence of similar outcome for most psychotherapies for a wide range of conditions and evidence that a substantial proportion of outcome change arises from generic mechanisms (Beutler, 1991; Castonguay & Beutler, 2006a; Luborsky, Singer, & Luborsky, 1975). However, generic mechanisms are not the whole story. There is also evidence—albeit more limited—that some domains of psychopathology respond better to some interventions than others, that is, outcome is domain specific (Piper & Joyce, 2001). This issue will be considered later.

The results of outcome studies have three implications. First, treatment needs to be structured specifically to BPD. Second, optimal use should be made of generic mechanisms (Livesley, 2003a; Meyer & Pilkonis, 2006). Third, it is useful to differentiate interventions based on generic mechanisms from specific interventions that target a particular component of the disorder.

Conceptual Limitations of Current Treatment Models

Each specialized treatment is based on a theory of BPD that guides treatment strategies. Although theories differ across treatments, all suffer from two limitations: 1. none account for all of the many biological and psychosocial factors implicated in the development of the disorder; 2. all offer one-dimensional explanations that emphasize a single underlying impairment.

Current theories stress the psychosocial origins of BPD. Heritable influences are usually acknowledged but they are not systematically incorporated into either the underlying model or treatment strategies. This is a serious limitation because BPD has a substantial heritable component (Distel, Trull, Derom, Thiery, Grimmer, et al., 2008; Torgerson, Lygren, Oien, Skre, Onstad, et al., 2000) and no aspect of borderline pathology seems free from genetic influence. This does not mean that psychotherapy is irrelevant or that personality cannot be changed. However, it does necessitate some rethinking of treatment goals and the changes that are feasible when treating heritable traits such as anxiousness, emotional lability, and insecure attachment that are central to the disorder. The biological basis of traits makes it more effective to work with traits (Paris, 1998) and promote more adaptive expression of traits than to attempt to change them in more fundamental ways (Livesley, 2003a).

Most theories assume that BPD involves a single impairment such as affect dysregulation, maladaptive cognitions, conflicted relationships, fragmented object relationships, mentalizing impairments, or self pathology. Consequently, different therapies emphasize different strategies and interventions. For example, because DBT (Linehan, 1993) assumes that affect regulation is the primary problem, emphasis is placed on developing emotional regulation skills. In contrast, MBT (Bateman & Fonagy, 2004) considers the central problem to be impaired mentalizing and focuses in increasing mentalizing capacity with the assumption that this will promote affect regulation. Given that BPD involves emotion dysregulation and impaired mentalizing, it may be more appropriate to combine interventions from these therapies than to rely on one of them. This also applies to the other therapies.

This suggests that treatment models need to incorporate a multidimensional conception of the disorder that recognizes the multiple etiological pathways along which it develops (Livesley, 2008). The implication is that generic interventions need to be supplemented with more specific interventions that target specific problems. The challenge is how to organize such an integrated approach so as to avoid therapy being a confusing mixture of conceptual models and interventions. This is a particular problem because BPD consists of more than dysfunctional emotions, cognitions, and affects. It also involves difficulty achieving coherent and integrated personality functioning that results in the failure to establish a coherent self structure and integrated representations of others. Hence, treatment needs to promote integration. It is not sufficient, therefore, to simply combine treatments. A more integrated approach is needed that combines an evidence-based model of the disorder with a framework for coordinating interventions.

Heterogeneity of Borderline Personality Disorder

A third concern about specialized treatments is limited recognition of the heterogeneity of borderline pathology. BPD is an amorphous diagnosis encompassing a wide range of features. Heterogeneity is partly a reflection of the tangled roots of current conceptions of the disorder in both classical phenomenology and psychoanalysis (Stone, 1980, 2010) and partly a function of the interconnectedness of personality characteristics and the extensive links between personality and general psychopathology. Overlap with other PDs, co-occurrence with other mental disorders, and wide differences across individuals in co-occurring personality characteristics create enormous heterogeneity in clinical presentations that presents a challenge to highly specialized, protocol driven treatments. The diagnosis, like many psychiatric diagnoses, is essentially a heuristic for organizing clinical information and guiding clinical decisions (Hyman, 2010; Livesley, 2003b) that unfortunately tends to be reified. This reification encourages a focus on what is considered core pathology and comparative neglect of other features. Hence the relatively narrow focus of some specialized therapies.

Heterogeneity is not simply a consequence of the *DSM-IV* requirement that 5 of 9 diagnostic criteria are necessary for diagnosis. It is also a consequence of the underlying structure of personality. Multivariate studies consistently show that four broad dimensions underlie disordered personality. These represent emotional dysregulation-dependency, psychopathy, social avoidance, and compulsivity with each factor defined by a cluster of primary traits. The emotional-dependency factor resembles *DSM-IV* BPD. The four-factor phenotypic structure reflects the genetic architecture of personality (Livesley, Jang, & Vernon, 1998). Behavioral genetic studies show the primary traits from a given domain are influenced by a single general genetic factor. Many primary traits are also affected by genetic variability specific to that trait. Consequently, the genetic architecture of personality disorder is complex: multiple genetic factors underlie personality traits with the magnitude of each factor varying across individuals. Environmental factors then interact with genetic influences to create enormous diversity in personality phenotypes such as BPD. The imposition of broad typal constructs onto this variability results in diagnostic heuristics that show little correspondence to actual clinical presentations. As Westen and Arkowitz-Weston (1998) noted, about 40% of patients being treated for PD could not be adequately described using *DSM-IV* diagnoses.

The four broad factors or domains of traits are not mutually exclusive but rather co-occur. Consequently, many patients with high levels of borderline traits (emotional dysregulation-dependency factor) also show high levels of one or more traits from other clusters. Hence, some BPD patients are highly impulsive (not merely in the sense that they self-harm but also in the sense that they do things on the spur of the moment), sensation-seeking, and reckless. In contrast, others are more socially avoidant. High levels of traits from other clusters exert powerful influences

on clinical presentations. The co-occurrence of sensation-seeking, for example, creates a craving for excitement that contributes to interpersonal crises and helps to stabilize maladaptive patterns. When sensation-seeking is combined with recklessness, treatment, especially in the early stages, is often dominated by recurrent crises characterized by "acting out" behaviors. A very different picture is presented by patients with socially avoidant traits. These increase fearfulness and apprehensiveness that hinders both the establishment of an effective relationship and attempts to encourage new experiences and new behaviors. These differing presentations frequently require different treatment strategies. Manual driven approaches can act like a blinder that limits recognition of other features and hence the need to accommodate heterogeneity.

Another aspect of heterogeneity that is neglected by specialized treatments is severity. Studies show that severity, not type of disorder, is the best predictor of outcome. Variables linked to severity such as psychological mindedness, dissociative tendencies, cognitive dysfunction when stressed, influence the ability to use specific interventions. Hence guidelines are needed about what strategies to use with different levels of severity.

Domains of Psychopathology

Heterogeneity among patients with BPD is complemented by extensive within-individual heterogeneity in problems and psychopathology. This diversity provides a cogent argument for combining effective methods from different therapies. Patients with BPD show features from at least seven domains of psychopathology: 1. symptoms such as dysphoria and deliberate self-harm; 2. dysregulated emotions; 3. maladaptive traits such as anxiousness, emotional lability, and insecure attachment; 4. conflicted interpersonal patterns; 5. self or identity pathology; 6. impaired metacognitive processes;

and 7. dysfunctional environmental circumstances (Livesley, 2003a; 2012).

This diversity highlights the need for interventions pertinent to each domain because outcome is domain specific (Piper & Joyce, 2001): interventions that work for one domain do not necessarily work for another. Specialized therapies are remiss in respect: one-dimensional explanations of borderline pathology leads to comparative neglect of other problems. Taken together, specialized treatments include interventions that address all domains, individually they do not.

Examination of effective methods for each domain and a rational analysis of the methods that appear to be relevant to each domain provide a framework for selecting specific interventions. The optimal strategy for treating symptoms and emotion dysregulation is probably a combination of medication and cognitive-behavioral interventions. Cognitive methods are also integral to treating the interpersonal domain. However, these usually need to be augmented with methods drawn from psychoanalytic and interpersonal reconstructive therapy (Benjamin, 2003) and strategies to enhance the ability to understand the mental states of self and others. Finally, changes to self pathology require an array of methods that increase self-knowledge and self-understanding and help to construct a new self-narrative.

Examination of the relationship between domains of psychopathology and optimal treatment methods highlights a limitation of specialized therapies: adherence to a single model means that effective methods may not be used simply because they belong to an alternative approach. It also points to recognizing the multidimensional nature of BPD. Consequently, a basic strategy of integrated treatment is to decompose the disorder into domains and target domains with appropriate interventions. This approach differs markedly from the more homogeneous model of psychopathology organized around a single primary impairment adopted by some specialized treatments.

GENERIC CHANGE MECHANISMS

Similar outcome across treatments led to the proposal that integrated treatment be organized around generic mechanisms supplemented, wherever appropriate, with specific interventions to treat focal problems. Implementation of this proposal requires delineation of generic change principles, the strategies for implementing these principles, and the interventions that operationalize these strategies (Beutler & Harwood, 2000). Generic mechanisms have a *supportive* component based on the treatment relationship and a *technical* component involving opportunities for new learning and to apply new skills (Beutler & Harwood, 2000; Lambert, 1992; Lambert & Bergen, 1994). This section examines the literature on generic mechanisms, including conclusions drawn from an analysis of effective change mechanisms by the joint Task Force of the Society for Clinical Psychology (Division 12 of the American Psychological Association) and the North American Society for Psychotherapy Research (Castonguay & Beutler, 2006b; Critchfield & Benjamin, 2006).

Conceptual Structure

The task force noted that all effective therapies for PD have a well-defined conceptual structure (Critchfield & Benjamin, 2006). This prompts the first principle: that treatment be based on an explicit conceptual model. The principle is supported by studies showing that although specialized treatments are more effective than TAU they are not more effective than well-structured care. The importance of a defined model is highlighted by a second general principle: that effective outcome requires a consistent therapeutic process. Consistency is only possible when the therapist has an explicit framework to guide responses to therapeutic events. These principles imply that a simple eclectic approach involving an array of effective interventions is not a viable alternative to specialized treatment. Technical integration alone cannot provide the conceptual framework needed for consistency.

Relationship Factors

Outcome studies also reveal the importance of a strong working alliance (Smith, Barrett, Benjamin, & Barber, 2006). Relationship factors have additional significance when treating BPD because rejection-sensitivity and mistrust hinder alliance formation. A consistent focus on obstacles to alliance formation offers ongoing opportunities to change interpersonal schemas associated with these problems. The evidence suggests that the alliance is fostered by a therapeutic stance based on Rogerian and self-psychology dimensions of empathy, warmth, genuineness, support, and validation. This stance also reduces disruptions to the alliance that result from a confrontational and challenging stance (Horowitz & Marmar, 1985). Establishing and maintaining an effective alliance is an ongoing challenge: fluctuations in the alliance are common, so therapists need to monitor the alliance closely and intervene promptly when problems arise (Safran, Muran, Samstag, & Stevens, 2002).

Therapist qualities related to an effective alliance include open-mindedness, flexibility, and creativity (Fernandez-Alvarez, Clarkin, Salguiero, & Critchfield, 2006)—qualities that contrast sharply with the idea of fixed protocols. These qualities are especially important when handling threatened therapy disruptions, crises, and patient difficulty in implementing change (Critchfield & Benjamin, 2006). At these times, rigidity and strong adherence to a fixed protocol is a hindrance. Although an explicit model is a prerequisite for effective outcome, the model has to permit the flexibility required to deal with the complex clinical problems that are an inevitable part of treating BPD.

Effective treatment also requires therapists who are comfortable with long-term, emotionally intense relationships and are able to manage strong feelings about the patient and treatment. A clearly indentified change principle linked to the relationship is patient–therapist agreement on treatment goals and how they will be achieved. Discussion of patient goals fosters collaboration, enhances engagement, and builds a commitment to change. The evidence also supports two other principles: outcome is better when the therapist has specific training in treating BPD, and effective treatment requires greater activity than is needed when treating other conditions (Critchfield & Benjamin, 2006).

Patient Variables

Many patient characteristics linked to outcome hinder alliance formation, most notably poor social skills, impaired object relationships, poor relationships in the nuclear family, pessimism, hopelessness, strong defensive behavior, low psychological mindedness, hostility, and perfectionism. These findings draw attention to the importance of tailoring treatment to the individual and to variables that therapists need to keep in mind when monitoring the alliance.

Another patient factor linked to outcome is motivation. The significance of motivation is highlighted by the high dropout rate associated with most treatments. Unfortunately, low motivation is common with BPD. It is not simply a consequence of denial or the ego-syntonicity of many behaviors that hinders problem recognition, but rather a more pervasive consequence of psychosocial adversity that produces feelings of helplessness, powerlessness, hopelessness, and passivity. Effective treatment, therefore, requires a therapeutic climate that enhances motivation and strategies to build a commitment to change. These strategies are needed throughout treatment from the very beginning when the patient is assessed. The problem of motivation also highlights the importance of an empathic stance: empathy helps to build motivation and predicts outcome (Linehan, Davison, Lynch, & Sanderson, 2006; Miller & Rollnick, 2002).

Effective Treatment Strategies

Outcome research has largely focused on the efficacy of specialized treatments. Less attention has been given to identifying the active ingredients of each approach or the most effective interventions for treating each domain of psychopathology. Nevertheless, the task force reached some general conclusions about effective strategies (Critchfield & Benjamin, 2006). Specifically, a goal-orientated approach is optimal. It is also helpful to give priority to presenting problems and to identifying maladaptive patterns of thinking, feeling, and acting that underlie and maintain problems. It also seems useful to focus directly on problems, symptoms, and major concerns from the outset and to explain how treatment may ameliorate these problems. Discussion of immediate concerns also promotes recognition of the cognitive-emotional factors underlying problem behavior and hence it begins the process of linking thoughts, feelings, actions, and experience. This is the first step in promoting more adaptive ways of thinking and acting—a strategy used by all effective treatments (Critchfield & Benjamin, 2006).

Emphasis on promoting more adaptive functioning is linked to another effective strategy: a consistent focus on change. The need to promote change is a challenge, given the prevalence of low motivation and passivity. The balance between acceptance and support and promotion of change used in DBT (Linehan, 1993) is a useful way to focus on change, while maintaining a supportive and validating stance. Problems arise when therapists focus primarily on only one pole of this dialectic.

A CONCEPTUAL FRAMEWORK FOR ORGANIZING INTEGRATED TREATMENT

Given the outcome literature and the results of systematic analyses of effective change mechanisms, it is clear that treatment should use all effective methods regardless of their conceptual origins. It is also clear that a conceptual framework is a prerequisite for effective outcomes. In fact, two frameworks are needed: one for describing and organizing the multifaceted pathology of BPD and a complementary framework for conceptualizing the treatment process. Although a detailed discussion of a framework for conceptualizing BPD is beyond the scope of this article, a brief outline is required to provide a context for understanding the proposed treatment model.

A FRAMEWORK FOR UNDERSTANDING BORDERLINE PERSONALITY DISORDER

Borderline personality disorder is primarily a pervasive regulation disorder involving emotional, interpersonal, self, cognitive, and behavioral dyscontrol with the first three being necessary for diagnosis and the other two common associated features that are not necessary for diagnosis. This conceptualization does not imply that the disorder is discrete: as discussed earlier the condition is assumed to be heterogeneous in psychopathology, associated features and disorders, and etiology. This conception is based on the assumption that personality is a loosely organized set of subsystems (Livesley, 2003a; Mayer, 2005; Vernon, 1964) with pathology involving most components.

The system is assumed to be organized around heritable predispositions that give rise to trait structure. In the case of BPD, salient traits are anxiousness, emotional lability, submissiveness, insecure attachment, cognitive dysregulation, and to a lesser degree social apprehensiveness. Anxiousness is assumed to be the keystone trait that influences and regulates the expression of all other traits in the constellation (Livesley, 2008). The emergence of these traits during development influences other parts of the personality system, especially the self and interpersonal systems. These interrelated systems are conceptualized as knowledge systems that organize information about the self and interpersonal world into a set of constructs or schemata that encode information, impose meaning on experience, and predict events.

The schemas of the self-system serve to organize self-referential knowledge into a hierarchical structure consisting of different views or representations of the self. Experiences, coherence, and personal unity and continuity that characterize adaptive self-functioning are assumed to be the experiential consequences of the interconnections among self-schemas (Toulmin, 1978) so that: the *more* self-referential knowledge is organized into a complex matrix, the *greater* the sense of integration and coherence (Horowitz, 1998). In a similar way, the interpersonal system is assumed to consist of schematic representations of other people and beliefs and expectations about the interpersonal world. These schemas are used to encode, appraise, and anticipate interpersonal events and to plan appropriate action. Formation of self and interpersonal knowledge systems depends upon a wide variety of basic cognitive processes that function to integrate and combine information into schemas such that any impairment in these processes (including memory functions) is assumed to increase the risk of personality pathology. Especially relevant to personality are metacognitive processes involved in self-reflection and understanding the mental states of self and others (Dimaggio, Semerari, Carcione, Nicolo, & Procacci, 2007; Fonagy, Gergely, Jurist, & Target, 2002).

The personality system also includes a variety of self-regulatory mechanisms that control and regulate emotional expression

and coordinate action. The environment also needs to be understood to be an important component of the system. Although the environment is often considered to be independent of the individual, this is not the case. Individuals tend to create and maintain their own environment by selecting situations and contexts that fit their personality, talents, interests, and values. These personal niches play an important role in maintaining adaptive and maladaptive behavioral patterns.

Psychoanalytic, cognitive, cognitive-behavioral, interpersonal, and constructionist models of personality and psychotherapy share the idea that cognitive-emotional structures used to interpret and organize information about the self, others, and the world are core features of personality. These structures are assumed to underlie most aspects of the personality system. Thus, personality is considered to be largely an information-processing, decision-making system. These structures are variously labeled object relationships, self and object representations, working models, and self-and-interpersonal schemas. The idea of cognitive structure is a potentially integrating concept and here the structures involved will be referred to as schemas and cognitive-emotional systems. As discussed, these structures are assumed to underlie the self and interpersonal systems and to form the psychological or behavioral component of traits. It follows that much of therapy involves modifying these structures whether they are involved in emotion regulation, interpersonal behavior, trait-based behavior, or self pathology.

A FRAMEWORK CONCEPTUALIZING TREATMENT

The treatment framework addresses the problem of coordinating an eclectic collection of interventions in two ways. First, interventions based on general change mechanisms are used to provide structure, support, build motivation, and explore thoughts and feelings associated with problem behaviors. Used throughout therapy, these interventions provide the basic structure to an integrated treatment that promotes a coherent and consistent process. Specific interventions are used only when the conditions established by the general strategies are met: that is, when there is a consistent treatment process, a good alliance, and a motivated patient. Specific methods vary throughout treatment as different problems come into focus. Pressure to change specific interventions in response to ever changing problems creates the possibility that treatment will become inconsistent and disorganized. This is dealt with through the second component of the treatment framework—the idea that most treatments follow a systematic progression of phases each focusing primarily of a different domain of psychopathology. Consequently, specific interventions vary in an orderly way across the phases of treatment.

General Treatment Strategies

The generic components of change are operationalized through 5 major strategies: 1. Establish the basic frame of therapy; 2. Build and maintain a collaborative treatment alliance; 3. Maintain a consistent treatment process; 4. Build motivation for change; 5. Promote self-reflection. The therapeutic frame is delineated by the therapeutic stance and treatment contract. Together, they establish the boundaries, create the tone of treatment, and structure patient–therapist interaction. Earlier the stance was defined in terms of support, empathy, and validation. The treatment contract rounds out the frame by establishing collaborative treatment goals and defining the therapist's and patient's roles in attaining goals.

The second strategy, building a collaborative alliance, recognizes that without an effective alliance little is achieved. When considering interventions to build collaboration, it is useful to conceptualize the alliance as having (a) a *perceptual* component in which patients see their therapists as helpful and see themselves as accepting help and (b) a *relationship* component, wherein patient and therapist work cooperatively to attain treatment goals (Luborsky, 1984). Interventions that build the perceptual component include establishing treatment and therapist credibility by communicating a sense of realistic hope and optimism; indicating acceptance of, and giving priority to, the patient's problems and concerns; supporting treatment goals; demonstrating a preparedness to work with the patient to address the presenting concerns; recognizing assets and strengths; and focusing on progress and achievements. Interventions that build the relationship component of the alliance include engaging the patient in a joint search to understand the meaning, significance, and, if needed, the origins of the patient's problems; helping the patient to learn new skills and encouraging their application inside and outside sessions; facilitating the therapeutic bond; and emphasizing the collaborative nature of treatment. These interventions help to establish an ongoing process that consistently counters many of the core beliefs underlying borderline pathology.

A collaborative alliance is facilitated by a validating strategy that builds the alliance through affirmation of the legitimacy of the patient's experiences. Validation serves multiple functions: it is inherently empathic and supportive; also it helps to counter earlier invalidating experiences (Linehan, 1993) and hence promotes self-validation, a prerequisite for constructing a more adaptive self-structure. The task is to validate experience without validating causes and consequences of experiences and responses that are invalid. This involves helping the patient to distinguish the experience from the reasons given for the experience and responses to it.

The central role of the alliance, coupled with the difficulty patients have with collaboration and trust, require constant monitoring of the alliance, bearing in mind that it is the patient's perception of the alliance and not the therapist's that predicts outcome. Disruptions to the alliance should be dealt with immediately. Again, the evidence suggests that the therapist's sensitivity to, and handling of, alliance-ruptures is critical to effective treatment. Alliance-ruptures are readily managed using the five-stage process described by Safran and colleagues (Safran, Muran, & Samstag, 1994; Safran et al., 2002). Repair to the alliance begins by drawing the patient's attention to any deterioration in the alliance. Subsequently, the reasons for the rupture and the patient's experience of what has happened are discussed and the patient is encouraged to express any negative feelings about the event. Then the therapist validates the patient's account of the experience. If these steps are not effective, attention focuses on how the patient is avoiding recognizing and exploring the rupture. Finally, there must be an acknowledgement of any contribution to the rupture from the therapist's side. The therapist then encourages discussion of the reasons why things went wrong and attempts to re-establish the bond. The value of this approach is that it uses a potentially negative event to enhance the alliance and to change maladaptive schemas related to mistrust and fear of rejection.

The third strategy—maintaining a consistent treatment process—reflects the emphasis that all effective treatments place on consistency (Critchfield & Benjamin, 2006) and the fact that patients often cite therapist consistency as a helpful factor (Livesley, 2007). Consistency is only possible when treatment is based on an explicit framework and a clearly defined therapeutic contract. Consistency is then simply a matter of adhering to the model and contract. Once achieved, consistency provides the structure needed to contain unstable emotions. This consistency also offers patients a stable *experience* of themselves in relationship with the therapist of a sort that can form the basis for constructing more stable and integrated representations of self and others. Adherence to the frame is often a challenge especially early in treatment, because labile affects, unstable self-states, distrust, fear of abandonment, and conflicts around dependency often contribute to behaviors that challenge the therapist's resolve to be consistent. Maintenance of consistency requires setting limits in a supportive way that does not compromise an empathic stance.

The fourth strategy—building motivation for change—is based on evidence that motivation predicts outcome. Motivation is essential for patients to pursue treatment and work on problems. Low motivation probably accounts for much of the difficulty observed in engaging and maintaining patients in treatment. Attempts by specialized therapies to address this problem have not been totally successful: even under the favorable conditions of a clinical trial, engagement is difficult. Poor motivation is inherent to BPD and hence low motivation cannot be contraindication for treatment. Instead, systematic attention has to be paid to strategies for *building* motivation (Miller & Rollnick, 2002; Rosengren, 2009). Unfortunately, there is little research on how to enhance motivation when treating BPD. This is a topic that warrants extensive study.

Building motivation begins by establishing collaborative goals and eliciting a commitment to work toward these goals. Since motivation fluctuates during treatment, these commitments need to be affirmed regularly when reviewing progress and whenever new goals are established. When motivation is poor, it seems best to maintain support and empathy while exploring the reasons for low motivation and its likely consequences (Linehan, Davison, Lynch, & Sanderson, 2006). Therapist flexibility at these times is often critical to resolving the therapeutic impasse (Critchfield & Benjamin, 2006).

The four strategies discussed thus far largely involve building or using the treatment relationship to establish conditions for change. The fifth strategy, increasing self-reflection, is more instrumental. Metacognitive impairments associated with BPD include difficulties in understanding mental states of self and others (Bateman & Fonagy, 2004;

Choi-Kain & Gunderson, 2008; Semerari, Carcione, Dimaggio, Nicolò, & Procacci, 2007) as well as more specific problems with recognizing and communicating about emotions (Nicolò, Semerari, Lysaker, et al., 2011) and awareness of a sense of agency (Dimaggio, Vanheule, Lysaker, Carcione, & Nicolò, 2009). Therapists' awareness of these impairments helps them to incorporate treatment methods to improve metacognitive functioning into the treatment process and to promote a more reflective stance that helps to delay the kind of emotional arousal that could rapidly spill into action. This decentering is fundamental to increasing emotional regulation and reducing interpersonal reactivity. It also lays the foundation for a more adaptive self structure.

SPECIFIC TREATMENT METHODS AND PHASES OF CHANGE

Specific interventions are only used when there is a good alliance and a motivated patient. The use of specific interventions is also influenced by severity of personality pathology and by the presence of personality features noted earlier that contribute to poor outcomes—the greater the severity, the greater the need for caution in using specific methods, especially those that lead to increased emotional arousal.

When selecting interventions to treat a given problem, is it helpful to distinguish the intervention from its associated theory. Thus, skill building interventions from DBT, mentalizing techniques from MBT, or specific cognitive methods from SFT may be used without adopting the underlying theory. Selection and coordination of specific treatment methods is facilitated by conceptualizing treatment as a series of phases, each being primarily concerned with a given domain of psychopathology: 1. Ensuring the *safety* of the patient and others; 2. *Containment* of symptoms, emotions, and impulses; 3. *Regulation and control* of emotions and impulses (including deliberate self-harm) by increasing self-regulation skills and strategies; 4. *Exploration and change* of the more stable cognitive-emotional structures underlying maladaptive behavior and interpersonal patterns; and 5. *Integration and synthesis* of a more adaptive self structure.

The idea of phases of change is based on evidence of the differences in stability and plasticity across domains (Tickle, Heatherton, & Wittenberg, 2001). This suggests a sequential strategy in which attention is given first the more readily changed components of personality pathology. Symptoms (e.g., dysphoria and self-harm) are highly plastic, tending to wax and wane naturally over time. An initial focus on symptoms is likely to produce positive results early in treatment that may be used to foster the alliance and also the motive for further change. Closely linked to symptoms are emotional regulation mechanisms. These are also relatively plastic and often improve rapidly. In contrast, interpersonal patterns and associated cognitive-emotional systems are more stable. More stable still are core self-schemas, problems of identity, and chronic problems with intimacy and attachment.

This hierarchy of stability is consistent with the general progression of treatment. Most treatments give priority to managing crises and containing emotions and impulses. Subsequently, attention is given to increasing emotional regulation partly because crises and associated self-harm and suicidality demand attention, and partly because it is difficult to work on other problems without a measure stability. Once emotional regulation improves and crises subside, treatment gradually progresses to exploring and changing the consequences of adversity and the cognitive-emotional structures (self and interpersonal schemas, object relationships, and so on) that underlie repetitive maladaptive interpersonal patterns. Finally, attention is given to constructing a more adaptive sense of identity or life script and to helping individuals to build a better life for themselves.

Phase 1. Safety

Treatment of severe BPD typically begins with a crisis characterized by emotional and behavioral instability that may include regressive and dissociated behavior and cognitive dysregulation involving impaired thinking and quasi-psychotic symptoms. At this time, the goal is to ensure the *safety* of the patient and others. This is largely achieved through structure and support.

Phase 2. Containment

Safety merges rapidly with the containment phase. Here, the goal is to settle unstable emotions and impulses and to restore behavioral control. The first two phases are largely crisis management designed to return patients to their pre-crisis level of functioning as soon as possible, prevent psychopathology escalating, and establish the foundation for longer-term treatment. However, with many cases, this phase may be extended. Containment is achieved through general mechanisms of support, empathy, and structure supplemented with medication as needed. Containment interventions are based on the idea that when in a crisis, the patient's primary concern is relief from the distress that often arises from feeling misunderstood (Joseph, 1983; Steiner, 1994). Consequently, the therapist's task is to acknowledge and align with the patient's distress. Containment is used throughout treatment whenever a crisis occurs or cognitive functioning is impaired due to intense emotions or dissociation. The only specific intervention used during this phase is medication to treat specific symptoms of impulsivity, affective lability, or cognitive dysregulation (Soloff, 2000).

Phase 3. Control and Regulation

Crisis resolution and greater stability usually lead to an improved alliance, making it then possible to use specific interventions aimed at reducing symptoms by increasing emotional control. This is best achieved with an array of cognitive-behavioral interventions, augmented with medication. Emphasis is placed on cognitive behavioral methods for two reasons. First, accumulating evidence testifies to the value of cognitive-behavioral therapies in treating these problems (Blum et al., 2008; Evans, Tyrer, Catalan, et al., 1999; Linehan, Armstrong, Suarez, Allmon, & Heard, 1991; Schmidt & Davidson, 2004). Second, evidence especially from forensic studies suggests that specific behavioral problems are best addressed directly using cognitive-behavioral methods (Lipsey, 1995).

During this phase, treatment is guided by the assumption that self-harm is the endpoint of a sequence that begins with a triggering event that is typically interpersonal. This arouses maladaptive schemas associated with fears of abandonment and rejection that in turn evoke an escalating dysphoric state. Deliberate self-harm is then considered to be a maladaptive way to self-regulate distress. The model is consistent with the assumptions of both DBT (Linehan, 1993) and TFP (Clarkin et al., 1999; see Swenson, 1989).

Treatment begins by helping the patient to become aware of this sequence by linking components in the chain. This increases *self-understanding* of the connections between problem behaviors, situational factors, emotional reactions, and associated cognitions that Critchfield and Benjamin (2006) found to be an important part of effective change. Subsequently, different parts of the chain are targeted with specific interventions.

When the sequence leading to crises is explored, the idea of reducing self-harming behaviors may be introduced with the goals of delaying self-harm when the urge is experienced and of reducing the frequency of self-harming acts rather than eliminating them. These related goals—modest yet attainable—increase the chances of a success that may then be used to build the alliance, enhance motivation, and increase self-efficacy. Behavioral interventions such as distraction, self-soothing, and response prevention are simple methods to use for this purpose. Psycho-education about the *sequence* leading to deliberate self-harm and about the *reasons* for self-harm helps both to strengthen the alliance and to reduce self-criticism. It also encourages discussion of alternative ways to handle distress, thus paving the way for introducing interventions to increase emotional control.

Steps to increase emotional control begin by helping the patient to identify emotions and recognize the nuances of emotional experience. Attention is also given to improving distress tolerance because patients are often remarkably "phobic" about negative emotions. Although cognitive therapies tend to promote emotion recognition and tolerance using set exercises, it is often more effective to incorporate these interventions into the process of therapy so that the therapeutic relationship can be used to modulate emotional arousal.

In tandem with these interventions, patients are encouraged to use self-soothing and distraction exercises at the first signs of distress. Simple relaxation methods may be introduced to self-manage emotions; attention-control is increased by teaching the patient how to divert attention from distressing thoughts rather than ruminating about them. Specific cognitive interventions are also used in helping the patient to change maladaptive thinking of the sort that tend to augment distress (such as rumination, catastrophizing, and self-invalidation).

Two other interventions are also useful during this phase. First, patients often benefit from learning more effective ways to seek help when a crisis looms. Most borderline patients only seek help *after* harming themselves, and many present in an angry, demanding manner that often alienates those they turn to for help. Second, many crises can be averted if patients learn to examine interpersonal situations more carefully and avoid personalizing situations so readily. For example, a patient may assume that a friend's reluctance to meet is a sign of "dislike." The patient may be slow to recognize that people have their own lives and may have prior commitments. Encouraging patients to question their interpretation of events often helps to restructure experiences and decrease maladaptive perceptions that trigger crises.

Throughout this phase, mentalizing interventions that build self-reflection and self-appraisal are also helpful. They help individuals to begin reflecting on their emotional distress rather than simply react to it. Hence they contribute to the ability to decenter from emotional experiences and help to build appraisal processes that are essential for increased self-regulation.

Phase 4. Exploration and Change

The goal of this phase is to explore and change the cognitive-emotional structures underlying symptoms and problems. Problems addressed during this phase include maladaptive interpersonal schemata and repetitive dysfunctional interpersonal patterns, maladaptive expression of traits (such as submissiveness and insecure attachment), and the personal and interpersonal consequences of trauma. Work on these problems invariably involves emotionally charged material, which is why this work is deferred until the patient is better able to handle distress.

The common elements to these problems are maladaptive cognitive-emotional structures. Consequently, treatment is largely focused on restructuring these schemas, using a combination of methods. Cognitive interventions continue to be important but these often need to be supplemented with methods drawn from psychoanalytic and interpersonal therapies. Psychodynamic strategies and methods are useful in managing tendencies to avoid or suppress exploration of painful issues. At the same time, focus on the patient's relationship with the therapist—as emphasized by psychodynamic treatments—helps identify broad patterns of thinking and relating. Once identified, these patterns are readily explored using the behavioral analyses favored by cognitive-behavioral therapy to clarify the various ways these patterns are expressed and also the environmental contingencies that evoke and maintain them.

Psychodynamic interventions also assume a larger role at this time because, as SFT stresses, the treatment relationship becomes the major vehicle for changing core schemas involving distrust, rejection, abandonment, and shame. Examination of the relationship established with the therapist captures the urgency of the moment and provides an opportunity to explore schema activation, the feelings evoked, and their impact on interpersonal behavior in real time. This is an especially useful way to change schemas (Young et al, 2003): many patients with BPD have difficulty using standard cognitive interventions (Layden, Newman, Freeman, & Morse, 1993) as shown by the poor outcome of short-term cognitive therapy (Cotteaux et al., 2009). The use of the treatment relationship to explore and change core maladaptive schemata offers a way to combine important ingredients of cognitive, interpersonal, and psychodynamic therapies. Lasting change in interpersonal behavior also depends on enhanced ability to understand the mental states of self and others. Although most therapies lead to increased self-understanding, MBT has developed effective strategies to enhance this capacity. Throughout this phase, attention is given to helping patients to identify their own and others' mental states and to put themselves in the role of the other in the various scenarios that form the treatment narrative.

Restructuring the cognitive-emotional systems that underlie many components of borderline pathology is also useful when treating maladaptive expressions of traits such as anxiousness, submissiveness, and insecure attachment. As noted earlier, the origins of these traits in genetic predispositions suggests that they are best managed by concentrating on changing the threshold of trait activation and the frequency and intensity of trait expression, and by promoting more adaptive behavioral expressions. These changes require modification in the cognitive structures underlying trait-based behaviors. For example, with emotional traits such as anxiousness, it is often possible to restructure beliefs about the threatening and malevolent nature of the world and about one's personal inability to cope with threats. The use of the anxiety-control skills learned earlier then help to control anxiety arousal. With traits such as submissiveness that are exacerbated by adversity and abuse, it is often possible to help patients to express the trait in more controlled and adaptive ways so that the tendency to be submissive need not contribute to the perpetuation of abusive relationships.

Phase 5. Integration and Synthesis

With many cases, treatment ends before the goal of constructing a more adaptive and integrated sense of self and identity is fully achieved. Nevertheless, most long-term treatments need to help patients to build a more productive life for themselves if treatment is going to lead to improvements in the quality of life. The ultimate, but rarely attained, goal is to help the individual to achieve more integrated personality functioning. This requires the synthesis of new processes and structures—including a more coherent identity, more integrated representations of others, and greater capacity for self-directedness. Unfortunately, there is little empirical evidence on the best ways to achieve these goals. However, much of the foundation is provided throughout therapy by interventions that (a) remove obstacles to self development, such as self-invalidating ways of thinking and that (b) increase self-knowledge. Any intervention that connects different aspects of self-experience and links this experience to events and behaviors will contribute to the cohesion and integration. At the same time, the continuous corrective experience established by the general treatment strategies promotes these developments by providing consistent and veridical feedback. These more general methods often have to be supplemented with methods from self psychology, constructionist approaches, and CAT (Ryle, 1995). These focus more directly on constructing a more adaptive self narrative. CAT, in particular, includes ideas and techniques to promote integration of disparate self-states and fragmented self structure that is central to BPD.

CONCLUDING COMMENTS

Over the last 20 years considerable progress has been made in treating BPD. We now have a repertoire of effective therapies and hence a substantial array of effective strategies and interventions. This is an impressive accomplishment, considering that not so long ago this condition was considered difficult to treat. Therapeutic nihilism prevailed. Unfortunately, all these treatments produce similar results and, rather disappointingly, they do not appear to produce better results than good quality care tailored to the disorder. This suggests the need to rethink the way we treat this disorder.

Currently, there are a variety of treatment options. Rather than viewing these options as alternative methods, the next iteration in treatment models needs to capture the essential ingredients common to all treatments and to identify specific components of each approach that are effective. Taken individually, all treatments have limitations; combined, they are likely to include most of the methods needed for comprehensive treatment. It is also apparent that the next iteration has to do a better job of accommodating the heterogeneity of the disorder. All current treatments and current diagnostic practices treat the condition as if it were a discrete entity with a single primary psychopathology. But this a complex disorder with a diverse etiology that is probably the end-result of multiple developmental paths. This complexity cannot be treated by a standard protocol that is applied to all cases.

Given the heterogeneity associated with the diagnosis, it is useful to recognize that any particular patient shows features shared with *all* other individuals with BPD, features shared with *some* but not all individuals, and features *unique* to the individual. Current conceptualizations of the disorder and treatments emphasize the universal features. However, a more nuanced understanding of individual patients is needed for effective treatment. This implies greater flexibility in treatment strategies than specialized treatments acknowledge. It also argues for treatment models with the flexibility to deal with both universal and common shared features while not losing sight of the unique aspects of each case.

REFERENCES

American Psychiatric Association. (2000). *Diagnostic and statistical manual of mental disorders* (4th ed., text rev.). Washington, DC: Author.

Bartak, A., Soeteman, D. I., Verheul, R., & Busschbach, J. J. V. (2007). Strengthening the status of psychotherapy for personality disorders: An integrated perspective on effects and costs. *Canadian Journal of Psychiatry, 52*, 803-810.

Bateman, A., & Fonagy, P. (2004). Psychotherapy for borderline personality disorder. Oxford: Oxford University Press.

Bateman, A., & Fonagy, P. (2009). Randomly controlled trial of outpatient mentalizing-based therapy versus structured clinical management for borderline personality disorder. *American Journal of Psychiatry, 166*, 1355-1364.

Benjamin, L. S. (2003). *Interpersonal reconstructive therapy.* New York: Guilford.

Beutler, L. E. (1991). Have all won and must all have prizes? Revisiting Luborsky et al.'s verdict. *Journal of Consulting and Clinical Psychology, 59*, 226-232.

Beutler, L. E., & Harwood, T.M. (2000). *Prescriptive psychotherapy.* Oxford: Oxford University Press.

Blum, N., St. John, D., Pfohl, B., Stuart, S., McCormick, B., Allen, J., Arndt, S., & Balck, D. W. (2008). Systems Training for Emotional Predicability and Problem Solving (STEPPS) for outpatients with borderline personality disorder: A randomized controlled trial and 1-year follow-up. *American Journal of Psychiatry, 165,* 468-478.

Castonguay, L. G., & Beutler, L. E. (2006a). Common and unique principles of therapeutic change: What do we know and what do we need to know? In L. G. Castonguay & L. E. Beutler (Eds.), *Principles of therapeutic change that work* (pp. 353-369). New York: Oxford University Press.

Castonguay, L. G., & Beutler, L. E. (Eds.). (2006b). *Principles of therapeutic change that work.* New York: Oxford University Press.

Chanen, A. M., Jackson, H. J., McCutcheon, L. K., Jovev, M., Dudgeon, P., Yuen, H. P., Germano, D., Nistico, H., McDougall, E., Weinstein, C., Clarkson, V., & McGorry, P. D. (2008). Early intervention for adolescents with borderline personality disorder using cognitive analytic therapy: Randomised controlled trial. British Journal of Psychiatry, 193, 477-484.

Choi-Kain, L. W., & Gunderson, J. G. (2008). Mentalization: Ontogeny, assessment and application in the treatment of borderline personality disorder. *American Journal of Psychiatry, 165,* 1127-1135.

Clarkin, J. F., Yeomans, F. E., & Kernberg, O. (1999). *Psychotherapy for borderline personality disorder.* New York: Wiley.

Cottraux, J., Note, I. D., Boutitie, F., Milliery, M., Genouihlac, V., Yao, S. N., et al. (2009). Cognitive versus Rogerian supportive therapy in borderline personality disorder. *Psychotherapy and Psychosomatics, 78,* 307-316.

Critchfield, K. L., & Benjamin, L. S. (2006) Integration of therapeutic factors in treating personality disorders. In L. G. Castonguay & L. E. Beutler (Eds.), *Principles of therapeutic change that work* (pp. 253-271). New York: Oxford University Press.

Dimaggio, G., Semerari, A., Carcione, A., Nicolo, G., & Procacci, M. (2007). *Psychotherapy of personality disorders: Metacognition, states of mind, and interpersonal cycles.* London: Routledge.

Dimaggio, G., Vanheule, S., Lysaker, P. H., Carcione, A., & Nicolò, G. (2009). Impaired self-reflection in psychiatric disorders among adults: A proposal for the existence of a network of semi independent functions. *Consciousness and Cognition, 18,* 653-664.

Distel, M. A., Trull, T. J., Derom, C. A., Thiery, E. W., Grimmer, M. A., Martin, N. G., Willemsen, G., & Boomsma, D. L. (2008). Heritability of borderline personality disorder features is similar across three countries. *Psychological Medicine, 38,* 1219-1229.

Doering, S., Hörz, S., Rentrop, M., Fischer-Kern, M., Schuster, P., Benecke, C., Buchheim, A., Mar-

tius, P., & Buchheim, P. (2010). Transference-focused psychotherapy v. treatment by community psychotherapists for borderline personality disorder: Randomised controlled trial. *British Journal of Psychiatry, 196,* 389-395.

Evans, K., Tyrer, P., Catalan, J., Schmidt, U., Davidson, K., Tata, P., Thornton, S., Barber, J., & Thompson, S. (1999). Manual assisted cognitive-behavioral therapy (MACT): A randomized controlled trial of a brief intervention with bibliotherapy in the treatment of recurrent deliberate self-harm. *Psychological Medicine, 29,* 19-25.

Fernandez-Alvarez, H., Clarkin, J. F., Salguiero, M., & Critchfield, K. L. (2006). Participant factors in treating personality disorders. In L. G. Castonguay & L. E. Beutler (Eds.), *Principles of therapeutic change that work* (pp. 203-218). New York: Oxford University Press.

Fonagy, P., Gergely, G., Jurist, E. L., & Target, M. (2002). *Affect regulation, mentalization, and the development of the self.* New York: Other Press.

Giesen-Bloo, J., van Dyck, R., Spinhoven, P., van Tilberg, W., Dirksen, C., van Asselt, T., Kremers, I., Nardort, M., & Arntz, A. (2006). Outpatient psychotherapy for borderline personality disorder: Randomized trial of schema-focused therapy vs transference-focused therapy. *Archives of General Psychiatry, 63,* 649-658.

Hermans, H. J. M., & Dimaggio, G. (Eds.). (2004). *The dialogical self in psychotherapy.* London: Brunner/Routledge.

Horowitz, M. J. (1998). *Cognitive psychodynamics: From conflict to character.* New York: Wiley.

Horowitz, M. J., & Marmar, C. (1985). The therapeutic alliance with difficult patients. In R. E. Hales & A. J. Frances (Eds.), *Psychiatric update: American Psychiatric Association Annual Review* (pp. 573-585). Washington, DC: American Psychiatric Association Press.

Hyman, S. (2010). The diagnosis of mental disorders: The problem of reification. *Annual Review of Clinical Psychology, 6,* 155-179.

Joseph, B. (1983). On understanding and not understanding: Some technical issues. *International Journal of Psychoanalysis, 64,* 291-298.

Lambert, M. J. (1992). Psychotherapy outcome research: Implications for integrative and electical therapists. In J. C. Norcross, M. R. Goldfried, et al. (Eds.), *Handbook of psychotherapy integration* (pp. 94-129). New York: Basic Books.

Lambert, M. J., & Bergen, A. E. (1994). The effectiveness of psychotherapy. In A. E. Bergin, S. L. Garfield, et al. (Eds.), *Handbook of psychotherapy and behavior change* (4th ed., pp. 143-189). New York: Wiley.

Layden, M. A., Newman, C. F., Freeman, A., & Morse, S. B. (1993). *Cognitive therapy of borderline personality disorder*. Needham Heights, MS: Allyn & Bacon.

Leichsenring, F., & Leibing, E. (2003). The effectiveness of psychodynamic therapy and cognitive behavior therapy in the treatment of personality disorders: A meta-analysis. American Journal of Psychiatry, 160, 1223-1232.

Linehan, M. M. (1993). *Cognitive-behavioural treatment of borderline personality disorder*. New York: Guilford.

Linehan, M. M, Armstrong, H. E., Suarez, A., Allmon, D., & Heard, H. (1991). Cognitive-behavioural treatment of chronically parasuicidal borderline patients. *Archives of General Psychiatry, 48,* 1060-1064.

Linehan, M. M., Comtois, K. A., Murray, A. M., Brown, M. Z., Gallop, R. J., Heard, H. L., Korslund, K. E., Tutek, D. A., Reynolds, S. K., & Lindenboim, N. (2006). Two-year randomized controlled trial and follow-up of dialectical behavior therapy *vs* therapy by experts for suicidal behaviors and borderline personality disorder. Archives of General Psychiatry, 63, 757-766.

Linehan, M. M., Davison, G. C., Lynch, T. R., & Sanderson, C. (2006). Techniques factors in treating personality disorders. In L. G. Castonguay & L. E. Beutler (Eds.), *Principles of therapeutic change that work* (pp. 239-252). New York: Oxford University Press.

Lipsey, M. W. (1995). What do we learn from 400 research studies on the effectiveness of treatment with juvenile delinquents? In J. McGuire (Ed.), *What works: Reducing reoffending: Guidelines from research and practice* (pp. 63-78). Oxford, England: Wiley.

Livesley, W. J. (2003a). *Practical management of personality disorder*. New York: Guilford.

Livesley, W. J. (2003b). Diagnostic dilemmas in the classification of personality disorder. In K. Phillips, M. First, & H. A. Pincus (Eds.), Advancing DSM: Dilemmas in psychiatric diagnosis (pp. 153-189). Washington, DC: American Psychiatric Association Press.

Livesley, W. J. (2007). Integrated therapy for complex cases of personality disorder. *Journal of Clinical Psychology: In Session, 64,* 207-221.

Livesley, W. J. (2008). Toward a genetically-informed model of borderline personality disorder. *Journal of Personality Disorders, 22,* 313-331.

Livesley, W. J. (2012). Integrated treatment: A conceptual framework for an evidence-based approach to the treatment of personality disorder. *Journal of Personality Disorders, 26,* 18-42.

Livesley, W. J., Jang, K. L., & Vernon, P. A. (1998). The phenotypic and genetic architecture of traits delineating personality disorder. *Archives of General Psychiatry, 55,* 941-948.

Luborsky, L. (1984). *Principles of psychoanalytic psychotherapy*. New York: Basic Books.

Luborsky, L., Singer, B., & Luborsky, L. (1975). Comparative studies of psychotherapies. *Archives of General Psychiatry, 32,* 995-1008.

Mayer, J. D. (2005). A tale of visions: Can a new view of personality help to integrate psychology? *American Psychologist, 60,* 294-307.

McMain, S. F., Links, P. S., Gnam, W. H., Guimond, T., Cardish, R. J., Korman, L., & Streiner, D. L. (2009). A randomized trial of dialectical behavior therapy versus general psychiatric management for borderline personality disorder. American Journal of Psychiatry, 166, 1365-1374.

Meyer, B., & Pilkonis, P. (2006). Developing treatments that bridge personality and psychopathology. In R. F. Krueger & J. L. Trackett (Eds.), *Personality and psychopathology* (pp. 262-291). New York: Guilford.

Miller, W. R., & Rollnick, S. (1991) *Motivational interviewing*. New York: Guilford.

Miller, W. R., & Rollnick, S. (2002). *Motivational interviewing: Preparing for change*. New York: Guilford.

Nicolò, G., Semerari, A., Lysaker, P. H., Dimaggio, G., Pedone, R., d'Angerio, S., & Carcione, A. (2011). Alexithymia in personality disorders: Correlations with symptoms and interpersonal functioning. *Psychiatry Research, 190,* 37-42.

Paris, J. (1998). *Working with traits*. Northvale, NJ: Aronson.

Piper, W. E., & Joyce, A. S. (2001). Psychosocial treatment outcome. In W. J. Livesley (Ed.), *Handbook of personality disorders*. New York: Guilford.

Rosengren, D. B., (2009). *Building motivational interviewing skills: A practitioner workbook*. New York: Guilford.

Ryle, A. (1975). *Cognitive analytic therapy and borderline personality disorder*. Chichester, England: Wiley.

Safran, J. D., Muran, J. C., & Samstag, L. W. (1994). Resolving therapeutic alliance ruptures: A task analytic investigation. In A. O. Horvath & L. S. Greenberg (Eds.), *The working alliance: Theory, research, and practice* (pp. 225-255). New York: Wiley.

Safran, J. D., Muran, J. C., Samstag, L. W., & Stevens, C. (2002). Repairing alliance ruptures. In J. C. Norcross (Ed.), *Psychotherapy relationships* that work: Therapist contributions and responsiveness to patients (pp. 235-254). New York: Oxford University Press.

Schmidt, U., & Davidson, K. (2004). Life after self-harm. Hove, UK: Brunner-Routledge.

Semerari, A., Carcione, A., Dimaggio, G., Nicolò, G., & Procacci, M. (2007) Understanding minds, different functions and different disorders? The contribution of psychotherapeutic research. Psychotherapy Research, 17, 106-119.

Smith, T. L., Barrett, M. S., Benjamin, L. S., & Barber, J. P. (2006). Relationship factors in treating personality disorders. In L. G. Castonguay & L. E. Beutler (Eds.), Principles of therapeutic change that work (pp. 219-238). New York: Oxford University Press.

Soloff, P. H. (2000). Psychopharmacology of borderline personality disorder. Psychiatric Clinics of North America, 23, 169-190.

Steiner, J. (1994). Patient-centered and analyst-centered interpretations: Some implications of containment and countertransference. Psychoanalytic Quarterly, 14, 406-422.

Stone, M. H., (1980). The borderline syndromes. New York: McGraw-Hill.

Stone, M. H. (2010). The diversity of borderline syndromes. In T. Millon, R. F. Krueger, & E. Si-monsen (Eds.), Contemporary directions in psychopathology (pp. 577-594). NewYork: Guilford.

Swenson, C. (1989). Kernberg and Linehan: Two approaches to the borderline patient. Journal of Personality Disorders, 3, 26-35.

Tickle, J. J., Heatherton, T. F., & Wittenberg, L. G. (2001). Can personality change? In W. J. Livesley (Ed.), Handbook of personality disorder (pp. 242-258). New York: Guilford. Press.

Torgersen, S., Lygren, S., Oien, P. A., Skre, I., Onstad, S., et al. (2000). A twin study of personality disorders. Comprehensive Psychiatry, 41, 416-425.

Toulmin, S. (1978). Self-knowledge and knowledge of the "self." In T. Mischel (Ed.), The self: Psychological and philosophical issues (pp. 291-317). Oxford: Oxford University Press.

Vernon, P. E. (1964). Personality assessment: A critical survey. London: Methuen.

Weston, D., & Arkowitz-Weston, L. (1998). Limitations of Axis II in diagnosing personality pathology in clinical practice. American Journal of Psychiatry, 155, 1767-1771.

Young, J. E., Klosko, J. S., & Weishaar, M. E. (2003). Schema therapy. New York: Guilford.

Borderline Patients 25 to 50 Years Later:
With Commentary on Outcome Factors

Michael H. Stone

Abstract: The current study concerns the long-term follow-up of 40 patients with borderline personality disorder. Sixteen were patients from the PI-500 study, formerly hospitalized at the New York State Psychiatric Institute. Twenty-four had been from the author's private practice 25 to 50 years ago. Twenty-one of the combined group had first been in treatment 50 years ago. This is believed to be the longest follow-up period recorded for borderline patients. The main results are that two-thirds of the patients eventually reached the level of either clinical remission or clinical recovery. Reaching recovery, in the patients now in their 60s and 70s, was associated with having life-long personality traits, as described in the Five-Factor Model, of Agreeableness and Conscientiousness. These traits conduced to better outcome in forming lasting relationships and in workplace success. In some of the patients, genetic vulnerability to mood disorder (recurrent unipolar depression; bipolar disorder) was associated with slower improvement or to poorer outcome. Incest by an older-generation relative appears as another negative prognostic factor. Psychotherapy for most of the patients had originally been psychoanalytically oriented ("expressive"), though circumstances and life crises often led to the use of supportive, psychopharmacological, and behavioral interventions as well.

In recent articles I discussed therapeutic factors relevant to borderline personality disorder (BPD), along with summaries of long-term follow-up studies of BPD (Stone, 2016, 2017). The earlier follow-up studies were retrospective in design; those based on the largest Ns, the largest percentages of traced patients, and the longest follow-up periods (10 to 25 years) were those of McGlashan (1986, 1993), carried out at Chestnut Lodge in Maryland, and Stone (1990), based on patients at the New York State Psychiatric Institute. A drawback in the retrospective approach lies in the dependence for data and impressions—upon the memories of the former patients and their relatives: memories that invariably will differ in reliability. In recent years follow-up studies of BPD patients have been launched using a prospective de-

sign, in which the patients agree during their index (usually, a hospital-based) treatment to be re-evaluated at discrete intervals, usually of a year or two. The assessments made by the team of evaluators, made at each interval, are thus less prone to the fallibility and vagaries of memory. The more prominent of these studies, some of which are now approaching 16 or more years of repeated assessments, include those of Gunderson, Stout, McGlashan et al. (2011); Gunderson, Stout, Shea et al. (2014)—the latter addressing the interaction of BPD and mood disorders, and also those from the McLean Hospital based group led by Zanarini (Zanarini, Frankenburg, Reich, & Fitzmaurice, 2012; Zanarini, Frankenburg, Reich, Wedig et al., 2015; Zanarini, Frankenburg, Wedig, & Fitzmaurice 2013).

Despite the superiority of the prospective approach with respect to uniformity of data gathering and accuracy of results, there are some caveats. Such studies are more readily carried out on samples of borderline patients first contacted during a hospital admission—where it is easier to assemble groups of therapists and evaluators, each using similar or standardized methodologies, interview techniques, questionnaires, etc. But there are many borderline patients who are never hospitalized—including those seen only in private practice, where long-term follow-up via standardized approaches is less feasible. Add to this: in the current generation, psychiatric hospitalizations (for patients of whatever diagnostic category) tend to be much shorter than were those upon which the earlier long-term studies were based. The BPD patients in the PI-500 study (Stone, 1980) spent on average 12.5 months (3 months to 3 years) on the unit. During this time familiarity and loyalties were often built up between patients, their parents, and staff that fostered a willingness on the part of the subsequently discharged patients and their families to share information about outcome with staff members conducting an evaluation many years later. A patient hospitalized for a week or two might be less likely to form the kind of positive relationships with staff upon which follow-up efforts—especially at long intervals—largely depend.

With regard to ultra-long follow-up studies—of 30 years and beyond—there are other obstacles to be overcome. The cost factors in obtaining a grant to underwrite a well-designed prospective study of 250 or 300 BPD patients, and of then conducting the study at appropriate (e.g., two-year) intervals—are formidable. Given the heterogeneity within any BPD sample, even an N of 300 patients would not do justice to all the variation with such a sample. As time went on, certain variables would likely emerge as quite important—whose significance was not foreseen at the outset. The BPD (and other) patients at the Chestnut Lodge and New York State Psychiatric Institute sites were born chiefly in the 1940s and 1950s. Fewer were from divorced families as would be the case with patients born after the 1960s surge in U.S. divorce rates. Marijuana abuse became frequent starting in the early 1960s, when abuse of cocaine, opiates, and the more exotic drugs (phencyclidine, methylene dioxy-methamphetamine or "Ecstasy," etc.) was still uncommon. Many BPD patients of the current and just-prior generations regularly abuse a much expanded menu of illicit drugs—which we did not foresee in the 60s and 70s. Researchers embarking on a long-term follow-up study today would fail to include outcome factors whose nature—unknown now, but deemed important by future researchers—will not have emerged until a decade or two hence.

THE FOLLOW-UP: 25 TO 50 YEARS

This report reflects follow-up material gathered from 40 BPD patients (diagnosed via *DSM-III* criteria; American Psychiatric Association, 1980). Of these, 18 had been seen initially at New York State Psychiatric Institute; 22 were from my private practice; 4 had become my private patients, having first been patients at Psychiatric Institute. The length of time between initial contact and most recent follow-up varied between 25 years (three examples), 30 years (four), 35 years (five), 40 years (five), 45 years (two) and 50 to 52 years (21 examples). The average was thus 40.5 years. The majority of the patients from 50 or more years ago were from the hospital group (15); the other 6 had been in private practice with me since 1965.

Although the data discussed here were primarily retrospective in nature, about a fourth of the patients could be understood as examples of a prospective approach. By "retrospective" I refer to recollections by the former patients of distant events and states of mind. By "prospective" I refer to material gathered at various intervals from the time of initial contact up to the present time. This latter group was composed of patients with whom I have exchanged Christmas letters for the last 50 years, by way of keeping in touch and learning of their life course during this long interval—or else have contacted by phone at varying intervals (usually one to three years).

Most of the patients are in their 60s or 70s. A 50-year follow-up requires a measure of longevity on the part of both the patients and the examiner. All but six of the patients are still alive. Besides the four who died of natural causes, one had committed suicide, another had been murdered.

The sex ratio of the patients was tilted, as is customarily the case in samples of BPD patients, toward females (cf. Widiger & Trull, 1991): 34, as against 6 males.

The section that follows contains brief clinical vignettes of former BPD patients from each of the six follow-up intervals: 25-year, 30-year...finishing with the 50-year group. To preserve confidentiality, names, occupations, and locales have been altered, as well as other identifying characteristics.

CLINICAL EXAMPLES

Follow-Up at 25 Years

Eleanor, a woman now in her 50s, was one of a large family originally from the northeast. Her father was an executive in an engineering company, whose work took him—and the family—to a variety of countries. In contrast to the father—an easy-going man of whom she was very fond, and who died when she was 15, her mother was punitive and rejecting. One of the patient's sisters and a maternal aunt had suffered depressions (not requiring hospitalization). While at college, she became depressed and made several (non–life-threatening) suicide gestures and was hospitalized on two occasions. Her therapist at the time made sexual overtures. This precipitated a third hospitalization and the termination with that therapist. I began

working with her when she then moved to New York. She worked in the financial industry, lived alone, and dated occasionally. Her depression was now of moderate degree, and was alleviated with an antidepressant. She took anxiolytics on an as-needed basis. After several years of twice-weekly therapy—psychoanalytically oriented with supportive interventions—she began a relationship with a divorced man. Uncertain about the solidity of the relationship, she maintained her own apartment for several years, until moving in with him two years ago—in what has now been a stable and pleasant relationship. In personality she was notably pessimistic and disgruntled in the past; she is now of a more cheerful disposition. She also found a more satisfying position in the food industry. I kept abreast of her progress, lately, via half-yearly phone calls.

Teresa, a woman now in her late 50s, was one of six children from a family many members of which were either bipolar, with irritable temperament and episodes of either manic "highs" or (more prolonged) depressions. The mother, during periods of psychosis, also had religious delusions. Teresa had a prickly personality: hypercritical, irascible, arrogant, and self-centered. She had a number of tempestuous relationships with men, never lasting more than a few years. She made a number of suicide attempts in her 20s, and abused a number of drugs: chiefly, alcohol, marijuana, and opiates. A bright woman, she had a master's degree in international relations, but her work history was sporadic. I worked with her briefly when she was in her mid-30s, but she quit after a year, not willing to take my recommendations about drug-rehabilitation programs such as Alcoholics Anonymous or Hazelden. As I learned from a sibling (through weekly sessions), she is still, 25 years later, functioning poorly, with continuing drug abuse and a meager work history.

Jeannine, a woman of 21, was mid-way through college when she sought help for depression, anxiety, and suicidal ideation—following a "summer romance" while on an extended vacation in the west. The man she had dated pressured her into a sexual relationship for which she felt disinclined, and then rejected her. Her father, a prosperous merchant, had divorced her mother when Jeannine was seven. She and an older sister then lived with their mother; her two brothers, with the father and his new wife. In her twice-weekly sessions she often mentioned her dreams—which she felt were God-inspired and prophetic, after the manner of Joseph's interpretation of the Pharaoh's dream in Gen. 41. In her first—and rather frightening—dream, she and her sister were in a bar in Texas, where an elderly man had been hanged from the ceiling, his body then dropping to the floor. She had no idea what the dream "foretold." I suspected it concerned her ambivalent feelings toward her father, whom she disliked as favoring her brothers, but upon whom she was financially dependent. Her relationships with men were in general characterized by a deep mistrust. She was also troubled as to a career choice. Offered a position in her father's business, she turned it down, not wishing to be in his "orbit." She did have an interest in a medicine, but the steps in becoming a physician seemed too long and too arduous. After two years in therapy, she did enroll in nursing school. In this area she was successful, such that 25 years later, as I learned recently from her mother, she was now the manager of a wellness clinic, and financially independent. She has remained single.

Follow-Up at 30 Years

Sharon was 25 when she began in therapy with me, after a lengthy stay at a hospital that had been prompted by depression and several suicide attempts. She had grown up the only child in a well-to-do family, raised chiefly by her mother, following the premature death of her father when Sharon was eight. Her mother was strict and punitive; questions about sex were taboo, and great emphasis was placed on being spotless-

ly clean. This seemed to underlay her germ avoidance, and her quasi-delusional fear that she could become "fat" if she so much as walked by a pregnant woman. Thrice-weekly sessions focusing on psychodynamics and the important conflicts proved helpful in lessening her depression. But exploring the link between the germ avoidance and her mother's prudery and fastidiousness did not alleviate the symptom. I tried instead to compel her to confront "germs" by having her touch paper money—ridden as they are with the germs of all the people who have handled the bills previously. I assured her that she "would live to see the morrow." After a time, she grew more relaxed about handing money—and other objects handled by the public (such as stair railings and bannisters). There was a downturn for a while when she dated a man who boasted of being a prosperous businessman. She contemplated marrying him, despite her mother's suspicion that he was not nearly so successful. The mother was correct: he was after her money. Sharon was devastated and felt suicidal. We had sessions daily for several weeks until she regained her composure. Not long after, she met a much more suitable man—whom she eventually married. I have kept in contact with her periodically, and know that at 30 years her outcome has been most favorable. They have a son who is about to enter college. Sharon became a social worker, and is largely free from the symptoms that were so apparent at the outset. She no longer experiences depression. One factor that may have tilted the balance in a favorable direction is her unfailing politeness and sweetness of personality—akin to the "agreeableness" factor emphasized by Widiger and Costa (2003). She seemed incapable of anger (unlike the more typical BPD patient in whom "inordinate anger" is a recurring feature)—even when made aware the first fiancé was a "gold digger," blaming herself and becoming suicidal instead. Fortunately, her life subsequently has gone smoothly, and she has rarely been confronted with situations, at least within the family, where anger would be an appropriate emotion.

Florence was in her late 40s when she was referred for therapy because of depression and alcoholism. Her husband came from a prestigious Italian family and they maintained several homes here and abroad. During the two years I worked with her, the marriage had grown turbulent. Alcohol had been a problem on and off in the early years of their marriage, but was now more acute. Her husband was often away on business; upon his return they would argue and even get a bit physical with one another. She felt lonely and neglected. Aside from these displays of temper, she was otherwise a woman of unusual graciousness and refinement. She had a good sense of humor, and also took my suggestions to heart and without complaint. I felt strongly she should enroll in Alcoholics Anonymous, and I located a church where meetings were held—that were attended by people from her social class. She was menopausal during this time, which appeared to have contributed to her storminess at home. With the help of AA she was able to put her alcohol problem behind her, and tranquility was restored between herself and her husband. She now took some post-graduate courses in music which helped fill out her day. She and her husband became involved in charitable work and were highly respected in the community. When contacted at year 30, she was asymptomatic, content with her life, and functioning at a high level.

Alice was 25 when she began in therapy with me, primarily for depression and suicidal ideation triggered by the death of her mother a few months before. Many members on both sides of her family had suffered from depressions, including both her parents and a maternal aunt. It became clear several months after we began our work that she was in the grips of a conviction—which at times had the force of delusion—that people were snickering about her as though she had been in the midst of an affair with several men of prominence in the community. Sometimes she felt that certain passages in maga-zines were making veiled allusions to these "affairs." The passages seemed to me quite free from innuendo of that sort, and it was clear she was not having sexual relations with anyone. Hospitalization was indicated, and she spent a month as an in-patient, receiving antipsychotic and also antidepressant medications. I have maintained contact with her at intervals over the years. She has never been able to work consistently at the level she maintained before her mother's death. Currently, 30 years later, she has a part-time job and does volunteer work in the afternoon. She has a boyfriend, and lives in the original family home, her father also having died in the intervening years. Her function remains at the "fair" level; she has not required hospitalization in the past 20 years. My information comes from yearly phone calls with her, plus additional contact, at less frequent intervals, with one of her sisters.

Louisa was 45 when she came for treatment—at the insistence of her husband toward whom she had begun to behave abusively over the past few months. Complaining he was inattentive and perhaps unfaithful, she would create scenes in which she tossed dinner plates at him or hurled to the floor a book he was reading. One of her children blocked her from making a suicide attempt. She had threatened to kill him and then herself. She told me she was desperate to preserve the marriage, yet could not grasp how her behavior was pushing her husband to dissolve it. Not heeding my warning, she threatened my life as well, and then broke several of her husband's cherished possessions. That led him to seek the divorce she dreaded. She then abruptly quit treatment. I learned via a chance encounter with one of her children seven years later that she had settled down and had found a new partner (as had her husband). A well-respected professional person before all the turbulence, she was able to restore her position, which she holds to this day, the drama of the events leading to the divorce now just a distant memory. According to her husband, who had contacted me initially, she had always been somewhat quick-tempered, but had become increasingly so as well as notably irritable and depressed during the time she had become menopausal—the year before he saw me in consultation, urging me to treat his wife for her depression and for the behaviors that were uncharacteristic of her usual self. It appeared that the hormonal changes that may accompany the perimenopausal phase might have affected her emotional state, aggravating her tendency to mood alterations and volatility. The clinical picture I witnessed, one of severe depression, self-damaging acts, and irritability met, albeit temporarily, the criteria for borderline personality disorder—granted that BPD would not have been diagnosed until the year before I saw her, and was no longer in evidence by the time I met with one of her children years later. The hormonal changes involved in menopause, estrogen, progesterone, follicle-stimulating hormone (FSH), and luteinizing hormone (LH; cf. Stöppler, 2016, cited below), were not assayed in this patient. Irritability, mood swings, depression, and exacerbation of pre-existing conditions are among the many symptoms that may accompany menopause (Sajatovic et al., 2006). Women who have experienced post-partum depression or who have bipolar disorder appear to be at risk for the more severe forms of menopausal symptoms (Robertson-Blackmore, Craddock, Walters, & Jones, 2008), especially depression or bipolar mood symptoms (Pearlstein, Rosen, & Stone, 1997; Rasgon, Shelton, & Halbreich, 2005). Louisa had bouts of irritability and depression in her 30s, but was not known to have manic symptoms. It remains more conjecture than established fact that Louisa's BPD-like symptoms were manifestations of this life-stage.

Follow-Up at 35 Years

Martha was 42 when she was referred to me for continuing psychoanalysis, after she quit seeing her previous analyst, whom she felt was not helping her. Both parents and a maternal uncle were all in treatment with Lithium for bipolar disorder. She considered her mother punitive and cruel. Her father had an incestuous relationship with her during her early years (roughly age 8 to 12), but as he was kind and generous toward her, she much preferred him despite the sexual molestation. Martha had never married. She worked as an administrative assistant in a large company, but did not advance very far since her coworkers found her short-tempered and hostile. She had frequent bouts of depression and had made a number of suicide gestures and threats for which she had been several times hospitalized. Her life was punctuated by a series of crises which demanded immediate attention, requiring supportive interventions on my part that, in her mind, interrupted the "purity" of a psychoanalytic approach. She once asked: "What the hell kind of therapy is this?" Her tendency to alienate people left her with few friends. She had not dated in many years; her longest sexual relationship had lasted only about two years. During the second year of my work with her, she phoned me at 6:30 in the evening of New Year's Eve, announcing that, "I'm going to kill myself!" I told her I would call the police and send them to her apartment, breaking down the door, if necessary, to make sure she was rescued. They did break the door, but she managed to convince them she wasn't all that serious about suicide. She was furious with me, and not much comforted by my interpretation that her threat was borne of envy—that while I was about to enjoy a pleasant evening on New Year's Eve, she was alone and unhappy in her apartment. I tried to help her understand that hers was not an adaptive way of dealing with the situation. A better solution would have been to have dinner with a friend, or, failing that, to immerse herself in the crowd on Times Square. But for her, self-pity and a bit of vengeance (hoping to ruin my evening) trumped the more adaptive alternatives. She remained an embittered person, quit therapy several months later, and continued to lead a solitary existence. When I attempted to reach her years later, I learned from her brother that she had recently died from coronary artery disease—at about 35 years from our initial contact.

Shirley was 20 when referred to me for psychotherapy and control of her eating disorder and depression. She had a mother and sister with recurrent depressions. Her anorexia began in her mid-teens, and was less of a problem when I first saw her. But she was beginning to behave erratically and to abuse alcohol and marijuana. Her moods fluctuated markedly from hypomanic and "wild" to depression and moments of suicidal ideation when things didn't go her way. She behaved provocatively with her boyfriend in a way that invited trouble. They would go to a bar, for example, where she would dance in a frenetic manner, continuing on tabletops. Forced to leave the bar, she would then have her boyfriend drive her back home—only to have him push her out of the car, making her hitchhike the rest of the way in the wee hours. Her parents and I staged a confrontation, insisting she join Alcoholics Anonymous and quit smoking marijuana. She quit AA after two meetings, and then became dependent on benzodiazepines (Valium). Left alone when her parents went on vacation, she became suicidal and was hospitalized. Acutely sensitive to the slightest decrease in the Valium dose, it took two months to taper her off the drug. I stopped treating her at that point, but she was more stable and got work in a gym, She moved into an apartment with a friend she met at the hospital. I would call every so often to see how she was doing, but then lost contact. When I finally reached her 35 years after our initial sessions, she was now off all drugs and was the manager of a Pilates gym in another state. She had not married but was supporting herself well and functioning overall at a good level.

Marjorie was one of two children who came from a well-to-do family from North Carolina. Whereas her father was kindly and indulgent, her mother was hypercritical and punitive, much more so toward Marjorie than toward her brother. She felt relief to go to college in New York—but became depressed and lonely, assuaging her loneliness in brief affairs with men that did not return her affection. She began to abuse alcohol, and made a serious suicide attempt with an overdose of acetaminophen, for which she was hospitalized. She started in therapy with me after she left the hospital, and also enrolled in a fashion institute. Suicidal ideation continued during the early months of treatment, sometimes accompanied by wrist-cutting. Those episodes usually occurred in the wake of a disappointment in a romantic relationship. Our psychotherapeutic work concentrated on her damaged self-image and how this predisposed her to affiliate with self-centered men who—perhaps because of her unusually sweet disposition—easily took advantage of her. In her first dream, she saw herself in a hotel where there was a glass wall separating her from an elderly man on the other side of the wall. Unable to reach him, in despair she walked up the stairs to a room on the second floor where she attempted to commit suicide. Her associations led her to dwell on her longing to be with her father—the one source of love in her family. Later she was aware also of a transference implication—with myself as a kindly but ultimately unobtainable man. Our work progressed to the point where, in the third year of therapy she met a divorced man ten years her elder, who was a more worthy person and ready for a committed relationship. They married and moved to a different state. Two years later they had a son. I have kept in Christmas-card contact with Marjorie ever since. She has been well all the years of her marriage, with no recurrence of symptoms. Her son is finishing college; her husband has retired from his business, and they now have the time for extended leisure trips. Her overall function has remained excellent.

I began treating Andrea when she was in her mid-20s. She had been hospitalized after a suicide attempt while at college. Afterward she worked in a business establishment, but was subject to depressions and suicidal ideation, the latter becoming at times (especially before her menses) intense enough to provoke thoughts of walking into oncoming traffic, hoping to be struck. Though her mother's favorite among four children, she felt starved for maternal affection, since her father commandeered his wife's time, going on long vacations just with her. This pattern underlay one of Andrea's chief problems: she dreaded the absences of her therapists (there had been several before me), since she assumed each therapist cared only for his wife and nothing for her. She tended to be jealous of the other woman in her workplace, and unself-confident with men. These tendencies diminished as therapy progressed. Her yearning for closeness with her mother was sometimes pictorialized in her dreams in a sexual way, which she found disturbing. Therapy shifted from analytically oriented to a more supportive mode. As her self-confidence improved she became more at ease with both her female friends and with men. Eventually she met a quite suitable man—whom she then married. She left therapy at that point, and we kept in touch at intervals over the years. She and her husband now have several grown children; her depressions have not recurred. Her course overall has been very good—and better than I originally expected.

Marianne was 18 when she began in therapy with me in the midst of a stormy relationship with a boyfriend, in the course of which she became depressed and unable to finish her first year of college. She had grown up cared for by relatives, after her parents divorced when she was three, and her mother, an alcoholic, was unable to function. Sessions were twice weekly. She felt empty and lonely, and, at first, went impulsively from one man to another—men who tended to mistreat or take advantage of her. She had ambitions as a writer, but found it difficult to finish any project. After returning to college, she was ultimately able to finish, later working as an executive assistant. Her work record was spotty, in part because recurring depressive symptoms made it difficult to work consistently, and at times took on the character of narcolepsy, such that stimu-

lant medications were needed to help her get through the work day. Therapy continued until her early 30s, when she met and married a suitable man. They moved to a different state. Several years later, she developed a painful condition, and became dependent on opiates—a habit she was not able to break until after some five years. We have kept in touch by phone or Christmas cards. In her late 30s she had a child, who has now become the focus of her life, which is now more stable than it had been in many years. Now in her early 50s, her current function is stable and good, no longer storm-tossed as it had been for many years.

Follow-Up at 40 Years

Vanessa was a college student of 20 when I began treating her. Her main problems were depression and bulimia. The latter symptom dominated her life, since she spent much time traveling to other cities to buy—and consume—large portions of food (later to be disgorged)—so that her classmates would not know of her eating disorder. She was one of four children in a family of immense "old-money" wealth. Between the father's business-, and the mother's social commitments, they spent little time with the children—who grew up in a kind of splendid isolation. Vanessa would often, when she was growing up, curl up in a distant part of the estate reading comic books by herself. Though hungry for affection and maternal care (for both of which food became the substitute), she seemed incapable of relating to others as individuals. They were nameless "objects." Her narcissism, though a dominant characteristic, seemed confined to the *DSM-IV* NPD trait: "*lacks empathy: is unwilling to recognize or identify with the feelings and needs of others*" (American Psychiatric Association, 1994, p. 661). During the half-year I worked with her, for example, she had for a time dated a young man from a well-to-do family whose means could in no way compare with her family's. They once spent a night in a small New England inn. When he responded "yes" to her question the next morning: "did you like it?" she wrote out a check to the owner and bought the inn for her boyfriend. She could not understand that he felt shocked and humiliated, and was baffled why he then broke off the relationship. And she could not understand my efforts to explain to her the young man's reaction to her cavalier gesture. She quit treatment. Half a year later, I chanced to see her at a restaurant. She did not remember my name. Many years later I came to learn, through an aunt, that her relationships, including several brief marriages, have remained shallow. But she is in good health and has an adequate social life.

Ursula came from a family several of whose members had mood disorders: a brother with bipolar disorder; a mother with recurrent depression. What brought her to treatment when she was 30 was a combination of depression and a troubled relationship with a boyfriend. Both worked in business corporations and had apartments near one another. Though engaged to be married, her fiancé was hesitant about setting a wedding date. There was a separate problem involving her parents. They were paying for her twice-weekly sessions, but she was scornful of them, accusing them of openly preferring her brother. A few weeks after starting therapy, she had gone home for a holiday and had taken some photos of her family. The atmosphere was hostile and there were many arguments. Upon her return she told me she was about to send to her parents photos she had made of them—in which she had cut out the eyes. I suggested strongly she not do that, but instead share with me why she was so angry as to carry through a vengeful act of that sort—especially as they were taking care of her therapy costs. Three days later I received a call from her mother, asking if I knew what her daughter had done. The mother was heartened to know that I had warned Ursula not to commit such a hostile act. This was the first of many such acts I became aware of as time went on. Ursula exerted a suffo-

cating kind of control over her fiancé, William, sneaking over to his place and peering through the keyhole to make sure he was not with another woman, alienating him from his friends, who disliked her, and criticizing his every gesture. Some months later William invited her to Thanksgiving dinner with his family. She announced to the assembled guests: "William has to marry me because he gave me herpes!" In reality he had contracted it from her, but I then insisted that he accompany her during her next session. He was a thoroughly decent, if rather passive, young man, whereas in her the absence of shame and the pathological lying bespoke antisocial traits I felt were beyond fixing. I then dismissed her from treatment—something I had done on only one other occasion. Ursula, as I learned from her previous fiancé, did eventually marry another man and is still working in her early 60s as an administrative assistant in a business firm.

When she first sought therapy, Helen was 27 and had just separated from an unhappy marriage in which her husband would often not speak to her for days or weeks at a time. There had been much emotional illness in her family: a mother and sister with recurrent depression and a paternal grandfather with bipolar disorder. He father had died of a heart attack, and had for a time abused alcohol and sleeping pills. Helen was depressed, had suicidal impulses, and abused alcohol. In her first dream she pictured herself in a hospital recovery room as though eviscerated, with several organs placed next to her on the stretcher. A doctor enters the room and reassures her, without much confidence that she would be "all right." Her associations centered on her father: she was his "favorite," yet she could not count on his support toward the end of his life because of his drug abuse. I suggested, on the transference side, that she must also have been quite nervous, putting herself in my hands: a total stranger whom she could scarcely trust to put herself together again. Her reflective capacity was quite good as was the working alliance that soon formed between us. But there were harrowing moments, as when she drove at a high speed after drinking, hoping she might "crash"—in a suicidal "accident"—several days after her divorce became final. She was hospitalized briefly after that episode, and then at my urging entered AA. She soon conquered her alcohol habit and has been sober ever since. A research assistant in a medical laboratory, she worked steadily; at the end of the second year of therapy she met an estimable man with a promising future—whom she then married. At this point 40 years later, they have led fulfilling and prosperous lives with their two children both of whom have graduated from professional schools. I have kept in contact with her, and also with her mother, at half-yearly to yearly intervals.

Colette came from a family with many mood-disordered persons on the maternal side: a mother and aunt with recurrent depressions, and another aunt with schizoaffective disorder. Her father had incestuous relations with her between the ages of 8 and 15. At 15 she made a suicide attempt and also told her mother about the father, after which the mother immediately sought divorce. Marrying at 22, she was markedly jealous, and suspected her husband of infidelity. When her suspicions were later actually verified, she experienced a number of dissociative episodes in which she would end up in a different city, and, using a false name, have sex with men she met in bars. She divorced from her husband then, but made another suicide attempt and was briefly hospitalized. An accomplished sculptress, she remarried several years later, but her husband died shortly thereafter. She then lived with her mother until the latter's death. Chronically anxious, she has relied on anxiolytic medications and leads a sheltered life, seldom venturing out. Now in her late 60s, her life course has shown fluctuations from good to fair, reaching remission from the more severe symptoms, but not reaching recovery. We have remained in touch via phone calls at six-month intervals.

Frances was one of two children born to a university professor and his wife, an interior decorator. She regarded her father as kindly and sympathetic; her mother, as aloof and scornful. Her paternal grandfather, who lived nearby, carried on an incestuous relationship with her from when she was 9 until 13. She told no one about this until she saw a therapist, shortly after finishing a college degree in fine arts, for treatment of depression and suicidal behavior. She had been hospitalized for three months following a suicide attempt with self-cutting and an overdose of Tylenol. The attempt had been triggered by a breakup with a boyfriend. I began treating her two years later, soon after she married. The marital relationship was stormy at first. One time in a fit of anger she threw her wedding ring out the window. It was never found. She threatened suicide again, and was hospitalized briefly and stabilized with antidepressants. When, during our sessions, we got on the subject of the incest, she would suddenly tune out, staring at the ceiling, mumbling nonsense words or else irrelevancies like grocery lists. I would clap my hands to awaken her from the dissociated state. Her attitude toward me, initially angry and untrusting, softened over time. Gifted in many artistic media, she was much appreciated in her community for her watercolor paintings. The marital difficulties were resolved over time, but her health failed. No longer able to come to my office, we have remained in touch via weekly phone sessions.

Follow-Up at 45 Years

Lenore showed serious emotional disturbances since childhood. She had frequent tantrums until she was 8 or 9, and these were replaced by marked obsessional behaviors, along with agoraphobia and school avoidance. She was considered "borderline" according to standards within child psychiatry, as set forth by Kernberg (1990) and Diepold (1992). The diagnosis remains controversial, since not all children thought to be "borderline" meet adult criteria for BPD as they enter their 20s (Lofgren, Bemporad, Lindem,

& O'Driscoll, 1991). At all events, Lenore refused to go to school altogether after her father died when she was 13. Her mother remarried three years later. Lenore had periods of hypomania amid more frequent periods of depression, and was treated (without much success) with thioridazine (Mellaril). By her late adolescence she was re-diagnosed as bipolar. At 20, she married a young man who was equally handicapped and who also abused drugs (which Lenore did not). He died of cancer a few years later, at which point she lived alone, and became hostile to her relatives to the point of threatening to poison her mother and sister, meantime attempting to seduce her step-father. She would call me several times a year, having gotten my name from a previous therapist. She tried to persuade me into sanctioning her plans of "getting back" at her mother and sister—which I of course declined. She was now living in a different state, and remained house-bound, never working nor engaged in any productive activity. Her borderline traits are admixed with prominent paranoid, antisocial, and narcissistic characteristics. She has at times spoken of suicidal thoughts, though has not acted on them. But 45 years later she is still a therapeutic failure and grossly dysfunctional. I hear from her about two to three times a year, and also from her mother—approximately once a year.

Valerie, a medical student in her mid-20s, was admitted to the hospital following a disappointment in a romantic relationship. In response to the break-up she became seriously depressed and made a suicide attempt with an overdose of barbiturates. After resuscitation in the emergency room, she was transferred to the psychiatric center. She remained there for eight months, receiving a combination of antidepressant medication and analytically oriented psychotherapy. Her recovery was gradual but substantial, and she was then able to finish medical school. She has done well since that time, with no more than occasional bouts of mild depression. At the 45-year mark, she is married with two grown children, still holding an administrative post in the neurology department of a teaching hospital. My current information comes from a colleague—her former therapist.

Follow-Up at 50 Years

Jeffrey came for therapy not of his own accord, but at the insistence of his parents. Owners of a large department store, the parents were greatly concerned that Jeffrey not only showed no interest in assuming a role in the family business, but had, already in his mid-20s, gotten into trouble with the law on several occasions—for driving while intoxicated, getting thrown out of restaurants for groping waitresses, and shoplifting. He was contemptuous toward his parents, who regarded him as defiant, disobedient, and impulsive since childhood. Though bright, he did poorly in school because of disruptive behavior and inattention. He was treated for ADHD with methylphenidate (Ritalin), but without favorable response. I saw him only four times, before he quit therapy. Three years later I learned about his status at that time, by the coincidence of my then working at a public hospital where his sister had been admitted. She had suffered a psychotic break in the aftermath of having been raped by her brother and two of his male companions. About ten years later I learned from his parents that he had moved to Las Vegas. He continued to get into trouble as an alcoholic, had been jailed briefly on several occasions for thefts and for acting as a procurer for prostitutes. When I traced him recently, 50 years after our initial contact, he was still in Las Vegas—less often in trouble with the law, probably because of having "aged out"—now that he is in his early 70s.

Beverly had been hospitalized 52 years ago when she was 15, shortly after the death of her father. She was agoraphobic, and was subject to frequent panic attacks and nightmares. Obsessive-compulsive disorder was an additional diagnosis to BPD—because of a pronounced hand-washing compulsion.

Fantasy and reality were blurred, often in the manner of "over-valued ideas," though at times she entertained thoughts that were delusional. She was convinced her father was not her real father, and after leaving the hospital, hired a detective to look into the matter. The detective could not corroborate her idea. She held a job only briefly, but after she was fired, she retreated to her apartment. She never answered the phone. Some years ago I traveled 200 miles hoping to meet with her to learn how she was doing. She was still housebound but did let me in to talk with her. To cope with her anxiety, she relied on benzodiazepines—which she had taken steadily for many years. She kept a diary in which she penned all sorts of accusations against her parents (who in reality had never been abusive). She attributed her agoraphobia, for example, to her parents having hanged her upside down when she was a toddler or to her having been placed in a play-pen when she was little. Her condition steadily deteriorated, and, as I learned from her brother several years ago, she was still house-bound and had committed suicide with an overdose of sleeping compounds and benzodiazepines.

Morton, a single man of 28, had been ordered by the court to seek treatment, after being arrested for exhibitionism at a school, where had had pulled down his pants, exposing his genitals to some adolescent girls. This had been his only brush with the law. He worked at a large airline company as a controller, making sure each aircraft was in good condition to fly. Obsessive-compulsive and perfectionistic by nature, he made many enemies among the pilots, since he would ground a plane if there were the tiniest thing wrong even with cabin lighting or other areas that had no bearing on the plane's basic function. He had never dated, confining his sexual activities to occasional encounters with prostitutes. His attitude toward women was negative at best; at times, bordering on hatred. The youngest of eight children in an immigrant family, he was taunted by his sisters for being "little." But his animosity was directed primarily at his mother, by whom he felt belittled and humiliated. His most searing childhood memory: he was walking downtown with his mother when he was seven. He told her: "Ma, I gotta pee!" Her response: "Go between the cars. You got nothin' to hide!" That incident became the dynamic underlying his exhibitionism, as became clear in the early phases of his therapy: he needed urgently to prove he *did* have something to hide. He reported a dream in which a huge volcano erupted, the flames and lava killing all the women. In the two-and-a-half years of our twice-weekly sessions, his attitude toward women gradually softened. He came to accept that, despite the experiences with his mother and sisters, there were women "out there" who were kind, trustworthy, and genuinely affectionate. As for his exhibitionism paraphilia, he never reoffended. After leaving treatment, he also left his job at the airport, and opened a business, in which he was quite successful. He married and had three children. Morton died two years ago at 78.

Sandra was 30 when hospitalized—for a severe anorexia nervosa in which she had lost a third of her weight down into the 80s. There was a pronounced paranoid cast to her personality. She was embittered, defiant, and uncooperative with the hospital staff, complaining that the doctors (most of whom were in the middle of their residency training) "played God" and were arrogant. She disliked the nurses as well. At first she refused to be weighed, and required considerable coaxing before she would drink her calorie-rich supplements. She made no friends on the unit, though she did enjoy occupational therapy where she learned to work with carpentry tools. Months later, when her weight was adequate and stable, she left the hospital and found a position in a wood-working establishment, where she was employed for many years until she retired. She took care of her mother until her mother's death, and now in her mid-80s lives by herself, describing herself as a "loner" who does not seek people out. I had reached her by phone a year before the writing of this article.

Caroline sought treatment 52 years ago because of difficulties in her marriage and anxiety concerning her young son. Her husband was an attorney in a highly regarded law firm. Although she had graduated with honors at college, he constantly put her down, disparaging her intellect and ignoring a comment she might make about an interesting fact she came across in a book or magazine. Sometimes adding insult to injury, he would tell her the same fact later, forgetting that she had told it to him three weeks before. He also wanted three more children besides the two that they had—which she felt would push her beyond her maternal capabilities. She had become anxious and at moments even suicidal in her thoughts—prompted by the feeling that she had somehow "damaged" her elder son (six at the time) because he had developed a small lesion on his penis. She attributed this to her having engaged in premarital sex with her husband shortly before their marriage—an act which she had been brought up to regard as a mortal sin. She worried that her son's penis would somehow be damaged or even lost—as God's punishment for her transgression. Treatment consisted of thrice-weekly analytically oriented psychotherapy. In a dream early in the course of her therapy she saw herself trying to swim across a narrow river—but before she got to the other side, a shark bit off her leg and she was then stranded, bleeding to death, awakening in a panic just before she "died" in the dream. Her association to crossing the river was leaving the marriage and getting to a new place where she could have a better life. But she viewed divorce itself as a sin, and worried what man would marry a woman with two small children. In time she began to realize that what had made her feel divorce was so dreadful a sin was not so much what was preached to her in church—so much as what she had absorbed from her mother's moral sternness and rigidity. This came through in another dream—in which she saw herself in Hell, being mercilessly beaten on her back with a rosary. But it was not the Devil wielding the rosary-whip, it was her mother. As she began to realize that the harshness of her own conscience stemmed primarily from her puritanical mother, rather than from God, she became less anxious—and more emboldened about ending her marriage. Therapy ended after three years. By that time she had divorced and had begun to form a relationship with another man—whom she later married. We have kept in contact via Christmas cards all of the 49 years since then. There have been no periods of depression, suicidal ideation, or panic since leaving treatment. Her progress has been remarkable. She earned a Ph.D., became a professor at a university—where she later assumed a high administrative position. Her sons both have executive positions in the business world. As she mentioned in her latest card (2016): "Somehow I have made it through these challenges. There is not an ache in my body. I don't even feel old yet."

Nancy had been hospitalized when she was 22 following a serious suicide attempt from an overdose of imipramine and alcohol. During her adolescence she had been molested sexually by an uncle who lived near her home—where he was a frequent guest. When she later summoned the courage to reveal this, the members of her immediate family accused her of lying and treated her harshly, assaulting her physically and forcing her to disclaim her accusation. She spent nearly a year at the hospital and was treated with a combination of twice-weekly psychotherapy and antidepressants. Her improvement was only moderate. After she was discharged, her course was not smooth. She worked on and off as a salesperson at a department store. But she has had periodic depressive episodes, some accompanied by suicide gestures, necessitating hospitalizations on two occasions. Her relationships with men were tenuous and brief; she never fully overcame the mistrust of men that had arisen out of the abuse and antagonism from her male relatives. At this point in her life, she is chronically unhappy though no longer suicidal. She has a small group of female friends, and gets by on disability recompense and a modest income from social security. My information comes from one of her former therapists who still sees her on a regular basis.

Rosalie was hospitalized at 20 for a depressive episode that had begun shortly after graduating from high school. She had been born in the U.S., and was living here mostly with relatives, since her parents spent the greater part of the year in Europe, where her father was the director of a school. She had done well academically, but felt isolated and lonely. Her depression became more intense as she entered college; she would indulge occasionally in what was called at the time "gentle wrist cutting"—where the cut did not go below the skin and resulted in little bleeding, but led, paradoxically, to a relief of psychic pain—and to relatively little of the physical pain one would ordinarily expect. Apart from missing her parents, whom she saw only a month or two out of the year, her life had been free of other untoward life events: there had been no verbal, physical, or sexual abuse, no serious illnesses, and no history of injuries or head trauma. After spending a year in the hospital, she was able to resume college, meanwhile continuing for several years to see a therapist and take an antidepressant. She completed a course in nursing school upon completion of college, and eventually became a nurse administrator of a hospital unit specializing in respiratory diseases—where she works to this day. Along the way, as I learned recently from her brother, she married and has a son who recently graduated from college. She has not suffered further bouts of depression, and never engaged in self-injurious behaviors once she left the psychiatric unit 50 years ago.

Jonathan had been hospitalized at 20 in the midst of a conflictual relationship with his mother, whom he regarded as excessively controlling. He became severely depressed, had suicidal ideation (though made no self-injurious acts), and was unable to continue his studies in his second year at college. As we observed him on the unit, he was often preoccupied with philosophical ruminations about the meaning of life, is there a soul, and if so, what happens to it after death? He responded well to a psychotherapy that combined supportive and analytically oriented elements, and required only a minimum of antidepressant and anxiolytic medications. He formed a relationship with one of the female patients on the unit. He was able to leave the hospital six months later around the same time she was also released. They married shortly thereafter. In the meantime he completed college and went on to medical school. The marriage ended several years later. At this time (50 years later), as I learned from a colleague who is treating him currently, he has an academic position in internal medicine at a hospital. He lives alone and has sought therapy once again, with the goal of resolving conflicts that, despite his success in the occupational sphere, have stood in the way of establishing companionable relationships.

Annette first became emotionally ill at the time of her parents' divorce when she was 14. She was depressed, unable to continue at school, became uncommunicative for long periods, and made several suicide gestures. She then lived mostly with her father, who lived off family money and didn't work. He lived a solitary life, and grew uncomfortable as his daughter wanted to leave the house to be with friends. As her illness increased in severity, she was sent to an adolescent treatment center, where she spent three years—before being transferred to yet another treatment center for another three years. She failed to improve, and was then hospitalized on our unit. She was severely agoraphobic, and could scarcely be persuaded to leave her room. She also became mute for long periods, which led the staff to consider her perhaps a catatonic schizophrenic. She was treated with anxiolytics, which proved to be of little help. In her second year on the unit I became her therapist. During our twice-weekly sessions she would glare at me with a hostile expression and not say a word. This went on for about four months, during which time I would make one stilted comment after the other about why I thought she might be so reluctant to talk. My approach was quite un-successful. At this point Dr. Harold Searles began coming to New York once a month to supervise residents on our unit. I chose to discuss Annette with him, but gave a garbled presentation, mixing up past history, her cur-rent behavior, the comments I had made—in a not very comprehensible jumble. Dr. Searles replied: "When I hear presentations about patients, about 20% of the time I can't make heads or tails of it—so I get to think-ing: maybe there's something about the pa-tient you cherish the way she is"—implying I don't want to get suggestions of the sort that might help her get better. I began then to re-call how much Annette resembled my moth-er, especially in mannerisms. My mother was at the time dying of cancer. Both she and An-nette had come from similar families, wore white gloves, and put great emphasis on social class and "correctness." I was, unwit-tingly, by doing nothing therapeutically use-ful, preserving Annette just as she was—as a substitute, however meager, for my mother once she died (which she did three months later). During my next session with Annette, I felt emboldened—to toss aside momentari-ly the methods I had been taught, and be just myself. I told her with some force: "I think if I don't hear a word out of your mouth, I'm going to *explode*!" She then said (the first words I had heard her say): "You too!?" She now began to talk easily and without hesita-tion. What emerged was how angry she had been for years at being a slave to her father's own agoraphobia, and to his insistence she not leave him even for a brief errand. Her phobia was based not on the usual fear of what might happen to her if she went out among people, but what her father might do to her if she left the house. Annette made a rapid recovery from this point on; she shed her hostile façade, beneath which was a truly cheerful and engaging personality. She was still reluctant to walk outside the hospital, so I hit upon a behavioral measure: I encour-aged her to walk with me to the bus stop near the hospital. She would board the bus and I would then run two blocks to the next

stop—and meet her when she got off; we would then walk back to the hospital. Soon thereafter, she was able to take the train to visit her mother—a hundred miles away. She felt anxiety at the half-way mark, when she was equidistant between the hospital and her mother's home. Four months later she was able to leave the hospital. She could walk to the store and back in the company of her puppy. In time she could walk alone with-out fear. She had a boyfriend she had known from before. Their friendship resumed, and later in the year they became engaged. She married when she was 22, and later had two children. She and I have kept in contact with Christmas cards every year for the past 52 years. Her course has not been without downturns. She divorced after five years and remarried several years later. By now she is a grandmother—and a great grandmother, helping to take care of the smaller children in her extended family. In her 50th Christmas card she wrote: "It's half a century! Doesn't feel like it! We are a fortunate generation. I appreciate so much how we've stayed in touch all these years…hope to continue many more."

By the time Beatrice was transferred to our unit, she had already been a patient at a different hospital for a year. The initial hos-pitalization had been prompted by her hav-ing run away from home when she was 15. She had been escaping sexual molestation by two close relatives, and after running from home, was rescued—and sent to a hospital in a benumbed state, barely able to talk. Any-one with a psychotic break in that era (the 1960s) was labeled "schizophrenic," and in her case the treatment consisted of multiple treatments of electroshock. These treatments had no ameliorative effect, instead causing a retrograde amnesia, blotting out her memo-ry of the traumata she had suffered. After a year, she was transferred to our hospital in the forlorn hope we might be able to have better luck with her treatment. We had no better success either, during the first year, since she did not establish a good relation-ship with her new therapist. She had already made a number of suicide attempts in the past, which she recorded in a diary she kept (which I still possess), written in a tiny script that can only be read under magnification. She was very demure and soft-spoken, to the point of near inaudibility; in personality, noticeably sweet and compliant. The therapist assigned to her during the second year turned out to be a much more appropriate choice. He also benefited from supervision with Dr. Searles, who, when he interviewed her, told her (as she sat rigidly in her chair with her hands folded) "sitting next to you, I feel like a dirty old man." This led to her willingness to share with her therapist the fact, hitherto concealed, that she had been sexually molested when in her early teens. Her self-destructiveness persisted for many months. She made suicide gestures within the hospital unit, especially when her therapist was on a brief vacation. On one occasion, she struck her head against the wall and had to be rescued by the nurses. On another, she threatened to jump off a bridge nearby the hospital. The latter was handled deftly by her therapist, who reassured her that he would summon the authorities to make sure there would be a net below to catch her before she plunged into the water. His intervention was meant to show her he cared about her enough to make sure she would remain safe. This latter intervention was in her third year of hospitalization, by which time, despite her fragility, she was ready for release. He continued to treat her in private practice for several years. By that time her progress was remarkable. She went to college, where she graduated with highest honors, and then went to graduate school, becoming a psychologist. She made a most suitable marriage, and later had two children. She wrote a book recently about her experiences before and during the hospitalizations—published at the 50-year mark from her treatment at Psychiatric Institute. In recent years, she and I have given lectures about her experience at several psychiatric centers. He former therapist (and my colleague at the hospital) have socialized and had dinners together, reminiscing about old times. Beatrice's story is unusual particularly because she progressed—under the impact of a successful therapy with a psychiatrist with whom she "clicked"—from seeming at first like a hopeless case of unavoidable suicide, to a woman who was able to rise above her destructive background all the way to a person of high function, free of bitterness with what had earlier befallen her.

BRIEF VIGNETTES

There are a number of other former patients, all representing 50-year follow-ups, whom I have chosen to describe only briefly: some are professionals in mental-health branches; others have become public figures. Two were private patients originally; the others had once been hospitalized at Psychiatric Institute. Within this group of 11 are 3 men and 8 women. Two have died recently; the others are in their late 60s or early 70s.

1. A woman had been hospitalized for depression and a series of suicide attempts following the death of her father during her teens. Several close relatives had recurrent depressions; her one sibling was normal. Her recuperation was slow, and she was hospitalized later on one other occasion. She became a mental-health professional, and had a long-term relationship with a man. She continued to work after his death, after which she became depressed again, albeit moderately. I maintained contact with her by means of phone calls at one- to two-year intervals. Her overall adjustment went from "good" to "fair."

2. A woman of 70 had been diagnosed during her adolescence as "borderline" while at the hospital. Her course, as it evolved, took on the symptomatology of bipolar disorder-2 (brief hypomanic episodes alternating with deeper depressions). There were

several close relatives with bipolar disorder. She has been able to work only sporadically, sometimes as a volunteer in charitable organizations. As I learned recently from meeting with both her and her mother, she lives alone and had never married. Her functional level has been at the "fair" level throughout.

3. A man now in his mid-70s had been depressed when hospitalized originally, and had engaged in a few self-injurious behaviors that were not very serious. He was already an accomplished artist when first admitted and was discharged as improved after a few months. Currently he is a well-known artist who exhibits in a prestigious gallery. His level has been consistently at the "excellent" level.

4. A woman with a mixture of borderline (affective) and schizotypal characteristics had never been hospitalized, but led a solitary and unhappy life, supported by family money. She lived next door to two famous theater directors, whose friendship she hoped to foster by leaving baked goods at their door. Neither responded to her gifts. She was a firm believer in astrology and was convinced she could predict the fate of others—if she knew not just the day, but the hour and minute of their birth. I once provided her with the precise birth times of two persons: one a hospitalized schizophrenic, the other, a high-functioning colleague—whose birth times were only a few minutes apart. She could not tell which was which, but held fast to her beliefs. Both her mother and brother had been hospitalized for long periods with schizophrenia. She eventually took some courses at a university but never worked. She died a few years ago in her mid-70s. Her adjustment level had been poor throughout her life.

5. A young woman was hospitalized on our unit at age 17 because of depression, panic episodes, and impulsive behaviors. After leaving the unit, she became a member of a religious cult in a different part of the country. After leaving the cult at the urging of her parents, she finished her schooling, and now has a position in the mental-health field. She is married with children, and has led a successful life for many years. Her level of function has been very good throughout all the intervening years, as I learned after speaking with her by phone last year.

6. After the divorce of her parents, a girl of 15 had become rebellious, had clashes with her mother and ran away. She began to use marijuana and occasionally cocaine. When found, she was hospitalized as a PINS case (person in need of supervision) on our unit—where she spent two years and completed high school. Because she made several suicide gestures while on the unit, the staff felt her prognosis was "unfavorable." In that their judgment proved quite wrong. After her release, she became a writer, with articles published in national magazines. She also wrote a book about her experiences at the hospital. Her overall adjustment has been consistently very good throughout her adult years. On two occasions recently she and I discussed her life course before a group of psychiatrists and other mental-health professionals.

7. A young man, a sophomore in college, had been admitted to our unit following a kind of existential crisis, preoccupied in an abstruse philosophical way about questions like "*What is the meaning of life?*" or "*Does God really exist?*" and so on. Though not directly suicidal, he was plagued with the question: "*Is life worth living?*" Abstractions of this sort filled his

mind after his girlfriend had broken off their relationship; he was then in a state of depression and confusion about his identity. After his release from the unit seven months later, his trajectory has been steadily upward; his recovery, excellent. Having spoken with him recently, I learned that he eventually earned an advanced degree in the mental-health field, married, and has been a respected practitioner for over 40 years.

8. An adolescent of 15 had experienced a series of traumata at the hands of her parents. She had been sexually molested by her father and abused physically by her mother. Reacting in anger, she hurled dishware and glasses against the wall, and cut her wrists—which led to her being hospitalized. Several relatives on both sides of the family had affective disorders. Her course was stormy at first, but she later settled down and was admired for her helpfulness to her fellow patients. At the end of the second year she finished high school and made a perfect score on her college-entrance tests, and was accepted to several colleges even though her return address was that of a psychiatric hospital. After her release she completed college—and then medical school, married, had two children. She became ill as she approached 70 and died—after a long and successful career in medicine. Before that, we had kept in touch by phone on a yearly basis.

9. Lonely and depressed during her first year at college, a young woman of 18 made a serious suicide attempt with an overdose of a sleeping compound. Her parents had divorced when she was four, and her mother, an imperious woman, blocked the father from having any access to their daughter. She spent two years on our unit. A meeting was arranged with her father.

It went badly because she felt he never cared to contact her, rather than that her mother had interfered. She aspired to a career in art or theater, but her talents lay elsewhere. Ten years after leaving the hospital she was reunited, this time amicably, with her father. She married, and became the proprietor of an art gallery. I learned through one of the other former patients who had kept in contact with her that her life has been tranquil and successful for the past 35 years, compatible with a *recovery* status.

10. A woman of 20 showed 6 of the 9 BPD traits in *DSM-IV*, especially inordinate anger, affective instability, and unstable interpersonal relationships. Her father, a wealthy manufacturer, alternated between dismissiveness and emotional supportiveness; her mother was shockingly contemptuous of her daughter, given to humiliating her in public and cursing at her with invective peppered with four-letter words. The woman's self-esteem was shattered, when with her parents she often used just as strong language back at them, and when with men, tended to be irritable, abrasive, and short-tempered. My efforts in therapy to help her relate to others in more measured tones was not successful. After college, her father set her up in a small clothing business, but this failed after a year-and-a-half. She then moved to a different state. I kept in touch periodically to see how she was doing. She never made a lasting relationship with the men she dated, and led a lonely life, depressed often, embittered always. Her father supported her. She took to abusing alcohol. I spoke to her every few months by phone to see how she was getting along, but then she no longer answered the phone. I then learned through the Internet at year 50 that in the year before,

she had attacked her father—then in his late 90s, and demented—with a broken beer bottle, causing him to scream—and bleed. She was arrested for "elder abuse," and spent a brief time in jail. I had felt her prognosis was not good; in the end, her outcome was worse than my pessimistic assumption.

11. A 24-year-old man in his second year of law school sought treatment for a combination of depression and impulsive behavior. In his despair over rejection in a romantic relationship, he took to driving recklessly and was arrested once for driving while intoxicated. Born when his father was in the army, he received little affection from his mother—who felt burdened by having to care for an infant by herself. She favored his older brother, even though by the time I worked with the law student, the brother had become a drug addict. Treatment was supportive at first, but transitioned into a predominantly analytically oriented mode thereafter. Identity issues were prominent in his therapy: because he was so different from his working-class family in intellectual interests and accomplishments, he felt like a "changeling"—as though a "substitute" child, not really a birth-child of his family. After he left treatment, we kept in touch at intervals over the years. Recently we spoke by phone and also exchanged letters by e-mail. He ultimately became partner in a prominent law-firm. Recently, for reasons of ill health, he retired from law practice, but devotes some time to charitable pursuits.

DISCUSSION

The 40 patients described here (29 in longer, 11 in shorter vignettes) represent a necessarily much shorter sample both of the old patients from the PI-500 study and from the early years of my private practice. A number of the former patients in either group have died; their parents (except for a small number in their 90s) have all died—and thus are no longer available as contacts with information about their children, or with information about their current whereabouts. The patients are less representative of borderline patients in the general public even than those from the PI-500, because the latter had all spent time in a psychiatric hospital, whereas there are many BPD patients who (a) seek treatment but are never hospitalized, or (b) never seek treatment at all. The socioeconomic group from which the PI-500 patients came was largely middle and upper-middle class (Stone, 1980); those from my private patients were mostly from upper-middle to upper class backgrounds: this is another way in which the sample is not representative of BPD patients in general. The data, as they have emerged, are nevertheless of some value, since the life course of the patients covers almost their entire life: most are now in their 70s and 80s. I do not anticipate a "60-Year Follow-Up," either for them—or for me. As for the hospitalized group, I have vivid recollections of all of those I was able to locate—thanks in good measure to their lengthy stays on the unit. Patients in the PI-500 spent from 3 months to 3 years on the unit (avg. 12.5 months), which was typical of specialized centers for treating BPD patients in that era (the 1960s/1970s)—such as those at Chestnut Lodge, McLean Hospital, Sheppard-Enoch Pratt, Menninger's, and elsewhere. Young psychiatrists and psychologists in the current era seldom have the opportunity to become so acquainted with their hospitalized BPD patients, now that the length of stay is measured more in days and weeks than in months and years. There is also a certain "authenticity" about the observations of one's personality in the elder years. Many BPD patients changed dramatically from 15 to 30; some changed substantially from 30 to 50. But how one is in personality and behavior at 70 makes for a definitive statement about—*how one is.*

All the former patients described here, with the exceptions of those I have called Ursula, Jeffrey, and Morton, had received psychotropic medications (chiefly antidepressants and anxiolytics, but in many: neuroleptics and mood stabilizers also) during various phases of their course. Though the emphasis in this report, in keeping with my own perspective and also with the preferred approach on the New York State Psychiatric Institute unit where most of the hospitalized patients had been treated, was on intensive psychotherapy, the medications played an important role in eventual outcome for many—sometimes, decisively so.

For those of us who evaluate BPD patients when we first get to know them, we usually make estimates regarding prognosis. The hospital staff at Psychiatric Institute routinely made such forecasts within a week or two of their hospitalization. I formed similar estimates after brief experience with my new patients. Some of the patients inspired optimism; others, pessimism. This clinical guesswork could be further categorized, in the light of long-term (25- to 50-year) follow-up, into compartments in the following manner:

A Those who were expected to do well...And ultimately did well

B Those who were expected to do well...But did better than expected

C Those who were expected to do well...But did worse than expected

D Those who were expected to do poorly...And who did poorly

E Those who were expected to do poorly...But who did better than expected

F Those who were expected to do poorly...But who did even worse than expected

Corresponding to the broad categories of "well" and poorly," are the *DSM Global Assessment of Functioning* (GAF) brackets:

"poor" (50 or less) and "fair" (51–60) versus "good/well" (61–70) and "very well/excellent" (71–80 and scores above 80). The 40 patients in the sample here could, in this manner, be divided into two main groups. Those in subgroups A, B, and E numbered 27 altogether. Those in subgroups C, D, and F numbered 13 in all. This meant in effect about twice as many were now doing "well" or better—than were in the less favorable categories (doing "fair," "poorly," or in the one case—dead by suicide).

One of the peculiarities of BPD, as described in *DSM* and elsewhere, is that the definition "...is based more on symptomatic behaviors (self-damaging acts, stormy relationships, brief psychotic episodes) than on true traits of personality (demandingness, unreasonableness, vehemence, manipulativeness, changeableness...)" (Stone, 2013, p. 362). But, as I mentioned elsewhere (Stone, 2016), the disconnect between limbic-system versus (delayed) frontal-lobe maturation characteristic of adolescence tends to lessen after about age 25, with the result that the dramatic (and often disagreeable) behaviors of BPD patients in their earlier years are less in evidence as the patients enter their 30s and beyond. The former patients in the present sample are mostly in their 60s and 70s, where the dramatic and identifying (as "borderline") behaviors are comparatively uncommon. What one sees instead are manifestations of the underlying personality traits—either as they always were, or as they changed gradually with the passage of time. Of the factors in the Five-Factor Model (*Neuroticism, Extraversion, Agreeableness, Conscientiousness,* and *Openness*), two have particular relevance vis-à-vis BPD patients; namely, Agreeableness and Conscientiousness. Agreeableness ("A") relates to the spectrum spanning compassion to antagonism. People high in "A" tend to be "...soft-hearted, good-natured, trusting, helpful, forgiving and altruistic, eager to help others, and empathic. Those low in 'A' tend to be cynical, rude, abrasive, suspicious, uncooperative, irritable, manipulative, vengeful and ruthless"

(Widiger & Costa, 2013, p. 4). Viewed in this light, there were 7 patients in the present sample who showed particularly low "agreeableness": Eleanor, Martha, Ursula, Lenore, Jeffrey, Beverly, and Sandra. Their current level of function was "poor" (in four cases), "fair" (in two), and "suicide" (one). Two, for example, were notably uncooperative (Eleanor and Sandra), one was vengeful (Lenore); another, extremely manipulative (Ursula); another, querulous (Martha), and another, antisocial (Jeffrey). Among those high in "A" were three who were strikingly good-natured (Florence, Helen, Caroline), one with a very trusting nature (Rosalie), and four whose personalities were remarkably "sweet" (gracious, gentle, soft-hearted, forgiving, amicable, kindly).

Conscientiousness (C) is another positive personality trait crucial to a successful life. Widiger and Costa mention several qualities under this heading: reliable, hard working, scrupulous, and persevering (as opposed to—aimless, lazy, negligent, and hedonistic; 2013, p. 4).

In the current sample, 12 of the former patients had personality configurations that were "high" on Agreeableness. All but one are now doing "as well as originally expected" (Group A) or "better than expected" (Group B), except for one patient who is currently doing "worse than originally expected" (Group C). The latter is a patient who is still depressed, not working, single, and supported by family. There were 13 patients considered "low" on Agreeableness: of these 10 were currently doing poorly. The three who were now doing "well, and better than expected" happened also to score "high" on Conscientiousness. These three included two males (Morton and Jonathan) and one woman (Louisa). From these findings it appears that the highs and lows of Agreeableness are strongly associated with favorable versus unfavorable outcomes in the long term—with only a few exceptions on either side.

Conscientiousness, in contrast, was in this series an even stronger predictor of eventual outcome. The 20 who were "high" on this measure are all doing well: 19 in either the "A" or "B" subgroups; the other, in group "E." The latter, Louisa, had been—and later resumed—her position as a well-respected professional, once through the turbulent years in her mid-40s. The 7 former patients who scored "low" on this dimension were now doing poorly—including the one who committed suicide, and the one who assaulted her father.

Another factor that affected long-term outcome in the present sample was the presence or absence of genetic vulnerability to an affective or cognitive (or mixed) disorder. The patients could be divided into two nearly equal groups: those with such vulnerability (N = 19) and the remainder without known vulnerability (N = 21). The "vulnerable" group consisted of 9 with one or more bipolar first-degree relatives; 7 with first-degree relatives with depressive disorders. An additional 3 had schizoaffective features in addition to the BPD; one of these patients had both a mother and brother chronically hospitalized for schizophrenia. The patients with genetic vulnerability tended to do poorly (12 out of 19), whereas those with no discernible vulnerability were mostly now doing well (18 out of 21). These results are depicted in Table 1.

A history of incest, particularly by a member of the older generation, is another factor that may have a bearing on long-term outcome in BPD patients. Five of the patients in this sample had been incest victims: three by a father, one by a grandfather, and one (Beatrice) by both a father and grandfather. Of the first four, two were now doing fairly well; two were doing poorly—but all four also had close relatives with affective disorder (bipolar in three cases; unipolar in the other). It is not easy to disentangle the effects of incest and heredity in the two women whose outcomes were not favorable. Beatrice, despite traumatization from two close relatives, and though dysfunctional during all her late adolescence, had two advantageous qualities: a "sweet" disposition (high on Agreeableness) and strong Conscientiousness. From one of

TABLE 1. Presence or Absence of Genetic Vulnerability to Major Affective or Cognitive Disorders

OUTCOMES (N = 40)

Outcome Groups	A, B, or E	C, D, or F	Total
Vulnerability present	7	12	19
Vulnerability absent	18	3	21
Total	25	15	40

Note. Outcomes A, B, and E represent favorable long-term outcome; C, D, and F—unfavorable outcome. Fisher's Exact Test, 2-tailed: $p = 0.0027$.

the most worrisome patients, she ultimately became one of the best functioning, even publishing a memoir of her experiences at the hospital.

Regarding *psychotherapy*, the patients can be placed in two main categories: those who had at one point or another been hospitalized, and those who had never been hospitalized even throughout the long follow-up years. Among those hospitalized, 16 had been at Psychiatric Institute originally (in the 1960s and early 1970s) and 11 at other hospitals (in five cases, *after* I had begun treating them). The unit at Psychiatric Institute specialized in psychoanalytically oriented psychotherapy. All the patients were treated by that method, in either twice-weekly sessions for the adults, or thrice-weekly sessions for the adolescents (specifically, those 18 or under). At one point or another, all the patients were also treated with supportive interventions, especially those involved in limit-setting for potentially self-destructive and other maladaptive behaviors. There were times when, for many of the patients, educational and behavioral interventions were also utilized. For those well enough to earn weekend passes, "limit-setting" might also consist of admonitions about returning to the unit on time, and to avoid situations like going to bars, having sex with another patient—or with strangers encountered on the outside. Few of the former PI patients required further hospitalization after discharge: only three of the 16 in the ensuing 25 to 50 years. Among my private patients there were three with whom analytically oriented psychotherapy could be carried out with only a few

shifts, during crises, into a more supportive mode. With Annette, for example, this shift was necessary during the time of her divorce from a husband who had become alcoholic. With Marjorie, the crisis involved her fiancé's insistence they not have children (he later relented and they had a child). A similar shift toward supportive therapy was necessary to help Andrea resolve certain conflicts during the time she was engaged to her future husband. Louisa's eventual recovery was a matter of getting past the extreme turbulence of her mid-40s, and later remarrying and resuming her profession—with no additional help from anyone.

A picture that begins to emerge from the study of ultra-long follow-up of BPD patients is that there is a multiplicity of factors—some destructive, others mollifying—that combine to either intensify or attenuate the pre- and post-natal factors operating in each patient. Furthermore, various neurophysiological, hormonal, and endocrine changes peculiar to the various life stages combine to make the passage through these stages either turbulent or chaotic, or else manageable or smooth. In the older literature on BPD, destructive mothers often took pride of place as prime etiologic factors in the genesis of the disorder. In the present sample I could identify at least ten mothers who were unusually cruel and destructive, especially the mother of the woman who assaulted her elderly father, and the man whose mother kept saying, "I wish you were never born." We do not know what confluence of protective and destructive factors drove the woman to violence and an empty life—and allowed the

TABLE 2. Original Diagnosis and Current Status of the BPD Patients in the Longer Vignettes

Vignette Name	Ever hosp'd ?	Associated diagnostic features	Current Status
Teresa	Yes	Narcissistic	Still dysfunctional
Eleanor	No	Depression	Recovery
Jeannine	No	Avoidant, depressive traits	Recovery
Sharon	Yes	Obsessive, depressive; anorexia nervosa	Recovery
Louisa	No	Paranoid, depressive	Recovery
Florence	No	Histrionic; alcoholism	Recovery
Alice	Yes	Schizotypal, depressive, avoidant	Still dysfunctional
Martha	Yes	Bipolar-II, paranoid, passive-aggressive	Dysfunctional; died
Shirley	Yes	Histrionic, narcissistic; substance abuse	Recovery
Marjorie	Yes	Depression	Recovery
Andria	Yes	Depression; passive-aggressive	Recovery
Marianne	No	Histrionic, depressive	Remission
Ursula	No	Paranoid, antisocial, passive-aggressive	Remission
Vanessa	No	Bulimarexia, depression, narcissism	Still dysfunctional
Helen	Yes	Depressive-masochistic traits	Recovery
Colette	Yes	Depression, histrionic, pathologic jealousy	Still dysfunctional
Frances	Yes	Depression, avoidant traits	Remission
Valerie	Yes	Depression, narcissistic traits	Recovery
Lenore	No	Paranoid, antisocial traits; depression	Still dysfunctional
Jeffrey	No	Antisocial, alcoholism	Still dysfunctional
Beverly	Yes	Schizotypal traits, agoraphobia, depression	Dysfunctional, died
Annette	Yes	Avoidant, agoraphobia	Recovery
Morton	No	Obsessive-compulsive, exhibitionism	Recovery
Nancy	Yes	Depression, avoidant	Still dysfunctional
Beatrice	Yes	Depression	Recovery
Rosalie	Yes	Depression	Recovery
Caroline	No	Depressive-masochistic traits	Recovery
Jonathan	Yes	Obsessive-compulsive	Recovery
Sandra	Yes	Anorexia nervosa, paranoid traits	Still dysfunctional

Note. The patients in this group were all evaluated by the author. All but 6 had also been his private patients. Eight of the patients (1 in the 45-year subgroup; 7 in the 50-year subgroup) had originally been seen and evaluated at the New York State Psychiatric Institute. The term "Remission" signified that at the time of follow-up they no longer met DSM criteria for BPD, though still had psychological problems of some significance. "Recovery"—signified that, in addition to remission-status, they were now functioning well in both the areas of Love (intimate partner and friendships) and Work (occupation and avocational pursuits). Dysfunctional signified that current function was fair to poor and that the criteria for BPD diagnosis were still met.

man to rise above his mother's hatred, and become a contented and highly successful attorney. As for the fathers, several of the patients had fathers who were rejecting though not cruel (Alice, Jeannine, Vanessa, Nancy). Father–daughter incest had occurred in four, but the fathers had not been abusive physically or verbally.

Giedd (2015) drew attention to the developmental disconnect between the (early) maturation of the limbic system and the (late) completion, around age 25, of myelination in the brain's frontal lobes that mediate self-control. This appears to contribute to (at best) the impetuosity of youth—or (at worst) to the impulsivity, and at times, the violence of persons in their adolescent and early adult years, such as is a common counterpart of borderline psychopathology. Among the more fragile borderline patients who managed to reach 30 (past, that is, the peak age of suicide in BPD: mid-20s), the now more fully myelinated frontal lobes (such as the dorsolateral prefrontal cortex helping to foster impulse control) contribute in many instances to a smoother life course: one in which the "inordinate anger" and "suicidal behaviors and gestures, and self-damaging acts" are

TABLE 3. Diagnosis and Current Status of the BPD Patients in the Briefer Vignettes

Vignette No.	Ever Hosp'd?	Associated Diagnostic Features	Current Status
1	Yes	Recurrent unipolar depression, dependent traits	Remission
2	Yes	Bipolar-II disorder	Still dysfunctional
3	Yes	Obsessive-compulsive traits	Recovery
4	No	Schizoaffective traits	Dysfunctional, died
5	Yes	Depressive-masochistic traits	Recovery
6	Yes	Depression, substance abuse	Recovery
7	Yes	Obsessive-compulsive traits	Recovery
8	Yes	Depression, oppositional-defiant traits	Recovery
9	Yes	Depression, histrionic	Recovery
10	No	Depression, passive-aggressive traits	Still dysfunctional
11	No	Depression, obsessive-compulsive traits	Recovery

Note. The patients in this group had all been evaluated by the author. Six had also been in private practice with the author. Eight of the patients had originally been seen and evaluated at the New York State Psychiatric Institute. The criteria for the terms Remission, Recovery, and Dysfunctional are the same as those described in Table 2.

now much less frequent, or which subside altogether. By the "middle" years from 45 to 60, hormonal changes contribute, usually, to a more tranquil adaptation in both women and men. In the case of Louisa, above, she was no longer consumed with impulses toward murder and suicide, and settled into a life of calmness and productivity. As the testosterone titer in Morton diminished, as it does in the later years, he was no longer preoccupied with dreams of volcanoes killing all the world's women; he settled down into running a business, marrying, and raising a family. At the 50-year mark only 7 of the sample's original 40 patients would still fulfill criteria for BPD; two were still significantly depressed, and one (Sandra) still had marked paranoid traits. The majority are now in states of either remission (no longer fulfilling BPD criteria, but still showing noticeable life problems, cognitive peculiarities, etc.) or recovery (leading largely successful lives in the areas of love and work emphasized by Freud)—as defined in a paper by Zanarini et al. (2012).

In just over half the borderline patients in the current study (21/40) the follow-up period reached 50 years. Their clinical status is such that 23 of the 40 are now in a state of recovery. Along the way, numerous factors

appear to have contributed to their improvement—and to their (a) no longer meeting diagnostic criteria for BPD ("remission"), and (b) achieving a state of general well-being ("recovery"). An additional four reached the level of remission. Altogether, two-thirds of the patients (27 of 40, or 67.5%) improved significantly during the follow-up period, which spanned 25 to 35 years in 12 persons; 40 to 50 years in the other 28. Among these ameliorating factors were the above-mentioned age-related physiological and hormonal changes; in addition, favorable life events, such as forming a good life partnership or marriage, achieving financial success at work or, in several cases, renown as a writer or artist.

These results are summarized in Table 2 for the patients of the longer vignettes (identified by their pseudonyms) and in Table 3 for those of the briefer vignettes (identified through numbers 1 to 11). For each of the 40 patients the main diagnostic impressions at the time of initial evaluation were my own. All but eight were my own patients; these remaining eight were patients seen at Psychiatric Institute—for whom I had made the initial diagnostic interview and assessment, or had been the unit director when the patient had been presented to the hospital staff for the first time (a formal gathering that took place two weeks after the patient had been admitted to the unit). The tables also indicate the current functional state for each of the former patients—as to whether they were now in a state of either clinical remission or recovery, or else were still dysfunctional.

Psychotherapy played a key role primarily in the early phases of this life-long process—helping the patients navigate the path between the impulsivity and suicide-proneness of their adolescence and 20s—and the more tranquil years of maturity and middle age. Few of the patients received only one mode of therapy. No one psychotherapeutic method proved universally applicable. The flexibility of the therapist and reliance on an integrated approach that borrowed at times from interventions that differed from those of one's main approach—was more important (and helpful) than a strict adherence to one method only (Gunderson, 2001; Judd & McGlashan, 2003; Livesley, 2008, 2012; Stone 2016). As Gunderson mentioned in his discussion of individual psychotherapies for borderline patients (2001, p. 274), "...patients who had a strong therapeutic alliance with their therapists did improve significantly in supportive therapy"—which was often admixed with the psychoanalytically oriented (or "expressive") therapy when the latter had been chosen at first as the main therapeutic mode. Citing Wallerstein's 1986 book about the Menninger Project concerning the treatment of borderline patients, Gunderson added that "...patients frequently switched between treatment modes and between therapists" (p. 274). Of the 40 patients in the current study, psychoanalytically oriented/ expressive therapy occupied a prominent role in the psychotherapeutic (as opposed to psychopharmacological and other) aspects of their treatment. But depending on the particularities of each patient, and the crises affecting their lives, supportive and behavioral interventions were often utilized as well, and at times became the mainstay of the psychotherapy. My own preference for the "expres-sive" psychotherapeutic approach has, for example, more to do with my psychoanalytic training and my cognitive style than with this approach being the only one capable of successful work with borderline patients. My half century in this field and my 50-year follow-up with a number of borderline patients have also taught me that, once the flamboyant symptoms of their earlier years have subsided (and when suicide has been avoided), the underlying personality traits—especially their degrees of agreeableness and conscientiousness—play an important role in determining whether the lives of the former patients end up years later as unrewarding—or, as is more often the case, recovered.

REFERENCES

American Psychiatric Association. (1980). *Diagnostic and statistical manual of mental disorders* (3rd ed.). Washington, DC: Author.

American Psychiatric Association. (1994). *Diagnostic and statistical manual of mental disorders* (4th ed.). Washington, DC: Author.

Diepold, B. (1992). Problems in diagnosis of borderline disorders in childhood. *Praxis Der Kinderpsychologie Und Kinderpsychiatrie, 41*, 207-214.

Giedd, J. N. (2015). The amazing teen brain. *Scientific American, 312*, 33-37.

Gunderson, J. G. (2001). *Borderline personality disorder: A clinical guide*. Washington, DC: American Psychiatric Press.

Gunderson, J. G., Stout, R. L., McGlashan, T. H., Shea, M. T., Morey, L. C., Grilo, C. M., Zanarini, M. C., Yen, S., Markowitz, J. C., Samislow, C., Ansell, E., Pinto, A., & Skodol, A. E. (2011). Ten-year course of borderline personality disorder: Psychopathology and function from the Collaborative Longitudinal Personality Disorders study. *Archives of General Psychiatry, 68*, 827-837.

Gunderson, J. G., Stout, R. L., Shea, T., Grilo, C. M., Markowitz, J. C., Morey, L. C., Sanislow, C., Yen, S., Zanarini, M. C., Keuroghlian, A. S., McGlashan, T. H., & Skodol, A. E. (2014). Interactions of borderline personality disorder and mood disorder over ten years. *Journal of Clinical Psychiatry, 75*, 829-834.

Judd, P. H., & McGlashan, T. H. (2003). *A developmental model of borderline personality disorder: Understanding variations in course and outcome*. Washington, DC: American Psychiatric Press.

Kernberg, P. (1990). Resolved: Borderline personality exists in children under twelve. Affirmative. *Journal of the American Academy of Child & Adolescent Psychiatry, 29,* 478-482.

Livesley, W. J. (2008). Integrated therapy for complex cases of personality disorder. *Journal of Clinical Psychology, 64,* 207-221.

Livesley, W. J. (2012). Moving beyond specialized therapies for borderline personality disorder: The importance of integrated domain-focused treatment. *Psychodynamic Psychiatry, 40,* 47-74.

Lofgren, D. P., Bemporad, J., Lindem, K., & O'Driscoll, G. (1991). A prospective follow-up study of so-called borderline children. *American Journal of Psychiatry, 148,* 1541-1547.

McGlashan, T. H. (1986). The Chestnut Lodge follow-up study: III. Long-term outcome of borderline personalities. *Archives of General Psychiatry, 43,* 20-30.

McGlashan, T. H. (1993). Implications of outcome research for the treatment of borderline personality disorder. In J. Paris (Ed.), *Borderline personality disorder: Etiology and treatment* (pp. 235-260). Washington, DC: American Psychiatric Press.

Pearlstein, T., Rosen, K., & Stone, A. B. (1997). Mood disorders and menopause. *Endocrinology Metabolism Clinics of North America, 26,* 279-294.

Rasgon, N., Shelton, S., & Halbreich, U. (2005). Perimenopausal mental disorders: Epidemiology and phenomenology. *CNS Spectrum, 10,* 471-478.

Robertson-Blackmore, E., Craddock, N., Walters, J., & Jones, I. (2008). Is the perimenopause a time of increased risk of recurrence in women with a history of bipolar affective post-partum psychosis? A case series. *Archives of Women's Mental Health, 11,* 75-78.

Sajatovic, M., Friedman, S. H., Schuermeyer, I. N., Safavi, R., Ignacio, R. V., Hays, R. W., West, J. A., & Blow, F. C. (2006). Menopause knowledge and subjective experience among peri- and postmenopausal women with bipolar disorder, schizophrenia and major depression. *Journal of Nervous and Mental Disorders, 194,* 173-178.

Stone, M. H. (1980). *The fate of borderlines.* New York: Guilford.

Stone, M. H. (1990). *The fate of borderline patients.* New York: Guilford.

Stone, M. F. (2013). Treatment of personality disorders from the perspective of the five-factor model. In T. A. Widiger & P. T. Costa, Jr. (Eds.), *Personality disorders and the five-factor model of personality* (3rd ed., pp. 349-373). Washington, DC: American Psychological Association.

Stone, M. H. (2016). Borderline personality disorder: Therapeutic factors. *Psychodynamic Psychiatry, 44,* 505-539.

Stone, M. H. (2017). Borderline personality disorder: Treatment from the contextual perspective. *Psychodynamic Psychiatry, 45,* 1-21.

Stöppler, M. (2016). Menopause: Nine symptoms to look for and age of transition. http://www.emedicinehealth.com/menopause/article_em.htm

Wallerstein, R. (1986). *Forty-two lives in treatment.* New York: Guilford.

Widiger, T. A., & Costa, P. T., Jr. (2003). Five-factor model personality disorder research. In P. T. Costa, Jr. & T. A. Widiger (Eds.), *Personality disorders and the five-factor model of personality* (2nd ed., pp. 59-87). Washington, DC: American Psychiatric Press.

Widiger, T. A., & Costa, P. T., Jr. (2013). Personality disorders and the five-factor model of personality: Rationale for the 3rd edition. In T. A. Widiger & P. T. Costa, Jr. (Eds.), *Personality disorders and the five-factor model of personality* (pp. 3-11). Washington, DC: American Psychological Association.

Widiger, T. A., & Trull, T. J. (1991). Diagnosis and clinical assessment. *Annual Review of Psychology, 42,* 109-133.

Zanarini, M. C., Frankenburg, F. R., Reich, D. B., & Fitzmaurice, G. (2012). Attainment and stability of sustained symptomatic remission and recovery among patients with borderline personality disorder and Axis II comparison subjects: A 16-year prospective follow-up study. *American Journal of Psychiatry, 169,* 476-483.

Zanarini, M. C., Frankenburg, F. R., Reich, D. B., Wedig, M. M., Conkey, L. C., & Fitzmaurice, G. (2015). The subsyndromal phenomenology of borderline personality disorder: A ten-year follow-up study. *American Journal of Psychiatry, 164,* 929-935.

Zanarini, M. C., Frankenburg, F. R., Wedig, M. M., & Fitzmaurice, G. (2013). Cognitive experiences reported by patients with borderline personality disorder and Axis II comparison subjects: A 16-year prospective follow-up study. *American Journal of Psychiatry, 170,* 671-679.

Pathological Narcissism and the Obstruction of Love

David Kealy and John S. Ogrodniczuk

Abstract: Pathological narcissism is a form of maladaptive self-regulation that impedes the capacity to love. Although narcissism is often construed as excessive self-love, individuals with pathological narcissism are impaired in being able to love themselves as well as others. With the subject of impaired love in mind, we review selected conceptualizations from an enormous and diverse psychodynamic literature on narcissism. Major theoretical approaches illustrate a number of psychodynamics associated with narcissistic self-regulatory problems. This paper provides a concise overview of major conceptual themes regarding pathological narcissism and impaired capacity to love.

The capacity to give and to receive love is arguably the most valuable acquisition available. Being able to love is so fundamental that it may be taken for granted; for those who possess this ability, loving may be akin to breathing, being really noticed only when jeopardized. Those who struggle to love and to feel loved may be acutely aware of painful feelings associated with their plight, while others may attempt to hide or override this difficulty. Symptoms, problem behaviors, or interpersonal challenges may ensue—the very issues that motivate many people to seek some form of psychosocial help. Psychodynamic clinicians have long seen beyond these presenting concerns to consider deeper issues, including obstacles to giving or receiving love. Narcissism—the modulation of self-image—has been one such issue. Indeed, clinicians of all theoretical orientations have become increasingly aware of the problems associated with pathological forms of narcissism. Recent volumes attest to both the continued clinical value of the narcissism construct as well as the theoretical complexity involved in understanding it (Campbell & Miller, 2011; Ogrodniczuk, 2013).

Pathological narcissism is commonly regarded as an impediment to love relations. Individuals who are considered to have narcissistic problems tend to be viewed as being in love with themselves, so much so that they are unable to pay attention to anyone else as a potential love object. This view, taken from the ancient Greek myth of Narcissus (who was so enraptured by his own image that he neglected the beseeching call of the nymph Echo and eventually perished), suggests that narcissistic individuals cannot tear themselves away from their own self-love to engage in love for another. Clinical discussions of narcissism also refer to its pernicious effects on love relations. Literature on narcissism in love relationships has emphasized the difficult attitudes and behaviors of individuals with pathological narcissism, and their impact on romantic partners and family members. These include self-absorption, insincere attention to a partner, and limited tolerance of genuine separateness and mutuality (Akhtar, 2009; Solomon, 1994), issues that can isolate and drive a partner away. Yet there is more at stake than a romantic relationship here: pathological narcissism is connected with an overall difficulty in the capacity to love. Indeed, it may be more fitting to say that pathological narcissism fundamentally *is* an impairment in the capacity to love. This includes not only love for others, but the capacity for self-love. Love for oneself is generally held to be an essential component of healthy psychosocial functioning, and theories of pathological narcissism at least implicitly speak to this ability being impaired, along with deficits in love relations with others.

Narcissism remains difficult to theorize. Multiple psychoanalytic perspectives have brought richness and depth to the concept, but have produced a somewhat confusing and muddled literature (Britton, 2004). Despite the important connection between narcissism and love, however, concise reviews of this theorizing are not available. The present paper is aimed at providing such an overview for clinicians who are likely to encounter clients whose impairments in loving are entwined with maladaptive narcissistic issues. Our discussion is, in the interest of succinctness, necessarily selective and cursory. It is not our intention to present a unified conceptualization: a varied theoretical contemplation allows for a more flexible understanding of pathological narcissism and its obstruction of love.

DEFINING NARCISSISM

Despite widespread colloquial use of the term, narcissism remains a notoriously slippery construct. Pulver (1970) highlighted the confusing and variable use of the term in psychoanalytic discourse: a sexual perversion, a developmental stage, a mode of relating to others, and a form of self-esteem functioning. Few people today talk about narcissism as either a sexual issue or a developmental stage. However, the term has also expanded into the field of social and personality psychology, as a trait domain that does not necessarily line up with clinical definitions of narcissistic pathology (Pincus & Lukowitsky, 2010). In clinical psychology and psychiatry, pathological narcissism is a significant form of mental disorder involving distorted self-esteem, diminished empathy toward others, and problematic attitudes such as envy and entitlement. Extreme expressions of this are recognized in formal psychiatric nosology as narcissistic personality disorder (NPD; American Psychiatric Association, 2013; World Health Organization, 2010); NPD is also represented in the *Psychodynamic Diagnostic Manual* (PDM Task Force, 2006).

Part of what makes the study of narcissism so difficult is the notion of narcissism being ubiquitous. Stolorow (1975) emphasized that narcissism refers simply to the maintenance of the self; any mental phenomenon that contributes to positive or stable self-regard can thus be considered narcissistic. Indeed, normal narcissism is thought to be essential for healthy functioning, involving a balanced amount of self-investment, positive appraisal, and self-preservation, all of which contribute to the achievement of personal goals, including love relations (Stone, 1998). Pathological narcissism, by contrast, involves a distortion of self-regard and a failure to maintain a positive sense of self. Although this often involves maladaptive efforts at self-enhancement—such as inflated views of the self and devalued views of others—the key issue is a deficiency in healthy self-regulation (Ronningstam, 2011).

PATHOLOGICAL NARCISSISM

Pincus and Lukowitsky (2010) define pathological narcissism as involving "significant regulatory deficits and maladaptive strategies to cope with disappointments and threats to a positive self-image" (p. 426). These self-regulatory deficits have been broadly delineated across two fundamental themes: grandiosity and vulnerability (Cain, Pincus, & Ansell, 2008). Grandiosity encompasses self-inflation, interpersonal domination and callousness, and fantasies of superiority. Vulnerability, on the other hand, refers to feelings of helplessness, suffering, and anxiety regarding threats to the self, reflecting inner feelings of inadequacy, emptiness, and shame. Although some individuals may exhibit more of one theme than another, these elements are frequently observed to comingle and fluctuate. As a clinical problem, pathological narcissism is associated with various other areas of psychopathology, including suicide (Ronningstam, Weinberg, & Maltsberger, 2008), co-morbid psychiatric conditions (Stinson, Dawson, Goldstein, Chou, Huang et al., 2008), interpersonal relationship problems (Ogrodniczuk et al., 2009), and emotional distress and functional impairment (Miller, Campbell, & Pilkonis, 2007).

LOVE DIVERTED: NARCISSISTIC EQUILIBRIUM

Psychoanalytic conceptualizations of narcissism have invariably drawn on a range of ideas developed by Freud, including theories of defense, unconscious mentation, and psychic structure. However, Freud himself wrote only one major treatise on narcissism in 1914, prior to his development of the structural model of the mind consisting of the id, ego, and superego. In "On narcissism: An introduction," Freud discussed narcissism in terms of the investment and allocation of psychic energy—the derivative of instinctual libidinal drive. Freud (1914) identified narcissism as a state of libidinal investment in the ego (at that time, the ego in Freud's writing had not been distinguished as a distinct psychic agency within his tripartite structural model).

Freud posited a universal, initial stage of primary narcissism: the infantile absorption in the fulfillment of bodily requirements, without awareness of externality. This experience is inevitably relinquished as the separateness from caregivers is gradually realized, necessitating investment in others. Freud suggested that for some individuals this encroachment of reality upon a blissful sense of omnipotence is too frustrating to bear. This gives rise to secondary narcissism—a reclaiming of psychic investment in the ego (self)—as a reaction to such frustration.

Freud's economic views of psychic energy led to the idea that only a finite quantity of libido is available for distribution. Secondary narcissism essentially removes psychic energy from the realm of interpersonal relations and redirects investment toward self-gratification and omnipotent fantasy. Love is thus forestalled due to there not being enough emotional currency to go around. In this model, pathological narcissism involves a concentration of biologically based emotional energy on the self. The reality of separateness and frustration is denied in an attempt to unconsciously recapture the fantasy of being "his majesty, the baby" (Freud, 1914, p. 91). This does not obviate engagement in what might appear to be love relationships. Indeed, Freud suggested that love relations may themselves be organized in ways that meet certain narcissistic functions. Thus, secondary narcissism influences the formations of relationships in that a partner may be unconsciously recruited to help restore narcissistic equilibrium. Freud described narcissistic object choice as the development of relations with others according to:

what he himself is (i.e., himself),

what he himself was,

what he himself would like to be,

someone who was once part of himself.
  (Freud, 1914)

The implication here is that the degree of narcissistic needs will influence the choice of partner. According to Freud, the feeling of being in love with someone may be determined by the nature of narcissistic self-regulatory need. Under the sway of intense narcissism, a partner is not loved for who they are uniquely, but for their representation of a real or imagined part of the self. Freud's position suggests that the degree of actual love involved is likely inversely related to the degree of secondary narcissism at play in the relationship. A relative absence of narcissistic problems can thus foster a sense of separateness, mutuality, and reciprocal valuation.

Clinical Vignette*

Jillian felt complete having Todd in her life. He was both charming and brash, implicitly demanding attention whenever he entered the room. Before meeting him, Jillian had felt empty and disconsolate, lacking in these characteristics she saw in Todd. It did not matter to her that he could be petulant and self-absorbed; indeed, she claimed to feel flattered by his insistent sexual requirements. Her compliance and deference to Todd facilitated a relationship that seemed to confer upon Jillian a sense of confidence and possibility that had always eluded her. She essentially found in Todd those qualities that she wished for herself, allowing her to establish a blissful sense of omnipotence. When he eventually discarded her, Jillian was left to painfully face the lack of reciprocity and true intimacy within their relationship: her investment in Todd's grandiosity had served her own self-regulatory needs, at the expense of a loving, mutual investment.

LOVE DESTROYED: NARCISSISTIC INTOLERANCE OF DEPENDENCE

Melanie Klein's attention to primitive mental states resulted in a conceptualization of pathological narcissism based on primary affects of love and hate. Although Klein did not directly use the terminology of narcissism, several Kleinian concepts essentially deal with narcissistic phenomena; these have subsequently been extended by other theories of pathological narcissism, most notably those of Otto Kernberg (1984). Klein (1946) took psychoanalytic theorizing further back in time to the inner world of the infant, emphasizing the infant's alternating experiences of love and hate, contentment and deprivation, and envy and gratitude. She contended that these primal anxieties are never fully resolved, and that adult psychopathology reflects a predominance of these anxieties and the primitive defences employed to deal with them.

Central to Kleinian theory is the idea of developmental positions (Segal, 1973), between which the individual fluctuates throughout life to a varying extent, rather than developmental stages through which the individual progresses epigenetically. The paranoid-schizoid position is the earliest and most primitive, representing the infant's experience of a chaotic world—at times blissful (as in after a satisfying feeding) and at times savagely depriving (as in the state of hunger or discomfort). Klein suggested that the infant attempts to manage his or her subjectivity through splitting: categorically separating experience so that, for instance, the nurturing breast is not simultaneously the same object that only moments earlier evoked the baby's desperate hunger. Klein used language such as "breast" (rather than mother) in part to convey that the paranoid-schizoid position is characterized by the experience of others as physical part-objects: essentially fulfill-

---

*All of our vignettes use composite cases and the removal or disguise of identifying information in order to preserve patient confidentiality.

ing needs rather than being experienced as whole persons (Ogden, 1986). In healthy development, this mode of functioning eventually recedes in favor of a capacity to experience others as separate, complex individuals. This phase, referred to as the depressive position, is associated with the growing recognition that the mother (caregiver, etc.) who frustrates is the same soothing mother who feeds and protects. The capacity for guilt and concern is ushered in as the infant gradually recognizes the effects and implications of his/her negative (e.g., angry, aggressive) feelings and fantasies towards caregivers. "Depressive" refers to the prospect of genuine concern and mourning for a separate person rather than a "part object" (Klein, 1946; Winnicott, 1955). This remains a somewhat precarious developmental achievement, in that one remains susceptible to slipping into the paranoid-schizoid position—the splitting up of difficult affective experiences—throughout life.

A Kleinian perspective on narcissism draws attention to the impediments associated with a limited achievement of the depressive position. Kernberg (1984) has particularly emphasized the difficulties in genuine sadness and mourning that are part of narcissistic character functioning. The potential for love is essentially destroyed by a lack of tolerance for dependence—even a mutual interdependence—on others as distinct individuals. Dependent, needy feelings are split off and defended against through grandiose attitudes and behaviors, and others may be dealt with as part-objects who can be used and then dropped. In this mode of narcissistic functioning, located in the paranoid-schizoid position, other people are not fully experienced as "both significant and separate" (Britton, 2004, p. 478). Although this "incapacity to depend" (Kernberg, 1984, p. 270) appears to be a form of self-absorption, it may more likely reflect a lack of real interest in one's own inner world. The inability to fully experience guilt and concern, often

regarded as a hallmark of narcissistic pathology, limits the prospect of love not only for others, but for oneself as an individual. Kernberg (1984) clarifies that pathological narcissism is not an over-investment in the self, but a distorted version of the self; *it is not a "real" self that is invested in.* How can one love oneself if one's shortcomings, failures, and transgressions cannot be tolerated? Through the splitting off of negative self-experience, the "grandiose self," like Klein's infant, averts guilt and mourning, and ultimately genuine love.

Clinical Vignette

Adam suffered from recurrent depressive episodes that he attributed to repeated maltreatment by other people. He felt his co-workers were incompetent, and would often attempt to corral them into working more effectively, only to become enraged at their contemptuous responses toward him. Adam's experience with his wife was similar: he saw himself as her supporter and champion, in the context of her chronic medical illness, yet he complained bitterly when she failed to implement his advice. Indeed, he perceived her, as he did his co-workers, as deliberately seeking to undermine and upset him. Adam could not acknowledge his dependent feelings in relation to his wife; he had split off his needy feelings and located them in her. Her attempts at refusing this role threatened to overturn his disavowal, adding fuel to his angry responses. He regarded his hostile reactions as purely justified by the rejection of his altruistic efforts, rather than as products of his mind that he might further understand. Although these dynamics maintained some narcissistic equilibrium for Adam, they occurred at the cost of marital harmony, nuanced emotional experience, and deepened knowledge of both his partner and himself.

LOVE EVADED: NARCISSISTIC ILLUSORY RELATIONS

Narcissistic investment in a distorted self-structure can also be regarded as a characteristic use of illusion as a means of self-regulation, an enactment of fantasy at the expense of reality. Stephen Mitchell (1986) highlighted the theme of illusion within major psychoanalytic theories of narcissism, emphasizing the role of illusion in both creativity and in defensive functioning, with illusion becoming particularly distorted in the service of narcissistic self-regulation. From this perspective, illusion can either promote growth and creative freedom or take a pathogenic turn toward the constriction of self-actualization and love. Mitchell suggests that the distortion of illusion is not limited to any particular developmental phase, rather that it is inextricably embedded within contexts of interpersonal relationships.

Interpersonal psychoanalytic theory, originating with the work of Harry Stack Sullivan (1953), conceives of the self as operating virtually entirely in accord with interpersonal relations within an interactional field. Sullivan suggested that anxiety can contagiously influence interpersonal interactions, necessitating ways of coping with or reducing anxiety. Although functionally similar to classical defense mechanisms, Sullivan's "security operations" serve not to ward off forbidden wishes but instead to manage the experience of the self in interpersonal relations. Of course, children are particularly susceptible to vulnerabilities in their self-experience, and Sullivan (1953) proposed that repeated, early anxiety-ridden interactions can infuse one's personality with negative representations known as "bad me" or "not me" experiences. These aspects of self-concept are prone to being painfully evoked in subsequent interpersonal relations, and hence motivate the development of security operations in order to stifle their emergence. Security operations can take various forms, not the least of which consist of grandiose and omnipotent illusions.

Although Sullivan did not specifically address narcissism, his formulations suggest that grandiose illusions may protect the individual from "bad me" representations. Narcissistically oriented "illusionary me-you patterns" (Bacal & Newman, 1990, p. 34) might involve an illusion of others as irrelevant, if not inferior, to the individual's self. Such an illusion would serve to cover over any anxiety regarding normative relational needs and the interpersonal risks associated with them. A reliance on illusions like this one, along with their behavioral expression, imposes obvious limitations on interpersonal interactions, and in particular the development of love relationships. Further, a person who relies on illusionary patterns is ultimately preventing the development of their own genuine resources and self-esteem (Mitchell, 1986).

While many narcissistic illusions contain brilliant or triumphant self-attributions, themes of failure and defeat can also reflect illusionary self-regulatory processes. Arnold Cooper described a variation of narcissistic pathology consisting of chronic self-defeating trends (Cooper, 2009). This narcissistic-masochistic character type tends to present with overt themes of vulnerability and deficiency. In Cooper's formulation, repetitive patterns of being hard-done-by, unappreciated, or rejected serve important narcissistic functions. Lurking beneath a chronic sense of injustice may be a covert sense of superiority associated with suffering wrongdoings and receiving little from life. Cooper proposed that the core of narcissistic-masochistic functioning involves an illusory notion that one is in control of one's own suffering. This illusion preserves a sense of autonomy and defends against anxiety over being helpless, envious, or rejected. By unconsciously engineering one's own failures, the individual can avert painful feelings of disappointment—and shame—that follow from hoping for, but not receiving, love or success. In a form of self-fulfilling prophecy, love relationships are suspiciously rendered as further injustices to be "collected," rather than engaged in afresh as potentially expansive connections.

Erich Fromm also cautioned against the role of narcissistic illusion in love relations, and ultimately in the broader social realm. Fromm (1955) argued that pathological narcissism entailed an illusory avoidance of universal existential realities. He suggested that psychological development is pervaded by anxieties regarding the transience of life and the limitations of human relatedness. In Fromm's view, the finitude and separateness of human existence is a basic but terrifying truth, from which one may seek refuge in illusionary attitudes. These attitudes, including the view of the self as a commodity, contribute to narcissistic pathology and the derailment of love and social harmony (Fromm, 1947).

Fromm (1976) argued that cultural values associated with consumerism promote an illusory notion of the self resting upon what one has, rather than upon one's intrinsic sense of being. The sense of having does not just apply to material goods: one can "have" a certain image or lifestyle. These do not constitute the "being" at the heart of the self. In Fromm's view, these window dressings of selfhood—possession of things or characteristics—reinforce the powerful illusion of having as the central aim of human existence. The cost of this for the individual is an ultimately fragile sense of self and a dilution of one's capacity to love and to create. Fromm suggested that loving and creating are fundamental, positive ways in which humankind can transcend the "passivity and accidentalness of existence" (Fromm, 1955, p. 35). Narcissistic withdrawal and destructiveness—substitutive escapes from existential reality—are the antithesis of creativity and love (Fromm, 1955).

Clinical Vignette

Amanda's relationship history had been a trail of disappointments. She had al-ternated between short-lived, intense flings with exciting men to unstable long-term involvements with marginally functioning men. The former type of relationship electrified her with an illusion of living the high life, but the reality proved to be far below Amanda's idealized expectations, and her enthusiasm quickly dissipated. Alternatively, being with lower-functioning partners had facilitated an aversion to "bad me" feelings: she felt superior by comparison, and protected from abandonment. Beneath a carefully managed exterior of cynicism and edginess, Amanda felt deeply insecure and self-critical. She conveyed an image of herself as a tough outsider through the use of provocative piercings and tattoos. After some time in therapy, Amanda's reliance on having this image lessened, and she questioned the self-regulatory illusions she had been pursuing in her relationships. She developed the capacity to become interested in a "normal" man, to feel relatively free to be herself with him, and to tolerate the inevitable ups and downs that ensued in their relationship.

LOVE SACRIFICED: NARCISSISTIC INTERNAL OBJECT RELATIONS

W. R. D. Fairbairn (1952) devoted his psychoanalytic career to the study of patients who keep love at bay through an absorption in their own inner world. Like Fromm and Sullivan, Fairbairn emphasized the use of illusion and the flight from psychological freedom associated with impeded love relations. Although couched in the language of schizoid disorders, Fairbairn's broad personality theory can be readily applied to narcissism. Indeed, his description of schizoid disorder bears a close resemblance to the vulnerable narcissism construct, and his ideas speak directly to the problem of narcissistically living in one's own mind (Ogden, 2010).

Fairbairn placed object relations—the quest for love for love's own sake—at the center of psychic life, giving primacy to the frustration of relational needs in the development of psychopathology. He regarded early object relations as being so fundamental that they are psychologically preserved at all costs, even at the expense of self-esteem and real relatedness (Fairbairn, 1952). When these early relationships are fraught with turmoil or trauma, the child must find a way to uphold the tie to his or her primary object(s) by an assumption of personal responsibility: far better to cast oneself as a defective unit under the care of ideal parents than face the idea of simply being subject to capriciously neglectful or savage parents (Bacal & Newman, 1990). Dissatisfying early relations are internalized in a self-preservative bid to stem further disappointment and traumatization. Part of this internalization involves the inner experience of "bad objects," the representatives of frustrating early relations that continue to haunt the traumatized individual. These internal object relations serve as templates that are subsequently imposed upon new interpersonal relationships; others are experienced more as aspects of internalized early relations than as they actually are.

Fairbairn's structural model is too elaborate to describe in detail here, but his ideas are particularly useful in explaining the persistence of narcissistic object relations in the face of new and potentially mutative experience. In his view, the schizoid/narcissistic self clings to what is known and reliable, rather than risk a dreaded failure anticipated in new forms of relatedness. An internal relationship with a rejecting inner object is felt to prevent abject desolation: any kind of object is better than none (Fairbairn, 1952; Ogden, 1986). Further, new relatedness constitutes a kind of uprising against internal objects, a destabilization for which the individual feels unprepared. Preservation of inner object relations can, under traumatic circumstances, involve an enduring sense of the self as shameful and bad, and subject to persistent criticism from a negative "internal saboteur" object representation. A neglected child, for example, may preserve an inner sense of having "good" parents by accepting responsibility for maltreatment: she concludes that she does not deserve to be loved, and incorporates this into her self-concept. Fairbairn felt that this internal sabotage would be unleashed on the self in response to any glimmer of hope that the self may feel worthy of love. Although grandiose attitudes may be engaged to counterbalance this situation, an underlying sense of bleakness often persists. Narcissistic love relations are frequently characterized as one-sided and superficial. In Fairbairn's view, this is likely reflective of pervasive feelings that one's love is fundamentally bad. Relational superficiality may thus be conceived of as a self-regulatory compromise between engagement and protection against being overwhelmed by bad objects, feelings of shame and inadequacy, and the potential loss of internal structure (Fairbairn, 1952; Ogden, 1986).

Bowlby's attachment theory, now a widely researched area in social psychology, extended Fairbairn's ideas regarding the impairment of self-esteem and love relations, and has been raised as a conceptualization of pathological narcissism (Bennett, 2006; Pistole, 1995). Bowlby (1988) emphasized the needs of infants and young children to experience physical proximity, safety, and loving affects with their caregivers or attachment figures. Like Fairbairn, Bowlby regarded inconsistent or unsafe attachment figures as contributing to the development of dysfunctional inner models of self and other, which are subsequently brought to bear on future attachment relationships. One of the strengths of attachment theory is the operationalization and empirical investigation of attachment styles according to the relative level of security. Such research has only recently turned to the issue of narcissism: a preliminary finding in a clinical sample indicates an association between narcissistic grandiosity and an anxious form of insecure attachment (Kealy et al., 2013). In other words, patients with narcissistic tendencies were found to struggle with fears of abandonment regarding love relationships.

Further empirical and conceptual development within attachment theory has focused on deficits in mentalization that are the consequences of attachment trauma, commonly observed among patients with borderline personality disorder. Mentalization is the capacity to think about mental states—one's own and those of others—and to reflect on the independence of minds. This ability develops within secure attachment relationships and is thought to provide the evolutionary advantage of being able to conceive of others' intentions in an interpersonal world (Fonagy, Gergely, Jurist, & Target, 2002). Inhibited mentalization is described in terms of particular modes of mental functioning (which occur naturally during early phases of development). Individuals with attachment trauma are more likely to slip into pre-mentalizing, "psychic equivalence" modes where thoughts are experienced concretely, non-symbolically, and with limited internal-external differentiation (Fonagy et al., 2002). Another mode, "pretend" functioning, involves a detachment from mental states, a sequestering of mental experiences as though having no connection with external reality.

Although this perspective on attachment-related mental functioning has not been explicitly applied to pathological narcissism, fluctuations between psychic equivalence and pretend modes may contribute to narcissistic functioning and impediments in love relations. An insistent entitlement and dominance, for example, may reflect a difficulty in understanding corresponding mental states such as desire or vulnerability. Instead, such attitudes may be experienced as based completely on external, veridical fact. One's demands for admiration, for example, might be perceived as legitimately deserved, rather than merely wished for, and thus requir-

ing of action. An insult to the self may be experienced as a deliberate, humiliating attack, rather than associated with any other motivation. Likewise, retaliation is felt to be concretely required: only physical action can rid the self of the intolerable sense of defeat (Fonagy et al., 2002).

Clinical Vignette

Jake was intellectually bright and talented in his work. He enjoyed fantasizing about a brilliant future in which he would shine in virtually any career he wanted—engineering, finance, technology—and he made no secret of these musings to those around him. At the same time, he harbored tremendous feelings of inadequacy. Jake's childhood occupation was to be his mother's confidante as she weathered brutal outbursts from his alcoholic father. He refused to allow any recognition of the burden associated with this role, or with other forms of emotional neglect. Indeed, he seemed to adopt an inner sense of deficiency in order to cleanse his mother's image. Yet there were scarcely any "good object" representations upon which to draw for the establishment of love relationships. Jake felt extremely uncomfortable approaching women that he thought would be interesting to talk to. He was convinced of an inability to sustain a meaningful connection, and despite his talents he could not imagine why any intelligent woman would be interested in him. He instead opted for an addictive relationship with pornography, about which he felt guilty and ashamed, along with dead-end liaisons that provided transient self-enhancement. Although he protested being locked in this pattern of (not) relating, Jake usually rebuffed those who tried to get to know him better, ultimately electing to perpetuate the closed system of his inner world.

LOVE UNDEVELOPED:
NARCISSISTIC (IM)MATURITY

Heinz Kohut (1971) provided one of the most pivotal and influential psychoanalytic formulations of narcissistic pathology. Along with Kernberg, Kohut helped to renew interest in narcissistic disorders in the late 20th century. Kohut placed narcissism as an essential component in the evolution of the self, a developmental pathway that distorts into pathology under unfavorable conditions (Kohut, 1971). His contributions ultimately evolved into a general model of psychopathology and psychotherapy known as self psychology, at the heart of which is the concept of the selfobject. A selfobject is an intrapsychic experience of an object (other person) that provides support or enhancement to the self. In other words, selfobjects are those individuals (and the subjective experience of them) who are sustaining to one's sense of selfhood, a type of relationship that is required in varying degrees throughout the lifespan.

The selfobject construct speaks to the need for essential, self-sustaining relational experiences, evoked through the empathic responsiveness of others (Kohut & Wolf, 1978). Mirroring selfobject experiences consist of caregiver responses that confirm for the child their own sense of greatness and vitality, such as a parent's beaming face as the child takes their first steps. The child also needs to be able to idealize their caregivers: experiences of identifying and merging with parents who are calm, effective, and reliable. Mirroring and idealizing selfobject experiences contribute to the development of ambitions and ideals. Together with a range of empathic responses, these selfobject relations provide the individual with a sense of strength and vitality with which to pursue desires and maintain values in the face of life's challenges. Under optimal conditions, early selfobject experiences are provided by parents through their natural empathic responsiveness toward the child. For example, a mother may have an innate sense of understanding for the need that her infant has to be spoken to in an engaging tone of voice; at other times, she might discern the child's distress and respond with an embrace that signals to the child that all is now well. Maturation brings different selfobject needs and therefore different responses: optimal selfobject experiences for an adolescent might include respect for privacy and independence.

Kohut drew attention to the crucial role of empathy in selfobject experience, in both healthy development and in the etiology of pathological narcissism (Kohut, 1971; Wolf, 1988). Like Fairbairn, he highlighted the difficulties caused by caregivers' empathic limitations with their children, often because of parents' own narcissistic issues. Though often subtle, empathic ruptures can impede the conditions required for the growth of the self. A preoccupied father, for example, may lack sufficient empathy for his son's need to experience the father's presence and devotion. A mother lacking in positive selfobject experiences may lose sight of her baby's need to "melt into" a calm mother, her own anxiety being the foremost priority for her. Kohut suggested that breaches of empathy are expectable and, under non-traumatic circumstances, contribute to the development of a sturdy self. Repeated, traumatic selfobject failures, however, lead to a fragile self that relies excessively on awkward mechanisms of preservation.

Because selfobject experiences are essential for the self's robustness and vitality, their absence or chronic frustration lead to feelings of deficiency and emptiness—positive selfobjects are not reliably available for internalization (Kohut & Wolf, 1978). Associated with this is a sense of profound shame and a propensity for the self to become fragmented upon future disruptions. Pathological grandiosity is deployed to compensate for this sense of vulnerability and defectiveness (Morrison, 1983), masking feelings of weakness with the transient glow of being superficially admired. Although grandiosity can cover over a sense of defect, this veneer may be pierced through by an insult or interpersonal letdown. For some, the ensuing fragmentation can lead to narcissistic rage, an aggression borne out of utter helplessness and deployed to restore a damaged self (Kohut, 1972). Narcissistic rage tendencies clearly represent extreme impairments in love relations, likely contributing to emotional and physical abuse.

The self-psychological perspective holds that the failure to internalize early selfobject relations accounts for deficiencies in the capacity to give and receive love. On one level, inadequate selfobject experience leaves the individual without an empathic foundation from which to draw and extend to a partner in a love relationship. At another level, a fragmentation-prone individual may be so preoccupied with obtaining narcissistic support that empathy toward a partner would be essentially thwarted; how can love be given when one's own self must be frantically held together? At yet another level, the shame associated with traumatic selfobject failure contributes to an avoidance of intimate, reciprocal relatedness. Mature relationships, with their attendant vulnerability, carry the threat of further selfobject failure as an inevitable aspect of the ups and downs of interdependency. Substitute selfobject stand-ins may instead be sought out and utilized to transiently restore or enhance a devitalized self.

Clinical Vignette

Cindy sought psychotherapy because of a steadily increasing feeling that her marriage was on the rocks. She had long perceived her husband Wayne as inconsiderate and unappreciative of her. Any expression of disagreement from him regarding her management of their children, her career, or their home would launch a dysphoric reaction that

would last for days. This was comparable to her family of origin: she had been either ignored or belittled by preoccupied, quarrelling parents. Cindy felt a need to hyperfunction at work, at home, and in social settings in order to avert any potential criticism and to reassure herself of her own value. This was coupled with a barely admissible desire that others would notice and admire her efforts. Her sensitivities to others' responses had fostered a stultified atmosphere in her marriage; Wayne tended to either avoid her or provide superficial responses that were minimally sustaining to Cindy's self-regard. Maintaining this status quo averted acute dysphoric episodes, but prevented more genuine interactions between them. In therapy, Cindy seemed to require a lengthy period of simply being empathically listened to—a reliable selfobject experience—before she was able to intuit her husband's experience and see that he actually didn't share her perfectionistic priorities.

CONCLUDING COMMENTS

The common view of narcissism is that it consists of over-indulgent self-love. The myth of Narcissus appears at first glance to depict this, in that Narcissus regards his own image as the only object worth desiring. Echo, however, can be viewed as having a similar narcissistic problem, despite her desire for Narcissus (Grenyer, 2013). In the ancient myth, Echo was obsessed with Narcissus and unable to develop a mature love for him. Indeed, she could not even speak her own words, but could merely repeat the words of admiration Narcissus was uttering to himself. In their own way, each character from the myth represents a different facet of impaired love and pathological narcissism (Grenyer, 2013). Fromm (1955) notes that, "what matters is the particular quality of loving, not the object" (p. 30). In Fromm's view, it is not enough to simply and only love another person; one must be capable of loving humanity, loving others as separate selves, and in so doing, loving oneself. Thus, narcissistic self-absorption is hardly a form of self-love. The conceptualizations covered here seem to unequivocally regard pathological narcissism as destructive to the love of others, and ultimately to the love of the self. Given the high value of love in human living, understanding and ameliorating pathological narcissism is crucial work. Such work may be extremely challenging, perhaps requiring multiple and/or sustained efforts from various health and social care providers, informal supports, and families. Yet the stakes are high, as Fromm points out: "In the experience of love lies the only answer to being human, lies sanity" (1955, p. 31).

REFERENCES

Akhtar, S. (2009). Love, sex, and marriage in the setting of a pathological narcissism. *Psychiatric Annals, 39*, 185-191.

American Psychiatric Association. (2013). *Diagnostic and statistical manual of mental disorders, 5th edition.* Arlington, VA: American Psychiatric Publishing.

Bacal, H. A, & Newman K. M. (1990). *Theories of object relations: Bridges to self psychology.* New York: Columbia University Press.

Bennett, S. (2006). Attachment theory and the research applied to the conceptualization and treatment of pathological narcissism. *Clinical Social Work Journal, 34*(1), 45-60.

Bowlby, J. (1988). *A secure base.* London: Routledge.

Britton, R. (2004). Narcissistic disorders in clinical practice. *Journal of Analytical Psychology, 49*, 477-490.

Cain N. M., Pincus, A. L., & Ansell, E. B. (2008). Narcissism at the crossroads: Phenotypic description of pathological narcissism across clinical theory, social/personality psychology, and psychiatric diagnosis. *Clinical Psychology Review, 28*, 638-656.

Campbell, W. K., & Miller, J. D. (2011). *The handbook of narcissism and narcissistic personality disorder: Theoretical approaches, empirical findings, and treatments.* Hoboken, NJ: Wiley.

Cooper, A. M. (2009). The narcissistic-masochistic character. *Psychiatric Annals, 39*, 904-912.

Fairbairn, W. R. D. (1952). *Psychoanalytic studies of the personality.* London: Routledge.

Fonagy, P., Gergely, G., Jurist, E. L., & Target, M. (2002). *Affect regulation, mentalization, and the development of the self.* New York: Other Press.

Freud, S. (1914/1957). On narcissism: An introduction. In J. Strachey (Ed.), *The standard edition of the complete psychological works of Sigmund Freud* (Vol. 14, pp. 66–102). London: Hogarth.

Fromm, E. (1947). *Man for himself.* New York: Holt, Rinehart and Winston

Fromm, E. (1955). *Sane society.* Florence, KY: Routledge.

Fromm, E. (1976). *To have or to be?* New York: Harper & Sons.

Grenyer, B. F. S. (2013). Historical overview of pathological narcissism. In J. S. Ogrodniczuk (Ed.), *Understanding and treating pathological narcissism* (pp. 15–26). Washington, DC: American Psychological Association.

Kealy, D., Ogrodniczuk, J. S., Joyce, A. S., Steinberg, P. I., & Piper, W. E. (2013). Narcissism and relational representations among psychiatric outpatients. *Journal of Personality Disorders.* doi: 10.1521.pedi_2013_27_084

Kernberg, O. F. (1984). *Severe personality disorders: Psychotherapeutic strategies.* New Haven, CT: Yale University Press.

Klein, M. H. (1946). Notes on some schizoid mechanisms. *International Journal of Psychoanalysis, 27*, 99-110.

Kohut, H. (1971). *The analysis of the self.* Chicago: University of Chicago Press.

Kohut H. (1972). Thoughts on narcissism and narcissistic rage. *Psychoanalytic Study of the Child, 27*, 360-400.

Kohut, H., & Wolf, E. S. (1978). The disorders of the self and their treatment: An outline. *International Journal of Psychoanalysis, 59*, 413-25.

Miller, J. D., Campbell, W. K., & Pilkonis, P. A. (2007). Narcissistic personality disorder: Relations with distress and functional impairment. *Comprehensive Psychiatry, 48*, 170-177.

Mitchell, S. A. (1986). The wings of Icarus: Illusion and the problem of narcissism. *Contemporary Psychoanalysis, 22*, 107-132.

Morrison, A. P. (1983). Shame, ideal self, and narcissism. *Contemporary Psychoanalysis, 19*, 295-318.

Ogden, T. H. (1986). *The matrix of the mind: Object relations and the psychoanalytic dialogue.* Northvale, NJ: Aronson.

Ogden, T. H. (2010). Why read Fairbairn? *International Journal of Psychoanalysis, 91*, 101-118.

Ogrodniczuk, J. S. (2013). *Understanding and treating pathological narcissism*. Washington, DC: American Psychological Association.

Ogrodniczuk, J. S., Piper, W. E., Joyce, A. S., Steinberg, P. I., & Duggal, S. (2009). Interpersonal problems associated with narcissism among psychiatric outpatients. *Journal of Psychiatric Research, 43*, 837-842.

PDM Task Force. (2006). *Psychodynamic diagnostic manual*. Silver Spring, MD: Alliance of Psychoanalytic Organizations.

Pincus, A. L., & Lukowitsky, M. R. (2010). Pathological narcissism and narcissistic personality disorder. *Annual Review of Clinical Psychology, 6*, 421-446.

Pistole, M. C. (1995). Adult attachment style and narcissistic vulnerability. *Psychoanalytic Psychology, 12*, 115-126.

Pulver, S. E. (1970). Narcissism: The term and the concept. *Journal of the American Psychoanalytic Association, 18*, 319-341.

Ronningstam, E. F. (2011). Narcissistic personality disorder: A clinical perspective. *Journal of Psychiatric Practice, 17*, 89-99.

Ronningstam, E. F., Weinberg, I., & Maltsberger, J. T. (2008). Eleven deaths of Mr. K: Contributing factors to suicide in narcissistic personalities. *Psychiatry, 71*, 169-182.

Segal, H. (1973). *Introduction to the work of Melanie Klein*. London: Hogarth.

Solomon, M. F. (1994). Narcissism and intimacy: Treating the wounded couple. *The Family Journal, 2*, 104-113.

Stinson, F. S., Dawson, D. A., Goldstein, R. B., Chou, S. P., Huang, B., et al. (2008). Prevalence, correlates, disability, and co-morbidity of DSM-IV Narcissistic Personality Disorder: Results from the Wave 2 National Epidemiologic Survey on Alcohol and Related Conditions. *Journal of Clinical Psychiatry, 69*, 1033-1045.

Stolorow, R. (1975). Toward a functional definition of narcissism. *International Journal of Psychoanalysis, 56*, 179-185.

Stone, M. (1998). Normal narcissism: An etiological and ethological perspective. In E. Ronningstam, (Ed.), *Disorders of narcissism: Diagnostic, clinical, and empirical implications*. Washington, DC: American Psychiatric Association.

Sullivan, H. S. (1953). *The interpersonal theory of psychiatry*. New York: Norton.

Winnicott, D. W. (1955). The depressive position in normal emotional development. *British Journal of Medical Psychology, 28*, 89-100.

Wolf, E. S. (1988). *Treating the self: Elements of clinical self psychology*. New York: Guilford.

World Health Organization. (2010). *ICD-10: International statistical classification of diseases and related health problems* (10th rev.). Geneva: World Health Organization.

Schizophrenia

Psychotherapy for Schizophrenia: A Review of Modalities and Their Evidence Base

Michael Brus, Vladan Novakovic, and Ahron Friedberg

Abstract: We reviewed the techniques and evidence base of four psychotherapeutic adjuncts to the pharmacological treatment of schizophrenia: Personal therapy, cognitive behavioral therapy, cognitive enhancement therapy, and psychodynamic psychotherapy. While there is a significant evidence base for the first three of these modalities, there is a paucity of research on psychodynamic treatments for schizophrenia. We review the history of psychodynamic treatment for schizophrenia and the ways in which it informs current treatment. In light of the limited efficacy of antipsychotic medications in the treatment of schizophrenic persons, there is increasing interest in the role of social and psychological approaches.

This article will review the technique and evidence base of four prominent psychotherapeutic adjuncts to the pharmacological treatment of schizophrenia: personal therapy, cognitive behavioral therapy, cognitive enhancement therapy, and psychodynamic psychotherapy. These modalities were chosen either because they have been systematically tested on schizophrenic populations or, in the case of psychodynamic therapy, because it has been a popular treatment historically and continues to inform current therapies. The review was prompted by accumulating evidence that many, if not most, patients with schizophrenia will not achieve remission with medication alone. As the American Psychiatric Association's practice guidelines for schizophrenia state:

> About 10%–30% of patients have little or no response to antipsychotic medications, and up to an additional 30% of patients have partial responses to treatment, meaning that they exhibit

improvement in psychopathology but continue to have mild to severe residual hallucinations or delusions. (Lehman, Lieberman et al., 2004, pp. 39-40)

In the NIMH-sponsored CATIE study of antipsychotic drugs, 74% of study participants discontinued their medication within 18 months, largely due to inefficacy or intolerable side effects (Lieberman et al., 2005).

NON-PSYCHODYNAMIC THERAPIES

Personal therapy (PT) for schizophrenia was developed by Hogarty et al. (1995) at the Western Psychiatric Institute. It was conceived as a multi-year treatment emphasizing psycho-education and behavior therapy. It was also designed to be distinct from traditional analytic therapy and case management. Where traditional analytic therapy for schizophrenia focuses on a historical investigation of the patient's development and its relation to defensive style, PT focuses on the recognition of current affect states. And where traditional case management focuses on environmental manipulation to reduce patient stress, PT focuses on the patient's affective and behavioral responses to stress, independent of their origin.

Patients in PT progress through three phases. Phase one emphasizes pro-social statements, appointment attendance, medication and housing stability, and minimization of hallucinations and delusions. Phase two emphasizes recognizing affective signs of decompensation, performing stress-breathing techniques to attenuate affective arousal, and role-playing social and vocational scenarios to teach conflict resolution. Phase three focuses on cognitive techniques for dealing with criticism, whole-body relaxation exercises, education about the need for long-term medication adherence, and limited social and vocational exposure.

A three-year trial of PT yielded promising but mixed results (Hogarty et al., 1997). Of 151 recently discharged patients with schizophrenia or schizoaffective disorder randomized to either PT or a competing therapy (family psycho-education, supportive therapy, or a combination treatment), PT reduced relapse and increased medication adherence in the subset of patients living with family. But in the subset living independently—who were older and more persistently ill—it increased relapse rates. For both subsets, PT improved work performance and interpersonal relationships more than the competing therapies, but it had few differential effects on symptom control. The social-adjustment benefits of supportive and family therapy peaked at 12 months, but those of PT were still rising after three years. The investigators concluded that PT has the potential to effect long-term gains in social adjustment for patients with stable living situations. However, for patients living independently, the anxiety of navigating new social roles, and the time required by therapists to secure day-to-day

resources for these patients, may limit its efficacy.

Since cognitive behavioral therapy (CBT) was first developed for depression by Aaron Beck in the 1970s, it has been adapted to treat many psychiatric illnesses, including schizophrenia. Early iterations of CBT for schizophrenia focused on behavioral strategies to improve social and independent-living skills, increase medication adherence, and attenuate negative symptoms (Tai & Turkington, 2009).

The positive symptoms of schizophrenia were initially not targeted by cognitive therapists, on the assumption that they were phenomenologically different from ordinary experience and therefore not amenable to the cognitive reframing strategies used to treat nonpsychotic illnesses. However, recent applications of cognitive therapy for psychosis attempt to make delusions and hallucinations amenable to treatment by conceptualizing them as either intrusive thoughts—akin to those occurring in obsessive-compulsive disorder—or as misinterpretations of ordinary experience. This attempt to normalize the perceptions of some schizophrenic patients can help patients avoid negative thought loops that worsen positive symptoms and can help them to reframe disorganized behaviors (such as social withdrawal) as compulsions based on a misinterpretation of environmental threats (Tai & Turkington, 2009).

A meta-analysis of seven controlled studies of cognitive treatment for chronic schizophrenia found a large mean effect size for decrease in psychotic symptoms from pre- to posttreatment (0.65; Gould, Mueser, Bolton, Mays, & Goff, 2001). In the subset of four studies that followed patients for more than six months posttreatment, the mean effect size was even larger (0.93). In this meta-analysis, cognitive treatments were defined as those targeting belief systems rather than information-processing abilities or behavior. The mean number of treatment sessions was 14, but there was no significant association between the number of sessions and outcome.

A trial of 422 community mental-health patients with schizophrenia randomized to either "brief CBT" (three-to-six hour-long sessions with a nurse who received ten days of training) or treatment as usual found significant effects on overall symptomatology, insight, and depression (Turkington, Kingdon, & Turner, 2002). One-year follow up found significant improvements in insight and negative symptoms, but not for overall symptomatology or depression (Turkington et al., 2006). Two-year follow-up found beneficial effects on relapse and rehospitalization but not on occupational recovery (Malik, Kingdon, Pelton, Mehta, & Turkington, 2009). The most recent consensus guidelines of the NIMH-sponsored Schizophrenia Patient Outcomes Research Team (PORT) recommend four to nine months of adjunctive cognitive therapy for schizophrenic patients with "persistent psychotic symptoms while receiving adequate pharmacotherapy" (Kreyenbuhl, Buchanan, Dickerson, & Dixon, 2010, p. 99).

A more recent contribution to the psychotherapy of schizophrenia is Hogarty and Flesher's (1999) cognitive enhancement therapy (CET). CET was developed as a way to help schizophrenic patients achieve the subtle cognitive skills necessary for socialization. Where previous therapies (including PT) focus on role play of stereotyped situations or rote instruction to prepare patients for social engagement, CET tries to promote socially adaptive cognitive qualities like initiative, spontaneity, flexibility, perspective-taking, and context appraisal through structured but unrehearsed activities.

Hogarty et al. (2004) conducted a two-year randomized controlled trial of CET on 132 stable outpatients with schizophrenia, most of whom were in their 30s and in complete or partial remission from positive symptoms. The therapy featured 75 hours of progressive computer exercises in attention, memory, and problem solving, which patients completed in pairs. Four to six months after the start of these exercises, groups of six patients each met for 1.5 hours a week to complete about 50 hours of social cognitive exercises, consisting of appraisal of affect and social contexts, practice initiating and maintaining conversations, play writing, and abstraction of themes from newspapers. The control group received enriched supportive therapy (EST), a variant of PT. At two years of treatment, the effect sizes of CET for measures of neurocognition, processing speed, cognitive style, social cognition, and social adjustment (but not for symptoms) were greater than one standard deviation from pretreatment, and exceeded those of EST by > 0.50.

A later study of 58 patients with early-course schizophrenia (mean illness duration about three years) randomized to CET and EST found differential effects in favor of CET at two years in social cognition, cognitive style, and functional indicators such as competitive employment, social functioning, global adjustment, and negative symptoms (Eack et al., 2009). These effects were broadly maintained at one year post-treatment (Eack, Greenwald, Hogarty, & Keshavan, 2010). Both of these CET studies (of chronic and of early-course patients) also showed beneficial effects of the control treatment, EST, that were not seen in the earlier studies of PT, EST's progenitor. The authors speculated that this anomaly may be due to the different populations studied—stable outpatients in the EST studies versus immediate post-discharge patients in the PT ones.

It should be noted that the generalizability of the studies referenced above is limited. While most of them included patients with schizoaffective disorder as well with schizophrenia, they mostly excluded patients who were abusing substances or not adherent to antipsychotic medication. Despite these limitations, PT, cognitive therapy for schizophrenia, and CET all show promise as psychotherapeutic adjuncts to established schizophrenia treatments like neuroleptics and case management.

PSYCHODYNAMIC
PSYCHOTHERAPY

Among the evidence-based psychotherapies for psychosis, is there a place for psychodynamic psychotherapy? The first PORT guidelines for schizophrenia treatment, in 1998, recommended against "psychotherapies adhering to a psychodynamic model." The authors admitted that "the scientific data on this issue are quite limited," but argued that "there is a consensus that psychotherapy that promotes regression and psychotic transference can be harmful to persons with schizophrenia" (Lehman, Steinwachs, & the Co-Investigators of the PORT Project, 1998, pp. 7-8). Starting in 2003, PORT guidelines dropped all recommendations against specific treatments, including the one discouraging psychodynamic therapy (Lehman, Kreyenbuhl, et al., 2004).

There is a long history of case reports documenting the dramatic recoveries of schizophrenic patients who underwent intensive psychoanalytic treatment. Analysts such as C. J. Jung (1909), Harry Stack Sullivan (1962), and Bertram P. Karon (1981) wrote about psychodynamic remedies for psychosis. Most prominently, *I Never Promised You a Rose Garden*, the semiautobiographical recovery novel of one of Frieda Fromm-Reichmann's schizophrenic patients, became a bestseller on its publication in 1964 (Greenberg, 1964). Most of these psychoanalytic histories are anecdotal and hail from the pre-*DSM-III* era, when the diagnosis of schizophrenia was highly unreliable (Kendell et al., 1971). There is, indeed, a dearth of high-quality, modern research on the efficacy of psychodynamics in schizophrenia.

However, recently some authors have attempted to bring psychodynamic principles back into a mainstream conversation that is often dominated by abstract models of cognitive remediation and symptom quantification. In his 2009 article on psychodynamic approaches to psychosis, Eric R. Marcus noted that

talking to the psychotic patient is important since there is no other way to understand that person's psychotic experience, and it is the emotional story that informs and reinforces the psychotic process. Working in conjunction with [other modalities], individual psychodynamic psychotherapy can serve to strengthen such dysfunctional aspects of the ego as boundary dissolution, reality testing, and the synthesizing functions that organize the patient's relationship to the world around him. (p. 148)

An exploration of future psychotherapy research directions in *Schizophrenia Bulletin* linked resurgent interest in patient-centered psychosis treatment—such as that found in the recovery movement—to the influence of psychodynamics. "Psychotherapy is not only about resolution of specific problems or impairments," the authors wrote. "People have always engaged in therapy for broader purposes, including 'becoming a better person,' 'understanding myself better,' and 'appreciating life more.' . . . Today we are rediscovering the importance and centrality of the 'person' in [schizophrenia], and this rediscovery will influence research on treatment, rehabilitation, and recovery in the foreseeable future" (Spaulding & Nolting, 2006, p. S102).

CONCLUSION

Prior to the pharmacological revolution, psychoanalysts had been consistently interested in working psychotherapeutically with psychotic patients. Partly as a result of mainstream psychoanalysis's focus on well-organized neurotic patients who could be treated in private office settings, and partly as a result of the pharmacological revolution and the movement toward descriptive psychiatry, psychoanalytically oriented discussions of psychosis treatment diminished. There was a short-lived wave of excessively optimistic hope among mental-health professionals that drugs would be found that would cure schizophrenia. Unfortunately that has not occurred. Despite their positive effects in a significant number of patients, antipsychotic medications leave many symptoms untreated and have serious side effects including tardive dyskinesia, extra-pyramidal symptoms, and metabolic dysfunction (Correll, Leucht, & Kane, 2004; Lieberman et al., 2005; Miller et al., 2008). Therefore, the mental health community is starting to turn its attention to two major areas in addition to pharmacotherapy: social interventions and psychotherapy. The modern understanding and treatment of schizophrenic patients, therefore, tends to be better informed by a biopsychosocial model rather than simply a medical-pharmacological paradigm.

REFERENCES

Correll, C. U., Leucht, S., & Kane, J. M. (2004). Lower risk for tardive dyskinesia associated with second-generation antipsychotics: A systematic review of 1-year studies. *American Journal of Psychiatry, 161,* 414-425.

Eack, S. M., Greenwald, D. P., Hogarty, S. S., Cooley, S. J., DiBarry, A. L., Montrose, D. M., & Keshavan, M. S. (2009). Cognitive enhancement therapy for early-course schizophrenia: Effects of a two-year randomized controlled trial. *Psychiatric Services, 60,* 1468-1476.

Eack, S. M., Greenwald, D. P., Hogarty, S. S., & Keshavan, M. S. (2010). One year durability of the effects of cognitive enhancement therapy on functional outcome in early schizophrenia. *Schizophrenia Research, 120,* 210-216.

Gould, R. A., Mueser, K. T., Bolton, E., Mays, V., & Goff, D. (2001). Cognitive therapy for psychosis in schizophrenia: An effect size analysis. *Schizophrenia Research, 48,* 335-342.

Greenberg, J. (1964). *I never promised you a rose garden.* New York: Henry Holt and Company.

Hogarty, G. E., & Flesher, S. (1999). Practice principles for cognitive enhancement therapy for schizophrenia. *Schizophrenia Bulletin, 25,* 693-708.

Hogarty, G. E., Flesher, S., Ulrich, R., Carter, M., Greenwald, D., Pogue-Geile, M., et al. (2004). Cognitive enhancement for schizophrenia: Effects of a two-tear randomized trial on cognition and behavior. *Archives of General Psychiatry, 61,* 866-876.

Hogarty, G. E., Greenwald, D., Ulrich, R. F., Kornblith, S. J., DiBarry, A. L., Cooley, S., et al. (1997). Three-year trials of personal therapy among schizophrenic patients living with or independent of family, II: Affects on adjustment of patients. *American Journal of Psychiatry, 154,* 1514-1524.

Hogarty, G. E., Kornblith, S. J., Greenwald, D., DiBarry, A. L., Cooley, S., Flesher, S., et al. (1995). Personal therapy: A disorder-relevant psychotherapy for schizophrenia. *Schizophrenia Bulletin, 21,* 379-393.

Hogarty, G. E., Kornblith, S. J., Greenwald, D., DiBarry, A. L., Cooley, S., Ulrich, R. F., et al. (1997). Three-year trials of personal therapy among schizophrenic patients living with or independent of family, I: Description of study and effects on relapse rates. *American Journal of Psychiatry, 154,* 1504-1513.

Jung, C. G. (1909). *The psychology of dementia praecox.* Toronto: University of Toronto Libraries.

Karon, B. P. (1981). *Psychotherapy of schizophrenia: The treatment of choice.* New York: Jason Aronson.

Kendell, R. E., Cooper, J. E., Gourlay, A. J., Copeland, J. R., Sharpe, L., & Gurland, B. J. (1971). Diagnostic criteria of American and British psychiatrists. *Archives of General Psychiatry, 25,* 123-130.

Kreyenbuhl, J., Buchanan, R. W., Dickerson, F. B., & Dixon, L. B. (2010). The schizophrenia patient outcomes research team: Updated treatment recommendations 2009. *Schizophrenia Bulletin, 36,* 94-103.

Lehman, A. F., Kreyenbuhl, J., Buchanan, R. W., Dickerson, F. B., Dixon, L. B., Goldberg, R., et al. (2004). The schizophrenia patient outcomes research team: Updated treatment recommendations 2003. *Schizophrenia Bulletin, 30,* 193-217.

Lehman, A. F., Lieberman, J. A., Dixon, L. B., McGlashan, T. H., Miller, A. L., Perkins, D. O., Kreyenbuhl, J., American Psychiatric Association, & Steering Committee on Practice Guidelines. (2004). Practice guideline for the treatment of patients with schizophrenia, second edition. *American Journal of Psychiatry, 161*(2 Suppl), 1-56.

Lehman, A. F., Steinwachs, D. M., & the Co-Investigators of the PORT Project. (1998). At issue: Translating research into practice: The schizophrenia patient outcomes research team treatment recommendations. *Schizophrenia Bulletin, 24,* 1-10.

Lieberman, J. A., Stroup, T. S., McEvoy, J. P., Swartz, M. S., Rosenheck, R. A., Perkins, D. O., et al. & Clinical Antipsychotic Trials of Intervention Effectiveness (CATIE) Investigators. (2005).

Effectiveness of antipsychotic drugs in patients with chronic schizophrenia. *New England Journal of Medicine, 353,* 1209-1223.

Malik, N., Kingdon, D., Pelton, J., Mehta, R., & Turkington, D. (2009). Effectiveness of brief cognitive-behavioral therapy for schizophrenia delivered by mental health nurses: Relapse and recovery at 24 months. *Journal of Clinical Psychiatry, 70,* 201-207.

Marcus, E. R. (2009). Psychodynamics of psychosis. In J. M. Barnhill (Ed.), *Approach to the psychiatric patient: Case-based essays* (pp. 146-148). Washington, DC: American Psychiatric Publishing.

Miller, D. D., Caroff, S. N., Davis, S. M., Rosenheck, R. A., McEvoy, J. P., Saltz, B. L., et al., & Clinical Antipsychotic Trials of Intervention Effectiveness (CATIE) Investigators. (2008). Extrapyramidal side effects of antipsychotics in a randomized controlled trial. *British Journal of Psychiatry, 193,* 279-288.

Spaulding, W., & Nolting, J. (2006). Psychotherapy for schizophrenia in the year 2030: Prognosis and prognostications. *Schizophrenia Bulletin, 32,* S94-S105.

Sullivan, H. S. (1962). *Schizophrenia as a human process.* New York: W.W. Norton.

Tai, S., & Turkington, D. (2009). The evolution of CBT for schizophrenia: Current practice and recent developments. *Schizophrenia Bulletin, 35,* 865-873.

Turkington, D., Kingdon, D., Rathod, S., Hammond, K., Pelton, J., & Mehta, R. (2006). Outcomes of an effectiveness trial for cognitive-behavioral intervention by mental health nurses in schizophrenia. *British Journal of Psychiatry, 189,* 36-40.

Turkington, D., Kingdon, D., & Turner, T. (2002). Effectiveness of brief cognitive-behavioral therapy intervention in the treatment of schizophrenia. *British Journal of Psychiatry, 180,* 523-527.

Somatic Symptom Disorders

A Psychodynamic Perspective on Treatment of Patients with Conversion and Other Somatoform Disorders

Marcia J. Kaplan

Abstract: Conversion disorder, the development of symptoms of neurological disease with no organic basis, is a challenge for mental health professionals to diagnose and treat effectively. There are well-established predisposing factors, such as female sex, childhood trauma, and alexithymia, but less clear is how to approach the subjective suffering that is symbolized with the symptom rather than consciously recognized. While there are overlapping comorbidities such as depression and anxiety that may be treated with medication, psychotherapy is the primary effective treatment for patients with adequate capacity to engage in the process. This article addresses means of identifying patients who might benefit from psychotherapy (along with medication in some instances) as well as some guidelines for conducting psychotherapy, with case examples.

Conversion disorder, or medically unexplained neurological symptoms, includes non-anatomically distributed sensory or motor abnormalities, seizures without corresponding EEG change, intractable headache, balance and movement disorders, blindness, deafness, aphonia, aphasia, memory loss, or other neurological disorders without evidence of organic cause. The phenomenon has been known throughout recorded human history. Somatization disorder is a related but distinct category of somatoform illness, with a wide variety of symptoms spanning many organ systems, often including pain and autonomic function. Both are defined in *DSM-5* (American Psychiatric Association, 2013) as "somatic symptom disorders" characterized by duration of symptoms and the impact of preoccupation with symptoms and suffering on the individual's life. While conversion disorder can be readily differentiated from somatization disorder, they share predisposing factors, clinical presentation, and aspects of treatment strategy.

HISTORICAL CONSIDERATIONS

The term "conversio" was used in the Middle Ages to refer to diseases attributed to suffocation of the womb (Jacquart & Thomasset, 1988) and Ferriar (1795) described conversion of diseases in reference to the development of non-organic symptoms that were "commonly void of danger." Conversion disorder in modern usage refers to Sigmund Freud's theory that unexplained neurological symptoms were derived from drive energy that could not be discharged by connection to a mental representation; instead, the energy was converted into a physical symptom that stood for an unconscious conflict, initially, specifically resulting from sexual seduction of the child by an adult. (Freud later abandoned the seduction theory as he recognized that fantasies of seduction could be as powerful as actual seduction.) Until late in the 19th century, hysteria referred to behavioral symptoms resulting from disease of the female reproductive system. (For a thorough historical review, see Mace, 1992.) Briquet was an early advocate of hysteria as a neurological disease, which was accepted by Charcot despite lack of evidence via the clinic-anatomical method of correlating symptoms in life with autopsy findings of corresponding lesions (Mai & Merskey, 1980). Charcot suggested a functional lesion, and his student Freud (1893) famously commented that "hysteria behaves as though anatomy did not exist." The *DSM* has progressively removed almost all vestige of traditional psychoanalytic language from the description of these disorders. In the *DSM-5*, conversion disorder is named functional neurological symptom disorder, though "conversion" is still mentioned alongside the new name. Somatization disorder, also known as Briquet's syndrome, has become somatic symptom disorder, and hypochondriasis is now called illness anxiety disorder. The idea of primary and secondary gain has been eliminated but there remains indirect acknowledgement of the unconscious nature of these disorders since malingering, a conscious creation of symptoms expressly for external reward, is not mentioned.

In distinction to conversion hysteria which was classified by Freud as a psychoneurosis, or a symptom related to unconscious conflicts regarding childhood sexual experience, somatization (similar to Freud's descriptions of neurasthenia and anxiety neurosis) was identified as *actual* neurosis, or symptoms from unprocessed anxiety caused by current day sexual experience (neurasthenia from excessive masturbation and anxiety neurosis from lack of orgasm), unrelated to unconscious conflict and without defensive significance (Freud, 1895). The presence or absence of underlying mental structure differentiates these conditions. Somatization occurs in individuals without adequate internal structure and representational capacity to allow for symbolization and connection of a physical symptom with an unconscious conflict. Freud pointed out that without this capacity, psychoanalysis is ineffective. These patients may have neurological symptoms as do those with conversion disorder, but always along with a wide array of symptoms affecting other organ systems. In general, somatization is considered resistant to benefit from psychoanalytic psychotherapy, though patients may benefit from supportive and cognitive behavioral approaches (Dinwiddie, 2013; Kent, Tomasson, & Coryell, 1995; Verhaeghe, Vanheule, & De Rick, 2007). In contrast, Dora's psychosomatic reaction to Herr K's efforts at seduction, leading to her attacks of gait instability and appendicitis symbolizing labor pains (i.e., conversion) served as a foundational example of the unconscious conflict that could be addressed with the talking cure.

EPIDEMIOLOGY AND PREDISPOSING FACTORS

Conversion disorder can develop across the lifespan but typically develops in young to middle adulthood (Feinstein, 2011; Tomasson & Kent, 1991). The occurrence of conversion symptoms in children is rare before the age of 10, but the majority of symptoms remit, and symptoms are often similar to those of an important adult in the child's life (Ani, Reading, Lynn, Forlee, & Garralda, 2013; Lehmkuhl, Blanz, Lehmkuhl, & Braun-Scharm, 1989; Reilly, Menlove, Fenton, & Das, 2013). Conversion disorder is strongly correlated with female sex, with prevalence estimates from 70% to 95%, and somatization disorder nearly always develops in young adult women (Brown & Lewis-Fernandez, 2011; Sar, Akyüz, Dogan, & Öztü, 2009). The lifetime prevalence in general populations has been reported from 0.3% to 48.7%, though high rates are based on questionnaire results rather than clinical assessment; conservative estimates for prevalence in the general population are 0.1% to 0.7% (Woolfolk & Allen, 2010). The rate in clinical populations is reported from 3.3% to 6.3%, while the rate in neurology clinics is reported from 14% to 33%, with rates as high as 40% in epilepsy monitoring units (Carson et al., 2000; Chand et al., 2000; Fink, Sorenson, Engberg, Holm, & Munk-Jorgensen, 1999; Snijders, de Leeuw, Klumpers, Kappelle, & van Gijn, 2004; Stone, Carson, Duncan, Roberts et al., 2009; Szaflarski, Ficker, Cahill, & Privitera, 2000). Eventual discovery of an organic cause of symptoms is generally very low (Mace & Trimble, 1996; Stone, Carson, Duncan, Coleman, & Roberts, 2009).

Childhood trauma is among the most robust predictors of conversion disorder (Arnold & Privitera, 2006; Fiszman, Alves-Leon, Nunes, D'Andrea, & Figueira, 2004; Kaplan et al., 2013; Lehmkuhl et al., 1989; Roelofs, Keijsers, Hoogduin, Naring, & Moene, 2002; Roelofs, Spinhoven, Sandijck, Moene, & Hoogduin, 2005; Sar, Akyuz, Kundakci, Kziltan, & Dogan, 2004). Childhood trauma is also strongly correlated with somatization disorder and dissociative disorders; a full investigation of the overlap of these disorders with conversion disorder is beyond the scope of this article but Roelofs and Spinhoven (2007) provide a thorough review. Janet believed that hereditary weakness predisposed traumatized individuals to enter a hypnoid state in which consciousness became strangulated and segregated, or dissociated, from ordinary consciousness; physical symptoms arise from the dissociated or strangulated memories unavailable to conscious processing (van der Kolk & van der Hart, 1989). The experience of current life stressors resonating with early childhood trauma is a well-documented foundation for the development of conversion disorder at a specific time in an individual's life (Aybek et al., 2014). As will be discussed below, developing a narrative about one's own life history with the symptoms seen in that context

is a useful psychotherapeutic strategy in conversion disorder, but much less so in somatization disorder.

It is difficult to identify the prevalence of conversion disorder among military veterans. Following World War II, Grinker and Spiegel (1945) reported five categories of stress reactions which included conversion states and psychosomatic reactions, but there is little published specifically regarding conversion disorder in combat veterans of wars since then, including Vietnam, the Gulf War, and Iraq/Afghanistan (of note is Lindy's *Vietnam: A Casebook*, 1987, which includes a case in which a Vietnam veteran experienced crushing pain in his chest that corresponded to the story of killing a child). Several authors have reported the correlation of combat trauma with posttraumatic stress disorder (PTSD), dissociation, and somatization (Marmar et al., 1994; van der Kolk et al., 1996; Yehuda, Southwick, & Giller, 1992), but studies have utilized self-report measures of dissociation and somatization, for example, the Dissociative Experiences Scale (DES; Bernstein & Putnam, 1986), or subsets of the MMPI-2-RF (Ben-Porath & Tellegen, 2008), that would not identify conversion disorder or differentiate it from other psychosomatic concerns. The presence of interpersonal trauma in early life predicts more severe symptoms of PTSD from combat trauma (Marmar et al., 1994). Similarly, Yehuda et al. (1992) report greater severity and morbidity from PTSD in soldiers exposed to brutal human death compared to those exposed to the threat of death from combat. Recent reviews of the psychological aftermath of the wars in Vietnam and the Middle East focus on PTSD, traumatic brain injury, substance abuse, and mood disorders; somatization is typically related to PTSD (Escalona, Achilles, Waitzkin, & Yager, 2004). Apparently, complaints about psychosomatic symptoms judged to be conversion are rare enough in current-day studies of veterans' mental disorders that the phenomenon is not considered in large scale reports (Taneilian & Jaycox, 2008).

MODERN THEORIES ABOUT CONVERSION ETIOLOGY

Later theorists on psychosomatic illness include the French school led by de M'Uzan and Marty (de M'Uzan, 1974; Marty & de M'Uzan, 1963) with their identification of a disorder of thought and language they called la pensee operatoire; patients suffered from a lack of fantasy, concreteness, and emotional deadness. Bucci (1997) and McDougall (1989) both postulate the requirement of language in the development of mental rather than physical symptoms. Sifneos (1996) coined the term alexithymia to describe patients without a capacity to identify or describe their feeling states. Taylor and Bagby (2013) developed further measures of alexithymia and created the most widely used self-report scale, the Toronto Alexithymia Scale (TAS). Meares et al. (2008) suggest stimulus entrapment, or the attention paid to a physical symptom, as the result of an unconscious fear of a much worse mental state of emptiness if the symptom is not available, especially in individuals with borderline personality disorder. Friston and colleagues (Edwards, Adams, Brown, Parees, & Friston, 2012) have developed a model for functional motor and sensory symptoms in line with computational models of a brain that is self-organizing and energy conserving. Patients' "top-down" attention to the idea of illness overwhelms "bottom-up" evidence from the internal body, leading to a symptom that feels involuntary.

FUNCTIONAL IMAGING STUDIES

The lack of CNS motor/sensory cortical or peripheral lesions identifiable through electrophysiological tests or CNS imaging is the most basic finding in conversion disorder, so researchers must attempt to locate defects in self-awareness or attention and in the processing of internal/external perception and intention. Non-invasive functional imaging such as fMRI, magnetoencephalography (MEG), single photon emission CT (SPECT), and positron emission tomography (PET) identify patterns of brain activity that might be correlated with maintenance of symptoms. Patients with specific conversion symptoms such as blindness, aphonia, sensory loss, or paralysis can be compared to healthy controls; resting and experimental states can also be compared within subjects. Studies that compared brain activity during efforts to move a paralyzed limb in conversion patients or to imagine movement of a hypnotically paralyzed limb in a healthy control subject show similar patterns of prefrontal cortical inhibition of motor and sensory cortex. The results are also consistent with a problem of attention, with disconnection between awareness, perception, and intention/volition. Several authors (Black, Seritan, Taber, & Hurley, 2004; Bryant & Das, 2012; De Lange, Roelofs, & Toni, 2008) have reviewed the possible conclusions from imaging experiments in the past decade.

TREATMENT CONSIDERATIONS

With sophisticated diagnostic technologies, it becomes easy to "prove" that a symptom is not organic, but this does not benefit the patient suffering with a medically unresolvable problem. Most patients with conversion symptoms resist recognition that problems originate in the psychic realm, much less accept referral for psychological treatments, and need to maintain the physical symptom along with the primary and secondary gains that accrue (Carson et al., 2000). Those patients able to consider the possibility that symptoms have to do with psychic conflict may improve and even have complete remission of conversion symptoms with psychotherapy, but at the risk of awareness of affective distress as the underlying conflicts become conscious. Patients with somatization typically have less capacity for symbolic thought, may be less inclined to enter psychotherapy and are less likely to have meaningful improvement; if one symptom improves in the course of psychotherapy, another worsens. Patients with psychosomatic symptoms of any type generally benefit subjectively from a sympathetic listener even if there is no change in perception of symptoms.

Just as there is a vast array of psychic characteristics of individuals with conversion and somatization symptoms, there are many approaches to treatment and many ways of measuring the outcome of treatment. Goals of treatment may include improvement in number and severity of psychosomatic symptoms, remission of psychosomatic symptoms, improved functioning in activities of daily life, better emotional coping skills, improvement in subjective quality of life, establishment of social support, improvement in comorbid symptoms of anxiety and/or depression, and reduced utilization of medical services. Psychodynamic approaches to conversion symptoms aim, in addition, for development of reflective function, construction of a narrative about oneself, development of greater awareness of underlying psychic conflicts, and capacity for self-analysis (Luyten & Van Houdenhove, 2013). Given that many patients with conversion symptoms have histories of significant trauma, efforts at construction of a narrative that includes recognition of childhood traumata should avoid exposing the patient to excessive regression and decompensation, which may occur with frequent sessions and development of intense negative transferences. Cognitive behavioral therapies do not expose patients to these risks and have been found to reduce the number of complaints and the severity of symptoms in patients with somatization (Allen, Woolfolk, Escobar, Gara, & Hamer, 2006; Sumathipala, Hewege, Hanwella, & Mann, 2000).

Studies have documented benefits from short-term cognitive and both short-term and long-term psychodynamic treatments (Abbass, Kisely, & Kroenke, 2009; Sattell et al., 2012). Short-term therapies are often helpful and effective for patients who are reluctant to engage in open-ended psychotherapy. Furthermore, for patients with limited health insurance benefits and no means to pay private fees, cost is a major source of resistance to staying with treatment. Patients able to maintain longer term treatment were found to improve more in terms of general functioning than those in short-term treatment in a recent meta-analysis (Koelen et al., 2014), which also found that cognitive and behavioral therapies and therapies focused on the body were not as effective in terms of general functioning compared to psychodynamic psychotherapy. Importantly, improvement in general functioning is not equivalent to improvement in specific symptoms, which did not typically remit with psychodynamic psychotherapy.

Choosing the approach to treatment is a complex decision that includes the therapist's tolerance for psychosomatic symptoms and assessment of the patient's capacity and willingness to engage in treatment. Mental health professionals are often exasperated by patients who don't show interest in their own psychic life, and many non-medical therapists fear they do not have the expertise to rule out organic illnesses, especially when symptoms worsen or new ones arise. Cognitive behavioral treatment may be manualized and time-limited, providing guidelines for therapists that may be welcome with this challenging group of patients. There are risks with psychodynamic psychotherapy, for example, regression and decompensation with overt discussion about childhood trauma, fear that talking about problems may threaten important dependency relationships, or efforts to please the therapist by losing a symptom that is then replaced by another. Severely traumatized somatizing patients may disclose multiple personalities in the course of treatment (Herman, 1997). Patients with addictions to narcotics and/or tranquilizers may have significant reluctance to improve if it means giving up depended-upon drugs.

When a patient comes for consultation, the therapist should offer reassurance that while there is no ready organic explanation for their symptoms, what the patient experiences is quite real and understandably distressing. Furthermore, it is important to make clear that removal of the symptom is not the goal of treatment; the goal is helping the patient understand and cope with the impact of the illness on important relationships and initiatives, which might lead to less suffering. The psychotherapist should identify complications like extensive dissociative spells, multiple personalities, drug dependence, etc., in order to determine whether working with the patient is feasible. There should be no reluctance to refer patients with symptoms that are overwhelming to the therapist, and obtaining consultation about the patient from a more experienced colleague can be very helpful.

Psychiatrists may be more favorably perceived that non-medical therapists in that they may prescribe medications for comorbid problems with mood and anxiety, which are common; *la belle indifference* may exist with respect to the meaning of somatic symptoms, but most patients are well aware of psychic distress, and welcome interventions that keep alive hope for a medical cause. Conversion symptoms do not respond directly to psychotropic medication, though anxiety and depression may be effectively treated, enabling patients to tolerate psychotherapy better. When symptoms do remit, it is the result of developing a narrative about oneself in the context of a relationship that alters the psychic economy in such a way that the symptoms are no longer necessary (Luyten, Van Houdenhove, Lemma, Target, & Fonagy, 2012).

Psychoanalysts are ideally prepared to work with conversion patients, since they are familiar with concepts such as attachment and mentalization, internal object representations, and psychic structure underlying symptoms and behavior (Luyten et al., 2012). Furthermore, psychoanalytically trained therapists are usually capable of tolerating the preoccupation with symptoms without feeling frustrated or angry with the patient.

Less experienced psychotherapists (as well as some neurologists and medical specialists) may feel unsure whether the symptoms have an organic basis, creating doubt in their own and the patient's mind whether psychotherapy has any relevance. As long as the patient has reassurance that an organic explanation can be found by the right expert, progress in psychotherapy is unlikely. But if symptoms can be granted existence whatever the cause, and if symptom removal is not the major focus of treatment, these patients have much to gain in psychotherapy. Attempts to avoid talking about the symptom, as in hoping it will go away with neglect, are doomed to failure. Maintaining interest in the patient's internal and external life should include talking about the symptom to the extent that the patient wants to focus on it.

Individuals with pain syndromes already prescribed high doses of narcotics are generally not treatable with psychotherapy. Narcotic-dependent patients usually have underlying problems with attachment, and may have few if any positive internal objects or identifications to build on. They often refuse permission for mental health professionals to contact the prescribing physician. Otherwise capable and ethical prescribing physicians may be unaware of that ongoing narcotic prescribing to a patient with non-cancer pain means involvement in a transference/countertransference enactment with the patient, and will not or cannot stop what they know to be inappropriate treatment. Supportive psychotherapy is reasonable, along with education about the effects of chronic narcotic use on mood and motivation that are often presenting problems.

Patients with conversion symptoms that do not involve pain, on the other hand, are typically eager for the mental health professional to discuss their problems with other treating physicians. Frequently conversion patients elicit contempt or avoidance by medical caretakers when their symptoms turn out to be without organic basis. On the other hand, they may elicit overinvolved efforts to care for patients that include prescribing unnecessary medications, including tranquilizers and narcotics. Often several medical specialists involved in treating the patient do not confer with one another, and the mental health professional (particularly the psychiatrist who speaks "medical" language) may provide important integration of the patient's diagnosis and treatment plan, as well as providing education and emotional support for other physicians coping with conversion patients.

There is a typical pattern to successful psychodynamic psychotherapy with patients with conversion symptoms. First, it is typical for patients to have experienced a proximal crisis or traumatic experience that resonates with unconscious childhood traumatic memories, the symptom appears since there is no other way to think about the disturbance. Patients may not fully recognize the impact of the old experience that the therapist understands to be the current crisis (i.e., la belle indifference) but it can be identified and tied to past history over time. Therapist expression of warm interest in the patient without either excessive attention to or avoidance of the symptom is critical to building an alliance. Clear direction that the therapist is interested in an investigative process of getting to know the patient, including childhood, important relationships, career or avocation, dreams, fantasies, etc., as well as psychic and physical symptoms, starts a process of constructing a narrative about the self.

Almost inevitably, after a honeymoon period of meeting without overt focus on symptoms or interference by the symptom, the patient sets up an unconscious test for the psychotherapist by having a serious setback of symptom worsening. This may involve after-hours phone calls from the patient or patient's family or from emergency room doctors. It is critical for the psychotherapist to maintain a steady curiosity about what might have happened to make the symptoms worse and to stick with the investigative attitude. Often this leads to productive discussion about how the symptom is experienced

or why it occurred when it did. Often, the beginning organization in the patient's mind of how he or she understands and feels about relationships with important people can be connected to the symptom. Primary gain through the symptom can be shifted to primary gain through feeling understood by the therapist and eventually, in relationships outside the consulting room.

Conversion patients sometimes achieve remission of symptoms via psychotherapy, but not without new psychic awareness of the very warded-off conflicts that now cause distress. Some patients develop overt depression as they gain awareness of conflicts and suffering that was formerly evaded by having the symptom. This sort of depression is possible to address with psychotherapy and/or medication, and is essentially evidence that the physical has been converted back to the psychic. Like any psychotherapy, there is a working-through period that takes time but that creates confidence as the patient sets up new ways of coping with painful feelings. Again, like any other form of psychotherapy, when the symptom has remitted and the patient has fashioned a new psychic equilibrium, some patients will terminate treatment without apparent sorrow at losing the therapist. Others will want to maintain a relationship in order to practice life without the symptom and share progress with the therapist. It is best to allow the patient to dictate the terms, which is an advantage of longer-term psychotherapy over briefer time-limited psychotherapy.

It is possible to identify general positive prognostic factors that help the psychotherapist make appropriate recommendations to the patient. Adequate maternal attachment, and some positive internalized objects and identifications are hopeful factors. Given the prevalence of childhood trauma, traumatic experiences that do not directly involve perpetration by the maternal caretaker are more workable in psychotherapy. Patients with some successes in relationships and/or career have advantages over those with severe lifelong inhibitions. Conversion symptoms that "tell a story" predict some capacity for symbolization that can be built on in psychotherapy. The recent onset of symptoms relative to consultation for psychotherapy, without the unconscious goal of becoming disabled, is a positive sign, and on the other hand, those with disability income or attempting to become disabled may be difficult to treat. Those patients without serious substance abuse or dependence are also more likely to have some ego strengths that can be built on.

General negative prognostic factors contrast to the good ones, and include those with significant maternal attachment problems, and few positive internal object representations or identifications. Serious childhood trauma that involves the maternal caretaker, including her refusal to acknowledge and stop abuse or help the patient with recovery, is obviously destructive to psychic development. This may be correlated with the patient's lack of success in relationships or career endeavors, as well as with serious substance dependence. A pattern of somatization with a long list of symptoms that do not tell a coherent story is evidence of the fragility of psychic structure that can be built on with the investigative and narrative-creating process. Finally, longstanding symptoms at the outset of psychotherapy referral, existing disability benefits, or an obvious goal of being declared disabled to get benefits, all point to poorer outcome.

These principles will be illustrated by case material from work with two patients, one male and one female, with conversion disorder who were cured of the conversion symptom. Both are patients for whom the primary diagnosis was conversion disorder at the time of presentation, though the first had depression in childhood; details about both individuals have been disguised to the extent that they should not be recognizable.

CASE EXAMPLES*

Mr. A

Mr. A, a man with childhood sexual abuse who was cured of psychogenic seizures, illustrates a group of individuals with significant childhood trauma never talked about out of fear and shame, but with good prognostic chances of recovery, given recent onset, young age, secure maternal attachment, some positive internal object representations and identifications, adequate functioning in relationship and occupational realms such that primary gain from being ill is not required for living a coherent life, lack of substance abuse or dependence, and lack of significant secondary gain from the symptoms.

Mr. A was 28 years old and dressed in grimy work clothes when he came for his first visit with me. He was a high school graduate who worked for a construction company. His wife, who worked as a secretary for a large corporation, wanted children and had started pressing about trying to conceive, but he did not feel ready. Mr. A had been sent to see me by the neurologist who explained to him that the spells he was having were caused by stress and maybe I could help him since the anti-epileptic medications probably wouldn't. Though clearly a friendly and guileless man, Mr. A was anxious about talking to me. He relaxed and grinned once I made it clear that I was interested in hearing about and trying to understand his problems. I was aware of slowing down my speech and choosing simple words in order to make him comfortable. I did not want to seem remote or haughty.

I asked him to tell me about himself. It didn't take long to summarize his work life, since he had held the same job since he graduated from high school, working on construction sites, which he generally enjoyed. He got along well enough with the other guys, but didn't really socialize much. He didn't like

---

*Identifying characteristics have been changed to protect patient privacy.

to drink alcohol and had never wanted to use drugs that might cause him to feel out of control. He'd married his high school sweetheart, and the two of them were very happy together. He enjoyed playing basketball with a local recreational team, and loved working on renovating the house he and his wife had been able to buy not long ago. His parents were alive and well, and he had two older brothers who worked on the family farm.

Mr. A grew up on the farm where his father's brothers also lived and worked. He and his brothers and male cousins played together after school on the farm. Mr. A liked school but did poorly in high school despite knowing he could have made good grades if he'd tried. In our first session, Mr. A denied overt trauma in childhood, though he did say that he felt his father had always been harder on him, expecting better grades and higher achievement than was expected of his brothers, who even now were always getting handouts. He remembered being depressed as a kid and reported that his mother had taken him to see a psychiatrist who didn't help much. He described the spells that involved shaking and passing out that had begun about two years prior to our meeting, and that had eventually been identified as psychogenic seizures in the epilepsy monitoring unit. He was worried about having another spell and had trouble sleeping, but was not overtly depressed. I suggested he take 25 mg of quetiapine to help him feel sleepy without causing him to get addicted to sleeping pills. He readily accepted medication, and reported that it worked well.

After our second session, Mr. A's mother called, at his request, to tell me more about his history. His mother had worked full time as a secretary when the kids were all in school, and left Mr. A and his brothers with their grandmother in the afternoons. Mr. A had been a normal, happy child until he developed encopresis around age seven. At eight years old, Mr. A attempted suicide for the first time, and was taken to a psychiatrist who was unable to identify a cause. After his third suicide attempt, Mr. A was hospitalized in a psychiatric unit where he admitted to being bullied by older boys at school because of the encopresis; he was known as "Stinky" by his classmates and could not control the soiling caused by leakage around the fecal mass he held in. His mother did not know what else might have happened to cause the trouble, but she knew that even after he stopped attempting suicide and withholding bowel movements, he was withdrawn and unhappy for the remainder of junior high and high school.

In the following session, I told Mr. A about my discussion with his mother and wondered if he remembered more that he might not have wanted to tell her. At that point, Mr. A tearfully told me about playing with his brothers and cousins in the barn when an older cousin grabbed Mr. A when the others left. The cousin took him up to the loft where he began subjecting Mr. A to anal penetration that went on for months, accompanied by threats of death if he told anyone. The cousin stopped seeking him out, most likely due to fear of discovery after Mr. A's suicide attempts. Mr. A had never told anyone about this, and stayed away from the cousin as much as he could. Mr. A got away from his family after high school rather than working on the farm like his brothers.

Shortly after this visit, Mr. A had a generalized tonic-clonic seizure while sitting in church. We talked about how embarrassing it was to have these spells in front of people and what might have been happening in his mind prior to having the spell. I wondered aloud if having had to hold all this pain and anger inside all these years, and having no way to ever express the bad feelings meant it could only come out this way, through the seizures. He agreed with me; he would have liked to have been able to tell someone about what his cousin did, and have someone do something about it, but felt sure he would be blamed or accused of lying by the grown-ups and subject to retaliation by the perpetrator. He knew that the cousin's father was the eldest of the three brothers and the one with the most authority in the family. Soon after we discussed this trauma, Mr. A told his parents what had happened, and they were appropriately supportive and sorry that they hadn't known and so couldn't have intervened. Mr. A felt relieved and heartened as his father seemed less critical and friendlier toward him.

I talked with Mr. A about his wife's interest in getting pregnant. He didn't have inhibitions about having intercourse with her, and they had been using condoms for years to prevent pregnancy. He enjoyed being married, but worried about how complicated life could become if there was a baby to care for. How would his wife continue to work and how could he manage the mortgage payments and house repairs with his meager income, much less the expense of a baby? And what kind of father would he be, since he had never really felt very close to his own father, and wasn't sure he would know what to do.

The spell in church turned out to be his last. He was sleeping well, and he wasn't as worried as he had been about the idea of having a baby. His wife had agreed to wait till they had more money saved up. Mr. A thought he would like to talk with a therapist but wanted to see someone he could afford to pay himself since his mother had been paying for his visits with me. I suggested some colleagues from his insurance list but did not make a formal referral. A follow-up letter from the neurologist a year later said he had been seizure-free for the interval, felt well, and was ready to be released from the neurologist's care.

Ms. B

Ms. B is a woman with emotional abuse and conversion disorder cured by psychotherapy. Like Mr. A, she has good prognostic chances given the recent onset, some positive internal object relationships and identifications, relatively secure maternal attachment, lack of substance abuse or dependence, and history of gratification from career, even if there are still serious problems in the realm of intimate relationships.

Primary gain was not ego-syntonic and there was not significant secondary gain.

Ms. B was 35 years old and divorced when she was referred by the epilepsy monitoring unit neurologist. She had been having what appeared to be tonic-clonic seizures for the past year, and when medication didn't stop them, had monitoring that showed them to be psychogenic. She was an only child, friendly, open, intelligent, and pretty, though considerably overweight. Her weight caused her parents enormous grief. She knew that there were probably psychological problems that caused her to binge eat, but she'd never felt motivated to look into them.

Ms. B had attempted to become independent by marrying a man she'd met while in college in another city. She dropped out of college and got a job doing administrative work in an office where she was well-liked and became a favorite of her male boss since she was so enthusiastic, efficient, and reliable. She genuinely enjoyed feeling helpful and knew she was appreciated. Ms. B and her husband spent their free time going to casinos after work, where they played slot machines and blackjack, and had amassed considerable debt on credit cards. She hated her husband's drinking and angry outbursts and when she started fearing for her physical safety, she left him to move back in with her parents so she could pay back the debt and figure out a new life on her own. The marriage was dissolved and she found administrative work similar to what she had done before. Instead of the good experience she'd had before, now Ms. B had problems managing the relationship with her female supervisor who counted on Ms. B's superior performance to make up for the supervisor's own inadequacies, and who also had begun to confide in Ms. B. Initially Ms. B was flattered by the extra attention but soon felt overwhelmed at being expected to do others' jobs in addition to her own. She was resentful of having to listen to her supervisor's problems, and tried to avoid her, which led to a retaliatory attack by the supervisor, increasing her workload and criticizing her to other employees. It was at this point that the seizures started.

Her mother was described as loving and supportive. She worked in a white collar administrative job, and was proud of the status this conferred and her mother often pointed out how much more genteel she was than her father. Ms. B hated her father, an uneducated laborer who had coarse manners and was given to angry rages. Her mother had long confided in Ms. B her anger and resentment toward the father, and Ms. B had always commiserated with her mother, since she too found her father infuriating. Ms. B knew her mother had always needed her to stay close and had cried for days before Ms. B left for college, begging her not to go, and later, to not marry her ex-husband. Ms. B had never identified the similarity of the relationships with her mother and supervisor but her eyes widened in amazement when I suggested a pattern. She had assumed that it was altogether normal for her mother to want to stay close to her daughter and blamed herself for being a difficult daughter even as she felt compelled to rebel against her mother's wishes that she stay close.

We agreed to meet for sessions on a weekly basis, to be paid for by her parents, since Ms. B was slowly paying off credit card debt and helping out by buying her own food and clothing. Her parents wanted her to stay with them forever, it seemed, though she dreamed of getting training to do hairdressing and a job in a salon that would allow her independence. Her mother agreed to help her with tuition but not until the existing debt was paid off. She hated her job but she couldn't afford to leave. Ms. B had a few high school girlfriends she spent time with, but her typical recreation was going to the neighborhood tavern after dinner. She enjoyed being one of the "regulars" there, and she was proud that she kept her spending and drinking to a minimum, since it was the fellowship and not the alcohol that appealed to her. Ms. B ate entire boxes of cookies at night to counter the anger and frustration she felt. She sometimes had thoughts about killing herself as

a way out of her predicament. We discussed her mood and functioning and decided that she might be better on an antidepressant. She began venlafaxine and did feel considerably better within a few weeks.

After three months of sessions without incident, Ms. B had a full-blown generalized tonic-clonic seizure followed by apparent brief loss of consciousness while at work that led to a dramatic scene as paramedics carried her out on a stretcher. At the next session, we talked more about the specific problems that might have been on her mind in the days before the spell. She was beginning to understand that she was in a struggle with her mother in a way she had never conceptualized before. Ms. B had always been the favorite of her maternal aunt, and her mother was clearly jealous of their closeness. Her aunt was always sympathetic and understanding while her mother was often critical and judgmental, especially about her weight. Ms. B often felt there was nothing she could do right in her mother's eyes, even though she usually believed she was guilty as charged. Ms. B went out for dinner with her aunt without inviting her mother along a week before the spell, which led to her mother retaliating by not speaking to her for several days. Furthermore, her mother resented Ms. B leaving to go to the tavern in the evenings rather than sitting with her mother to watch TV shows.

Ms. B and I had a good rapport, and she clearly enjoyed coming in to investigate matters that had never seemed relevant or possible to discuss. She spent many hours reconstructing the relationship with her mother from earliest memory, and was often surprised at my reframing of it as emotionally abusive. In a striking example, she recounted returning home from school as a third grader, after a much anticipated parade that morning in front of all the kids' parents. She found her mother crying at the kitchen table because Ms. B had been too shy to look up as she marched by with all the grown-ups around. Her mother had been eagerly waiting for her to make eye contact and acknowledge her presence, and attacked Ms. B for humiliating her by failing to do so. Ms. B was stunned and felt she had done something terribly wrong to her mother, though she didn't know how to overcome her shyness or repair the problem. She had never thought of this experience as evidence of a problem in the relationship with her mother, but had assumed this to be expectable maternal behavior of a mother who loved her very much. Now she began to put a different picture together, and could see how she might have distorted relationships with other important people, like her supervisor and ex-husband, based on the assumptions and conflicts about autonomy that she had grown up with.

Ms. B repaired her standing in the office after what turned out to have been her last seizure, by working hard to avoid entanglements and asking the boss for a new supervisor to report to. She got along well with her new supervisor and co-workers; when she entered cosmetology school, she was asked to keep her job on a part-time basis, since she was so efficient; this suited her as the income helped defray expenses. She tried out dating a man she met at the bar, and shared with me her disappointment as they got closer and he began disciplining her about her eating and weight. She was sorry to see it end, but also did not want to feel criticized and bossed around. I never mentioned her weight, assuming that Ms. B was not ready to look into this aspect of her psychic functioning.

After two years of work together, Ms. B had consolidated a better understanding of herself. She had no further psychogenic seizures, and was ready to stop weekly sessions, though she wanted to maintain occasional contact so we could talk about her progress. That has continued on a yearly basis for the past several years and the news is always good. We conclude each visit with Ms. B reminding me, "I came in here thinking my father was the problem, and all along, it was really my mother!"

SUMMARY AND CONCLUSION

When previously well-functioning individuals develop conversion symptoms, it is safe to assume that an old conflict related to childhood traumatic experience has been revived by more recent trauma that cannot be addressed with conscious thought. There may be genetic factors still not well understood, that confirm Janet's idea of an inherited weakness predisposing to conversion, such as brain connectivity, telomere length, methylation patterns, and parental exposure to traumatic stress (Clark, DeYoung et al., 2013; Gweon, Dodell-Feder, Bedny, & Saxe, 2012; Malan, Hemmings, Kidd, Martin, & Seedat, 2011; Szyf, 2014). With help from a psychotherapist to develop a narrative about one's life experiences and the current experience of an old conflict, the conversion symptom is no longer necessary and forward development is again possible, albeit with the acceptance and mourning necessary for progress in any form of psychoanalytic psychotherapy.

Patients who come to psychotherapists with conversion symptoms and histories of less successful adaptation to life, serious attachment problems, and few positive identifications or representations, are a challenge to treat, as they have little to build on. Primary gain from the conversion symptom has provided some relief and secondary gain may be considerable. Even so, helping these more impaired patients create an orderly narrative about themselves often leads to improvement. Those with narcotic addictions are especially unlikely to get real benefit from psychotherapy.

APPENDIX: GUIDELINES FOR CLINICAL WORK WITH CONVERSION DISORDER

General Positive Prognostic Factors

1. Adequate maternal attachment, and some positive internalized objects and identifications.

2. Childhood trauma that does not involve maternal caretaker.

3. Some successes in relationships and/or career.

4. Recent onset of symptom relative to consultation for psychotherapy, without obvious goal of becoming disabled.

5. Conversion symptom that "tells a story."

6. Lack of serious substance abuse or dependence.

General Negative Prognostic Factors

1. Significant maternal attachment problems, few positive internal object representations or identifications.

2. Serious childhood trauma that involves maternal caretaker, including parental refusal to acknowledge and stop abuse, or help with recovery.

3. Little success in relationships or career endeavors.

4. Longstanding symptoms, existing disability benefits, or obvious goal of being declared disabled to get benefits.

5. Somatization pattern with long list of symptoms that do not tell a coherent story.

6. Substance abuse and dependence.

General Principles for the Psychotherapist

1. Open expression of interest, sympathetic stance, and non-partisan approach to physical symptoms. Other physicians may be engaged to pursue new symptoms or worsening existing symptoms so they do not become the sole focus of psychological work.

2. Ask permission to talk with the referring physician or doctor treating the symptoms. The psychiatrist may become the orchestrator of a number of specialists who are each consulting on a particular problem but not communicating with others. This is often an excellent way for both the psychiatrist and other treating physicians to gain experience with what constitutes conversion or somatization.

3. Maintain awareness of the development of transference but emphasis of transference feelings does not often lead to productive deepening. Obvious expression of negative transference that threatens therapy should be addressed openly and sympathetically. Most important is the treatment alliance, based on the positive transference that enables patients to maintain hope and continue to investigate.

4. Elicit a thorough history of psychiatric illness that includes past history from earliest childhood to the present. It is not unusual to hear a history of serious childhood trauma and family history of mood, anxiety and substance abuse problems. Treat comorbid symptoms of depression or anxiety aggressively. Haphazard medication efforts by non-psychiatrists are typical, and often include SSRI antidepressants, benzodiazepines, and narcotics. It is useful to tell patients that regular use of benzodiazepines and narcotics may lead to worse depression and lack of energy and motivation. Remission of underlying depression, which might require use of antidepressants, antipsychotics, or mood stabilizers, and stimulants, may lead to surprising improvement in physical symptoms.

5. Remain interested in discussion about the symptoms; inevitably, once the patient feels safe with the therapist, the symptom will be experienced at full intensity, probably testing whether the therapist will maintain positive regard. This leads to further discussion of the timing and associated thoughts and feelings related to symptoms.

6. Maintain a steady focus on the history and current day qualities of important relationships. The therapist's interest and sustained attention generally elicits a good flow of information and associations. If the patient has dreams or nightmares, ask for details and interpret broad themes. Empathic efforts to re-state historical information can have a powerful effect on individuals who have lived without the experience of empathic attunement. The therapist's expression of understanding how painful life has been and how the patient is blameless in developing symptoms that express that pain will cement the alliance.

7. Whenever possible, educate patients about the impact of attachment problems and overt trauma on the child, illustrating with examples from the patient's experience. The goal of treatment is typically not the development of insight through self-discovery and analysis of transference as it might be with a healthy neurotic individual. Establishing a positive relationship that allows for giving the patient a framework for understanding life experiences and putting together a life narrative is the active element.

REFERENCES

Abbass, A., Kisely, S., & Kroenke, K. (2009). Short-term psychodynamic psychotherapy for somatic disorders. *Psychotherapy and Psychosomatics, 78*, 265-274.

Allen, L. A., Woolfolk, R. L., Escobar, J. I., Gara, M. A., & Hamer, R. M. (2006). Cognitive-behavioral therapy for somatization disorder: A randomized controlled trial. *Archives of Internal Medicine, 166*, 1512-1518.

American Psychiatric Association. (2013). *Diagnostic and statistical manual of mental disorders* (5th ed.). Arlington, VA: American Psychiatric Publishing.

Ani, C., Reading, R., Lynn, R., Forlee, S., & Garralda, E. (2013). Incidence and 12-month outcome of non-transient childhood conversion disorder in the U.K. and Ireland. *British Journal of Psychiatry, 202*, 413-418.

Arnold, L. M., & Privitera, M. D. (2006). Psychopathology and trauma in epileptic and psychogenic seizure patients. *Psychosomatics, 37*, 438-443.

Aybek, S., Nicholson, T. R., Zelaya, F., O'Daly, O. G., Craig, T. J., et al. (2014). Neural correlates of recall of life events in conversion disorder. *JAMA Psychiatry, 71*, 52-60.

Ben-Porath, Y. S., & Tellegen, A. (2008). *Minnesota Multiphasic Personality Inventory-2 Restructured Form* (MMPI-2-RF). Minneapolis: University of Minnesota Press.

Bernstein, E. M., & Putnam, F. (1986). Development, reliability and validity of a dissociation scale. *Journal of Nervous Mental Disease, 174*, 727-735.

Black, D. N., Seritan, A. L., Taber, K. H., & Hurley, R. A. (2004). Conversion hysteria: Lessons from functional imaging. *Journal of Neuropsychiatry, 16*, 245-251.

Brown, R. J., & Lewis-Fernandez, R. (2011). Culture and conversion disorder: Implications for DSM-V. *Psychiatry, 74*, 187-206.

Bryant, R. A., & Das, P. (2012). The neural circuitry of conversion disorder and its recovery. *Journal of Abnormal Psychology, 121*, 289-296.

Bucci, W. (1997). Symptoms and symbols: A multiple code theory of somatization. *Psychoanalytic Inquiry, 17*, 151-172.

Carson, A. J., Ringbauer, B., McKenzie, L, Warlow, C., & Sharpe, M. (2000). Neurological disease, emotional disorder, and disability: They are related: A study of 300 consecutive new referrals to a neurology outpatient department. *Journal of Neurology, Neurosurgery and Psychiatry, 68*, 202-206.

Carson, A. J., Ringbauer, B., Stone J., McKenzie, L., Warlow, C., et al. (2000). Do medically unexplained symptoms matter? A prospective cohort study of 300 new referrals to neurology outpatient clinics. *Journal of Neurology, Neurosurgery and Psychiatry, 68*, 207-210.

Chand, S. P., Al-Hussaini, A. A., Martin, R., Mustapha, S., Zaidan, Z., et al. (2000). Dissociative disorders in the Sultanate of Oman. *Acta Psychiatrica Scandinavica, 102*, 185-187.

Clark, R., DeYoung, C. G,. Sponheim, S. R., Bender, T. L., Polusny, M., et al. (2013). Predicting post-traumatic stress disorder in veterans: Interaction of traumatic load with COMT gene variation. *Journal of Psychiatric Research, 47*, 1849-1856.

De Lange, F. P., Roelofs, K., & Toni, I. (2008). Motor imagery: A window into the mechanisms and alterations of the motor system. *Cortex, 44*, 494-506.

de M'Uzan, M. (1974). Psychodynamic mechanisms in psychosomatic symptom formation. *Psychotherapy and Psychosomatics, 23*, 103-110.

Dinwiddie, S. H. (2013). Somatization disorder: Past, present and future. *Psychiatric Annals, 43*, 78-83.

Edwards, M. J., Adams, R. A., Brown, H., Parees, I., & Friston, K. J. (2012). A Bayesian account of "hysteria." *Brain, 135,* 3495-3512.

Escalona, R., Achilles, G., Waitzkin, H., & Yager, J. (2004). PTSD and somatization in women treated at a VA primary care clinic. *Psychosomatics: Journal of Consultation Liaison Psychiatry, 45,* 291-296.

Escobar, J. I., Gara, M. I., Diaz-Martinez, A. M., Interian, A., Warman, M., et al. (2007). Effectiveness of a time-limited cognitive behavior therapy-type intervention among primary care patients with medically unexplained symptoms. *Annals of Family Medicine, 5,* 328-335.

Feinstein, A. (2011). Conversion disorder: Advances in our understanding. *Canadian Medical Association Journal, 183,* 915-920.

Ferriar, J. (1795). *Medical histories and reflections, vol. II.* London: Cadell and Davies.

Fink, P., Sorenson, L., Engberg, M., Holm, M., & Munk-Jorgensen, P. (1999). Somatization in primary care. Prevalence, health care utilization and general practitioner recognition. *Psychosomatics: Journal of Consultation Liaison Psychiatry, 40,* 330-338.

Fiszman, A., Alves-Leon, S. V., Nunes, R. G., D'Andrea, I., & Figueira, I. (2004). Traumatic events and posttraumatic stress disorder in patients with psychogenic nonepileptic seizures: A critical review. *Epilepsy and Behavior, 5,* 818-825.

Freud, S. (1893). Some points for a comparative study of organic and motor paralyses. In J. Strachey (Ed. & Trans.), *The standard edition of the complete psychological works of Sigmund Freud* (vol. I, pp. 160-172). London: Hogarth Press.

Freud, S. (1895). On the grounds for detaching a particular syndrome from neurasthenia under the description "anxiety neurosis." In J. Strachey (Ed. & Trans.), *The standard edition of the complete psychological works of Sigmund Freud* (vol. III). London: Hogarth Press.

Grinker, R. R., & Spiegel, J. P. (1945). *Men under stress.* Philadelphia: Blakiston Press.

Gweon, H., Dodell Feder, D., Bedny, M., & Saxe, R. (2012). Theory of mind performance in children correlates with functional specialization of a brain region for thinking about thoughts. *Child Development, 83,* 1853-1868.

Herman, J. L. (1997). Trauma and recovery (p. 124). New York: Basic Books.

Jacquart, D., & Thomasset, C. (1988). *Sexuality and medicine in the middle ages* (p. 175). London: Pollity Press.

Kaplan, M. J., Dwivedi, A. K., Privitera, M. D., Isaacs, K., Hughes, C., & Bowman, M. (2013). Comparisons of childhood trauma, alexithymia,

and defensive styles in patients with psychogenic non-epileptic seizures vs. epilepsy: Implications for the etiology of conversion disorder. *Journal of Psychosomatic Research, 75,* 142-146.

Kent, D. A., Tomasson, K., & Coryell, W. (1995). Course and outcome of conversion and somatization disorders: A four-year follow-up. *Psychosomatics: Journal of Consultation Liaison Psychiatry, 36,* 138-144.

Koelen, J. A., Houtveen, J. H., Abbass, A., Luyten, P., et al. (2014). Effectiveness of psychotherapy for severe somatoform disorder: Meta-analysis. *British Journal of Psychiatry, 204,* 12-19.

Lehmkuhl, G., Blanz, B., Lehmkuhl, U., & Braun-Scharm, H. (1989). Conversion disorder (*DSM-III* 300.11): Symptomatology and course in childhood and adolescence. *European Archives of Psychiatry and Neurological Sciences, 238,* 155-160.

Lindy, J. D. (1987). Vietnam: A Casebook. New York: Routledge.

Luyten, P., & Van Houdenhove, B. (2013). Common and specific factors in the psychotherapeutic treatment of patients suffering from chronic fatigue and pain. *Journal of Psychotherapy Integration, 23,* 14-27.

Luyten, P., Van Houdenhove, B., Lemma, A., Target, M., & Fonagy, P. (2012). A mentalization-based approach to the understanding and treatment of functional somatic disorder. *Psychoanalytic Psychotherapy, 26,* 121-140.

Mace, C. J. (1992). Hysterical conversion, I: A history. *British Journal of Psychiatry, 161,* 369-377.

Mace, C. J., & Trimble, M. R. (1996). Ten-year prognosis of conversion disorder. *British Journal of Psychiatry, 169,* 282-288.

Mai, F. M., & Merskey, H. (1980). Briquet's treatise on hysteria. *Archives of General Psychiatry, 37,* 1401-1405.

Malan, S., Hemmings, S., Kidd, M., Martin, L., & Seedat, S. (2011). Investigation of telomere length and psychological stress in rape victims. *Depression and Anxiety, 28,* 1081-1085.

Marmar, C. R., Weiss, D. S., Schlenger, W. E., Fairbank, J. A., Jordan, K., et al. (1994). Peritraumatic dissociation and posttraumatic stress in male Vietnam theater veterans. *American Journal of Psychiatry, 151,* 902-907.

Marty, P., & de M'Uzan, M. (1963). Operational thinking. In D. Birksted-Breen, S. Flanders, A. Gibeault (Eds.); D. Alcorn, S. Leighton, & A. Weller (Trans.), *Reading French psychoanalysis* (pp. 449-458). New York: Routledge/Taylor & Francis Group.

McDougall, J. (1989). *Theaters of the body: A psychoanalytic approach to psychosomatic illness.* New York: Norton.

Meares, R., Gerull, F., Korner, A., Melkonian, D., Stevenson, J., et al. (2008). Somatization and stimulus entrapment. *Journal of American Academy of Psychoanalysis and Dynamic Psychiatry,* 36,165-180.

Reilly, C., Menlove, L., Fenton, V., & Das, K. B. (2013). Psychogenic non-epileptic seizures in children: A review. *Epilepsia, 54,* 1715-1724.

Roelofs, K., Keijsers, G. P. J., Hoogduin, K. E. L., Naring, G. W. B., & Moene, F. C. (2002). Childhood abuse in patients with conversion disorder. *American Journal of Psychiatry, 159,* 1908-1913.

Roelofs, K., & Spinhoven, P. (2007). Trauma and medically unexplained symptoms: Towards an integration of cognitive and neuro-biological accounts. *Clinical Psychology Review, 27,* 798-820.

Roelofs, K., Spinhoven, P., Sandijck, P., Moene, F. C., & Hoogduin, K. E. L. (2005). The impact of early trauma and recent life-events on symptom severity in patients with conversion disorder. *Journal of Nervous and Mental Disease, 193,* 508-514.

Sar, V., Akyüz, G., Dogan, O., & Öztü, E. (2009). The prevalence of conversion symptoms in women from a general Turkish population. *Psychosomatics: Journal of Consultation Liaison Psychiatry, 50,* 50-58.

Sar, V., Akyuz, G., Kundakci, T., Kiziltan, E., & Dogan, O. (2004). Childhood trauma, dissociation and psychiatric co-morbidity in patients with conversion disorder. *American Journal of Psychiatry, 161,* 2271-2276.

Sattel, H., Lahmann, H., Gundel, E., Guthrie, E., Kruse, J., et al. (2012). Brief psychodynamic interpersonal psychotherapy for patients with multisomatoform disorder: Randomized controlled trial. *British Journal of Psychiatry, 100,* 60-67.

Sifneos, P. E. (1996). Alexithymia: Past and present. *American Journal of Psychiatry, 153,* 137-142.

Snijders, T. J., de Leeuw, F. E., Klumpers, U. M., Kappelle, L. J., & van Gijn, K. (2004). Prevalence and predictors of unexplained neurological symptoms in an academic neurology outpatient clinic—an observational study. *Journal of Neurology, 251,* 66-71.

Stone, J., Carson, A., Duncan, R., Coleman, C., & Roberts, R. (2009). Symptoms "unexplained by organic disease" in 1144 new neurology outpatients: How often does the diagnosis change at follow-up? *Brain, 132,* 2878-2888.

Stone, J., Carson, A., Duncan, R., Roberts, R., Warlow, C., et al. (2009). Who is referred to neurology clinics? *Clinical Neurology and Neurosurgery, 112,* 747-751.

Sumathipala, A., Hewege, S., Hanwella, R., & Mann, A. H. (2000). Randomized controlled trial of cognitive behaviour therapy for repeated consultations for medically unexplained complaints: A feasibility study in Sri Lanka. *Psychological Medicine, 30,* 747-757.

Szaflarski, J. P., Ficker, D. M., Cahill, W. T., & Privitera, M. D. (2000). Four-year incidence of psychogenic nonepileptic seizures in adults in Hamilton County, OH. *Neurology, 55,* 1561-1563.

Szyf, M. (2014). Lamarck revisited: Epigenetic inheritance of ancestral odor fear conditioning. *Nature Neuroscience, 17,* 2-4.

Taneilian, T., & Jaycox, L. (2008). *Invisible wounds of war.* Santa Monica, CA: RAND Corporation.

Taylor, G. J., & Bagby, R. M. (2013). Psychoanalysis and empirical research: The example of alexithymia. *Journal of the American Psychoanalytic Association, 61,* 99-133.

Tomasson, K., & Kent, D. (1991). Somatization and conversion disorders: Comorbidity and demographics at presentation. *Acta Psychiatrica Scandinavica, 84,* 288-293.

Van der Kolk, B. A., Pelcovitz, D., Roth, S., Mandel, F., MacFarlane, A., & Herman, J. L. (1996). Dissociation, somatization, and affect dysregulation: The complexity of adaptation to trauma. *American Journal of Psychiatry, 153*(suppl.), 83-93.

Van der Kolk, B. A., & van der Hart, O. (1989). Pierre Janet and the breakdown of adaptation in psychological trauma. *American Journal of Psychiatry, 146,* 1530-1540.

Verhaeghe, P., Vanheule, S., & De Rick, A. (2007). Actual neurosis as the underlying psychic structure of panic disorder, somatization, and somatoform disorder: An integration of Freudian and attachment perspectives. *Psychoanalytic Quarterly, 76,* 1317-1350.

Woolfolk, R. L., & Allen, L. A. (2010). Affective-cognitive behavioral therapy for somatization disorder. *Journal of Cognitive Psychotherapy, 24,* 116-131.

Yehuda, R., Southwick, S. M., & Giller, E. L. (1992). Exposure to atrocities and severity of chronic posttraumatic stress disorder in Vietnam combat veterans. *American Journal of Psychiatry, 149,* 333-336.

Substance-Related and Addictive Disorders

Further Evidence of Self-Medication: Personality Factors Influencing Drug Choice in Substance Use Disorders

Lindsey Colman McKernan, Michael R. Nash, William H. Gottdiener, Scott E. Anderson, Warren E. Lambert, and Erika R. Carr

Abstract: According to Khantzian's (2003) self-medication hypothesis (SMH), substance dependence is a compensatory means to modulate affects and self-soothe in response to distressing psychological states. Khantzian asserts: (1) Drugs become addicting because they have the power to alleviate, remove, or change human psychological suffering, and (2) There is a considerable degree of specificity in a person's choice of drugs because of unique psychological and physiological effects. The SMH has received criticism for its variable empirical support, particularly in terms of the drug-specificity aspect of Khantzian's hypothesis. We posit that previous empirical examinations of the SMH have been compromised by methodological limitations. Also, more recent findings supporting the SMH have yet to be replicated. Addressing previous limitations to the research, this project tested this theory in a treatment sample of treatment-seeking individuals with substance dependence ($N = 304$), using more heterogeneous, personality-driven measures that are theory-congruent. Using an algorithm based on medical records, individuals were reliably classified as being addicted to a depressant, stimulant, or opiate by two independent raters. Theory-based a priori predictions were that the three groups would exhibit differences in personality characteristics and emotional-regulation strategies. Specifically, our hypotheses entailed that when compared against each other: (1) Individuals with a central nervous system (CNS) depressant as drug of choice (DOC) will exhibit defenses of repression, over-controlling anger, and emotional inhibition to avoid acknowledging their depression; (2) Individuals with an opiate as DOC will exhibit higher levels of aggression, hostility, depression, and trauma, greater deficits in ego functioning, and externalizing/antisocial behavior connected to their use; and (3) Individuals with a stimulant as DOC will experience anhedonia, paranoia, have a propensity to mania, and display lower levels of emotional inhibition. MANOVAs were used to test three hypotheses regarding drug group differences on the personality variables that were in keeping with the SMH. The MANOVAs for Hypothesis I (Depressant group) and Hypothesis II (Opiate group) were statistically significant. Findings partially support the SMH, particularly in its characterization of personality functioning in those addicted to depressants and opiates.

Khantzian's (1985, 1997, 2003) self-medication hypothesis (SMH) of substance use is an attractive and intuitively compelling theory of substance use among patients and clinicians, offering a compassionate and relatable explanation for the emotional pain that individuals with substance use disorders (SUDs) experience. The SMH postulates that suffering is at the heart of SUDs, where individuals use substances to modulate painful affect and to self-soothe unmanageable psychological states (Khantzian, 2003, 2012). For clinicians from a range of theoretical perspectives, the SMH provides an empathic platform to explore the interplay between mood states and substance use, promote understanding and acceptance, and address the affective components that are contributing to patterns of use in psychotherapy (Blume, Schmaling, & Marlatt, 2000; Khantzian, 2012; Khantzian & Albanese, 2008). In spite of its popularity, the SMH has received criticism for its variable empirical support (Darke, 2012), with authors calling for revisions, and in one case "abandonment" of the SMH entirely (Dupont & Gold, 2007; Henwood & Padgett, 2007; Lembke, 2012).

Substance Dependence and Self-Regulation

Khantzian (2012) conceptualizes substance dependence broadly as a self-regulation disorder, where individuals with SUDs suffer because they cannot or do not regulate their emotions, self-esteem, relationships, or behavior. For example, behavioral (self-care) dysregulation includes an inability to draw cause/consequence relationships in the face of risk (Khantzian, 1997, 2012). These self-regulation difficulties are associated with a significant amount of psychological turmoil. The self-medication hypothesis posits that (1) individuals use substances to alleviate psychological suffering and (2) gravitate toward particular drugs as a result of their physiological and psychological effects (drug-specificity). Khantzian postulates that substances

function to relieve suffering and to help the individual exercise control over the experience of helplessness that accompanies confusing and uncontrollable affect (Khantzian, 2012, 2013; Suh, Ruffins, Robins, Albenese, & Khantzian, 2008). In addition, the ability of substances to temporarily alter distressing states powerfully reinforces dependence on the substance and further erodes existing coping capacities (Blume, Schmaling, & Marlatt, 2000; Khantzian, 2012). Taken together with genetic and environmental influences, these self-regulation vulnerabilities increase the chance of substance dependence.

Khantzian believes there is a significant amount of specificity in what drives a person to a particular substance. The SMH posits that several factors influence what drug appeals most to a person, including the chief effect or action of the drug, the personality of the individual, the inner states of their distress, and the availability of the substance (Khantzian & Albenese, 2008). Based on these interactions, the SMH categorizes substances into three groups:

Central Nervous System (CNS) Depressants. Depressants (alcohol, barbiturates, and benzodiazepines) have amnestic properties as well as relaxant and sedative-hypnotic effects (Parrott, Morinan, Moss, & Scholey, 2004). At low concentrations, due to inhibiting norepinephrine transmission and increasing dopamine and fluidity of cell membranes, alcohol can have excitant or "disinhibitory" effects, reducing perceived anxiety, social inhibition, and fostering feelings of closeness with others (Benton, 1988; Kushner, Abrams, & Borchardt, 2000; Parrott et al., 2004; Winger, Woods, & Hoffmann, 2004). Although initially producing euphoria, as concentrations increase, alcohol has overall depressant and sedative effects (Grant & Harford, 1995). Alcohol withdrawal is also associated with re-inducing norepinephrine systems in the brain, which may serve to generate anxiety, often driving an individual to drink to relieve the anxiogenic effects (Kushner et al., 2000). Barbiturates follow the same course, although in pill form, and are used less now than historically in exchange for benzodiazepines (Winger et al., 2004). According to the SMH, individuals dependent upon depressants tend to inhibit and over-contain their experience of emotions, utilizing rigid defenses of repression and denial (Khantzian & Albanese, 2008; Suh, Ruffins, Robins, Albanese, & Khantzian, 2008). The "cutting off" and unacknowledgement of emotions leads to emptiness and isolation, predisposing individuals to depression. As such, alcohol serves to soften this defensive structure and allows individuals to temporarily relieve emotional tension (Khantzian, 1997, 1999).

Opiates/Narcotics/Analgesics. Opiates produce a high by altering the release and reuptake of neurotransmitters in the brain, generating slowing and analgesic effects. Initially, the ingestion of narcotics (e.g., heroin) gives an individual an extremely preoccupying rush of pleasure, followed by drowsiness, reduced sensitivity to stimuli, reduced anxiety/inhibition, muscle relaxation, pain relief, and slowed respiration (Caan, 2002; Parrott et al., 2004). Anecdotal reported effects of opiates include feeling safe, comforted, and immune to life's pains, miseries, and humiliations (Caan, 2002). The SMH proposes that individuals gravitate toward opiates primarily to manage intense and often disorganizing feelings of anger due to their calming and "normalizing" effects (Khantzian, 1997). Through extensive clinical observations ("practice-based evidence"), Khantzian (1985) noted a strong association between opioid use and traumatic backgrounds. Accordingly, the SMH states that opioids act specifically to reverse regressive states by softening otherwise intolerable feelings of aggression, rage, and/or related depression often associated with the experience of trauma, loss, or painful disappointment (Khantzian, 1999; Khantzian & Albanese, 2008).

Central Nervous System Stimulants. When ingested, cocaine and amphetamines lead to increased dopamine and noradrenaline activity, due to the drug blocking dopamine transporters and reuptake of neurotransmitters into synaptic terminals (Volkow, Fowler, Wang, & Swanson 2004; Winger et al., 2004). This stimulation heightens alertness, decreases sleep and appetite, increases locomotor activity, and intensifies mood states (Parrott et al., 2004; Winger et al., 2004). The initial effects of cocaine are reported as very positive, including increased energy, feeling powerful, confident, and lively, and experiencing the world as more interesting and pleasurable (Parrott et al., 2004). The SMH identifies two types of cocaine abusers: "low energy" and "high energy" individuals (Khantzian & Albanese, 2008). Both types of users appear to be avoiding affect related to depression. "Low energy" cocaine abusers experience chronic feelings of boredom, dysphoria, or fatigue—mirroring a depressive state. For these individuals, cocaine acts as a means to increase energy and counter anhedonia. Conversely, the "high energy" class of individuals possess a magnified need for elation and excitement. "High energy" users are thought of using cocaine as a "flight from depression," by living a restless lifestyle, and maintaining feelings of hypomania. Additionally, Khantzian (1997) noted that in some individuals, stimulants can paradoxically calm and counter ADHD-related symptoms.

Previous Research and Controversy

The SMH is criticized in the literature primarily due to research not demonstrating a causal link between psychological disorders and the development/maintenance of SUDs and the lack of empirical support for the drug specificity aspect of the SMH (Lembke, 2012). In addition, researchers question the notion that substances act to relieve psychological distress, as they often do the reverse (Dupont & Gold, 2007). While empirical investigations have demonstrated higher levels of psychopathology in SUDs, Khantzian's drug specificity predictions have been less successful when empirically tested. Studies have consistently demonstrated higher rates of psychiatric co-morbidity in individuals diagnosed with a SUD, and increased rates of childhood trauma, maltreatment, and/or adversity among substance abusers (Grant et al., 2004; Sihna, 2008). When administering structured interviews to assess onset of psychiatric symptoms relative to substance use, researchers found that substance dependence followed the onset of a psychiatric disorder, such as depression preceding alcohol dependence (Abraham & Fava, 1999; Deykin, Levy, & Wells, 1987). However, these only suggest, and cannot prove causality.

Studies specifically examining self-medication have found higher levels of psychological distress in substance abusers, with individuals reporting using substances to cope with painful affect, anxiety, hyper-arousal associated with PTSD, and/or depressive symptoms (Aharonovich, Nguyen, & Nunes, 2001; Craig, 1988; Henwood & Padgett, 2007; Robinson, Sareen, Cox, & Bolton, 2011; Shipherd, Stafford, & Tanner, 2005; Weiss, Griffin, & Mirin, 1992). Multiple empirical investigations of drug specificity according to the SMH could not support this aspect of the hypothesis (Aharonovich et al., 2001; Castaneda, 1994; Greene, Adyanthaya, Morse, & Davis, 1993; Hall & Queener, 2007; Weiss et al., 1992). An early investigation linking personality traits to drug use found distinct personality differences among drug users, particularly among barbiturate users, who displayed higher levels of emotional distress and reported decreased anxiety following drug use (Crain, Ertel, & Gorman, 1975). These authors concluded that barbiturate users may gravitate toward this particular drug out of a personal need to avoid cognitive activity and social interaction. Using methods that target underlying affective constructs in personality functioning, a more recent investigation found partial support for the SMH, with lower depression and repression predicting alcohol dependence, cynicism predicting opioid dependence, and higher levels of psychomotor acceleration predicting cocaine dependence (Suh et al., 2008).

Limitations of Previous Research

The above examinations of the drug-specificity aspect of the SMH have several methodological limitations that warrant consideration, including issues in assessing drug of choice, measurement, power, and generalizability. Studies (Aharonovich et al. 2001; Castaneda, 1994; Hall & Queener, 2007) based drug of choice on self-reported use. According to a 24-study meta-analysis of self-reported drug use among high-risk populations, self-reported drug use is extremely unreliable (Kappa = .42), variable, and under-reported, particularly in post-treatment follow-up visits and out-of-treatment populations (Magura & Kang, 1996). These authors suggest that along with self-reported use, drug dependency research should routinely include an appropriate biological test to increase validity of reports. This is particularly relevant in assessing drug preference when individuals are abusing multiple classes of drugs, a point of the specificity hypothesis that has drawn criticism in the past (Lembke, 2012).

With regard to measurement, previous studies utilized strictly self-report measures and/or instruments that target major psychiatric symptom categories to measure distress, narrative responses to questions, and one using a new and unreliable measure to assess for emotionality relative to substance use (Ahoronovich et al., 2001; Castaneda, 1994; Hall & Queener, 2007; Weiss et al., 1992). The clinical scales of the Minnesota Multiphasic Personality Inventory–2 (MMPI-II; Butcher, Dahlstrom, Graham, Tellegen, & Kaemmer, 1989) used by Greene and colleagues (1993) are heterogeneous in nature and multidimensional, with symptom overlap. The SMH focuses on characterological functioning in SUDs, such as affect regulation and psychological defense. These concepts are subtle and difficult to capture, and could have easily been missed by heterogeneous measures or narratives. Lastly, sample characteristics in the research indicate limited power and generalizability. Sample sizes in these studies were as low as 20 to 29 participants in each drug group (Aharonovich et al., 2001; Greene et al., 1993), and three studies utilized mostly men—one with participants each carrying a personality disorder diagnosis (Aharonovich et al., 2001; Castaneda, 1994; Schinka, Curtiss, & Mulloy, 1994).

After raising concerns with the assessments used in previous studies to assess the drug specificity aspect of the SMH, Suh and colleagues (2008) used content, supplementary, and Harris-Lingoes scales of the MMPI-II instead of the previously investigated clinical diagnostic scales (Butcher, Graham, Williams, & Ben-Porath, 1990). These scales are considered homogeneous and provide the clinical descriptions and underlying factors of the syndromes assessed by the standard clinical scales, such as traits and attitudes (Hathaway & McKinley, 1989). Using these scales, Suh et al. (2008) found evidence in partial support of the hypothesis, finding alcohol users to have a greater tendency to over-control their anger, use repression, and refrain from acknowledging their emotions; heroin users had a tendency to experience higher levels of anger, trauma, and negativity; and cocaine users were more apt to maintain restless and exhilarating psychological states.

Rationale for the Current Study and Hypotheses

We believe previous methodological limitations compromised investigation of the SMH, and the earlier described limitations could be addressed in three ways using: (1) multiple points of data/raters to determine drug of choice (DOC), increasing reliability; (2) a larger sample, increasing power, and (3) theory-driven measures to capture

the underlying affective and defensive (characterological) functioning of individuals diagnosed with a SUD. To reliably determine DOC, we used multiple points of treatment data, including biological measures (urinalysis), and created a decision-making process, or algorithm, for multiple raters to follow to determine an individual's DOC. We believe that following this algorithm strengthens the analysis by accounting for poly-drug use and supplementing individuals' self-report of drug use, which has been found unreliable and variable when used alone (Magura & Kang, 1996).

The SMH has only been tested once with the Personality Assessment Inventory (PAI; Morey, 1991), which was too broad when used alone (Schinka et al., 1994), and has yet to be tested with the Young Schema Questionnaire (YSQ; Young, 2005) both of which function to assess characterological problems and modes of affect regulation unique to the individual. Often, researchers have not had the ability to assess alcohol use disorders and SUDs concurrently (Aharonovich et al., 2001; Greene et al., 1993; Hall & Queener, 2007). The assessments used in this study more accurately pertain to the theory, and could provide insight into its validity, or perhaps into areas that need re-evaluating to better distinguish between substance use groups. Furthermore, Suh and colleagues' (2008) findings using different assessments have yet to be replicated. Replication in research is essential for theoretical development through confirmation and disconfirmation of results, building a knowledge base that aids in the construction of new and the refinement of old psychological theories (Brandt et al., 2014).

After creating an algorithm for multiple raters to reliably determine DOC, we conducted this project as a partial replication and expansion of Suh et al.'s (2008) study, using a large clinical inpatient treatment sample with drastically different demographics. We had the opportunity to use multiple personality assessments, in order to assess the applicability of the theory across measures. If psychological attributes and patterns in personality functioning exist that distinguish depressant, stimulant, and opiate dependency from each other, and if we can detect these patterns, we then have usable scaffolding upon which we can add to models of acquisition of SUDs, its maintenance, and treatment. Analyzing psychological, personality, and maladaptive schema data concomitantly might further this process. The hypotheses of this study have been broken down into three substance categories derived from the SMH. We hypothesize that when compared against each other, each drug category will demonstrate differences in emotional regulation and psychological defenses. Specifically, we expect that when compared against each other:

(1) Individuals with a CNS depressant as DOC will exhibit defenses of repression, over-controlling anger, and emotional inhibition to avoid acknowledging their depression; through demonstrating higher levels of Repression (R; MMPI-II), Over-controlled Hostility (O-H; MMPI-II), and Emotional Inhibition (EI; YSQ), and lower levels of Subjective Depression (Dep-1; MMPI-II), Paranoia (PAR; PAI), and Aggression (AGG; PAI) on assessment measures.

(2) Individuals with an opiate as DOC will exhibit higher levels of aggression, hostility, depression, and trauma, greater deficits in ego functioning, and externalizing/antisocial behavior connected to their use; through demonstrating higher levels of Posttraumatic Stress (Pk; MMPI-II), Subjective Depression (Dep-1; MMPI-II), Cynicism (CYN; MMPI-II), Aggression (AGG; PAI), Antisocial Tendencies (ANT; PAI), and Insufficient Self-Control (ISC; YSQ); and lower levels of Ego Strength (ES; MMPI-II) on assessment measures.

(3) Individuals with a Stimulant as DOC will experience anhedonia, paranoia, have a propensity to mania, and display lower levels of emotional inhibition through exhibiting higher levels of Psychomotor Acceleration (Ma2; MMPI-II), Subjective Depression (Dep-1; MMPI-II), Cynicism (CYN; MMPI-

II), Paranoia (PAR; PAI), and Insufficient Self-Control (ISC; YSQ) on assessment measures.

METHOD

After Institutional Review Board approval, archival data were gathered from a treatment facility for substance abuse and dependence located in the Southeast United States. Program participants included insured, contract-based, and private-pay clients primarily from the treatment facility's region. Participants engaged in a variety of inpatient, intensive outpatient, and/or outpatient treatment programs, with stays generally ranging from 1–3 months. Medical record data was gathered from 2007–2009 program participants, including demographic information, medical and treatment history, drug screens, treatment participation, and psychological assessments. Upon admission to treatment, all patients engaged in numerous semi-structured interviews with staff and medical professionals and completed an assessment battery. Initially, individuals were assessed for withdrawal using the Clinical Opiate Withdrawal Scale (COWS; Wesson & Ling, 2003) and Clinical Institute Withdrawal Assessment of Alcohol Scale (CIWA-Ar; Sullivan, Sykora, Schneiderman, Naranjo, & Sellers, 1989), and those identified as experiencing withdrawal were monitored and did not complete assessments until deemed medically and psychiatrically stable.

Measurements

Minnesota Multiphasic Personality Inventory–2nd Edition (MMPI-II). The MMPI-II (Hathaway & McKinley, 1989) is a 567-item self-administered questionnaire in true/false format that assesses the existence of various forms of Axis-I psychopathology. The MMPI-II is frequently used to assess psychopathology in clinical and research settings because of its high reliability and validity

(Butcher et al., 1989; Butcher & Williams, 2000; Greene, 1991). The standard clinical scales of the MMPI-II have been shown to accurately identify diagnoses, but are insufficient in assessing unique, affect-related constructs due to their heterogeneous and multidimensional contents (Suh et al., 2008). Therefore, in this investigation, subscales from the supplementary, content, and Harris-Lingoes scales of the MMPI-II were used (Butcher et al., 1990; Butcher & Williams, 2000; Graham, 2002; Greene, 2000). These scales are more relevant in terms of the SMH as they are heterogeneous and assess more intricate psychological constructs, characteristics, clinical descriptions and underlying factors of syndromes assessed by the standard clinical scales of the MMPI-II. For analysis, we used the specific subscales of (1) Subjective Depression (Dep-1), depression, anergia, and anhedonia; (2) Cynicism (CYN), anger and negative feelings toward self/others; (3) Psychomotor Acceleration (Ma2), a proclivity for increased energy, restlessness, and excitement; (4) Posttraumatic Stress (Pk), trauma, emotional turmoil, intrusive thoughts, and feeling misunderstood/mistreated; (5) Repression (R), the tendency to avoid or deny unpleasant affect; (6) Ego Strength (ES), adaptability, resiliency, and personal resourcefulness; and (7) Over-controlled Hostility (O-H), the rigid inhibition of frustration (Hathaway & McKinley, 1989). The subscales used in this investigation have all shown high reliability and validity, internal consistency, and construct validity (Ben-Porath, McCully, & Graham, 2000; Graham, 2002; Lilienfeld, 1999; Spiro, Butcher, Levenson, Aldwin, & Bose, 2000).

Personality Assessment Inventory (PAI). The PAI (Morey, 1991) is a 344-item self-report measure of personality in which examinees select the response that best pertains to them, endorsing a statement as not at all true, slightly true, mainly true, or very true. Test–retest reliability of the PAI demonstrated that the instrument taps relatively enduring patient characteristics rather than current clinical state alone (Morey, 1991; Parker, Daleiden, & Simpson, 1999). The PAI consists of 22 scales that provide a comprehensive overview of psychopathology in adults, and has been shown to be a reliable measure of psychopathology (Hopwood, Baker, & Morey, 2008; Morey 1991, 1996), with adequate convergent and discriminant validity in its substance use subscales when compared to other measures of SUDs (Parker et al., 1999). To analyze constructs relevant to self-medication, we used the specific subscales of (1) Paranoid (PAR), a tendency for vigilance, resentment, and a readiness to spot inequities in the way one is treated; (2) Antisocial features (ANT), egocentricity, adventuresomeness, and low empathy; and (3) Aggression (AGG), assertiveness, poor anger control, and/or a proclivity for violence (Morey, 1991).

Young Schema Questionnaire–3rd Edition, Long Form (YSQ-L3). The YSQ-L3 (Young, 2005) is a 232-item self-administered questionnaire that assesses for the presence of Early Maladaptive Schemas. The items are answered on a 6-point scale, with higher item scores (ranging from 1–6) reflecting a more unhealthy level of a particular maladaptive schema. The YSQ-L3 measures 18 cognitive schemas across five separate domains. Evidence supports the reliability and validity of this measure (Lee, Taylor, & Dunn, 1999; Oei & Barnoff, 2007; Schmidt, Joiner, Young, & Telch, 1995; Waller, Meyer, & Ohanian, 2001). For the purpose of this study, we used specific schemas of (1) Emotional Inhibition (EI), excessive inhibition of spontaneous action, feeling, or communication; and (2) Insufficient Self-Control (ISC), pervasive difficulty or refusal to control/delay frustration or restrain emotions and impulses (Young, Klosko, & Weishaar, 2003).

Substance Abuse Subtle Screening Inventory–3 (SASSI-3). The SASSI-3 (Miller, 1999) is a 94-item true/false questionnaire assessing for the possibility of a substance use disorder in individuals. The SASSI has two sides, with questions on the first side producing eight empirically derived scales that discriminate between known groups of substance abusers and persons who do not have a substance use problem. The second side assesses for a client's willingness to admit alcohol or drug abuse problems (Lazowski, Miller, Boye, & Miller, 1998). Both sides are taken into account when assessing for abuse/dependence problems. The SASSI has a *DSM-IV* substance dependence diagnostic criterion correspondence rate of 94%, excellent test–retest reliability, and is considered a valid and reliable measure of detecting substance dependence in respondents in multiple settings (Lazowski et al., 1998).

Addiction Severity Index, 5th Ed. (ASI). The ASI (McLellan et al., 1992) is a well-known and widely used structured interview designed to assess the severity of drug and alcohol use by analyzing addiction-related impairment in seven areas of functioning: medical, psychological, family/social, legal, employment, alcohol, and drug. The reliability and validity of this measure in treated substance abusers have been well documented (Appleby, 1997; Argeriou, McCarty, Mulvey, & Daley, 1994; McLellan et al., 1992).

Medical Records Information. Data was gathered from two sources in medical history, including a patient's initial history and physical exam (H&P) and urinanalysis reports upon intake. Initial H&P exams were conducted by medical professionals, where information pertaining to self-reported drug of choice, drug use history, treatment history, and familial drug history was gathered. In addition to other data, this medical information was reviewed by raters when evaluating patients' drug of choice.

Procedure

The information collected came from patients' medical records and assessments recorded via computer systems at the treatment facility, which was condensed into a database using SPSS 18.0. Patients from different treatment programs were included, and also those that did not finish treatment, relapsed, or left against medical advise (AMA). Per validity and reliability standards of both assessments, patients with incomplete or invalid assessments on the MMPI-II [Lie Scale (L) > 70, Infrequency (F) > 99, or Defensiveness (K) > 80)] and PAI [Negative Impression Management (NIM) > 93 or Infrequency (INF) > 82)] were excluded from analysis, reducing the subject pool from an initial $N = 450$ to $N = 332$.

Determining Drug of Choice. In order to accurately and reliably determine each patient's DOC to the best extent possible, multiple points of information pertaining to substance use was separated and independently analyzed by two raters. We collected information generated from the patient's personal assessment of their drug preference and reported use patterns, medical data, and substance-use variables from objective psychological assessments administered at treatment outset. More specifically, we extracted the following information: self-reported DOC, usage reported upon intake (substance tolerance), substance usage history, treatment history, urinalysis, discharge diagnosis (given by a licensed clinical psychologist and two board-certified physicians), and substance use scales from the SASSI, PAI, and ASI. Once the information was gathered, we compared self-reported DOC against medical data and assessment records, and created a stepwise decision-making process to determine drug preference when discrepancies in information existed. We first took the self-reported DOC into account, and then compared this against corroborating information, such as discharge diagnosis. If these pieces of information were congruent, we then concluded the DOC to be the self-reported DOC. When discrepancies existed, individuals reported multiple DOCs, carried multiple SUD diagnoses, and/or in situations of polysubstance use, we incorporated additional information in order to arrive at a decision, including viewing urinalysis reports, considering pre-treatment use/tolerance levels, and relevant substance-use assessment variables.

For example, if an individual identified their DOC as "beer" on their initial intake assessment, and was diagnosed upon discharge with "alcohol dependence" (and no other substance use diagnosis), their DOC was determined to be alcohol and they were categorized into the "CNS depressant" group. If an individual identified a DOC as "heroin," and was given a diagnosis of "opiate dependence" and "alcohol abuse," their DOC was determined to be heroin and they were categorized into the "Opiate" group. If an individual identified their DOC as "beer" and carried more than one substance use dependence or polysubstance dependence diagnosis, we would assess recent usage patterns, urinalysis reports, and assessment variables to distinguish if a preference for one substance over another could be determined. The algorithm we developed to determine drug of choice is too complicated and lengthy to fully present in the body of this article. A detailed description is appended in supplementary materials (see Appendixes A and B.

Using this algorithm, individuals were categorized into one of five drug-of-choice groups: (1) Depressant (alcohol, benzodiazepines, barbiturates), (2) Opiate (narcotics, analgesics), (3) Stimulant (cocaine, amphetamines), (4) Marijuana, and (5) Indeterminate. Any instance after reviewing data/following the algorithm where a rater felt it impossible to confidently determine a drug-of-choice category, that individual was automatically classified as "Indeterminate." For analysis, only the Depressant, Opiate, and Stimulant groups (#1–3) were used, due to their relevance to the SMH, reducing the sample from $N = 332$ to $N = 304$. An interrater reliability analysis using Cohen's Kappa and standards outlined by Shrout and Fleiss (1979) was performed to determine consistency among raters prior to analyzing data.

Data Analysis. Included in the data analysis were 304 individuals with valid assessments classified with depressants, opiates, or stimulants as their DOC. Independent samples *t*-tests were used to assess for variable differences by gender, and chi square analyses to assess for group differences by gender. Using 5 of the 6 MMPI-II variables initially investigated by Suh et al. (2008), we also included variables from additional personality-driven assessments that are congruent with the conceptual basis of the SMH. In total we selected 12 theory-congruent variables to compare between groups from the MMPI-II (Dep-1, O-H, Pk, CYN, Ma2, R, ES), PAI (PAR, AGG, ANT), and YSQ (EI, ISC). We tested the SMH by taking each DOC group, selecting the relevant scales that were hypothesized to distinguish that group from the others, and using multivariate analysis to test whether each group's score on those variables really does set them apart. Using combinations of variables across categories, we chose to conduct three MANOVAs for analysis (IV: DOC group, DV: personality variables) in order to assess whether each group differs from the other two groups on the variables predicted (i.e., depressants group vs. combined opiates/stimulants groups; opiates group vs. combined depressants/stimulants groups; and stimulants group vs. combined depressants/opiates groups). Hotelling's T (1931), or multivariate analysis, was chosen as the primary analysis because it most concisely and powerfully tests the theory-driven notion that each DOC group differs from the other two groups across combinations of specific personality variables while controlling for Type I error.

If multivariate analysis demonstrated statistical significance, we followed with univariate analysis to determine whether the directionality of each variable was as predicted, and to clarify what might be "driving" the relationships between personality and drug of choice. With this analysis being multivariate, effect sizes are reported as partial η^2, or partial eta squared. Effect sizes of partial η^2, according to Cohen (1988), fall within the following parameters: 0.0099 = small effect, 0.0588 = medium effect, and 0.1379 = large effect.

RESULTS

Patient Demographics

The sample consisted of 232 males (69.9%) and 100 females (29.9%). Age ranged from 17–71 years old ($M = 37.7$, $SD = 12.34$). Ethnic distribution consisted of 301 Caucasians (90.1%), 11 African Americans (3.3%), 5 Native Americans (1.5%), 3 identified as "Other" (0.6%), and 12 chose not to answer (3.6%). Distribution of relationship status was 120 married (35.9%), 108 single (32.3%), 58 divorced (17.4%), 24 separated (7.2%), 5 widowed (1.5%), 4 engaged (1.2%), 1 partnered (0.3%), and 12 chose not to answer (3.6%).

Treatment Demographics

In regards to the longest period of past sobriety, 105 individuals reported less than 1 month (32.0%), 39 as 1–3 months (11.7%), 32 as 4–6 months (9.6%), 40 as 6 months to 1 year (12.0%), 42 as 1–3 years (12.6%), 32 as five years or more (9.6%), and 42 did not answer (12.6%). Total time spent in current treatment ranged from 1–381 days ($M = 59.6$; $SD = 49.8$). Of those who entered current treatment, 235 completed their stay (70.4%), 48 left against medical advice (14.4%), 43 were "Administratively Discharged" for rule violations (12.9%), and 6 were "Therapeutically Discharged" to a higher level of medical or psychiatric care (1.8%).

Assessing Drug of Choice

Using the algorithm described above, individuals were categorized into one of five conditions by two independent raters. Each rater was given 70 randomly selected cases to test inter-rater reliability, classifying over 20% of the sample to provide adequate power. Using Cohen's Kappa, we demonstrated a rater agreement of 0.91, $p < .001$, which is considered "very good agreement" (Altman, 1991; Fleiss & Cohen, 1973). Of the cases assessed, 174 individuals were identified as preferring "Depressants" (52.1%), 96 as preferring "Opiates" (28.7%), 34 as preferring "Stimulants" (10.2%), 15 as "Marijuana" (4.5%), and 11 as "Indeterminate" (3.3%).

Gender Differences

According to independent samples t-tests with a Bonferroni correction of $p < .004$, females exhibited significantly higher levels of Subjective Depression than males, Dep-1: Female (F) Mean = 67.98 ($SD = 15.16$); Male (M) Mean = 61.24 ($SD = 14.36$). This is consistent with previous research that females have higher rates of depression than males (Nolen-Hoeksema & Hilt, 2009). Chi square analysis indicated that gender did not significantly differ between drug-of-choice groups (chi square = 0.73, $df = 2$, $p = .69$).

Hypothesis I: CNS Depressants versus Other. Per Khantzian (2003), individuals preferring depressants are emotionally over-controlled and inhibitive. As such, we anticipated depressant SUDs to reflect this style of emotional functioning in higher levels of Repression (R; MMPI-II), Over-controlled Hostility (O-H; MMPI-II), and Emotional Inhibition (EI; YSQ), while reporting lower levels of Anhedonia (Dep-1; MMPI-II), Paranoia (PAR; PAI), and Aggression (AGG; PAI) when compared to other drug groups. In our first analysis, those in the Depressant group were coded as "1," and Opiate or Stimulant groups as "0."

Because this hypothesis specifies six comparisons, we first tested the omnibus model using a MANOVA comparing depressant users to other users across all the proposed in-

Table 1. Hypothesis I: Univariate Analysis of the 6 Measures Hypothesized to
Differentiate Depressant Group from Other (Opiate/Stimulant) Groups, and Directionality

Variable	Depressant Mean	Other Mean	F	p	Partial η²	Predicted Direction?
Paranoia	50.20 (10.54)	55.52 (10.95)	16.34	.001	.057	Yes
Aggression	50.20 (12.64)	53.58 (14.18)	4.29	.039	.016	Yes
Repression	53.29 (10.01)	53.17 (10.38)	0.004	.953	< .001	Yes
Over-Controlled Hostility	51.78 (9.62)	48.27 (10.49)	8.17	.005	.029	Yes
Subjective Depression	61.38 (14.63)	67.68 (14.45)	12.43	.001	.044	Yes
Emotional Inhibition	9.87 (13.45)	8.92 (10.45)	0.39	.531	< .001	Yes

dices, taken together. The overall model was statistically significant, indicating that across the six measures taken together, the Depressant group and Other group responded differently: $F(6, 266) = 5.27$, $p < .001$; Hotelling's Trace = .12, partial η^2 = .11.

Table 1 summarizes the six univariate differences on the criterion variable, specifying differences, and their directionality. As per Table 1, four of the six univariate comparisons were statistically significant, and all group differences were in the hypothesized direction. Specifically, the Depressant group significantly differed from Other groups in their levels of Paranoia, $F(1, 266) = 16.34$, $p < .001$, partial η^2 = .06; Subjective Depression, $F(1, 266) = 12.43$, $p < .001$, partial η^2 = .04; Over-controlled Hostility, $F(1, 266) = 8.17$, $p = .005$, partial η^2 = .03; and Aggression, $F(1, 266) = 4.29$, $p = .039$, partial η^2 = .02. In sum, the depressant group exhibited lower levels of paranoia, aggression, and depression and higher levels of over-controlled hostility when compared to other substance users. No significant differences were observed in levels of repression or emotional inhibition. This partially supports the SMH in regard to drug specificity of depressant users, in that the groups function differently with regard to emotionality and defense, but not entirely as predicted by SMH.

Hypothesis 2: Opiate versus Other. Per Khantzian (1999), individuals identified as

preferring opiates struggle to regulate intense affect, are increasingly aggressive/hostile, experience depression and trauma, and display antisocial behavior in conjunction with their use. Accordingly, we anticipated those identified as preferring opiates to reflect this style of emotional functioning by having higher levels of reported Posttraumatic Stress (Pk; MMPI-II), Anhedonia (Dep-1; MMPI-II), Cynicism (CYN; MMPI-II), Antisocial Tendencies (ANT; PAI), Aggression (AGG; PAI) and Insufficient-Self Control (ISC; YSQ) than other substance users, while having lower levels of Ego Strength (ES; MMPI-II). In the second multivariate analysis, we coded individuals in the Opiate group as "1," and Depressant/Stimulant group as "0."

The second multivariate analysis indicated the overall model as significant, meaning that across the seven measures combined, the Opiate group and Other group responded differently, $F(7, 263) = 5.29$, $p < .001$, Hotelling's Trace = .14, partial η^2 = .12. Table 2 summarizes the seven univariate analyses, indicating significance and directionality. As per Table 2, five of the seven univariate comparisons were statistically significant, and all group differences occurred in the hypothesized direction. Specifically, Opiate SUDs differed significantly on their levels of Posttraumatic Stress, $F(1, 263) = 6.91$, $p = .01$, partial η^2 = .03; Subjective Depression, $F(1, 263) = 7.68$, $p = .006$, partial η^2 = .03; Cyni-

Table 2. Hypothesis II: Univariate Analysis of the Seven Measures Hypothesized to Differentiate Opiate Group from Other (Depressant/Stimulant) Groups, and Directionality

Variable	Opiate Mean	Other Mean	F	p	Partial η^2	Predicted Direction?
Posttraumatic Stress	65.39 (14.79)	60.18 (15.29)	6.91	.009	.025	Yes
Subjective Depression	67.66 (14.58)	62.34 (14.71)	7.68	.006	.028	Yes
Cynicism	54.16 (9.62)	49.51 (10.17)	12.66	.001	.045	Yes
Ego Strength	39.26 (13.50)	42.96 (13.50)	4.38	.037	.016	Yes
Insufficient Self-Control	26.95 (22.66)	23.42 (21.30)	1.54	.216	.006	Yes
Aggression	53.52 (14.99)	50.63 (12.55)	2.73	.100	.010	Yes
Antisocial Tendencies	63.74 (13.16)	56.44 (11.05)	22.56	.001	.077	Yes

cism, $F(1, 263) = 12.66$ $p < .001$, partial $\eta^2 = .05$; Ego Strength, $F(1, 263) = 4.38$, $p = .04$, partial $\eta^2 = .02$; and Antisocial Tendencies, $F(1, 263) = 22.56$, $p < .001$, partial $\eta^2 = .08$. In sum, the Opiate group displayed higher levels of Posttraumatic Stress, Subjective Depression, Cynicism, and Antisocial Behavior and lower levels of Ego Strength when compared to other groups. No significant differences were observed for the Opiate group on levels of Insufficient Self-Control or Aggression. This partially supports the SMH, in that the groups function differently with regard to emotionality and defense, but not entirely as predicted by the SMH.

Hypothesis 3: CNS Stimulants versus Other. The third hypothesis pertained to Stimulant SUDs. As per the SMH (Khantzian, 1999), we hypothesized that when compared to other groups, Stimulant SUDs experience anhedonia, have a propensity to mania, paranoia, and aggression, and struggle to regulate their emotions. We anticipated these differences to be reflected through higher levels of Hypomania (Ma2; MMPI-II), Subjective Depression (Dep-1; MMPI-II); Cynicism (CYN; MMPI-II), Paranoia (PAR; PAI), and Insuffi-

cient-Self Control (ISC; YSQ). For the third multivariate analysis, we coded individuals identified as addicted to a Stimulant as "1" and Opiate/Depressant SUDs as "0."

The third multivariate analysis indicated that across the combined five measures, Stimulant SUDs do not respond differently than Other SUDs, $F(5, 265) = 0.50$, $p = .77$, Hotelling's Trace = .01, partial $\eta^2 = .01$. With regard to the Stimulant group, there were no significant differences between groups, and the SMH was not supported.

Post-Hoc Discriminant Function Analysis

We elected to conduct a post-hoc discriminant analysis (DA; Khattree & Naik, 2000) in an attempt to better understand the underlying functions that distinguish Depressant and Opiate users from each other in our sample through examining their unique profiles together. Discriminant analysis allows researchers to determine the underlying dimensionality of the data and the interrelationships among variables. We used the following significant predictor variables from the previous analysis: Antisocial Ten-

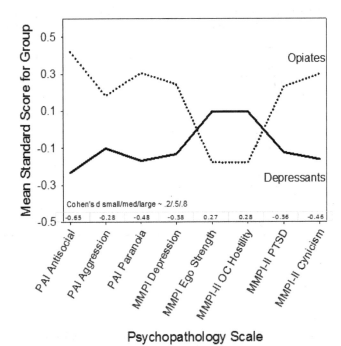

FIGURE 1. Discriminant function analysis: Profiles of Depressant and Opiate groups. Note. Small numbers above X-Axis are the effect size of the group difference, Cohen's $d = (X1 - X2) / SD_{pooled}$. According to Cohen, small/medium/large ~ .2/.5/.8.

dencies, Paranoia, Aggression, Cynicism, Depression, Trauma, Over-controlled Hostility, and Ego Strength. The last result is a profile of differences between the Opiate and Depressant groups. We turned to descriptive multivariate modeling to see if there is a clinical profile that makes theoretical sense. Discriminate analysis is an ordinary least squares model much like linear regression: $Y_1 = B_0 + X_1B_1 + X_2B_2 + ... + X_N B_N$. However, in discriminant analysis the outcome Y is a category with two or more classes. First, as shown in Table 3, we ran eight independent t-tests using both traditional and bootstrap t-tests (Efron, 1993). Ignoring multiple testing in the left column, all eight t-tests were significant ($p < .05$). With bootstrap correction (Westfall & Young, 1993) five of eight tests were significant.

Next, we ran a discriminant function with SAS CANDISC in which X_1, $X_2...X_8$ were the eight personality variable scores shown in Table 3. The eight scores were z-scores (Mean = 0.00, SD = 1.00), letting us view group differences as Cohen's d effect sizes. The model had a significant canonical correlation, $r = 0.33$, $p > .0001$, suggesting that a statistically significant profile exists. Cohen (1992) suggests that $r = 0.30$ is a "medium" effect size. Effect sizes of the variables ranged from 0.27 to 0.65. Figure 1 displays the profiles of both Depressant and Opiate users on the eight personality variables.

DISCUSSION AND CONCLUSION

The omnibus theory that individuals with SUDs differ in their emotional and characterological functioning based on drug of choice was supported for those preferring Depressants and Opiates. Taken together, findings support the notion that the SMH in-

Table 3. Significance of Differences between Groups

Scale	Raw P	Bootstrap P
PAI Antisocial	< .0001	< .0001
PAI Aggression	0.03	0.14
PAI Paranoia	0.002	0.001
MMPI-II Depression	0.004	0.03
MMPI-II Ego Strength	0.04	0.20
MMPI-II OC Hostility	0.04	0.19
MMPI-II PTSD	0.01	0.046
MMPI-II Cynicism	0.0004	0.003

Note. Distribution-free bootstrap re-sampling ran nonparametric t-test 10,000 times for each variable.

forms us about how personality is associated with drug of choice. Across the three hypotheses, there were 18 predictions (six for Hypothesis I; seven for Hypothesis II; and five for Hypothesis III). Of the 18 group comparisons, 17 were in the predicted direction; 9 were significantly different differences; and the a-priori MANOVA for Hypotheses I and II were statistically significant.

Group 1 (Depressants)

According to Khantzian (2003), individuals addicted to a depressant (alcohol, benzodiazepine, or barbiturate) inhibit and over-contain their emotional experience, using rigid defenses such as repression and denial. The use of a depressant acts to soften this rigid defensive structure and reduce an individual's internal tension state. Operating in this manner, alcohol users are notoriously alexithymic and present with flattened or "cut off" affect, and following extended periods of sobriety (Aguilar de Arcos, Verdejo-Garcia, Peralta-Ramirez, Sanchez-Barrera, & Perez-Garcia, 2005; de Timary, Luts, Hers, & Luminet, 2008). Identifying these concepts in subscales of the MMPI-II, PAI, and YSQ, we believed depressant users would differ on assessments when compared to other drug users, and in six specific areas.

In partial support of the first hypothesis, multivariate analysis indicated that Depressant SUDs respond differently than Other SUDs across the six predicted scales taken together. Group differences on all six of the relevant scales were in the predicted direction, four significantly. Specifically, as predicted, the Depressant group presented with significantly lower levels of Paranoia, Depression, and Aggression, and significantly higher levels of Over-controlled Hostility when compared to other SUDs. The Depressant group also had higher, but not significant, levels of both Emotional Inhibition and Repression.

According to research, those with an alcohol use disorder experience higher rates of depressive disorders than the general population, and at elevated levels among treatment seekers (Grant et al., 2004; Lynskey, 1998). With these statistics in mind, one might anticipate higher reflections on assessments that pertain to depressive experience. In our sample, and accordance with the SMH, these scores were lower and in the nonclinical range on the MMPI-II. Overall, the group reported lower levels of symptomology/psychopathology than other groups. We believe this reflects a dismissal of affect or denial. Taken with findings from Suh et al. (2008), there is building evidence that a denial-based defensive system is characteristic of alcohol abusers. Surprisingly, we did not find repression or emotional inhibition to significantly differ between drug groups. We believe this may be a function of the population studied. Depressant users seeking treatment are considered to have higher occurrences of psychopathology (Grant et al., 2004), and in being an "acute" population, could also reflect under-developed, faltering, or regressed psychological defenses. In creating his hierarchy of ego defenses, Valliant (1994) characterized repression and isolation of affect as more developed, or "neurotic" defenses than that of denial, which is considered more primitive. This is also supported by Kernberg (1975), who theorized denial to function at different levels, where primitive levels of denial are akin to splitting-off experiences and higher levels of denial are related to repression.

Group 2 (Opiates)

The SMH (Khantzian, 1999) posits that individuals identified as addicted to an opiate, narcotic, or analgesic use the drug to attenuate feelings of aggression, rage, and depression often associated with trauma. Opiate SUDs rarely possess a defensive structure able to regulate overwhelming emotion. Instead, there is collapse (i.e., psychic trauma; Dodes, 1990; Khantzian, 1999). Opiates act as a coping mechanism and mute psychic pain, blunt acute helplessness, and give temporary relief to a compromised ego structure (Dodes, 2009; Khantzian, 1999; Wurmser, 1974). In comparing assessments, we anticipated Opiate SUDs to reflect emotional hypersensitivity, poor emotional control, and a higher incidence of trauma than their counterparts.

In partial support of the second hypothesis, multivariate analysis indicated that Opiate SUDs respond differently than Other SUDs across the seven predicted scales taken together. Five of the seven predictor variables were significant, and all group differences were in the hypothesized direction. We found opiate SUDs to display significantly higher levels of Subjective Depression, Cynicism, Antisocial Tendencies, and Posttraumatic Stress than other groups. Concurrent with the SMH, the Opiate group also had significantly lower levels of Ego Strength

than other SUDs. In particular, Cynicism and Antisocial attitudes seem to be driving this relationship. Both scales are associated with skepticism and mistrust of others, which may relate to early trauma, which is thought of as integral to understanding opiate SUDs (Darke, 2012).

Group 3 (Stimulants)

Identifying both "high" and "low" energy users, the SMH posits that the need to regulate inner emptiness, boredom, and depressive states or to maintain restlessness drives individuals to the energizing effects of cocaine (Khantzian & Albanese, 2008; Suh et al., 2008). Conceptualizing cocaine use as a "flight from depression," we anticipated that this group would be increasingly disinhibited, risk taking, and display higher levels of depression, a lack of self-control, and restlessness when compared to other groups. Multivariate analysis of the Stimulant group did not confirm predicted differences between stimulant users and other SUDs.

It is tempting to attribute the failure of Hypothesis III to low power ($n = 34$). Still, the group differences were very small, even if four of the five were in the predicted direction. Even *with* more power, the effect size is anemic. More likely these findings reflect either a mistranslation of the theory, or a failure of the theory itself. With Khantzian proposing two "types" of stimulant users (one "low" depressed, and one "high" manic), we might better have *first* investigated to see if cocaine SUDs do indeed have different response styles. If "low" and "high" energy groups exist, their response styles would perhaps differ in their levels of hypomania, risk taking, and depression. As no previous research has translated the theory in this manner, we believe it might be an area for further investigation to ascertain whether a mistranslation has muddled empirical findings. Recent research (Suh et al., 2008) providing empirical support for the SMH found Psychomotor Acceleration (Ma2, MMPI-II) to predict stimulant SUDs, which we could not replicate. The same study did not observe any significant findings surrounding cocaine disorders and depression, and suggested using alternative scales to capture the relationship (which we did, and still found no significance).

Since the introduction of the SMH, research has demonstrated a rise in rates of antisocial personality disorder among treatment-seeking cocaine users, which is now thought to affect between 45–55% of patients (Poling, Kosten, & Sofuoglu, 2007; Rounsaville et al., 1991). Also, individuals dependent on cocaine have demonstrated higher rates of childhood ADHD, estimated at 35%, and reportedly use cocaine to treat their symptoms (Carroll & Rounsaville, 1993). Theorists agree that stimulant SUDs display higher levels of sensation/stimulus-seeking behavior and impulsivity, which also reflect antisocial and/or attention-disordered traits (Khantzian, 1999; Poling, Kosten, & Sofuoglu, 2007). This also provides an alternative explanation for why Suh et al. (2008) found Psychomotor Acceleration to be related to cocaine SUDs. According to Hathaway and McKinley (1989), individuals scoring high in Psychomotor Acceleration are tense, restless, and excited and may seek out risk, excitement, or danger as a way of overcoming boredom. This can be interpreted as a "flight from depression," but also could be due to an attention deficit or related to antisocial tendencies. Although our sample size was small, with the alternative explanations posed and changes in the population's epidemiology and treatment-seeking characteristics documented, further research and possible revisions to this aspect of Khantizian's theory may be necessary. In sum, it may be that the psychological makeup of stimulant SUDs is more heterogeneous than other substance use groups, thus presenting a special challenge for theory and research.

Discriminant Function Analysis

Post-hoc discriminant function analysis details the nature of differences between opiate and depressant users, when considered together. The profiles of Depressant and Opiate groups along the significant personality variables taken from our first analysis (Figure 1) demonstrate sizeable differences among areas of emotionality and interpersonal volatility. In comparison, the Opiate group appears more dysregulated in general, where affective experience may be felt more intensely than those who use depressants. We believe the nature of these differences has important implications for treatment.

Previous work on testing the SMH has had limited success (e.g., Castaneda, 1994; Craig et al., 1988; Green et al., 1993), which may be due to incorrect assessment of emotional constructs and use of broad assessments incapable of recognizing nuances between groups (Suh et al., 2008). More recent work providing support for Self-Medication (Suh et al., 2008), including this project, used assessments that better targeted the underlying emotional functioning of SUDs, where differences between groups linger.

Of note was our ability to accurately assess each individual's drug of choice. A finalized diagnosis was also used after each individual had gone through treatment, which allowed for the potential minimization of problems at treatment entry to subside, though notably had been a concern in previous studies. With dual raters, our reliability was very strong (91%). The most challenging cases to categorize were those with complex polysubstance dependence, which generally fell in the "undifferentiated" category ($N = 11$).

Study Limitations

Hypothesis testing in this population was a difficult endeavor due to the inability to assess individuals after a long period of abstinence or observe pre-addiction personality/psychopathology. Therefore, it is possible that extended drug use or withdrawal drove or altered a person's presentation. In addition, some individuals were likely taking psychiatric and medical medications at the time of being assessed, which could have influenced their presentation on assessments. However, individuals experiencing withdrawal symptoms were identified upon treatment entry and adequately medicated/detoxified prior to completing assessment measures, which helped account for that possibility, along with the elimination of invalid assessments from the sample. Also, researchers have found that even after an extended period of sobriety, substance abusers remained deficient in their emotional regulation abilities, and that psychiatric illnesses such as depression and posttraumatic stress generally precede substance use (Deykin, Levy, & Wells, 1987; Jacobsen, Southwick, & Kosten, 2001; Thorberg & Lyvers, 2005). Still, this remains a limitation of the study. A longstanding debate in the substance use and personality literature is the notion of causality, or possibility that extensive drug use alters personality characteristics. These conclusions are also limited by the sample's retrospective and cross-sectional design. Due to the study's retrospective nature, we were unable to interview subjects directly, which would have strengthened our assessment of drug of choice by providing important subjective information on access to substances and conscious experience that influence drug choice. Lastly, we recognize that personality components reflect one of many pieces of a complex interplay of factors that propel the acquisition and maintenance of a particular substance dependency. In order to thoroughly understand the impact of emotionality on drug of choice, longitudinal studies are necessary.

Future Research

Although having similar project aims, this investigation used more varied measures

and had strikingly different sample characteristics than Suh et al. (2008), and offers additional promising evidence for the SMH. The sample for this investigation was primarily White, well educated, mostly employed, health insured, and enrolled in inpatient treatment. For Suh et al. (2008), the sample had a richer ethnic distribution, were of lower socioeconomic status, varying education levels, and of an outpatient population. Both studies, although characteristically diverse, provide support for the SMH. This further highlights the need for continued use of the Harris-Lingoes and Content scales of the MMPI-II in future research, particularly for replication purposes in refining the SMH (Brandt et al., 2014). Additional research could also help clarify differences found in this Stimulant population compared to Suh et al. (2008), to determine whether the current findings are due to differences in sample characteristics, mistranslation of theory, or perhaps reflect the hypothesized changing nature of the Stimulant SUDs from depressed to antisocial characters.

Difficulties in self-regulation are core to the SMH, and remain major risk factors for relapses post-treatment, and helping individuals understand their use in relation to their interpersonal/intrapsychic world could help reduce this risk (Sinha, 2008). Approaching patients from an empathic and humanized perspective provides powerful reparation to the alienation, shame, and stigmatization associated with SUDs, and is critical to developing the therapeutic relationship in a population highly vulnerable to treatment attrition (Curran, Kirchner, Worley, Rookey & Booth, 2002; Khantzian, 2012). Clinicians can use this theory to deepen their understanding of patients through drug preference and guide intervention strategies. The differences observed between opiate and depressant disorders in personality could direct clinicians on how to approach self-regulation with each population. Specifically, those preferring opiates may need to focus on containment and emotional titration, while fostering awareness of emotional processes with depressant users. For both groups, of great importance is the understanding of current defenses, their maladaptive nature, and replacing them with more evolved and adaptive coping skills.

APPENDIX A. STEPS TO ASSESS DRUG OF CHOICE (DOC)

Information required:

- Self-reported DOC as recorded on initial assessment by MD on History and Physical
- Diagnoses given by treatment team at discharge (Clinical Director and MD)
- History of use as determined on History and Physical in initial assessment
- Drug Screen: **Be aware that *alcohol* will likely NOT be positive on a drug screen, as it can be cleared from an individual's system within 24 hours. Therefore, in conditions concerning alcohol, this item needs to be interpreted as such. Also, *marijuana* stays in an individual's system for up to 30 days after use, whereas opiates and benzodiazepines have a much shorter half-life in the body. Take this into account as individuals will stay positive for THC longer than other drugs. Also, beware if an individual is going through *medical detoxification* or *withdrawing* that there is a chance they are given *benzodiazepines* to control symptoms (keep an eye out for *DSM* 292.xx codes for withdrawals in diagnoses and/ or detoxification conditions).
- Clinical Variables from objective assessment data:
    - PAI drug
    - PAI alcohol
    - ASI drug
    - ASI alcohol
    - SASSI FVA
    - SASSI FVOD
- Drug amount used as reported in History and Physical

Objectives:

- Note the substance
- Categorize into the following 6 conditions:
    - 1 = CNS Depressants (Alcohol, Benzodiazepines, Barbiturates)
    - 2 = Opiates, Narcotics, and Analgesics
    - 3 = CNS Stimulants
    - 4 = Marijuana

5 = Cannot Determine DOC due to complex poly-substance dependence or "other" drug that does not fit into a category
   –This condition is reserved for individuals who are heavy poly-drug users that do not have a distinguishable preference for one drug over another
   –Also, individuals that claim no DOC and have no diagnosis fit into this category
   –Occasionally, individuals claiming behavioral addictions such as "sex addiction" or "gambling addiction" fall into this category
6 = Not enough information to determine DOC
   –This condition is reserved for individuals missing vital information (e.g., H&P, diagnosis, drug screen) that make determining a DOC impossible

APPENDIX B
PROCEDURE FOR RATER TO FOLLOW:

As per "steps" described (in detail) previously:

   1 = Self-reported DOC in History and Physical
   2 = Diagnosis given by treatment team
   3 = Self-reported use at the time of treatment entry, including amounts,
      in History and Physical
   4 = Drug Screen
   5 = Clinical Variables
   6 = Amount of use reported in initial assessment

Condition A:
   If 1 = X and 2 = X, then DOC = X.

Condition B:
   If 1 = X and 2 = Polysubstance, then
      a. Review 3. If 3 is positive for X, then DOC = X.
      b. If 3 is negative for X, review 4. If 4 is positive for X, then DOC = X.
      c. If 3 and 4 are negative for X, but both positive for Y, then DOC = Y.
      i. Under this condition, corroborate information by reviewing 5 and 6 (a–f). If one of the variables (a–f) is clinically significant, then DOC = Y.
      d. If 1 and 3 and 4 are both positive for multiple substances, review information from

6. Determine DOC by reviewing amount of drugs used per patient report. If severity of use is indistinguishable between drugs, then no DOC can be reported.

Condition C:
If 1 = X, Y, and 2 = X, then DOC = X.

If 1 = X, Y, and 2 = Y, then DOC = Y.

If 1 = X, Y, Z, and 2 = X only, then DOC = X. (This is for all cases where information from 1 contains multiple drugs with only one diagnosis given. If the individual does not have a diagnosis for these drugs it is likely they were used recreationally or abused, and the individual's dependence on a substance falls more into one specific category as determined by treatment team throughout that individual's course of treatment.)

If 1 = X, Y, and 2 = X *dependence* and Y *abuse*, then DOC = X.

If 1 = X, Y, and 2 = X *abuse* and Y *dependence*, then DOC = Y.

Condition D:
If 1 = X, Y, and 2 = X, Y, then:

a. Review 3. If 3 is only positive for one (X or Y), then the substance 3 is positive for becomes that individual's DOC.

  i. IF 3 is positive for both X and Y, but has a "2" instead of a "1" for either X or Y, then defer to the drug that has a "1" on History and Physical. This is likely a situation where a patient received a diagnosis of drug dependence based on history (and is not currently "choosing" this drug).

b. If 3 is positive for both X and Y, review 4. If only one of these substances is positive on 4, then that substance becomes the individual's DOC.

  i. HOWEVER if either X or Y is reported as *alcohol*, it is likely that this will not show on 4 (drug screen). Therefore, skip to 5 and/or 6. Compare the drug and alcohol variables (a–f) for clinical significance.

  ii. If both substances on 4 are positive for X and Y, then record both drugs as DOC and note that in the database, so we can look at #6.

     a. These individuals will be flagged and looked back into their H&P/Drug Screen to review levels of the drug in their system and amount of use. If one substance is substantially

higher than the other (respectively), that that substance becomes the individual's DOC. Otherwise, it is inconclusive.

Condition E:
If 1 = X, 2 = Y, and 3 = Y (not X), then DOC = Y.

If 1 = X, 2 = Y, and 3 is positive for X and Y (or polysubstance), then:

a. Review 4. If 4 is positive for one of X or Y, then that substance would become DOC.

  i. If either X or Y is *alcohol*, skip 4 and move to 5. Compare the drug and alcohol variables (a–f) for clinical significance. If more variables relating to alcohol are significant, then that becomes the individual's DOC (and vice-versa). If all variables are clinically significant, then no drug of choice can be determined.

     a. If no discernment can be made from this information, move to information from #6 and flag this in the database.

b. Review information from 6. Determine DOC by reviewing amount of drugs used per patient report. If severity of use is indistinguishable between drugs, then no DOC can be reported.

c. If no DOC can be determined, and X and Y are both substances that fall in the same group (e.g., CNS depressants such as alcohol and a benzodiazepine), then the individual can still be grouped for the study, with no determined DOC.

Condition F:
If 1 = X, 2 = Y, but 3 and 4 = X (not Y), then DOC = X.

If 1 = X and 2 = Y, review 3.

a. If 3 is positive for X (not Y), then DOC = X.

b. If 3 is positive for both X and Y, review 4.

c. If 4 is positive for one of X or Y, then DOC is that substance.

  i. However, in the case of alcohol being X, move on to 5. If more variables relating to alcohol are significant, then that becomes the individual's DOC (and vice-versa). If all variables are clinically significant, then no drug of choice can be determined.

  ii. If no DOC can be determined, and X and Y are both substances that fall in the same group (e.g., CNS depressants), then the individual can still be grouped for the study, with no determined DOC.

Condition G:

If 1 = X, Y

AND

2 = X, Y

AND

Both 3 and 4 are positive for X and Y

THEN

Review information from 6. Determine DOC by reviewing amount of drugs used per patient report. If severity of use is indistinguishable between drugs, then no DOC can be reported.

Condition H:

If 1 = X, X, and Y (e.g., multiple substances within same use category, such as two different types of opiates) AND 2 = X, then DOC = X.

If 1 = X, X, and Y, and 2 = Poly-substance, then DOC = X.

If 1 = X, X, and Y, and 2 = X, Y, then review 3. If 3 is positive for only X, then DOC = X.

a. If 3 is positive for X and Y, review 4.

b. If 4 is positive for X and Y (minus situations when alcohol/marijuana are involved), skip to 5/6 and follow the same procedure of flagging this in your database.

c. If 4 is positive for only one of X or Y (minus alcohol/marijuana), then that becomes the individual's DOC.

REFERENCES

Abraham, H. D., & Fava, M. (1999). Order of onset of substance abuse and depression in a sample of depressed outpatients. *Comprehensive Psychiatry, 40*, 44-50. doi: 10.1016 /S0010-440X(99)90076-7

Aguilar de Arcos, F., Verdejo-Garcia, A., Peralta-Ramirez, M. I., Sanchez-Barrera, M., & Perez-Garcia, M. (2005). Experience of emotions in substance abuser exposed to images containing neutral, positive, and negative affective stimuli. *Drug and Alcohol Dependence, 78*, 159-167. doi: 10.1016/j.drugalcdep.2004.10.010

Aharonovich, E., Nguyen, M. S., & Nunes, E. V. (2001). Anger and depressive states among treatment-seeking drug abusers: Testing the psychopharmacological specificity hypothesis. *The American Journal on Addictions, 10*, 327-334. doi: 10.1080/aja.10.4.327.334

Altman, D. G. (1991). *Practical statistics for medical research.* London: Chapman and Hall.

Appleby, L. (1997). Assessing substance use in multiproblem patients: Reliability and validity of the Addiction Severity Index (ASI) in a mental hospital population. *Journal of Nervous and Mental Disease, 185*, 159-165. doi: 10.1097/00005053-199703000-00005

Argeriou, M., McCarty, D., Mulvey, K., & Daley, M. (1994). Use of the addiction severity index with homeless substance abusers. *Journal of Substance Abuse Treatment, 11*, 359-365. doi: 10.1016/0740-5472(94)90046-9

Ben-Porath, Y. S., McCully, E., & Graham, J. R. (2000). Incremental validity of the MMPI-II content scales in the assessment of personality and psychopathology by self-report. In J. N. Butcher (Ed.), *Basic sources on the MMPI-II* (pp. 343-357). Minneapolis: University of Minnesota Press.

Benton, D. (1988). The role of opiate mechanisms in social relationships. In M. Ladler (Ed.), *The psychopharmacology of addiction.* New York: Oxford University Press.

Blume, A. W., Schmaling, K. B., & Marlatt, G. A. (2000). Revisiting the self-medication hypothesis from a behavioral perspective. *Cognitive and Behavioral Practice, 7*, 379-384. doi: 10.1016/S1077-7229(00)80048-6

Brandt, M. J., IJzerman, H., Dijksterhuis, A., Farach, F. J., Geller, J., Giner-Sorella, R., et al. (2014). The replication recipe: What makes for a convincing replication? *Journal of Experimental Social Psychology, 50*, 217-224. doi: 10.1016/j.jesp.2013.10.005

Butcher, J. N., Dahlstrom, W. G., Graham, J. R., Tellegen, A., & Kaemmer, B. (1989). *Minnesota Multiphasic Personality Inventory-2 (MMPI-II): Manual for administration and scoring.* Minneapolis: University of Minnesota Press.

Butcher, J. N., Graham, J. R., Williams, C. L., & Ben-Porath, Y. S. (1990). *Development and use of the MMPI-II content scales.* Minneapolis, MN: University of Minnesota Press.

Butcher, J. N., & Williams, C. L. (Eds.). (2000). *Essentials of MMPI-II and MMPI-A interpretation* (Vol. 2). Minneapolis, MN: University of Minnesota Press.

Caan, W. (2002). The nature of heroin and cocaine dependence. In W. Caan & J. de Belleroche (Eds.), *Drink, drugs and dependence: From science to clinical practice.* New York: Routledge.

Carroll, K. M., & Rounsaville, B. J. (1993). History and significance of childhood attention deficit disorder in treatment-seeking cocaine abusers. *Comprehensive Psychiatry, 34*, 75-82. doi: 10.1016/0010-440X(93)90050-E

Castaneda, R. (1994). Empirical assessment of the self-medication hypothesis among dually diagnosed inpatients. *Comprehensive Psychiatry, 35*, 180-184. doi: 10.1016/0010-440X(94)90189-9

Cohen, J. (1988). *Statistical power: Analysis for the behavioral sciences* (2nd ed.). Hillsdale, NJ: Erlbaum.

Cohen, J. (1992). A power primer. *Psychological Bulletin, 112*(1), 155-159. doi: 10.1037//0033-2909.112.1.155

Craig, R. J. (1988). Psychological functioning of cocaine free-basers derived from objective psychological tests. *Journal of Clinical Psychology, 44*, 599-606. doi: 10.1002/1097-4679(198807)44:4<599::AID-JCLP2270440417>3.0.CO

Crain, W. C., Ertel, D., & Gorman, B. S. (1975). Personality correlates of drug preference among college undergraduates. *The International Journal of the Addictions, 10*, 849-856.

Curran, G. M., Kirchner, J. E., Worley, M., Rookey, C., & Booth, B. M. (2002). Depressive symptomology and early attrition from intensive outpatient substance use treatment. *Journal of Behavioral Health Services and Research, 29*, 138-143. doi: 10.1007/BF02287700

Darke, S. (2012). Pathways to heroin dependence: Time to re-appraise self-medication. *Addiction, 108*, 659-667. doi: 10.1111/j.1360-0443.2012.04001.x

de Timary, P., Luts, A., Hers, D., & Luminet, O. (2008). Absolute and relative stability of alexithymia in alcoholic inpatients undergoing alcohol withdrawal: Relationship to depression and anxiety. *Psychiatry Research, 157*, 105-113. doi: 10.1016/j.psychres.2006.12.008

Deykin, E. Y., Levy, J. C., & Wells, V. (1987). Adolescent depression, alcohol and drug abuse. *American Journal of Public Health, 77*(2), 178-182. doi: 10.2105/AJPH.77.2.178

Dodes, L. M. (1990). Addiction, helplessness, and narcissistic rage. *Psychoanalytic Quarterly, 59*, 398-419.

Dodes, L. M. (2009). Addiction as a psychological symptom. *Psychodynamic Practice, 15*, 381-393. doi: 10.1080/14753630903230468

Dupont, R. L., & Gold, M. S. (2007). Comorbidity and "self-medication." *Journal of Addictive Diseases, 26*, 13-23. doi: 10.1300/J069v26S01_03

Efron, B. T. R. (1993). *An introduction to the bootstrap*. Boca Raton, FL: Chapman and Hall/CRC.

Fleiss, J. L., & Cohen, J. (1973). The equivalence of weighted kappa and the intraclass correlation coefficient as measures of reliability. *Educational and Psychological Measurement, 33*, 613-619. doi: 10.1177/001316447303300309

Graham, J. R. (2002). *MMPI-II: Assessing personality and psychopathology (Vol. 4)*. New York: Oxford University Press.

Grant, B. F., & Harford, T. C. (1995). Comorbidity between DSM-IV alcohol use disorders and major depression: Results of a national survey. *Drug and Alcohol Dependence, 39*, 197-206. doi: 10.1016/0376-8716(95)01160-4

Grant, B. F., Stinson, F. S., Dawson, D. A., Chou, S. P., Dufour, M. C., Compton, W., et al. (2004). Prevalence and co-occurrence of substance use disorders and independent mood and anxiety disorders: Results from the National Epidemiologic Survey on Alcohol and Related Conditions. *Archives of General Psychiatry, 61*, 807-816. doi: 10.1001/archpsyc.61.8.807

Greene, R. L. (1991). *MMPI-II/MMPI: An interpretative manual*. Boston: Allyn and Bacon.

Greene, R. L. (2000). *The MMPI-II: An interpretative manual (Vol. 2)*. Boston: Allyn and Bacon.

Greene, R. L., Adyanthaya, A. E., Morse, R. M., & Davis, L. J. (1993). Personality variables in cocaine- and marijuana-dependent patients. *Journal of Personality Assessment, 67*, 224-230. doi: 10.1207/s15327752jpa6102_2

Hall, D. H., & Queener, J. E. (2007). Self-medication hypothesis of substance use: Testing Khantzian's updated theory. *Journal of Psychoactive Drugs, 39*, 151-158. doi: 10.1080/02791072.2007.10399873

Hathaway, S. R., & McKinley, J. C. (1989). *Minnesota Multiphasic Personality Inventory-2 (MMPI-II)*. Minneapolis, MN: University of Minnesota Press.

Henwood, B., & Padgett, D. K. (2007). Reevaluating the self-medication hypothesis among the dually diagnosed. *The American Journal of Addictions, 16*, 160-165. doi: 10.1080/10550490701375368

Hopwood, C. J., Baker, K. L., & Morey, L. C. (2008). Personality and drugs of choice. *Personality and Individual Differences, 44*, 1413-1421. doi: 10.1016/j.paid.2007.12.009

Hotelling, H. (1931). The generalization of Student's ratio. *Annals of Mathematical Statistics, 2*, 360-378. doi: 10.1214/aoms/1177732979

Jacobsen, L. K., Southwick, S. M., & Kosten, T. R. (2001). Substance use disorders in patients with post-traumatic stress disorder: A review of the literature. *American Journal of Psychiatry, 158*, 1184-1190. doi: 10.1176/appi.ajp.158.8.1184

Kernberg, O. F. (1975). *Borderline conditions and pathological narcissism*. New York: Jason Aronson.

Khantzian, E. J. (1985). The self-medication hypothesis of addictive disorders: Focus on heroin and cocaine dependence. *American Journal of Psychiatry, 142*, 1259-1264.

Khantzian, E. J. (1997). The self-medication hypothesis of substance use disorders: A reconsideration and recent applications. *Harvard Review of Psychiatry, 4*, 231-244. doi: 10.3109/10673229709030550

Khantzian, E. J. (1999). *Treating addiction as a human process.* Northvale, NJ: Jason Aronson.

Khantzian, E. J. (2003). Understanding addictive vulnerability. *Neuro-Psychoanalysis, 5*, 5-21. doi: 10.1080/15294145.2003.10773403

Khantzian, E. J. (2012). Reflections on treating addictive disorders: A psychodynamic perspective. *The American Journal on Addictions, 21*, 274-279. doi: 10.1111/j.1521-0391.2012.00234.x

Khantzian, E. J. (2013). Addiction as a self-regulation disorder and the role of self-medication. *Addiction, 108*, 668-669. doi: 10.1111/add.12004

Khantzian, E. J., & Albenese, M. J. (2008). *Understanding addiction as self medication: Finding hope behind the pain.* New York: Rowman and Littlefield.

Khattree, R., & Naik, D. N. (2000). *Multivariate data reduction and discrimination with SAS software.* Cary, NC: SAS Institute.

Kushner, M. G., Abrams, K., & Borchardt, C. (2000). The relationship between anxiety disorders and alcohol use disorders: A review of major perspectives and findings. *Clinical Psychology Review, 20*, 149-171. doi: 10.1016/S0272-7358(99)00027-6

Lazowski, L. E., Miller, F. G., Boye, M. W., & Miller, G. A. (1998). Efficacy of the Substance Abuse Subtle Screening Inventory-3 (SASSI-3) in identifying substance dependence disorders in clinical settings. *Journal of Personality Assessment, 71*, 114-128. doi: 10.1207/s15327752jpa7101_8

Lee, C. W., Taylor, G., & Dunn, J. (1999). Factor structure of the Schema Questionnaire in a large clinic sample. *Cognitive Therapy and Research, 23*, 441-451. doi: 0.1023/A:1018712202933

Lembke, A. (2012). Time to abandon the self-medication hypothesis in patients with psychiatric disorders. *The American Journal of Drug and Alcohol Abuse, 38*, 524-529. doi: 10.3109/00952990.2012.694532

Lilienfeld, S. O. (1999). The relation of the MMPI-II Pd Harris-Lingoes subscales to psychopathy, psychopathy facets, and antisocial behav-

ior: Implications for clinical practice. *Journal of Clinical Psychology, 55*, 241-255. doi: 10.1002/(SICI)1097-4679(199902)55:2

Lynskey, M. T. (1998). The comorbidity of alcohol dependence and affective disorders: Treatment implications. *Drug and Alcohol Dependence, 52*, 201-209. doi: 10.1016/S0376-8716(98)00095-7

Magura, S., & Kang, S. Y. (1996). Validity of self-reported drug use in high risk populations: A meta-analytical review. *Substance Use and Misuse, 31*, 1131-1153. doi: 10.3109/10826089609063969

McLellan, A. T., Kushner, H., Metzger, D., Peters, R., Smith, I., Grissom, G., et al. (1992). The fifth edition of the Addiction Severity Index (ASI). *Journal of Substance Abuse Treatment, 9*, 199-213. doi: 10.1016/0740-5472(92)90062-S

Miller, G. A. (1999). *The SASSI manual: Substance abuse measures* (2nd ed.). Springville, IN: SASSI Institute.

Morey, L. (1991). *The Personality Assessment Inventory: Professional manual (PAI).* Odessa, FL: Psychological Assessment Resources.

Morey, L. (1996). *An interpretative guide to the Personality Assessment Inventory (PAI).* Odessa, FL: Psychological Assessment Resources.

Nolen-Hoeksema, S., & Hilt, L. M. (2009). Gender differences in depression. In I. H. Gotlib & C. L. Hammen (Eds.), *Handbook of depression* (2nd ed., pp. 386-404). New York: Guilford.

Oei, T. P. S., & Baranoff, J. (2007). Young Schema Questionnaire (YSQ): Review of psychometric and measurement issues. *Australian Journal of Psychology, 59*, 78-86. doi: 10.1080/00049530601148397

Parker, J. D., Daleiden, E. L., & Simpson, C. A. (1999). Personality Assessment Inventory (PAI) substance-use scales: Convergent and discriminant relations with the Addiction Severity Index (ASI) in a residential chemical dependence treatment setting. *Psychological Assessment, 11*, 507-513. doi: 10.1037/1040-3590.11.4.507

Parrott, A., Morinan, A., Moss, M., & Scholey, A. (2004). *Understanding drugs and behavior.* Chichester, England: Wiley.

Poling, J., Kosten, T. R., & Sofuoglu, M. (2007). Treatment outcome predictors for cocaine dependence. *The American Journal of Drug and Alcohol Abuse, 33*, 191-206. doi: 10.1080/00952990701199416

Robinson, J., Sareen, J., Cox, B. J., & Bolton, J. M. (2011). Role of self-medication in the development of comorbid anxiety and substance use disorders. *Archives of General Psychiatry, 68,* 800-807. doi: 10.1001/archgenpsychiatry.2011.75

Rounsaville, B. J., Anton, S. F., Carroll, K., Budde, D., Prusoff, B. A., & Gawin, F. (1991). Psychiatric diagnoses of treatment-seeking cocaine abusers. *Archives of General Psychiatry, 48,* 43-51. doi: 10.1001/archpsyc.1991.01810250045005

Schinka, J. A., Curtiss, G., & Mulloy, J. M. (1994). Personality variables and self-medication in substance abuse. *Journal of Personality Assessment, 63,* 413-422. doi: 10.1207/s15327752jpa6303_2

Schmidt, N. B., Joiner, T. E., Young, J. E., & Telch, M. J. (1995). The Schema Questionnaire: Investigation of psychometric properties and hierarchical structure of a measure of maladaptive schemas. *Cognitive Therapy and Research, 19,* 295-321. doi: 10.1007/BF02230402

Shipherd, J. C., Stafford, J., & Tanner, L. R. (2005). Predicting alcohol and drug abuse in Persian Gulf War veterans: What role do PTSD symptoms play? *Addictive Behaviors, 30,* 595-599. doi: 10.1016/j.addbeh.2004.07.004

Shrout, P. E., & Fleiss, J. L. (1979). Interclass correlations: Uses in assessing rater reliability. *Psychological Bulletin, 86*(2), 420-428. doi: 10.1037/0033-2909.86.2.420

Sinha, R. (2008). Chronic stress, drug use, and vulnerability to addiction. *Annals of the New York Academy of Sciences, 1141,* 105-130. doi: 10.1196/annals.1441.030

Spiro, A., Butcher, J. N., Levenson, M. R., Aldwin, C. M., & Bose, R (2000). Change and stability in personality: A five-year study of the MMPI-2 in older men. In J. N. Butcher (Ed.), *Basic sources on the MMPI-2* (pp. 443-462). Minneapolis, MN: University of Minnesota Press.

Suh, J., Ruffins, S., Robins, C. E., Albenese, M. J., & Khantzian, E. J. (2008). Self-medication hypothesis: Connecting affect experience and drug choice. *Psychoanalytic Psychology, 25,* 518-532. doi: 10.1037/0736-9735.25.3.518

Sullivan, J. T., Sykora, K., Schneiderman, J., Naranjo, C. A., & Sellers, E. M (1989). Assessment of alcohol withdrawal: The revised Clinical Institute Withdrawal Assessment for Alcohol scale (CIWA-Ar). *British Journal of Addiction, 84,* 1353-1357. doi: 10.1111/j.1360-0443.1989.tb00737.x

Thorberg, F. A., & Lyvers, M. (2005). Attachment, fear of intimacy and differentiation of self among clients in substance disorder treatment facilities. *Addictive Behaviors, 31,* 732- 737. doi: 0.1016/j.addbeh.2005.05.050

Valliant, G. E. (1994). Ego mechanisms of defense and personality psychopathology. *Journal of Abnormal Psychology, 103,* 44-50. doi: 10.1037/0021-843X.103.1.44

Volkow, N. D., Fowler, J. S., Wang, G. J., & Swanson, J. M. (2004). Dopamine in drug abuse and addiction: Results from imaging studies and treatment implications. *Molecular Psychiatry, 9,* 557-569. doi: 10.1038/sj.mp.4001507

Waller, G., Meyer, C., & Ohanian, V. (2001). Psychometric properties of the long and short versions of the Young Schema Questionnaire (YSQ): Core beliefs among bulimic and comparison women. *Cognitive Therapy and Research, 25,* 137-147. doi: 10.1023/A:1026487018110

Weiss, R. D., Griffin, M. L., & Mirin, S. M. (1992). Drug abuse as self-medication for depression: An empirical study. *American Journal of Drug and Alcohol Abuse, 18,* 121-129. doi: 10.1177/026988119801200116

Wesson, D. R., & Ling, W. (2003). Clinical Opiate Withdrawal Scale (COWS). *Journal of Psychoactive Drugs, 35,* 253-260. doi: 10.1080/02791072.2003.10400007

Westfall, P. H., & Young, S. S. (1993). *Resampling-based multiple testing: Examples and methods for p-value adjustment.* New York: Wiley.

Winger, G., Woods, J. H., & Hofmann, F. (2004). *A handbook on drug and alcohol abuse: The biomedical aspects (4th ed.).* New York: Oxford University Press.

Wurmser, L. (1974). Psychoanalytic considerations of the etiology of compulsive drug use. *Journal of American Psychoanalytic Association, 22,* 820-843. doi: 10.1177/000306517402200407

Young, J. E. (2005). *Young Schema Questionnaire–3rd Edition Long Form.* New York: The Schema Therapy Institute.

Young, J. E., Klosko, J. S., & Weishaar, M. E. (2003). *Schema therapy: A practitioner's guide.* New York: Guilford.

Trauma and Stressor-Related Disorders

Psychodynamic Treatment of Combat Veterans with PTSD at Risk for Suicide

Herbert Hendin

Abstract: Posttraumatic stress disorder is a condition associated with suicide in both military personnel and combat veterans. Most veterans with PTSD, however, are not at risk of suicide. The major factor distinguishing those who attempted or were preoccupied with suicide is persistent severe guilt over behavior in combat while emotionally out of control. A 12-session short-term, psychodynamic psychotherapy, presented here, showed promise of success in dissipating the guilt from combat-related actions in veterans of the war in Vietnam. Preliminary work with combat veterans of the wars in Iraq and Afghanistan indicates it may be equally successful in treating them. Basic aspects of the psychodynamic approach could also be incorporated into current therapies and should improve their ability to treat veterans with PTSD at risk for suicide. Case examples are provided.

Although storytellers and writers going back to Homer described the profound psychological effects of war on those who fought, it was not until World War I that psychiatrists in Austria and Germany began to describe in detail the traumatic reactions to combat. They concluded that combat trauma involved a breaking through of the individual's defense against stimuli (*reitzschutz*). "Traumatic neurosis" was the result of fright (*schreck*)—a condition occurring when one encountered a danger without being adequately prepared. The repetitive nightmares seen in the disorder were considered an attempt to be prepared after the fact, to dissipate by repetition the anxiety generated by the experience (Ferenczi, Abraham, Simmel, Jones, & Freud, 1921).

Abram Kardiner's work with World War I veterans, and subsequent collaboration with Spiegel who worked with World War II veterans, clearly delineated the symptoms of posttraumatic stress disorder (Kardiner

& Spiegel, 1947). Although he acknowledged *reitzschutz* theory as a starting point for his own thinking, he incorporated traumatic stress into an adaptational frame of reference. Kardiner saw trauma as an alteration in the individual's usual environment in which the adaptive maneuvers suitable to previous situations no longer sufficed. With the balance between the individual and his or her adaptive equipment broken, a new adaptation was not possible, and the individual accommodated his or her shrunken inner resources with the development of symptoms.

Kardiner described the features of what was then called traumatic war neurosis: fixation on the trauma, repetitive nightmares, irritability, exaggerated reactions to unexpected noise (startle reactions), proclivity to explosive, aggressive behavior, and a contraction of the general level of functioning, including intellectual ability. He also saw loss of interest in activity as a result of the breakup of organized channels of action that were replaced by periodic outbursts of disorganized aggression. The internal conception of the self became altered, confidence was lost, the world was seen as a hostile place, and the patient lived in perpetual dread of being overwhelmed (Kardiner & Spiegel, 1947). The symptoms Kardiner described were subsequently categorized for use in a civilian population in the American Psychiatric Association's (APA) *Diagnostic and Statistical Manual of Mental Disorders* that became the basis for the diagnosis of PTSD.

The Vietnam veterans seen shortly after the war were diagnosed on the basis of *DSM-III* (APA, 1980) criteria. PTSD is a different disorder in a veterans' population, if only because of the veterans' sustained exposure to many traumas. This led VA researchers to want to develop their own instrument to diagnose PTSD. When *DSM-IV* was introduced they developed the Post-traumatic Stress Checklist–Military (PCL-M; Weathers et al., 2013), which was conceptually compatible with *DSM-IV*, but is in questionnaire form and is focused more on evaluating the severity of the impact on the veteran's adaptation. Since *DSM-5* (APA, 2013) was introduced the VA uses it to make the diagnosis. There was no compatible version of the PCL-M so the version developed earlier is still being used for research.

As early as the end of the 19th century the effect of combat in contributing to suicide was recognized by the French sociologist, Emil Durkheim, who reported that suicide rates among European military men were up to ten times greater than those among male civilians of comparable age (Durkheim, 1951). Only after the war in Vietnam were systematic analyses undertaken in the United States that confirmed a higher rate of suicide among men who had served in the military than among other men of the same age (Centers for Disease Control, 1987; U.S. House of Representatives, Committee on Veteran Affairs, 1978). Clinicians who worked closely with men who saw considerable combat in Vietnam noted that suicidal behavior was frequently a manifestation of what came to

be known as Posttraumatic Stress Disorder (PTSD) (Jury, 1979; Kolb, 1986; Lipkin, Blank, Parson, & Smith, 1982; Stuen & Solberg, 1972). Vietnam veterans with PTSD have been shown to be four times more likely to die by suicide than veterans without PTSD (Bullman & Kang, 1996).

A 7-year research and treatment project begun in 1978 at a Veterans Administration medical center, consisting of combat veterans of the Vietnam War with PTSD and designed to determine who were at risk for suicide, laid the groundwork for the material in this article (Hendin & Pollinger Haas, 1984a, 1984b). Research done at the Michael DeBakey VA Medical Center in Houston, Texas, which focused on veterans of the wars in Iraq and Afghanistan built on this work (Hendin, Al Jurdi, Houck, Hughes, & Turner, 2010).

POSTTRAUMATIC STRESS DISORDER AND THE RISK FOR SUICIDE

The study of Vietnam combat veterans with PTSD provided insight into some of the factors associated with suicide among them. One hundred combat veterans with PTSD completed a comprehensive questionnaire and five semi-structured interviews which we have described in detail elsewhere (Hendin & Haas, 1991). The interviews elicited additional information about the individual's life before and after his service in Vietnam. None of the veterans had made a suicide attempt or been preoccupied with suicide prior to their combat experience.

Persistent severe guilt over combat experiences was found to be the major factor differentiating veterans who had attempted suicide and those who were seriously preoccupied with suicide from those veterans who were neither (Hendin & Haas, 1991). Nineteen of the 100 combat veterans with PTSD had attempted suicide at least once since returning from Vietnam. Guilt related to combat actions was significantly marked in all 19 of the suicide attempters but in only 32 of the 66 non-suicidal veterans (x^2 = 14.24; df = 1, p < 0.001). Fifteen veterans, who had not attempted suicide, had been seriously preoccupied with suicide since they left the service. Guilt was also marked in 12 of these 15 veterans compared to the 66 non-suicidal veterans (x^2 = 3.71; df = 1, p = .05). Although anxiety, survivor guilt, and depression marked those at risk for suicide, combat guilt was the strongest predictor when all four were entered into a logistic regression simultaneously.

Although logistic regression analysis did not identify survivor guilt as a significant predictor of suicide attempts, additional one-way analysis provided evidence of the importance of the concurrent presence of the two types of guilt. Forty of the 100 veterans studied, for example, showed both marked guilt about combat actions and marked survivor guilt. Among the group, 14 (35%) had made a suicide attempt. By contrast, none of the 30 veterans who showed neither marked combat guilt nor survivor guilt had attempted suicide (x^2 = 13.3, df = 1, p < .001). The findings suggest that the combination of these two types of guilt play a significant role in determining suicidal risk among patients.

Moreover, among the 17 veterans who had killed civilians while feeling out of control and felt guilty about such actions but were not suicidal only two had survivor guilt. By contrast 9 of the 12 suicide attempters who had killed civilians while feeling out of control experienced survivor guilt in addition to guilt over their combat actions (x^2 = 12.21, df = 1, p < .001).

The combat experiences of the suicidal veterans were examined for possible determinants of their guilt. The chaotic nature of guerilla warfare in Vietnam, the uncertainty about who was the enemy, the emphasis on body counts, and the Vietcong's use of women, children, and the elderly as combatants contributed to combat actions about which veterans felt severe guilt.

The Vietcong, for example, would strip an American soldier they had killed and hang his naked body from a tree with his genitals stuffed into his mouth. Such tactics, designed to frighten soldiers, also infuriated them and contributed to atrocities on both sides.

MEANING OF COMBAT

How each veteran experienced the combat events, that is, the meaning of the combat experience to the veteran, was integral in determining the nature of the guilt and the risk for suicidal behavior. The term *meaning of combat* refers to the *subjective, often unconscious perception* of the traumatic event, and includes the affective state of the veteran before the event took place, when it took place, and the affects experienced subsequently.

Repetitive nightmares and re-experiencing symptoms are cardinal symptoms of PTSD. Both are valuable tools in determining the meaning of the experience to the veteran (Hendin & Pollinger Haas, 1984a). The following case example is illustrative.

Case 1*

Throughout his tour, Greg L. thought he would be killed in action. The thought was comforting to him because it would enable him to avoid having his friends, family, and fiancée discover that he had lost control of his anger and killed without reason in Vietnam. During the last two weeks of his tour, when he learned that he was not going to be assigned to any more combat missions, he tried to kill himself with an overdose of drugs.

He had been an artillery spotter in Vietnam. He was preoccupied with a memory of a friendly village that he and his sergeant had helped to destroy in a contest designed to see who could call in the best coordinates.

Names and details have been changed to protect patient privacy.

Through his binoculars, Greg had watched with excitement as the shells landed. As the village was being destroyed he saw an old woman with betel nut stains on her teeth running in his direction. She was shaking her arms trying to get him to stop the shelling. As she ran toward him, she was killed by an artillery round.

After he returned to the United States, Greg was tormented by a painful recurring nightmare that expressed his intense guilt over the destruction of the village. In the dream he is captured by South Vietnamese villagers, strung on a pole like a pig carcass, and paraded around the village so that everyone can curse him, spit on him, hit him, and throw stones at him. The old woman with the betel nut-stained teeth is taunting him. The villagers hold him responsible for all the death and destruction in their village. He knows they are going to kill him.

Greg made a second suicide attempt during a re-experiencing event in which he thought he saw the villagers covered in blood. He cut his wrists, and described feeling a sense of relief as the blood spurted out. Both the nightmare and the reliving experience express his sense of guilt and need for punishment.

The nightmares of most veterans with PTSD correspond closely with the combat experiences and the terror over being killed that they engender. Veterans who have severe guilt over their combat are more likely to experience nightmares that reflect guilt, are punitive in nature, and indicate risk for suicide. Greg's experience of feeling out of control while in Vietnam was usual among the suicide attempters. Sixteen of the 19 suicide attempters (82%) had felt out of control as a result of excessive fear or rage during their tours of duty, including the situations in which their anger led to deaths about which they felt guilty (Hendin & Haas, 1991). Veterans like Greg, who felt out of control while in combat, and remained so in civilian life, are the most difficult to involve in treatment, so it was not surprising that Greg turned down the offer of short-term psychotherapy that was available to participants in the re-

search project. During the course of study, three of the veterans who also felt out of control, and did not accept the offer of treatment, did kill themselves (Hendin, 2014).

RECOGNIZING THE VETERAN AT RISK FOR SUICIDE

Treating the veteran at risk for suicide requires identifying correctly those veterans who are at risk. In a previous study with patients who were not veterans, detailed data was obtained from therapists of patients who committed suicide while in treatment with them. Written responses to questionnaires and subsequent personal interviews with the therapist were used to determine what patients were feeling and experiencing in their lives immediately before their suicides (Hendin, Maltsberger, Lipschitz, Haas, & Kyle, 2001). The data was contrasted with data from the same therapists on their comparably depressed patients who were not suicidal. We found that the suicides were preceded by a time-limited suicide crisis that was marked by three factors: a precipitating event, behavioral changes, and intense affective states.

Intense affective states that were intolerable and uncontrollable proved to be the factor most related to suicide (Hendin, Maltsberger, & Szanto, 2007). The uncontrollable nature of the affects engendered fear on the part of the patients that they were fragmenting, that is, "falling apart." Nine affects were examined: anxiety, rage, desperation, abandonment, loneliness, hopelessness, self-hatred, guilt, and humiliation. A striking contrast was observed in the patients who went on to suicide and the comparably depressed patients who were not suicidal. Just before death the suicides averaged more than three times the number of intense affects than comparably depressed non-suicidal patients. These differences remained when controlled for severity of depression, psychiatric disorders, and borderline personality disorders.

That work made it possible to develop the Affective States Questionnaire (ASQ), which prospectively showed its ability to predict short-term, 3-month risk for suicidal behavior among a population of 240 outpatient and inpatient veterans, not selected for the presence of PTSD or the risk for suicide. Recognizing the intense, overwhelming emotional states that leave patients feeling out of control in a crisis period immediately preceding their suicidal behavior is critical in this process (Hendin, Al Jurdi, Houck, Hughes, & Turner, 2010).

Other instruments used in our work beside the ASQ and the PCL-M to determine both suicide risk and progress in treatment are the Quick Inventory of Depressive Symptoms (QIDS), the Modified Sheehan Disability Scale which asks questions as to whether the veteran's symptoms are disrupting his ability to work, his social life, his family/home responsibilities, and the Columbia Suicide Severity Rating Scale (C-SSRS) which tracks suicidal behavior.

TREATING THE VETERAN WITH PTSD AT RISK FOR SUICIDE

Earlier concepts of the unconscious that are outdated have been supplanted by modern psychodynamics that has recognized its underlying, enduring, conceptual contributions to our understanding and ability to treat mental illness and, in particular, the role of the unconscious in influencing behavior, the value of dreams, and the nature of the relationship with the therapist doing the treatment. Even slight differences in the dream and the actual experience can be helpful in understanding the nature of the experience and making treatment possible. Tom B. is an example.

Case 2

Troubled by violent impulses toward his family as well as suicidal thoughts, Tom's entire post-combat life had been pervaded by PTSD. For years he had suppressed the symptoms with drugs, which he began using since he returned from Vietnam. He stopped, because he felt they were destroying his body, but he then became aware of his preoccupation with Vietnam and the disturbing nature of his nightmares. Tom had one recurrent nightmare that he said "...scares the hell out of me. It's so real but I don't know if it actually happened." In the dream he is carrying the dead body of a young woman and trying to bury it so no one can find it. Upon waking from this dream he would sense that he had some involvement in the girl's death, but would be unable to recall what it was. When asked if he had ever raped any Vietnamese women, Tom replied that he had not. When asked if he had ever witnessed a rape, he said that he had.

His squad had been assigned to secure the entrance to a tunnel complex while four men from another squad went underground to explore the tunnels. His squad was in radio contact with the other squad and learned that they had found a Vietcong hospital base. A short while later Tom heard shouting and the sounds of grenades exploding. The four men came out of the tunnel dragging a French nurse who was bleeding from arm wounds. Each of the four raped the nurse while Tom's squad watched. When the last man was finished he pulled out his knife and killed the woman. When this happened Tom and his squad departed; he never knew how the men disposed of the nurse's body. He did know that when the four soldiers reported the incident they made no mention of taking anyone alive. Tom claimed to have had no particular reaction to the event. He admitted that he had been sexually excited while watching what had happened, but he had never connected the episode with his nightmare.

Tom was seen for several months of short-term psychotherapy while he explored and processed the emotions connected with his nightmare. Just as in the dream where he was carrying and trying to find a place to bury a woman's dead body, he had tried for years to bury the entire experience. Although he had succeeded on a conscious level, the burden of guilt he was nonetheless carrying is evident in his dream. In therapy he was able to connect it with the rape and killing of the nurse he had witnessed, to recognize that he was a "participant" in her rape, and to experience the emotions connected with it. He was then able to accept that, although he had reason to feel guilty, there was no need to let it affect the rest of his life. He stopped having the nightmares, became less angry with his family, no longer had thoughts of suicide, and had remained so on follow-up a year later.

Tom's treatment involved: a focus on his affect and the expression of emotions; exploration of his attempts to avoid distressing thoughts and feelings; focus on interpersonal relations (primarily with his family); focus on the therapeutic relationship; and exploration of dreams. (His early life experiences while growing up and pre-combat did not indicate that either he or his family had any psychiatric problems so we did not explore these relationships).

Tom had been treated with behavioral therapy and medication without any improvement before he was referred to the research and treatment program. His nightmare, however, had been treated only as a symptom to be suppressed with sleeping medication rather than an opening to unconscious feelings that were troubling him (Hendin, 2014).

Like Tom, a number of the veterans we saw had been referred to us after they had been treated with behavioral therapy without improvement. Their nightmares would have alerted the therapist to their guilt but were treated as symptoms that needed to be repressed. The veterans had not been recruited for treatment but we offered it to those who needed it and wanted it. We were able to relieve the guilt of these veterans and eliminated their suicide risk which also made it easier to address other PTSD symptoms. Although the prediction factor was established in a controlled study, the treatment success

was not and we only had a one-year follow-up.

Tom's therapy was not likely to succeed while he was still abusing substances. Substance abuse and/or difficulty functioning—at work and in family and social relations—increase the risk for suicide (Hendin, Al Jurdi, Houck, Hughes, & Turner, 2010). For substance abusing veterans with PTSD at risk for suicide, enrollment in a program treating substance abuse probably needs to be a requirement for participation in a psychodynamic treatment.

ALIENATION

Combat veterans with and without PTSD often feel alienated from society and believe—not incorrectly—that people cannot understand them or their experience. The stress of their exposure to sustained violence is often heightened by the feeling that the war was unwinnable. In Vietnam that view was intensified by fighting to take over territory, winning it, and then being ordered to leave it to be re-occupied by the enemy. Their sense of futility was further exacerbated by the soldiers being reduced to counting the number of those who had been killed as a way of measuring success. The favorite phrase of Vietnam combat veterans to describe their combat is "it don't mean nothing." Despite the differences in the wars, combat veterans of the wars in Iraq and Afghanistan have had a similar reaction.

These veterans, however, had bonded with combat comrades in a way they often cannot do at home, even with other veterans. Some re-enlist for that reason. It is important for any therapist who wants to treat combat veterans, to become familiar with their experiences and culture. *Achilles in Vietnam: Combat Trauma and the Undoing of Character* by VA psychiatrist Jonathan Shay (1994) provides an excellent description and analysis of the effect of combat on veterans. Prize-winning fiction by combat veterans of both wars based on their own experiences provides a moving sense of their emotions. *Paco's Story* (Heinemann, 1987) is a National Book Award winning novel of the aftermath of war for a veteran whose scars suggest a map of Vietnam which still dominates his physical and emotional life. Heinemann's earlier novel, *Close Quarters* (1975), is a vivid rendering of combat situations so intense they drive soldiers toward out-of-control violence and nightmares of dying and searching for their own body among the dead. *Redeployment*, a collection of short fiction by Phil Klay (2014), won the National Book Award for its power in exploring both combat in the Iraq war and its aftermath back home.

GOALS AND TIME FRAME FOR TREATMENT

The following is a summary of the goals and time frame for treatment in a 12-session psychodynamic psychotherapy. Starting with the first session, a core of trust between the therapist and the veteran must be established for therapy to be effective. This can be conveyed while eliciting the veteran's chief complaints, combat history, and any past relevant family history. The therapist needs to be calm, nonjudgmental, and confident, a figure with whom the veteran can connect and one he can respect.

Rapport can be facilitated by the therapist's ability to discuss the veteran's deployment in the service (branch of service, years served, what units he was in, his assignment, and how he felt about it). It helps to know, for example, the difference between a squad (9–20 soldiers), a platoon (25–60 soldiers, 2–4 squads), and a company (70–250 soldiers, 2–6 platoons); to know that an IED is an improvised explosive device with a detonator, commonly used in guerilla warfare; an MRAP is a Mine-Resistant Ambush Protected Vehicle designed to protect against IEDs; a Humvee is a High-Mobility Multipurpose Wheeled Vehicle, a light truck that has no

armored protection. Conversation could also involve more casual subjects—the veteran's interests, hobbies, skills, family, and children.

If a good contact has been made, by the fourth session the most traumatic combat experience of the veteran can usually be elicited and the feelings about it before, during, and afterward, as well as any recurrent nightmare connected with it, can be addressed. Keep in mind, however, that this is not an exposure therapy—you are not going to have the veteran repeat many times what he told you with a view to deconditioning him to his experience.

The veteran will have learned in the referral interview and in the process of informed consent that if he completes six sessions plus an assessment to evaluate his progress, his contribution to our research will be recognized with a framed plaque. There will be further recognition if he repeats this process at the completion of treatment (12 sessions).

Although there will be an early focus on guilt over combat experiences, the veteran is likely to bring up other problems at the same time and they will be discussed in the same session. The therapist needs to learn what the veteran's life is like between his sessions. If the veteran is severely distressed during the week, the therapist should recommend activities that will both relieve anxiety and improve mood. For veterans this is most apt to be running, gym, exercises, swimming, yoga, and scuba diving. The last six sessions will be largely divided between relieving guilt related to combat experiences, dealing with problems related to emotional control, and dealing with interpersonal relationship problems.

The last two sessions of therapy will also deal with the transition to the end of treatment. Although we expect to dissipate or diminish the veterans' risk for suicidal behavior, in a 12-session therapy relationship problems are not likely to be completely resolved. But the veteran will have been given an approach that he can utilize in dealing with them.

The therapist will discuss with him the two follow-ups that will be done at a 3-month and 6-month session after treatment is completed. Instruments assessing whether progress is being maintained will be administered by a research assistant. During those visits the therapist will see the veteran. Many of the veterans will want the therapist's advice regarding other therapies the VA has to offer.

TREATING COMBAT VETERANS OF THE WARS IN IRAQ AND AFGHANISTAN WITH PTSD AND AT RISK FOR SUICIDE

There is a significant difference in the population that served in the Vietnam War and the wars in Iraq and Afghanistan. The veterans of the war in Vietnam were drafted, their average age was 20, and they rarely had histories of depression or suicidal behavior prior to the war. Veterans of the wars in Iraq and Afghanistan were volunteers, their average age was 28, and they frequently had histories of pre-combat mental illness including suicidal behavior (LeardMann, Powell, Smith, Bell, Smith et al., 2013). In cases we have seen, their enlistment was often a way of trying to provide structure to their lives which left them vulnerable when it did not work.

The combat experiences of Vietnam veterans also differed significantly from the experiences of veterans of the wars in Iraq and Afghanistan, where IEDs were a principal cause of traumatic brain injury (TBI). Veterans with TBI are also more likely to die by suicide than those without TBI (Brenner, Ignacio, & Blow, 2011). Guilt over the killing of noncombatants is less likely to play a role in their suicide than it is with Vietnam veterans who experienced the chaotic combat firefights and sustained guerilla warfare of the war in Vietnam. Iraq veterans with experiences roughly comparable to those of Vietnam veterans usually fought in battles, like those in Fallujah, Ramadi, and Nasiriya,

in which sustained firefights (over months and years) in cities and within buildings led to actions in which women and children were killed and situations where soldiers felt guilt afterward. Multiple deployments, however, that characterized the wars in Iraq and Afghanistan have been shown to contribute to veterans' physical and mental health problems (Kline, Falca-Dodsin, Sussner, Ciccone, Chandler et al., 2010) and appear to be contributing to suicide independent of combat exposure.

Therapy often flounders when the veteran shares disturbing specifics of his combat tour. The therapist may inadvertently respond with revulsion, anger, or fear. More frequently the therapist's discomfort is communicated in the need to convey understanding before he is in a position to do so. It is the therapist's discomfort rather than what is specifically said that the veteran responds to, only increasing his distress.

It is better for the therapist to accept and respect the veteran's guilt, to acknowledge the pain of the experience, to indicate that he has already punished himself enough, and to work to not let that event continue to define his life. Telling a veteran who appropriately feels guilty over his behavior in combat, "Those things happen in war," is counterproductive.

Another principle of psychodynamic therapy applicable in treating non-veterans as well as veterans, and of use in eliciting the combat experiences of veterans, is not to accept all statements made by patients at face value.

Examples

One patient seen in Boston in his initial session after saying hello to his therapist said, "I want you to know I am not a Boston Red Sox fan." Most people probably know of Boston's passionate devotion to the Red Sox in both good times and bad. That he was letting his therapist know that he was a contrarian became more evident in his therapy.

A patient dreamed of saving his child from drowning. He interprets the dream as saving his child from danger, saying he worries that something bad will happen to her. In his sessions he had been expressing his anger with his child for the child's impact on his relationship with his wife. In the therapy he came to understand his dream as both expressing his anger and denying it at the same time: he is the author of the dream and he put the child in a life-threatening situation. Nor does the dream mean he actually wants the child to die. The discussion of the dream made it possible for him to recognize and resolve the difficulties he was having in being a father.

Knowledge of this principle will help therapists deal with one of the most common obstacles to eliciting combat experiences from veterans. Veterans will often relate a somewhat troubling experience to avoid discussing some other one that is far more disturbing. That is either a plea bargain and/or a test of what the therapist's response will be. A common traumatic memory used by veterans of the war in Iraq is of shooting and killing drivers who do not stop at checkpoints—learning later from other passengers that the driver could not see or could not read the checkpoint sign.

Jack B, a veteran of the war in Iraq, related an incident in which he shot and killed an old man who did not stop at a checkpoint sign. From other passengers in the car he learned that the man had not seen the sign. The veteran described this as his most disturbing experience. It was pointed out to him that while he had killed someone he had not needed to kill, he had done so inadvertently while following military procedures. He was asked if he was more disturbed by any killing he had done when he was not following military procedures. He then revealed that he had killed a captured prisoner of war.

Therapists learn more when they ask about the veteran's nightmares. A veteran of the Iraq war who had also killed a captured prisoner said it did not bother him because "everybody did it." He had a recurrent nightmare, however, in which he is captured and killed by Iraqi soldiers. When this contradiction was pointed out it enabled the therapist to help him deal with his guilt.

The relationship between the veteran and the therapist plays a key role in the healing process of veterans who have PTSD, and this is particularly true for those who have severe combat guilt and are at risk of suicide. The veteran needs to forgive himself for the behavior that triggered his guilt and the self-punitive way it is expressed. When the veteran feels relief at having shared the experience with a trusted therapist, the therapist is in a position to give him "permission" to forgive himself, to resolve problems that have developed in the course of the illness, and to go on with his life. Guilt is an emotion that can be harmful when it is self-punitive, but it can be a powerful force for changing the direction of one's life.

LOSS OF EMOTIONAL CONTROL

A high percentage of the veterans who are guilty over behavior in combat were emotionally out of control when the behavior occurred. For many, that lack of control remains after they return to civilian life, placing them at high risk for suicide, and is a major complication of treatment. Beside guilt, other emotions that have been linked to suicide are anxiety, rage, hopelessness, and desperation. Therapists need to ascertain what the veterans are feeling their anxiety, rage, hopelessness, or desperation about. Working with veterans to dissipate or control these emotions utilizes behavioral techniques:

Anger

- Uncontrolled anger and impulsively expressed rage is a major problem complicating the family and social relationships of veterans with PTSD.

- Establish with whom the veterans are angry, what they are angry about, and how they are expressing it.
- Encourage the veterans to take time before expressing their anger.
- Suggesting that "holding your anger" is analogous to "holding your fire" when in combat has proven helpful.
- Sessions must be used to help the veterans to deal with their anger effectively rather than destructively.

Hopelessness

- Hopelessness is best addressed by asking what the veteran feels hopeless about.
- After learning the source of the patient's hopelessness, the therapist should express confidence that they can work together to deal with the problems.
- Progress in treatment will reduce hopelessness.
- Veterans may resign themselves to being in a hopeless situation and tolerate it for years.
- Hopelessness, and other affects, evolve to desperation just prior to a suicide.

Desperation

- A serious short-term risk factor for suicide is desperation, emotional pain (anguish) that the veteran cannot tolerate, driving a need for *immediate relief*.
- Desperate veterans have high levels of anxiety and are apt to feel they are falling apart.
- The therapist must ask the veteran what is making him feel that way. If the veteran is in immediate danger, the therapist must arrange for his hospitalization.
- Hospitalization needs to be presented as something being done short-term to help the veteran feel better.

- Unless they are asking for hospitalization, avoid the mistake of suggesting that hospitalization is needed to prevent their suicide—suicidal veterans may not want to give up the freedom to end their lives.

Anxiety

- Veterans who exhibit desperation have a great deal of anxiety.
- Anxiety has also been shown to increase the risk of suicide in patients who are depressed.
- Anxiety and anger have a reciprocal relationship with suppressed anger underlying the anxiety and vice versa. The veteran who worried about something bad happening to his child while he was trying to suppress his rage toward her is an example.
- Helping the veteran to be conscious of this will to help him cope with both emotions.

DISCUSSION

Both the VA and the Defense Department have expressed concern that the current treatments are not slowing the rate of suicide among the active military and combat veterans with PTSD (Frances, 2012; Shinseki, 2010). Exposure therapy, cognitive behavioral therapy (CBT), and dialectical behavioral therapy (DBT) are the treatments of choice of the VA for veterans with PTSD. Although they have shown some ability to reduce PTSD symptoms, they have not shown the ability to prevent suicidal behavior in this population. These therapies would be more successful in treating veterans with PTSD at risk for suicide if they incorporated some simple psychodynamic principles.

In the past few decades the efficacy of psychodynamic therapy with *non-veteran* psychiatric patients has been tested in controlled studies and in meta-analyses (Shedler, 2010).

Psychodynamic therapy has been shown to be as effective, and sometimes more so, than the behavioral therapies. Studies of the outcomes of cognitive therapy and short-term psychodynamic therapy indicate that cognitive therapy owed its effectiveness to the therapists' *utilization of psychodynamic principles* (Ablon & Jones, 1998; Jones & Pulos, 1993). Perhaps most important, the beneficial effects of psychodynamic therapy have been shown, more than other therapies, not only to endure but to increase with time (Anderson & Lambert, 1995; Leichsenring & Rabung, 2008).

More than 10 years ago psychoanalysts working in the Department of Veterans Affairs recognized that psychodynamic therapy made it possible to move beyond patients' symptoms, and to treat veterans as individuals in the context of their own life stories (Kudler, 2007). It was summarized succinctly: "With psychodynamics you get to know the patient not just the diagnosis." The VA, however, has not adopted psychodynamic therapy despite the evidence of its value. Nevertheless, the VA does not prevent the therapists who have some training in psychodynamic therapy to use it in their treatment of veterans. This has permitted us to conduct a training project in the Bronx and Manhattan VAs, where therapists who have had some training in psychodynamic therapy are intensively supervised when treating veterans who are severely disturbed over their behavior in combat, whether or not they have PTSD or are at risk for suicide.

Psychodynamic therapy also utilizes techniques of behavioral therapies, so the training has appeal to behavioral therapists who can improve their skills with this training. As VA therapists incorporate psychodynamics into their approach more veterans will receive the treatment they need. It may also increase the likelihood that the VA will be more receptive to accepting psychodynamic therapy and funding research with regard to it.

SUMMARY AND CONCLUSIONS

This unique 12-session short-term psychodynamic treatment targets the guilt from combat-related experiences that underlies suicidal behavior in combat veterans with PTSD who are most at risk. Their risk of suicide is intensified if they also have survivor guilt. The treatment has shown promise in successfully treating Vietnam veterans whose behavior in chaotic firefights aroused their guilt. Preliminary work with veterans of the wars in Iraq and Afghanistan indicate it may be equally effective in treating them. The treatment defines the meaning of combat to the veteran with the aid of the veterans' nightmares and enables the therapist to relieve their guilt. As that occurs it is easier to help the veteran deal with his other PTSD symptoms. The VA should embrace this psychodynamic therapy.

REFERENCES

Ablon, J. S., & Jones, E. E. (1998). How expert clinicians' prototypes of an ideal treatment correlate with outcome in psychodynamic and cognitive-behavioral therapy. *Psychotherapy Research, 8,* 71-83. https://doi.org/10.1080/105033098123 31332207

American Psychiatric Association. (1980). *Diagnostic and statistical manual of mental disorders* (3rd ed.). Washington, DC: Author.

American Psychiatric Association. (2013). *Diagnostic and statistical manual of mental disorders* (5th ed.). Arlington, VA: Author.

Anderson, E. M., & Lambert, M. J. (1995). Short-term dynamically oriented psychotherapy: A review and meta-analysis. *Clinical Psychology Review, 15*(6), 503-514.

Brenner, L. A., Ignacio, R. V., & Blow, F. C. (2011). Suicide and traumatic brain injury among individuals seeking Veterans Health Administration services. *Journal of Head Trauma Rehabilitation, 26,* 257-264.

Bullman, T. A., & Kang, H. K (1996). The risk of suicide among wounded Vietnam veterans. *American Journal of Public Health, 86,* 662-667.

Centers for Disease Control. (1987). Postservice mortality among Vietnam veterans. *JAMA, 257*, 790-795.

Durkheim, E. (1951). *Suicide.* Glencoe, IL: Free Press.

Ferenczi, S., Abraham, K., Simmel, E., Jones, E., & Freud, S. (1921). *Psychoanalysis and the war neuroses.* London: Psychoanalytic Press.

Frances, A. (2013, March 27). The epidemic of suicide in the military. *Huffpost Healthy Living.* www.huffingtonpost.com/section/healthy-living

Heinemann, L. (1975). *Close quarters.* New York: Vintage.

Heinemann, L. (1987). *Paco's story.* New York: Vintage.

Hendin, H. (2014). An innovative approach to treating combat veterans with PTSD at risk for suicide. *Suicide and Life-Threatening Behavior, 44*(5), 582-590.

Hendin, H., Al Jurdi, R. K., Houck, P. R., Hughes, S., & Turner, J. B. (2010). Role of intense affects in predicting short-term risk for suicidal behavior: A prospective study. *Journal of Nervous and Mental Disease, 198*, 220-225.

Hendin, H., & Haas, A. P. (1991). Suicide and guilt as manifestations of PTSD in Vietnam combat veterans. *American Journal of Psychiatry, 148*, 586-591.

Hendin, H., Maltsberger, J. T., Lipschitz, A., Haas, A. P., & Kyle, J. (2001). Recognizing and responding to a suicide crisis. *Suicide and Life-Threatening Behavior, 34*, 115-128.

Hendin, H., Maltsberger, J. T., & Szanto, K. (2007). The role of intense affective states in signaling a suicide crisis. *Journal of Nervous and Mental Disease, 195*, 363-368.

Hendin, H., & Pollinger Haas, A. (1984a). Combat adaptations of Vietnam veterans without posttraumatic stress disorders. *American Journal of Psychiatry, 141*, 956-960.

Hendin, H., & Pollinger Haas, A. (1984b). *Wounds of war: The psychological aftermath of combat in Vietnam.* New York: Basic Books.

Jones, E. E., & Pulos, S. M. (1993). Comparing the process in psychodynamic and cognitive behavioral therapies. *Journal of Consulting and Clinical Psychology, 61,* 306-316. https://doi.org/10.1037/0022-006x.61.2.306

Jury, D. (1979). The forgotten warriors: New concern for the Vietnam veteran. *Behavioral Medicine, 6,* 38-41.

Kardiner, A., & Spiegel, H. (1947). *War stress and neurotic illness.* New York: Hoeber.

Klay, P. (2014). *Redeployment.* New York: Penguin.

Kline, A., Falca-Dodsin, M., Sussner, B., Ciccone, D. S., Chandler, H., Callahan, L., & Losonzy, M. (2010). Effects of repeated deployment to Iraq and Afghanistan on the health of New Jersey Army National Guard troops. Implications for military readiness. *American Journal of Public Health, 100,* 276-283.

Kolb, L. C. (1986). Post-traumatic stress disorder in Vietnam veterans (editorial). *New England Journal of Medicine, 3,* 641-642.

Kudler, H. (2007). The need for psychodynamic principles in outreach to new combat veterans and their families. *Journal of the American Academy of Psychoanalysis and Dynamic Psychiatry, 35,* 39-50.

Kuehn, B. M. (2010). Military probes epidemic of suicide: Mental health issues remain prevalent. *JAMA, 304,* 1427-1430.

LeardMann, C., Powell, T. M., Smith, T. C., Bell, M. R., Smith, B., Boyko, E. J., Tomoko, I, H., Gackstetter, G. D., Ghamsary, M., & Hoge, C. W. (2013). Risk factors associated with suicide in current and former U.S. military personnel. *JAMA, 310,* 406-505.

Leichsenring, F., & Rabung, S. (2008). Effectiveness of long-term psychodynamic psychotherapy: A meta-analysis. *Journal of the American Medical Association, 300,* 1551-1565.

Lipkin, J. O., Blank, A. S., Parson, E. R., & Smith, J. (1982). Vietnam veterans and posttraumatic stress disorder. *Hospital and Community Psychiatry, 33,* 908-912.

Sareen, J., Cox, B. J., Afifi, T. O., Stein, M. B., Belik, S., Meadows, G., & Shedler, J. (2010). The efficacy of psychodynamic therapy. *American Psychological Association, 65*(2), 98-109.

Shay, J. (1994). *Achilles in Vietnam: Combat trauma and the undoing of character.* New York: Scribner.

Shedler, J. (2010). The efficacy of psychodynamic therapy. *American Psychological Association,* 65(2), 98-109.

Shinseki, E. (2010, November 12). Suicide rates soar among U.S. vets. *Military.com.* www.military.com

Smith, T. C., Ryan, M. A. K., Wingard, D. L., Slymen, D. J., Sallis, J. F., & Kritz-Silverstein, D. (2008). New onset and persistent symptoms of posttraumatic stress disorder self-reported after deployment and combat exposure: Prospective population-based U.S. military cohort study. *BMJ, 336,* 366-371.

Stuen, M. R., & Solberg, K. B. (1972). The Vietnam veteran: Characteristics and needs. In L. I. Sherman & E. M. Caffey (Eds.), *The Vietnam veteran in contemporary society.* Washington, DC: Veterans Administration.

U.S. House of Representatives, Committee on Veterans Affairs. (1978). *Presidential review memorandum on Vietnam-era veterans: House report 38.* Washington, DC: U.S. Government Printing Office.

Weathers, F.W., Litz, B.T., Keane, T.M., Palmieri, P.A., Marx, B.P., & Schnurr, P.P. (2013). *The PTSD Checklist for DSM-5 (PCL-5).* Scale available from the National Center for PTSD at www.ptsd.va.gov.

The Cost of Chronic Stress in Childhood: Understanding and Applying the Concept of Allostatic Load

Debra A. Katz, Ginny Sprang, and Circe Cooke

Abstract: This article explores the concept of allostatic load and its utility as an integrative framework for thinking about the impact of chronic stress on children and adolescents. Allostatic load refers to the failure or exhaustion of normal physiologic processes that occurs in response to severe, frequent, or chronic stressors. This persistent physiologic dysregulation may lead to secondary health problems such as immunosuppression, obesity, atherosclerosis, and hypertension. Allostatic load can be measured and followed as a composite index of a group of physiologic parameters which fall outside of a normal range. Although research regarding allostatic load in children is limited, this article explores relevant studies and identifies ways in which the concept of allostatic load can be used to broaden approaches to assessment, case formulation, and treatment in children. The concept of allostatic load may be of particular interest to psychodynamic psychiatrists in recognizing the ways in which chronic stress and adverse childhood experiences lead not only to negative psychological sequelae but also to long-term health consequences including the possibility of premature death. It underscores the importance of monitoring patients' physical as well as psychological health and thinking about the complex interrelations between the two.

The concept of "stress" is difficult to define and measure. It has been used to refer to a real or imagined threat to the psychological or physical integrity of an individual or to the impact of "stressors" (e.g., environmental, psychological, or biological events) on emotional, behavioral, or physiologic functioning. Stress may be viewed as beneficial when it is of tolerable duration and leads to growth, mastery, and increased competence or as detrimental when it is severe, prolonged, or recurrent and overwhelms or impairs psychological or physiological coping abilities. What are the long-term physical and mental health effects of chronic stress on children? How can clinicians integrate an understanding of the impact of cumulative stress into their assessments, formulations,

prevention efforts, and treatment plans? Research on factors such as trauma, attachment, gene-environment interactions, risk and protective factors, psychosocial adversity, and physical illness have broadened the scope of child evaluations, however, understanding and quantifying their impact, or the "stress" they cause, on a child's current problems or potential to develop future problems has been a challenge. Psychiatrists are asked to evaluate psychosocial stressors as part of their multiaxial diagnostic assessment of each patient, however, the clinical usefulness, reliability, and validity of Axis IV assessment has been questioned (Skodol, 1991). In this article, we introduce the concepts of allostasis and allostatic load which we believe provide a helpful, integrative framework for thinking about the impact of stress on children and adolescents. Becoming acquainted with the concept of allostatic load allows clinicians to become aware of the ways in which chronic stress and adverse childhood experiences lead to long-term health consequences and contribute to premature death.

DEFINITIONS

Allostasis refers to the ability of complex physiological systems to "maintain stability or homeostasis through change" by adapting to physical, psychosocial, and environmental challenges (Sterling & Eyer, 1988). Changing internal and external demands lead to regulation of metabolic activities within multiple physiological systems such as cardiovascular, neuronal, immunologic, and endocrine. Allostasis involves adaptation by an organism to different situations by altering its internal parameters in order to maintain normal function or stability. While homeostasis focuses on isolated feedback loops, allostasis emphasizes multiple interacting physiologic systems along with brain and nervous system control over the body's responses. The concept of allostasis also includes the ability to anticipate stressors as opposed to solely reacting in response to them as well as the ability to show variability in response and complex responses through neurologic control of multiple physiologic systems.

Allostatic load refers to the failure or compromise of normal allostatic processes leading to chronic dysregulation of physiologic systems. Severe, frequent, or chronic challenges lead to cumulative strain over time on multiple organs and tissues which can be measured as allostatic load. For example, secretion of catecholamines and cortisol may be associated with healthy adaptation to an acute stressor (allostasis), but prolonged or severe stress may result in persistently abnormal catecholamine and cortisol levels. This chronic physiologic dysregulation, or

allostatic load, may lead to secondary health problems such as immunosuppression, obesity, atherosclerosis, and hypertension and has been associated with impaired physical and cognitive functioning and increased mortality in adulthood (McEwen, 2000; Seemen, McEwen, Rowe, & Singer, 2001).

Allostatic load involves the brain. The brain reacts to internal and external experiences by modulating physiologic and behavioral responses and, in turn, is changed structurally and chemically by these experiences (McEwen, 2000). Psychological traits such as hostility or anxiety influence both the perception of what is stressful as well as the response to stress and therefore impact on allostatic load. Psychiatric disorders constitute a form of allostatic load through factors such as altered responsiveness to stressful experience, impaired social interaction, and abnormal mood as well as through their associated neurochemical and structural brain changes. For example, dysregulation of the hypothalamic-pituatary-adrenal (HPA) system, as is seen in depression, has powerful and enduring effects on the brain and has been associated with structural brain changes such as hippocampal atrophy (Videbech & Ravnikilde, 2004).

Genetics exert a powerful effect on both the propensity to develop psychiatric and medical illnesses, including the disorders associated with allostatic load, but may also influence allostatic load in indirect ways. For example, Kendler, Karkowski, and Prescott (1999) have shown that while stressful experiences play a key role in precipitating depression, individuals who are genetically at risk for depression actually segregate themselves into higher risk environments. These findings illustrate the complexity of the gene-environment interaction and the multiple influences on the development of disease states associated with allostatic load. Behavioral and social factors may also constitute forms of allostatic load. Stress-related behaviors such as smoking, drinking, and overeating impact on health outcome and risk over time and social factors such as socioeconomic sta-

Table 1. Measures of Allostatic Load

Primary Mediators	Function
Cortisol	*Hypothalamic-pituitary-adrenal (HPA) activation*
Dehyroepiandrosterone sulphate (DHEA-S)	*HPA antagonism*
Epinephrine and norepinephrine	*Sympathetic system activation*
Secondary Outcomes	
Systolic and diastolic blood pressure	*Cardiovascular activity index*
Waist-hip ratio or body mass index (BMI)	*Metabolic function index*
High-density lipoprotein (HDL) & total-HDL cholesterol ratio	*Atherosclerotic risk index*
Glycosylated hemoglobin	*Glucose metabolism index*

tus have been shown to be strongly associated with morbidity and mortality. Finally, early adverse life experiences such as neglect or trauma profoundly and oftentimes permanently impact on brain circuitry involved in the stress response (Bremner, 2003) and contribute to the wide range of psychiatric and medical disorders that are commonly seen in this population in adult life (Anda et al., 2006).

HOW IS ALLOSTATIC LOAD MEASURED?

The physiologic parameters that reflect allostatic load differ across studies but are generally divided into *primary mediators*, such as norepinephrine, which regulate a variety of cellular events, and *secondary outcomes*, such as blood pressure, which reflect the cumulative effects of the primary mediators (Table 1; Clark, Bond, & Hecker, 2007). *Tertiary outcomes* are the actual disorders (e.g., hypertension, diabetes, atherosclerosis) that arise from allostatic load. The allostatic load score is typically calculated by summing the number of parameters which fall into the highest risk quartile. Thus if 10 physiologic indicators of risk are measured, the allostatic load score could range from 0–10. While there is not yet consensus on which of these parameters are most useful to measure in children, there is recognition

that allostatic load provides a way of assessing physiologic "wear and tear" across multiple systems. By combining a broad range of biological risk factors into a composite score for allostatic load, clinicians have a comprehensive way to assess and follow a patient's risk for a variety of stress-exacerbated diseases. This allows for assessment of risk in healthy individuals before the development of disease as well as an assessment of stress burden in patients with multiple mental or physical health diagnoses.

RESEARCH ON ALLOSTATIC LOAD IN CHILDREN AND ADOLESCENTS

The Adverse Childhood Experiences (ACE) study clearly demonstrated the connection between negative psychological experiences in childhood with physical and mental health problems in adulthood. This large epidemiologic study showed that as the number of adverse childhood experiences increased, the risk for serious psychiatric and physical health problems in adulthood increased in a parallel fashion (Anda et al., 2006). This corresponds with exposure of the developing brain to physiologic mediators of the stress response with resulting dysregulation of multiple brain structures and functions. A longitudinal study of over 10,000 children followed from birth into middle adulthood demonstrated a correlation between internalizing and externalizing behaviors during childhood and increased mortality risk in adulthood thus confirming the serious health risks of childhood psychopathology (Jokela, Ferrie, & Kivimaki, 2009) Although these studies demonstrate a correlation between a variety of adverse childhood experiences and symptoms and morbidity and mortality in adulthood, they do not delineate or follow the stepwise physiologic changes that occur in response to the chronic stressors studied.

Research on allostatic load in children and adolescents is limited but studies have correlated allostatic load with factors such as early menarche (Allsworth, Weitzen, & Boardman, 2005), household density (Johnston-Brooks, Lewis, Evans, & Whalen, 1998), violence (Murali & Chen, 2005), lower parent education (Goodman, McEwen, Bin, Dolan, & Adler, 2005), and adolescent alcohol use (Zimmerman, Blomeyer, Laucht, & Mann, 2007). Allostatic load has also been implicated as a mechanism in the development and perpetuation of eating disorders (Halmi, 2009). However, it is hard to separate out specific risk factors that lead to allostatic load when looking at the total stress burden on an individual child. Utilizing the concept of cumulative risk exposure, Evans (2003) found that allostatic load increased with elevated cumulative risk exposure in a group of rural elementary-school children. Cumulative risk included physical factors such as crowding, noise, and housing quality, psychosocial factors such as child separation, family turmoil, and exposure to violence and home environment factors such as poverty, single parenthood, and maternal high school educational status. Children with greater cumulative risk exposure had more psychological distress, lower perceptions of self-worth, increased self-regulatory behavior problems, and learned helplessness. As these children were followed into adolescence (Evans, Kim, Ting, Tesher, & Shannis, 2007), the effect of elevated cumulative risk continued to be correlated with increased allostatic load. A recent study has correlated the chronic stress caused by childhood poverty with impairments in working memory in young adulthood (Evans & Schamberg, 2009). Chronic stress as measured by allostatic load in this study is thought to be an important factor accounting for the income-achievement gap. In a follow-up study of children with elevated cumulative risk who were followed into adolescence, maternal responsiveness was identified as a protective factor in buffering the impact of allostatic load (Evans, Kim, Ting, Tesher, & Shannis, 2007). This suggests that enhancing parent–child relationships, an important aspect of clinical work with children, can significantly impact on allostatic load. However, this also suggests that children who experience disruptions in caretaking and attachment or who experience unresponsive or harsh parenting may be even more susceptible to the effects of cumulative risk exposure and allostatic load.

Early relationships and security or insecurity of attachment may influence vulnerability to allostatic load. In a study of over 100 mother-infant pairs (Hill-Soderlund et al., 2008), infants classified as insecure-avoidant showed greatest evidence of allostatic load as measured by sympathetic and parasympathetic responses to separation and reunion. Although all mothers demonstrated physiological changes with attempts to regulate their infant's distress, mothers of securely attached infants showed the greatest physiological responses. This may seem surprising but these increased reactions, most evident during the last reunion episode suggest a greater attempt at interactive repair in this securely attached group of mothers. These findings illustrate the importance and impact of the earliest attachment relationships on physiologic responses to psychosocial stress in both infants and mothers and lend support to the importance of early intervention in clinical work with children. These findings should be interpreted with caution since further work needs to be done to correlate these findings in infancy with long-term negative health effects and allostatic load in adulthood. However, it has been shown that *adults* with insecure-avoidant attachment patterns tend to suppress negative emotion and forego or avoid social support leading to increased risk for the development and continuation of physical health problems (Kotler, Buzwell, Romeo, & Bowland, 1994). The interconnections between attachment profile and physiologic changes leading to allostatic load have yet to be worked out fully, but these findings underscore the importance of early parent–child relationships in impacting on physical as well as psychological health and the tremendous effect that clinicians can have by addressing dysfunctional relationships early in life.

HOW CAN CLINICIANS USE THE CONCEPT OF ALLOSTATIC LOAD?

Assessment

There is not consensus on how best to assess allostatic load in children, and research in this area is still in its infancy. However, there are a variety of ways the clinician can establish a baseline and follow parameters associated with allostatic load. Measuring primary mediators such as overnight cortisol, epinephrine, and norepinephrine is generally not realistic. Assessing secondary outcomes such as blood pressure, waist-hip ratio, blood lipids, and glycosylated hemoglobin can easily be done in an office setting and may provide useful information about overall health status especially if followed over time. Psychiatrists or other mental health clinicians may not typically obtain this information about their patients, but it may prove useful both for following overall cardiovascular health status as well as in considering allostatic load. It is important to remember that it is not one set of measurements at one point in time that is important in allostatic load but rather the small, incre-

mental changes over time that elevate a child into high risk groups for each parameter. This makes the need for long-term continuity of care especially important for patients at risk. Given the early stages of research on allostatic load in children, there is a need to gather data as to how often measurements should be made, which measurements are most helpful and how to understand the association of these measurements with long-term morbidity in children with psychiatric disorders.

Case Formulation

The concepts of allostasis and allostatic load do not attempt to neglect important aspects of a child's experience (e.g., intrapsychic, family, school) or to replace useful models of case formulation such as the biopsychosocial model or the "four Ps" model (predisposing, precipitating, perpetuating, protective). The goal of all case formulation is to develop a set of hypotheses about the etiology and range of influences on the patient's presenting problems which will hopefully lead to a set of specific, individualized treatment recommendations.

Utilizing the concepts of allostasis and allostatic load broadens and deepens the clinician's formulation regarding the impact of external challenges that children confront and their potential for permanently dysregulating multiple physiologic systems leading to chronic impairment of mental and physical health. It allows the clinician to think more broadly about a variety of interventions, including those that seem somewhat simple or minor, and the significant impact they may have on long-term health. For example, low socioeconomic status, crowded living conditions, and single parenthood are not just social stressors but can be thought of as powerful contributors to allostatic load and overall child health. Likewise, psychological stressors such as exposure to violence, multiple foster care placements, or harsh parenting carry risk not only for psychological well-being but may also impact on physical health and morbidity from chronic illness through their impact on the neuroendocrine system and the brain. Dysregulation of the HPA axis from depression may not be recognized as a "biological" factor in a traditional biopsychosocial formulation but does lead to ongoing neurochemical and structural brain changes as well as to emotional and behavioral alterations that impact on the ability to respond adaptively to future stressors. It therefore becomes important as a clinician to think not just of typical stressors in each of the biological, psychological, and social domains but to think broadly and creatively regarding each of these and to pay careful attention to cumulative risk for all children. Stressors that have been associated with allostatic load in children that clinicians may not routinely think about might include physical crowding in the home, exposure to excessive noise, poor housing quality, current or prior episodes of living in poverty, and parental high school dropout status. Insecure-avoidant attachment, early menarche, and frequent school absences due to illness have also been correlated with allostatic load in children. Much more work needs to be done to elucidate information that could be obtained from a clinical history that might reflect or be associated with allostatic load but current research suggests intriguing possibilities.

Risk and Intervention

Allostatic load reflects a confluence or convergence of risk factors and emphasizes the idea that cumulative wear and tear on the body over time results in a series of seemingly small physiologic changes (e.g., mild elevations in blood pressure, glucose, or lipids) that have the potential to impact on long-term health. Each small change in a physiologic parameter results in a small increase in morbidity and mortality, but, when changes in individual parameters are combined collectively over time, marked increases in morbidity, mortality, and psychosocial dysfunction are seen. Clinicians are in the unique position of being able to impact on allostatic load before these changes become fixed or irreversible. Psychodynamically oriented clinicians who typically work with patients over longer periods of time may have special opportunity to not only effect psychological change but to impact on allostatic load. Thus what may appear as seemingly small interventions such as referring a caretaker for treatment of depression or encouraging a child to participate in a sport to increase exercise and social interaction can have significant mental and physical health benefits. While enhancing maternal responsiveness is one factor that has been shown to reduce allostatic load (Evans, Kim, Ting, Tesher, & Shannis, 2007) other general interventions that may be helpful (but which psychodynamic clinicians may discount as important) include encouraging patients to reduce unhealthy behaviors such as smoking or overeating, ensuring adequate sleep, enhancing social connections, promoting cardiovascular health through exercise and diet, and working to enhance self-esteem and social success (McEwen, 2007). Children in out-of-home care may be especially vulnerable to allostatic load through the effects of early trauma, disrupted attachment relationships, and exposure to violence and substance abuse. It is especially important for clinicians to advocate for placement safety and stability and to minimize violence exposure and opportunities for retraumatization to reduce allostatic load in this vulnerable population (Sprang, Katz, & Cooke, 2009). On a broader social level, allostatic load can be reduced by advocating for services and policies such as access to health care, education, and housing that support children and families.

Physicians typically obtain physical examination and laboratory measurements as a way to assess potential risks or side effects of medications, but it may be helpful as well to consider this data in light of allostatic load. Since allostatic load is affected by both psychological and physical stressors, a child's weight gain and elevated blood glucose may be due in part to elevated stress hormones in response to psychiatric illness or to psychological distress from recent events in addition to the primary side effects of medication. Psychiatric medications may exert a positive or negative impact on allostatic load. Neurotransmitter systems in the brain are altered by psychiatric medications which may, in the case of an illness like major depression, reduce allostatic load through reversal of adverse chemical or structural brain changes (McEwen, 2007). Allostatic load may be increased through the effects of medication on cardiovascular parameters such as blood pressure or on blood glucose or lipids. Because the origins of allostatic load are multidetermined and interconnected, improvements due to medication in one system do not always translate into improvements in other systems or in overall allostatic load. Thus the issues regarding allostatic load and medications are complex and necessitate a full consideration of both psychiatric benefit and medical risk.

The concept of allostatic load offers advantages over a risk-resilience model. Instead of attempting to correlate individual risk and protective factors with a vast array of psychiatric and medical diseases, allostatic load provides a way of measuring a composite index of stress burden on an individual—the allostatic load score—and allows the clinician to follow that score over time. In addition, some risks carry more weight than others and some periods of development are more vulnerable than others. There is significant evidence that early traumatic experiences are especially important and may initiate a cascade of physiological and psychological processes that alter behavior as well as the structure and function of the brain (Bremner, 2003). These early experiences, which may be seen by psychodynamically oriented clinicians as primarily having psychological im-

pact, carry tremendous risk for the development and persistence of allostatic load into adulthood necessitating close mental and physical health follow-up.

Allostatic load does not differentiate between or privilege the social, psychological, or biological causes of stress burden on an individual but attempts in a rough way to quantify it. This allows the clinician to creatively decide how to intervene to lessen allostatic load. These interventions may include ongoing psychotherapy or other forms of psychiatric treatment but may also include efforts not directly related to the problem at hand. For example, encouraging a parent to find appropriate housing may significantly reduce household density, noise, and exposure to violence which may ultimately impact on allostatic load. These ideas validate some of the efforts clinicians make on behalf of patients that are outside the scope of typical professional interventions.

Challenges and Future Directions

There are a number of challenges involved in attempting to utilize the concept of allostatic load with patients. Most of the research on allostatic load has been done with adults and much more work is needed to understand the development and progression of allostatic load in children. Further research is needed to operationalize which measures of allostatic load are most helpful in children, how to obtain these measures in busy clinical settings, which disease states correlate most strongly with different allostatic load profiles and how to manage individuals with elevated scores. The association of allostatic load with larger societal issues such as socioeconomic inequality makes it important for clinicians to be aware of their own attitudes and prejudices toward patients whose backgrounds may involve risk factors for high allostatic load. Because allostatic load is a composite index, the exact cause of an individual's stress burden is not clear when they have an elevated score. This may therefore make it difficult to develop specific interventions to reduce allostatic load. Much more work needs to be done to understand, delineate, and quantify the impact of multiple stressors on allostatic load.

REFERENCES

Allsworth, J. E., Weitzen, S., & Boardman, L. A. (2005). Early age at menarche and allostatic load: Data from the Third National Health and Nutrition Examination survey. *Annals of Epidemiology, 15*, 438-444.

Anda, R. F., Felitti, V. F., Bremner, J. D., et al. (2006). The enduring effects of abuse and related adverse experiences in childhood: A convergence of evidence from neurobiology and epidemiology. *European Archives of Psychiatry and Clinical Neuroscience, 256*, 174-186.

Bremner, J. D. (2003). Long-term effects of childhood abuse on brain and neurobiology. *Child and Adolescent Psychiatric Clinics of North America, 12*, 271-292.

Clark, M. S., Bond, M. J., & Hecker, J. R. (2007). Environmental stress, psychological stress and allostatic load. *Psychology, Health & Medicine, 12*, 18-30.

Evans, G. W. (2003). A multimethodological analysis of cumulative risk and allostatic load among rural children. *Developmental Psychology, 39*, 924-933.

Evans, G. W., Kim, P., Ting, A. H., Tesher, H. B., & Shannis, D. (2007). Cumulative risk, responsiveness and allostatic load among young adolescents. *Developmental Psychology, 43*, 341-351.

Evans, G. W., & Schamberg, M. A. (2009). Childhood poverty, chronic stress, and adult working memory. *Proceedings of the National Academy of Sciences, 106*, 6545-6549.

Goodman, E., McEwen, B. S., Bin, H., Dolan, L., & Adler, N. E. (2005). Social inequalities in biomarkers of cardiovascular risk in adolescence. *Psychosomatic Medicine, 67*, 9-15.

Halmi, K. A. (2009). Perplexities and provocations of eating disorders. *Journal of Child Psychology and Psychiatry, 50*, 163-169.

Hill-Soderlund, A. L., Mills-Koonce, W. R., Propper, C., Calkins, S. D., Granger, D.A., Moore, G.A., et al. (2008). Parasympathetic and sympathetic responses to the strange situation in infants and mothers from avoidant and securely attached dyads. *Developmental Psychobiology, 50*, 361-376.

Johnston-Brooks, C. H., Lewis, M. A., Evans, G. W., & Whalen, C. K. (1998). Chronic stress and illness in children: The role of allostatic load. *Psychosomatic Medicine, 60*, 597-603.

Jokela, M., Ferrie, J., & Kivimaki, M. (2009). Childhood problem behaviors and death by midlife: The British National Child Development Study. *Journal of the American Academy of Child and Adolescent Psychiatry, 48*, 19-24.

Kendler, K. S., Karkowski, L. M., & Prescott, C. A. (1999). Causal relationship between stressful life events and the onset of major depression. *American Journal of Psychiatry, 156*, 837-841.

Kotler, T., Buzwell, S., Romeo, Y., & Boland, J. (1994). Avoidant attachment as a risk factor for health. *British Journal of Medical Psychology, 67*, 237-245.

McEwen, B. (2007). Physiology and neurobiology of stress and adaptation: Central role of the brain. *Physiological Reviews, 87*, 873-904.

McEwen, B. S. (2000). Allostasis and allostatic load: Implications for neuropsychopharmacology. *Neuropsychopharmacology, 22*, 108-124.

Murali, R., & Chen, E. (2005). Exposure to cardiovascular and neuroendocrine measures in adolescents. *Annals of Behavioral Medicine, 30*, 155-163.

Seeman, T. E., McEwen, B. S., Rowe, J. W., & Singer, B. H. (2001). Allostatic load as a marker of cumulative biological risk: MacArthur studies of successful aging. *Proceedings of the National Academy of Sciences of the United States of America, 98*, 4770-4775.

Skodol, A. E. (1991). Axis IV: A reliable and valid measure of psychosocial stressors? *Comprehensive Psychiatry, 32*, 503-15.

Sprang, G., Katz, D. A., & Cooke, C. (2009). Allostatic load: Considering the burden of cumulative trauma on children in foster care. *Journal of Child and Adolescent Trauma, 2*, 242-252.

Sterling, P., & Eyer, J. (1988). Allostasis: A new paradigm to explain arousal pathology. In S. Fisher & J. Reason (Eds.), *Handbook of Life Stress, Cognition and Health, 34*, 629-649.

Videbech, P., & Ravnikilde, B. (2004). Hippocampal volume and depression: A meta-analysis of MRI studies. *American Journal of Psychiatry, 161*, 1957-1966.

Zimmerman, U. S., Blomeyer, D., Laucht, M., & Mann, K. F. (2007). How gene-stress-behavior interactions can promote adolescent alcohol use: The roles of predrinking allostatic load and childhood behavior disorders. *Pharmacology, Biochemistry & Behavior, 86*, 246-262.

Part 3
Psychodynamic Psychiatry
in Special Populations

Richard C. Friedman, MD, Jennifer I. Downey, MD and César A. Alfonso, MD

PARENT-INFANT
PSYCHODYNAMIC THERAPIES

Salomonsson, from the Karolinska Institute in Stockholm, provides an overview of psychotherapies for parent-infant dyads with particular attention to how psychodynamic interventions may benefit certain families. Salomonsson's own recent research adds to the evidence-base literature on psychodynamic therapies, after a randomized controlled trial of mother infant psychoanalytic treatment compared to routine wellness pediatric care in child health centers in Sweden showed improvement in maternal wellbeing (anxiety, depression, ambivalence about motherhood) in the experimental and control group, and gains in infant health (targeting difficulties with feeding or weaning, poor sleep, gaze avoidance and mood instability) in infants who received psychotherapy treatment but not in infants who received routine pediatric supportive care. The psychodynamic dyadic intervention tested was intensive and time limited, with 2-3 times a week sessions over a period of 2-3 months examining verbal and nonverbal mother-infant communication processes looking at how interactive mismatches relate to emotional disorders in infants, and how intrapsychic conflict of the parent can engulf and disturb the infant causing a cycle of emotional distress.

Therapeutic nursery settings and dyadic family therapies for preverbal children that are primarily psychoeducational, expressive and supportive have been shown to be of great help to mothers and caregivers. These include interaction guidance for parents with limited insight and parent-infant psychotherapy with an ego-psychology supportive framework, both developed by Fraiberg in the 1980s at the University of Michigan. Inadequate attachments in these approaches are understood as originating from unconscious displaced parental conflicts that negatively impact quality of caregiving. Cramer and colleagues in Geneva, a decade later, further developed Fraiberg's approach examining outcomes when parents treat infants as narcissistic extensions of themselves, helping caregivers with this problematic dynamic. Lebovici at the Centre Albert Binet in Paris was the first to carefully examine enactments and countertransferences in parent infant therapies. Beebe and Lachman in New York introduced the concept of co-constructing interactions, when parents monitor and regulate their inner state while simultaneously tracking and attending the infant's communications and actions. Beebe's elegant work looks at micro-processes and nuances of dyadic experiences. Johan Norman, a Swedish analyst, proposed that a therapeutic relationship could be established between an infant and an analyst in the presence of the mother or parent. Relating to babies in their own right through verbal and nonverbal containment and empathic validation, and recognizing them as subjects can have a profound impact on the parent as well. Another innovative approach, the Watch, Wait and Wonder parent-infant therapy developed in Toronto is based on attachment theory and allows the infant to lead the treatment, with the parent asked to get down on the floor and observe and interact with the baby only at the baby's initiative, similar to what play therapy does with older children, in order to gain insight into the infant's inner world and needs. The therapist engages in this therapy modality in a parallel process of observation and reflection. Parent-infant therapies, especially those that are psychodynamically informed, have gained an important place in promoting healthcare, secure attachments and emotional well being of infants. Public health initiatives to make these time-limited therapies available to infants and families at risk will follow as these evidence-based therapies continue to gain recognition and acceptance.

WORKING WITH CHILDREN AND RISK

The need to characterize childhood precursors of adult psychopathology has been apparent throughout the history of psychiatry. One of Freud's most important contributions for example was his recognition that childhood experience influences adult experience and behavior. It stands to reason that the earlier in life psychopathology can be identified, the sooner it can be treated and ameliorated or extinguished.

Kestenbaum, from Columbia University, was among the first to identify and discuss the diagnosis and treatment of children who were not psychotic but had psychopathology that foretold later occurring adult psychiatric disorders. In her chapter on childhood precursors of Personality Disorders, Kestenbaum notes that only one childhood disorder is known to predict an adult Personality Disorder. Conduct Disorder of Childhood has been demonstrated to predict the occurrence of Antisocial Personality Disorder during adulthood.

Kestenbaum discusses the history of psychiatric thought about genetic and environmental influences on behavior, summarizing the contributions of Kernberg and Chazen, Thomas and Ches, Kagan, Kendler and others.

She reviews attachment theory and stresses the need to foster the capacity for secure attachment in therapeutic work. Importantly, Kestenbaum emphasizes that assessment of peer play behavior is crucially important in understanding childhood psychodynamics and psychopathology in contrast to assessment of adult behavior.

Kestenbaum comments on the use of dimensional perspectives for clarifying influences on the development of psychopathology from childhood through adulthood. She notes that dimensional perspectives are emphasized in DSM-V.

Despite advances in clarifying relationships between childhood state-trait behavior, psychological symptoms, and adult Personality Disorders many important questions remain to be explored by clinical research in the future.

PSYCHODYNAMIC ASPECTS OF THE CLINICAL CARE OF SPOUSES OF THE MEDICALLY ILL

Ingram, from New York Medical College and the American Institute for Psychoanalysis, conducted systematic interviews of mental health clinicians caring for spouses of the medically ill. Chronic conditions reported in this sample were Huntington's disease, multiple sclerosis, Parkinson's disease, amyotrophic lateral sclerosis, chronic fatigue syndrome, Crohn's disease, chronic obstructive pulmonary disease, cancer, heart disease with congestive heart failure, and multiple traumatic injuries with disabling sequelae. In a previous study, Ingram conducted interviews of clinicians treating spouses of persons with dementia. Both surveys resulted in a library of case vignettes that enrich the psychodynamic psychiatry literature, with astute observations and thoughtful peer supervision.

Although illness is part of the life cycle, chronic and debilitating conditions, especially if disfiguring, with uncertain prognosis, incapacitating and associated with social stigma are experienced as dehumanizing and cause distress in affected individuals and their loved ones. In the Holmes and Rahe Social Readjustment Rating Scale, ill health of a family member has a valence score of 44, compared to 53 for personal illness and 100 for death of a spouse. It is important to note that the magnitude of psychological distress experienced by spousal caregivers may threaten the integrity of their own health. Ingram's interviews of therapists of spousal caregivers identified important psychodynamic factors that either facilitate or impede the therapeutic alliance when caring for caretakers.

Therapists of caregivers of persons with dementia reported dissociative reactions, denial and the impulse to disengage, with a tendency to undervalue the spousal attachment bond. Premature recommendations for home care, assisted living and residential care reflect therapeutic misalignment and failure of empathy. Ingram illustrates the importance of Racker's conceptualization of concordant and complementary countertransferences and how unconscious forces may lead to collusion with denial, endorsement of pathological caregiving and symmetrical identification with states of helplessness in therapists who work with spousal caregivers of the medically ill. Value conflicts between therapists and caretakers around issues such as transparent communication, discordant involvement of other family members, fidelity, ambivalent feelings towards spouses, and expression of affects of rage, guilt and shame need to be carefully evaluated to facilitate working through, attain symptomatic reduction and strengthen the therapeutic alliance.

WORKING WITH SURVIVORS OF INTIMATE PARTNER VIOLENCE

Human violence is predominately perpetrated by males. Throughout human history, since records have been kept males have invariably been found to be more violent than females.

This is the case with respect to Intimate Partner Violence (IPV) the subject of the chapter by Levendosky, Lannert and Yalch from Michigan State University. Men often attack each other but sadly they also frequently attack women. Levendosky, Lannert and Yalch note that 25% of women in an adult relationship with a male partner have been violently assaulted. As is the case with many other forms of violence women sometimes attack their partners but the lifetime prevalence of male victims is only 7.6% and the physical and psychological damage tends to be less severe. This chapter is focused on violence committed by men toward women.

Many of these women are mothers of young children. As might be expected mothers who are victims of violence often become impaired in their capacity to be caregivers. Their children tend to suffer psychological impairments as well hence IPV leads to intergenerational psychopathology.

Diverse psychological symptoms and syndromes my be provoked by IPV including Post-Traumatic Syndrome, depression, anxiety, substance abuse and other disorders.

Children of women who have experienced IPV may be at increased risk of perpetration and victimization. If IPV occurs during pregnancy the resultant maternal stress and dysphoria may adversely influence the developing fetus and the post-natal behavior of the child.

Because of the frequency of IPV and its malignant effects on mother, child and family unit mental health professionals should systematically inquire about its occurrence in routine diagnostic assessments and during psychotherapeutic treatment.

WORKING WITH CRIMINAL OFFENDERS IN FORENSIC SETTINGS

Mulay, Kelly, and Cain from Long Island University argue that psychodynamic psychotherapy is under-utilized in prisons. They note that jails contain a disproportionally large number of mentally ill inmates. Many of the incarcerated mentally ill suffer from psychoses, bipolar disorder, serious addictions, suicidal depressions, and multiple disorders simultaneously.

Although some prisoners have antisocial personality disorder, most do not. Some have committed serious crimes and may be career criminals. Others are simply people who for one reason or another have broken the law and in some cases become entangled in a web of legal and bureaucratic machinery. It is important to be aware of gender differences when thinking about the institutional treatment of the mentally ill. Men with certain types of psychiatric disorders are likely to be imprisoned, whereas women are more like to be treated in hospitals and clinics. This is probably primarily because men are more violent than women but may also reflect gender differences in relational style as well. In any case, a psychotherapist who works in jails must be prepared to treat men with multiple psychiatric diagnoses and predilections toward violence.

The vast majority of mentally ill inmates do not receive appropriate counseling services. Mulay, Kelly, and Cain note that psychodynamic psychotherapy is effective across diverse diagnoses and point out that lengthy sentences of many prisoners make them candidates for such treatment. They suggest ways in which psychodynamic psychotherapy could be studied should it be implemented. In order to fully understand their reasoning, however, social context must be taken into account. What are prisons actually like? In fact, standards of care are often low because of limited resources. Many clinicians experience burnout and there are too few therapists to treat all those in need.

The authors' scholarly review of psychopathology in the prison population is helpful but their discussion of treatment applies to a hypothetical ideal scenario. Resources devoted to treating the mentally ill in prisons reflect social- political attitudes of American society as a whole. Groups without political power tend to be resource poor. This not only includes the incarcerated but also the very young, the seriously impoverished and the mentally ill in state hospitals. Adequate mental health services in prison require trained staff and also a physically safe environment for all.

Although long-term psychotherapy may be helpful for some patients, this is only one of many treatment options to be found under the general umbrella of psychodynamic psychiatry. This includes intensive psychodynamic short-term psychotherapy, combined pharmacotherapy and psychotherapy, group therapy, and other therapeutic modalities as well. If resources were generally available, it might then be practical to implement psychodynamic concepts that are theoretically useful.

WORKING WITH THE ELDERLY

Schacther, Kächele and Schachter, affiliated with Columbia University and the International Psychoanalytic University in Berlin, describe important themes and modifications of technique in the psychodynamic treatment of elderly persons. Eriksonian developmental tasks relevant in this phase of life include generativity vs. stagnation and integrity vs. despair. Life's meaningfulness can erode if losses of friends, spouses and close relatives cause depressive cognitive distortions, leading to despair, apathy, withdrawal and even suicidality. Psychoanalysts beginning with Abraham over a century ago recognized how valuable treatment can be in late life. As Schachter, Kächele and Schachter point out, however, there is a paucity of literature dedicated to the subject and most psychoanalytic training institutes fail to offer students didactic guidance.

The magnitude of losses in late life could encompass loss of loved ones and friends, loss of parenting gratification, loss of physical vitality, loss of cognitive functions, sensory loss, loss of professional identity, social status, and income. Depressive syndromes often follow loss and further complicate adjustment and adaptation. Fromm-Reichman and Sullivan brought the affective constellation and experiences of loneliness to the attention of the psychiatric community with important early publications on this subject.

Schachter, Kächele and Schachter describe two modifications in the psychoanalytic treatment of elderly persons. One is to incorporate directive guidance when appropriate, especially by offering patients recommendations to strengthen social networks and increase meaningful and stimulating prosocial activities. Cabaniss and Gabbard describe psychodynamic psychotherapy as a process conducted along a supportive, expressive, and exploratory continuum. Supportive interventions with vulnerable populations are always adequate. The other recommendation Schachter, Kächele and Schachter provide is to offer post-termination contacts after satisfactory completion of analytic treatment. Olarte had similarly proposed intermittent psychodynamic psychotherapy visits as an alternative to a linear analytic treatment frame that has a beginning, middle and categorical end. Termination is thus reframed in a manner similar to the medical paradigm where psychotherapy visits are always welcome as needed. Loss of support is associated with negative affects and existential concerns in the last phase of life and the psychodynamic psychiatrist is well equipped to provide support and assistance with the developmental challenges of this critical period.

Psychodynamic Therapies with Infants and Parents: A Critical Review of Treatment Methods

Björn Salomonsson

Abstract: The theory of psychoanalysis has always relied on speculations about the infant's mind, but its clinical practice was slow in taking an interest in babies and their parents. The therapy methods that nevertheless have evolved during the last 50 years differ in their emphasis on support or insight, which roles they attribute to mother and baby in therapy, and to what extent they focus on the unconscious influences in mother and baby, respectively. They also differ to what extent their theories rely on classical psychoanalysis, attachment psychology, developmental psychology, and infant research. Each method also contains assumptions, most often tacit, about which kinds of samples for which they are most suited.

The article describes the most well-known modes of psychodynamic therapy with infants and parents (PTIP). There is a certain emphasis on methods that are less known to the U.S. readership, such as the French and Scandinavian traditions. It submits them and the other methods to a critical review.

From early on in the history of psychoanalysis, clinicians sought to modify its classical technique. Their aim was to reach patient categories beyond those that Freud and his contemporaries were treating. Their efforts resulted in therapy modes with a decreased frequency and duration, such as brief and focal psychotherapy. They also gave rise to techniques for psychotic and borderline patients, as well as groups and couples. One of the last patient categories to be reached by such efforts was the mother–infant dyad. Parent–infant psychotherapy was introduced on both sides of the Atlantic by Fraiberg (1980) and Dolto (1982, 1985) half a century ago. Today it is gaining increasing interest among psychoanalytic therapists. This article will review and delineate methods with a psychoanalytic focus on the internal worlds of infant and parent and their interaction. A second article will report on results from

quantitative studies and how they might help develop therapy techniques further. The acronym PTIP will cover the various modes of Psychodynamic Therapy with Infants and Parents. There will be some emphasis on two therapy traditions that are less well known to the American readership; those suggested by French-speaking analysts (Cramer & Palacio Espasa, 1993; Dolto, 1982; Lebovici & Stoléru, 2003) and one devised by a Swedish analyst, Johan Norman (2001).

Two limitations will be pointed out at the start, which will lead to the article's two major questions. The American literature often uses "infant" for children up to 2–3 years of age. In contrast, European authors generally restrict it to pre-verbal children. The Latin word *in-fans* means "speechless" or "not talking." In agreement with Winnicott (1960) the term infancy will be referred to as "the phase prior to word presentation and the use of word symbols" (p. 588), and to therapies with babies up to 12, or at the most 18, months of age in company with a parent. This brings us to our first major question; can one really call an "in-fans" a therapy patient? Does he take part in the therapeutic process and is he affected by it? The survey of PTIP methods will provide different answers.

Second, the article focuses on methods based on psychoanalytic or psychodynamic theory (these terms will be used interchangeably). This theory describes man as struggling with unconscious urges that impact on his/her character, relationships, interests, passions, conscious attitudes, and cognitive capacities. Consequently, methods will be omitted if their main aim is to support the mother's ego and encourage her to change her behavior with the baby. Though they are widely used in child health care settings, for example, developmental guidance (Lojkasek, Cohen, & Muir, 1994), infant massage (Field, 2000), interaction guidance (McDonough, 2004), and Marte Meo (Aarts, 2000), they will not be covered here. The focus will be on therapy forms that help mother to get in contact with unconscious ambivalence toward her child, her partner, or her maternal role and also—to a varying extent—help the baby to get in contact with his unconscious affects. The last clause brings us to our second major question; psychodynamic therapy focuses on the patient's conflicts between conscious and unconscious urges. In contrast, far from all therapists would agree that this applies to an infant in therapy. The question is thus if unconscious factors, in the dynamic and/or the systematic sense, may be at work in a baby. The theories behind all PTIP methods agree that the *parent's* involvement constitutes a mix of conscious strivings to bond with the child and provide a fertile ground for attachment—and unconscious urges stemming from his/her childhood. Therapy often reveals a clash between these strivings. In contrast, few methods speak of similar factors in the *baby*. As we will see,

different positions on this point will affect therapeutic technique.

All PTIP modes build on classical psychoanalytic theory—sometimes in agreement with it, sometimes in increasing disagreement. Traditionally, it has regarded the mother as the primary object. She, or rather her body parts or functions, are involved in the baby's fantasies—or whatever term used to cover his primeval mental activities. This maternal primacy is stated more or less explicitly by all PTIP theories and is also reflected in the dominance of mothers and babies in case presentations. We will now begin with a survey of Freud's assumptions about the infant mind and their importance to his theoretical edifice. This will be contrasted with a realization that it took many years for analysts to devote their therapeutic efforts to clinical babies. Some reasons for this will be suggested.

THE FREUDIAN BABY

Freud did not work therapeutically with babies but was a keen observer of everyday interactions with their mothers. He used such observations to speculate on what went on in their internal worlds. These speculations in fact played a major role in his theoretical edifice. We will exemplify with the concept of *representations*. In the "Project for a Scientific Psychology" (Freud, 1895) he describes how the baby experiences satisfaction—a psychological event—in physiological terms; as a neuronal discharge. But his description of such experiences includes an interactive dimension; it presupposes an "alteration in the external world (supply of nourishment, proximity of the sexual object)" (p. 318) via "extraneous help," that is, by "an experienced person" who gets drawn to the child's state. Freud actually describes a relationship; a baby keeps crying until his mother listens and comforts him.

Freud's neurophysiological terminology may obscure to the modern reader his position that the infant forms representations of the mother. When a baby communicates his distress to "the helpful person" (obviously Freud's term for the mother) he will perceive her as hostile. Freud links the baby's painful experiences with his perception of a "hostile object" (pp. 320, 322, etc.). He then suggests that the baby is disinclined to keep the hostile mnemic image cathected, a process which he names a "primary defence [fending off]" (p. 322). The baby thus has representations of a hostile object who cannot comfort him—and he will defend himself against retaining them. "The Interpretation of Dreams" (Freud, 1900) contains similar references, though here Freud prefers the term *wish*; this is an effort at re-establishing "the situation of the original satisfaction. An impulse of this kind is what we call a wish" (pp. 565–566). Evidently, to recall a satisfying memory implies to re-evoke its representation. It arises from biological needs, it is charged with affects, and it involves an object.

The Freudian baby is thus from the very start a psychological being; disturbing events in his somatic being are not only *registered* biologically but also *experienced* subjectively. These biological events and their concomitant experiences are handled through interactions with the mother, which leave traces in the baby's mind. Truly, Freud wavers between describing the infant as being governed by biological forces and psychological motives. In a passage on infantile sexuality (Freud, 1905), it remains unclear if any representational activity is involved when the baby is "sinking back satiated from the breast and falling asleep with flushed cheeks and a blissful smile" (p. 182). Things become clearer when he writes about "infants in arms" (Freud, 1925–1926, p. 138). He suggests their anxiety arises when they are separated from the mother. As long as he labels this an "automatic phenomenon" and a "rescuing signal," he is applying biological terms. However, he also applies psychologi-

cal terms when stating that the anxiety is a "product of the infant's *mental* helplessness" (p. 138, italics added), and that it is countered by repeated experiences of satisfaction which sum up to create the maternal *object*. "This object, whenever the infant feels a need, receives an intense cathexis which might be described as a 'longing' one" (p. 170). To sum up, Freud suggests two kinds of infant representations; a positive longing image of a mother who will provide satisfaction, and a negative hostile image of a mother who does not take away his suffering. The baby wants to do away with the latter, a process labelled defense.

Freud returns to the topic of representations in "The Unconscious" (Freud, 1915b), where he differentiates thing- from word-presentations. He suggests that all representations originate as unconscious thing-presentations. They are "the first and true object-cathexes" (p. 201) and thus the only ones existent in the infant's mind. When they get linked with "the residues of perceptions of words" (p. 202), word-presentations emerge. This linking "is not yet the same thing as becoming conscious, but only makes it possible to become so." Freud's division creates problems, as Maze and Henry (1996) have remarked. A baby has many conscious representations; mother's voice, a dog's barking, the scent of milk, etc. Since he cannot yet link words to them we cannot, according to Freud, label them conscious because "objects cannot become conscious through the medium of their own perceptual residues" (1915b, p. 202). Yet it is hard to deny that a baby who smiles at his mother is conscious that she is someone special or, to put it more generally, that the "thing" mother in front of his eyes differs from other "things" he is looking at, such as the ceiling or the lamp. To put it in imaginative words: "I know *she* is there and that *she* is different from the '*it-s*' around me, but I neither know what *she* nor the *it-s* are called."

In addition to a shift in the concept of representations, Freud's 1915 papers (1915a, 1915b) —compared with "The Project" (1895)—also imply a shift in the concept of defense; now it becomes tied to the aim of keeping *verbal* representations out of awareness. In "The Project" he had suggested that already the preverbal infant could defend himself against unpleasant experiences. Freud now suggests that "an instinct can never become an object of consciousness— only the idea that represents the instinct can" (1915b, p. 177). Ideas are thought-processes that can be verbalized. The aim of repression is now viewed as twofold; to keep out of awareness both the ideational content and the affective and unpleasant component. Freud refers here to a more "sophisticated" version of repression, one that is a key component in neurotic children and adults rather than in normal crying babies.

"The Unconscious" may give us the impression that Freud thought the differentiation between thing- and word-presentations was clear-cut. However, a close reading reveals that he noted that word-presentations also contain sense-perceptions. Though a baby does not understand a word's literal meaning, he may be attentive to its "sound-image" (1915b, p. 210), or its "thing-like" quality assembled from "auditory, visual and kinaesthetic elements" (p. 210). Thus, the dividing line between pre-representational and representational life is indistinct—and it does *not* coincide with the child's acquisition of language. We are returning to our first question; if a baby is sensitive to the thing-like qualities of words, perhaps a therapist's interventions might touch him. The question is; in what ways? As we will see, different PTIP modes look at this issue from various perspectives.

The concept of representation has been chosen to illustrate how important Freud's infant observations and speculations were to his metapsychology. Other such concepts

include the dream psychology (1900), the formation of the unconscious (1915b), the pleasure principle (1920), primal repression and repression proper (1915a), the primary and secondary processes (1911), and infantile sexuality (1905). To Freud there was a straight, albeit subterranean, line running from the internal world of the infant to that of the adult. Our adult character is "based on the memory-traces of our impressions . . . The impressions which have had the greatest effect on us—those of our earliest youth— are precisely the ones which scarcely ever become conscious" (1900, p. 539).

PSYCHODYNAMIC THERAPIES WITH INFANTS (PTIP)

We have established that Freudian theory is firmly anchored in speculations on the internal world of the infant. This young creature is emotionally affected by biological events and also by the people around him; especially his mother seeks to silence his unpleasant experiences and offer him pleasant ones instead. In other words, Freud's baby is involved in passionate relationships from very early on—though specific dates of development are rarely provided. He also intuits that there is an infant-like remnant in every adult's personality. This might explain why psychoanalysts have been reluctant to treat babies and why it took such a long time for PTIP to develop. When a therapist is working with a baby, countertransference may be overwhelming. She or he is prone to a "massive identification with the child . . . it is not always easy to control one's reactions to [the baby's] positive or negative provocations" (Watillon, 1993, p. 1045). The analyst may shun his/her own primitive reactions to a screaming or subdued baby and to a helpless or rejecting mother.

The notion of psychoanalysis as a "talking cure" utilizing words as the major channel of communication has led to the mistake, according to Olinick (1985), that the primary data in psychoanalysis are words rather than "representations or signifiers of process" (p. 500). This might have prevented them from viewing the baby as a patient with whom they may communicate. One would expect that the one analytic school that continued and substantially enlarged Freud's baby speculations, the Kleinian school, would have promoted PTIP. In reality however, when Kleinian and post-Kleinian analysts speak of the infant world they often refer to infant-*like* parts of the verbal child's or the adult's personality, especially as it emerges in the transference (Joseph, 1985; Meltzer, 1992; O'Shaugnessy, 1988). As for analysts with an ego-psychological orientation, they warn against attributing mental capacities lying outside the baby's developmental timetable (Fonagy, 1996). They rely on developmental models delineating how behavior and facultative capacities "change in a regular way over the early years in accord with emergent maturational biological changes in the context of a range of environmental prods" (Shapiro, 2013, p. 8). Their apprehension of "adultomorphizing" the baby (Peterfreund, 1978; Stern, 1985) makes them reluctant to view the baby as an active participant in psychotherapy.

Another reason for the relatively slow development of PTIP might simply be organizational. Many analysts work in private practice and are contacted by people who acknowledge their emotional suffering. In contrast, many "baby worries" emerge at a visit to the Child Health Center. A mother might complain about her child's somatic health or development without feeling that she needs psychotherapy herself (Stern, 1995). Alternatively, she might feel depressed or anxious and be suggested individual psychotherapy or pharmacological treatment. Neither case will result in a joint mother–infant treatment.

Nevertheless, though the delivery of PTIP was protracted several methods have now seen the day. The major methods will be introduced with some critical reflections added. Each caption contains the name of its major author. This should not make us overlook that many of their followers have published independent papers and books.

INFANT-PARENT PSYCHOTHERAPY

Like many PTIP innovators Selma Fraiberg was a psychoanalyst. She formulated three intervention modes: brief crisis interventions, interaction guidance-supportive treatments, and infant–parent psychotherapy. The first was used for treating problems arising from a "circumscribed set of external events and when the parents' psychological capacities suggest that they can make use of a brief focused intervention" (1989, p. 60). To illustrate; a well-functioning couple who were very anxious about their newborn's well-being suffered from an unresolved mourning of another baby who had died earlier. After a few sessions, the parents' mourning was worked through and they could attach to the newborn as a separate young person. The second mode, interaction guidance, aimed at guiding and scaffolding parents with a limited psychological-mindedness. It was based on a psychoanalytic understanding of the family members but did not aim at fundamentally altering their psychodynamics. In lieu of using transference interpretations that might derail the parents' equilibrium, this was more of an "educational technique" (Sherick, 2009, p. 231). Similar techniques adopting a "non-authoritative therapeutic stance, using treatment goals identified by the parents, emphasizing already-existing family strengths, increasing parents' satisfaction and enjoyment from interaction with their infants, and suggesting alternative interpretations of the infants' behavior" (Vik & Braten, 2009, p. 290) have been developed by Aarts (2000), Beebe (2003), and McDonough (2004).

Infant–parent psychotherapy, Fraiberg's third therapy mode, was a clear-cut example of PTIP. She applied it to cases where the baby reminded his parents of "an aspect of the parental self that is repudiated or negated" (1989, p. 60), for example a childhood memory of a rejecting parent or a competing sibling. This unconscious "ghost in the nursery" marred the parent's interactions with the baby, who then got engulfed in the parental neurosis. This might result in emotional disturbances in the baby. To illustrate, one mother had a five-month-old listless and subdued girl whom the mother felt did not attach well to her. Therapy revealed that the mother had been abandoned during *her* mother's postpartum psychosis. An extramarital affair had added an obsessive guilt that wiped out any joy at being a mother. A hypothesis was formed: "When this mother's own cries are heard [by the therapist], she will hear her child's cries" (1980, p. 109). The therapist promoted the emerging mother–baby attachment by encouraging the mother to talk about how she had felt abandoned during childhood. Thus, "the pathology which had spread to embrace the baby" (p. 111) could be withdrawn from the child.

Our first major question in the article's beginning concerned the role of the "infans" in therapy. Fraiberg regarded him as a "catalyst" (1989, p. 53) who intensified the emotional climate and sometimes also engaged in "eloquent dialogue" with the family members and the therapist. She did not, however, aim at becoming a specific relational figure for the baby. The intention behind the baby-therapist dialogues was rather to bypass the mother's customary perceptions of her baby, influenced as they were by her "ghosts." If such bypass was successful, their relationship might improve. Fraiberg's followers continue to explore such parental perceptions in terms of "negative attributions" onto the child (Silverman & Lieberman, 1999). A mother might, for example, complain that her baby is whining. Therapy reveals that her reproaches emanate from an unconscious suspicion that she is a cry-baby herself. When the little one internalizes her attributions and his self-image becomes that

of a "whiner," the negative attribution has been "successful" from the mother's perspective. She will feel less ashamed of her weakness—but the baby will find no way out of his whining and the mother's reproaches.

A recent monograph describes this therapy mode in depth (Lieberman & Van Horn, 2008). It has been subjected to at least three randomized outcome trials (RCT; Cohen et al., 1999; Lieberman, Weston, & Pawl, 1991; Robert-Tissot et al., 1996) to be reported in the second article. Suffice it to say here that Fraiberg's method proved to be about as efficacious as Interaction Guidance (the study by Robert-Tissot et al.) and Watch, Wait, and Wonder (the study by Cohen et al.), though the effects were slower in coming. Compared with a non-intervention group, its results were superior (the study by Lieberman et al.).

As a clinician Fraiberg was deeply sensitive to the plight of parents and a keen and empathic observer of infants. She did not extend her closeness to the baby into also addressing him in order to build up a therapeutic relationship. She restricted the ghost metaphor to unconscious structures in the *parent*—not in the *baby*. Reverting to our second major question, one could claim that this was because she did not think a baby possessed an Unconscious. Actually, Fraiberg was ambivalent about this issue. She did think that a baby as young as three months of age can erect a "pathological defense" (Fraiberg, 1982), such as avoiding the mother's eyes. This behavior served to specifically ward off the perception of a primary object that was eliciting pain and distress in the infant. She objected to calling it a defense mechanism, because the baby's ego was too immature for such an advanced mental activity. Then again, when explaining the phenomenon she used terms like "signal anxiety" and even "psychic conflict." These terms indicate her view that a baby might be influenced by unconscious experiences, though evidently she found it hard to integrate her clinical observations with her ego-psychological framework. She viewed pathology as the result of a mutual influence of unconscious aspects within mother *and* baby, though she was aware that they were neither on par nor identical; the baby is less mature than mother and interprets the world in his own right.

INFANT–PARENT PSYCHOTHERAPY

The therapists of the "Geneva school" are affiliated to the University of Geneva. They have worked with less disadvantaged families than Fraiberg. Its main figure is Bertrand Cramer. Though he trained for a decade in the U.S., the major clinical works by him and his associate Francisco Palacio Espasa were published in French (Cramer & Palacio Espasa, 1993; Manzano, Palacio Espasa, & Zilkha, 1999). Some papers and a book (Cramer, 1997, 1998; Espasa & Alcorn, 2004) as well as a succinct introduction (Zlot, 2007) were published in English.

The dividing line between the traditions of Fraiberg and Cramer/Palacio Espasa is subtle. The Swiss therapists focus more on the mother's psychopathology and also address it more consistently, for example, her masochistic and narcissistic issues. Yet, this focus on "the conflicts of parenthood" (Zlot, 2007, p. 14) does not make them overlook the dynamics behind the *infant's* symptoms, which might express "a repressed tendency in the parent" (Cramer & Palacio Espasa, 1993, p. 85). This creates a "core conflictual relationship" between the baby and the repressed part of his parent, which will be enacted in therapy and become its focus. Its pathogenic mechanism may originate in the mother's anxiety and guilt; if she has not managed to mourn her own childhood injuries, resentment may color her expectations from the baby. This comes very close to Fraiberg's notion of the "ghost in the nursery." But, the Geneva therapists rather describe it as the mother's "narcissistic scenarios" (Manzano et al., 1999), which prevent her from seeing the baby in his own right. As a result, the child becomes involved in a relationship he cannot comprehend. The therapist confronts the mother about her misperceptions. By including the baby in his "joint focal attention" (Cramer, 1998, p. 156), he also observes the baby's reactions. Therapy should promote insight about "the mother-infant *relationship* in order to liberate it from projective distortions" (Cramer & Palacio Espasa, 1993, p. 84).

The Geneva therapists seem to regard the baby as less of an active therapy participant than did Fraiberg. When one baby reacts to an emotionally charged comment by the mother, the authors merely name such instances "chronological coincidences" (Cramer & Palacio Espasa, 1993, p. 84). Addressing our question about unconscious strata in the baby, the Swiss therapists seem uncomfortable with applying it to babies.

THERAPEUTIC CONSULTATIONS WITH BABIES

We are now moving to the French arena. Serge Lebovici headed the Centre Alfred Binet, a child psychiatric outpatient clinic in Paris, and was active there between 1980 and 2000, the year of his demise. He was the president of the International Psychoanalytic Association 1973–1977. His interventions were akin to Winnicott's therapeutic consultations (1971) and Fraiberg's brief crisis interventions (1989). We recognize Fraiberg's thinking when reading that the "mother's internal reality, her unconscious, constitutes the first world offered to the baby" (Lebovici & Stoléru, 2003, p. 289). Whereas Fraiberg often suggested that the mother's *trauma* might build up to forming the "ghost in the nursery," Lebovici focused more on fantasies stemming from her *infantile sexuality*. These differences could depend on divergent theoretical foci, with Fraiberg being oriented toward ego-psychology and Lebovici to drive psychology. He often interpreted to mothers how their unconscious sexuality colored the relationship with the baby. For example, one mother sought help for her seven-month-old son's insomnia. In treatment, it emerged that she had become frigid because she kept thinking about him while making love to her husband (p. 283). Lebovici noted that she held him in a way that only allowed the boy to look at the wall behind her, which distressed him. He suggested that she hold him with a hand between his thighs. Now, the boy calmed down and the eyes of mother and son met. Lebovici thus linked the boy's insomnia and distress not only with the mother–infant interactive *behavior* but also with how it was compromised by the mother's sexual *fantasies*.

Perhaps Lebovici's most interesting contribution (2000) was to unravel what happens in the mind of the PTIP therapist, notably his *enactment* (Fr: *l énaction*) and *metaphorizing function*. The two are constituents of the empathic function, which rests on two pillars; the analyst's parental function and creativity. Already Emde (1990), among many authors, had suggested that the therapist's empathy is rooted in, and similar to, "the mutuality experiences provided within the early mother-child relationship" (p. 884). Lebovici added that empathy also involves the therapist's creativity. An empathic response consists not only in "feeling into" the patient but also in "forgetting about oneself" (2000, p. 227) and letting one's associative processes interact with the patient's. This would correspond to a mother's committed smalltalk with her baby. Widlöcher (2001) has called this aspect of empathy "co-thinking"; it is a "process of communication" involving "the reciprocal development of associative activity" (p. 254) between therapist and patient.

The term "co-thinking" (Fr: *co-pensé*) resembles Beebe and Lachmann's (2002) notion of "co-constructing interactions." The latter concept relies on mother–infant research and covers how we humans are "always monitoring and regulating our inner state at the same time as we are tracking our partner's words and actions" (p. 26). The term co-thinking focuses on what happens in the therapist's mind and here, according to Lebovici, enactment and metaphor occupy special positions. Enactment refers to spontaneous sensations in his body—sometimes acted out in a spontaneous gesture—which might indicate an unacknowledged affect in mother or child. A therapist's spontaneous metaphor might reveal what he or she assumes—unconsciously rather than consciously—is going on between mother and infant. If he submits it to the mother it might also help improve her symbolizing capacities and liberate similar dawning capacities in the baby, according to Lebovici.

To illustrate a metaphor in PTIP, an example of Lebovici's technique from a DVD with English subtitles (Casanova, 2000) will be referred. A mother in treatment with her husband and their six-month-old daughter says her baby is constantly curled up against her breast. She describes them as an idealized unit, but Lebovici's countertransference indicates that she is annoyed with being a mother. He tells her, "It's as if you were holding a steering-wheel in your hands but it, not you, is driving the car." At first, she takes this metaphor to portray her vexation that the child is "holding the steering-wheel." Then her comments open up in an unexpected direction. She starts crying and tells of her guilt feelings about her elder son. He was involved in an accident resulting in a cerebral handicap. The steering-wheel of the family car had prevented the parents from observing when he fell into the water.

One could suspect that the link between Lebovici's steering-wheel metaphor and the mother's sad story was coincidental. However, he claimed that such metaphors often conveyed relevant information because they functioned as tools for circumventing the resistances in the countertransference. In such a situation, the imagery of a metaphor might clarify what was indistinct in the analyst's thinking. To assess if it revealed something important about the patient's internal world, it must be followed up during the session. As it happened, the steering-wheel metaphor opened up to this mother talking about guilt feelings vis-à-vis her handicapped son and how they disturbed the relationship with her little girl.

Concerning our question about the "infans" in treatment, Lebovici suggested that the baby should be present in the session since this enabled the therapist to probe into the unconscious meanings of the parent's spontaneous behavior or comments. Another reason was that the baby's presence stimulated the therapist's metaphoric function. In contrast, he was not prone to intervene *to* the baby. Concerning a baby's Unconscious, he would probably have agreed that it exists from very early on, but he would never have agreed with his compatriot Dolto that a baby can understand verbal import. It is time to turn to this clinician.

DIRECT AND BRIEF THERAPY WITH BABY AND MOTHER

Françoise Dolto was a Parisian psychoanalyst who was active from the 1940s up to the 1980s. Two books were translated into English; her dissertation (Dolto, 1971a) and a case study of an adolescent, "Dominique" (1971b). In another English volume various authors describe her work and biography (Hall, Hivernel, & Morgan, 2009). Long before researchers like Beebe (Beebe & Lachmann, 2002), Sander (Condon & Sander, 1974), Stern (1985), and Trevarthen (Trevarthen & Aitken, 2001), she spoke of the young infant's ability and efforts at communicating with his caretakers. In contrast to them and other PTIP therapists, Dolto was convinced that a baby may understand some literal meaning of the therapist's words. Her work has met with severe criticism by some American analysts (Anthony, 1974; Axelrad, 1960), albeit not specifically concerning her PTIP method. They claim that she is omniscient and that she makes sweeping and prejudiced generalizations. Before concluding whether such critique should be directed to her PTIP method as well, it is necessary to

know more about it and its theoretical foundations.

Here is one example of her clinical work (Dolto, 1985): A mother at the delivery ward with her fourth child learns from her husband that things are not going well with the children at home. Her worries are aggravated by the news that her own mother has died. At this point the newborn stops breastfeeding and Dolto is called in for a consultation. She addresses the baby: "Everything was OK when you were inside Mom's tummy. Then you were born . . . Mom had milk and you were calling for it . . . One day you heard, together with Mom, it was Dad who told you, that things weren't going well at home. Maybe you told yourself 'Poor little Mom, I'd better get back into her tummy, 'cause everything went well as long as I was there'" (p. 211). Dolto thought the baby's refusal to suckle resonated with the mother's mourning and worries about the home situation. She even argued that the girl understood the therapeutic intervention verbally. Dolto asked the girl to nod if she had understood. When the girl turned her head toward Dolto, she took this as a confirmation. Already here, we can establish that at this point Dolto was wrong; an overwhelming body of research (for a summary, see Karmiloff & Karmiloff-Smith, 2001) refutes that a young baby can understand spoken words literally. Thus, the reason that she turned her head toward Dolto could not be that she had understood her words.

Before taking a more general stand on Dolto's PTIP method, let us go deeper into her arguments. She was convinced that when parents conceal the truth about embarrassing facts, it may stunt the baby's development. In the vignette, Dolto guessed that the mother tried to protect her baby by hiding that she was mourning her mother and worrying about the older siblings' well-being. This created a paradoxical situation to the girl who, perhaps, was sensitive to the painful affects beneath the mother's well-meaning efforts at caretaking. Another paradoxical situation is when parents conceal that Daddy is not the biological father. A child may sense something on an unconscious level and suffer until the double-entendre is revealed.

Most PTIP therapists would agree that already a baby may intuit that "something is wrong" and that the parents are inauthentic. Fraiberg and Cramer would no doubt agree that such a situation might constitute a ghost in the nursery and thus be harrowing to the baby. However, they would have talked to the *parents*, not the child, about it. Dolto's reason for addressing the child was that the parental superego had been imposed on the child, with the result that "instinctual urges whose affects have not succeeded in expressing themselves . . . disturb the child's somatic and cognitive functioning and engender anxiety . . . [The therapist's] role consists in re-establishing the flow between all this" (Dolto, 1982, p. 30). This, she claimed, should be done directly with the child.

It is easy to argue that such sensitivity to parental skewed communication may exist in older children—but not in babies of some months of age, let alone in a newborn as referred to above. This question touches on a greater issue, namely, how one regards the infant's self development. This is a vast topic, and only the views of Winnicott and Dolto will be compared here. Winnicott speaks of the baby's absolute dependence which the good-enough mother must meet in order for the *true self* to emerge in a healthy and spontaneous way. In Dolto's view, parents and infants are caught up in a "complex and ambiguous web of competing and conflicting demands and desires. There is little certainty about who or what is good, or good enough" (Bacon, 2002, p. 260). The infant's self is "fragmented and fragmentary, held together and made meaningful not by an inside 'truth' [corresponding to Winnicott's true self], but, like words in a sentence, by law or grammar or force" (p. 260). Indeed, the infant does not speak but he is "continuously being formed in and informed by language and speaking" (p. 260).

Dolto's mistake in attributing linguistic comprehension to a young baby unfortunately clouds another important angle of investigation. This is hinted at in the last sentence by Bacon above, that *the baby is formed in and informed by language*. The question is thus if language might have another function in the baby's development than to convey lexical meaning. Dolto's answer is that maturation comes about only to the extent that he manages to substitute his *désir* with demands that are acceptable to the community, and that this substitution comes about through the adult's spoken words which introduce the child to the symbolic order. Already "before the age of words, the presence of a mother speaking to her infant is a nourishment more valuable than the milk she offers at the breast" (Dolto, 1994). The ultimate aim with mother's talking is to institute "symboligenic castration," which helps the child "displace his drive towards another object" (Dolto, 1982, p. 48). Dolto's term castration thus takes on a wider meaning than in Freud's writings. It implies that "at each decisive moment of the child's development [he must suffer] a rupture, a separation from the mother to whom he is attached, in a vital dyad which always risks becoming harmful if he absorbs himself in it completely" (de Sauverzac, 1993, p. 198, quoted in Dollander & de Tychey, 2004). Castration will thus help the child enter the symbolic community. This happens, for example, when a child begins to accept that the *milk* is offered and thence belongs to him whereas the *breast* belongs to the mother. Not until the child accepts this can he be weaned successfully, learn to speak, and express what he wants from the world.

To claim that a child must displace his drive impulses for development to proceed optimally is, evidently, part of the Freudian canon. Why then should a therapist use *words* to stimulate this process? Parents have many ways of communicating with their babies. They speak, frown, shake their head, sigh, get tense, smile, raise their voice, giggle, etc. This might lead us to oust verbal communication from any prime position in the world of communication. Perhaps the infant simply experiences words according to the present emotional quality of his interactions with the parent; as a comforter, an intimidation, or a captivating sound (Markova & Legerstee, 2006). However, infant research (Gervain, Macagno, Cogoi, Peña, & Mehler, 2008) indicates that very young babies regard speech as a special mode of communicating. The newborn is more sensitive to perceptual patterns typical of infant-directed speech, like *mama* and *dada*. Two-month-olds show a brain lateralization similar to that of adults when they listen to speech (Gervain & Mehler, 2010). Young infants also grasp that words, in contrast to general sounds, can be used for categorizing objects (Ferry, Hespos, & Waxman, 2010). It is as if the baby were thinking when his parent is speaking: "It is something special, this combination of facial movements and peculiar sounds that I cannot produce. It seems to indicate something, but I just don't get it."

In the PTIP session, the therapist's position is different from that of the mother. The latter is entangled in a relationship disorder with her baby, which diminishes her possibilities of understanding what takes place on an emotional level and of addressing her baby about it. The therapist is in a better position to understand the emotional background to the baby's plight and, to use Dolto's expression, *parler vrai* to baby and mother about it. To sum up, some of Dolto's conclusions were simply wrong; a very young infant has no lexical language comprehension and one cannot take his/her nod as a proof of the correctness of an interpretation. However, this does not automatically annihilate the rationale in speaking with the baby about painful matters. To frame this in terms of the article's two questions, Dolto would have argued that a baby's unconscious forces contribute to the pathology as long as his instinctual urges do not get a satisfactory outlet. Second, he needs to be addressed in a PTIP process and thus be introduced into the symbolic order.

MOTHER–INFANT PSYCHOANALYTIC TREATMENT

Another analyst who would also have answered the article's two questions in the affirmative, though relying on another theoretical framework and with different arguments than Dolto, was Johan Norman. His writings follow in the traditions of Freud, Klein, Bion, and Meltzer. His basic tenets were "(1) that a relationship can be established between the infant and the analyst; (2) that the infant has a primordial subjectivity and self as a basis for intersubjectivity and for the search for containment; (3) that the infant has an unique flexibility in changing representations of itself and others that comes to an end as the ego develops, and (4) that the infant is able to process certain aspects of language" (Norman, 2001, p. 85). His technique, Mother–Infant Psychoanalytic treatment (MIP), utilized the "disability" of every infant, that is, the fact that the ego is immature. This made a baby prone to become involved in an emotional disturbance with mother—but also to look for containment from whoever offered it. This immaturity was thus a window of chance for undoing the effects of trauma. Norman thought, just like Fraiberg, that a baby may contribute actively to parent–infant pathology but he went one step further and addressed, not so much the parents but more so the baby, about these processes. He did not, however, agree with Dolto that a baby understands the lexical meaning of words. Another difference was that he worked in lengthy treatments to contain the baby's agony thoroughly, whereas Dolto worked in brief consultations.

Norman's 2001 paper contains a case of six-month-old "Lisa" in therapy with her mother. Mother became depressed after delivery and was in hospital and received ECT and medication during Lisa's third and fourth months of life. When the two came for therapy mother was still depressed. She complained that the girl had not recognized her when she returned from the hospital. This could be interpreted as Lisa's initial reaction to the long separation, but Norman noticed that Lisa was still avoiding mother's eyes. It was thus an instance of gaze avoidance (Fraiberg, 1982). Norman greeted the girl and told her his name. As he noticed her attention he continued: "You don't seem afraid of me when we talk to each other, but I see that you avoid looking at Mother" (p. 89). He then told Lisa that mother had been away from her in a hospital, that she was avoiding mother whom she felt was ruined, and that she was afraid of her ruined mother. Norman noticed that Lisa was looking at him attentively while avoiding Mum's eyes. During this first session, Lisa began to seek contact with mother by sucking her blouse. Mother made vague efforts at comforting Lisa and then looked out the window. Norman had referred mother to therapy of her own but concluded that the ensuing improvement of her mood did not result so much from that treatment. It rather emerged because "Lisa had managed to wake her mother up" (p. 89), which was a result of his containment of the baby's pain of separation and dread of rejection.

Therapeutic progress was dramatic though not sudden; mother and baby started paying attention to each other in a new way and the girl began looking into her mother's eyes. The mother's condition improved partially and the girl's avoidant behavior disappeared. Norman describes the vicious interactive circle:

> Lisa's mother had a psychic pain that she could not bear. As Lisa's distress and sense of rejection increased her mother's own distress and pain, the mother was reluctant to open up the emotional links. As a defence against pain, Lisa's mother was rejecting Lisa. The mother's capacity to symbolize was severely impaired and with that her capacity to metabolise Lisa's distress. Both Lisa and her mother appeared to feel threatened by the other's pain and rejection. They were locked in mutual avoidance. (p. 90)

This formulation coincides with the views of Fraiberg and Cramer. Cramer, however, might focus more on the mother's pathology, for example, the narcissistic affront engendered by the child's rejection. Fraiberg would have recognized Lisa's avoidance of mother but she would probably not have addressed the girl as directly. Her focus would rather be to help mother understand which "ghosts" were marring her contact with the baby.

Another difference between Norman's and Fraiberg's work was that his technique presupposed that the mother was highly motivated and willing to leave the baby "in his hands." Fraiberg's patients were often less advantaged from an educational and socioeconomic perspective. This might lead a mother to a diminished motivation for insight-oriented work and to an increased wish for support and attention of her own from the therapist. To such a mother, his baby focus might perhaps be felt as an abandonment.

Norman's technique was often questioned with the argument that babies did not understand what he was saying to them. His method of containing the infant's anxiety evidently implied an effort at directly modifying her internal mental state. This raises fundamental problems not only about the child's capacity of comprehending words, but also of her capacity of memorizing interventions and subjecting them to cognitive elaboration. If we, however, make explicit on which levels of signification the analyst-baby interchange takes place, some of the "mystery" about these treatments vanish. Semiotic theory emphasizes that human communication takes place at various levels, among which the verbal is only one. Today many analysts use concepts coined by the American philosopher of semiotics C. S. Peirce (Kloesel & Houser, 1992; Muller & Brent, 2000) to explicate what takes place between them and their adult patients (Chinen, 1987; da Rocha Barros & da Rocha Barros, 2011; Gammelgaard, 1998; Goetzmann & Schwegler, 2004; Grotstein, 1980, 1997;

Martindale, 1975; Muller, 1996; Muller & Brent, 2000; Olds, 2000; Van Buren, 1993). For example, rather than seeing the drive as a psychobiological force as did Freud, they see it as a "messenger of information" (Grotstein, 1980). In order to further our understanding of the therapeutic process in MIP, two papers were written (Salomonsson, 2007a, 2007b) which apply semiotic theory to such treatments. They analyze in detail the various levels of signification in the interactions between analyst, infant, and mother. A similar perspective is in fact applied by infant researchers who apply a microanalysis to mother–infant interactions (Beebe & Lachmann, 2014; Tronick, 2007). Without using a semiotic conceptual apparatus, they investigate nonverbal mother–baby communication and how repeated interactive mismatches may lead to emotional disorders in the child.

When describing the therapeutic process, most PTIP therapists do not use psychoanalytic concepts as much as those stemming from attachment theory and developmental research. Norman, in contrast, used Bion's concepts such as the model of container/contained, the function of reverie in transforming beta- to alpha-elements, etc. (Bion, 1962, 1965, 1970). He also used some Freudian concepts such as primal repression (Freud, 1915a, 1915b) to explain incipient psychopathology of the baby. It is relevant to study if other classical concepts may help us understand further infant pathology and the PTIP process. It has been suggested that the sexuality of mother *and* infant may play a role in breast-feeding problems (Salomonsson, 2012). Another example is a study of primal repression (Salomonsson, 2014). That article argues that unless a PTIP is instituted early, vicious interactions like the ones between Lisa and her mother may become "fossilized" into primal repressions. Temporary states of suffering in the baby may then develop into recalcitrant character traits, for example, of nervousness or gloominess. Another paper (Salomonsson, 2013) investigates the role of transference in PTIP. It has been found that a baby in MIP sometimes develops a specific relational behavior with the analyst. The paper clarifies the conditions for calling such phenomena transference from the baby to the therapist.

THE INFANT AS SUBJECT

In Melbourne there is a group of PTIP therapists, many of whom are psychoanalysts. They work at the Royal Children's Hospital and their infant patients often suffer from physical illness. Their work contains similarities with Norman's technique, such as an emphasis on dialogue with the baby. One example is when a therapist not only explains to the parents that their child is cross but also address the young, as when telling a 14-month-old boy: "You're cross—and it'll be all right" (Thomson Salo, 2007, p. 964). On a note similar to Norman, the therapist tries to "understand the infant's experience in order to enter treatment through the infant's world rather than primarily through the parents' representations" (p. 965). The aim of relating to babies in their own right, or recognizing them as a subject, is to bring about a "change in their thinking, feelings and behaviour, and the parents as well" (p. 965).

The infant focus applied by these clinicians (Thomson Salo, 2007; Thomson Salo & Paul, 2001; Thomson Salo et al., 1999) is, however, not identical to that of Norman. They work directly with the infant to enable the *parents* "see more easily that their fantasies of having totally damaged or killed off the infant are not reality" (Thomson Salo et al., 1999, p. 59). This comes close to Fraiberg's "ghosts" and Cramer's "parental projections." Ann Morgan suggests that the therapist should make contact with the baby to understand "the experience from inside the infant's world rather than looking from outside as if it were inexplicable" (in Thomson Salo & Paul, 2001, p. 15). This comes about through a mutual infant–therapist fascination, in which the baby is viewed "as a subject in her own right which then allows a gap to be created between mother and baby" (p. 14). Such a gap has previously not existed because the parent has identified the baby with "some internal object in the parent's mind rather than [having built] an empathic relationship with the infant" (p. 18). Once again, we hear echoes of Fraiberg and Cramer. Having created such a space by addressing the baby, the therapist works with parental projections and also "with the infant so that the mother sees her differently . . . the therapist becomes a container for the hate and the toxic projections for which the infant was previously the receptacle" (p. 18).

We note a difference compared with Norman's stance; a therapist who is making a link with a baby is not necessarily encouraging the baby's stormy feelings to flourish vis-à-vis mother *and* therapist. If an infant is a subject "entitled to an intervention in [his] own right" (Thomson Salo, 2007, p. 961), the question is if this implies that one regards— or does not regard—the infant's communications as directed toward the therapist. This question is essential once we focus on the baby's negative emotions. Paul and Thomson Salo (in Pozzi-Monzo & Tydeman, 2007) describe how "some infants relate positively to us from the first, as though they have left aside the difficulties with their parents" (p. 145). This suggests a more supportive stance than that of Norman. He would probably have suspected that the baby was warding off some taxing emotion, which risked being overlooked by the clinician.

WATCH, WAIT, AND WONDER

This technique (WWW; Lojkasek et al., 1994) originated from the Hincks-Dellcrest Center in Toronto. It has been compared with Fraiberg's mother–infant psychotherapy in an RCT (Cohen, Lojkasek, Muir, Muir, & Parker, 2002; Cohen et al., 1999), which will be referred to more fully in the second article. Suffice it to state here that the WWW method seemed quicker in creating positive outcomes than Fraiberg's method. The Toronto clinicians' method proceeds from their observations that most PTIP techniques focus on changing the *mother's* behavior with, or representations of, her infant. To emphasize their different perspective, they describe their method as being *infant-led*.

One important foundation of the WWW is attachment theory; if a mother does not perceive and respond to her baby's signals, a secure attachment will not develop. This theory acknowledges how important the caregiver's physical presence is to the baby. Therefore, the authors emphasize the mother's participation in sessions, and they agree with many of the previous authors that her interaction with, and view of, the baby may be marred by her ghosts (Fraiberg), attributions (Lieberman), projections (Cramer), or fantasies (Lebovici). Importantly however, they criticize these methods for overlooking the importance of the *infant's* presence and participation in therapy.

To allow the infant to lead the session the mother is asked to get down on the floor, observe the baby, and interact with him though only at his initiative. Her role is compared to that of a play therapist with an older child; she becomes an "observer of her infant's activity, potentially gaining insight into the infant's inner world and relational needs" (Cohen et al., 1999, p. 433). The baby inspires the mother to observe, reflect and change her ways with him. He will have "the therapeutic experience of negotiating his relationship with his mother, and thus begins to master his environment" (p. 433). The therapist, finally, "engages in a parallel process of watching, waiting, and wondering about the interactions between mother and infant" (p. 437). He or she empowers the mother to describe how she experiences her infant's play and their relationship. This allows her "to examine her internal working models of her relationship with her infant and to modify or revise them to be more in line with her new experiences" (Lojkasek et al., 1994, p. 214). This work occurs during the second half of the session, when therapist and mother discuss what transpired between her and the baby.

The emphasis on the infant's presence and activity, and the advice for the adults to follow his lead, might lead one into thinking that the WWW method is similar to Norman's approach. However, there are clear-cut differences which emerge from the following quotation:

> The therapist does not instruct, give advice, or *interpret* the infant's activity or play but *provides a safe, supportive environment* . . . so that the mother can express her own observations, thoughts, feelings, and interpretations of her infant's activity and their relationship. The mother and the therapist *discuss the mother's observations of her infant's activity* and attempt to understand the themes and relational issues that the infant is trying to master, focusing on the inevitable problems that emerge as the mother begins to struggle with following her infant's lead. (Cohen et al., 1999, p. 434)

The added italics indicate that the therapist neither addresses the baby directly nor interprets the meaning behind his activity. Rather, he or she and the mother discuss what they think the baby is doing.

THE PIP TEAM AT THE ANNA FREUD CENTRE

Another technique influenced by attachment theory is Parent–Infant Psychotherapy (PIP) at the Anna Freud Centre in London. A volume by this group (Baradon et al., 2005) illustrates a trend among some present-day PTIP therapists; they wish to integrate Freudian metapsychology with infant research, attachment theory, and developmental psychology, but they do not always acknowledge that this creates theoretical tensions. The authors use a "psychoanalytic framework," which assumes that "unconscious material is to be addressed because it shapes the pathology" (p. 33). Accordingly, they suggest that "the bulk of interventions will address impingements of conflict, phantasy, negative affect and maladaptive defences" (p. 33). This amounts to a classical Freudian approach, but beyond this statement they mostly speak of promoting "the parent-infant relationship in order to facilitate infant development" (p. 25), and supporting the baby's "attachment needs" toward his "caregivers" (p. 8).

These British authors view the baby as propelled by a *need* to engage a *caregiver* to help him with *attachment* and *emotional regulation*. They are more hesitant to attribute to him a *wish* to enroll a parental *object* to become the target of his *drives*. Consequently, the words "drive" and "object" are rarely mentioned. Thus, the Freudian influence on their frame of reference is not conspicuous. This also becomes evident in their use of the term sexuality, by which they refer to that of the mother, not of the child. Indeed, this restriction applies to most authors cited earlier (Salomonsson, 2012).

Like many therapists presented so far, the PIP therapists also focus on the baby. Their aim is not so much to interpret *to the baby* what might go on in his mind. It is rather to promote his efficacy in engaging his parent's care. The baby is regarded as a "partner in the therapeutic process" (p. 79); when a therapist engages directly with the baby her aim is to "scaffold [the baby's] communications . . . and represent them to her parents" (p. 75). The overall aim is to support the baby's "beginning mentalization and emotional regulation" (p. 75). The therapist observes the infant's contact with her as evidenced by his voice, facial expressions, and eye contact. The use of countertransference to understand therapeutic processes is also emphasized. Video-recordings are sometimes used (Woodhead, Bland, & Baradon, 2006) to clarify to parents how they interact with the child.

THE IMPACT OF THE SETTING AND THE CLINICAL SAMPLE

This survey has been cursory and simplified, with many legitimate candidates excluded due to considerations of space. Another fact needs emphasis as well; almost all the referred authors worked in public health clinics, though in varying settings with different samples. Fraiberg founded in 1972 an infant mental health program in Ann Arbor, which later moved to San Francisco. Some years later Cramer founded a similar center in Geneva. Dolto's "Maisons Vertes," which are still in operation, were walk-in facilities where mothers with babies could receive instant psychotherapeutic interventions on a brief and improvised note. As for Norman, when he started working with babies he was a consultant analyst at a Child Health Center in Stockholm, but his published cases were drawn mainly from his private practice. This enabled lengthy high-frequency treatments, a modality he strongly recommended: "The analytical setting, with its containment of the strong emotional expressions in both mother and infant [is a] prerequisite for the process to evolve and for the working through" (Norman, 2004).

The various forms of PTIP were devised for patients living under different circumstances. Many of Norman's parents seemed reasonably well motivated and psychologically minded. In this, we recognize similarities with the Geneva sample. In contrast, Fraiberg often treated adolescent or immigrant mothers with a low educational and economic status (Dowling, 1982), which also seems to apply to the PIP team in London. The Melbourne therapists treat severely sick children and their parents. Such factors will influence the parents' trust in the clinician, motivation for analytic work, and economic and practical means of taking part in therapy. These differences make it hard to compare the methods. This overview is therefore but a skeleton that helps us understand the major questions that any PTIP method must face. When we try to imagine how various authors have approached them, we should also recall that their ways of working were probably not always "according to the book." Norman's technique had more supportive elements, and he addressed the mother's suffering more consistently, than what emerged in his writings. Similar discrepancies could most probably be found among the other authors.

CONCLUSIONS

Two major questions were formulated initially: (1) Which role does a PTIP mode attribute to a baby in therapy? (2) If it claims to work by helping parents come to grips with their unconscious attitudes toward the baby, does it speak of similar struggles in the infant? Does it even speak of an Unconscious in the infant? The survey indicates that all PTIP therapists view the baby's participation as essential. They wish him to be affected by the therapeutic process, and they seek to comprehend his nonverbal communication to help the process evolve. The main dividing line is (a) if they regard him as a *catalyst* fuelling the therapeutic process in the mother, or

(b) as someone who needs to *communicate with* the therapist. Whichever alternative the therapist opts for, it has repercussions on question (1) and on his technique. In model (a), he is more prone to talk to the mother *about* her baby. Model (b) will lead him more into talking *to* the baby about her suffering. Improvement will be seen as coming not only via the mother's changed perception of her baby but also via the baby's direct contact with the therapist which, in its turn, helps change his relationship with the mother.

As for question (2), no author seems comfortable with attributing to a baby an Unconscious in the *systematic* sense. Norman, however, assumed that "the infant has an unconscious in the *dynamic* sense of the word" (2004, p. 1107, italics added). Questions (1) and (2) are in fact related. The more a therapist is prone to speak of unconscious forces at work in a baby, the more he will intervene directly to the young. If he thinks the baby harbors conflicting affects vis-à-vis mother, then addressing both participants seems logical. Norman's case of Lisa is a case to the point. He did not think that the depressive mother's lack of emotional availability was the only root to the problem. He also thought the girl was active in avoiding mother's eyes.

Cases of gaze avoidance are suitable for discussing further question (2). Most clinicians would not use the term "unconscious" in connection with a baby, except for Dolto and Norman, whereas Fraiberg was ambivalent. She wrote (1982) that "something within us resists the word [defense] and its connotations" (p. 614), but she did regard a baby's gaze avoidance as the result of a defensive process. The issue can be resolved if one studies existent definitions of the defense concept. Traditionally, it has been defined as a process by which a conscious mental instance wards off an unconscious instinctual urge. Laplanche and Pontalis (1973) regard defense in a more general way, as a "group of operations aimed at the reduction and elimination of any change liable to threaten the *integrity and stability of the bio-psychological individual*" (p. 103, italics added). Fraiberg's and Norman's descriptions of gaze avoidance comply with this criterion; the interactive flow between mother and child has been disrupted, which frightens the baby. Therefore she shuns that part of mother which is the central medium of communication and which conveys her depressive ambivalence toward the child; her eyes.

Laplanche and Pontalis add that a defense is not only directed "towards internal excitation (instinct)" but also toward those "representations (memories, phantasies) [which] this excitation is bound to and to any situation that is unpleasurable for the ego as a result of its incompatibility with the individual's equilibrium and, to that extent, liable to spark off the excitation. Unpleasurable affects, which serve as motives or signals for defence, may also become its object" (p. 104). Fraiberg would agree that her gaze-avoiding babies had unpleasant representations of a depressed mother, and that their avoidance aimed to minimize the risk of having them sparked off once again. This position is actually an extension of Freud's position in "The Project" (1895) referred to above; an object who cannot satisfy the baby is perceived as hostile. Freud's notion of satisfaction was bound up with the provision of food and shelter but today, not the least thanks to infant research, we know that the baby also seeks to regulate affects in cooperation with the parent. Fraiberg's and Norman's babies avoided mother's eyes because depression prevented her from regulating the baby's affects. Therapies revealed that mother's conscious wishes of loving and caring for her baby clashed with unconscious wishes of being alone, staying aloof, or rejecting the child. This ambivalence created out of mother a Gestalt that frightened the child who, in response, rejected mother. Thereby the baby became a frightening Gestalt to the mother who took the gaze avoidance as a proof that the child did not love her.

Any PTIP therapist would agree that such a mother is caught up in an unconscious conflict with her child. Many, however, would claim that the child is *not* capable of having a similar conflict. This article indicates that such a view departs from basic assertions in Freudian theory. It is often claimed that the reluctance to attribute unconscious forces to a young baby relies on the notion that her ego is too immature to produce such advanced mental operations. This was Fraiberg's argument—whence she proceeded to describe precisely such phenomena. Another explanation to this reluctance is related to the influence of infant research. Stern (1985) agrees with object relations theoreticians that the baby has a "very active subjective life, filled with changing passions and confusions" (p. 44). However, to him such descriptions only concern "internal state fluctuations and social relatedness that could contribute to a sense of self" (p. 44). He disagrees that a baby experiences the world in terms of pleasure/unpleasure. He also objects to the notion that trauma and high-intensity affects play a crucial role in constituting the baby's self, and that they result in representations of a "good" and "bad" mother. Consequently, Stern's term infantile vitality affects does not "reflect the categorical content of an experience" (Sandler, Sandler, & Davies, 2000, p. 86).

Stern suggests that sleep or feeding problems during "the formative phase of core relatedness," from about three months onward, "are not signs or symptoms of any intrapsychic conflict within the infant . . . They are the accurate reflection of an ongoing interactive reality, manifestations of a problematic interpersonal exchange, *not psychopathology of a psychodynamic nature* (Stern, 1985, p. 202, italics added). If Norman's six-month-old Lisa is too old to apply to Stern's description this is not so for a similar case of Fraiberg (1982); that boy was three months old. Stern thus indirectly helps us realize that Fraiberg thought of gaze avoidance as indeed reflecting a psychodynamic pathology to which unconscious forces within baby and mother alike were contributing factors. Actually, this formulation parallels descriptions by Beebe and Lachmann (2014), despite the fact that they do not use psychoanalytic terminology. They microanalyze videos of four-month-old babies and speculate that their interactions with mother emanate from "expectancies." These patterns "repeat over time and form generalized action-sequence procedural memories. These expectancies involve anticipation of what will happen, as well as memories of what has generally happened in the past" (p. 3). The term "unconscious" is absent but we can infer it; the expectancies of babies with gaze avoidance and feeding problems may emanate from unpleasant memories of being with mother. The infants shun her eyes or breasts, and PTIP treatment allows us to infer the unconscious dynamics behind such symptoms.

It is true that unconscious forces cannot be revealed directly. The therapist needs a setting to *interpret* the unconscious meaning behind the patient's symptom. Therefore, mundane observations of babies provide no proofs of unconscious influence. We observe a crying baby on the bus and infer that he is hungry. So does the mother and starts breastfeeding him. If he calms down, we will never know whether his crying was indeed motivated by hunger or by some unconscious conflict. Another baby does not look Mum in the eyes and we infer that he is shy. Perhaps, however, his avoidance reflects a conflict with his mother. If she seeks help with a PTIP therapist, and if they get in good contact and mother is motivated, they may uncover unconscious affects and fantasies in all the three relationships between mother, infant, and therapist. Sometimes the baby will show that the intervention, or to put it more cautiously, the containment has affected him. This he will demonstrate via smiling, playing, laughing, new bodily movements—or if his psychic pain has been addressed—via crying and screaming. He neither speaks nor understands words, but he has a mind that seeks to avoid unpleasure, experience pleasure, and create relationships that help him reach these goals. This article has pointed to the need of investigating if such assets may be used in PTIP to a greater extent than is done today.

REFERENCES

Aarts, M. (2000). *Marte Meo: Basic manual.* Harderwijk, Netherlands: Aarts Productions.

Anthony, E. J. (1974). Dominique: The analysis of an adolescent: By Françoise Dolto. (Book review). *Psychoanalytic Quarterly, 43,* 681-684.

Axelrad, S. (1960). On some uses of psychoanalysis. *Journal of the American Psychoanalytic Association, 8,* 175-218.

Bacon, R. J. (2002). Winnicott revisited: A point of view. *Free Associations, 9B,* 250-270.

Baradon, T., Broughton, C., Gibbs, I., James, J., Joyce, A., & Woodhead, J. (2005). *The practice of psychoanalytic parent-infant psychotherapy—Claiming the baby.* London: Routledge.

Beebe, B. (2003). Brief mother-infant treatment: Psychoanalytically informed video feedback. *Infant Mental Health Journal, 24*(1), 24-52.

Beebe, B., & Lachmann, F. (2002). *Infant research and adult treatment: Co-constructing interactions.* Hillsdale, NJ: Analytic Press.

Beebe, B., & Lachmann, F. (2014). *The origins of attachment. Infant research and adult treatment.* New York: Routledge.

Bion, W. R. (1962). *Learning from experience.* London: Karnac Books.

Bion, W. R. (1965). *Transformations.* London: Karnac Books.

Bion, W. R. (1970). *Attention and interpretation.* London: Karnac Books.

Casanova, A. (2000). Serge Lebovici. *Eléments de la psychopathologie du bébé (Elements of infantile psychopathology).* DVD. France.

Chinen, A. B. (1987). Symbolic modes in object relations: A semiotic perspective. *Psychoanalysis and Contemporary Thought, 10,* 373-406.

Cohen, N. J., Lojkasek, M., Muir, E., Muir, R., & Parker, C. J. (2002). Six-month follow-up of two mother-infant psychotherapies: Convergence of therapeutic outcomes. *Infant Mental Health Journal, 23*(4), 361-380.

Cohen, N. J., Muir, E., Parker, C. J., Brown, M., Lojkasek, M., Muir, R., & Barwick, M. (1999). Watch, wait and wonder: Testing the effectiveness of a new approach to mother-infant psychotherapy. *Infant Mental Health Journal, 20*(4), 429-451.

Condon, W. S., & Sander, L. W. (1974). Neonate movement is synchronized with adult speech: Interactional participation and language acquisition. *Science, 183*(4120), 99-101.

Cramer, B. (1997). *The scripts parents write and the roles babies play.* Northvale, NJ: Jason Aronson.

Cramer, B. (1998). Mother-infant psychotherapies: A widening scope in technique. *Infant Mental Health Journal, 19*(2), 151-167.

Cramer, B., & Palacio Espasa, F. (1993). *La pratique des psychothérapies mères-bébés. Études cliniques et techniques (The practice of mother-infant psychotherapies. Clinical and technical studies).* Paris: Presses Universitaires de France.

da Rocha Barros, E. M., & da Rocha Barros, E. L. (2011). Reflections on the clinical implications of symbolism. *International Journal of Psychoanalysis, 92*(4), 879-901.

de Sauverzac, J. F. (1993). *Françoise Dolto.* Paris: Champs Flammarion.

Dollander, M., & de Tychey, C. (2004). Affective development, education and prevention: A psychodynamic model. *Psychoanalytic Review, 91,* 257-270.

Dolto, F. (1971a). *Psychoanalysis and paediatrics: Key psychoanalytic concepts with sixteen clinical observations of children* (F. Hivernel & F. Sinclair, Trans.). London: Karnac.

Dolto, F. (1971b). *Dominique: The analysis of an adolescent.* New York: Outerbridge & Lazard.

Dolto, F. (1982). *Séminaires de psychanalyse d'enfant, vol. 1 (Seminars on child psychoanalysis, vol. 1).* Paris: Editions du Seuil.

Dolto, F. (1985). *Séminaires de psychanalyse d'enfant, vol. 2 (Seminars on child psychoanalysis, vol. 2).* Paris: Editions du Seuil.

Dolto, F. (1994). *Solitude.* Paris: Gallimard.

Dowling, S. (1982). Review of "Clinical studies in infant mental health. The first year of life": Edited by Selma Fraiberg. *Psychoanalytic Quarterly, 51,* 430-434.

Emde, R. N. (1990). Mobilizing fundamental modes of development: Empathic availability and therapeutic action. *Journal of the American Psychoanalytic Association, 38*(4), 881-913.

Espasa, F. P., & Alcorn, D. (2004). Parent-infant psychotherapy, the transition to parenthood and parental narcissism: Implications for treatment. *Journal of Child Psychotherapy, 30*(2), 155-171.

Ferry, A. L., Hespos, S. J., & Waxman, S. R. (2010). Categorization in 3- and 4-month-old infants: An advantage of words over tones. *Child Development, 81*, 472-479.

Field, T. (2000). Infant massage therapy. In C. H. J. Zeanah (Ed.), *Handbook of infant mental health* (pp. 494-500). New York: Guilford.

Fonagy, P. (1996). Discussion of Peter Wolff's paper "Infant observation and psychoanalysis." *Journal of the American Psychoanalytic Association, 44*(2), 404-422.

Fraiberg, S. (1980). *Clinical studies in infant mental health*. New York: Basic Books.

Fraiberg, S. (1982). Pathological defenses in infancy. *Psychoanalytic Quarterly, 51*(4), 612-635.

Fraiberg, S. (1989). *Assessment and therapy of disturbances in infancy*. Northvale, NJ: Jason Aronson.

Freud, S. (1895). Project for a scientific psychology. In J. Strachey (Ed. & Trans.), *The standard edition of the complete psychological works of Sigmund Freud* (Vol. 1). London: Hogarth Press.

Freud, S. (1900). The interpretation of dreams. In J. Strachey (Ed. & Trans.), *The standard edition of the complete psychological works of Sigmund Freud* (Vol. 4-5). London: Hogarth Press.

Freud, S. (1905). Three essays on sexuality. In J. Strachey (Ed. & Trans.), *The standard edition of the complete psychological works of Sigmund Freud* (Vol. 7, pp. 123-246). London: Hogarth Press.

Freud, S. (1911). Formulations on the two principles of mental functioning. In J. Strachey (Ed. & Trans.), *The standard edition of the complete psychological works of Sigmund Freud* (Vol. 12, pp. 213-226). London: Hogarth Press.

Freud, S. (1915a). Repression. In J. Strachey (Ed. & Trans.), *The standard edition of the complete psychological works of Sigmund Freud* (Vol. 14, pp. 141-158). London: Hogarth Press.

Freud, S. (1915b). The unconscious. In J. Strachey (Ed. & Trans.), *The standard edition of the complete psychological works of Sigmund Freud* (Vol. 14, pp. 159-216). London: Hogarth Press.

Freud, S. (1920). Beyond the pleasure principle. In J. Strachey (Ed. & Trans.), *The standard edition of the complete psychological works of Sigmund Freud* (Vol. 18, pp. 1-64). London: Hogarth Press.

Freud, S. (1925-1926). Inhibitions, symptoms and anxiety. In J. Strachey (Ed. & Trans.), *The standard edition of the complete psychological*

works of Sigmund Freud (Vol. 20, pp. 87-178). London: Hogarth Press.

Gammelgaard, J. (1998). Metaphors of listening. *Scandinavian Psychoanalytic Review, 21*(2), 151-167.

Gervain, J., Macagno, F., Cogoi, S., Peña, M., & Mehler, J. (2008). The neonate brain detects speech structure. *Proceedings of the National Academy of Sciences of the United States of America, 105*, 14222-14227.

Gervain, J., & Mehler, J. (2010). Speech perception and language acquisition in the first year of life. *Annual Review of Psychology, 61*, 191-218.

Goetzmann, L., & Schwegler, K. (2004). Semiotic aspects of the countertransference: Some observations on the concepts of the "immediate object" and the "interpretant" in the work of Charles S. Peirce. *International Journal of Psychoanalysis, 85*(6), 1423-1438.

Grotstein, J. (1980). A proposed revision of the psychoanalytic concept of primitive mental states—Part I. Introduction to a newer psychoanalytic metapsychology. *Contemporary Psychoanalysis, 16*, 479-546.

Grotstein, J. (1997). Integrating one-person and two-person psychologies: Autochthony and alterity in counterpoint. *Psychoanalytic Quarterly, 66*, 403-430.

Hall, G., Hivernel, F., & Morgan, S. (Eds.). (2009). *Theory and practise in child psychoanalysis: An introduction to Françoise Dolto's work*. London: Karnac.

Joseph, B. (1985). Transference: The total situation. *International Journal of Psychoanalysis, 66*, 447-454.

Karmiloff, K., & Karmiloff-Smith, A. (2001). *Pathways to language*. Cambridge, MA: Harvard University Press.

Kloesel, C., & Houser, N. (Eds.). (1992). *The essential Peirce, vol. 1: 1867-1893*. Bloomington, IN: Indiana University Press.

Laplanche, J., & Pontalis, J. B. (1973). *The language of psychoanalysis*. London: Hogarth Press.

Lebovici, S. (2000). La consultation thérapeutique et les interventions métaphorisantes (The therapeutic consultation and the metaphorizing interventions). In M. Maury & M. Lamour (Eds.), *Alliances autour du bébé. De la recherche à la clinique (Alliances around the baby. From research to clinic*; pp. 250). Paris: Presses Universitaires de France.

Lebovici, S., & Stoléru, S. (2003). *Le nourisson, sa mère et le psychanalyste. Les interactions précoces (The baby, his mother and the psychoanalyst. Early interactions)*. Paris: Bayard.

Lieberman, A. F., & Van Horn, P. (2008). *Psychotherapy with infants and young children—Repairing the effects of stress and trauma on early attachment*. New York: Guilford.

Lieberman, A. F., Weston, D. R., & Pawl, J. H. (1991). Preventive intervention and outcome with anxiously attached dyads. *Child Development, 62*(1), 199-209.

Lojkasek, M., Cohen, N. J., & Muir, E. (1994). Where is the infant in infant intervention? A review of the literature on changing troubled mother-infant relationships. *Psychotherapy: Theory, Research, Practice, Training, 31*(1), 208-220.

Manzano, J., Palacio Espasa, F., & Zilkha, N. (1999). *Les scénarios narcissiques de la parentalité. Clinique de la consultation thérapeutique (The narcisstic scenarios of parenthood. The clinic of therapeutic consultations)*. Paris: PUF, le Fil Rouge.

Markova, G., & Legerstee, M. (2006). Contingency, imitation, and affect sharing: Foundations of infants' social awareness. *Developmental Psychology, 42*(1), 132-141.

Martindale, C. (1975). The grammar of altered states of consciousness: A semiotic reinterpretation of aspects of psychoanalytic theory. *Psychoanalysis and Contemporary Science, 4*, 331-354.

Maze, J. R., & Henry, R. M. (1996). Problems in the concept of repression and proposals for their resolution. *International Journal of Psychoanalysis, 77*(6), 1085-1100.

McDonough, S. (2004). Interaction guidance. Promoting and nurturing the caregiving relationship. In A. J. Sameroff, S. C. McDonough, & K. L. Rosenblum (Eds.), *Treating parent-infant relationship problems* (pp. 79-96). New York: Guilford.

Meltzer, D. (1992). *The claustrum*. Perthshire, Scotland: Clunie Press.

Muller, J. (1996). *Beyond the psychoanalytic dyad*. New York: Routledge.

Muller, J., & Brent, J. (2000). *Peirce, semiotics, and psychoanalysis*. Baltimore & London: The John Hopkins University Press.

Norman, J. (2001). The psychoanalyst and the baby: A new look at work with infants. *International Journal of Psychoanalysis, 82*(1), 83-100.

Norman, J. (2004). Transformations of early infantile experiences: A 6-month-old in psychoanalysis. *International Journal of Psychoanalysis, 85*(5), 1103-1122.

Olds, D. D. (2000). A semiotic model of mind. *Journal of the American Psychoanalytic Association, 48*, 497-529.

Olinick, S. L. (1985). The primary data of psychoanalysis. *Contemporary Psychoanalysis, 21*, 492-500.

O'Shaugnessy, E. (1988). W. R. Bion's theory of thinking and new techniques in child analysis. In E. Bott Spillius (Ed.), *Melanie Klein today. Developments in theory and practice. Volume 2: Mainly practice* (pp. 177-190). London: Tavistock/Routledge.

Peterfreund, E. (1978). Some critical comments on psychoanalytic conceptualizations of infancy. *International Journal of Psychoanalysis, 59*, 427-441.

Pozzi-Monzo, M. E., & Tydeman, B. (Eds.). (2007). *Innovations in parent-infant psychotherapy*. London: Karnac Books.

Robert-Tissot, C., Cramer, B., Stern, D. N., Scrpa, S. R., Bachmann, J.-P., Palacio-Espasa, F., et al. (1996). Outcome evaluation in brief mother-infant psychotherapies: Report on 75 cases. *Infant Mental Health Journal, 17*(2), 97-114.

Salomonsson, B. (2007a). Semiotic transformations in psychoanalysis with infants and adults. *International Journal of Psychoanalysis, 88*(5), 1201-1221.

Salomonsson, B. (2007b). "Talk to me baby, tell me what's the matter now." Semiotic and developmental perspectives on communication in psychoanalytic infant treatment. *International Journal of Psychoanalysis, 88*(1), 127-146.

Salomonsson, B. (2012). Has infantile sexuality anything to do with infants? *International Journal of Psychoanalysis, 93*(3), 631-647.

Salomonsson, B. (2013). Transferences in parent-infant psychoanalytic treatments. *International Journal of Psychoanalysis, 94*(4), 767-792.

Salomonsson, B. (2014). *Psychoanalytic therapy with infants and parents: Practice, theory and results*. London: Routledge.

Sandler, J., Sandler, A.-M., & Davies, R. (Eds.). (2000). *Clinical and observational psychoanalytical research: Roots of a controversy*. London: Karnac Books.

Shapiro, T. (2013). *Discussion of Salomonsson's paper on transferences in infancy*. New York. Association for Psychoanalytic Medicine. Columbia University Center for Psychoanalytic Training and Research.

Sherick, I. (2009). A proposal to revive "Parent Guidance": An illustration of a brief intervention with the mother of a toddler. *Psychoanalytic Study of the Child, 64,* 229-246.

Silverman, R., & Lieberman, A. (1999). Negative maternal attributions, projective identification, and the intergenerational transmission of violent relational patterns. *Psychoanalytic Dialogues, 9*(2), 161-186.

Stern, D. N. (1985). *The interpersonal world of the infant.* New York: Basic Books.

Stern, D. N. (1995). *The motherhood constellation: A unified view of parent-infant psychotherapy.* London: Karnac Books.

Thomson Salo, F. (2007). Recognizing the infant as subject in infant-parent psychotherapy. *International Journal of Psychoanalysis, 88,* 961-979.

Thomson Salo, F., & Paul, C. (2001). Some principles of infant-parent psychotherapy. Ann Morgan's contribution. *The Signal. The World Association for Infant Mental Health, 9*(1-2), 14-19.

Thomson Salo, F., Paul, C., Morgan, A., Jones, S., Jordan, B., Meehan, M., & Morse, S. (1999). "Free to be playful": Therapeutic work with infants. *Infant Observation, 31*(1), 47-62.

Trevarthen, C., & Aitken, K. J. (2001). Infant intersubjectivity: Research, theory, and clinical applications. *Journal of Child Psychology and Psychiatry and Allied Disciplines, 42*(1), 3-48.

Tronick, E. (2007). *The neurobehavioral and social-emotional development of infants and children.* New York: Norton.

Van Buren, J. (1993). Mother-infant semiotics: Intuition and the development of human subjectivity—Klein/Lacan: Fantasy and meaning. *Journal of the American Academy of Psychoanalysis and Dynamic Psychiatry, 21*(4), 567-580.

Vik, K., & Braten, S. (2009). Video interaction guidance inviting transcendence of postpartum depressed mothers' self-centered state and holding behavior. *Infant Mental Health Journal, 30*(3), 287-300.

Watillon, A. (1993). The dynamics of psychoanalytic therapies of the early parent-child relationship. *International Journal of Psychoanalysis, 74,* 1037-1048.

Widlöcher, D. (2001). The treatment of affects: An interdisciplinary issue. *The Psychoanalytic Quarterly, 70*(1), 243-264.

Winnicott, D. W. (1960). The theory of the parent-infant relationship. *International Journal of Psychoanalysis, 41,* 585-595.

Winnicott, D. W. (1971). *Therapeutic consultations in child psychiatry.* London: Hogarth Press.

Woodhead, J., Bland, K., & Baradon, T. (2006). Focusing the lens: The use of digital video in the practice and evaluation of parental infant psychotherapy. *Infant Observation, 9*(2), 139-150.

Zlot, S. (2007). The parenthood conflict in the light of mother-infant psychotherapy. *Mellanrummet, 16,* 11-22.

Childhood Precursors of Personality Disorders: Evaluation and Treatment

Clarice J. Kestenbaum

The term "borderline," though originally confined to adult patients, began to be applied about a generation ago also to children, thanks in part to the work of Paulina Kernberg (1990), and, around the same period, Kenneth Robson (1983). In the chapter I had contributed to Robson's book I expressed my reservations about the term in relation to child psychiatry, drawing attention to the following problem:

> ... the seriously disturbed child who is not psychotic may be exhibiting the prodromata of a future major psychiatric disorder (i.e., Axis I), that may have constitutional underpinnings. It is better, in my opinion, to consider such a child as on the way to becoming schizophrenic, for example, or manic-depressive, rather than borderline ... The importance of early assessment has preventive implications ... and we might be able to identify the constitutionally vulnerable child and provide specific treatment modalities best suited to avert or ameliorate the condition. (Kestenbaum, 1983, p. 51)

In that chapter I presented seven children who were given the diagnosis "borderline" according to criteria developed by Vela, Gottlieb, and Gottlieb (1983), and whom I had personally evaluated later during the course of a 10- to 25-year follow-up. Of the seven, three of the patients in adult life were in the schizophrenic spectrum, two would be classified today as bipolar, one developed into antisocial personality disorder. The seventh had become a well-functioning psychoanalytic patient.

Currently, *DSM-V* (APA, in press) is under review. Dimensional models are now being developed; personality disorders may well serve as laboratories to test trait-based paradigms within a dimensional framework.

Some key questions: What is the optimal representation of a patient's personality characteristics? Under what circumstances are traits considered pathological? We tend, for example, to consider certain traits as pathological by their very nature (cruelty, mendacity); others, only when noted in an exaggerated form (politeness, shyness ...).

The personality disorders of the current *DSM* (1994), with its ten categories subsumed under three "Clusters," usually become recognizable during adolescence or early adult life. Some children come to exhibit a variety of traits subsumed under any or all of the three clusters. As to the question whether the age for establishing a personality disorder should be lowered, it is of interest that the only childhood disorder demonstrated to be reliably predictive of an adult personality disorder (Antisocial Personality Disorder) is Conduct Disorder of Childhood (Pardini & Fite, 2010). Even that evolution, however, is not inevitable, since it can at times be circumvented by appropriate therapy.

How, then, should we evaluate symptomatic children who appear in our offices, and what diagnostic label should we apply? Here one draws attention to *constitution*, implying inborn temperamental characteristics that, together with certain patterns developing postnatally (the *environmental factors*), give rise to the concept of personality (Kagan, 1998). Commonly encountered variants in temperament, such as the *easy* child, the *slow-to-warm-up* child, and the *difficult* child, were described by Thomas and Chess (1977). These authors enumerated nine temperamental dimensions, as indicated below:

(1) activity level

(2) regularity of basic functions, i.e., sleep, hunger, bowel function

(3) approach and withdrawal style

(4) adaptation to new situations

(5) stimulus reactivity

(6) energy level responsiveness

(7) overt mood (happy, sad, irritable)

(8) distractibility

(9) attention span

Thomas and Chess relied heavily on questionnaires administered to parents; Kagan and his colleagues extended the earlier research by studying the babies themselves. Kagan was interested primarily in two qualities—the *cautious* compared with the *bold* child (subsequently labeled "inhibited" and "uninhibited").

Differences in neurochemistry and associated neurophysiology were found to correlate with certain temperamental variations. Among these neurophysiological differences, it was noted that newborns with high plasma levels of dopamine- -hydroxylase (DBH) were unusually sensitive to lights, sounds, and (at five months) new faces. Kagan characterized such infants as "overly responsive to stimulation" (Kagan, 1998, p. 52). At age one, some of these children were noted to be highly fearful and separation-anxious—the same sorts of children described years ago as showing "unusual sensitivities" (Bergman & Escalona, 1943).

In contrast, certain babies with *low* levels of DBH, and, related to this, lower sympa-

thetic reactivity, might be unusually fearless, and show little concern about punishment. This physiological variant has been found to predispose to conduct disorder in children (especially in boys), some of whom emerge in adolescence as aggressive and antisocial (Gabel, Stadler, Bjorn, Shindledecker, & Bowen, 1993). Recently startle-reflex has been studied, as yet another temperamental "marker": startle-reactions tend to be diminished in children who go on to develop antisocial personality, but exaggerated in those with anxiety disorders (Reeb-Sutherland et al., 2009). Genetic variants have also been implicated not only in Conduct Disorder, but also in Attention Deficit Hyperactivity Disorder (ADDH), both with heritability estimates of 40 to 50% or greater (Monteaux, Biederman, Doyle, Mick, & Faraone, 2009).

In the continuing search for genetic underpinnings to the various personality variations, Kendler and his group have postulated that many Axis I and Axis II psychiatric disorders have an underlying structure that reflects two major dimensions: *internalizing* versus *externalizing*. Their results, based on a study of 2,111 young Norwegian adult monozygotic and dizygotic twin pairs, led them to conclude that genetic factors outweighed the environmental vis-à-vis the organization into coherent diagnostic groups such as we now utilize (Kendler et al., 2011). Four major factors emerged from their study: Factor-1 (symptom-disorder) Internalizing and Factor-1 Externalizing; also Factor-2 (personality disorder) Internalizing and Factor-2 Externalizing. Examples, as seen in this light, include panic disorder (Factor-1 Internalizing), conduct disorder (Factor-1 Externalizing), avoidant personality (Factor-2 Internalizing), and borderline personality (Factor-2 Externalizing). Antisocial personality, though placed in Axis 2 in *DSM*, maps best on Factor-1 Externalizing, just as does its childhood counterpart: "conduct disorder."

In general, the genetic and neurophysiological research over the past two decades have discredited to the earlier notions that we were born with a tabula rasa upon which the environment gradually imprinted its patterns specific to each individual—ideas once popularized by Watson and Skinner (Skinner, 1938; Watson & Raynor, 1920).

Most current developmental researchers accept the concept of gene-environment interaction. Among the more prominent figures in this field are Avshalom Caspi and Terry Moffit, who have shown, for example, how the relative weights of these factors help account for the difference between the so-called life-course persistent versus adolescent-limited types of early appearing antisocial behaviors (Moffitt & Caspi, 2001).

What seems to be of increasing importance to the nature of the caregivers' (i.e., mothers') expectations and the innate temperament of the child, is a *poor fit*, as Chess noted decades earlier. For example, a high energy, outgoing boy and a perfectionistic, demanding mother who cannot tolerate her toddler's curiosity and motion-proneness might lead to continual friction (with unpleasant consequences for both parties).

ATTACHMENT THEORY

Advances in understanding personality and its predisposing factors have not been limited to genetics and neurophysiology. On the psychoanalytic side, research on the origins and development of *attachment style* has also contributed to our understanding of normal and abnormal personality in adults and children. The ways in which ideal mother–infant interaction fostered the development of secure attachment in growing children and in adults had been described by Bowlby (1969), carried further by Winnicott of the British Objects Relation School (cf. Sutherland, 1980), and objectified via rating scales by Mary Main and her colleagues (Behrens, Hesse, & Main, 2007). The manner in which infants learn, via interaction with the mother, the various emotional states

(joy, sadness, anger, guilt, etc.) has been highlighted by Izard (1972).

In England Peter Fonagy, Mary Target and their group, using Main's Adult Attachment Interview, have shown the connection between various symptom disorders and corresponding attachment styles (Fonagy et al., 1996). Anxiety disorders, for example, were often found in connection with unresolved or preoccupied attachment styles, as were many patients with borderline personality. Secure attachment is recognized as a crucial first step in socialization. In children and adolescents who lack secure attachment, one of the important goals in psychotherapy is first to identify the abnormalities of attachment; then, to foster the development of secure attachment via the therapeutic work.

RELATIONSHIPS WITH PEERS

One of the difficulties besetting the adoption of acceptable criteria for "borderline" personality in children, in contrast to adults, is the lack of close counterparts within the child population—to certain descriptors of (adult) Borderline Personality Disorder (BPD). The item in *DSM-IV*: "a pattern of unstable and intense interpersonal relationships characterized by alternating between extremes of idealization and devaluation" is not readily translatable at the child level. (The item is more easily discernible in romantic relationships gone wrong). The stormy relationships of BPD may, however, be witnessed *in statu nascendi* in certain abnormalities in children's *peer relationships*.

For this reason I always question children closely about their peer relationships. It is not enough for children to say they have "10 or 12 friends," then naming all the other children in their class. One must assess the *quality* of the friendships via such questions such as "what is the difference between a friend and a best friend?" Or: "Can you tell your best friend your secrets?" From their answers we learn how important close friendships are (usually with children of the same sex), and whether their friendships are relatively harmonious or instead highly volatile and changeable. We learn whether they have no real friends at all. The absence of friends, or serious problems in the area of peer relationships, may point to the presence of an "intermediate" level of personality pathology in a child—akin to what might be considered "borderline" in late adolescence or young adults. But it must not be assumed that such abnormalities in children will necessarily evolve, as they pass age 18, into the types of relational pathology we associate with BPD.

THE DIAGNOSTIC EVALUATION

The diagnostic evaluation has always been the crucial first step of the psychiatric treatment plan. In contrast to the assessment of an adult (where the chief informant is usually just the patient), the task facing the child psychiatric interviewer is far more complex. The interviewer must take into account the child's age, cognitive level of development, and willingness to discuss problems. The examination of the child alone rarely, if ever, can serve as the only source of information sufficient to make a diagnosis; but the examiner can certainly form a valuable diagnostic impression. Information is also needed that the child cannot supply: a developmental history (including genetic background), a broad understanding of the home environment, and some knowledge of the significant people in the child's life. A thorough assessment of the school and other aspects of the child's world often are needed for a comprehensive evaluation, including current or past events (e.g., the death of a parent, effects of divorce, or a traumatic event such as a fire or automobile accident) that may have a lasting impact on future development.

School reports as well as pediatric records (including a neurologic examination when indicated) may be sent to the diagnostician prior to the first visit. A psychological evaluation already may have been obtained or may be requested by the evaluator. Evaluation of family functioning is important. A family interview is often required to determine the quality of the parent–child "fit."

By way illustrating these points, I have provided three clinical vignettes of children—each representing one of the three Axis II Clusters. Although the symptoms in several may appear identical, the underlying psychopathology is markedly different for each child, pointing to a future personality disorder that will be different for each.

The following cases involved, for the most part, a psychodynamic therapeutic approach. At times I employed other modalities as well, such as dialectical behavior therapy, pharmacotherapy, and family therapy. In this age of evidence-based psychological treatments, we still find that empirical evidence supports the efficacy of psychodynamic psychotherapy (Shedler, 2010). Similarly, Gerber et al. (2011) noted that existing randomized controlled trials of psychodynamic psychotherapy have been promising and appear sufficient to make this of therapy empirically validated. Even a generation ago, Barrnett and his colleagues (Barrnett, Docherty, & Frommelt, 1991) proposed that the key to successful outcome lay in the choice of therapist trained in a particular therapeutic paradigm, using procedures applied to specific problems. Child psychiatrists, to an extent greater than is so with most adult psychiatrists, need this kind of familiarity with multimodal treatments, even while psychodynamic psychotherapy remains the foundation, upon which the other therapies are built.

The principles of psychodynamic therapy are the same for children as they are for adults, with, as I hope to show with the vignettes, certain modifications. The child's play, for example, rather than his dreams, becomes the "royal road" to uncovering unconscious conflicts. Anna Freud noted long ago (1966) that the child "sees the therapist, *in part*, as a transference object, but also as a new object, an object of externalization of inter- and intra-systemic conflicts, and an auxiliary ego." There is, moreover, a non-transference relationship in the psychoanalytic situation, the "real" relationship. This is a necessary component of any successful therapy—in other words, transference *plus*. With children the "plus" is a far more significant factor than with adults.

The child best suited for psychodynamic therapy is the one who comes for treatment because of specific symptoms: phobias, compulsive rituals, school avoidance, separation anxiety, childhood depression, and the like—but free of psychosis. Merely changing the environment such as moving to a different neighborhood or school setting will not change that child's representational world nor enable him to work through an unresolved trauma. A child must be able to tolerate some frustration in the therapeutic situation and to control impulses by translating his feelings into play or words, not action.

THE VIGNETTES*

1. Roger, Age 7, Cluster C (Possible Future Obsessive-Compulsive, Avoidant, Dependent Personality Disorders)

Roger came to my attention when the guidance counselor of his private boy's school suggested his parents call me. The parents were concerned about Roger who seemed frightened much of the time, especially at bedtime. An "easy child" at first, he began early in life to experience intense separation anxiety. Nightmares occurred several times a week. At school he was fearful of being alone or of going unaccompanied on

expeditions throughout the school building. He frequently clutched at his penis. At other times, he wandered about the classroom, was often inattentive in class, and called out answers out of turn. Sometimes he got into fights with other boys. He had had three playground accidents requiring stitches, and had once suffered a fractured foot when at age 6 he impulsively ran into the street and was struck by a taxi.

According to his father, his son had always been an active child but that his fearfulness seemed to increase rather than disappear with age. This symptom became worse after the father had been suddenly hospitalized with meningitis the past summer. Roger's nightmares made him too frightened to remain in his room at night; he now insisted on sleeping with his mother. After the father's return, Roger was displaced to his own room. The second night he was ordered out of the parents' bedroom. Roger told his father, "I wish you died when you were sick." Later, he said he was sorry for saying such a terrible thing, but his night monsters continued. Roger became increasingly anxious, not only at night, but at school. Always an active child, he was now easily distracted and, it seemed at times, almost unable to sit still.

During our first session, Roger mentioned that lately he didn't like to play much. When I asked: "Is that because of the worries?" he said: "I keep thinking about the monsters."

The "Monsters" were not hallucinations, as it turned out, but true figments of his imagination "inside my head, like my thoughts." At first, they bothered him at night, but recently they followed him into school cloakrooms and closets, such as the one in my office. When I suggested he draw me a picture of the "monsters," he was most reluctant, as though any such picture would reignite his fears. But, with some encouragement, he gradually put to-

---

*All names and details have been changed to protect privacy.

gether a picture of an ugly monster with sharp fangs, black blood—who eats children. The monster was then subdued with knives and flames. As a final measure, I encouraged Roger to shred the picture in little pieces and toss it away—which he did with great glee. For a further step in helping him to convert an anxiety-producing conflict into one he could now resolve and master, I suggested to his mother that she allow him to place another monster-picture under his pillow, with the instruction that if he had a bad dream, he then "kill" the monster (by adding in a gun that shoots it), and tear up and toss away the picture.

Several weeks later the boy informed me that the picture remained under the pillow, but the nightmares had disappeared. The mechanism we had devised to help him gain control—was working well.

During the few remaining months of the spring school term, I consulted frequently with Roger's teacher. She noted that he was far less fearful, was more relaxed in class. Separation anxiety was much diminished, but Roger still seemed inordinately concerned about loss, death, and dying. He was quite upset when his hamster died, saying: "It reminds me of the time Daddy was in the hospital. I got hit by a car and had to have three stitches in the emergency room, that same year my great-grandmother died, and my aunt and uncle got divorced." Roger was able for the first time to discuss his father's hospitalization. I pointed out that most of children of five believe somehow that they are responsible in some way. "If I had been good, God wouldn't have let that happen," he told me. At my urging, he drew a picture of his concept of Heaven and Hell, adding that his notion was that if you were good you went to Heaven, but if you were bad, you went to Hell. Because he sometimes had "bad thoughts" (such as when he wished his father dead), he assumed he was destined for the bad place. I shared with him my contrasting philosophy; namely, that *actions* are what really count, not words

or thoughts. Having spoken with the father, I also reassured him that his father felt the same way and did not hold his son's "bad thoughts" against him.

Roger seemed comforted by our discussions. Soon afterwards he began spending more time with his father (who was quite pleased by his son's progress)—playing baseball, going with him to movies, and even helping him around the yard. Roger stopped treatment at the end of the school year. He was doing well at home, in school, and at summer camp, his first extended stay away from home. The symptoms which had brought him to treatment had long since disappeared. A five-year follow-up report describes a bright, popular, competent 14-year-old without major problems, who is functioning well without the need for constant presence of an adult. Ten years later I heard that he had had a brilliant college career, and was engaged to be married. The year of psychotherapy had clearly helped him back onto the proper developmental path, having lowered his anxieties, lessened his shyness, and reduced his reliance on obsessive-compulsive thoughts and rituals.

2. Mona, Age 6, Cluster A (Schizotypal Personality Traits)

Mona was referred for treatment because of school refusal, extreme shyness, inconsistent schoolwork habits, and a diminished pleasure sense. Symptoms included enuresis, phobic-level fear of the dark and of animals, and a belief that the eyes in photos and paintings could follow her around the room. She had no friends.

Her mother had "emotional problems" (consisting largely of agoraphobia), and the maternal grandfather was alcoholic and paranoid; that grandfather's brother had died in a mental institution.

Mona's language development was marked by a belated ability for verbal communication (though her comprehension seemed adequate), and she showed considerable separation anxiety and tantrums. On neuropsychological evaluation her full-scale IQ was 115, but with noticeable subtest scatter. Peculiar percepts were noted on projective tests: monsters, dragons, skeletons, staring eyes—reminiscent of (adult) "paranoid personality."

In her twice-weekly sessions, she at first avoided eye contact, thinking that "looks could kill." In Mona's stories and drawings fire, explosions, death, and destruction were typical themes. To a drawing of a girl, she said: "The girl is all bad, she has no friends and she hates everyone." In doll-play she once said that "if you eat something you don't like, your head will fall off."

Eventually becoming more trusting in her therapy, she began to acquire friends. Bizarre notions appeared in her stories; in one story she pictured a girl who "didn't want to come out of her mother's tummy; she had two brains—one of which turns itself off when she wants to go into her secret world."

After several years of treatment, she was troubled by her budding sexuality; she experienced moments of depersonalization. Her fears of the pubertal changes were heralded by odd fantasies, in one of which she had an abortion, but pushed the abortus back inside, turned herself inside out; her ovaries then walked outside on two little legs.

I encouraged Mona to use her rich imagination to create stories that could more appropriately be shared with her teachers. Altogether, I worked with her in twice-weekly therapy until she was 13 years old. Eventually Mona became editor of the school newspaper. The family moved when Mona was 14. When I contacted her later, she had adjusted well to college and later found employment in a school library. She married a physician, continued to write—for a local newspaper—and never experienced a psychotic breakdown.

3. Jason, Age 10, Cluster B (Oppositional-Defiant Disorder and Narcissistic Personality)

Jason's birth was uncomplicated; he was not abused physically or verbally by either parent. In his latency years he would say "no" to whatever his mother asked of him, and he had often been suspended at school for getting into fights. He had no friends and had been rude to his teachers. He lied about having done his homework and earned a bad reputation for stealing games and other items from classmates' backpacks (acknowledgement for which he vigorously denied). He was particularly intolerant of ever losing a game, becoming tantrumy and combative.

Jason tended to blame everyone else—his classmates and teachers—for his problems, calling them "morons." At first I accepted his externalizing without challenging his views. By way of exploring his intolerance of losing, I decided to play checkers with him, letting him win the first two games. When I won the third game, Jason became angry and wanted to leave the session. This spelled out one of his major problems: an inability to be a good sport. Many of the next sessions were devoted to helping Jason develop the ability to lose a game—with grace. Initially, for example, he regarded putting on a good face when he lost as "lying." Later we played ping-pong. Again he won games at first, but once, as a kind of test, I threw my paddle across the room after I'd lost. His reaction: "Boy, you sure are a poor loser!" Fortunately, he was able to see the connection between my staged reaction and his usual reaction.

A turning point in Jason's treatment occurred when, after initial refusal, his father finally came to a session: he started to play ping-pong with his son, determined, to judge his face, to "kill" his son at ping-pong. But at that moment his back gave out and he fell to the floor in pain—and had to be taken to hospital by ambulance. Afterwards Jason asked me in a flash of insight:

"Do you think dad has a problem about losing like I used to have?" From then on Jason was more tractable, made a few friends, and did well academically. When I contacted him years later, I learned that he had gone on to medical school. Later still, he sent me an invitation to his wedding.

DISCUSSION

In an earlier article (Kestenbaum, 1983), I had expressed my disinclination to label children with a *DSM* personality disorder, meantime granting that *seriously* disturbed children (some of whom had begun to be designated "borderline") may be exhibiting the prodromata of one or another major psychiatric disorder. Such disorders usually have distinct genetic or constitutional underpinnings. Our knowledge base in relation to these genetic and neurophysiological factors having been amplified considerably in the intervening quarter century, that earlier view requires modification. There may indeed be a justification for inclusion in the forthcoming *DSM-V* of a section devoted to personality disorders in childhood and adolescence, particularly one that relies on a dimensional model (or on a combination dimensional/categorical model) rather than on a purely categorical approach (Rottman, Ahn, Sanioslow, & Kim, 2009). We recognize more than was once the case that the fewer adverse environmental factors are present (neglect, abuse, early loss of a parent . . .), the more weight must attach to heredity and constitution—in the assessment of disturbed children. The vignettes given above were chosen to highlight this distinction, since all three children came from intact upper-middle-class families where neglect and abuse were either minimal or altogether absent. There was also the mitigating factor that all three children (even the one with conduct disorder) had adequate reflective capacity of a sort that enhanced their ability to work cooperatively in the therapeutic encounter (cf. Fonagy & Target,

1997; Muir, 1995). In all the three cases I described a strong neurobiological base was apparent, but each child also showed good reflective capacity. The vignettes also illustrate one of the three major developmental tracts encountered in child psychiatry vis-à-vis personality disorder. One track (exemplified in the vignettes) concerns children who appear to have a personality disorder, but in whom personality disorder is either no longer discernible or else much attenuated as they emerge into adulthood. A second track concerns those whose apparent personality disorder is simply the childhood stage of a lifelong disorder. Finally, we encounter children who appear fairly normal throughout their early years, but who go on—often in response to harsh environmental circumstances—to develop a personality disorder that becomes evident in their adult years. As for children from the first two tracks, psychiatric evaluation should take into consideration genetic and environmental risk factors (and their various combinations) so that appropriate interventions can be instituted as early as possible.

COMMENTS ON THE CHILDHOOD PRODROMATA OF THE CLUSTER-RELATED DISORDERS

Cluster "A": The "Eccentric" Cluster

Certain traits, when displayed during childhood or adolescence in a fairly pronounced form, are considered harbingers of one or another Cluster "A" disorder: schizoid, schizotypal, or paranoid. These disorders are characterized by peculiarities of cognition, especially schizotypal PD—the disorder most clearly linked genetically to schizophrenia. There may be a surplus of paranoid and schizoid persons in the families of schizophrenics, but there are other routes to those two disorders besides a genetic link to schizophrenia. Schizophrenics and those with less severe forms of what Meehl had called schizotaxia (1962)—the neurointegrative underpinning to schizophrenia-like conditions—are also prone to a deficit in the capacity to experience pleasure (anhedonia), as emphasized by Harrow, Grinker, & Holzman, (1977). By no means do all children manifesting some of the traits linked to schizophrenia (marked introversion, eccentricity of thought, aloofness . . .) develop the psychosis later on. In the stress-diathesis model proposed by Gottesman and Schields (1972), intervening factors may minimize the risk, or, in the presence of chaotic homelife or early drug abuse, maximize the risk for eventual schizophrenic breakdown (Erlenmeyer-Kimling, Kestenbaum, Bird, & Hildoff, 1984; McGorry, McKenzie, Jackson, Waddell, & Curry, 2000). Children with autism-spectrum disorders and Asperger's syndrome also show peculiarities of cognition, along with an empathic handicap that renders them less able to grasp the emotional states of others and to relate to others appropriately in social settings. Yet they are usually *not* on the same genetic track as those predisposed to schizophrenia. They only appear to be in the "schizophrenia spectrum" to those less familiar with the syndrome, because of their inability to understand the feeling states of others and their inability to tune in to others. Unable to socialize or to make small talk, Asperger persons (there will be more male than female) often become social isolates, acting in peculiar ways that are reminiscent of certain schizophrenic persons with similar social handicaps and peculiar behaviors. Simon Baron-Cohen (2011) has written an excellent monograph on empathy, highlighting the differences between two types of persons, each with major deficits in empathy. The psychopath and the person with Asperger's both have "zero-empathy" in Baron-Cohen's schema. But the psychopath, while he may have a bit of cognitive empathy (ability to recognized facial expressions) has no compassion. This is "zero-empathy-Negative." The psychopath is capable of exploitation and even cruelty. In Asperger's one sees severe impairment of cognitive empathy, but usually a capacity for compassion; exploitation and cruelty are not accompanying attributes. This is "zero-empathy-Positive (Chapters 3 and 4).

Whereas gene-environment interactions have been studied for decades, particularly with regard to the schizophrenias, early interventions for "pre-schizophrenic" and other cognitive disorders in children have only recently received scientific scrutiny (Falloon, Kydd, Coverdale, & Laidlaw, 1996).

Therapists who work with schizophrenic children of any age must be sensitive to individual differences in capacity, motivation, and level of communication. They must be aware that an outburst of rage may reflect (as one common dynamic) intolerance of being alone, that obsessional rituals may be an attempt to ward off imagined dangers, and that reality testing is, by definition, poor. Ego integration is at best faulty, with sharply contradictory and unassimilated attitudes about the self causing confusion and bewilderment. The schizophrenic child lacks the ability to distinguish fantasy from reality. Frustration tolerance is invariably low. Common defenses against overwhelming anxiety include denial, projection, and withdrawal. There is rarely a sense of humor, so that jokes are taken at their most concrete level, an attitude which most normal children will not tolerate.

Therapy with such children, according to Escalona (1964), has taken two directions: "expressive" and "suppressive." "Expressive" therapy, derived from concepts inherent in the psychoanalysis of neurotic individuals, permits the expression of previously unconscious material. Suppressive therapy is better at keeping the prepsychotic child grounded in the "here and now."

Cluster "B" Disorders: The "Dramatic Cluster"

DSM-IV recognizes four disorders in this "Dramatic" Cluster: histrionic, borderline, antisocial, and narcissistic. As for Antisocial Personality, Kernberg and Chazen (1991) observed that children with conduct disorder were particularly at risk for developing antisocial traits or even the full disorder (Kernberg & Chazen, 1991). They described two subtypes: an *aggressive-socialized* and an *aggressive-non-socialized*. Antisocial personality has been linked in part to genetic predisposition via allelic peculiarities in the catechol-O-methyl-transferase gene (Langley, Heron, O'Donovan, Owen, & Thapar, 2010) that appears to underlie deficits in executive control and social understanding. On the environmental side, adolescents with these tendencies are over-represented in foster care settings, and are prone to run afoul of the juvenile justice system.

Efforts had been made in the past to create a definition of "borderline personality" applicable to children, analogous to the *DSM* definition of BPD. This was prompted in part by the observation that certain children, while clearly not enduringly psychotic, were nevertheless more psychologically aberrant and ill—than were the more ordinary child-cases seen in clinics or private practice. Indeed, the three vignettes provided above all concerned children in this intermediate zone of psychopathology. But there is no solid connection between children labeled "borderline" in this broad and imprecise way—and adult BPD: many of the so-called borderline children emerge in adulthood in unpredictable ways, only a portion of whom could reasonably meet adult *DSM* criteria for BPD.

Thomas Insel, director of NIMH, has emphasized that mental disorders are brain disorders, in which behavior and cognition are the last to change (Moran, 2011). Diagnosis has hitherto been based primarily on those latter-day abnormalities. Viewed in this light, "borderline" is better understood as an endophenotype, recognizable in adulthood, but which had been preceded by many different genetic and environmental pathways during the course of development. In the case of ADD/H, as Moran mentions in his review, Insel underlines the importance of delays in cortical maturation in the prefrontal regions (important in attentional and motor-planning processes)—which are occurring well before a child is diagnosed (via certain behaviors) with attention-deficit/hyperactivity.

The "Dramatic Cluster" also contains antisocial personality (ASPD), also better understood as an endophenotype to which many etiological sources converge. We now distinguish, for example, between lifelong/persistent antisociality versus the adolescent-onset variety (Pardini & Fite, 2010). It now appears that in callous-unemotional children (most of whom will be boys) their reduced amygdalar response to fearful expressions is primarily related to genetic peculiarities (Marsh et al., 2008). This is not to deny that adolescent-onset antisocial traits may also have genetic underpinnings, but here highly traumatic and disruptive home environments appear to play a greater role in the "nature-nurture" balance—than do genetic factors. As might be expected, young persons in the callous-unemotional group tended to be more prone to predatory aggression (and eventual psychopathy) and less responsive to treatment efforts (Fontaine, McCrory, Boivin, Moffitt, & Viding, 2011; Masi et al., 2011).

Cluster "C" Disorders: The "Anxious" Cluster

Hereditary factors are said to account for about half the variance in personality disorders (Cloninger, 1986; Plomin & Reade, 1991). But viewed from the perspective of cultural norms, the disorders of Clusters A and B represent greater deviations from adaptive, quasi-normal personality, and it is not surprising that more abnormalities have been noted via such measures as MRI and neurotransmitter assay in, for example, schizotypal, antisocial, and borderline disorders than in obsessive-compulsive and dependent subtypes. Anxious-Cluster persons tend to show what Cloninger has spoken of as "harm-avoidance"—for which comparatively elevated levels of brain serotonin may be a factor. Hoarding and compulsive rituals in children may be viewed as early signs of obsessive-compulsive disorder (OCD). Over a third of persons with OCD also will meet criteria for obsessive-compulsive personality disorder (OCPD); prognostically, the (OCPD) trait of perfectionism predicted worse treatment outcome for OCD (Pinto, Liebowitz, Foa, & Simpson, 2011). Some now speak of an obsessive-compulsive "spectrum"—with key traits of perfectionism and rigidity, and key symptoms of compulsive behaviors and ego-alien obsessional thoughts—with common etiological factors. These are said to arise from a combination of genetic predispositions and non-shared environmental factors held in common, rather than being the expression of nonspecific influences (Taylor, Asmundson, & Jang, 2011). Presumably, the brain changes associated with OCD (in frontal-striatal-thalamic areas) are more pronounced than would be found in children or adults with only OCPD traits (cf. Chiu et al., 2011; MacMaster, O'Neill, & Rosenberg, 2008).

Dependent and Avoidant personality disorders are predicted, in Cloninger's schema, to show high "harm-avoidance" (and correspondingly high serotonergic activity) and high "reward dependence" (associated with low basal noradrenergic activity). But the kinds of brain-tract and limbic-system peculiarities associated with OCD have not been demonstrated in dependent/avoidant personalities. Lately, dissatisfaction has even been expressed concerning the very retention of Dependent PD in *DSM-V*, given that the traits of dependence and submission which, when "excessive" in American culture earn the label Dependent PD—may

be well within cultural norms in Chinese (as well as in Japanese and other) cultures.

We should also note that, from the standpoint of psychotherapy, children, adolescents, and adults with the Anxious-Cluster disorders and allied configurations such as "depressive-masochistic" (O. Kernberg, 1992, pp. 36-41) generally show greater reflective capacity or psychological mindedness than is seen in, say, antisocial, narcissistic, and paranoid personalities. For this reason, they will often respond better to our psychotherapeutic interventions and have better outcomes. The children in the clinical vignettes above, each representing a different personality Cluster, all ultimately had favorable outcomes—but "Roger" (from the Anxious Cluster) was the most amenable to treatment. None were antisocial, let alone in trouble with the law. A full discussion of treatment for antisocial children and adolescents: which ones are amenable to currently available methods; which ones are not—lies beyond the scope of this article. Earlier works by August Aichhorn (1925) and Melitta Schmideberg (1959) focused on youthful offenders who are nevertheless reachable by psychotherapeutic (including behavioral) means. Among the child and adolescent patients currently, the most challenging from a therapeutic standpoint are the "callous-unemotional" youths, many of whom are identifiable as psychopathic personalities as they enter adulthood.

COMMENT

I had earlier expressed the view that children should not be labeled with any *DSM* personality disorder, granted that certain seriously disturbed children could be said to exhibit prodromata of a future psychiatric disorder (Kestenbaum, 1983). The future disorder might be limited to what is now considered a "symptom" disorder (such as anorexia, depression, or agoraphobia) or might emerge as a personality disorder—or as a mixed condition embodying both symptom and personality elements. It would be common to see a constitutional underpinning to whatever condition is observed during the childhood period.

Given the explosion of information on many fronts, particularly in regard to genetic research, over the past two decades, I now see a justification for the inclusion of personality disorders in childhood and adolescence—in the forthcoming 5th edition of *DSM*. Such inclusion is all the more acceptable now that a dimensional approach has been adopted, amplifying the purely categorical approach of the previous editions (Rottman et al., 2009). The three vignettes described above all had a strong neurobiological base; they could not be understood purely on an environmental ("nurture" as opposed to "nature") basis. Every evaluation in child psychiatry should take into consideration genetic as well as environmental risk factors so that appropriate interventions can be instituted as early as possible. With children whom clinicians label "borderline," genetic and constitutional (usually meaning "in utero") factors are almost always an important part of the picture. Trauma may also be an important factor, as in the case of incest or parental cruelty. Even in the absence of recognizable "nature" factors, "nurture"-related stresses, if severe and protracted enough, can by themselves set in motion the development of a future personality disorder.

REFERENCES

Aichhorn, A. (1925). *Die verwahrloste Jugend* [The Wayward Youth]. Vienna: Int. Psychoanalytische Verlag.

American Psychiatric Association. (1994). *Diagnostic and statistical manual of mental disorders* (4th ed.). Washington, DC: American Psychiatric Association.

American Psychiatric Association. (in press). *Diagnostic and statistical manual of mental disorders* (5th ed.). Washington, DC: American Psychiatric Association.

Baron-Cohen, S. (2011). *The science of evil: On empathy and the origins of cruelty*. New York: Basic Books.

Barrnett, R. J., Docherty, J. P., & Frommelt, G. M. (1991). A review of child psychotherapy research since 1963. *Journal of the American Academy of Child and Adolescent Psychiatry, 30*, 1-14.

Behrens, K. Y., Hesse, E., & Main, M. (2007). Mothers' attachment status as determined by the Adult Attachment Interview (AAI) predicts their 6-year-olds' reunion responses. *Developmental Psychology, 43*, 1553-1567.

Bergman, P., & Escalona, S. K. (1943). Unusual sensitivities in very young children. *The Psychoanalytic Study of the Child, 3-4*, 335-352.

Bleuler, E. (1911). *Dementia praecox or the group of schizophrenias*. New York: International Universities Press.

Bowlby, J. (1969). *Attachment* (Parts I and II). New York: Basic Books.

Chiu, C. H., Lo, Y. C., Tang, H. S., Liu, I. C., Chiang, W. Y., Yeh, F. C., Jaw, F. S., & Tseng, W. Y. (2011). White matter abnormalities of fronto-striato-thalamic circuitry in obsessive-compulsive disorder: A study using diffusion spectrum imaging tractography. *Psychiatry Research, 192*, 176-182.

Cloninger, C. R. (1986). A unified biosocial theory of personality and its role in the development of anxiety states. *Psychiatric Developments, 3*, 167-226.

Erlenmeyer-Kimling, L., Kestenbaum, C. J., Bird, H., & Hildoff, U. (1984). Assessment of the New York high-risk subjects in Sample A—who are now clinically deviant. In N. F. Watt, E. J. Anthony, L. Wynne, & J. Roff (Eds.), *Children at risk for schizophrenia: A longitudinal perspective* (pp. 227-239). New York: Cambridge University press.

Escalona, S. (1964). Some considerations regarding psychotherapy with psychotic children. In M. R. Haworth (Ed.), *Child psychotherapy* (pp. 50-58). New York: Basic Books.

Falloon, I. R., Kydd, R. R., Coverdale, J. H., & Laidlaw, T. M. (1996). Early detection and intervention for initial episodes of schizophrenia. *Schizophrenia Bulletin, 22*(2), 271-282.

Fonagy, P., Leigh, T., Steele, M., Steele, H., Kennedy, R., Mattoon, G., Target, M., & Gerber, A. (1996). The relation of attachment status, psychiatric classification, and response to psychotherapy. *Journal of Consulting and Clinical Psychology, 64*, 22-31.

Fonagy, P., & Target, M. (1997). Attachment and reflective function: Their role in self-organization. *Developmental Psychopathology, 9*, 679-700.

Fontaine, N. M., McCrory, E. J., Boivin, M., Moffitt, T. E., & Viding, E. (2011). Predictors and outcomes of joint trajectories of callous-unemotional traits and conduct problems in childhood. *Journal of Abnormal Psychology*. [Feb. 21, E-publication]

Freud, A. (1966). A short history of child analysis. *Psychoanalytic Study of the Child, 21*, 7-14.

Gabel, S., Stadler, J., Bjorn, J., Shindledecker, R., & Bowden, C. (1993). Dopamine-beta-hydroxylase in behaviorally disturbed youth. *Biological Psychiatry, 34*, 434-442.

Gerber, A. J., Kocsis, J. H., Milrod, B. L., Roose, S. P., Barber, J. P., Thase, M. E., Perkins, P., & Leon, A. C. (2011). A quality-based review of randomized controlled trials of psychodynamic psychotherapy. *American Journal of Psychiatry, 168*, 19-28.

Gottesman, I. I., & Shields, J. (1972). *Schizophrenia and genetics: A twin study vantage point.* New York: Academic.

Harrow, M., Grinker, R. R., Holzman, P. S., & Kayton, L. (1977). Anhedonia and schizophrenia. *American Journal of Psychiatry, 134*(7), 794-797.

Izard, C. E. (1972). *The face of emotion.* New York: Appleton-Century-Crofts.

Kagan, J. (1998). *Galen's prophesy: Temperament in human nature* (pp. xvii). New York: Basic Books.

Kendler, K. S., Aggen, S. H., Knudsen, G. P., R ysamb, E., Neale, M. C., & Reichborn-Kjennerud, T. (2011). The structure of genetic and environmental risk factors for syndromal and subsyndromal common *DSM-IV* axis I and all axis II disorders. *American Journal of Psychiatry, 168*(1), 29-39.

Kernberg, O. F. (1992). *Aggression in personality disorders and perversions.* New Haven: Yale University Press.

Kernberg, P. F. (1990). Borderline personality exists in children under twelve. *Journal of the American Academy of Child and Adolescent Psychiatry, 29*, 478-482.

Kernberg, P. F., & Chazan, S. E. (1991). *Children with conduct disorders. A psychotherapy manual.* New York: Basic Books.

Kestenbaum, C. J. (1978). Childhood psychosis: Psychotherapy. In B. E. Wolman, J. Egan, & A. O. Ross (Eds.), *Handbook of treatment of mental disorders in childhood and adolescence* (pp. 354-384). Englewood Cliffs, NJ: Prentice-Hall.

Kestenbaum, C. J. (1983). The borderline child at risk for major psychiatric disorder in adult life: Seven case reports with follow-up. In K. S. Robson (Ed.), *The borderline child* (pp. 49-81). New York: McGraw-Hill.

Kraepelin, E. (1896). *Dementia praecox and paraphrenia.* Chicago, IL: Chicago Medical Book Company.

Langley, K., Heron, J., O'Donovan, M. C., Owen, M. J., & Thapar, A. (2010). Genotype link with extreme antisocial behavior: The contribution of cognitive pathways. *Archives of General Psychiatry, 67*(12), 1317-1323.

MacMaster, F. P., O'Neill, J., & Rosenberg, D. R. (2008). Brain imaging in pediatric obsessive-compulsive disorder. *Journal of the American Academy of Child and Adolescent Psychiatry, 47*, 1262-1272.

Marsh, A. A., Finger, E. C., Mitchell, D. G., Sims, C., Kosson, D. S., Towbin, K. E., Liebenluft, E., Pine, D. S., & Blair, R. J. (2008). Reduced amygdalar response to fearful expressions in children and adolescents with callous-unemotional traits and disruptive behavior disorders. *American Journal of Psychiatry, 165*, 712-720.

Masi, G., Manfredi, A., Milone, A., Muratori, P., Polidori, L., Ruglioni, L., & Muratori, F. (2011). Predictors of non-response to psychosocial treatment in children and adolescents with disruptive behavior disorders. *Journal of Child and Adolescent Psychopharmacology, 21*, 51-55.

McGorry, P. D., McKenzie, D., Jackson, H. J., Waddell, F., & Curry, C. (2000). Can we improve the diagnostic efficiency and predictive power of prodromal symptoms for schizophrenia? *Schizophrenia Research, 42*(2), 91-100.

Meehl, P. E. (1962). Schizotaxia, schizotypy, schizophrenia. *American Psychologist, 17*, 827-838.

Moffitt, T. E., & Caspi, A. (2001). Childhood predictors differentiate life-course persistent and adolescent-limited pathways among males and females. *Development and Psychopathology, 13*, 355-375.

Monteaux, M. C., Biederman, J., Doyle, A. E., Mick, E., & Faraone, S. V. (2009). Genetic risk for conduct disorder symptom subtypes in an ADHD sample: Specificity to aggressive symptoms. *Journal of the American Academy of Child and Adolescenat Psychiatry, 48*(7), 757-764.

Moran, M. (2011). Brain, gene discoveries drive new concept of mental illness. *Psychiatric News, 46*(12), 29.

Muir, R. C. (1995). Transpersonal processes: A bridge between object relations and attachment theory in normal and psychopathological development. *British Journal of Medical Psychology, 68*, 243-257.

Pardini, D. A., & Fite, P. J. (2010). Symptoms of conduct disorder, oppositional defiant disorder, attention-deficit/hyperactivity disorder, and callous-unemotional traits as unique predictors of psychosocial maladjustment in boys: Advancing an evidence base for *DSM-V. Journal of the American Academy of Child and Adolescent Psychiatry, 49*, 1134-1144.

Pinto, A., Liebowitz, M. R., Foa, E. B., & Simpson, H. B. (2011). Obsessive compulsive personality disorder as a predictor of exposure and ritual prevention outcome for obsessive compulsive disorder. *Behavior Research and Therapy, 49*, 453-458.

Plomin, R., & Reade, R. (1991). Human behavioral genetics. *Annual Review of Psychology, 442*, 161-190.

Reeb-Sutherland, B. C., Helfinstein, S. M., Degnan, K. A., Pérez-Edgar, K., Henderson, H. A., Lissek, S., Chronis-Tuscano, A., Grillon, C., Pine, D. S., & Fox, N. A. (2009). Startle response in behaviorally inhibited adolescents with a lifetime occurrence of anxiety disorders. *Journal of the American Academy of Child and Adolescent Psychiatry, 48*(6), 610-617.

Robson, K. S. (1967). The role of eye to eye contact in maternal-infant attachment. *Journal of Child Psychology and Psychiatry, 8*, 13-25.

Robson, K. S. (1983). *The borderline child.* New York: McGraw Hill.

Rottman, B. M., Ahn, W. K., Sanioslow, C. A., & Kim, N. S. (2009). Can clinicians recognize *DSM-IV* personality disorders from Five-Factor Model descriptions of patient cases? *American Journal of Psychiatry, 166*, 427-433.

Schmideberg, M. (1959). Psychiatric treatment of offenders. *Mental Hygiene, 43*, 407-411.

Shedler, J. (2010). The efficacy of psychodynamic psychotherapy. *American Psychologist, 65*(2), 98-109.

Skinner, B. F. (1938). *The behavior of organisms.* New York: Appleton-Century.

Stone, M. H. (2012). Disorder in the domain of personality disorders. *Psychodynamic Psychiatry, 40*(1), 23-45.

Sutherland, J. D. (1980). The British object-relations theorists: Balint, Winnicott, Fairbairn, Guntrip. *Journal of the American Psychoanalytic Association, 28*, 829-860.

Taylor, S., Asmundson, G. J., & Jang, K. L. (2011). Etiology of obsessive-compulsive symptoms and obsessive-compulsive personality traits: Common genes, mostly different environments. *Depression and Anxiety.* [July 18, 2011, E-publication ahead of print]

Thomas, A., & Chess, S. (1977). *Temperament and development.* New York: Bruner-Mazel.

Vela, R., Gottlieb, H., & Gottlieb, R. (1983). Borderline syndromes in childhood: A critical review. In K. S. Robson (Ed.), *The borderline child* (pp. 31-48). New York: McGraw Hill.

Watson, J. B., & Raynor, R. (1920). Conditioned emotional reactions. *Journal of Experimental Psychology, 3*, 1-14.

How Clinicians Feel about Working with Spouses of the Chronically Ill

Douglas H. Ingram

Abstract: Clinicians who provide psychotherapy to spouses or partners of the chronically ill were solicited through listserves of psychodynamic and other organizations. The current report excluded those therapists working with spouses of dementia patients. Interviews were conducted with clinicians who responded. The interviews highlight the challenges commonly encountered by psychotherapeutic work with this cohort of therapy patients. A comparison is drawn that shows both overlap and distinctions between the experiences of those therapists engaging with spouses of chronically ill patients without a dementing process and those working with spouses of chronically ill patients who do suffer from a dementing process.

Several years ago, I began working in psychodynamic therapy with two men facing the same overwhelming stress.* They were referred separately and were unacquainted. Each man was successful in his life's work and each had an enduring lifelong marriage with children and grandchildren. Whatever other matters they were facing, they suffered a common life circumstance. The wife of each was suffering from dementia: the wife of one had Alzheimer's and the wife of the other had Parkinson's with severe impairment of motoric, affective, and cognitive functions.

I found professional fulfillment in offering a steadying presence for them when they were overcome with helplessness, fear, rage, guilt, and uncertainty. I felt keenly the poignancy of their circumstances. Discussions with colleagues proved helpful. Though I prescribed psychotropic medica-

tion (low-dose benzodiazepines), medication was decidedly beside the point.

I wondered whether other therapists working with caregivers of dementing spouses had experiences similar to mine. I posted an e-mail on numerous LISTSERVs soliciting clinicians who worked with persons who were caring for spouses or partners with dementia. I also solicited professional colleagues and recruited others who heard of this project by word-of-mouth. I found that some therapists reported occasional mild dissociative reactions in their sessions, not dissimilar from my own, and perhaps best described as awe and amazement. Some therapists experienced denial and the impulse to disengage, including the tendency to undervalue the spousal attachment bond, to prematurely recommend the hiring of aides, respites away from the ill spouse, and residential placement. I also found challenges to the therapist's value

---

*Names and details have been changed to protect patient privacy.

system, and, finally, difficulties these therapists encountered with the spousal caregiver's rage and potential violence (Ingram, 2014).

A commentary by Richard C. Friedman (2014) accompanied the report in publication. Friedman stated, "Most of the issues discussed in this article are not specific to patients with neurocognitive disorders... Therapists' empathic capacity toward caretakers of cancer or stroke patients for example, or those with a variety of terminal or chronic debilitating illnesses may be strained in a similar manner" (p. 305). While this is undeniable, I wondered about the extent of the overlap. How is the experience of therapists working with spouses of demented patients different from, or the same as, the experience of therapists working with spouses of the chronically ill but for whom dementia does not figure prominently? I decided to consider these questions using the same methodology as before (see Appendices A and B).

As in the prior exploration, my purpose in the current project was to use an open-ended psychodynamic orientation to interview therapists who have the experience I was seeking. The interviews were based on generally accepted psychodynamic paradigms of motivation and emphasized conscious and (inferred) unconscious attitudes, feelings, and beliefs of therapists. These were usually stimulated by unconsciously motivated behaviors of caregivers toward the ill spouse and/or were involved in coping with anxiety, anger, and/or depression mobilized by the caregiving situation. The interviews were not recorded and were 45–75 minutes' duration. I chose to exclude therapists treating spouses of those with primary psychiatric disorders, or those whose patients' spouses faced near-term mortality. My interest was in comparing the experiences of therapists working with caregivers whose spouses presented an ongoing chronic disorder where neither the immediacy of death nor psychiatric disorder would be complicating variables. As in

the prior exploration, this undertaking was focused on the experience of therapists, not the spousal caregivers or the ill patients.

I interviewed 12 clinicians who broadly met the project criteria. One was excluded because of excessive guardedness and refusal or inability to report meaningful subjective experiences of his work in therapy. Four were social workers, four were psychiatrists, two were Ph.D.-level psychologists, and one was a marriage and family counselor. Of the group, nine were psychodynamically trained. Several stated they were certified in psychoanalysis. Often the respondents had substantial professional experience with spouses of chronically ill persons. One respondent, a psychiatrist with extensive experience in independent-living and assisted-living facilities, reported on his work with numerous spouses of the chronically ill. Afflictions reported of ill spouses by the therapists interviewed included Huntington's disease, multiple sclerosis, Parkinson's disease, amyotrophic lateral sclerosis, chronic fatigue syndrome, Crohn's disease, chronic obstructive pulmonary disease, cancer, heart disease with congestive heart failure, and multiple traumatic injuries with disabling sequelae. Although several of these illnesses may progress toward dementia, the respondents recognized that we were excluding dementia in the ill spouse. To meet the criteria I had established, dementia must not yet have become evident. The level of impairment and disability needed be continuously present and figuring prominently in the life of the marriage. That these criteria were met was established in my interviews with the respondents.

My interviews were by telephone and were aimed at eliciting therapists' subjective experiences that emerged in their work with spousal caregiver patients. Follow-up discussions and correspondence were conducted to verify accuracy of reports and to ensure sufficient disguise in order to protect patient privacy. The reports that follow below were each approved for possible publication by the interviewees. All subjects gave verbal consent and approval through e-mail for interview material to be published and discussed.

An unexpected finding was that three therapists whom I personally contacted simply had not registered that one or more of their patients were partnered with a chronically ill person. Of the three, two agreed to be interviewed. One declined for unstated reasons. It appeared that the therapeutic engagement for these therapists was not so intently focused on the burdens of spousal caregiving as to warrant special recognition. By this I mean that they were aware of the chronic illness in an intellectual sense, but viewed it as not being of particular significance from an emotional perspective. They did not assign weight to it in assessing their patients' subjective experience. These two therapists acknowledged that they were more concerned with their patients' characterologic issues and regarded the stress of caring for a chronically ill spouse as simply another circumstance in which these issues were evident.

IMPACT OF THE THERAPISTS' PERSONAL EXPERIENCE ON THEIR WORK IN THERAPY WITH SPOUSES OF THE CHRONICALLY ILL

Although most respondents reported no motivation to provide therapy with spouses of the chronically ill, 5 of the 11 indicated how their experience with their own chronically ill family members affected their work. One therapist stated:

Report 1: My father had heart attacks every year from my age of 13 until he died when I was 21. As a consequence, I think I understand my patient's terror of her husband's illness. I push it away sometimes. I don't want that terror triggered in me. The specter of death hung over me as a girl—I was very affected and frightened. My father said, as he was

brought away on a gurney on one occasion, "You caused this!" He was right. I felt that I contributed to his illness—I would fight with him about things like coming home later at night than he demanded. I was rebellious and fought with him as teenagers will do with their parents. Maybe I was more rebellious than most. I called his doctor once and asked if I was making my father worse. The doctor agreed! Now, with my patient, I feel she contributes to her husband's illness insofar as she disappoints and angers him. When she tells me about upsetting him, I get angry (an internal state, only) at her lack of empathy. I guess that in this, I am identified with my father.

Another therapist also commented on how his personal history impacts his work with his patients:

Report 2: My mother was chronically depressed and hampered in her motherhood as a result. My wife has chronic back problems with psychological overlay. These experiences in my own life have attuned me to the psychological issues that often occur for a person who provides care to an ill spouse. It gives me a quicker sense of the dynamic operations in destructive codependent caregiving. I have experienced a sense of the profound tragedy in which one can spend much of one's life providing needless care for a mostly factitious illness. The hovering caregiver provides a necessary audience in these circumstances. Sometimes, a simple statement can work wonders: "You can get angry at her even though she is sick." That turns out for me to be the rewarding part of the work with the caregivers. I have two women and one man who are caregivers of non-demented, chronically ill spouses. I regard the work I do as situationally focused dynamic therapy. To try to ameliorate disordered caregiving can be a challenge. Sometimes, delightedly, it succeeds.

A third respondent joined in his patient's denial as a result of his personal experience:

Report 3: A patient came to see me because of anxiety and depressed mood triggered by his wife's condition. His wife's Parkinsonism was characterized by muscle rigidity and impairment in walking. I found myself less focused on his wife's condition than on his communication style which inexplicably concerned me. In the early phase of treatment, my patient often became excited about what seemed like minor bureaucratic side benefits of his wife's disability. I'd feel alienated from him at those times. I saw this enthusiasm as a manic defense against underlying depression. He would move about almost hyperactively while he talked, his hands flying as if to illustrate his words. I saw him every other week and he focused on successful activities they had shared. I was waiting around for him to talk about himself rather than about her management of her disability, but he preferred not to.

There was a personal component in my response to this patient. At the time, my wife's uncle had advanced Parkinson's. My patient's happy-go-lucky mannerisms put me off. They felt off-base. Through my wife's uncle's deterioration, I felt I could see what the future held. I saw the horror of my uncle's condition, and I had that in mind when I saw my patient. His apparent denial of what was likely to happen in the future was alienating for me. I found myself taking a parental posture in this, thinking—better that you don't see what's coming down the pike. In protecting him from the future, I joined him in his manic denial. Once I became aware of this countertransference I was able to appreciate the importance of his defenses. I was less reactive, more supportive, and my patient, in turn was less strident in repressing depressed feelings.

Another therapist, a former caregiver to a husband with Huntington's disease (HD) offered the following:

Report 4: I come from 25 years of police work. I have a different skin because of that professional history. It may be thicker than the average therapist. Nothing surprises me. Caregiving was and is exhaustive. My husband was ill for 17 years with HD. The last 7 years of his life were unbearable. I was a police officer, the parent of two young children, and my husband's caregiver. I had no time for self-care. I suffered from acute major depression, a result of caregiver burnout. I had depleted my internal resources. It took one year of antidepressant medication and psychotherapy to stabilize me. But even with that help there was still only slight relief. I was starved for self-care. I had a career-ending injury in 2005 that led to forced retirement as an officer from the police department. In retrospect, that injury and numerous surgeries plus recuperation gave me the gift of time with my husband in his final years. My husband died in February 2008. Because of HD, I am now a Marriage and Family Therapist and Certified Thanatologist. I run bereavement groups around the state of Connecticut and I am the Huntington's Disease Society of America-CT Affiliate Caregiver support group leader for four support groups within the state. I work with my HD support groups as a spouse/caregiver/widow/survivor who had a husband who died with HD. I see spouses and family members struggling with caregiving for their loved ones with HD in all stages. I see examples of destructive codependent caregiving in both HD support groups and some of my bereavement groups.

Another therapist, working with a man whose wife has Parkinson's disease reports that her own husband has had multiple sclerosis for 20 years, as well as cardiac problems:

Report 5: My husband's condition had gotten worse. He had not worked for the past decade. He walked with difficulty. We used a scooter or a wheelchair. As a result, I had quite a lot of empathy for my patient who was a caregiver to his chronically ill wife. It was a feeling of love and entrapment, both, he said. He was physically turned off to his wife and acknowledged fantasies about me and other women, and he felt guilty about it (my slip!—he didn't actually say that. My thing? I suppose so.). *Interviewer: Had you asked him if he feels guilty?*

I did not ask him—that might strike awfully close to home. This was an area that was not explored because—this situation, my treatment of him, hit closer to home than my usual work with patients. Earlier, I tried to reassure him that his fantasies about me and other women were ways of thinking about matters that would not come to pass, so the fantasies—because they would not be enacted—were very understandable and, in our therapy sessions, acceptable to disclose. He responded by missing his appointment the following week. He claimed illness. Also, he explained that fantasies were preludes to behavior. *Interviewer: For him they are rehearsals for performance. Imagine telling a performer that he is rehearsing for a performance that will never go on?!* We can regard my statement about fantasies as a way to reassure him—and to reassure me—that nothing will happen. I suppose this should be counted as a countertransference enactment.

HOW DO THERAPISTS COPE WITH THEIR REACTIONS IN WORKING WITH SPOUSAL CAREGIVERS?

Effective psychodynamic therapy relies in some measure on identification with the patient (Racker, 1968). In two reports (1 and 12, to be presented below), the therapist has an experience akin to that of the ill spouse. Regardless, the effective psychic metabolizing of matters that impinge on the therapist is necessary for therapy to proceed. We may ask, what are the adaptive defensive operations that enable therapists to maintain psychic stability in order to apply their skills? More specifically for the purposes of this exploration, what are the adaptive operations that are brought to bear by therapists in work with spouses of chronically ill, non-demented persons?

The following categories of adaptive operations are somewhat arbitrary.

Obsessional Defensive Operations

As defined here, obsessional defensive operations include the broad array of both pathological and healthy psychic means to engage and manage anxiety arising from threats that have their origins in both external reality and inner conflict. Obsessional operations may range from, say, reliance on thought with isolation of affect on the pathological end of the spectrum to mindfulness and deliberate self-analysis on the healthier end of the spectrum (cf. A. Freud, 1937; Salzman, 1968; Vaillant, 1992).

In the following, the therapist decides to turn to an explicit code, the Caregiver's Bill of Rights (Horne, 1985). In brief, this code affirms the right of the caregiver to care for oneself, seek help, experience difficult feelings such as anger, receive consideration from loved ones, and to appreciate one's own courage in the face of adversity.

Report 6: My patient's husband had Huntington's disease and she regarded herself as needing to help. If only she tried harder, she would succeed. I saw her as having a major anxiety disorder. She cancelled appointments with me. Sometimes, she frustrated me but I did like her a lot. Yet I was unable to get her to see that this disorder will not get better. I was a gentle confronter. My frustrations, which I felt with her, came under control. I gave her the Caregiver's Bill of Rights and this was a new concept for her. It helped her and it helped me. Gradually she began to see her husband's diagnosis more accurately and to better understand the chronicity and eventual outcome of this devastating illness. Though she continued to over-function, she appeared to understand that her efforts would not result in his improvement. She was increasingly able to self-care, spending more time doing what she enjoys and spending more time with her children and grandchildren.

Humor

Although humor may endorse defensive denial, humor may also serve the humanizing supportive engagement between patient and therapist, diminishing the immediacy and threat evoked in the therapist by the patient's situational difficulties.

> *Report 7:* I worked with a woman whose husband fell off a ladder and sustained severe head trauma and spinal injury. She blamed herself and struggled with the conflict of whether to leave him or stay. I was drawn into the depths of her conflict. I could not know what direction to support. She had run a business that supported the household and which she gave up to care for him. She became obsessively concerned that he would get an infection from caregivers. She could be very funny, mostly through self-deprecation. Sometimes, I joined her in laughter. Our use of humor did not especially lead to a loss of focus. Rather, it was often a way to encourage her continued self-exploration. I never initiated a humorous aside, but would react to hers spontaneously. I found that our shared humor advanced the therapeutic process. Eventually, she left her husband.

Projective Identification

In its broadest interpretation, projective identification refers to the therapist's intense experience of affective matter, which is primarily experienced by the patient who however is not aware of this. First described by the child psychoanalyst Melanie Klein (1946), projective identification refers to the infant's unconsciously externalizing to another person hostile internal objects with their associated affects, impulses, and cognitive content. These hostile objects had been internalized into the ego, but actually threaten the unity of the ego. Hence, they are projected outward and are no longer part of the infant's self-experience. Many clinicians have come to regard this process as occurring in people of all ages. When this defense mechanism does occur in therapy, a patient projects aspects of core feelings and conflicts into a therapist. The patient is not aware that this unconscious process is occurring. As illustrated in the clinical reports below, the therapist then experiences and is tempted to behave in a fashion similar to the conflictual object that the patient had internalized. Put differently, the therapist comes to identify with the projected part (Grotstein, 1994; Meissner, 1980; Ogden, 1979). The recognition by the therapist that this transpersonal process is occurring can lead to enhanced understanding of the patient. The effectiveness of therapeutic work may then be informed by forbearance, compassion, and interpretive effectiveness.

In the following instance, projective identification is recognized by the therapist but does not lead immediately to interpretive effectiveness:

> *Report 8:* I was working with a woman in her 50s. Her husband was diagnosed with MS a few years before. She felt completely responsible for her husband and I could not get her to take care of herself. She supported his denial. The husband had issues beyond the MS. One time, she fell and broke her knee cap. He was not willing to help her. She could not express or experience her anger. I felt anger in myself, interpreting it as a proxy for her anger that was repressed. I said, "That must make you angry." That proved of little value. She continued to deny feeling angry.

The following example also shows the capacity for the therapist to recognize projective identification, and likewise shows that doing so does not assure success in therapeutic work:

> *Report 9:* I will describe one of my least satisfying cases, that of a physician who in her compliance was quietly difficult. I saw her once weekly for about a

year. She came because her husband, a brilliant professor of mathematics, had developed a progressively debilitating neurological disease which was gradually rendering him physically disabled. Their life had become limited in all respects, and she felt guilty about her resentment of his dependency on her and the way it limited her living a full life. She expressed her distaste for his drooling and "eating in a way that looked disgusting." There were few ways he could help with all the tasks that were now on her shoulders, and she was violently angry about how little help there was from anyone in his family. She felt I wasn't helpful: I was just telling her what she already knew. I wondered if she felt competitive with me, resentful of what I appeared to have and needed to defeat me. It was never clear what she wanted from me. When she came, she had said she wanted to talk, but talking wasn't making her feel better. I believed that I was feeling what she was unable to feel—helpless and inadequate. I regarded this as a projective identification that I do not believe I identified for her clearly enough. It seemed impossible to bring it to a surface so that it could be explored. After a summer break, she didn't come back, saying therapy wasn't helping her.

The successful recognition of projective identification leads in the next example to the determined decision of the therapist to content himself with the role of bearing witness:

Report 10: My patient was skeptical that his wife had chronic fatigue syndrome. He regarded that diagnosis as buttressing her huge complaints about him and the world. He tended to regard her illness as a passive-aggressive adaptation. I experienced him as afraid of her, as weak and fearful, yet tenacious about the marriage. When I'd point out that perhaps he could stand up to her, he'd say, "You don't get it!" I was frustrated in my therapeutic ambition, a frustration in the countertransference that I believed paralleled his frustration with his wife. Like him, I felt defeated. I did ask him why he was

coming to therapy since my counsel was off target. He said that he would feel it a defeat if he left therapy, an attitude that also described why he would not leave his marriage.

It seemed to me that the best I could do, at least for now, was to bear witness to his suffering. Cynicism had become his adaptive attitude. Comments or therapeutic moves that assaulted this cynical attitude were threatening to him. My bearing witness served to provide an external auditor. By my willingness to continue as this man's therapist, I may be regarded as endorsing my patient's cynical worldview. Yet, there seemed little alternative and it did provide a level of stability for him.

When projective identification is adequately appreciated, the sense of mutual engagement is more patently evident. The experience of the therapist may parallel that of the patient. The identification is concordant with the self experience of the patient (Racker, 1968):

Report 11: He had come to accept his wife's problem and yet he was afraid that she would die and he would be left alone. He did love his wife. At times, he seemed to be in some denial about her illness. At those times, he tended not to talk about it. He tried to get her to try doing things. When he talked about it, I sometimes had this visceral feeling that part of him was "leaving"—suddenly he seemed so young and vulnerable. When I expressed this, he said, yes, that was how he felt. Mostly, at those times, I felt bad about his feeling helpless, and I also felt helpless. I think there was a parallel process there.

As in report 1 above, the therapist may identify with the ill spouse:

Report 12: In the course of treating a couple in marriage therapy, I held several individual sessions with the 50-year-old husband whose wife had been diagnosed with metastatic breast cancer. In the couple's sessions, she expressed ongoing concerns that her husband was not attentive or responsive to her feelings of anxiety and pessimism. The husband was a highly anxious, obsessional individual, perfectionistic—and with a harsh superego. With his wife he was in persistent denial and always explicitly positive, much like a football coach rallying his team. In response, she would feel unrecognized and unsupported. He loved her dearly and she knew it. I saw his defensive denial as a consequence of his own early history of abandonment and of his helplessness in the face of her diagnosis. I tried to help him see the defenses at work within him. Sometimes it became frustrating. His capacity for empathy was impaired by his fear of losing her. As a result, I could empathically engage with his wife more effectively than he could. I was aware that there may have been a competitive edge to it for me—an acting-in. And, I felt some toward him in my identification with her. Since his empathic engagement with her was impaired and mine was not, it was not surprising that I found myself thinking, "I could be a better partner to his wife."

Soon after, I discovered that I could put this realization of my own countertransference in the service of my work with him. I could better appreciate how his denial was functioning and empathically join with him to gain a realistic sense of just how ill she was.

My joining with him clearly enabled the patient to be more self-reflective about the essence of his defensive reactions to his wife. This was probably related to a lessening of his needing to unconsciously defend himself against my own unwitting communication of negative and competitive reactions.

Supervisory Assistance

Turning to a colleague or supervisor to help deal effectively with therapeutic challenges was the approach followed in a problem arising in an erotic transference and countertransference:

Report 13: I had been working with a vigorous elderly man whose wife had developed Parkinson's several years earlier. Incorporating magical thinking, he imagined his wife's condition to be psychological. He presented with neck pain that, in the absence of medical findings he believed to be related to unconscious material. He denied it had anything to do with his wife's condition. He was educated and successful in his professional life. When he first came to see me, he was emotionally very volatile. He cried and said, "What if I fell in love with you—I can see that happening?" I said that we'd talk about it. The erotic transference continued and entered into every session. He felt sexually very robust. Though I wondered if there were frontal lobe problems, I also knew his entire life was replete with sexualized issues involving women.

He and his wife had been married 50 years or more. He had had no sexual relations with her for 10 years. He masturbated sometimes and had a prostitute some months before his work began with me. He found his wife's body repellent. *Interviewer: How did his erotic transference affect you?* I was nonplussed and contacted a supervisor wanting help in containing the patient's sexual desires toward me yet doing it so as not to shame the patient. I contained it. At the same time, I found myself thinking a lot more than usual about what I would wear on the days of my sessions with him. I felt flattered. He was distinguished and successful. For me, his attraction to me was frankly seductive. I contained it successfully…I think.

HOW DO THERAPISTS FEEL ABOUT WORKING WITH SPOUSES OF THE NON-DEMENTED CHRONICALLY ILL?

In this exploration, I considered therapists' experiences in their work with patients whose spouses were afflicted with chronic illnesses that were neither psychiatric, neurocognitive, nor near-term fatal. An early finding during the selection process was the relative non-salience of the caregiving burdens in the experience of therapists' work with spousal caregivers. Therapists who were personally addressed by the author or whose relationship with the author led to review of their practice rolls with these questions in mind discovered that indeed they were working with patients married to chronically ill persons. This may reflect a denial or minimization of the impact of chronic illness that both the spousal caregiver and the therapist share.

This relative lack of salience is noted (report 3) by the clinician who found himself "waiting around for [my patient] to talk about himself rather than [his wife's] disability." Although his patient spoke incessantly about his wife's Parkinsonism, the locus of concern for the clinician is his patient's manic denial and his own willingness to support that denial as a consequence of the clinician's personal family experience with Parkinson's. Similarly, the clinician who recognized that his patient's cynicism was paramount (10) and whose therapeutic plan moved toward "bearing witness" regarded the matter as characterologic, not situational.

Focus on patient character structure rather than the painful circumstance of that patient's chronically ill spouse is likewise observed in reports 2 and 4. Both clinicians offer supportive help and attend to what the clinician of report 2 describes as "situationally focused dynamic therapy," but both are concerned about what they refer to as "destructive codependence." Codependency is a concept arising from within the self-help movement and understood in the self psychology literature as counterdependency. In the present context, the caregiver is understood as suffering from profound object hunger and relies desperately on the ill spouse to provide archaic self-selfobject needs (Cooper, 1992; Kohut, 1971). Mahr has applied the term "pathological caregiving" to this disordered pairing of ill spouse

and caregiver (2014, personal communication). The therapists of reports 2 and 4 address situational concerns in order to mitigate the expression of underlying character pathology. Of note is that these two clinicians appear to have occupied through many years of their lives the role of caregiver to chronically ill spouses. They expressed more strongly than others in the project a concern about what they refer to as destructive codependence.

The voluntary willingness of therapists to be interviewed, as in any similar methodology, raises the question, Why would they? What is salient about the project that a clinician would be prompted to participate? Of the 11 participants, five had personal experiences with chronically ill relatives. These experiences rendered their feelings with their patients more compelling. Of note is of the five, three clinicians arguably felt a more immediate compassion for their spousal caregiver patients (reports 3, 4, and 5). The therapy provided by the author of report 3 was shaped by his relative's deteriorating Parkinsonism. Marriage to a man with Huntington's disease and a caregiver, herself, shaped the life of the author of report 4 leading to professional work as a counselor to support groups. Likewise, the author of report 5 is the caregiver of a husband with multiple sclerosis.

However, for the therapist having experience as a caregiver to the chronically ill does not necessarily confer concordant identifications and associated compassionate regard for patients who are spousal caregivers. The author of report 1 states that her adolescent rebelliousness worsened her father's chronic cardiac condition leading in her report of the clinical relationship to feel angry with a patient who upsets the patient's ill husband. The author of report 2 had a depressed mother and a wife with back problems. He is keenly aware of "the profound tragedy" of needless caregiving.

Adaptive defensive operations are a ubiquitous constant of psychic operations. For the author of report 6, reliance on an external code, the Caregiver's Bill of Rights (Horne, 1985) provided authority beyond that conferred transferentially in the therapeutic relationship. Other reporters did not turn to an external code relying instead on the transference to provide the necessary authority to say, for example, "It is acceptable for you to feel anger, here." The communion provided by the enjoyment of shared humor was central to the clinician in her report 7. Recognition that projective identification was utilized as a defensive operation by the patient, that the therapist was a recipient of repressed and projected affect and associated cognition, proved helpful for the authors of reports 8, 9, and 10. The conscious experience of helplessness, experienced symmetrically between patient and therapist characterized the reported aspect of the work of the author in report 11.

As is likely the case with each patient who consults us, our own life experiences impinge significantly in our understanding and approach to our work. The recognition that this is inevitable, that neutrality is a problematic concept, has been a source of consternation and contention within psychoanalytic circles (Greenberg, 2001; Hoffer, 1985; Zachrisson, 2008). The impact of the therapist's past is evident in most of the reports. The therapists fully own that this is the case. The therapists who voluntarily participated had done so largely because its focus touched them. As a consequence, the lessons to be drawn are uncertain. As psychodynamic therapists, we bring who we are to the work we do. So, too, do the therapists who participated. Beyond that tired cliché, a commonality mostly endorsed through a review of the vignettes is the tendency among these therapists to regard their patients' characterological matters as deserving attention, the illness of the

spouse serving as a substrate or medium through which these characterological features are highlighted and become the object of therapeutic attention.

WORKING WITH SPOUSES OF DEMENTIA PATIENTS COMPARED WITH WORKING WITH SPOUSES OF CHRONICALLY ILL PATIENTS WITHOUT DEMENTIA

Those patients whose spouses suffer from dementia, regardless of the etiology of the dementia, share a specific commonality: the loss of the psychic integrity of a life partner. The loss is gradual and progressive in most instances. The therapist who accompanies the patient through the decline of the patient's partner likewise endures in concordant identifications with the patient an intensity of painful subjective experiences (Ingram, 2014). The therapist may be struck that the bond between his or her patient and dementing partner can be so profound that the therapist may experience mildly dissociative reactions or denial that the bond could possibly be as strong as it seems. The therapist, seeking to mitigate his or her own subjective distress, may prematurely recommend residential placement for the ill spouse, the introduction of a health care aide, and social outreach. In other words, unable to empathically tolerate the patient's struggle with the anguish of caring for the demented partner, the therapist too quickly engages in problem solving. Also, the therapist's personal values may be affronted by the well spouse's use of "white lies" or the quest for intimate personal and sexual relations outside the marital union. The most economical theoretical formulation for these difficulties is found in attachment theory. The threat to the bond of attachment occasioned by the dementing process can trigger a protest in the spousal caregiver so intense that it may threaten to become violent.

Where chronic illness occurs, and dementia is specifically excluded, the issues encountered by the spousal caregiver are far more varied than is found among spousal caregivers of demented partners. Similarly, the impact of these patients' caregiving burdens on the therapist is also more varied. The outcome in each instance of that vast array of chronic illnesses further impacts how that illness will be experienced by the ill spouse, the spousal caregiver (who is the patient in therapy), and the therapist. Is the patient on a downhill course leading to psychiatric and neurocognitive difficulties as in Huntington's disease and often multiple sclerosis? Is the course unlikely to be accompanied by significant cognitive decline as in diabetes, ALS, congestive heart failure, or COPD? Is mortality lurking as with metastatic cancer? Put differently, the heterogeneity entailed by non-dementing chronic illness is so much greater than that of a neurocognitive-based dementia that to compare the two groups is troublesome, comparing a basket of apples with a basket containing not only apples, but also oranges, pears, and grapes.

Briefly put, there are areas of overlap in the subjective experience of the two groups of therapists, as Friedman (2014) points out. However, therapists of spouses of the chronically ill non-demented are more likely to be directed toward characterologic issues exacerbated by situational stress. Therapists of the spouses of those afflicted with a dementing process are impacted far more by the circumstances arising from the threat to a primal attachment bond. Whereas counterdependency (so-called codependency) or pathological caregiving (Mahr, 2014, personal communication) is noted to be a finding by the therapists of the spouses of the chronically ill non-demented, this concern never arose among therapists of spouses in the dementia group. In general, the salience or penetrating immediacy of the therapists' experiences in the dementia group is far greater than that of the non-demented chronically ill.

CONCLUSION

The current exploration is an attempt to elaborate on Friedman's commentary to a prior report (Ingram, 2014). In that earlier exploration, I considered how therapists feel in their work with patients whose spouses were afflicted with neurocognitive disorders leading to progressive dementia. Friedman (2014) noted that the observations in that report may also apply at times to therapists of spouses of the non-demented chronically ill. This follow-up project sought to focus on the extent of overlap. I interviewed therapists of patients whose spouses are chronically ill, but where dementia is absent.

Both explorations depended on the willingness of therapists' responding to listserve solicitations to be interviewed about their work with partners of the chronically ill, each considering respectively partners with and without dementia. The methodology was the same for both. The bias created by the process of self-selection and the limited number of respondents need to be considered in evaluating the validity of both reports.

Nevertheless, these explorations suggest that in general the salience for therapists of patients whose spouses are suffering from dementia is qualitatively different from and greater than the salience for therapists of patients whose spouses suffer from chronic illness without dementia. Whereas therapists in the first group responded with considerable intensity to the attachment threat in their patients to dementia in their partners, the therapists of the second group showed greater interest in characterologic issues that render their patients susceptible to the burden of caregiving. In fact, for this latter group of therapists the burden of caregiving may seem to be yet another expression of life's difficulties that call on the susceptible individual to develop adaptive strategies. By contrast, the existential threat arising as a life partner fades through dementia is the primary factor that animates the therapist's experience in the first group.

To paraphrase a comment of one of the two men I described in the introduction of this article, pushing an otherwise healthy spouse in a wheelchair is altogether different from the sorrowful frustration of a spouse's vacant gaze and from the wracking grief of a loved one's diminishment. For the therapist, too, the treatment of the spouse who is pushing the wheelchair is likely to feel different from the treatment of the spouse whose partner is cognitively fading.

REFERENCES

Cooper, J. (1992). Chapter 8 codependency: A self-psychological perspective. *Progress in Self Psychology, 8,* 141-163.

Freud, A. (1937). *The ego and mechanisms of defense.* London: Hogarth.

Friedman, R. C. (2014). Commentary on how clinicians feel about working in therapy with spouses of dementia patients. *Psychodynamic Psychiatry, 42*(2), 305.

Greenberg, J. (2001). The analyst's participation: A new look. *Journal of the American Psychoanalytic Association, 49,* 359-381.

Grotstein, J. (1994). Projective identification and countertransference: A brief commentary on their relationship. *Contemporary Psychoanalysis, 30,* 578-592.

Ingram, D. (2014). How clinicians feel about working in therapy with spouses of dementia patients. *Psychodynamic Psychiatry, 42*(2), 287-304.

Hoffer, A. (1985). Toward a definition of psychoanalytic neutrality. *Journal of the American Psychoanalytic Association, 33,* 771-795.

Horne, J. (1985). *Caregiving: Helping an aged loved one.* AARP Books. For the Caregiver's Bill of Rights see http://www.caregivers.utah.gov/bill_of_rights.htm.

Klein, M. (1946). Notes on some schizoid mechanisms. *International Journal of Psychoanalysis, 27,* 99-110.

Kohut, H. (1971). *The analysis of the self.* New York: International Universities Press.

Meissner, W. (1980). A note on projective identification. *Journal of the American Psychoanalytic Association, 28,* 43-66.

Ogden, T. (1979). On projective identification. *International Journal of Psychoanalysis, 60,* 357-373.

Pausig, D. (2014). *An affair worth remembering with Huntington's disease, incurable love and intimacy during an incurable illness.* Retrieved from www.lulu.com/content/15318021.

Racker, H. (1968). *Transference and countertransference.* New York: International Universities Press.

Salzman, L. (1968). *The obsessive personality.* New York: Science House.

Vaillant, G. (1992). *Ego mechanisms of defense: A guide for clinicians and researchers.* Arlington, VA: American Psychiatric Publishing.

Zachrisson, A. (2008). Neutrality, tenderness and the analyst's subjectivity: Reflections on the analytic relationship. *Scandinavian Psychoanalytic Review, 31,* 86-94.

APPENDIX A

The following is the basic letter soliciting therapists for the project, modified to suit the LISTSERV where it would be appear:

Dear Colleague:

I am researching the experience of psychodynamically oriented clinicians who have worked in therapy with the husbands, wives, or longtime partners of those with significant chronic illness.

My interest is in learning about the experiences that working with "spousal caregivers" can produce for the therapist. What is the impact of the caregiving dimension in the patient's life for the therapist?

This inquiry is directed to therapists working with caregivers whose ill spouses do not suffer from a dementing process. The current research is a companion to a study that considered therapists' experiences with patients whose spouses suffer from neurocognitive impairment. The current study asks for therapists' experiences of patients whose spouses are chronically ill, but with disorders in which dementia is absent. This research is methodologically the same as in the prior study and is drawn from interviews with clinicians. Confidentiality is assured.

In this study, chronic illness is defined as a persistent, possibly progressive, non-psychiatric disorder accompanied by pain, personal, social, or occupational limitation of no less than 2 years' duration. Included is the full spectrum of medical disorders in which neurocognitive impairment is absent.

If you have worked with a patient whose spouse suffers from chronic illness without dementia, I would like to speak with you. Please contact me at [contact information]. Thank you.

APPENDIX B

The letter soliciting therapists was posted on the LISTSERVs of the following: American Institute for Psychoanalysis of the Karen Horney Institute and Center, American Psychoanalytic Association, New York Medical College Department of Psychiatry, American Academy of Psychoanalysis and Dynamic Psychiatry, Jack Drescher's LISTSERV, William Alanson White Institute, New York University Postdoctoral Program in Psychotherapy and Psychoanalysis, American College of Psychoanalysts, the Metropolitan Institute for Training in Psychoanalytic Psychotherapy, the New York Psychodynamic Psychiatry Study Group, The National MS Society, and the ALS Association.

The following is a partial list of those who helped make this project possible: Jean M. Baxendale, M.S.W.; Lynne Kwalwasser, Ph.D.; Patricia Brody, L.C.S.W.R.; Debbie Pausig, M.F.T., C.T., C.C.T.P.; John Stine, M.D., Nathan Horwitz, C.S.W., Jack Drescher, M.D., Richard Zuckerberg, Ph.D., Greg Mahr, M.D., and Robert Fenster, M.D.

The Effects of Intimate Partner Violence on Women and Child Survivors: An Attachment Perspective

Alytia A. Levendosky, Brittany Lannert, and Matthew Yalch

Abstract: Approximately 25% of women in the United States report having experienced intimate partner violence (IPV) in an adult relationship with a male partner. For affected women, IPV has been shown to increase the risk of psychopathology such as depression, anxiety, and symptoms of posttraumatic stress. Further, studies suggest that the risk of IPV (victimization or perpetration) may be carried intergenerationally, and children exposed to IPV are at a greater risk of both attachment insecurity and internalizing/externalizing problems. The authors employ an attachment perspective to describe how insecure/non-balanced working models of the relational self and others may be evoked by, elicit, or exacerbate maladaptive outcomes following experiences of IPV for mothers and their children. This article draws on both rich theory and empirical evidence in a discussion of attachment patterns in violent relationships, psychopathological outcomes for exposed women, disruptions in the caregiving relationship that may confer risk to children of exposed mothers, and the biological, social, and attachment risk factors for children exposed to IPV. A clinical case example is presented and discussed in the context of attachment theory.

Intimate partner violence (IPV) is a common phenomenon in the U.S., with a 25% lifetime prevalence rate reported by women (Tjaden & Thoennes, 2000). Although IPV may be also be perpetrated by women toward men, it is less frequent (prevalence rate at 7.6%), and less severe in its physical and psychological effects on the male victims (Tjaden & Thoennes, 2000). Thus, for the purposes of this article, we are defining IPV as violence perpetrated by a male against his female romantic partner. Women who are mothers of young children are at particularly high risk, as violence is much higher in younger men, declining with age after about 25 (Peters, Shackelford, & Buss, 2002). Numerous studies have documented that IPV is a traumatic event which negatively affects women and children's mental health. Specifically, women experiencing IPV report high rates of depression, anxiety, PTSD, as well as substance abuse, and suicide attempts (for reviews, see Golding, 1999; Taft, Watkins, Stafford, Street, & Monson, 2011). Children who live in homes with IPV (whether or not they directly witness the IPV) have higher rates of internalizing and externalizing behaviors, depressive symptoms, conduct problems, and attention problems, including clinical levels of disorders (for reviews see Evans, Davies, & DiLillo, 2008; Kitzmann, Gaylord, Holt, & Kenny, 2003; Wolfe, Crooks, Lee, McIntyre-Smith, & Jaffe, 2003). The current article reviews the research findings on the effects of intimate partner violence on women and children and, based primarily on the first author's prior empirical and theoretical work with colleagues (G. Anne Bogat, Alexander von Eye, William Davidson, and Alissa Huth-Bocks), proposes a model informed by attachment theory to explain the mechanisms through which intimate partner violence may affect children living in these homes and may inform our understanding of the mechanisms involved in the intergenerational transmission of intimate partner violence. In brief: IPV necessarily involves betrayal within an intimate, significant relationship. The model proposed in this article suggests that this betrayal serves to damage the internal working models of the woman survivor. When this woman has a child or is pregnant with a child, the development of her internal working models for herself (as mother) and for her child (as other) are thus negatively influenced by her damaged internal working models in her romantic relationship. This, in turn, influences her parenting behaviors, which then affects the child's development of internal working models of himself and other, and eventually his emotional and behavioral regulation. Thus, we see damage to internal working models passing across generations in the context of IPV, negatively influencing social and emotional functioning of women (both as individuals and as mothers) and children.

Prior to more fully describing the model of the mechanisms involved in the effects of IPV on women and children, it is important to explain the developmental model of normative social and emotional development as understood through the mother–child relationship. First, we will briefly describe the attachment perspective on the romantic relationship that yields the eventual mother–child relationship. In a romantic relationship, each romantic partner serves as an attachment figure for the other, mutually providing attachment and caregiving in times of stress (Bartholomew & Allison, 2006; Feeney, 2008). Moreover, attachment theorists propose that individuals' internal working models from childhood are projected onto their romantic relationships as adults (Hazan, Campa, & Gur-Yaish, 2006). These working models provide the template for how these individuals conduct themselves and relate to their partners within these relationships. The working model also includes expectations of these relationships that promote selective attention for expected relational patterns, which further reinforce these expectations (Collins & Read, 1994). As in childhood, these working models and expectations of caregiving within adult romantic attachments are particularly important under conditions of stress, during which the need for interpersonal security is intensified (Simpson & Rholes, 1994). Two dimensions of adult romantic attachment have been identified, attachment anxiety and attachment avoidance (Brennan, Wu, & Loev, 1998). The anxious and avoidant dimensions of attachment are orthogonal and specific attachment patterns are combinations of different levels of these dimensions. A combination of low levels of both dimensions is associated with the secure attachment functioning in adult romantic relationships. In contrast, insecure romantic attachments are defined in terms of excesses in anxiety or avoidance or both. Specifically, the preoccupied attachment pattern is associated with high anxiety and low avoidance, the dismissing-avoidant pattern is associated with low anxiety and high avoidance, and the fearful-avoidant pattern is associated with both high anxiety and high avoidance.

The mother–child relationship begins during pregnancy when the mother's caregiving system develops to maturity through the transactions between the physiological and psychological changes which accompany pregnancy (George & Solomon, 2008). The caregiving system is complementary to the attachment system. The attachment system evolved to obtain protection by ensuring proximity of the child to the caregiver and the caregiving system evolved to provide that protection and nurturance. These complementary systems thus ensure the survival of the offspring. Importantly, the psychological relationship that begins during pregnancy develops concurrently with the physiological relationship between mother and fetus which begins at conception and continues beyond birth, not only through breast-feeding, but also through maternal influences on physiological, emotional, and behavioral regulation. This physiological connection between mother and fetus is another way that IPV during pregnancy may affect the developing offspring, through prenatal programming of the HPA axis, (hypothalamic-pituitary-adrenal axis) a major stress response system in the body (Wadhwa, 2005). Thus, there are both psychological and physiological effects of prenatal IPV on the mother–child relationship and child outcomes.

During pregnancy, as part of the caregiving system, mothers develop maternal representations of the self and of the infant by reworking existing internal working models (George & Solomon, 2008; Leckman, Feldman, Swain, & Mayes, 2007; Stern, 1995; Winnicott, 1965). Maternal representations are a form of internal working model which include attributions, expectations, and affect related to the self as mother and the fetus as the mother's child. As defined by Zeanah and Benoit (1995), maternal representations may be categorized into balanced and non-balanced categories roughly analogous to secure and insecure attachment models, distinguished by the level of emotional and psychological engagement with the expected child, rigidity or flexibility of representations, and positive and negative beliefs about the expected child. Non-balanced representations may be further classified as *disengaged*, reflecting low psychological involvement and limited affective engagement, or *distorted*, reflecting significant disruptions in internal representations of reality, the self as caregiver, and the child. Given the dynamic nature of the process of maternal representation development, these models are sensitive to distortion due to external stressors, partic-

ularly during their initial formation in the late prenatal period (Slade & Cohen, 1996; Winnicott, 1960).

The period following birth was named by Winnicott as "primary maternal preoccupation" which described the mother and baby's symbiotic existence lasting approximately two to three months (1965). During these early months, the baby is fully dependent upon his caregivers to respond to all of his physical and psychological needs. The mother's ability to anticipate her infant's needs allows him to slowly begin to recognize the source of his own needs, for example, hunger, warmth, sleep. It is during the second half of the first year of life, while the baby continues to be physically dependent upon the caregivers, that the child's attachment relationships begin to form (Ainsworth, 1967; Bowlby, 1969, 1982). The infant's experience of the mother's responsiveness to him begins to form a cognitive and emotional template, called an internal working model/representation, of himself in relationship to significant others and significant others in relationship to himself (Bowlby, 1969, 1982).

The security of attachment, a behavioral manifestation of these internal working models, can be measured using the Strange Situation procedure. Children's behaviors in this 21-minute paradigm, in which the child is alternately with the mother, a stranger (experimenter), and by himself, are categorized into secure or one of three types of insecure attachment classifications— avoidant, ambivalent, and disorganized. The series of episodes is considered mildly to moderately stressful for the young child and, thus, induces particular attachment behaviors, such as crying, clinging, and withdrawal. In a low-risk population, about 65% of infants are classified as secure, 20–25% as avoidant, and 10–15% as ambivalent and less than 1% are disorganized.

A securely attached infant is upset by his mother's departure, but is quickly and easily comforted by her return and returns to exploratory behavior (Slade & Aber, 1992).

His mother is consistently responsive and sensitive to his needs, so that he feels safe in her presence and distressed by her absence. An avoidantly attached infant does not appear upset by his mother's departure and ignores her upon her return. He maintains exploratory behavior with or without the presence of his mother. He has adjusted to a mother who is consistently unresponsive to his needs and so he does not turn to her in conditions of stress, but rather relies on himself. The ambivalently attached child is quite distressed by his mother's departure, but is not easily soothed upon her return; instead, he clings to her, fussing, and will not return to exploratory behavior. The mother of an ambivalently attached child is inconsistent in her responsiveness and sensitivity to her child's needs—sometimes she responds quickly and at other times does not. This child fears the mother's departure and is not easily soothed upon her return because he cannot count on his mother's responsiveness to him, although he hopes for it because sometimes she is.

Finally, the disorganized child shows traumatized behaviors in his mother's departure and return in the Strange Situation—such as freezing, fear, disorientation, and switching between running to her and running away from her (Main & Solomon, 1990). This child's mother has typically been traumatized herself and so often behaves in either frightened or frightening ways with him (Main & Hesse, 1990). This child has not developed a consistent strategy to handle stress and separation in the context of relationships and thus is most likely at risk. The coexistence of a traumatized mother and an insecurely or disorganized attached infant leads the mother–infant dyad to have reduced flexibility in responding to challenges because the infant does not have a secure base to which to return in stressful experiences and has to learn to self-regulate without the typical scaffolding provided by the caregiver. This situation is commonly seen in families with IPV, as will be shown below.

During a traumatic experience, such as IPV, the attachment security system is evoked and the victim (i.e., woman/mother) of the trauma seeks protection from further trauma. However, since IPV inherently involves betrayal of trust within an intimate relationship, the woman finds herself in a psychological "double bind." Her attachment figure is the same as the perpetrator of the trauma. This is similar to the position of abused children. For a woman abused as a child, this betrayal in her adult intimate relationship reifies what she already "knows" about intimate relationships—they hurt. Her damaged internal working models of self and others are reinforced by the adult romantic relationship. For the woman who was not abused as a child, who has healthy internal working models, she begins to question her views of what to expect in intimate relationships. If she stays for long enough, her internal working models of adult intimate relationships will be altered to include a view of herself as victim and the other as perpetrator. Thus, the romantic relationship, rather than serving as a secure attachment system for the two partners, involves the projection and projective identifications of damaged working models in both partners. The damaged internal working models (whether due only to current or to both current and past trauma) leave the woman at higher risk for psychopathology, particularly under conditions of stress, such as ongoing IPV. Common outcomes for women include depression, PTSD, and anxiety disorders (e.g., Dutton et al., 2006; Koss, Bailey, Yuan, Herrara, & Lichter, 2003; Pico-Alfonso et al., 2006; Taft, Resnick, Watkins, & Panuzio, 2009). Complex PTSD as conceptualized by Herman (1992) has suggested that the combination of current and past chronic interpersonal trauma (most commonly child abuse and intimate partner violence) leaves women vulnerable for damage across a wide range of domains of functioning, including psychopathology and personality changes.

In the context of a relationship characterized by intimate partner violence, many women become pregnant and raise children. The first author's prior work (with previously mentioned colleagues) has demonstrated that the woman's caregiving representations, as characterized by maternal internal working models developed during the second trimester of pregnancy, are damaged by the experience of intimate partner violence during the pregnancy (Huth-Bocks, Levendosky, Bogat, & von Eye, 2004; Huth-Bocks, Levendosky, Theran, & Bogat, 2004). Thus, a mechanism for the intergenerational transmission of violence is proposed. Intimate partner violence is conceptualized not only as an assault on the woman, but on the caregiving system as a whole. Due to the violence, the mother becomes fearful and overwhelmed and is likely to thus respond to her infant's distress with either projective identification, where the infant is perceived to be helpless and vulnerable like herself, or with projection, in which the infant is perceived to be like the abuser—aggressive and hostile. These psychological distortions lead to parenting behaviors which either lack sensitivity or are inconsistent in responsiveness. This parenting behavior with the developing infant then sets in motion the development of insecure or disorganized attachment in the child and so the cycle of violence is likely to continue.

Insecure and disorganized attachment, in combination with witnessing trauma (i.e., intimate partner violence), puts the developing child at risk for a wide variety of psychopathologies, including depression, anxiety, PTSD, and aggressive behaviors (e.g., Graham-Bermann, Gruber, Howell, & Girz, 2009; Holt, Buckley, & Whelan, 2008; Levendosky, Bogat, & Martinez-Torteya, in press). This is perhaps best conceptualized by developmental trauma disorder which conceptualizes the damage seen in children experiencing chronic trauma in a wide variety of domains, for example, affective, social, behavioral, and biological, as all being related to the trauma, as opposed to discrete disorders (van der Kolk, 2005). In addition, relational trauma is seen in young children whose mothers are exposed to trauma and the infants and toddlers experience the mother's emotional dysregulation as she is unable to help them learn to self-regulate (Dayton, Bogat, & Levendosky, 2012; Levendosky, Leahy, Bogat, Davidson, & von Eye, 2006). Finally, children growing up in homes with IPV are at higher risk of being involved as either perpetrators or victims in violent intimate relationships.

This article reviews the empirical literature from an attachment perspective on the effects of IPV on women and children. We begin with the romantic relationship and then move to the parenting relationship, focusing initially on the intergenerational transmission of internal working models and concluding with the empirical findings about children's developmental outcomes. Findings from the empirical literature are interpreted in the context of attachment theory.

ATTACHMENT PROCESSES AND ABUSIVE INTIMATE RELATIONSHIPS

At its most readily observable level, IPV occurs within and is a manifestation of the romantic relationship shared by two adults. Accordingly, IPV has a number of ramifications for dynamics of the romantic attachment. Specifically, IPV creates a double-pronged assault on this relationship, both introducing stress to the attachment bond and compromising the role of the person within this bond who provides security to such stresses (i.e., the other, abusive, partner). The experience of a violent romantic partner places women in a role of helpless passivity, similar to that of an abused child, in which she feels like a victim and envisions her male partner as the powerful perpetrator. For the woman who has experienced IPV, her concept of herself in relation to the abusive partner has implications for the attachment bond with this partner. However, attachment within romantic relationships necessarily involves two people, and the quality of that attachment is thought to be the result of the individual contributions of each participant in the relationship (Collins, Guichard, Ford, & Feeney, 2006).

In the case of the violent relationship, the internal working models of both partners are, or may eventually become, damaged (Zosky, 2003). This damage may take a variety of forms and manifest itself in a variety of ways. One example is the damaged working models of the abusive male partner. His own working model may include a view of himself as a victimized, abused child (and, indeed, abuse experienced as a child predicts male perpetration of IPV as an adult; Gómez, 2011). As Zosky (2003) suggests, the abusive man splits this sense of victimization away from himself and projects it onto his partner. In turn, as he abuses his partner, he is also harming himself, thus re-enacting the abuse of his childhood. Regardless of her early life abuse history, a woman may identify with this projection, taking on not only the functional role of the abused child, but also the psychological identity of this child. The perpetrator of IPV may also incorporate into his working model of romantic relations the role of the violent male partner, which he internalized following his witnessing of IPV between his mother and father as a child. In this case, the abuse of a partner would take the form of dysfunctional means of conflict resolution transmitted intergenerationally by imitation rather than by projection, although the two are not mutually exclusive.

The woman in the IPV relationship will also suffer damage to her internal working models. Many of the women in IPV relationships have experienced physical, psychological, or sexual abuse as children (DiLillo, Giuffre, Tremblay, & Peterson, 2001). In the woman who has experienced child abuse at the hands of her parents, an expectation may already exist that she is a victim who will inevitably receive abuse. In such cases, the experience of IPV may confirm the expectations of these women's internal working models. A woman who was abused as a child may quickly fall into this role again in a relationship with a violent man. She may also project her internalized representation of the abusive parent onto her male partner, a role with which he readily identifies in his perpetration of further abuse directed toward her.

However, some women in IPV relationships in adulthood are experiencing abuse for the first time. As Herman (1992) suggests, the accumulation of the sustained abuse of IPV over time may result in an alteration of the internal working model of romantic relationships for the woman who has experienced IPV, modifying this model to include herself as victim and her partner as abuser, even without previous history of child abuse. Thus, for a woman without a history of child abuse, this projective identification may occur such that the role of victim is projected onto her by her violent male partner which she, in turn, internalizes. With the violent relationship dynamic established, the behaviors of IPV can be understood in terms of their function.

In the context of attachment theory, the behaviors that constitute IPV are further conceptualized as extreme and maladaptive forms of behavior used in order to regulate proximity with the caregiver (Bartholomew & Allison, 2006; Bowlby, 1984; Mayseless, 1991). Further, these behaviors are manifestations of attachment insecurity. Both physical and psychological violence toward women are more common among men with insecure attachments than among men with secure attachments (Dutton, Saunders, Starzomski, & Bartholomew, 1994; Henderson, Bartholomew, Trinke, & Kwong, 2005). A number of studies also indicate that violent male partners exhibit less adaptive and more aggressive behaviors toward their romantic partners than do nonviolent men, who exhibit more secure attachment behavior (Babcock, Jacobson, Gottman, & Yerington, 2000; Bookwala & Zdaniuk, 1998; Holtzworth-Monroe, Stuart, & Hutchinson, 1997; Kesner & McKenry, 1998; Mahalik, Aldarondo, Gilbert-Gokhale, & Shore, 2005; Tweed & Dutton, 1998).

More specifically, in their qualitative study on the behaviors of partners with varying romantic attachment styles, Allison and colleagues (Allison, Bartholomew, Mayseless, & Dutton, 2008) characterized the violence within romantic dyads as insecure attachment behaviors aimed either at pursuing one's partner or distancing oneself from him or her. These two aims can be classified as reactions to disruptions in one or both of two dimensions of attachment (anxiety and avoidance). Using these dimensions of attachment, one may better understand the violent behavior exhibited by men within romantic relationships.

Attachment anxiety is associated with a feeling that the caregiver is or will be unavailable to provide security for the recipient of care. Extreme feelings of attachment anxiety (i.e., a pervasive feeling that one will be abandoned by one's caregiver) can manifest as anger in the form of what Bowlby (1988) called protest behavior, or angry behavior aimed at preventing or curtailing abandonment. This is reflected in a number of studies suggesting that attachment anxiety among men is associated with more aggression toward female partners (Bookwala, 2002; Bookwala & Zdaniuk, 1998; Kesner & McKenry, 1998). More specifically, anxiety over abandonment is associated with men's utilization of violence behaviors with their partners (Holtzworth-Munroe et al., 1997; Roberts & Noller, 1998), further indicating that IPV perpetrated by men may have the goal of making their female partners stay with them. This violent protest behavior is particularly likely if the male partner has not only high attachment anxiety, but also has an angry temperament (Follingstad, Bradley, Helff, & Laughlin, 2002).

A male's violent behavior toward a female partner can also be associated with

efforts to psychologically distance himself from her (i.e., attachment avoidance). Silverman (2011) explains that this avoidant distancing may serve a dual purpose, protecting the male from potential abuses at the hands of his intimate caregiver, as well as regulating the fear, anger, and other emotions he experiences when engaged in an intimate caregiving relationship. These emotions are not only aversive, but also overstimulating for him. Violence stemming from attachment avoidance may manifest itself in a different way. Gormley (2005), for example, suggests that there is a difference between "burning hot" motivations for violent behavior within romantic relationships (e.g., reacting spontaneously to abandonment) and "burning cold," which is more associated with grudge-holding. This latter form may be more associated with attachment avoidance. Attachment avoidance among men is associated with psychological abuse of female partners (Lafontaine & Lussier, 2005), specifically under conditions of high stress (Gormley & Lopez, 2010). Attachment avoidance is also associated with increases in coercive sexual behavior within romantic relationships (Smallbone & Dadds, 2001), which can also result in a psychological distancing between the male and female partners in the relationship.

Although preoccupied attachment (high anxiety, low avoidance) is the adult pattern of attachment most closely linked with IPV perpetration among men (Henderson et al., 2005), IPV may also be a function of a mismatch in the attachment style of the male perpetrator and that of the female partner. For example, a male with high attachment anxiety may perpetrate physical violence against his partner in response to her exhibiting what he perceives as dismissing behaviors. In contrast, another male with a dismissing attachment style might psychologically and sexually abuse his partner following her own anxiety-related protest behaviors. There is some evidence suggesting that this may be the case. Doumas and colleagues (Doumas, Pearson, Elgin, & McKinley, 2008), for example, found that not only did attachment anxiety on the part of the female partner predict male-perpetrated violence, but so did the interaction between female attachment anxiety and male attachment avoidance. Similarly, Bookwala (2002) found that rating oneself as fearfully (i.e., anxiously) attached and one's partner as preoccupied was predictive of more reports of IPV. In sum, research suggests that IPV influences on the dynamics of romantic relationship on the level of internal working models. The influence of IPV is also experienced at the level of the individual, for example, in the effects on women's mental health.

PSYCHOLOGICAL SEQUELAE OF IPV WITHIN AN ATTACHMENT FRAMEWORK

Damage to the internal working models of women who have experienced IPV not only leaves these working models susceptible to further damage within romantic relationships, but also has devastating effects on women's individual psychological functioning in the form of mental health symptoms (Golding, 1999; Taft, Watkins, Stafford, Street, & Monson, 2011). IPV also involves the betrayal of trust within an intimate interpersonal relationship, which is associated with more severe forms of psychological symptoms (Freyd, 1996). IPV is also often chronic and repetitive (Baum, O'Keefe, & Davidson, 1990; Woods & Campbell, 1993), characteristics that Herman (1992) suggests are associated with more severe psychopathological symptoms (e.g., mood dysregulation, cognitive disruption, and physiological hyperarousal) than more time-limited forms of trauma.

The attachment system is activated by the experience of stress, during which time the attached person returns to the secure base of their caregiver for comfort and security (Bowlby, 1969). Within the context of the ro-

mantic relationship, the woman's partner is viewed as this secure base to which she can return at times of insecurity. If the caregiver within this relationship is abusive, then not only is a women endangered, but the secure base to which she would return for protection from this danger is also absent. This may lead to an amplification of the effects of other life stressors for the woman who has experienced IPV and the mental health symptoms that are often associated with them. This leaves women who have experienced IPV vulnerable to a number of psychological problems. Research suggests that women who have experienced IPV show more anxious, depressive, and posttraumatic symptoms than women without history of abuse (Pico-Alfonso et al., 2006).

Anxiety plays a crucial role in the psychological experience of the woman who has experienced IPV. Her own internal working model, damaged from the abuse within her romantic relationship, will almost inevitably contain an element of anxiety. Depending on the attachment style of her partner, attachment anxiety is also likely to be projected onto her and she may, in turn, identify with this anxiety. It follows from this that women who have experienced IPV are at increased risk of exhibiting symptoms of anxiety. Indeed, IPV is associated with high levels of state anxiety among women who experience it (Mertin & Mohr, 2000; Pico-Alfonso et al., 2006). Women who have experienced IPV also exhibit higher levels of phobic anxiety (Dorahy, Lewis, & Wolfe, 2007) and there is evidence that among women residing in a shelter that women who have experienced IPV exhibit diagnostic rates of phobias over eight times the rate of the general U.S. population (Helfrich, Fujiura, & Rutkowski-Kmitta, 2008). Generalized anxiety disorder and obsessive compulsive disorder also have high incidence rates among women who have experienced IPV (Ehrensaft, Moffitt, & Caspi, 2006; Gleason, 1993).

Like anxiety, mood disturbance has a close association with attachment insecurity. Bowlby (1982) proposed that depression was a common sequelae following either the inability to form a secure attachment or upon the loss of a previously established attachment. Women exposed to IPV experience both of these preconditions. For women whose internal working models entail an expectation for a relationship with a loving and nurturant partner, there is a sense of loss when this expectation is replaced with the reality of an abusive partner. For women both with and without histories of abuse, there is an inability to form a secure attachment with the violent male partner. As with symptoms of anxiety, it is no surprise that women who have experienced IPV exhibit high levels of depressive symptoms. Depressive symptoms are some of the most prevalent mental health problems reported by women who have experienced IPV (Bean & Möller, 2002). Some studies suggest that over a third of women who have experienced IPV meet diagnostic criteria for major depressive disorder (Nixon, Resick, & Nishith, 2004). Greater frequency, duration, and severity of violence experienced (including psychological and sexual abuse along with the physical violence) is associated with more depressive symptoms (Bogat, Levendosky, DeJonghe, Davidson, & von Eye, 2004; Bogat, Levendosky, Theran, von Eye, & Davidson, 2003; Kernic, Holt, Stoner, Wolf, & Rivara, 2003). Additionally, the more severe the violence, the more severe the depressive symptoms the women experienced (Taft, Vogt, Mechanic, & Resick, 2007).

Depression has effects not only on the individual, but also on that individual's relationship with others, through access to social support networks and employing social skills when interfacing with these networks (Joiner & Timmons, 2010). The interpersonal ramifications of depression can be conceptualized as extensions of the damage to the woman's internal working models of self and others. Research suggests that women who have experienced IPV report lower levels of social support and satisfac-

tion than women who have not (Thompson et al. 2000). One reason for this is that the male partners of women who experienced IPV often directly attempt to disrupt the social support networks of their female partners (Walker, 1979). This disruption serves to maintain the woman's depressive symptoms, as she does not have access to her social support which could help buffer the psychological effects of IPV (Beeble, Bybee, Sullivan, & Adams, 2009; Levendosky et al., 2004; Trotter, Bogat, & Levendosky, 2004).

IPV is not only stressful; it is traumatic. Within the framework of attachment theory, the traumatic nature of IPV can be conceptualized as having two origins. First, there is dissonance between the comfort, love, and security expected and desired in the romantic attachment bond and what is experienced within the violent romantic relationship. This dissonance itself results in a clash between expectation and reality, which can result in psychological trauma (Janoff-Bulman, 1992). This dissonance is especially pronounced among women whose internal working models of intimate relationships have not been damaged by prior abuse (e.g., in childhood). However, women whose internal working models were already damaged by earlier childhood abuse or other trauma are at an even greater risk of Posttraumatic Stress Disorder (PTSD) as a result of their previous traumatic experience. In these cases, IPV exacerbates and compounds the effects of the woman's prior trauma. Second, regardless of the working models women may have regarding the romantic attachment relationship, IPV inherently denies psychological and emotional union with the other person, which also further exerts traumatic psychological effects on the woman who has experienced IPV.

The trauma inherent to the experience of IPV is reflected in high levels of PTSD and PTSD symptoms among women experiencing IPV (Sharhabani-Arzy, Amir, Kotler, & Liran, 2003). Recency and severity of the most recent abusive event is associated with severity of PTSD symptomatology

(Astin, Lawrence, & Foy, 1993). This is especially the case with psychological forms of IPV, which research suggests exert a stronger influence on the development of PTSD symptoms among women who have experienced IPV than physical or sexual forms of IPV (Norwood & Murphy, 2011). Even among women who have experienced other forms of interpersonal trauma (e.g., child physical or sexual abuse), IPV provides a unique contribution to PTSD symptomatology (Becker, Stuewig, & McCloskey, 2010). For example, a study by Griffing and colleagues (2006) indicates that IPV exposure increments the effects of child sexual abuse in the prediction of hyperarousal symptoms and, among women with histories of child abuse (sexual or physical), is the only significant predictor of avoidance symptoms. Moreover, research suggests that women who have experienced IPV and who develop PTSD exhibit increased sensitivity to anxiety, thus rendering them more vulnerable to future mental health problems (Lang, Kennedy, & Stein, 2002). Attachment anxiety and dependency within the context of attachment were also vulnerability factors for PTSD in the presence of IPV, although PTSD symptoms were not associated with increased exposure to IPV (Sonis, 2007).

IPV exerts a number of pernicious psychological effects on women exposed to it, ranging from PTSD to anxiety to depression. However, there are additional ramifications of IPV when the woman who experiences it is a mother because of its effects on her parenting and the child's development. Thus, damage from IPV can be transmitted across generations.

THE INTERGENERATIONAL TRANSMISSION OF IPV

In general, studies examining the occurrence of intimate partner violence across generations have found an association, generally weak to moderate, between growing up in a home in which IPV occurs and experiencing IPV as an adult (Stith et al., 2000). The majority of studies examining the intergenerational transmission of IPV have focused on the effects of directly or indirectly witnessing violence as a child or adolescent on later adult experiences of intimate partner violence (Black, Oberlander, Lewis, Knight, Zolotor, Litrownik et al., 2009; Cannon, Bonomi, Anderson, & Rivara, 2009; Kerley, Xu, Sirisunyaluck, & Alley, 2010; Renner & Slack, 2006; Smith, Ireland, Park, Elwyn, & Thornberry, 2011). These studies have more commonly focused on the transmission of perpetration rather than the transmission of victimization risk (e.g., Cui, Durtschi, Donnellan, Lorenz, & Conger, 2010), and have most frequently examined the relationship between direct exposure to parental violence as reported by individuals and their adult experiences of perpetration or victimization (e.g., Black et al., 2009; Cannon et al., 2009). Studies assessing intergenerational transmission of risk have often adopted a social learning theory approach to explaining these phenomena, proposing that observational learning mechanisms account for the majority of variation in adult outcomes (Kerley et al., 2010).

However, there is also evidence that children of women experiencing intimate partner violence may acquire an increased risk of perpetration and victimization not only through direct observation of violence, but also through dynamic processes of interaction with exposed caregivers (Levendosky et al., 2006; Osofsky, 2003; Renner & Slack, 2006). In brief, children raised in a home in which IPV occurs may be understood as experiencing its effects through a variety of pathways, including direct exposure, impairments in caregiver mental health and parenting, and the internalization of overtly and covertly expressed maternal representations. Children may become vulnerable to experiencing IPV later in life due to the disorganizing effects that IPV exerts on maternal caregiving functions of attachment representations and parenting behaviors

(Levendosky et al., 2006; Lyons-Ruth, Yellin, Melnick, & Atwood, 2005), which subsequently disrupt the child's earliest systems of attachment and internal representations of self and others (Huth-Bocks, Levendosky, Bogat, & von Eye, 2004; Huth-Bocks, Levendosky, Theran, & Bogat, 2004). In particular, the use of defense mechanisms such as projection and projective identification may disrupt attachment processes through alterations in parent–child interactions, and these projections may further become internalized and enacted in adulthood.

One of the pathways by which IPV impacts early psychological functioning is through its disruptive effects on the maternal caregiving system and its reciprocal processes of infant attachment (Huth-Bocks, Levendosky, Bogat, & von Eye, 2004; Huth-Bocks, Levendosky, Theran, & Bogat, 2004; Solomon & George, 1996). The adult caregiving system is comprised of motivational strategies of infant care that are guided by internalized representations of the self as caregiver and of the infant (Solomon & George, 1996; Zeanah & Benoit, 1995). These strategies are themselves guided by the mother's own history of attachment and early caregiver interactions (Crandell, Fitzgerald, & Whipple, 1997; Slade & Cohen, 1996; Winnicott, 1960), such that the mother enacts internalized representations of self-other interactions, and this enactment in parenting behaviors shapes the development of the infant's internalized representations and attachment style (Zeanah, Benoit, Hirshberg, Barton, & Regan, 1994). Given that attachment insecurity is associated with involvement in violent intimate relationships in adulthood (Allison et al., 2008; Babcock et al., 2000), the disruptive effects of IPV on maternal caregiving representations and concomitant distortions in the infant's working attachment models may serve as a mechanism through which experiences of intimate partner violence are transmitted across generations. Further, as attachment styles may change within the context of a violent relationship, changes in

the early attachment relationship are likely to parallel the processes of change in adult relationships.

Qualitative examination of interviews with mothers experiencing IPV illustrates the distorting impact of maternal ego defenses on caregiving representations (for examples of narratives, see Huth-Bocks, Levendosky, Theran, & Bogat, 2004). Mothers may use neurotic defenses such as dissociation, withdrawal, and isolation to distance themselves from potentially painful emotional experiences of evaluating relationships, and thus disengage from psychological connection with their child. The narratives of disengaged women are marked by lack of involvement with the child, vagueness, and/or lack of integration of ideas. Mothers experiencing IPV may also engage in more immature defense mechanisms such as idealization, in which they project excessive positive qualities (e.g., self-reliance) on the self or the child. In some cases, more pathological defense mechanisms such as delusional projection, distortion, and splitting may be employed in the development of maternal representations, resulting in significant distortions to internal narratives of self and other (Zeanah & Benoit, 1995). Maternal representations whose narratives reflect more immature and pathological defenses, such as projection and splitting, are more likely to be classified as distorted.

Projection and projective identification may play key roles in shaping maternal representations of the infant and infant attachment, given the nature of intimate partner violence as an interpersonal stressor in the context of intimate relationships. Mothers in IPV relationships may find themselves unable to cope with powerful feelings of shame, helplessness, or fear, and so may project these unacceptable feelings onto their children. In doing so, they may perceive their children as exceedingly helpless and unable to cope. Conversely, they may project internal models of intimate relationships—in which the other is abusive—onto this new caregiving relationship, and so be more likely to perceive their children as aggressive, hostile, or inclined to hurt or reject them. This use of projection allows abused mothers to defend against threatening and inaccessible thoughts, feelings, or attributes while engaged in interactions with their children. For example, a mother who is unable to access her own feelings of warmth and nurturance may project the caretaking role onto her child, while a mother who rejects or is unable to access her own feelings of rage at the situation may project overly assertive qualities onto her child and encourage or overlook aggressive behavior.

These defensive strategies, and concurrent disruptions to maternal representations, have implications for parenting behaviors (Dayton et al., 2010; George & Solomon, 2008; Lyons-Ruth et al., 2005; Renner, 2009). How the maternal defenses of projection and projective identification affect parenting has been less studied, but is suggested by a theoretical understanding of ego defense functioning. In general, these defenses seem likely to shape maternal representations, which have been shown to predict later parenting behaviors and child attachment (Dayton et al., 2010; Huth-Bocks, Levendosky, Bogat, & von Eye, 2004). The impact of IPV on child attachment is explored more fully below. Mothers who perceive themselves as helpless and unable to protect or provide for her children, particularly those who experienced early attachment disruptions themselves, may withdraw from the caregiving relationship and abdicate parenting duties, resulting in emotional and potentially physical neglect (George & Solomon, 2008). Conversely, an extreme case of projective identification may lead a mother to enact the belief that her child is not capable of self-care, asserting appropriate boundaries, or engaging in healthy relationships, and these beliefs may become internalized by the child in such a way as to promote the development of avoidant and fearful patterns of interaction

with the world. In cases in which mothers project aggressive qualities of the abuser (or unacceptable feelings of rage and aggression within the self) onto their children, they may overtly or covertly reject the child, responding with hostility or limited affect to the child's efforts to elicit caregiving behaviors (Lyons-Ruth et al., 2005). This hostility may, in some cases, reach the level of abuse. Intimate partner violence in the first six months of life has been shown to predict an increased risk of child maltreatment in early childhood (McGuigan & Pratt, 2001), and research indicates that approximately 30–60% of children living in homes with intimate partner violence also experience child maltreatment and abuse (Osofsky, 2003). Parental maltreatment has been consistently implicated in the incidence of later experiences of violent victimization in dating and marital relationships (Kwong, Bartholomew, Henderson, & Trinke, 2003; Renner & Slack, 2006; Wekerle & Wolfe, 1998). Regardless of whether or not maladaptive parenting behaviors reach the level of abuse, however, there is evidence that early maternal representations of the self and child have direct implications for early parenting behaviors; Dayton and colleagues (2010) examined the relationship between prenatal maternal representations as measured by the Working Model of the Child Interview (WMCI; Zeanah & Benoit, 1995) and parenting behaviors at age one as observed in coded video interactions and found that mothers with distorted maternal representations were more likely to express hostility in interactions with their children, while mothers who exhibited disengaged representations of their children were more behaviorally controlling with their infants.

In summary, research and theory on childhood development within a context of intimate partner violence suggest that children are exposed to a range of psychological effects independent of the child directly witnessing violence. These effects occur via disruptions to attachment and parenting, which are shaped by the dynamic psychological processes of the mother as she interprets, processes, and responds to experiences of violence. As a consequence of disturbances in maternal representations and parenting, children are at increased risk for the development of insecure attachments and distorted representations of self and other within attachment contexts, which has significant implications for the risk of becoming engaged in and remaining within an abusive relationship as an adult. However, living in an environment of IPV also has significant direct effects on children, which may be buffered or exacerbated by the supportiveness of the parenting and attachment context.

CHILDREN'S FUNCTIONING

A number of recent meta-analyses and literature reviews have concluded that children exposed to intimate partner violence have higher rates of behavior problems than children who are in nonviolent homes (Chan & Yeung, 2009; Evans et al., 2008; Holt et al., 2008; Kitzmann et al., 2003; Sternberg, Baradaran, Abbott, Lamb, & Guterman, 2006; Wolfe et al., 2003). The problems include externalizing behaviors, such as aggression, attention problems, oppositional behaviors, and delinquency (e.g., Davis & Carlson, 1987; Fantuzzo, DePaola, Lambert, Martino, Anderson, & Sutton, 1991; Graham-Bermann & Levendosky, 1998a; Hughes, 1988; Levendosky, Leahy, Bogat, Davidson, & von Eye, 2006; Martinez-Torteya, Field, Bogat, Levendosky, Davidson, & von Eye, 2009) and internalizing symptoms, such as depression, and anxiety (e.g., Grych, Jouriles, Swank, McDonald, & Norwood, 2000; Hughes, 1988; Martinez-Torteya, Bogat, von Eye, & Levendosky, 2009; Martinez-Torteya, Bogat, Levendosky & von Eye, 2012). In addition, these children are at risk for trauma-related symptoms and

disorders, including PTSD and dissociative symptoms (Bogat, DeJonghe, Levendosky, Davidson, & von Eye, 2006; Graham-Bermann & Levendosky, 1998b; Levendosky et al., in press; Levendosky, Huth-Bocks, Semel, & Shapiro, 2002).

From a developmental perspective, there is some indication from a mega-analysis (Sternberg et al., 2006) that age may play an important role in the effects of witnessing IPV such that older children exposed to IPV are at higher risk to develop externalizing disorders. In contrast, age does not moderate the effects of IPV on internalizing disorders (Sternberg et al., 2006), such that children at all ages were at higher risk for internalizing disorders if exposed to IPV. In addition, normative developmental differences across childhood (e.g., dating during adolescence; development of attachment in infancy) are negatively affected during these particular childhood periods. For example, dating violence is higher in adolescents exposed to IPV compared with non-exposed adolescents (Levendosky, Huth-Bocks, Semel, & Shapiro, 2002; McCloskey & Lichter, 2003). In addition, as will be discussed below, attachment security is negatively affected by IPV (Huth-Bocks, Levendosky, Bogat, & von Eye, 2004; Huth-Bocks, Theran, Levendosky, & Bogat, 2011).

It is important to acknowledge that children exposed to IPV are also at risk for exposure to other forms of family violence, such as child maltreatment (Holt et al., 2008; McDonald, Jouriles, Tart, & Minze, 2009). We propose that children exposed to IPV (and other forms of family violence) are at high risk for behavioral and emotional disorders primarily due to the disruption of their attachment relationships. A baby forms attachment relationships with all significant caregivers during infancy and early childhood. The disruption in these relationships, caused by the violence, then disrupts the child's development of self-regulation, as well as disrupts the ability to develop healthy internal working models of the self and other. The attachment relationship begins, for the child, at the moment of birth.

Rates of insecure attachment in infants and toddlers are much higher in children exposed to family violence than in nonviolent homes. Youngblade and Belsky (1989) aggregated the findings from studies of abused and neglected children ages 12–24 months and compared them with the control children in these studies. They found that 65% of abused and neglected children had insecure attachments, while only 31% of the low-risk control children had insecure attachments. In addition to direct maltreatment, witnessing intimate partner violence has also been shown to be related to child attachment insecurity (Huth-Bocks, Levendosky, Bogat, & von Eye, 2004). Further, the trajectory of intimate partner violence from pregnancy through age four has been shown to be related to the stability or change in attachment security from age one to age four; such that those whose mothers continued to be abused were more likely to continue to have insecure or disorganized attachments at age four, compared with mothers who were no longer abused (Levendosky, Bogat, Huth-Bocks, Rosenblum, & von Eye, 2011). While most studies of attachment in maltreated children have been conducted with children ages 12–24 months, attachment behavior and the attachment relationship with the primary caregiver remains a significant part of the child's life throughout early childhood (Bowlby, 1969). Longitudinal studies find that attachment security is fairly stable from infancy through preschool age with rates of 58–69%, including in violent families, (Barnett, Ganiban, & Cicchetti, 1999; Easterbrooks, 1989; Egeland & Farber, 1984), thus indicating that early infant attachment is still relevant during the preschool years.

Thus far, we have discussed and reviewed the findings related to the child's attachment to the mother. The attachment relationship to the father or father-figure in a home characterized by intimate partner violence is likely to be significantly damaged by the aggression to the mother, though this is theoretical at this point, since there have been no studies of child–father attachment in families with IPV. Attachment relationships may be damaged with both parents through projective and projective identification processes described earlier. The child may develop internal working models of himself and others as aggressor and victim, enacting the projective and/or projective identification processes, which may influence the later development of behavior disorders. The lack of studies of child–father attachment in IPV families represents a gap in the literature; however, many researchers in this area are reluctant to involve fathers in their research due to concerns about the woman's exposure to more abuse based on the partner/father's knowledge of the focus of the study.

In addition to attachment security, IPV may also traumatize children by causing them to fear for the physical and/or psychological integrity of their mother. This is particularly frightening for young children, who are both more likely to be in homes with IPV (Fantuzzo, Boruch, Beriama, Atkins, & Marcus, 1997) and are more emotionally dependent upon their mothers. Relational PTSD is theorized to explain the high association between maternal and child PTSD in very young children (Scheeringa & Zeanah, 2001). Scheeringa and Zeenah propose that in situations where mothers experience trauma, relational PTSD can result—a situation in which the emotional relationship between the mother and child exacerbates the trauma symptoms of each of them. Some research supports this theory, finding that for young children, compared with older children, PTSD symptoms may be more highly related to the severity of the mother's trauma symptoms, rather than the frequency of witnessing IPV (or other traumas; Bogat et al., 2006; Levendosky et al., in press; Scheeringa & Zeanah, 2001). Thus, the child's ability to self-regulate may be impaired whether or not he witnesses the violence directly. The mother's affective dysregulation, as manifested by PTSD, can impair her capacity to respond sensitively to her child, and thus lead to the child's difficulty in affective regulation.

Children who witness the violence to their mother are likely to be traumatized and may develop symptoms of PTSD. The child's experience is that the entire world is ending if the mother's life is threatened and the security of the attachment system is not held firm. Further, research suggests that simply witnessing IPV is associated with PTSD symptoms among children (e.g., Jarvis, Gordon, & Novaco, 2005; Kilpatrick & Williams, 1997). However, while these studies generally find that mothers and/or children report high rates of PTSD symptoms, low rates of PTSD diagnosis are reported for children. Across studies of children, the rates of children who endorsed symptoms in each of the criteria sets were as follows: 52–85% for re-experiencing, 3–98% for avoidance, and 31–73% for arousal, while the rates of PTSD diagnosis reported were between 3–25% (Graham-Bermann, DeVoe, Mattis, Lynch, & Thomas, 2006; Graham-Bermann & Levendosky, 1998b; Levendosky et al., 2002; Mertin & Mohr, 2002; Rossman, Bingham, & Emde, 1997). The great variability in symptom rates across studies can be accounted for both by assessment measure and developmental age of the children assessed with older children reporting more symptoms.

Finally, another route to dysregulated affect is through prenatal exposure to intimate partner violence. The mechanism through prenatal representations was discussed earlier. In addition, recent research on prenatal programming suggests that exposure to IPV during pregnancy can have long-lasting effects on the child's affect regulation. There are a number of studies that indicate that prenatal maternal stress or anxiety negatively affect the developing fetus and the child, postnatally (for a review, see O'Donnell, O'Conner, & Glover, 2009). The perinatal period is a sensitive period for the development of the HPA axis,

but in addition, neural systems involved in the processes of attention, memory, and self-regulation are, in particular, adversely affected by stress. Thus, exposure to stress (including IPV) so early in development could shape the functionality of brain regions which are fundamental to executive functioning. Consistent with these possible mechanisms (i.e., HPA axis dysregulation, negative effects on development of cortical systems), children from these pregnancies are at higher risk for difficult temperament, attention and learning problems, mood and anxiety disorders, and conduct disorders (for reviews, see Glover, 2011; Glover, O'Connor, & O'Donnell, 2009; Weinstock, 2008). The infant's physiology, including the HPA axis, is important because it plays an important role in the development of self-regulation and some research and theory (Schore, 2009) demonstrates that the attunement between the mother and child, influenced by each of their physiologies, will help the child develop self-regulation—one of the primary goals of the holding relationship, along with establishing healthy internal working models of self and other. During early infancy, the functioning of the HPA axis evolves dynamically in response to the emerging biological maturation of the infant as well as to attentive, soothing caregiving. If the maternal-infant affect system is dysregulated, the infant may develop an impaired emotion regulation system, biologically and behaviorally. While it has not been explored, there are likely intersections between the developing prenatal representations and the maternal (and fetal) response to prenatal IPV. Dysregulation to both of these systems and their interactions would predict emotional and behavioral problems in infants and young children.

One additional potential mediator of the relationship between growing up in violent homes with impairments in caregiving and abusive relational dynamics in adulthood is the development of an increased sensitivity to rejection (Feldman & Downey, 1994; Pietrzak, Downey, & Ayduk, 2005; Romero-

Canyas, Downey, Berenson et al., 2010; Volz & Kerig, 2010). Parental rejection, whether overt (as expressed in physical or emotional maltreatment) or covert (as expressed in physical or emotional neglect), becomes internalized within the attachment narratives of maltreated children. The child develops an acute sensitivity to potential experiences of rejection, the expectation of which may be highly affect-laden given their origins within the most basic attachment relationships. This is a very similar construct to attachment anxiety and the child's response may be considered to be analogous to protest behaviors as a protection from rejection. Consequently, the child begins to perceive experiences of rejection as likely, to see potential dating partners as sources of both affection and potential emotional pain, and to experience the self as abhorrent or flawed and therefore likely to elicit rejection from others. As an adult, these children may maintain insecure attachment styles with avoidant or ambivalent styles predominating (Feldman & Downey, 1994; Volz & Kerig, 2010). They may become hypersensitive to perceived cues of rejection and to react with intense emotional outbursts when they expect rejection is imminent, projecting past experiences of parental rejection on immediate partner interactions and experiencing strong affective reactions to real or perceived neglect or abuse (Pietrzak et al., 2005; Romero-Canyas, Downey, Berenson et al., 2010). They may also be more prone to self-silencing behaviors, in which they—fearing the pain and loss of rejection—are reluctant to confront or address potential problems within a relationship (Harper, Dickson, & Welsh, 2006). Further, individuals sensitive to potential rejection may act in submissive or ingratiating ways in order to avoid rejection experiences, and this may be particularly true for women socialized in agreeableness (Romero-Canyas, Downey, Reddy et al., 2010). Emotional outbursts in response to real or perceived rejection, as well as reluctance to address potential problems in a relationship may actually increase

rejection on the part of others and may be utilized against victims of intimate partner violence by emotionally and psychologically abusive partners as tools to undermine the woman's self-esteem and minimize abusive behaviors. In combination, hypersensitivity to the potential rejection of an attachment partner may simultaneously normalize these experiences of neglect and abuse as an inherent element of attachment relationships while making it more difficult for women experiencing intimate partner violence to sever their relationship, given that the roots of their attachment representations stem from the most primitive emotional experiences of their earliest experiences of self and other. Thus attachment anxiety due to witnessing IPV can directly affect the development of romantic relationships during adolescence into early adulthood.

Thus, we can conclude that children exposed to IPV are at high risk for a wide variety of behavior problems and even clinical disorders. While many do not meet criteria for PTSD, the standard disorder associated with experiencing trauma, a newly proposed disorder, Developmental Trauma Disorder (DTD; van der Kolk, 2005), may help to address the very significant problem that many children exposed to traumatic events, including witnessing IPV, do not meet criteria for PTSD, and instead receive diagnoses unrelated to trauma, including disorders of mood, anxiety, or conduct. Van der Kolk (2005) proposed that these children exposed to IPV who have clinical levels of psychopathology are suffering from posttraumatic symptoms/disorders and thus are being mistreated by interventions designed for diagnoses of ADHD or depression in the absence of traumatic origin.

CASE ILLUSTRATION AND CLINICAL IMPLICATIONS

The trauma of intimate partner violence, in combination with the loss of security and trust in intimate relationships, can place women and their families at higher risk for psychopathology, particularly depression and PTSD. Disorganization in implicit working models of others likewise may place women experiencing intimate partner violence at greater risk for insecure or disorganized relationships, including further experiences of violence. These processes have implications for clinicians working with women and children who have directly experienced, been exposed to, or been raised by those experiencing intimate partner violence. The following case draws upon many relevant aspects of our present discussion:

Katherine (age 52) presented to psychotherapy with the second author (clinical supervision provided by the first author) for concerns about depression and anxiety. She reported strong feelings of helplessness, indecisiveness, and hopelessness. She described severe physical abuse, neglect, and sexual assault, beginning as early as infancy. In her household, she said, children were "to be seen, and never heard," to be used, but not wanted or loved—and the family's submission was enforced by a cold and controlling father. Her father's control of her mother was absolute, she reported, and she witnessed numerous incidents of physical and sexual assault perpetrated by her father against her mother. Katherine fled the household at age 13. As a teenager, she lived a transient life, living with friends, in shelters, or on the street, and experiencing further sexual abuse and assaults. As an adult, she was involved in a series of violent romantic relationships. An early marriage ended when her husband threatened to light both her and her daughter on fire, and Katherine fled the home with her daugh-

ter during the night and moved across the country. Katherine reported feeling absolutely confident in this decision and proud of her choice to protect her daughter and self by leaving, and reported that her ability to nurture and protect her daughter was a source of self-respect and pride for her. The precipitating factor in her decision to seek psychotherapy, she said, was the report of her (now adult) daughter that she had experienced sexual abuse from a family member in childhood. Katherine found this news devastating, and felt she had failed as a mother.

In sessions, Katherine spoke softly in a childlike voice and dressed herself in bright pastel clothing with emblems of butterflies and kittens. She rapidly formed an attachment to the therapist, expressing frequent gratitude for the clinician's time and seemingly projecting a wide range of positive qualities onto the clinician. Although the clinician was considerably younger, Katherine seemed to interact with the clinician as a child would with a caregiver; she expressed feelings of helplessness and dependence, often asking the clinician to help her in making daily decisions, and seemed vigilant for any sign of the clinician's approval or rejection. She responded to positive or encouraging comments from the therapist with a broad smile, tucking her head into her chest as if overwhelmed by the prospect of praise. Katherine also reported developing sudden strong attachments to others, particularly those she believed could teach her or guide her in some way, and described one such new acquaintance as the wisest, kindest, most kindred soul she could imagine. At the same time, she struggled to identify positive qualities in herself. At intake, she was involved in a relationship with a man that she initially described in positive, even effusive terms; as therapy progressed, however, she revealed incidents of violence occurring within a persistent pattern of psy-

---

All names and details have been changed o protect patient privacy.l

chological control, emotional abuse, sexual coercion, and physical assault. When asked about her feelings about these incidents, Katherine seemed visibly conflicted and was initially prone to either defending the virtues of her partner, pointing out her perceived role in evoking the abuse, or changing the subject suddenly.

Like many women who have experienced intimate partner violence, Katherine experienced forms of abuse early in life, in particular abuse from a parent that violated the security and trust of the caregiving relationship and led to dysregulation in affective responses and coping processes. The emotional neglect she experienced deprived her of needed opportunities for positive reflection and nurturance. The physical and sexual abuse she experienced, in combination with frequently witnessing a pattern of violence by her father against her mother, led her to internalize a working model of relationships in which pain, rejection, and fear were part and parcel of intimacy and dependence. Further, like many children whose earliest caregiving relationships are marked by inconsistent responsiveness, neglect, or abuse, Katherine was placed in a double bind: physically and emotionally dependent on those who harmed her, she internalized experiences of the "good" and "bad" caregiver but was unable to integrate these into a cohesive whole. Thus Katherine's emotional and interpersonal life was marked by splitting and its extremes: unable to integrate the painful actions of her caregivers with her dependence on them, she projected positive characteristics of the "good" object onto her caregivers and internalized the "bad" object as herself. She likewise internalized the projections of her parents, which implicitly and explicitly communicated the belief that she was incompetent, unwanted, and unworthy. Like many who develop such distorted working models of self and others, Katherine struggled to maintain relationships with others and responded to perceived slights or rejections with the extreme anger or hurt char-

acteristic of high attachment anxiety, often severing the relationship entirely. Her traumatic past, distorted and dysthymic self-image, continued re-enactments of abuse in current relationships, and limited social support placed Katherine at a high risk for psychopathology such as depression and anxiety. As a mother, Katherine projected her feelings of helplessness onto her daughter and doubled her efforts to protect and provide for her daughter. Thus, knowledge of her daughter's experiences of abuse invoked unacceptable feelings of helplessness and a longing for protection.

Treatment focused on encouraging Katherine to explore her traumatic interpersonal history and subsequent internalized threatening object representations of others within the context of a supportive and safe relationship. In addition, enactment of Katherine's attachment history within the therapeutic relationship offered opportunities for her to experience alternatives to firmly entrenched experiences of authoritarian control and dependence. The clinician made efforts not to engender her helplessness by assuming responsibility for decisions, despite Katherine's repeated efforts. Instead, the therapist assumed limited functions of the caregiving relationship relevant to those Katherine was denied: providing warmth, acceptance, and unconditional positive regard, while also communicating a belief that Katherine could meet developmentally appropriate expectations for self-care and self-efficacy. As she internalized the positive regard and acceptance of the clinician, her own sense of value and self-worth increased, and she began to reinterpret her role in past relationships, the quality of her current relationship and her perceptions of her partner. Her mood and functioning improved, and she began to experiment with new hobbies and developing new skills. After some time, Katherine made the decision to leave her partner, moved, and began—in her words—to assume control over herself and her life. In Katherine's case, an understanding of the underlying processes of attachment and associated working models of self and others in intimate relationships allowed the clinician to identify her conflicts and unmet needs. This knowledge also allowed the clinician to monitor the parallel processes of the therapeutic relationship and to provide alternative, nurturing interactions while preventing re-enactment of internalized models of excessive dependence, disregarded emotional and physical boundaries, rejection, shame, and pain. The manifestation of attachment disruptions following IPV may not necessarily parallel Katherine's presentation but, as discussed above, may vary greatly across individuals and circumstances—but an understanding of the disruptive effects of IPV on the intrapsychic attachment models of women and children can prove an invaluable guide to case formulation and treatment planning.

Intimate partner violence is fundamentally a violation of the security of an intimate relationship, and as such it exerts deleterious effects on women and their children through disruptions in systems of relating to others and representations of self and other in relational contexts. The insecurity in attachment engendered by these violations reflects underlying working models of self and other that begin to develop within the context of the earliest caregiving relationship. For women who have experienced abuse in early relationships, anxious or avoidant patterns of attachment are projected onto the current relationship and reinforced by further victimization. For women who enter violent relationships with a secure attachment style, the trauma of violence and violations in trust may lead to distortions in working models. These damaged working models, in combination with the stress of victimization, place women experiencing IPV at a greater risk for psychopathology such as anxiety, depression, and posttraumatic stress disorder. As mothers, women with anxious or avoidant attachment histories are more likely to transfer underlying distortions in working models across generations through impairments

in caregiving, which may be exacerbated by concomitant psychopathology. Through processes of projection and projective identification, women in violent romantic relationships may transfer vulnerability for insecure attachment (and future violence) through inconsistent, hostile, or distant interactions with their children. Similarly, children may be directly exposed to IPV within the household and suffer negative outcomes due to the combination of vulnerability due to insecure attachment and the traumatic stress of witnessing violence directly. They are consequently at increased risk of involvement in violent relationships as adults, either as perpetrators or victims. Thus, the relational nature of IPV leads to transmittable distortions in working models and attachment that can place multiple generations at increased risk of victimization and psychopathology.

Although the theory and research reviewed above provides a starting point for understanding the attachment processes in families experiencing IPV, there are some theoretical and empirical limitations to this review. First, although this review attempts to address the clinical applications of attachment and IPV, it is limited in its ability to inform treatment planning due to a variety of factors. In particular, it is unable to make predictions about the focus of treatment with women experiencing IPV, particularly in cases in which there exists a complex history of trauma. Whether the present, more proximal trauma of IPV, or more distal, early traumas such as childhood maltreatment should serve as the treatment focus is unclear. Likewise, attachment and working model–focused treatments may not appeal to all women experiencing intimate partner violence, and data on treatment acceptability under these circumstances is lacking. A second major clinical limitation lies in working with individuals at risk for the intergenerational transmission of violence. Although the intergenerational transmission of IPV through representations is suggested by attachment theory, these mechanisms are not yet well understood and research is limited. Attachment theorists suggest that working models of self and other developed in infancy persist into adulthood (Hazan et al., 2006), however, prospective longitudinal studies of attachment from infancy into adulthood are few in number, and there are no extant studies involving families experiencing IPV. Similarly, there are no studies of father–infant attachment in households experiencing IPV, limiting our understanding of the effects of the father–infant relationship on increasing or reducing risk for negative outcomes.

Intimate partner violence is a common experience for adult women in romantic relationships, and has significant effects on women as individuals and as mothers. In addition to increased risk of psychopathology, women experiencing IPV are at increased risk for disruptions in internal working models and behavioral attachment systems that may increase risk for negative outcomes for themselves and their children. A theoretical and empirical understanding of these processes both informs directions for further research and has implications for clinicians working with women and their families in a context of IPV.

REFERENCES

Ainsworth, M. D. S. (1967). *Infancy in Uganda: Infant care and the growth of love.* Baltimore: Johns Hopkins University Press.

Allison, C. J., Bartholomew, K., Mayseless, O., & Dutton, D. G. (2008). Love as a battlefield: Attachment and relationship dynamics in couples identified for male partner violence. *Journal of Family Issues, 29*(1), 125-150.

Astin, M. C., Lawrence, K. J., & Foy, D. W. (1993). Posttraumatic stress disorder among battered women: Risk and resiliency factors. *Violence and Victims, 8*(1), 17-28.

Babcock, J. C., Jacobsen, N. S., Gottman, J. M., & Yerington, T. P. (2000). Attachment, emotion regulation, and the function of marital violence: Differences between secure, preoccupied, and dismissing violent and nonviolent husbands. *Journal of Family Violence, 15*(4), 391-409.

Barnett, D., Ganiban, J., & Cicchetti, D. (1999). Maltreatment, negative expressivity, and the development of type D attachments from 12 to 24 months of age. In J. I. Vondra & D. Barnett (Eds.), Atypical attachment in infancy and early childhood among children at developmental risk (pp. 97-118). *Monographs of the Society for Research in Child Development, 64,* (Serial No. 258).

Bartholomew, K., & Allison, C. J. (2006). An attachment perspective on abusive dynamics in intimate relationships. In M. Mikulincer & G. S. Goodman (Eds.), *Dynamics of romantic love: Attachment, caregiving, and sex* (pp. 102-127). New York: Guilford.

Baum, A., O'Keeffe, M. K., & Davidson, L. M. (1990). Acute stressors and chronic response: The case of traumatic stress. *Journal of Applied Social Psychology, 20*(20), 1643-1654.

Bean, J., & Möller, A. T. (2002). Posttraumatic stress and depressive symptoms in a sample of battered women from South Africa. *Psychological Reports, 90,* 750-752.

Becker, K. D., Stuewig, J., & McCloskey, L. A. (2010). Traumatic stress symptoms of women exposed to different forms of childhood victimization and intimate partner violence. *Journal of Interpersonal Violence, 25*(9), 1699-1715.

Beeble, M. L., Bybee, D., Sullivan, C. M., & Adams, A. E. (2009). Main, mediating, and moderating effects of social support on the well-being of survivors of intimate partner violence across 2 years. *Journal of Consulting and Clinical Psychology, 77*(4), 718-729.

Black, M.M., Oberlander, S.E., Lewis, T., Knight, E.D., Zolotor, M.D., Litrownik, A.J., et al. (2009). A prospective investigation of sexual intercourse among adolescents maltreated prior to age 12. *Pediatrics, 124,* 941-949.

Black, D. S., Sussman, S., & Unger, J. B. (2010). A further look at the intergenerational transmission of violence: Witnessing interparental violence in emerging adulthood. *Journal of Interpersonal Violence, 25*(6), 1022-1042.

Bogat, G. A., Levendosky, A. A., DeJonghe, E., Davidson, W. S., & von Eye, A. (2004). Pathways of suffering: The temporal effects of domestic violence on women's mental health. *Maltrattamento e abuso all'infanzia, 6*(2), 97-112.

Bogat, G. A., Levendosky, A. A., Theran, S., von Eye, A., & Davidson, W. S. (2003). Predicting the psychosocial effects of interpersonal partner violence (IPV): How much does a woman's history of IPV matter? *Journal of Interpersonal Violence, 18*(11), 1271-1291.

Bogat, G. A., DeJonghe, E. S., Levendosky, A. A., Davidson, W. S., & von Eye, A. (2006). Trauma symptoms among infants who witness intimate partner violence toward their mothers. *Child Abuse & Neglect: The International Journal, 30,* 109-125.

Bookwala, J. (2002). The role of own and perceived partner attachment in relationship aggression. *Journal of Interpersonal Violence, 17(1),* 84-100.

Bookwala, J., & Zdaniuk, B. (1998). Adult attachment styles and aggressive behavior within dating relationships. *Journal of Social and Personal Relationships, 15(2),* 175-190.

Bowlby, J. (1969). *Attachment and loss, Vol. I. Attachment.* London: Hogarth.

Bowlby, J. (1980). *Attachment and loss, Vol. III. Loss: Sadness and depression.* New York: Basic Books.

Bowlby, J. (1982). *Attachment and loss. Vol. I: Attachment, 2nd Edition.* New York: Basic Books.

Bowlby, J. (1984). Violence in the family as a disorder of the attachment and caregiving systems. *The American Journal of Psychoanalysis, 44(1),* 9-27.

Bowlby, J. (1988). *A secure base: Parent-child attachment and healthy human development.* New York: Basic Books.

Brennan, K. A., Wu, S., & Loev, J. (1998). Adult romantic attachment and individual differences in attitudes toward physical contact in the context of adult romantic relationships. In J. A. Simpson & W. S. Rholes (Eds.), *Attachment theory and close relationships.* New York: Guilford.

Cannon, E. A., Bonomi, A. E., Anderson, M. L., & Rivara, F. P. (2009). The intergenerational transmission of witnessing intimate partner violence. *Archives of Pediatrics and Adolescent Medicine, 163(8),* 706-708.

Chan, Y., & Yeung, J. W. (2009). Children living with violence within the family and its sequel: A meta-analysis from 1995–2006. *Aggression and Violent Behavior, 14(5),* 313-322.

Collins, N. L., Guichard, A. C., Ford, M. B., & Feeney, B. C. (2006). Responding to need in intimate relationships: Normative processes and individual differences. In M. Mikulincer & G. S. Goodman (Eds.), *Dynamics of romantic love: Attachment, caregiving, and sex* (pp. 149-189). New York: Guilford.

Collins, N. L., & Read, S. J. (1994). Cognitive representations of attachment: The structure and function of working models. In K. Bartholomew & D. Perlman (Eds.), *Attachment processes in adulthood.* London, England: Jessica Kingsley Publishers.

Crandell, L. E., Fitzgerald, H. E., & Whipple, E. E. (1997). Dyadic synchrony in parent-child interactions: A link with maternal representations of attachment relationships. *Infant Mental Health Journal, 18(3),* 247-264.

Cui, M., Durtschi, J. A., Donnellan, M. B., Lorenz, F. O., & Conger, R. D. (2010). Intergenerational transmission of relationship aggression: A prospective longitudinal study. *Journal of Family Psychology, 24(6),* 688-697.

Davis, L. V., & Carlson, B. E. (1987). Observation of spouse abuse: What happens to the children? *Journal of Interpersonal Violence, 2,* 278-291.

Dayton, C. J., Bogat, G. A., & Levendosky, A. A. (2012). *Pregnancy, parenting and violence: The development and maintenance of early child externalizing behaviors when violence begins at the beginning.* Unpublished manuscript, under review.

Dayton, C. J., Levendosky, A. A., Davidson, W. S., & Bogat, G. A. (2010). The child as held in the mind of the mother: The influence of prenatal maternal representations on parenting behaviors. *Infant Mental Health Journal, 31,* 220-241.

DiLillo, D., Giuffre, D., Tremblay, G. C., & Peterson, L. (2001). A closer look at the nature of intimate partner violence reported by women with a history of child sexual abuse. *Journal of Interpersonal Violence, 16(2),* 116-132.

Dorahy, M. J., Lewis, C. A., & Wolfe, F. A. M. (2007). Psychological distress associated with intimate partner violence in Northern Ireland. *Current Psychology: A Journal for Diverse Perspectives on Diverse Psychological Issues, 25(4),* 295-305.

Doumas, D. M., Pearson, C. L., Elgin, J. E., & McKinley, L. L. (2008). Adult attachment as a risk factor for intimate partner violence: The "mispairing" of partners' attachment styles. *Journal of Interpersonal Violence, 23(5),* 616-634.

Dutton, M. A., Green, B. L., Kaltman, S. L., Roesch, D. M., Zeffiro, T. A., & Krause, E. D. (2006). Intimate partner violence, PTSD, and adverse health outcomes. *Journal of Interpersonal Violence, 21,* 955-968.

Dutton, D. G., Saunders, K., Starzomski, A., & Bartholomew, K. (1994). Intimacy-anger and insecure attachment as precursors of abuse in intimate relationships. *Journal of Applied Social Psychology, 24(15),* 1367-1386.

Easterbrooks, M. A. (1989). Quality of attachment to mother and to father: Effects of perinatal risk status. *Child Development, 60,* 825-830.

Egeland, B., & Farber, E. A. (1984). Infant-mother attachment: Factors related to its development and changes over time. *Child Development, 55,* 753-771.

Ehrensaft, M. K., Moffitt, T. E., & Caspi, A. (2006). Is intimate partner violence followed by an increased risk of psychiatric disorders among women but not among men? A longitudinal cohort study. *American Journal of Psychiatry, 163,* 885-892.

Evans, S. E., Davies, C., & DiLillo, D. (2008). Exposure to intimate partner violence: A meta-analysis of child and adolescent outcomes. *Aggression and violent behavior, 13,* 131-140.

Fantuzzo, J., Boruch, R., Beriama, A., Atkins, M., & Marcus, S. (1997). IPV and children: Prevalence and risk in five major U.S. cities. *Journal of the American Academy of Child and Adolescent Psychiatry, 36*(1), 116-122.

Fantuzzo, J. W., DePaola, L. M., Lambert, L., Martino, T., Anderson, & Sutton. (1991). Effects of interparental violence on the psychological adjustment and competencies of young children. *Journal of Consulting & Clinical Psychology, 59*(2), 258-265.

Feeney, J. A. (2008). Adult romantic attachment: Developments in the study of couple relationships. In J. Cassidy & P. Shaver (Eds.), *Handbook of attachment: Theory, research, and clinical applications* (2nd ed., pp. 456-481). New York: Guilford.

Feldman, S., & Downey, G. (1994). Rejection sensitivity as a mediator of the impact of childhood exposure to family violence on adult attachment behavior. *Development and Psychopathology, 6,* 231-247.

Follingstad, D. R., Bradley, R. G., Helff, C. M., & Laughlin, J. E. (2002). A model for predicting dating violence: Anxious attachment, angry temperament and need for relationship control. *Violence and Victims, 17*(1), 35-48.

Freyd, J. J. (1996). *Betrayal trauma: The logic of forgetting childhood abuse.* Cambridge, MA: Harvard University Press.

George, C., & Solomon, J. (2008). The caregiving system: A behavioral systems approach to parenting. In J. Cassidy & P. R. Shaver (Eds.), *Handbook of attachment: Theory, research, and clinical applications* (pp. 833-856). New York: Guilford.

Gleason, W. J. (1993). Mental disorders in battered women: An empirical study. *Violence and Victims, 8*(1), 53-68.

Glover, V. (2011). Annual research review: Prenatal stress and the origins of psychopathology: An evolutionary perspective. *Journal of Child Psychology and Psychiatry, 52,* 356-367.

Glover, V., O'Connor, T. G., & O'Donnell, K. (2009). Prenatal stress and the programming of the HPA axis. *Neuroscience and Biobehavioral Reviews, 35,* 17-22.

Golding, J. M. (1999). Intimate partner violence as a risk factor for mental disorders: A meta-analysis. *Journal of Family Violence, 14*(2), 99-132.

Gómez, A. M. (2011). Testing the cycle of violence hypothesis: Child abuse and adolescent dating violence as predictors of intimate partner violence in young adulthood. *Youth & Society, 43*(1), 171-192.

Gormley, B. (2005). An adult attachment theoretical perspective of gender symmetry in intimate partner violence. *Sex Roles, 52*(11-12), 785-795.

Gormley, B., & Lopez, F. G. (2010). Psychological abuse perpetration in college dating relationships: Contributions of gender, stress, and adult attachment orientations. *Journal of Interpersonal Violence, 25*(2), 204-218.

Graham-Bermann, S., De Voe, E. R., Mattis, J. S., Lynch, S., & Thomas, S. A. (2006). Ecological predictors of traumatic stress symptoms in Caucasian and ethnic minority children exposed to intimate partner violence. *Violence Against Women, 12*(7), 663-692.

Graham-Bermann, S. A., Gruber, G., Howell, K., & Girz, L. (2009). Factors discriminating among profiles of resilience and psychopathology in children exposed to intimate partner violence (IPV). *Child Abuse and Neglect, 33,* 648-660.

Graham-Bermann, S. A., & Levendosky, A. A. (1998a). The social functioning of preschool-age children whose mothers are emotionally and physically abused. *Journal of Emotional Abuse, 1*(1), 5-84.

Graham-Bermann S. A., & Levendosky A. A. (1998b). Traumatic stress symptoms in children of battered women. *Journal of Interpersonal Violence, 13,* 111-128.

Griffing, S., Lewis, C. S., Chu, M., Sage, R. E., Madry, L., & Primm, B. J. (2006). Exposure to interpersonal violence as a predictor of PTSD symptomatology in intimate partner violence survivors. *Journal of Interpersonal Violence, 21*(7), 936-954.

Grych, J. H., Jouriles, E. N., Swank, P. R., McDonald, R., & Norwood, W. D. (2000). Patterns of adjustment among children of battered women. *Journal of Consulting and Clinical Psychology, 68*(1), 84-94.

Harper, M. S., Dickson, J. W., & Welsh, D. P. (2006). Self-silencing and rejection sensitivity in adolescent romantic relationships. *Journal of Youth and Adolescence, 35*(3), 435-443.

Hazan, C., Campa, M., & Gur-Yaish, N. (2006). What is adult attachment? In M. Mikulincer & G. S. Goodman (Eds.), *Dynamics of romantic love: Attachment, caregiving, and sex*. New York: Guilford.

Helfrich, C. A., Fujiura, G. T., & Rutkowski-Kmitta, V. (2008). Mental health disorders and functioning of women in intimate partner violence shelters. *Journal of Interpersonal Violence, 23*(4), 437-453.

Henderson, A. J. Z., Bartholomew, K., Trinke, S. J., & Kwong, M. J. (2005). When loving means hurting: An exploration of attachment and intimate abuse in a community sample. *Journal of Family Violence, 20(4)*, 219-230.

Herman, J. L. (1992). *Trauma and recovery: The aftermath of violence from domestic abuse to political terror*. New York: Basic Books.

Holt, S. B., Buckley, H., & Whelan, S. (2008). The impact of exposure to domestic violence on children and young people: A review of the literature. *Child Abuse and Neglect, 32*, 797-810.

Holtzworth-Munroe, A., Stuart, G. L., & Hutchinson, G. (1997). Violent versus nonviolent husbands: Differences in attachment patterns, dependency, and jealousy. *Journal of Family Psychology, 11*(3), 314-331.

Hughes, H. M. (1988). Psychological and behavioral correlates of family violence in child witnesses and victims. *American Journal of Orthopsychiatry, 58*(1), 77-90.

Huth-Bocks, A. C., Levendosky, A. A., Bogat, G. A., & von Eye, A. (2004). The impact of maternal characteristics and contextual variables on infant-mother attachment. *Child Development, 75*(2), 480-496.

Huth-Bocks, A. C., Levendosky, A. A., Theran, S. A., & Bogat, G. A. (2004). The impact of intimate partner violence on mothers' prenatal representations of their infants. *Infant Mental Health Journal, 25*, 79-98.

Huth-Bocks, A. C., Theran, S. A., Levendosky, A. A., & Bogat, G. A. (2011). A social-contextual understanding of concordance and discordance between maternal prenatal representations of the infant and infant-mother attachment. *Infant Mental Health Journal, 32*, 405-426.

Janoff-Bulman, R. (1992). *Shattered assumptions: Towards a new psychology of trauma*. New York: Free Press.

Jarvis, K. L., Gordon, E. E., & Novaco, R. W. (2005). Psychological distress of children and mothers in intimate partner violence emergency shelters. *Journal of Family Violence, 20*(6), 389-402.

Joiner, T. E., & Timmons, K. A. (2010). Depression in its interpersonal context. In I. H. Gotlib & C. L. Hammen (Eds.), *Handbook of depression* (pp. 322-339). New York: Guilford.

Kerley, K. R., Xu, X., Sirisunyaluck, B., & Alley, J. M. (2010). Exposure to family violence in childhood and intimate partner perpetration or victimization in adulthood: Exploring intergenerational transmission in urban Thailand. *Journal of Family Violence, 25*(3), 337-347.

Kernic, M. A., Holt, V. L., Stoner, J. A., Wolf, M. E., & Rivara, F. P. (2003). Resolution of depression among victims of intimate partner violence: Is cessation of violence enough? *Violence and Victims, 18*(2), 115-129.

Kesner, J. E., & McKenry, P. C. (1998). The role of childhood attachment factors in predicting male violence toward female intimates. *Journal of Family Violence, 13*(4), 417-432.

Kilpatrick, K. L., & Williams, L. M. (1997). Posttraumatic stress disorder in child witnesses to intimate partner violence. *American Journal of Orthopsychiatry, 67*, 639-644.

Kitzmann, K. M., Gaylord, N. K., Holt, A. R., & Kenny, E. D. (2003). Child witnesses to intimate partner violence: A meta-analytic review. *Journal of Consulting and Clinical Psychology, 71*(2), 339-352.

Koss, M. P., Bailey, J. A., Yuan, N. P., Herrera, V. M., & Lichter, E. L. (2003). Depression and PTSD in survivors of male violence: Research and training initiatives to facilitate recovery. *Psychology of Women Quarterly, 27*, 130-142.

Kwong, M. J., Bartholomew, K., Henderson, A. J. Z., & Trinke, S. J. (2003). The intergenerational transmission of relationship violence. *Journal of Family Psychology, 17*(3), 288-301.

Lafontaine, M., & Lussier, Y. (2005). Does anger towards the partner mediate and moderate the link between romantic attachment and intimate violence? *Journal of Family Violence, 20*(6), 349-361.

Lang, A. J., Kennedy, C. M., & Stein, M. B. (2002). Anxiety sensitivity and PTSD among female victims of intimate partner violence. *Depression and Anxiety, 16*(2), 77-83.

Leckman, J. F., Feldman, R., Swain, J. E., & Mayes, L. C. (2007). Primary parental preoccupation: Revisited. In L. Mayes, P. Fonagy, & M. Target (Eds.), *Developmental science and psychoanalysis: Integration and innovation* (pp. 89-108). London: Karnac.

Levendosky, A. A., Bogat, G. A., Huth-Bocks, A., Rosenblum, K., & von Eye, A. (2011). The effects of intimate partner violence on the stability of attachment from infancy to preschool. *Journal of Clinical Child and Adolescent Psychology, 40,* 398-410.

Levendosky, A. A., Bogat, G. A., & Martinez-Torteya, C. (in press). PTSD symptoms in young children exposed to intimate partner violence. *Violence Against Women.*

Levendosky, A. A., Bogat, G. A., Theran, S. A., Trotter, J. S., von Eye, A., & Davidson, W. S. (2004). The social networks of women experiencing intimate partner violence. *American Journal of Community Psychology, 34*(1/2), 95-109.

Levendosky, A. A., Huth-Bocks, A. C., Semel, M. A., & Shapiro, D. L. (2002). Trauma symptoms in preschool-age children exposed to intimate partner violence. *Journal of Interpersonal Violence, 17,* 150-164.

Levendosky, A. A., Leahy, K. L., Bogat, G. A., Davidson, W. S., & von Eye, A. (2006). Intimate partner violence, maternal parenting, maternal mental health, and infant externalizing behavior. *Journal of Family Psychology, 20,* 544-552.

Lyons-Ruth, K., Yellin, C., Melnick, S., & Atwood, G. (2005). Expanding the concept of unresolved mental states: Hostile/helpless states of mind on the Adult Attachment Interview (AAI) are associated with disrupted mother-infant communication and infant disorganization. *Development and Psychopathology, 17,* 1-23.

Mahalik, J. R., Aldarondo, E., Gilbert-Gokhale, S., & Shore, E. (2005). The role of insecure attachment and gender role stress in predicting controlling behaviors in men who batter. *Journal of Interpersonal Violence, 20*(5), 617-631.

Main, M., & Hesse, E. (1990). Parents' unresolved traumatic experiences are related to infant disorganized attachment status: Is frightened and/or frightening parental behavior the linking mechanism? In M. T. Greenberg, D. Cicchetti, & M. E. Cummings (Eds.), *Attachment in the preschool years: Theory, research, and intervention* (pp. 161-182). Chicago: University of Chicago Press.

Main, M., & Solomon, J. (1990). Procedures for identifying infants as disorganized/disoriented during the Ainsworth Strange Situation. In M. T. Greenberg, D. Cicchetti, & M. E. Cummings (Eds.), *Attachment in the preschool years: Theory, research, and intervention* (pp. 121-160). Chicago: University of Chicago Press.

Martinez-Torteya, C., Bogat, G. A., Levendosky, A. A., & von Eye, A. (2012). *Childhood depression: The influence of HPA-Axis reactivity and prenatal intimate partner violence.* Unpublished manuscript.

Martinez-Torteya, C., Bogat, G. A., von Eye, A., & Levendosky, A. A. (2009) Resilience among children exposed to intimate partner violence:

The role of protective and vulnerability factors. *Child Development, 80,* 562-577.

Martinez-Torteya, C., Field, L., Bogat, G. A., Levendosky, A., von Eye, A., & Davidson, W. S. II (2009, May). *Prenatal exposure to domestic violence predicts infants' internalization behaviors and temperamental difficulties.* Poster presented at the annual meeting of the Association for Psychological Science, San Francisco, CA.

Mayseless, O. (1991). Adult attachment patterns and courtship violence. *Family Relations: An Interdisciplinary Journal of Applied Family Studies, 40*(1), 21-28.

McCloskey, L. A., & Lichter, E. L. (2003). The contribution of marital violence to adolescents' aggression across different relationships. *Journal of Interpersonal Violence, 18,* 390-412.

McDonald, R., Jouriles, E. N., Tart, C. D., & Minze, L. (2009). Children's adjustment problems in families characterized by men's severe violence toward women: Does other family violence matter? *Child Abuse and Neglect, 33,* 94-101.

McGuigan, W. M., & Pratt, C. C. (2001). The predictive impact of intimate partner violence on three types of child maltreatment. *Child Abuse and Neglect, 25*(7), 869-883.

Mertin, P., & Mohr, P. B. (2001). A follow-up study of posttraumatic stress disorder, anxiety, and depression in Australian victims of intimate partner violence. *Violence and Victims, 16*(6), 645-654.

Mertin, P., & Mohr, P. B. (2002). Incidence and correlates of posttrauma symptoms in children from backgrounds of intimate partner violence. *Violence and Victims, 17*(5), 555-567.

Nixon, R. D. V., Resick, P. A., & Nishith, P. (2004). An exploration of comorbid depression among female victims of intimate partner violence with posttraumatic stress disorder. *Journal of Affective Disorders, 82*(2), 315-320.

Norwood, A., & Murphy, C. (2011, August 22). What forms of abuse correlate with PTSD symptoms in partners of men being treated for intimate partner violence. *Psychological Trauma: Theory, Research, Practice, and Policy.* Advanced online publication. doi: 10.1037/a0025232

O'Donnell, K., O'Connor, T. G., & Glover, V. (2009). Prenatal stress and neurodevelopment of the child: Focus on the HPA axis and role of the placenta. *Developmental Neuroscience, 31,* 285-292.

Osofsky, J. D. (2003). Prevalence of children's exposure to intimate partner violence and child maltreatment: Implications for prevention and intervention. *Clinical Child and Family Psychology Review, 6*(3), 161-170.

Peters, J., Shackelford, T. K., & Buss, D. M. (2002). Understanding intimate partner violence against women: Using evolutionary psychology to extend the feminist functional analysis. *Violence and Victims, 17,* 255-264.

Pico-Alfonso, M. A., Garcia-Linares, M. I., Celda-Navarro, N., Blasco-Ros, C., Echeburúa, E., & Martinez, M. (2006). The impact of physical, psychological, and sexual intimate male partner violence on women's mental health: Depressive symptoms, posttraumatic stress disorder, state anxiety, and suicide. *Journal of Women's Health, 15*(5), 599-611.

Pietrzak, J., Downey, G., & Ayduk, O. (2005). Interpersonal cognition. In M. W. Baldwin (Ed.), *Interpersonal cognition* (pp. 62-84). New York: Guilford.

Renner, L. M. (2009). Intimate partner violence victimization and parenting stress: Assessing the mediating role of depressive symptoms. *Violence Against Women, 15*(11), 1380-1401.

Renner, L. M., & Slack, K. S. (2006). Intimate partner violence and child maltreatment: Understanding intra- and intergenerational connections. *Child Abuse and Neglect, 30*(6), 599-617.

Roberts, N., & Noller, P. (1998). The associations between adult attachment and couple violence: The role of communication patterns and relationship satisfaction. In W. S. Rholes & J. A. Simpson (Eds.), *Attachment theory and close relationships* (pp. 317-350). New York: Guilford.

Romero-Canyas, R., Downey, G., Berenson, K., Ayduk, O., & King, N. J. (2010). Rejection sensitivity and the rejection-hostility link in romantic relationships. *Journal of Personality, 78*(1), 119-148.

Romero-Canyas, R., Downey, G., Reddy, K. S., Rodriguez, S., Cavanaugh, E. J., & Pelayo, R. (2010). Paying to belong: When does rejection trigger ingratiation? *Journal of Personality and Social Psychology, 99*(5), 802-823.

Rossman, B. B. R., Bingham, R. D., & Emde, R. N. (1997). Symptomatology and adaptive functioning for children exposed to normative stressors, dog attack, and parental violence. *Journal of the American Academy of Child & Adolescent Psychiatry, 36*(8), 1089-1097.

Scheeringa, M. S., & Zeanah, C. H. (2001). A relational perspective on PTSD in early childhood. *Journal of Traumatic Stress, 14*(4), 799-815.

Schore, A. N. (2009). Relational trauma and the developing right brain. *Annals of the New York Academy of Sciences, 1159,* 189-203.

Sharhabani-Arzy, R., Amir, M., Kotler, M., & Liran, R. (2003). The toll of intimate partner violence: PTSD among battered women in an Is-raeli sample. *Journal of Interpersonal Violence, 18*(11), 1335-1346.

Silverman, D. K. (2011). A clinical case of an avoidant attachment. *Psychoanalytic Psychology, 28*(2), 293-310.

Simpson, J. A., & Rholes, W. S. (1994). Stress and secure base relationships in adulthood. In K. Bartholomew & D. Perlman (Eds.), *Attachment processes in adult relationships.* London: Jessica Kingsley Publishers.

Slade, A., & Aber, J. L. (1992). Attachments, drives, and development: Conflicts and convergences in theory. In J. W. Barron & M. N. Eagle (Eds.), *Interface of psychoanalysis and psychology* (pp. 154-185). Washington, DC: American Psychological Association.

Slade, A., & Cohen, L. J. (1996). The process of parenting and remembrance of things past. *Infant Mental Health Journal, 17,* 217-238.

Smallbone, S. W., & Dadds, M. R. (2001). Further evidence for a relationship between attachment insecurity and coercive sexual behavior in nonoffenders. *Journal of Interpersonal Violence, 16*(1), 22-35.

Smith, C. A., Ireland, T. O., Park, A., Elwyn, L., & Thornberry, T. P. (2011). Intergenerational continuities and discontinuities in intimate partner violence: A two-generational prospective study. *Journal of Interpersonal Violence, 26*(18), 3720-3752.

Solomon, J., & George, C. (1996). Defining the caregiving system: Towards a theory of caregiving. *Infant Mental Health Journal, 17,* 183-197.

Sonis, J. (2007). Posttraumatic stress disorder does not increase recurrent intimate partner violence. *Journal of Psychological Trauma, 6*(4), 27-48.

Stern, D. (1995). *The motherhood constellation: A unified view of parent-infant psychotherapy.* New York: Basic Books.

Sternberg, K. J., Baradaran, L. P., Abbott, C. B., Lamb, M. E., & Guterman, E. (2006). Type of violence, age, and gender differences in the effects of family violence on children's behavior problems: A mega-analysis. *Developmental Review, 26,* 89-112.

Stith, S. M., Rosen, K. H., Middleton, K. A., Busch, A. L., Lundeberg, K., & Carlton, R. P. (2000). The intergenerational transmission of spouse abuse: A meta-analysis. *Journal of Marriage and the Family, 62,* 640-654.

Taft, C. T., Resick, Watkins, L. E., & Panuzio, J. (2009). An investigation of posttraumatic stress disorder and depressive symptomatology among female victims of interpersonal trauma. *Journal of Family Violence, 24,* 407-415.

Taft, C. T., Vogt, D. S., Mechanic, M. B., & Resick, P. A. (2007). Posttraumatic stress disorder and physical health symptoms among women seeking help for relationship aggression. *Journal of Family Psychology, 21*(3), 354-362.

Taft, C. T., Watkins, L. E., Stafford, J., Street, A. E., & Monson, C. M. (2011). Posttraumatic stress disorder and intimate relationship problems: A meta-analysis. *Journal of Consulting and Clinical Psychology, 79*(1), 22-33.

Tjaden, P., & Thoennes, N. (2000). Prevalence and consequences of male-to-female and female-to-male intimate partner violence as measured by the National Violence Against Women Survey. *Violence Against Women, 6*, 142-161.

Thompson, M. P., Kaslow, N. J., Kingree, J. B., Rashid, A., Puett, R., Jacobs, D., & Matthews, A. (2000). Partner violence, social support, and distress among inner-city African American women. *American Journal of Community Psychology, 28*(1), 127-143.

Trotter, J. L., Bogat, G. A., & Levendosky, A. A. (2004). Risk and protective factors for pregnant women experiencing psychological abuse. *Journal of Emotional Abuse, 4*(2), 53-70.

Tweed, R. G., & Dutton, D. G. (1998). A comparison of impulsive and instrumental subgroups of batterers. *Violence and Victims, 13*(3), 217-230.

van der Kolk, B. A. (2005). Developmental trauma disorder: toward a rational diagnosis for children with complex trauma histories. *Psychiatric Annals, 35*, 401-408.

van der Kolk, B., Roth, S., Pelcovitz, D., Sunday, S., & Spinazzola, J. (2005). Disorders of extreme stress: The empirical foundation of a complex adaptation to trauma. *Journal of Traumatic Stress, 18*(5), 389-399.

Volz, A. R., & Kerig, P. K. (2010). Relational dynamics associated with adolescent dating violence: The roles of rejection sensitivity and relational insecurity. *Journal of Aggression, Maltreatment, and Trauma, 19*(6), 587-602.

Wadhwa, P. D. (2005). Psychoneuroendocrine processes in human pregnancy influence fetal development and health. *Psychoneuroendocrinology, 30*, 724-743.

Walker, L. E. (1979). *The battered woman.* New York: Harper & Row.

Weinstock, M. (2008). The long-term behavioural consequences of prenatal stress. *Neuroscience and Biobehavioral Reviews, 32*, 1073-1086.

Wekerle, C., & Wolfe, D. A. (1998). The role of child maltreatment and attachment style in adolescent relationship violence. *Development and Psychopathology, 10*, 571-586.

Winnicott, D. W. (1960). The theory of the parent-infant relationship. *International Journal of Psychoanalysis, 41*, 585-595.

Winnicott, D. W. (1965). *The maturational process and the facilitating environment.* New York: International Universities Press.

Wolfe, D. A., Crooks, C. V., Lee, V., McIntyre-Smith, A., & Jaffe, P. G. (2003). The effects of children's exposure to intimate partner violence: A meta-analysis and critique. *Clinical Child and Family Psychology Review, 6*, 171-187.

Woods, S. J., & Campbell, J. C. (1993). Posttraumatic stress in battered women: Does the diagnosis fit? *Issues in Mental Health Nursing, 14*(2), 173-186.

Youngblade, L. M., & Belsky, J. (1989). Child maltreatment, infant-parent attachment security, and dysfunctional peer relationships in toddlerhood. *Topics in Early Childhood Special Education, 9*, 1-15.

Zeanah, C. H., & Benoit, D. (1995). Clinical applications of a parent perception interview in infant mental health. *Child and Adolescent Psychiatric Clinics of North America, 4*, 539-554.

Zeanah, C. H., Benoit, D., Hirshberg, L., Barton, M. L., & Regan, C. (1994). Mothers' representations of their infants are concordant with infant attachment classifications. *Developmental Issues in Psychiatry and Psychology, 1*, 9-18.

Zosky, D. L. (2003). Projective identification as a contributor to intimate partner violence. *Clinical Social Work Journal, 31*(4), 419-431.

Psychodynamic Treatment of the Criminal Offender: Making the Case for Longer-Term Treatment in a Longer-Term Setting

Abby L. Mulay, Elspeth Kelly, and Nicole M. Cain

Abstract: In recent years, prisons and jails have become de facto psychiatric hospitals, responsible for the care and treatment of individuals with serious mental illness. Historically, cognitive-behaviorally informed therapeutic approaches have been the treatment of choice among mental health practitioners in correctional settings. However, inmate-clients often present with complex diagnostic issues that are arguably better served by long-term treatment options, such as psychodynamic psychotherapy. We first review the nature of psychotherapy in the correctional setting, as well as treatment barriers and challenges faced by both mental health providers and inmate-clients. We then review treatment studies that examine the efficacy of various therapeutic techniques in correctional/forensic contexts. Finally, we argue that, due to the complex nature of psychopathology, average length of time incarcerated, and treatment issues that arise in this multifaceted and challenging setting, mental health treatment providers should consider providing psychodynamic treatment modalities when working with incarcerated individuals. We also argue that more research is needed to examine the efficacy of these treatment approaches with inmate-clients.

Individuals with serious mental illness in the United States are ten times more likely to reside in correctional facilities than in state psychiatric hospitals (Torrey et al., 2014). A special report released by the Bureau of Justice Statistics (Ditton, 1999) estimated that 16.2% of prisoners in correctional facilities have a mental illness, with 10% of inmates reporting a "mental or emotional condition," and another 10% reporting a history of at least one overnight stay in a psychiatric facility. These results are also echoed in the state system: Cook County Jail in Chicago, for example, houses between 10,000 and 12,000 inmates, approximately one-third of whom have received a psychiatric diagnosis (Kuehn, 2014). Because of the staggering rates of psychiatric illness in the United States prison system, correctional facilities have become the leading providers of mental health services.

The correctional environment can exacerbate mental health symptoms, as well as engender risks for first episodes of serious mental illness (Galanek, 2013). Inmates also tend to present with complex diagnostic issues and are held for extended period of time. For example, one study found that the average length of stay in jail was 151 days, with substance abuse, psychosis, and bipolar disorder as the most commonly reported psychiatric diagnoses (Robst, Constantine, Andel, Boaz, & Howe, 2011). As such, it could be argued that inmates are the ideal candidates for psychodynamic psychotherapy. Although rooted in the concepts and traditions of classic psychoanalysis (Shedler, 2010), modern-day psychodynamic treatment approaches are increasingly being examined within the context of research; in fact, several psychodynamic treatment approaches have demonstrated strong empirical support in the treatment of a wide range of symptoms (for a recent review, see Fonagy, 2015). In this article, we first present background information regarding mental illness in the correctional system, as well as treatment issues relevant to this specialized population. Second, we review evidence surrounding the efficacy of both cognitive-behavioral and psychodynamic treatment approaches within jails and prisons. Finally, we argue that longer-term, psychodynamic treatment approaches may be applied in correctional institutions, though further research is vital in order to determine the efficacy of these approaches with incarcerated individuals.

PSYCHIATRIC ILLNESS IN THE U.S. CORRECTIONAL SYSTEM

Psychopathology, Psychotherapy, and the Correctional Setting

The most common psychiatric diagnoses within the correctional system are schizophrenia, depression, and bipolar disorder (American Psychiatric Association, 2004; Gordon, 2002), and it is estimated that approximately 35% of offenders likely carry a diagnosis of antisocial personality disorder (Black, Gunter, Loveless, Allen, & Sieleni, 2010). Substance use also remains a significant concern, with an estimated 56% of inmates meeting criteria for substance abuse or dependence (Mumola & Karberg, 2006). The treatment of choice for these disorders is psychological therapy or counseling (e.g., Brus, Novakovic, & Friedberg, 2012; Dakwar & Levin, 2013; Duggan, 2009; Karyota-

ki et al., 2016; Peters et al., 2014), yet many inmates do not receive psychological treatment during incarceration. In fact, research suggests that only 13% of the total inmate population receives recurring psychological therapy from a trained professional, with rates highest in both female-only confinement and maximum/high-security facilities (Beck & Maruschak, 2000). Inmates in the federal system are more likely to seek out individual counseling services, when compared to state prison inmates (Gonzalez & Connell, 2014). Group psychotherapy for problematic substance use appears to be the most readily available form of treatment in jails/prisons (e.g., Kelly & Welsh, 2016), yet inmates report a preference for individual psychotherapy (Morgan, Rozycki, & Wilson, 2004; Steffan & Morgan, 2005). Despite this finding, the majority of inmates report being pleased with the mental health treatment that they receive during incarceration (Way, Sawyer, Kahkejian, Moffitt, & Lilly, 2007).

Few studies have explored the characteristics of mental health workers in the correctional setting. MacKain, Myers, Ostapiej, and Newman (2010) examined characteristics of correctional mental health care providers in North Carolina. About 47% were female, master's level clinicians (73%), with reported salaries ranging from $51,000 to $60,0000. Correctional facilities often report that they are understaffed and subsequently unable to provide adequate training to mental health employees (e.g., Olver, Preston, Camilleri, Helmus, & Starzomski, 2011). Psychologists working in the correctional environment also tend to report high levels of burnout and low levels of job satisfaction (Senter, Morgan, Serna-McDonald, & Bewley, 2010).

Treatment with Medication

In addition to psychotherapy, the mental health issues of inmates are often treated with a wide range of psychotropic medications. Upon admission, it has been found that approximately 18% of federal and state inmates are already taking some sort of psychotropic medication (Gonzales & Connell, 2014). Although research examining the use of psychotropic medication in United States jails and prisons is scarce, a recent study conducted in England by Hassan, Senior, Frisher, Edge, and Shaw (2014) found that psychotropic medications were prescribed to 19.6% of male prisoners and 44% of female prisoners. Of those taking psychotropic medication, most inmates were prescribed only one psychotropic medication (67.2%), with antidepressants being the most commonly prescribed (13.8% of male inmates and 33.4% of women inmates). Within the United States, Veysey, Stenius, Mazade, and Schacht (2007) mailed surveys to all prisons and jails with a capacity of 1,000 or above. Of the 54 completed surveys, results revealed that an average of 219 prison inmates and 182 jail detainees received some sort of psychiatric medication, which corresponded to 83% of individuals receiving psychiatric intervention. It has also been found that inmates with schizophrenia are most likely to be prescribed psychotropic medication (Gonzales & Connell, 2014). While some have expressed concern that there is an over-reliance upon psychiatric medication in the correctional setting (Hassan, Edge, Senior, & Shaw, 2013), the decision to prescribe medication is generally based upon appropriate clinical factors, such as presenting psychopathology, rather than as a way in which to exert control over the inmate (Sommers & Baskin, 1991).

With regard to medication adherence, Baillargeon, Contreras, Grady, Black, and Murray (2000) surveyed a large sample of Texas prisoners with depression. Results revealed that medication adherence was significantly associated with male gender, while White and Black prisoners were more adherent than their Hispanic counterparts. However, medication non-adherence remains a significant problem among inmates, and it has been associated with violence among forensic psychiatric patients with psychotic disorders (Alia-Klein, O'Rourke, Goldstein, & Malaspina, 2007). While inmates may elect to take psychotropic medication, inmates may also be administered psychotropic medication against their will. As outlined in the landmark case, *Washington v. Harper* (1990), inmates may be administered psychotropic medication against their will if they are deemed a danger to self or other, or if the psychotropic medication is in the best interest of the overall health of the inmate. Although recent research suggests that involuntary medication does not decrease inpatient hospital stays for inmates, it does appear to decrease the number of disciplinary infractions among inmates taking antipsychotic medication (Salem, Kushnier, Dorio, & Reeves, 2015). Staff and inmates alike have also expressed support for the use of involuntary treatment approaches in the treatment of high-risk individuals (e.g., Hogan, Barton-Beliessa, & Lambert, 2015).

TREATMENT BARRIERS IN THE CORRECTIONAL SETTING

Provider Treatment Barriers

Generally speaking, correctional mental health providers believe that they are providing a useful service to their inmate-clients (Bewley & Morgan, 2011). Despite the availability of psychological treatment, psychotherapists face a significant number of challenges when attempting to deliver quality mental health care in the correctional setting. The role of the prison psychologist is generally centered on ongoing risk assessment (Forrester, MacLennan, Slade, Brown, & Exworthy, 2014) and crisis intervention (Huffman, 2006), rather than individual or group psychotherapy. It has also been suggested that the correctional environment itself fosters negative staff attitudes toward inmates, including the belief that if staff members show empathy and kindness toward an inmate, they put themselves at risk of being "conned" (e.g., Farkas, 2010). The therapist in the correctional setting may therefore not allow for or possibly impede, either knowingly or unknowingly, the development of a therapeutic alliance with an inmate-client, for fear of negative consequences.

Inmate Treatment Barriers

In addition to provider treatment barriers, inmates are hesitant to seek psychological services for a variety of reasons. In order to systematically assess for potential treatment barriers, Morgan, Steffan, Shaw, and Wilson (2007) surveyed 418 inmates from varying security levels (i.e., the reception unit, minimum security, and maximum security). Inmates were presented with a three-page survey, intended to assess experience with and attitudes toward mental health treatment. Results revealed four specific reasons why inmates were hesitant to seek mental health services: the desire to protect oneself (e.g., the desire to maintain confidentiality, the avoidance of appearing weak to others), practical barriers (e.g., lack of knowledge about how to obtain treatment), the preference to rely on one's self or close friends, and not having faith in staff's ability to help. Inmate demographic characteristics also appear to play a role in who seeks treatment; for example, older inmates are less likely to seek out mental health services, when compared to their younger counterparts (Mitchell & Latchford, 2010; Skogstad, Deane, & Spicer, 2006), and those with less serious psychopathology are more likely to seek out services (Faust & Magaletta, 2010).

Correctional facilities also engender an inherent power differential between the staff and inmates—the imprisoning and the imprisoned. It has long been recognized that this disparity of power frequently results in the unjust treatment of prisoners (e.g., Brenner, 2010; Haney, Banks, & Zimbardo, 1973), which has likely instilled a sense of mistrust in incarcerated individu-

als. Rhodes (2004) noted that the toxic correctional environment is "bound to cause harm" (p. 119). Although it is a popular belief among laypeople that the correctional environment should be harsh and punishing, poor environmental conditions (e.g., unclean living conditions) are associated with higher rates of violence (Bierie, 2012). Consequences of this long history of inmate maltreatment have likely resulted in a pervasive culture of mistrust of prison staff among inmates.

Mistrust might also be warranted because patient/therapist confidentiality in the correctional setting differs from the therapeutic relationship in the community. In the majority of states, psychotherapists must abide by the "duty to protect," which was born out of *Tarasoff v. Regents of the University of California* (1976). As such, a psychotherapist is legally obligated to breach confidentiality when the patient poses a clear and imminent threat to the safety of an identified individual. Similar guidelines require mental health professionals to breach confidentiality when the patient expresses the well-thought out intent and plan to commit suicide. According to the task force on jails and prisons assembled by the American Psychiatric Association (APA; 2000), psychiatrists working in the correctional environment should do their best to adhere to the confidentiality standards that are observed in the community. However, APA asserts that confidentiality should be broken when an inmate poses a clear risk of escape from the institution, or when an inmate is responsible to creating chaos within the institution. In cases of conflict between the inmate and the institution, the mental health worker is required to report illegal activities and/or potential threats (Krupers, 2005). Many also report a willingness to breach confidentiality if they believe that an inmate is in danger of harming himself or herself, or if an inmate has been the victim of some form of abuse (Elger, Handtke, & Wangmo, 2015). It is not surprising that an inmate may be hesitant to seek out mental health services, for fear that honesty may result in a behavioral infraction or the perception that the inmate is weak. Consequently, inmates should be fully informed of the limits to confidentiality in the correctional setting (Pinta, 2010).

Guidelines have also been put forth by the International Association for Correctional and Forensic Psychology (IACFP). Much like the APA, the IACFP also recommends that correctional psychologists adhere to community confidentiality standards to the best of their ability (for further information, see IACFP Practice Standards Committee, 2010). The correctional mental health worker should not assume any dual roles that overlap with other institutional duties (e.g., custody), as involvement in such activities could pose a risk of harm to inmate-clients. Although the correctional mental health worker is employed by the correctional facility, providers are expected to advocate for the highest quality of mental health services available to their inmate-clients.

Social and racial differences between staff and inmates, and the long history of racism and race-based mistreatment (e.g., Johnson, 2001; Markus, 2009; Reasons, 1974; Trulson, Marquart, Hemmens, & Carroll, 2008), compound inmates' difficulty in seeking psychological services. According to statistics released by the Bureau of Justice in 2013 (Carson, 2014), non-Hispanic Blacks (37%) comprise the largest portion of male inmates under state or federal jurisdiction, compared to non-Hispanic Whites (32%) and Hispanics (22%). Although the majority of female prisoners identify as White, the rate of imprisonment for Black females (113 per 100,000) is twice that of White females (51 per 100,000; Carson, 2014). Mental health workers in the correctional setting overwhelmingly identify as White (Senter, Morgan, Serna-McDonald, & Bewley, 2010), which may dissuade an inmate from seeking psychological services.

Krupers (2005) also argues that prison fosters a type of hegemonic masculinity known as "toxic masculinity." He defines toxic masculinity as a hyper-masculine trait that both emphasizes competition, dominance, violence, and the subjugation of women and the LGBTQ community, and disavows any emotional expression, with the exception of anger. Krupers asserts that engaging in psychotherapy directly contradicts toxic masculinity, as it communicates to both oneself and one's fellow inmates that there is something that the individual needs help with, which can be perceived of as a sign of weakness. This is particularly dangerous, as being perceived as "weak in the head" (p. 720) by others may incite targeted violence, as toxic masculinity encourages dominance over one's "weaker" peers. In contrast to male prisoners, female prisoners report difficulty trusting others, which impacts their willingness to seek treatment (Cantora, Mellow, & Schlager, 2016).

CAN OFFENDERS WITH MENTAL ILLNESS BE TREATED?

Once an inmate-client decides to seek treatment, research is mixed regarding the success of treatment for this specialized population. Some research suggests that participation in mental health treatment during incarceration is an effective strategy in the reduction of misconduct (Houser, Blasko, & Belenko, 2014), as well as recidivism upon release (Fisher et al., 2014). Abarcen, Gallo, Looman, and Goodwill (2016) examined the effectiveness of psychological treatment in the reduction of recidivism within a Canadian sample of criminal offenders considered at high risk for engaging in future criminal behaviors. Participants were federal offenders who were housed in a minimum-security institution with access to the community. The authors coded whether the study participants received no treatment, "moderate" treatment (i.e., 19 sessions or fewer), and "high" treatment (i.e., 20 sessions or more). Treatment was broadly defined as individual therapy sessions. Results showed that participants in the "moderate" group were 7.7 times less likely to reoffend when compared to the no treatment group, while participants in the "high" treatment condition were 11.6 times less likely to reoffend when compared to the no treatment group. These results suggest that psychotherapy may significantly reduce criminal recidivism.

Other research studies, in contrast, have not produced such an optimistic view of the potential long-term results of psychotherapy in the correctional setting. Morgan et al. (2012), for example, used meta-analytic techniques to examine the effectiveness of mental health treatment for offenders with mental illness. The majority (56.3%) of treatments examined by the authors were structured in nature, often utilizing a formalized treatment manual. Treatments ranged in length from 1.5 weeks to 78 weeks ($M = 24.9$; $SD = 27.2$), while total number of sessions ranged from 3 to 20 ($M = 11.8$; $SD = 7$). Overall, the authors found no evidence for decreased rates of criminal recidivism following treatment. The authors were, however, able to find other more immediate benefits of treatment, including a significant reduction in patients' overall levels of distress, as well as improvements in their ability to cope and institutional adjustment. It therefore remains unclear whether using structured interventions within the forensic or correctional setting is effective in the reduction of later criminal offending.

TREATMENT MODALITIES IN THE CORRECTIONAL SETTING

Cognitive Behavioral Therapy (CBT)

In order to address issues faced by criminal offenders with mental illness, mental health providers in the forensic and/or correctional setting tend to rely upon highly structured, cognitive behaviorally informed treatment modalities (e.g., Campbell

et al., 2016; Cohen & Harvey, 2016; Gannon et al., 2015; Lanza, Garcia, Lamelas, & González-Menéndez, 2014; Needham et al., 2015; Zlotnick, Johnson, & Najavits, 2009; Zlotnick, Najavits, Rohsenow, & Johnson, 2003). In fact, an overwhelming number of correctional psychologists identify as cognitive-behavioral practitioners (Bewely & Morgan, 2011; Boothby & Clements, 2000), yet these numbers may actually reflect the nature of the setting, rather than practitioner preference. For example, cognitive behavioral treatments tend to elicit symptom reduction in a relatively short amount of time (e.g., Feeney, Connor, Young, Tucker, & McPherson, 2006; Jones & Clausen, 2013; Naeem et al., 2015; Wu, Li, & Cho, 2014). It is therefore not surprising that correctional psychotherapists frequently utilize these intervention strategies, given the nature of the correctional setting, including the large numbers of individuals with severe psychiatric disorders (Kuehn, 2014), the pressure upon correctional psychologists and other mental health professionals to perform administrative duties (Boothby & Clements, 2000), and overall levels of occupational burnout (Senter et al., 2010).

As such, research remains focused on the efficacy of CBT approaches in the correctional setting. Wolff, Frueh, Shi, and Schumann (2012), for example, examined the effectiveness of Seeking Safety, a manualized cognitive-behavioral treatment, within a sample of incarcerated women with comorbid posttraumatic stress disorder and substance-use disorders. Although Seeking Safety was originally designed to include both individual and group components, the authors utilized the group therapy component only. Results revealed that, among the 74 women who completed the intervention, there were significant reductions in psychopathology and PTSD symptoms, and the majority of participants reported that they found the intervention to be helpful. Similarly, Glowe-Kollisch et al. (2014) administered an intervention to jail inmates housed in mental observation units. The authors drew upon the tenants of CBT, including motivational interviewing, social learning, and coping skills, in the design of their six-week treatment program. Topics such as engagement in treatment, medication compliance, coping skills, emotions, and symptom awareness were discussed. When study participants ($N = 218$) were compared with an earlier cohort of patients who were also residing on mental observation units, results revealed significant reductions in all domains assessed, including self-injurious behaviors, the need for use of force, the number of infractions, the need for suicide watch, and recidivism. However, when the authors compared the inmates who participated in the study to those who declined to participate but were living in the mental observation units at the same time, only time spent on suicide watch and recidivism were significantly lower. Mennicke, Tripodi, Veeh, Wilke, and Kennedy (2015) examined whether inmates exposed to a domestic violence treatment program showed improvements in recidivism following release. The authors evaluated STOP (i.e., survey, think, options, and prevention) and Change Direction, which is a 20-week, manualized CBT program with both group and individual components. The program aims to reduce attitudes related to the commission of domestic violence and prevent future incarceration. Results revealed significant improvements in attitudes toward women and criminogenic thinking following participation in the program. With regard to recidivism, although there were no significant differences at five- and seven-year follow-up points, there was some evidence for an overall reduction in reoffending.

Research has also examined the efficacy of Dialectical Behavior Therapy (DBT; Linehan, 1993, 2015), a cognitive-behaviorally informed intervention that is often used to treat complex and difficult psychopathology (for a review, see Berzins & Trestman, 2004). Nee and Farman (2005) examined a DBT pilot program with female prisoners in custody within the United Kingdom prison system. All participants ($N = 30$) met diagnostic criteria for borderline personality disorder. Despite the small sample size, the authors found significant improvements in self-esteem, impulsivity, and dissociative experiences. A similar study, conducted by Evershed et al. (2003) in the United States, found an 18-month treatment based on DBT to be effective in reducing participants' violent incidents and experience of anger and hostility. Despite the significant findings, however, Evershed et al.'s findings should be interpreted with caution due to a number of limitations, most notably its small sample size ($N = 8$). Within a sample of 63 incarcerated participants, Shelton, Sampl, Kesten, Zhang, and Trestman (2009) administered a twice-weekly, 16-week DBT group intervention, also intended to address problematic anger. The authors noted significant improvements in affect, aggression, and coping styles. Although CBT and DBT have been demonstrated as efficacious in the correctional setting, these treatments tend to focus upon behavioral issues (e.g., problematic anger responses, criminogenic risk factors), rather than the complex emotional issues often faced by incarcerated individuals that could be effectively addressed using longer-term treatment modalities.

Psychodynamic Treatment Approaches

Due to the complex combination of severe psychopathology and criminal behaviors, some have argued that the offender with mental illness requires more than a time-limited intervention (McGauley & Bartlett, 2015). From this reasoning, it can be argued that more offenders would benefit if they had access to longer-term, comprehensive psychotherapeutic treatments, so long as that treatment could be expected to conclude before the offender's sentence is complete. According to a recent report, the average length of stay for federal prisoners is 37.5 months

(Motivans, 2015), more than enough time to allow for psychodynamic interventions, as these treatments tend to range in length from 12 to 34 months (see Leichsenring & Rabung, 2011).

However, only a handful of studies have focused on psychodynamic treatment in the forensic or correctional setting. Moreover, many of these studies are limited by their reliance on qualitative methods, such as case reviews and theoretical discussions. For example, Ware, Wilson, Tapp, and Moore (2016) conducted qualitative interviews with four forensic male patients housed in a secure hospital who had completed an 18-month program of group and individual mentalization-based therapy (MBT). MBT is a psychoanalytic treatment approach that promotes the development of mentalization, or the ability to understand one's own internal state, as well as the internal states of others (Allen, Fonagy, & Bateman, 2008). Two participants had a diagnosis of schizophrenia (paranoid type), one participant had a diagnosis of borderline personality disorder, and one participant had a diagnosis of personality disorder not otherwise specified. Overall, these four participants reported that, following MBT, they were better able to manage problematic behaviors and emotions. They were also able to process past violent events, which led to the development of empathy. This qualitative study by Ware and colleagues demonstrates that longer-term treatment can successfully be implemented in the forensic setting.

Similarly, Sleed, Baradon, and Fonagy (2013) examined whether an attachment-based group intervention, which was designed for mothers and babies held in prison, could successfully improve the capacity for reflective functioning, parent–infant interactions, depression, and maternal object relations. The intervention, known as New Beginnings, consisted of two, 2-hour sessions per day, one day per week, for eight weeks. Baradon, Fonagy, Bland, Lénárd, and Sleed (2008) provide an overview of the New Beginnings intervention; specifically, session topics are intended to trigger the attachment relationship between the mother and infant, including the pregnancy, the extended family of the infant, childhood experiences of the mother, the mother's perceptions of the infant, the experience of being a mother, and the mother's future goals for both herself and the infant. Informational handouts and worksheets, and homework assignments are also included in the intervention, which are included so that the mothers involved can reflect upon the study materials at a later date. Although psychiatric diagnostic information was not included in the study, mothers in the control condition demonstrated a worsening in their reflective functioning. The authors suggested that the prison environment may account for this decline, as separation between the mother and infant is a common occurrence during incarceration. In contrast, maternal levels of sensitivity and attunement (e.g., non-intrusiveness, consistency in responding to the infant) remained consistent in the intervention group. However, it is important to note that, due to the short-term nature of the intervention and the study design, it is unknown whether the treatment effects held beyond the two-month follow-up period.

Finally, Smith (1999) reported that, in her work as a counselor at a larger correctional institution, she focuses upon understanding the unconscious conflicts of her female inmate-clients. Unfortunately, she did not provide a detailed description outlining *how* she implemented this strategy with inmate-clients, nor did she report the diagnoses that she worked with in the correctional setting. As such, the empirical literature on the effectiveness of long-term psychodynamic approaches in the correctional setting is limited, despite growing evidence that psychodynamic treatments are effective (e.g., Bateman & Fonagy, 2013; Clarkin, Levy, Lenzenweger, & Kernberg, 2007; Diamond et al., 2013; Leichsenring, Leweke, Klein, & Steinert, 2015; Leichsenring & Rabung, 2008; Milrod et al., 2007; Shedler, 2010) and may be ideal for the correctional setting, especially given the challenging issues clinicians often face when working with this population.

CONSIDERATIONS WHEN WORKING WITH OFFENDERS WITH MENTAL ILLNESS

Boundaries

Regardless of theoretical orientation, mental health practitioners in the correctional setting are encouraged to maintain strict boundaries with their inmate-clients. Marquat, Barnhill, and Balshaw-Biddle (2001) defined boundary violations as "actions which blur, minimize, or disrupt professional distance between" (p. 878) an individual in a professional role and the individual who receives the professional service. Such violations not only violate the ethical code of conduct that psychologists typically abide by (American Psychological Association, 2010), but they also undermine the security and stability of the correctional institution (Blackburn, Fowler, Mullings, & Marquart, 2011). It has also been suggested that prison and jail employees may be especially prone to boundary violations, due to the atmosphere of deprivation engendered by the correctional environment (Worley, 2016; Worley & Worley, 2016). The correctional atmosphere may be difficult for the correctional employee to withstand, thus leading to the desire to connect with others, even if that other is an inmate.

It is also important for the correctional mental health worker to keep in mind that, inmates, for a variety of reasons, might actually welcome boundary violations. Incarcerated individuals may exploit prison guards in an effort to profit in some way (e.g., developing a relationship with a prison guard to obtain cigarettes), while some inmates may engage in behaviors as a way in which to purposely tax the prison environment (e.g., putting a staff member into a compromising situation, which puts both the job security of the employee, as well as the security of the institution, at risk; Worley, Marquart, & Mullings, 2003). While the majority of inmates in the United States prison system are not permitted to have sexual relationships with individuals residing in the community (i.e., conjugal visits; Carlson, 2015), inmates may seek out sexual relationships with prison staff or guards, often due to the social isolation that commonly accompanies higher levels of security. Carcedo, López, Orgaz, Toth, and Fernández-Rouco (2008) interviewed 188 male and female prison inmates and found that inmates' psychological health was associated with their levels of social loneliness and sexual satisfaction. Thus, while boundary violations may be viewed from a negative light from an organization that mandates rules and order, these violations may be viewed as inmates' attempts as enhancing their own psychological health through decreasing social isolation. Younger inmates, as well as inmates who receive more disciplinary infractions, are more likely to seek out consensual sexual relationships during incarceration (Tewskbury & Connor, 2014). Mental health providers are therefore cautioned to maintain awareness of their relationship with their inmate-clients, in order to avoid potentially dangerous or damaging situations.

Transference

Transference was first described by Sigmund Freud (1912, 1914, 1940) as the phenomenon by which the patient projects feelings about a past figure—commonly a parent or another important figure from the patient's childhood—onto the analyst. Thus, should a patient have experienced trauma at the hands of abusive parents, he or she may, similarly, experience the therapist as abusive, while demonstrating difficulty viewing the therapist as a trustworthy figure. The issue of transference is particularly relevant to the correctional setting, as incarcerated individuals commonly report traumatic early experiences. For example, a survey conducted by Harlow (1999) on behalf of the U.S. Department of Justice, found alarming rates of physical and/or sexual abuse in correctional populations. Results revealed that over half (57.2%) of female state prison inmates reported a history of abuse, with 36.7% experiencing this abuse before the age of 18. Within a sample of 100 men who were being held in a county jail, a staggering 59% reported some form of childhood sexual abuse (Johnson, Ross, Taylor, Williams, Carvajal, & Peters, 2005). Because of these early traumatic experiences, inmates with a history of abuse may have learned to experience authority figures as violent and unsafe, and may, consequently, have difficulty engaging in the therapeutic relationship. Gill (1982) advised mental health professionals to not only understand patients' reactions to their therapist as merely a prototype of a past relationship, but to also question their own role in the making of this reaction. Extending and refining Freud's definition of transference, Gill (1982) noted, "Only if he [the analyst] considers himself a blank screen could he conceive of a patient's responses being dictated [solely] from within the patient" (p. 112). From this perspective, therapists should also question whether they, too, might be contributing to patients' difficulties in confiding their histories to the therapist, as there may

be very real repercussions for doing so. Unbeknownst to the correctional psychologist, he or she may represent a parental figure to the inmate-client, which could activate material that lies underneath the inmate-client's conscious awareness.

Issues of social class may also contribute to transferential reactions of the inmate-client. It is possible that mental health workers in correctional facilities may experience inmate-clients' fantasies that they are "only doing the job for the money." It is beyond the scope of this article to articulate the reasons that draw mental health workers to the correctional setting, but financial compensation in the correctional environment is undoubtedly low on the list. This type of assertion may, instead, be indicative of a transferential reaction. For example, an inmate-client who has felt mistreated or taken advantage of by authority figures in his past may have more difficulty trusting in his mental health workers' presumably good intentions in the present. It is also worth noting the realities that may contribute to this mistrust. A mental health worker's average salary of $50,000 to $60,000 (MacKain et al., 2010) towers over the inmate-client's wage of $0.23 to $1.15 per hour in prison (U.S. Department of Justice, 2009), and will likely exceed the inmate-client's income once they enter the community. Additionally, there is an unfortunate history in the United States of healthcare professionals abusing their rights to advance their own professions (e.g., Tuskegee syphilis experiment; Centers for Disease Control and Prevention, 2016), which may contribute to an overarching mistrust of the healthcare community.

There is a rich tradition of empirical support for the construct of transference, across both clinical and social psychology (e.g., Anderson & Berk, 1998; Anderson, Glassman, Chen, & Cole, 1995; Fried, Crits-Christoph, & Luboksky, 1992; Høglend et al., 2008). Studies that have examined the construct of transference in the correctional setting have done so in an unsystematic fashion, generally using case studies to illustrate their points (e.g., Collier, 2015; Elliot, 2011; Pelladeau & De Kernier, 2015). Due to this dearth of empirical support, we argue that transference should be examined within the correctional setting, which can be achieved using relatively simple data collection methods (e.g., self-report measures). It should also be noted that many psychodynamic treatment approaches are specifically designed to target issues related to transference.

Countertransference

Although many definitions exist, countertransference can be broadly defined as when the client/patient provokes unconscious feelings within the mental health treatment provider (Knott, 2016). Aviv and Springmann (1990) distinguished between three types of countertransference: *therapist induced* (i.e., the manifestation of the therapist's personality traits and unconscious conflicts), *client/patient induced* (i.e., countertransference attitudes that are engendered by the client/patient), and *combined countertransference* (i.e., when therapist- and client/patient-induced are interwoven with one another). Although not commonly referred to in the cognitive-behavioral literature, it has been argued that the examination of countertransference remains an important aspect of all therapeutic techniques, including CBT (e.g., Prasko et al., 2010), yet psychodynamically oriented practitioners tend to be more aware of and in tune with their internal reactions to clients or patients (Gordon et al., 2016).

Regardless of theoretical orientation, therapists in the correctional or forensic setting will likely experience complex internal reactions to their clients, which may influence therapists' behavior toward the client, or even the choice of intervention. For example, is not uncommon for a correctional therapist to encounter an inmate-client who is incarcerated for a violent offense. While special consideration might be given to the exploration of the potential meaning of the illegal act from the offender's perspective (Yakeley & Adshead, 2013), the examination of difficult case material may elicit negative reactions by the psychotherapist, including feelings of victimization, intimidation, humiliation, and/or exploitation (Springmann, 1988). The mental health practitioner is therefore encouraged to monitor his or her own reactions to inmate-clients and case material, as well as seek out supervision or consultation as needed.

Specific to the forensic setting, Protter and Travin (1983) delineated four unique countertransference "response sets" and argued that exploring one's specific countertransference to a patient may aid clinicians in their diagnosis and treatment. In the *Mad-or-Bad* response, clinicians may focus on the patient's antisocial qualities at the expense of acknowledging further psychiatric disturbances. The authors suggested that this is the result of the clinician feeling manipulated or controlled by the patient's antisocial qualities, followed by an experience of anger in response to this uncomfortable experience, and finally resulting in a desire to simply "dismiss" the patient as "bad" (e.g., a psychopath) rather than "mad" (e.g., psychiatrically ill in other ways, as well). They also suggested that there is something inherently seductive about focusing on antisocial qualities, which commonly results in the clinician colluding with patients' desires to keep their more severe psychopathology hidden.

Clinicians whose countertransference is consistent with the *Moralistic-Punitive* response tend to respond to patients' criminal behaviors with excessive punitive condemnation. Protter and Travin (1983) posited that this is likely due to the near prolific experience of being victim, or knowing a victim, of a crime, but warned that this punitive response may impede the development of a therapeutic relationship. Rather, they encouraged clinicians to maintain an open mind, while perhaps acknowledging to an extent their honest reactions to the crimes.

Protter and Travin (1983) also noted that, because many clinicians are afraid of patients who inappropriately express anger, aggression, and violence, they might unknowingly discourage patients from even exploring any underlying aggressive impulses. The consequences of such countertransference, included within the *Violence and Aggression* response set, may communicate to patients that their aggressive impulses are unmanageable and unsafe, which may hinder the valuable exploration of such underlying urges. The authors warned, however, that if clinicians find that they are actively discouraging a patient from expressing aggression, this countertransferential reaction may indicate that the patient is unable to express anger in an appropriate way, and may suggest the utility of including addition staff during sessions to ensure safety.

Finally, the authors also discussed a *Periodic Negative* response set, which includes the clinician's intermittent negative responses to patients with severe personality disorders. Protter and Travin (1983) suggested that these negative responses are in response to patients' primitive mental operations (e.g., splitting, projection), but encouraged clinicians to also evaluate to what extent their negative responses to the patients may be the result of their own histories so as to decide whether they are capable of working with that specific patient.

Thus, mental health providers in the correctional setting experience countertransference reactions that are not only elicited by the inmate-client, but also by the nature of the crime committed, as well as the punitive environment in which they practice. It may also be difficult for some clinicians to separate inmate-clients from their criminal offense histories. Mental health providers are encouraged to remain vigilant when working with this population and to closely monitor their countertransference reactions, seeking supervision or consultation when needed.

Taken together, the complex considerations when working with offenders with mental illness, such as boundary violations, transference, and countertransference, lend themselves to longer-term, psychodynamically oriented treatment modalities, rather than short-term, symptom driven interventions. However, more research is needed to examine the effectiveness of longer-term psychodynamic interventions in the correctional setting.

CONCLUSIONS

The United States is currently facing a mental health crisis, which is undoubtedly experienced by correctional facilities across the country. For a variety of reasons that are beyond the scope of this review article (e.g., deinstitutionalization, the "War on Drugs"), correctional facilities have become the leading provider of mental health services to disenfranchised populations. As previously discussed, mental health workers in the correctional environment tend to report high levels of burnout and frustration (e.g., Oser, Biebel, Pullen, & Harp, 2013; Perkins & Oser, 2014; Senter et al., 2010). Research also points to a shortage of adequately trained correctional mental health professionals (Olver et al., 2011). Job dissatisfaction, coupled with inadequate staffing and training, results in mental health workers' inability to provide quality mental health services to their inmate-clients, including longer-term psychodynamic psychotherapy. Instead, most correctional institutions rely upon shorter-term CBT-informed approaches in the treatment of inmate psychopathology, and research undoubtedly points to the effectiveness of these treatments. However, we argue that the complex nature of the correctional environment, coupled with the diagnoses commonly seen in the correctional setting, call for a more in-depth and holistic approach to inmate psychiatric treatment.

CBT interventions in the correctional setting tend to focus on problematic and overt criminogenic behaviors (e.g., anger management, reduction of recidivism), rather than the complex issues (e.g., trauma, personality pathology, attachment insecurity) that many inmate-clients bring with them to the correctional context. From this perspective, it is easy to think of the criminal offender as just that—an individual defined by his or her criminal past. Although reducing recidivism should undoubtedly be one goal of a psychological treatment in the correctional setting, inmate-clients also experience significant mental health issues, independent of their criminal offense histories. Of note, inmates report high rates of childhood physical and sexual abuse (Harlow, 1999; Johnson et al., 2005), which has likely left an imprint upon their psychological functioning. Moreover, many inmates report difficult life experiences, including poor socioeconomic conditions (Friestad, 2010), feelings of shame and stigma as a result of being labeled a "criminal" (West, Mulay, DeLuca, O'Donovon, & Yanos, 2016), and substance abuse (Facchin & Margola, 2016). Therefore, we argue that a comprehensive and long-term treatment approach—one that addresses factors beyond that of criminogenic risk—is vital to successful psychological treatment in the correctional setting.

Longer-term psychodynamic treatment approaches are uniquely designed to target complex treatment issues faced by both inmate-clients and their mental health providers. Importantly, these treatment modalities elicit long-term and lasting structural change within the individual, rather than short-term symptom reduction (e.g., Fjeldstand, Høglend, & Lorentzen, 2016; Huber, Henrich, Clarkin, & Klug, 2013; Leichsenring, Abbass, Luyten, Hilsenroth, & Rabung, 2013; Lindfors, Knekt, Virtala, & Laaksonen, 2012). Psychodynamic treatment approaches have been shown to successfully target serious symptomology, in-

cluding psychosis (e.g., Rosenbaum et al., 2012) and personality pathology (e.g., Clarkin et al., 2001), both of which are commonly reported by inmate-clients in correctional institutions. As such, we argue that these treatments have the potential to ultimately reduce recidivism; if the inmate-client receives longer-term psychotherapy during incarceration, there is a greater likelihood of improved functioning in the community upon release, which may lead to decreased engagement in criminal behaviors. However, further research is needed to investigate the efficacy of long-term psychodynamic treatments in the correctional setting.

Toward this aim, there are several measures that could easily be implemented in a correction setting to empirically examine the process and outcome of long-term psychodynamic psychotherapy. For example, the Adult Attachment Interview (AAI; George, Kaplan, & Main, 1985) has been used in the forensic context (e.g., Frodi, Dernevik, Sepa, Philipson, & Bragesjö, 2001; Levinson & Fonagy, 2004) and has been shown to successfully distinguish between a clinical sample of individuals who committed a sex offense and a comparable sample of non-clinical individuals (Grattagliano et al., 2015). In addition, Fonagy, Target, Steele, and Steele (1998) have developed a protocol to assess mentalization (or reflective function) in conjunction with the AAI. Fonagy and colleagues have used this protocol to assess change in mentalization with forensic and correctional samples (e.g., Levinson & Fonagy, 2004; Sleed et al., 2013). We encourage psychodynamic researchers to utilize these measures in the correctional setting to examine the efficacy of psychodynamic psychotherapy with this population.

Finally, it is also important for any psychotherapy research being done in the correctional setting to assess the working alliance, or the establishment of a positive relationship between the client/patient and the therapist (e.g., Bordin, 1979). The working alliance is an integral component of all psychotherapy, but is especially important in psychodynamic psychotherapy. The most common measure of the working alliance is the Working Alliance Inventory (WAI; Horvath & Greenberg, 1989), which has already been successfully implemented by researchers in correctional and forensic settings (e.g., Blasko & Jeglic, 2016; Donnelly et al., 2011; West, Vayshenker, Rotter, & Yanos, 2015). We argue that the examination of the working alliance is especially important in the correctional setting, due to the complex issues surrounding boundaries, transference, and countertransference that arise. As noted previously, the prison environment offers significant challenges that are often not faced by mental health practitioners in a general community setting (e.g., the frequency and intensity of boundary violations), and the examination of the working alliance within the prison environment may help clinicians to better understand these complex treatment issues.

In sum, we argue that, due to the treatment issues that typically arise in the correctional setting, as well as the average length of stay for inmates in Unites States prisons, a longer-term treatment approach will likely benefit the inmate-client seeking psychological services. However, we acknowledge that there is a dearth of literature examining these important issues, and we encourage researchers to explore the utility of psychodynamic approaches in the correctional setting.

REFERENCES

Abracen, J., Gallo, A., Looman, J., & Goodwill, A. (2016). Individual community-based treatment of offenders with mental illness: Relationship to recidivism. *Journal of Interpersonal Violence, 31*(10), 1842-1858. https://doi.org/10.1177/0886260515570745

Alia-Klein, N., O'Rourke, T. M., Goldstein, R. Z., & Malaspina, D. (2007). Insight into illness and adherence to psychotropic medications are separately associated with violence severity in a forensic sample. *Aggressive Behavior, 33*(1), 86-96. https://doi.org/10.1002/ab.20170

Allen, J. G., Fonagy, P., & Bateman, A. W. (2008). *Mentalizing in clinical practice.* Arlington, VA: American Psychiatric Association.

American Psychiatric Association. (2000). *Psychiatric services in jails and prisons: A task force report of the American Psychiatric Association.* Washington, DC: Author.

American Psychiatric Association. (2004). *Mental illness and the criminal justice system: Redirecting resources toward treatment, not containment.* Arlington, VA: Author.

American Psychological Association. (2010). *American Psychological Association ethical principles of psychologists and code of conduct.* Retrieved from http://www.apa.org/ethics/code/

Andersen, S. M., & Berk, M. S. (1998). Transference in everyday experience: Implications of experimental research for relevant clinical phenomena. *Review of General Psychology, 2*(1), 81-120. https://doi.org/10.1037/1089-2680.2.1.81

Andersen, S. M., Glassman, N. S., Chen, S., & Cole, S. W. (1995). Transference in social perception: The role of chronic accessibility in significant-other representations. *Journal of Personality and Social Psychology, 69*(1), 41-57. https://doi.org/10.1037/0022-3514.69.1.41

Aviv, A., & Springmann, R. R. (1990). Negative countertransference and negative therapeutic reactions: Prognostic indicators in the analysis of severe psychopathology. *Contemporary Psychoanalysis, 26*(4), 692-715. https://doi.org/10.1080/00107530.1990.10746686

Baillargeon, J., Contreras, S., Grady, J. J., Black, S. A., & Murray, O. (2000). Compliance with antidepressant medication among prison inmates with depressive disorders. *Psychiatric Services, 51*(11), 1444-1446. https://doi.org/10.1176/appi.ps.51.11.1444

Baradon, T., Fonagy, P., Bland, K., Lénárd, K., & Sleed, M. (2008). New Beginnings—An experience-based programme addressing the attachment relationship between mothers and their babies in prisons. *Journal of Child Psychotherapy, 34*(2), 240-258. https://doi.org/10.1080/00754170802208065

Batcup, D. C. (2013). A discussion of the dance movement psychotherapy literature relative to prisons and medium secure units. *Body, Movement and Dance in Psychotherapy, 8*(1), 5-16. https://doi.org/10.1080/17432979.2012.693895

Bateman, A., & Fonagy, P. (2013). Mentalization-based treatment. *Psychoanalytic Inquiry, 33*(6), 595-613. https://doi.org/10.1080/07351690.2013.835170

Bateman, A. W., & Fonagy, P. (2003). The development of an attachment-based treatment pro-

Berzins, L. G., & Trestman, R. L. (2004). The development and implementation of dialectical behavior therapy in forensic settings. *The International Journal of Forensic Mental Health, 3*(1), 93-103. https://doi.org/10.1080/14999013.2004.10471199

Bewley, M. T., & Morgan, R. D. (2011). A national survey of mental health services available to offenders with mental illness: Who is doing what? *Law and Human Behavior, 35*(5), 351-363. https://doi.org/10.1007/s10979-010-9242-4

Bierie, D. M. (2012). Is tougher better? The impact of physical prison conditions on inmate violence. *International Journal of Offender Therapy and Comparative Criminology, 56*(3), 338-355. https://doi.org/10.1177/0306624X11405157

Black, D. W., Gunter, T., Loveless, P., Allen, J., & Sieleni, B. (2010). Antisocial personality disorder in incarcerated offenders: Psychiatric comorbidity and quality of life. *Annals of Clinical Psychiatry, 22*(2), 113-120.

Blackburn, A. G., Fowler, S. K., Mullings, J. L., & Marquart, J. W. (2011). When boundaries are broken: Inmate perceptions of correctional staff boundary violations. *Deviant Behavior, 32*(4), 351-378. https://doi.org/10.1080/01639621003748837

Blasko, B. L., & Jeglic, E. L. (2016). Sexual offenders' perceptions of the client–therapist relationship: The role of risk. *Sexual Abuse: Journal of Research and Treatment, 28*(4), 271-290. https://doi.org/10.1177/1079063214529802

Boothby, J. L., & Clements, C. B. (2000). A national survey of correctional psychologists. *Criminal Justice and Behavior, 27*(6), 716-732. https://doi.org/10.1177/0093854800027006003

Bordin, E. S. (1979). The generalizability of the psychoanalytic concept of the working alliance. *Psychotherapy: Theory, Research and Practice, 16*(3), 252-260. https://doi.org/10.1037/h0085885

Breiner, M. J., Tuomisto, L., Bouyea, E., Gussak, D. E., & Aufderheide, D. (2012). Creating an art therapy anger management protocol for male inmates through a collaborative relationship. *International Journal of Offender Therapy and Comparative Criminology, 56*(7), 1124-1143. https://doi.org/10.1177/0306624X11417362

Brenner, G. H. (2010). The expected psychiatric impact of detention in Guantanamo Bay, Cuba, and related considerations. *Journal of Trauma and Dissociation, 11*(4), 469-487. https://doi.org/10.1080/15299732.2010.496074

Brus, M., Novakovic, V., & Friedberg, A. (2012). Psychotherapy for schizophrenia: A review of modalities and their evidence base. *Psychody-*namic Psychiatry, 40*(4), 609-616. https://doi.org/10.1521/pdps.2012.40.4.609

Caligor, E. (2005). Treatment manuals for long-term psychodynamic psychotherapy and psychoanalysis. *Clinical Neuroscience Research, 4*(5-6), 387-398. https://doi.org/10.1016/j.cnr.2005.03.012

Campbell, C. A., Albert, I., Jarrett, M., Byrne, M., Roberts, A., Phillip, P., Huddy, V., & Valmaggia, L. (2016). Treating multiple incident post-traumatic stress disorder (PTSD) in an inner city London prison: The need for an evidence base. *Behavioural and Cognitive Psychotherapy, 44*(1), 112-117. https://doi.org/10.1017/S135246581500003X

Cantora, A., Mellow, J., & Schlager, M. D. (2016). Social relationships and group dynamics inside a community correction facility for women. *International Journal of Offender Therapy and Comparative Criminology, 60*(9), 1016-1035. https://doi.org/10.1177/0306624X15591805

Carcedo, R. J., López, F., Orgaz, M. B., Toth, K., & Fernández-Rouco, N. (2008). Men and women in the same prison: Interpersonal needs and psychological health of prison inmates. *International Journal of Offender Therapy and Comparative Criminology, 52*(6), 641-657. https://doi.org/10.1177/0306624X07311596

Carlson, P. M. (2015). *Prison and jail administration: Practice and theory.* Burlington, MA: Jones and Bartlett Learning.

Carson, E. A. (2014). *Prisoners in 2013.* Washington, DC: Bureau of Justice Statistics.

Centers for Disease Control and Prevention. (2016). *U.S. Public Health Service Syphilis Study at Tuskegee.* Retrieved from https://www.cdc.gov/tuskegee/timeline.htm

Clarkin, J. F., Foelsch, P. A., Levy, K. N., Hull, J. W., Delaney, J. C., & Kernberg, O. F. (2001). The development of a psychodynamic treatment for patients with borderline personality disorder: A preliminary study of behavioral change. *Journal of Personality Disorders, 15*(6), 487-495. https://doi.org/10.1521/pedi.15.6.487.19190

Clarkin, J. F., Levy, K. N., Lenzenweger, M. F., & Kernberg, O. F. (2007). Evaluating three treatments for borderline personality disorder: A multiwave study. *The American Journal of Psychiatry, 164*(6), 922-928. https://doi.org/10.1176/appi.ajp.164.6.922

Cohen, G., & Harvey, J. (2016). The use of psychological interventions for adult male sex offenders with a learning disability: A systematic review. *Journal of Sexual Aggression, 22*(2), 206-223. https://doi.org/10.1080/13552600.2015.1077279

Collier, J. (2015). 3 man unlock: Out of sight, out of mind. Art psychotherapy with a woman with severe and dangerous personality disorder in prison. *Psychoanalytic Psychotherapy, 29*(3), 243-261. https://doi.org/10.1080/02668734.201 4.997835

Dakwar, E., & Levin, F. R. (2013). Individual mindfulness-based psychotherapy for cannabis or cocaine dependence: A pilot feasibility trial. *The American Journal on Addictions, 22*(6), 521-526. https://doi.org/10.1111/j.1521-0391.2013.12036.x

Diamond, D., Yeomans, F. E., Stern, B., Levy, K. N., Hörz, S., Doering, S., Fischer-Kern, M., Delaney, J., & Clarkin, J. F. (2013). Transference focused psychotherapy for patients with comorbid narcissistic and borderline personality disorder. *Psychoanalytic Inquiry, 33*(6), 527-551. https://doi.org/10.1080/07351690.2013.815087

Ditton, P. M. (1999). *Mental health and treatment of inmates and probationers* (Special report). Washington, DC: Bureau of Justice Statistics.

Donnelly, V., Lynch, A., Devlin, C., Naughton, L., Gibbons, O., Mohan, D., & Kennedy, H. G. (2011). Therapeutic alliance in forensic mental health: Coercion, consent and recovery. *Irish Journal of Psychological Medicine, 28*(1), 21-28. https://doi.org/10.1017/S0790966700011861

Duggan, C. (2009). A treatment guideline for people with antisocial personality disorder: Overcoming attitudinal barriers and evidential limitations. *Criminal Behaviour and Mental Health, 19*(4), 219-223. https://doi.org/10.1002/cbm.726

Elger, B. S., Handtke, V., & Wangmo, T. (2015). Paternalistic breaches of confidentiality in prison: Mental health professionals' attitudes and justifications. *Journal of Medical Ethics: Journal of the Institute of Medical Ethics, 41*(6), 496-500. https://doi.org/10.1136/medethics-2013-101981

Elliott, S. (2011). "Blind spots": Shame, jealousy and envy as hidden aspects within forensic psychotherapy. *European Journal of Psychotherapy and Counseling, 13*(4), 357-369. https://doi.org/1 0.1080/13642537.2011.625199

Evershed, S., Tennant, A., Boomer, D., Rees, A., Barkham, M., & Watson, A. (2003). Practice-based outcomes of dialectical behaviour therapy (DBT) targeting anger and violence, with male forensic patients: A pragmatic and non-contemporaneous comparison. *Criminal Behaviour and Mental Health, 13*(3), 198-213.

Facchin, F., & Margola, D. (2016). Researching lived experience of drugs and crime: A phenomenological study of drug-dependent inmates. *Qualitative Health Research, 26*(12), 1627-1637. https://doi.org/10.1177/1049732315617443

Farkas, M. A. (2010). Rehabilitation in the criminal justice system: Improving service delivery and potential therapeutic outcomes. *International Journal of Offender Therapy and Comparative Criminology, 54*(3), 287-288. https://doi.org/10.1177/0306624X10369823

Faust, E., & Magaletta, P. R. (2010). Factors predicting levels of female inmates' use of psychological services. *Psychological Services, 7*(1), 1-10. https://doi.org/10.1037/a0018439

Feeney, G. X., Connor, J. P., Young, R. M., Tucker, J., & McPherson, A. (2006). Improvement in measures of psychological distress amongst amphetamine misusers treated with brief cognitive-behavioural therapy (CBT). *Addictive Behaviors, 31*(10), 1833-1843. https://doi.org/10.1016/j.addbeh.2005.12.026

Fisher, W. H., Hartwell, S. W., Deng, X., Pinals, D. A., Fulwiler, C., & Roy-Bujnowski, K. (2014). Recidivism among released state prison inmates who received mental health treatment while incarcerated. *Crime and Delinquency, 60*(6), 811-832. https://doi.org/10.1177/0011128714541204

Fjeldstad, A., Høglend, P., & Lorentzen, S. (2016). Presence of personality disorder moderates the long-term effects of short-term and long-term psychodynamic group therapy: A 7-year follow-up of a randomized clinical trial. *Group Dynamics: Theory, Research, and Practice, 20*(4), 294-309. https://doi.org/10.1037/gdn0000055

Fonagy, P. (2015). The effectiveness of psychodynamic psychotherapies: An update. *World Psychiatry, 14*(2), 137-150. https://doi.org/10.1002/wps.20235

Fonagy, P., Target, M., Steele, H., & Steele, M. (1998). *Reflective-functioning manual: Version 5 for application to Adult Attachment Interview* (AAI). Retrieved from: http://mentalizacion.com.ar/images/notas/Reflective%20Functioning%20Manual.pdf

Forrester, A., MacLennan, F., Slade, K., Brown, P., & Exworthy, T. (2014). Improving access to psychological therapies in prisons. *Criminal Behaviour and Mental Health, 24*(3), 163-168. https://doi.org/10.1002/cbm.1898

Freud, S. (1912). The dynamics of transference. In J. Strachey (Ed. & Trans.), *The standard edition of the complete psychological works of Sigmund Freud* (Vol. XI). London: Hogarth Press.

Freud, S. (1914). Remembering, repeating, and working-through (further recommendations on the technique of psychoanalysis II). In J. Strachey (Ed. & Trans.), *The standard edition of the complete psychological works of Sigmund Freud* (Vol. XI). London: Hogarth Press.

Freud, S. (1940). *An outline of psychoanalysis.* Eastford, CT: Martino Fine Books.

Fried, D., Crits-Christoph, P., & Luborsky, L. (1992). The first empirical demonstration of transference in psychotherapy. *Journal of Nervous and Mental Disease, 180*(5), 326-331. https://doi.org/10.1097/00005053-199205000-00007

Friestad, C. (2010). Socio-economic status and health in a marginalized group: The role of subjective social status among prison inmates. *European Journal of Public Health, 20*(6), 655-658. https://doi.org/10.1093/eurpub/ckp242

Frodi, A., Dernevik, M., Sepa, A., Philipson, J., & Bragesjö, M. (2001). Current attachment representations of incarcerated offenders varying in degree of psychopathy. *Attachment and Human Development, 3*(3), 269-283. https://doi.org/10.1080/14616730110096889

Galanek, J. D. (2013). The cultural construction of mental illness in prison: A perfect storm of pathology. *Culture, Medicine and Psychiatry, 37*(1), 195-225. https://doi.org/10.1007/s11013-012-9295-6

Gannon, T. A., Alleyne, E., Butler, H., Danby, H., Kapoor, A., Lovell, T., Mozova, K., Spruin, E., Tostevin, T., Tyler, N., & Ó Ciardha, C. (2015). Specialist group therapy for psychological factors associated with firesetting: Evidence of a treatment effect from a non-randomized trial with male prisoners. *Behaviour Research and Therapy, 73*, 42-51. https://doi.org/10.1016/j.brat.2015.07.007

George, C., Kaplan, N., & Main, M. (1985). *The Berkeley Adult Attachment Interview (AAI): Interview protocol.* Berkeley, CA: University of California, Department of Psychology.

Gill, M. M. (1982). *Analysis of transference I: Theory and technique.* New York: International Universities Press.

Glowa-Kollisch, S., Lim, S., Summers, C., Cohen, L., Selling, D., & Venters, H. (2014). Beyond the bridge: Evaluating a novel mental health program in the New York City jail system. *American Journal of Public Health, 104*(11), 2212-2218. https://doi.org/10.2105/AJPH.2014.302126

Gonzalez, J. R., & Connell, N. M. (2014). Mental health of prisoners: Identifying barriers to mental health treatment and medication continuity. *American Journal of Public Health, 104*(12), 2328-2333. https://doi.org/10.2105/AJPH.2014.302043

Gordon, H. (2002). Suicide in secure psychiatric facilities. *Advances in Psychiatric Treatment, 8*(6), 408-417. https://doi.org/10.1192/apt.8.6.408

Gordon, R. M., Gazzillo, F., Blake, A., Bornstein, R. F., Etzi, J., Lingiardi, V., McWIlliams, N., Rothery, C., & Tasso, A. F. (2016). The relationship between theoretical orientation and countertransference expectations: Implications for ethical dilemmas and risk management. *Clinical Psychology and Psychotherapy, 23*(3), 236-245. https://doi.org/10.1002/cpp.1951

Grattagliano, I., Cassibba, R., Costantini, A., Laquale, G. M., Latrofa, A., Papagna, S., Sette, G., Taurino, A., & Terlizzi, M. (2015). Attachment models in incarcerated sex offenders: A preliminary Italian study using the Adult Attachment Interview (AAI). *Journal of Forensic Sciences, 60*(Suppl 1), S138-S142. https://doi.org/10.1111/1556-4029.12652

Gregory, R. J., & Remen, A. L. (2008). A manual-based psychodynamic therapy for treatment-resistant borderline personality disorder. *Psychotherapy: Theory, Research, Practice, Training, 45*(1), 15-27. https://doi.org/10.1037/0033-3204.45.1.15

Gussak, D. (2007). The effectiveness of art therapy in reducing depression in prison populations. *International Journal of Offender Therapy and Comparative Criminology, 51*(4), 444-460. https://doi.org/10.1177/0306624X06294137

Haney, C., Banks, C., & Zimbardo, P. (1973). Interpersonal dynamics in a simulated prison. *International Journal of Criminology and Penology, 1*, 69-97.

Harlow C. (1999). *Prior abuses reported by inmates and probationers.* Washington, DC: Bureau of Justice Statistics.

Hassan, L., Edge, D., Senior, J., & Shaw, J. (2013). Staff and patient perspectives on the purpose of psychotropic prescribing in prisons: Care or control? *General Hospital Psychiatry, 35*(4), 433-438. https://doi.org/10.1016/j.genhospsych.2013.01.012

Hassan, L., Senior, J., Frisher, M., Edge, D., & Shaw, J. (2014). A comparison of psychotropic medication prescribing patterns in East of England prisons and the general population. *Journal of Psychopharmacology, 28*(4), 357-362. https://doi.org/10.1177/0269881114523863

Hogan, N. L., Barton-Bellessa, S. M., & Lambert, E. G. (2015). Forced to CHANGE: Staff and inmate perceptions of involuntary treatment and its effects. *Applied Psychology in Criminal Justice, 11*(1), 19-39.

Høglend, P., Bøgwald, K., Amlo, S., Marble, A., Ulberg, R., Sjaastad, M. C., Sørbye, Ø., Heyderdahl, O., & Johansson, P. (2008). Transference interpretations in dynamic psychotherapy: Do they really yield sustained effects? *The American Journal of Psychiatry, 165*(6), 763-771. https://doi.org/10.1176/appi.ajp.2008.07061028

Horvath, A. O., & Greenberg, L. S. (1989). Development and validation of the Working Alliance Inventory (WAI). *Journal of Counseling Psychology, 36*(2), 223-233. https://doi.org/10.1037/0022-0167.36.2.223

Houser, K. A., Blasko, B. L., & Belenko, S. (2014). The effects of treatment exposure on prison misconduct for female prisoners with substance use, mental health, and co-occurring disorders. *Criminal Justice Studies: A Critical Journal of Crime, Law and Society, 27*(1), 43-62.

Huber, D., Henrich, G., Clarkin, J., & Klug, G. (2013). Psychoanalytic versus psychodynamic therapy for depression: A three-year follow-up study. *Psychiatry: Interpersonal and Biological Processes, 76*(2), 132-149. https://doi.org/10.1521/psyc.2013.76.2.132

Huffman, E. G. (2006). Psychotherapy in prison: The frame imprisoned. *Clinical Social Work Journal, 34*(3), 319-333. https://doi.org/10.1007/s10615-005-0022-4

IACFP Practice Standards Committee. (2010). Standards for psychology services in jails, prisons, correctional facilities, and agencies: International Association for Correctional and Forensic Psychology (formerly American Association for Correctional Psychology). *Criminal Justice and Behavior, 37*(7), 749-808. https://doi.org/10.1177/0093854810368253

Johnson, J. G. (2001). Violence in prison systems: An African American tragedy. *Journal of Human Behavior in the Social Environment, 4*(2-3), 105-128. https://doi.org/10.1300/J137v04n02_06

Johnson, R. J., Ross, M. W., Taylor, W. C., Williams, M. L., Carvajal, R. I., & Peters, R. J. (2005). A history of drug use and childhood sexual abuse among incarcerated males in a county jail. *Substance Use and Misuse, 40*(2), 211-229. https://doi.org/10.1081/JA-200048457

Jones, A., & Clausen, L. (2013). The efficacy of a brief group CBT program in treating patients diagnosed with bulimia nervosa: A brief report. *International Journal of Eating Disorders, 46*(6), 560-562. https://doi.org/10.1002/eat.22120

Karyotaki, E., Smit, Y., de Beurs, D. P., Henningsen, K. H., Robays, J., Huibers, M. H., Weitz, K., & Cuijpers, P. (2016). The long-term efficacy of acute-phase psychotherapy for depression: A meta-analysis of randomized trials. *Depression and Anxiety, 33*(5), 370-383. https://doi.org/10.1002/da.22491

Kelly, C. E., & Welsh, W. N. (2016). Examining treatment climate across prison-based substance abuse treatment groups. *Substance Use and Misuse, 51*(7), 902-911. https://doi.org/10.3109/10826084.2016.1155621

Kernberg, O. F. (2016). New developments in transference focused psychotherapy. *The International Journal of Psychoanalysis, 97*(2), 385-407. https://doi.org/10.1111/1745-8315.12289

Kita, E. (2011). Potential and possibility: Psychodynamic psychotherapy and social change with incarcerated patients. *Clinical Social Work Journal, 39*(1), 9-17. https://doi.org/10.1007/s10615-010-0268-3

Knott, H. (2016). Countertransference and projective identification revisited and applied to the practice of group analytic supervision. *International Journal of Group Psychotherapy, 66*(3), 323-337.

Koch, S. C., Ostermann, T., Steinhage, A., Kende, P., Haller, K., & Chyle, F. (2015). Breaking barriers: Evaluating an arts-based emotion regulation training in prison. *The Arts in Psychotherapy, 42*, 41-49. https://doi.org/10.1016/j.aip.2014.10.008

Krupers, T. A. (2005). Toxic masculinity as a barrier to mental health treatment in prison. *Journal of Clinical Psychology, 61*(6), 713-724. https://doi.org/10.1002/jclp.20105

Kuehn, B. M. (2014). Criminal justice becomes front line for mental health care. *JAMA, 311*(19), 1953-1954. https://doi.org/10.1001/jama.2014.4578

Lanza, P. V., García, P. F., Lamelas, F. R., & González-Menéndez, A. (2014). Acceptance and commitment therapy versus cognitive behavioral therapy in the treatment of substance use disorder with incarcerated women. *Journal of Clinical Psychology, 70*(7), 644-657. https://doi.org/10.1002/jclp.22060

Leichsenring, F., Abbass, A., Luyten, P., Hilsenroth, M., & Rabung, S. (2013). The emerging evidence for long-term psychodynamic therapy. *Psychodynamic Psychiatry, 41*(3), 361-384. https://doi.org/10.1521/pdps.2013.41.3.361

Leichsenring, F., Leweke, F., Klein, S., & Steinert, C. (2015). The empirical status of psychodynamic psychotherapy—An update: Bambi's alive and kicking. *Psychotherapy and Psychosomatics, 84*(3), 129-148. https://doi.org/10.1159/000376584

Leichsenring, F., & Rabung, S. (2008). Effectiveness of long-term psychodynamic psychotherapy: A meta-analysis. *The Journal of the American Medical Association, 300*(13), 1551-1565. https://doi.org/10.1001/jama.300.13.1551

Leichsenring, F., & Rabung, S. (2011). Long-term psychodynamic psychotherapy in complex mental disorders: Update of a meta-analysis. *The British Journal of Psychiatry, 199*(1), 15-22. https://doi.org/10.1192/bjp.bp.110.082776

Levinson, A., & Fonagy, P. (2004). Offending and attachment: The relationship between interpersonal awareness and offending in a prison population with psychiatric disorder. *Canadian Journal of Psychoanalysis/Revue Canadienne De Psychanalyse, 12*(2), 225-251.

Lindfors, O., Knekt, P., Virtala, E., & Laaksonen, M. A. (2012). The effectiveness of solution-focused therapy and short- and long-term psychodynamic psychotherapy on self-concept during a 3-year follow-up. *Journal of Nervous and Mental Disease, 200*(11), 946-953. https://doi.org/10.1097/NMD.0b013e3182718c6b

Linehan, M. M. (1993). *Cognitive-behavioral treatment of borderline personality disorder.* New York: Guilford.

Linehan, M. M. (2015). *DBT skills training manual* (2nd ed.). New York: Guilford.

MacKain, S. J., Myers, B., Ostapiej, L., & Newman, R. A. (2010). Job satisfaction among psychologists working in state prisons: The relative impact of facets assessing economics, management, relationships, and perceived organizational support. *Criminal Justice and Behavior, 37*(3), 306-318. https://doi.org/10.1177/0093854809357420

Marcus, K. L. (2009). Jailhouse Islamophobia: Anti-Muslim discrimination in American prisons. *Race and Social Problems, 1*(1), 36-44. https://doi.org/10.1007/s12552-009-9003-5

Marquart, J. W., Barnhill, M. B., & Balshaw-Biddle, K. (2001). Fatal attraction: An analysis of employee boundary violations in a southern prison system. 1995-1988. *Justice Quarterly, 18*(4), 877-910. https://doi.org/10.1080/07418820100095121

McGauley, G., & Bartlett, A. (2015). Striking a balance: The contribution of forensic psychotherapy to imprisoned women and their environment. *International Journal of Applied Psychoanalytic Studies, 12*(2), 106-121. https://doi.org/10.1002/aps.1443

Mennicke, A. M., Tripodi, S. J., Veeh, C. A., Wilke, D. J., & Kennedy, S. C. (2015). Assessing attitude and reincarceration outcomes associated with in-prison domestic violence treatment program completion. *Journal of Offender Rehabilitation, 54*(7), 465-485. https://doi.org/10.1080/10509674.2015.1076103

Milliken, R. (2002). Dance/movement therapy as a creative arts therapy approach in prison to the treatment of violence. *The Arts in Psychotherapy, 29*(4), 203-206. https://doi.org/10.1016/S0197-4556(02)00151-X

Mitchell, J., & Latchford, G. (2010). Prisoner perspectives on mental health problems and help-seeking. *Journal of Forensic Psychiatry and Psychology, 21*(5), 773-788. https://doi.org/10.1080/14789949.2010.488697

Milrod, B., Leon, A. C., Busch, F., Rudden, M., Schwalberg, M., Clarkin, J., Aronson, A., Singer, M., Turchin, W., Klass, E. T., Graf, E., Teres, J. T., & Shear, M. K. (2007). A randomized controlled clinical trial of psychoanalytic psychotherapy for panic disorder. *The American Journal of Psychiatry, 164*(2), 265-272. https://doi.org/10.1176/appi.ajp.164.2.265

Morgan, R. D., Flora, D. B., Kroner, D. G., Mills, J. F., Varghese, F., & Steffan, J. S. (2012). Treating offenders with mental illness: A research synthesis. *Law and Human Behavior, 36*(1), 37-50. https://doi.org/10.1037/h0093964

Morgan, R. D., Rozycki, A. T., & Wilson, S. (2004). Inmate perceptions of mental health services. *Professional Psychology: Research and Practice, 35*(4), 389-396. https://doi.org/0.1037/0735-7028.35.4.389

Morgan, R. D., Steffan, J., Shaw, L. B., & Wilson, S. (2007). Needs for and barriers to correctional mental health services: Inmate perceptions. *Psychiatric Services, 58*(9), 1181-1186. https://doi.org/10.1176/appi.ps.58.9.1181

Motivans, M. (2015). *Federal justice statistics, 2012-statistical tables.* Washington, DC: Bureau of Justice Statistics.

Mumola, C. J., & Karberg, J. C. (2006). *Drug use and dependence, state and federal prisoners, 2004* (Special report). Washington, DC: Bureau of Justice Statistics.

Naeem, F., Gul, M., Irfan, M., Munshi, T., Asif, A., Rashid, S., Khan, M. N. S., Ghani, S., Malik, A., Aslam, M., Farooq, S., & Ayub, M. (2015). Brief Culturally adapted CBT (CaCBT) for depression: A randomized controlled trial from Pakistan. *Journal of Affective Disorders, 177*, 101-107. https://doi.org/10.1016/j.jad.2015.02.0

Nee, C., & Farman, S. (2005). Female prisoners with borderline personality disorder: Some promising treatment developments. *Criminal Behaviour and Mental Health, 15*(1), 2-16. https://doi.org/10.1002/cbm.33

Needham, M., Gummerum, M., Mandeville-Norden, R., Rakestrow-Dickens, J., Mewse, A., Barnes, A., & Hanoch, Y. (2015). Association between three different cognitive behavioral alcohol treatment programs and recidivism rates among male offenders: Findings from the United Kingdom. *Alcoholism: Clinical and Experimental Research, 39*(6), 1100-1107. https://doi.org/10.1111/acer.12738

Olver, M. E., Preston, D. L., Camilleri, J. A., Helmus, L., & Starzomski, A. (2011). A survey of clinical psychology training in Canadian federal corrections: Implications for psychologist recruitment and retention. *Canadian Psychology/Psychologie Canadienne, 52*(4), 310-320. https://doi.org/10.1037/a0024586

Oser, C. B., Biebel, E. P., Pullen, E., & Harp, K. H. (2013). Causes, consequences, and prevention of burnout among substance abuse treatment counselors: A rural versus urban comparison. *Journal of Psychoactive Drugs, 45*(1), 17-27. https://doi.org/10.1080/02791072.2013.763558

Pelladeau, E., & De Kernier, N. (2015). Psychothérapie en milieu carcéral. Le cadre à l'épreuve de l'emprise. [Psychotherapy in a prison environment. The setting tested in a grip]. *Psychothérapies, 35*(3), 173-183. https://doi.org/10.3917/psys.153.0173

Perkins, E. B., & Oser, C. B. (2014). Job frustration in substance abuse counselors working with offenders in prisons versus community settings. *International Journal of Offender Therapy and Comparative Criminology, 58*(6), 718-734. https://doi.org/10.1177/0306624X13479347

Peters, A., Sylvia, L. G., da Silva Magalhães, P. V., Miklowitz, D. J., Frank, E., Otto, M. W., Hanse, N. S., Dougherty, D. D., Berk, M., Nierenberg, A. A., & Deckersbach, T. (2014). Age at onset, course of illness and response to psychotherapy in bipolar disorder: Results from the Systematic Treatment Enhancement Program for Bipolar Disorder (STEP-BD). *Psychological Medicine, 44*(16), 3455-3467. https://doi.org/10.1017/S0033291714000804

Pinta, E. R. (2010). Tarasoff duties in prisons: Community standards with certain twists. *Psychiatric Quarterly, 81*(2), 177-182. https://doi.org/10.1007/s11126-010-9127-1

Prasko, J., Diveky, T., Grambal, A., Kamaradova, D., Monzy, P., Sigmundova, Z., Slepecky, M., & Vyskocilova, J. (2010). Transference and countertransference in cognitive behavioral therapy. *Biomedical Papers, 154*(3), 189-197.

Protter, B., & Travin, S. (1983). The significance of countertransference and related issues in a multiservice court clinic. *Journal of the American Academy of Psychiatry and the Law Online, 11*(3), 223-230.

Reasons, C. (1974). Racism, prisons, and prisoners' rights. *Issues in Criminology, 9*(2), 3-20.

Rhodes, L. A. (2004). *Total confinement: Madness and reason in the maximum security prison.* Berkley, CA: University of California Press.

Robst, J., Constantine, R., Andel, R., Boaz, T., & Howe, A. (2011). Factors related to criminal justice expenditure trajectories for adults with serious mental illness. *Criminal Behaviour and Mental Health, 21*(5), 350-362. https://doi.org/10.1002/cbm.817

Rosenbaum, B., Harder, S., Knudsen, P., Køster, A., Lajer, M., Lindhardt, A., Valbak, K., & Winther, G. (2012). Supportive psychodynamic psychotherapy versus treatment as usual for first-episode psychosis: Two-year outcome. *Psychiatry: Interpersonal and Biological Processes, 75*(4), 331-341. https://doi.org/10.1521/psyc.2012.75.4.331

Salem, A., Kushnier, A., Dorio, N., & Reeves, R. (2015). Nonemergency involuntary antipsychotic medication in prison: Effects on prison inpatient days and disciplinary charges. *Journal of the American Academy of Psychiatry and the Law, 43*(2), 159-164.

Senter, A., Morgan, R. D., Serna-McDonald, C., & Bewley, M. (2010). Correctional psychologist burnout, job satisfaction, and life satisfaction. *Psychological Services, 7*(3), 190-201. https://doi.org/10.1037/a0020433

Shedler, J. (2010). The efficacy of psychodynamic psychotherapy. *American Psychologist, 65*(2), 98-109. https://doi.org/10.1037/a0018378

Shelton, D., Sampl, S., Kesten, K. L., Zhang, W., & Trestman, R. L. (2009). Treatment of impulsive aggression in correctional settings. *Behavioral Sciences and the Law, 27*(5), 787-800. https://doi.org/10.1002/bsl.889

Senter, A., Morgan, R. D., Serna-McDonald, C., & Bewley, M. (2010). Correctional psychologist burnout, job satisfaction, and life satisfaction. *Psychological Services, 7*(3), 190-201. https://doi.org/10.1037/a0020433

Skogstad, P., Deane, F. P., & Spicer, J. (2006). Social-cognitive determinants of help-seeking for mental health problems among prison inmates. *Criminal Behaviour and Mental Health, 16*(1), 43-59. https://doi.org/10.1002/cbm.54

Sleed, M., Baradon, T., & Fonagy, P. (2013). New beginnings for mothers and babies in prison: A cluster randomized controlled trial. *Attachment and Human Development, 15*(4), 349-367. https://doi.org/10.1080/14616734.2013.782651

Smith, L. (1999). Individual and institutional defenses against primitive anxieties: Counseling in prison. *Psychodynamic Counseling, 5*(4), 429-442. https://doi.org/10.1080/13533339908404981

Sommers, I., & Baskin, D. R. (1991). Assessing the appropriateness of the prescription of psychiatric medications in prison. *Journal of Nervous and Mental Disease, 179*(5), 267-273. https://doi.org/10.1097/00005053-199105000-00004

Springmann, R. R. (1988). Countertransference as an indicator in victimology. *Contemporary Psychoanalysis, 24*(2), 341-349. https://doi.org/10.1080/00107530.1988.10746249

Steffan, J. S., & Morgan, R. D. (2005). Meeting the needs of mentally ill offenders: Inmate service utilization. *Corrections Today, 67*(1), 38-41.

Tarasoff v. Regents of the University of California, 131 Cal. Rptr. 14 (Cal. 1976).

Tewksbury, R., & Connor, D. P. (2014). Who is having sex inside prison? *Deviant Behavior, 35*(12), 993-1005. https://doi.org/10.1080/01639625.2014.901078

Torrey, E. F., Zdanowicz, M. T., Kennard, A. D., Lamb, H. R., Eslinger, D. F., Biasotti, M. C., & Fuller, D. A. (2014). The treatment of persons with mental illness in prisons and jails: A state survey. Retrieved from http://s3.documentcloud.org/documents/1095566/persons-with-mental-illness-in-jails-and-prisons-2.pdf

Trulson, C. R., Marquart, J. W., Hemmens, C., & Carroll, L. (2008). Racial desegregation in prisons. *The Prison Journal, 88*(2), 270-299. https://doi.org/10.1177/0032885508319208

United States Department of Justice. (2009). *FPI Annual Report 2009*. Retrieved from https://www.prisonlegalnews.org/media/publications/federal_prison_industries_inc_annu al_report_2009.pdf

Veysey, B. M., Stenius, V., Mazade, N., & Schacht, L. (2007). Costs, control or just good clinical practice? The use of antipsychotic medications and formulary decision-making in large U.S. prisons and jails. *Journal of Offender Rehabilitation, 45*(1-2), 189-206. https://doi.org/10.1300/J076v45n01_13

Ware, A., Wilson, C., Tapp, J., & Moore, E. (2016). Mentalisation-based therapy (MBT) in a high-secure hospital setting: Expert by experience feedback on participation. *Journal of Forensic Psychiatry and Psychology, 27*(5), 722-744. https://doi.org/10.1080/14789949.2016.1174725

Washington v. Harper, 494 US 210 (1990).

Way, B. B., Sawyer, D. A., Kahkejian, D., Moffitt, C., & Lilly, S. N. (2007). State prison mental health services recipients perception of care survey. *Psychiatric Quarterly, 78*(4), 269-277. https://doi.org/10.1007/s11126-007-9048-9

West, M. L., Mulay, A. L., DeLuca, J. S., O'Donovon, K., & Yanos, P. T. (2016). Forensic psychiatric experiences, stigma, and self-concept: Qualitative findings. *American Journal of Psychiatric Rehabilitation*. (Manuscript under review)

West, M. L., Vayshenker, B., Rotter, M., & Yanos, P. T. (2015). The influence of mental illness and criminality self-stigmas and racial self-concept on outcomes in a forensic psychiatric sample. *Psychiatric Rehabilitation Journal, 38*(2), 150-157. https://doi.org/10.1037/prj0000133

Wolff, N., Frueh, B. C., Shi, J., & Schumann, B. E. (2012). Effectiveness of cognitive- behavioral trauma treatment for incarcerated women with mental illnesses and substance abuse disorders. *Journal of Anxiety Disorders, 26*(7), 703-710. https://doi.org/10.1016/j.janxdis.2012.06.001

Worley, R. M. (2016). Memoirs of a guard-researcher: Deconstructing the games inmates play behind the prison walls. *Deviant Behavior, 37*(11), 1215-1226. https://doi.org/10.1080/01639625.2016.1170541

Worley, R., Marquart, J. W., & Mullings, J. L. (2003). Prison guard predators: An analysis of inmates who established inappropriate relationships with prison staff, 1995-1998. *Deviant Behavior, 24*(2), 175-194. https://doi.org/10.1080/01639620390117237

Worley, R. M., & Worley, V. B. (2016). The economics of "crossing over": Examining the link between correctional officer pay and guard–inmate boundary violations. *Deviant Behavior, 37*(1), 16-29. https://doi.org/10.1080/01639625.2014.982781

Wu, K. K., Li, F. W., & Cho, V. W. (2014). A randomized controlled trial of the effectiveness of brief-CBT for patients with symptoms of posttraumatic stress following a motor vehicle crash. *Behavioural and Cognitive Psychotherapy, 42*(1), 31-47. https://doi.org/10.1017/S1352465812000859

Yakeley, J., & Adshead, G. (2013). Locks, keys, and security of mind: Psychodynamic approaches to forensic psychiatry. *Journal of the American Academy of Psychiatry and the Law, 41*(1), 38-45.

Zlotnick, C., Johnson, J., & Najavits, L. M. (2009). Randomized controlled pilot study of cognitive-behavioral therapy in a sample of incarcerated women with substance use disorder and PTSD. *Behavior Therapy, 40*(4), 325-336. https://doi.org/10.1016/j.beth.2008.09.004

Zlotnick, C., Najavits, L. M., Rohsenow, D. J., & Johnson, D. M. (2003). A cognitive-behavioral treatment for incarcerated women with substance abuse disorder and posttraumatic stress disorder: Findings from a pilot study. *Journal of Substance Abuse Treatment, 25*(2), 99-105. https://doi.org/10.1016/S0740-5472(03)00106-5

Psychotherapeutic/Psychoanalytic Treatment of the Elderly

Joseph Schachter, Horst Kächele, and Judith S. Schachter

Abstract: Elderly patients who may have been able to deal satisfactorily with earlier periods of stress may find that in later life they are impacted by an array of devastating losses and crises subverting their abilities to adapt satisfactorily. Psychotherapeutic/psychoanalytic treatment has been demonstrated to be helpful to many elderly patients, especially if the psychotherapist/psychoanalyst chooses to relax a traditional analytic stance and actively engage the patient with the exploration of new relationships and activities that may relieve any residual loneliness. We also propose that an alternative concept of termination be considered, one that includes the possibility of post-termination follow-up contacts between patient and analyst. We detail the advantages for both patient and analyst of this concept, which may be particularly useful for elderly patients.

We know of no consensus definition of "elderly;" it varies with epoch and society. While defined as ages 55 and older in Freud's day, post-industrial retirement and government programs have moved the marker to 65. The American Psychoanalytic Association, for example, proscribes a training analyst from beginning a training analysis with a new candidate once the training analyst is 70 and a half years old, presumably to protect the candidate from loss. One concept of old age places it at those ages nearing or surpassing the average life span of human beings. Wikipedia reports that white Americans born in 2010 are expected to live until age 75.9; African Americans to live to 75.1 years; and Hispanic Americans to 81.2 years. We arbitrarily suggest (for this paper) that the elderly be considered 75 years or older.

Psychotherapists/psychoanalysts treat individuals, and the concept of statistical averages has limited meaning. Many individuals today live far beyond age 75, and this group is the focus of our paper. Psychotherapeutic/psychoanalytic treatment of the elderly revealed problematic attitudes at its start, since Freud (1905) believed that psychoanalysis was not appropriate for his age group (facing age 50) and beyond: "On the one hand near or above fifty the elasticity of the mental processes, on which the treatment depends, is, as a rule, lacking" (p. 264). Freud may also have been influenced by his assumption that libidinal activity was sharply diminished in this age group, and therefore, access to and the interpretation of those libidinal conflicts he considered central to analytic treatment might not be feasible. Abraham (1919), however, fourteen years later, wrote about the value of psychoanalysis with patients "of advanced years." Recently, Settlage (1996) felt that the matter had been settled by the subsequent reported treatment experiences of analysts: "The myth of the unsuitability of middle-aged and elderly individuals for psychoanalytic treatment has been dispelled" (p. 548; Cath, 1990; Cath & Miller, 1986; Coltart, 1991; Crusey, 1985; Dunn, 1997; Griffin & Grunes, 1987; Kahana, 1993; Limentani, 1995; Lipson, 2002; Nemiroff & Colarusso, 1985, 1990; Panel Report, 1986; Sandler, 1984; Segal, 1958; Simburg, 1985; Wagner, 2005). Erikson (1959) and Erikson, Erikson, & Kivnick (1986) included old age in articulation of lifecycle stages, and Settlage added that, "The concept of adult development, including in old age, has received increasing exposition and acceptance" (Crusey, 1985; Gould, 1990; Griffin & Grunes, 1990; Levinson, 1985; Nemiroff & Colarusso, 1981, 1985, 1990; Settlage, 1996; Simberg, 1985).

Settlage (1996) graphically described two periods of psychotherapeutic/psychoanalytic treatment of a woman poet at ages 94 and 99 years. In his discussion, he considered whether the described treatment was psychoanalysis:

> I believe that psychoanalysis as a method of treatment is most cogently defined by its therapeutic action—by structural change resulting from the engagement and progression of psychoanalytic therapeutic process.
>
> The patient clearly had the capacities needed for optimal participation in psychoanalytic work: the ability to form a therapeutic relationship, psychological mindedness, abstraction, introspection, reflection, appreciation of symbolic representation and tolerance of surfacing memories, fantasies and feelings. Although the analytic couch and the usual frequency of four or five sessions a week were not employed, the treatment had the hallmarks of psychoanalytic work: free association, the use of dreams, transference, transference interpretation, resistance to the exposure of repressed mental content, insight, the resolution and working through of intra-psychic conflict and change in psychic structure. By these criteria, the work with this patient was psychoanalysis. (p. 558)

We believe that the relationship between psychotherapy and psychoanalysis is quantitative rather than qualitative.

Granting such, the treatment supports the observation that chronological age by itself is not an index of suitability or unsuitability for psychotherapy/psychoanalysis (Simburg, 1985). There is no evidence that the psychotherapeutic/psychoanalytic process is age-related; the psychotherapeutic/ psychoanalytic process may take place throughout life. Simburg characterizes psychotherapy/psychoanalysis as dealing with repressed infantile issues and later life-course issues. "Human object need and its derivative, transference, remain constant, insistent, and enduring throughout life" (Cath, in Panel Report, 1986, p. 164). Whereas physical strength diminishes with age, the intensity of the unconscious mind remains "timelessly intact" (Crusey, 1985).

Despite this growing acceptance of the value of treatment of the elderly, evidence suggests that psychotherapeutic/psychoanalytic treatment of the elderly remains limited. For example, a review of Psychoanalytic Electronic Publishing (PEP) yields only 24 papers about the elderly, in contrast with 248 about adolescents and 1,244 about children. In addition, it is noteworthy that while many American Psychoanalytic Association institutes and others provide courses about the treatment of children, adolescents, and adults, few provide a course in the treatment of the elderly. Our survey of institutes indicated that one provided a study group and another offered an elective course; 14 institutes provided neither a course nor a study group. In sum, none of the 16 responding institutes provided a required course in psychoanalytic treatment of the elderly.

THE ELDERLY ARE SUBJECTED TO A DEVASTATING ARRAY OF LOSSES

Settlage (1996) notes that the losses of old age have been documented and underscored (Berezin & Cath, 1965; Cath, 1962; Crusey, 1985; Goin, 1990; Hildebrand, 1985; King, 1980; Pollock, 1977; Sandler, 1984). The range of disturbing losses, taken together, may be relatively unique to this phase of development, except in wartime, natural disasters, or epidemics: loss of loved ones and/or of friends, loss of parenting gratification, loss of health including physical prowess, vision, hearing, and memory, loss of professional identity, loss of social status and income, and loss of self-esteem. In vulnerable individuals, such losses may produce depression at any age, and they are often accompanied by the risk of suicide. The Centers for Disease Control and Prevention note that more people die of suicide yearly than in car accidents, with suicide predominantly weighted toward both ends of the life arc: teenagers and the elderly. Of 100,000 people ages 65 and over, 14.9 died by suicide in 2007 compared to the 11.3 for our national average (Home Health and Education Publications). Elderly white men have the highest rate, 29 per 100,000.

THE NATURE OF LONELINESS

Loneliness is often a cardinal concern in the treatment of the elderly, and it warrants some reflections on the concept. Fromm-Reichmann's (1990) paper about loneliness, although it focused on its psychotic dimension, brought the concept of loneliness to analysts' attention as a facet of distress. Albert Murray in an interview described it graphically: "But nothing hurts quite like the loss of old friends. There are ways to cope at the time they die. But weeks and months later you realize you can't phone them and talk: Duke Ellington, Romare Bearden, Ralph Ellison, Alfred Kazin, Robert Penn Warren, Joseph Mitchell. It's hard to believe they're all gone" (Watkins, 2013, p. A15). Sullivan (1953) clearly articulated how hard it may be to define loneliness: "I, in common apparently with all the denizens of the English-speaking world, feel inadequate to communicate a really clear impression of the experience of loneliness in its quintessential force" (pp. 260-261).

Given marked variations both in biological endowment and in child rearing customs, we can assume a characterological variation in the need for relationships and intimacy, and pleasure or tolerance of being alone. Sullivan (1953) described loneliness as "the exceedingly unpleasant and driving experience connected with inadequate discharge of the need for human intimacy" (p. 290). Loneliness is caused thus not by being alone but by being without some internally defined needed relationship. Weiss (1973) reports, similarly, that loneliness syndromes give rise to yearning for the relationship—an intimacy, a friendship, a relationship with kin—that would provide whatever is at the moment insufficient. This form of loneliness, based on the absence of a close emotional attachment to another human, can only be remedied by the integration of another emotional attachment or the reintegration of the one that had been lost. Some people may find comfort with pets or nature and not need psychotherapeutic/psychoanalytic treatment. However, we are often confronted with those who may experience the loneliness of emotional isolation, of utter aloneness, whether or not the companionship of others is, in fact, accessible to them, and it is they who seek and are suitable for intensive analytic work throughout the age range. In contrast, the specific form of loneliness associated with the absence of an engaging social network—the "loneliness of social isolation"—can be remedied only by access to such a network. Since both elderly men and women are especially vulnerable to the loss of critically important social ties and to physical isolation, they are, therefore, at increased risk for loneliness. Weiss concludes that, "It is easy to see the lonely as out of step, as unwilling to make necessary overtures to others, as lacking in qualities necessary to satisfactory human relations. In this way we blame even as we purport to explain" (pp. 74-75).

DEALING WITH THE DISTURBING LOSSES OF THE ELDERLY

As we grow up, multiple non-family members play increasingly supportive roles in our lives, beginning in infancy with nannies, grandparents, babysitters and childcare workers, followed by teachers, friends, neighbors, coaches, and mentors, and then often spouse(s), new family members, and colleagues. The influence of family of origin members usually declines throughout life; the influence and importance of friends waxes in adolescence and increases again in the elderly period when, in a mobile society, friends and not family may well be the primary sources of love, care, and support (Cath, 1997).

Both Fleming (1972) and Bowlby (1973) asserted that we all need to feel confident that there are one or more trusted persons that will come to our aid should difficulties arise. Buechler (1997) adds that in both attachment theory and the Sullivanian understanding of the human condition "we are struggling to maintain the security we need as a base from which to venture into the unknown" (pp. 160-161).

PSYCHOANALYTIC TREATMENT OF THE ELDERLY

A subset of elderly patients who had developed reasonably satisfactory adaptations to the vicissitudes of earlier periods of development, with or without therapeutic interventions, may find the host of challenges and stresses of this new stage exceeding their adaptive capacities. Numerous reports document that psychotherapeutic/psychoanalytic treatment can be extremely helpful and beneficial to the elderly (references cited earlier by Settlage, 1996). A-M. Sandler (1984), importantly, points out that "some psychotherapists/analysts treating elderly patients may be too eager to discard the impact of external events and view the presenting symptoms entirely as a result of the breakdown of the mental agencies of the individual" (p. 473). We conceive that the elderly person may previously have achieved a reasonably adequate adaptation, but defenses may no longer be adequate for the new developmental tasks and losses of being elderly. In addition, awareness of the shortness of time ahead may provide impetus for seeking help. Sandler concluded that, "Mrs. A's illness should not be understood as due to the emergence of a neurosis ... To me it seems evident that Mrs. A became depressed because she found herself unable to cope with the internal stresses and conflicts aroused in her by the process of aging" (pp. 488-489). Nemiroff and Colarusso (1985) similarly view the treatment of older patients as specific to this discrete phase of development. Valenstein (2000) is even more focused and in agreement with our views when he describes that, "the transference serves two purposes: for reality-based attachment needs, where it is pivotally restitutional for the object-deprived older patient who has fewer opportunities for new attachments; and also, as far as feasible, for the facultative recapitulations of the past and their understanding as they experientially unfold" (p. 1583). He adds that in working with the older patient, "we are more accepting and inclined to be more responsive to the older patient's needs for attachment and support, even though that may depart in some measure from the priority traditionally given the analysis of the transference in its recapitulations of past conflicts and relationships" (pp. 1584-1585).

CHANGING THE ROLE OF THE ANALYST AND THE FRAME OF TREATMENT

We propose that after the apparent completion of extensive and intensive psychotherapeutic/analytic work to repair endogenous, narcissistic, neurotic roots of loneliness, with or without supplementary pharmaceutical help, if the patient remains troubled by persistent feelings of reality-based loneliness, the psychotherapist/analyst may utilize a modified stance that actively suggests the remedial development of new friends and activities to remedy this loneliness, while exploring any resistances to that suggestion. Although we have not collected data about the effect of such a suggestion on treatment outcome, we do not anticipate a significant negative impact while a positive outcome is plausible. We hope psychotherapists/analysts will consider applying this suggestion in stalemated treatments in which an isolated patient remains troubled by persistent feelings of loneliness. If tried, we hope that the results of such efforts will be reported.

Weinberg (1989) proposed this transition for the analyst to become the "ambassador" of friendship, a role possibly doubly difficult for an analyst unaccustomed to taking such an active role in treatment and, perhaps due to age, background, and personality thus unfamiliar with both the complexities of friendship in later life and local resources. The need for, and even the concept of generating friendships may be a challenge for both analyst and patient, possibly more so for some male analysts and male patient dyads, since usually at every life stage women focus more on and have more friendships than men.

Weiss (1973) prescribes, "I can offer no method for ending loneliness other than the formation of new relationships that might

repair the deficit responsible for the loneliness. And I think this solution ordinarily is not easy" (p. 231). A campaign of search for a single attachment figure is a risky enterprise simply in terms of the likelihood of success. Patients who enter treatment hoping to find a replacement for a lost attachment figure constitute therapeutic problems because of the limited probability of success. Rather, the focus should be revised to developing relationships with several others, engagement with various activities, and membership in networks *on bases valid in themselves*. Cacioppo and Patrick (2008) similarly advise, "Don't focus on trying to find the love of your life or to reinvent yourself all at once. Just slip a toe into the water. Play with the idea of trying to get small doses of the positive sensations that come from positive social interactions" (p. 237).

Just as some psychotherapists/analysts have acknowledged the limits of their pharmaceutical knowledge and have become comfortable in seeking consultation for pharmaceutical treatment, they may now need to acknowledge limited knowledge in social networking. Referring the patient to an experienced social worker or to a reputable service center may provide the necessary auxiliary support.

While we think that psychotherapists/analysts should always be prepared to seek outside help for problems beyond their expertise, this need may arise more frequently in the treatment of the elderly, with their multiplicity of losses, illnesses, and stresses. The transference significance of the analyst turning to outside help may provide a bridge for the patient's own outreach and recognition of limits. The psychotherapist/psychoanalyst may be supported by a functioning, trustful therapeutic alliance with the patient, which may help the patient deal with the ensuing concerns, negative reactions, and failures in response to the analyst's suggestion.

TERMINATION OF PSYCHOTHERAPEUTIC/ PSYCHOANALYTIC TREATMENT OF THE ELDERLY

Traditional psychoanalytic theory prescribes total patient-analyst separation after termination to support mourning the loss of the analyst. There is no evidence that total separation influences mourning, or that occasional post-termination patient-analyst contact inhibits mourning (Craige, 2002). Based on an empirical clinical interview study, Kantrowitz (2014) agrees and notes that post-analytic experiences of grief and extended periods of mourning were not less intense for analysands who were part of the analytic community than for those who were not. She also notes that for some patients completing treatment was a very hard won achievement, and when it occurred, joy, not grief, predominated in their feelings about ending; mourning was not the predominant emotion. She adds that older people may be more reluctant to end their analyses and feel more grief at ending them since the experience is likely compounded by the actual or expectable loss of others who are emotionally important to them. In general, in her cohort, the way individuals remembered their analysis was affected by their post-treatment contact with their former analyst. Some analysands clearly felt that later contact with the former analyst was sustaining, though this was less likely to be true for analyst/patients. Further, she concluded that each analysis and each ending is shaped by the nature of the particular issues of the analysand and the particular analytic dyad.

Schachter and Kächele (2013) presented an alternative concept of termination: If during the termination phase the patient has not considered the possibility of post-termination contact with the analyst, at an appropriate time the analyst should question why this has not been discussed. After an analytic exploration, the analyst may propose the possibility of occasional post-termination patient-analyst contacts and the benefits of such meetings. Kantrowitz believes that unless the former analysands chose to re-contact their former analysts, they would be left on their own to assimilate post-analytic experiences that might be unexpected, painful, or confusing. The decision about whether to plan such follow-up contacts should be a mutually agreed upon one. We believe that such contacts may provide the patient with the following benefits: 1) may enable the patient to re-experience the analyst's caring (especially relevant for elderly patients previously vulnerable to loneliness; such contacts may occur informally, spontaneously with elderly patients); 2) may reinvigorate helpful introjections of the analyst; and 3) may provide additional opportunity to deal with unresolved idealization of the analyst, if appropriate. Such follow-up contacts may also provide the analyst with information about the inevitable post-termination changes in the patient's life, positive and negative, which may help the analyst revise and improve his/her conceptions of the course of the analytic treatment. Since the follow-up contacts may be of use and of interest to the analyst as well as the patient, we suggest that the analyst not charge for these follow-up contacts. The frame of the follow-up contacts has been modified from that of the treatment itself, becoming perhaps more person-to-person, with the patient's needs and welfare remaining paramount. Follow-up meetings may have to take place in other settings, hospital rooms or other venues, while maintaining the professional roles.

There are no data available to compare the therapeutic effects of traditional concepts of termination to those of Schachter and Kächele. One study reported that psychotherapist/analyst–initiated follow-up contacts were beneficial to patients (Schachter, Martin, Gundle, & O'Neil, 1997). "In the first case the meetings facilitated the patient's re-entering treatment, leading to significant further growth. In the second and third cases, the meetings re-ignited mourning for the analyst and furthered analytic gains. The authors' overall impression was that the post-termination contacts were helpful for all three patients" (p. 1193).

Next, a clinical example of patient-initiated post-termination contact with an older patient is summarized. The treatment of a previously analyzed, childless mental health professional suffering through a second failing marriage was assumed on a face-to-face basis at the patient's request. The patient's first analyst had been a well-known older male; his current analyst, JSS, was a woman, new to the analytic community, with a child analytic background and a focus, in this psychoanalytic therapy, on attachment and caretaking by the patient's mother, who had lost both parents early and had felt compelled to prepare her only son to become an orphan. The father was seen as an active intelligent man whose first wife had died and abandoned their son to relatives. The patient himself had been sent to live for some time with an aunt who ran a Depression-era boarding house while his parents were ill.

As a boy, the patient rose to the challenge of raising himself, abandoning his parents before they might have abandoned him. He found a way to support himself successfully at boarding school, college, and graduate school. He remained relatively isolated, although he was superficially adept both socially and professionally throughout a career in the armed services and thereafter. After several years of therapy, he chose to return to an analytic schedule on the couch, during which he dealt with his narcissistic injuries, his hypochondriasis and isolation, and his fear of angering his attachment object, elicited when his analyst drank iced tea during a session. His father became a more understandable and significant figure, and the patient subsequently accepted responsibility for his aging mother and placed her in a nursing home close to his home. Meanwhile, he divorced, suffered the rage of and a narcissistic injury at the hands of his grown adopted stepsons who rejected him,

and found and married a warm successful woman with adult children and grandchildren. Midpoint in this analytic phase, when he was well past 75, I asked him if I could present our analytic work in a European discussion group, and he agreed. Both of us were disappointed when the discussion focused almost entirely on the ethics of analyzing an elderly patient.

Termination took place after a two-year discussion, when the psychotherapist/ analyst retired and relocated. The patient requested post-termination contacts, and they were arranged by e-mail and took place at approximately six-month intervals at his choice of restaurants in her city, except on the rare occasions when the analyst returned to their old city to visit friends. On those occasions, they also met at restaurants. The patient always paid for their meals, and no fee was charged. They both enjoyed food and were comfortable together. When he became seriously ill, the analyst increased the frequency of visits in both cities. The last two sessions took place in his home where, for the first time, the analyst met his wife and helped support her utilization of home hospice care. Their last meeting was clearly a farewell. The patient summoned all his strength and walked the analyst to her car, while pulling his IV line behind him.

In a general statement, Kantrowiz (2014) concludes that nowadays psychotherapists/analysts believe post-treatment returns may be helpful, and certainly are not viewed as harmful to patients' therapeutic gains.

CONCLUSION

Old age is the last developmental stage. The elderly may be subjected to a devastating array of losses and crises that exceed the scope and nature of those they managed satisfactorily in earlier stages. Widespread losses may generate intensely distressing feelings of loneliness and depression and call upon the universal need to know that there is at least one trusted person who will come to help when difficulties arise. Loss of support may be difficult when the elderly are experiencing feelings of loneliness, and the psychotherapist/analyst may, realistically, then provide one such anchor.

If intensive psychotherapeutic/psychoanalytic work with an elderly patient has proven helpful but left the patient isolated, with remaining painful feelings of loneliness, the psychotherapist/analyst has the option of enlarging the treatment by actively suggesting that the patient consider developing new relationships, interests, and activities. Further, proposed periodic post-termination patient-analyst follow-up contacts, in addition to providing the advantages delineated, can provide a form of maintenance therapy and caring which may assist the patient in continuing endeavors to avoid the persistence of loneliness by supporting new relationships and activities.

REFERENCES

Abraham, K. (1919). The applicability of psychoanalytic treatment to patients at an advanced age. *Selected papers* (pp. 312-317). London: Hogarth, 1927.

Berezin, M. A., & Cath, S. H. (1965). *Geriatric psychiatry: Grief, loss and emotional disorders in the aging process.* New York: International Universities Press.

Bowlby, J. (1973). *Attachment and loss. Vol. 2: Separation, anxiety and anger.* New York: Basic Books.

Buechler, S. (1997). Book review: Attachment theory as a secure base for psychoanalytic exploration: A review of attachment theory: Social, developmental and clinical perspectives. *Contemporary Psychoanalysis, 33,* 157-161.

Cacioppo, J. T., & Patrick, W. (2008). *Loneliness. Human nature and the need for social connection.* New York: Norton.

Cath, S. H. (1962). Some dynamics of middle and later years: A study of depletion and restitution. In M. A. Berezin & S. H. Cath (Eds.), *Geriatric psychiatry: Grief, loss, and emotional disorders in*

the aging process (pp. 21-72). New York: International Universities Press.

Cath, S. H. (1990). Book review: Treating the elderly with psychotherapy: The scope for change in later life. *Psychoanalytic Quarterly, 59,* 143-147.

Cath, S. H. (1997). Loss and restitution in later life. In S. Akhtar & S. Kramer (Eds.), *The seasons of life: Separation-individuation perspectives* (pp. 129-156). Northvale, NY: Aronson.

Cath, S., & Miller, L. E. (1986). The psychoanalysis of the older patient. *Journal of the American Psychoanalytic Association, 34,* 163-177.

Coltart, N. E. (1991). The analysis of an elderly patient. *International Journal of Psychoanalysis, 72,* 209-219.

Craige, H. (2002). Mourning analysis: The post-termination phase. *Journal of the American Psychoanalytic Association, 50,* 507-550.

Crusey, J. E. (1985). Short-term dynamic psychotherapy with a sixty-two-year-old man. In R. A. Nemiroff & C. A. Colarrusso (Eds.), *The race against time: Psychotherapy and psychoanalysis in the second half of life* (pp. 147-166). New York: Plenum.

Dunn, J. (1997). Book review: Psychotherapy with the elderly. *Psychoanalytic Quarterly, 66,* 368-369.

Erikson, E. H. (1959). *Identity and the life cycle. Selected papers.* New York: International Universities Press.

Erikson, E. H., Erikson, J. M., & Kivnick, H. Q. (1986). *Vital involvement in old age.* New York: Norton.

Fleming, J. (1972). Early object deprivation and transference phenomena: The working alliance. *Psychoanalytic Quarterly, 41,* 23-49.

Freud, S. (1905). On psychotherapy. SE vol. VII, pp. 255-268.

Fromm-Reichmann, F. (1990). Loneliness. *Contemporary Psychoanalysis, 26,* 305-329.

Goin, M. K. (1990). Emotional survival and the aging body. In R. A. Nemiroff & C. A. Colarusso (Eds.), *New dimensions in adult development* (pp. 518-529). New York: Basic Books.

Gould, R. L. (1990). Clinical lessons from adult developmental theory. In R. A. Nemiroff & C. A. Colarusso (Eds.), *New dimensions in adult development* (pp. 345-370). New York: Basic Books.

Griffin, B. P., & Grunes, J. M. (1987). The aged in psychotherapy: Psychodynamic contributions to the treatment process. In J. Sadavoy & M. Leszcz (Eds.), *Treating the elderly with psychotherapy* (pp. 312-344). Madison, CT: International Universities Press.

Griffin, B. P., & Grunes, J. M. (1990). A developmental approach to psychoanalytic psychotherapy with the aged. In R. A. Nemiroff & C. A. Colarusso (Eds.), *New dimensions in adult development* (pp. 267-287). New York: Basic Books.

Hildebrand, H. P. (1985). Object loss and development in the second half of life. In R. A. Nemiroff & C. A. Colarusso (Eds.), *The race against time: Psychotherapy and psychoanalysis in the second half of life* (pp. 211-227). New York: Plenum.

Home Health and Education Publications. National Institute of Mental Health, Bethesda, MD.

Kahana, R. J. (1993). The psychotherapy of the elderly self. *International Journal of Psychoanalysis, 74*, 1087-1088.

Kantrowitz, J. L. (2014). *Myths of termination.* New York: Routledge.

King, P. (1980). The life cycle as indicated by the nature of the transference in the psychoanalysis of the middle-aged and the elderly. *International Journal of Psychoanalysis, 61*, 153-160.

Levinson, G. A. (1985). New beginnings at seventy: A decade of psychotherapy in late adulthood. In R. A. Nemiroff & C. A. Colarusso (Eds.), *The race against time: Psychotherapy and psychoanalysis in the second half of life* (pp. 171-188). New York: Plenum.

Limentani, A. (1995). Creativity and the third age. *International Journal of Psychoanalysis, 76*, 825-833.

Lipson, C. (2002). Psychoanalysis in later life. *Psychoanalytic Quarterly, 71*, 751-775.

Nemiroff, R. A., & Colarusso, C. A. (1981). *Adult development: A new dimension in psychodynamic theory and practice.* New York: Plenum.

Nemiroff, R. A., & Colarusso, C. A. (Eds.). (1985). *The race against time: Psychotherapy and psychoanalysis in the second half of life.* New York: Plenum.

Nemiroff, R. A., & Colarusso, C. A. (1990). *New dimensions in adult development.* New York: Basic Books.

Panel Report. (1986). The psychoanalysis of the older patient (Reported by N.E. Miller). *Journal of the American Psychoanalytic Association, 34*, 163-177.

Pollock, G. H. (1977). The mourning process and creative organizational change. *Journal of the American Psychoanalytic Association, 25*, 3-34.

Sandler, A-M. (1984). Problems of development and adaptation in an elderly patient. *Psychoanalytic Study of the Child, 39*, 471-489.

Schachter, J., Martin, G. C., Gundle, M. J., & O'Neil, M. K. (1997). Clinical experience with psychoanalytic post-termination meetings. *International Journal of Psychoanalysis, 78*, 1193-1198.

Schachter, J., & Kächele, H. (2013). An alternative conception of termination and follow-up. *Psychoanalytic Review, 100*, 423-452.

Segal, H. (1958). Fear of death: Notes on the analysis of an old man. *International Journal of Psychoanalysis, 39*, 178-181.

Settlage, C. F. (1996). Transcending old age. *International Journal of Psychoanalysis, 77*, 547-564.

Simberg, E. J. (1985). Psychoanalysis of the older patient. *Journal of the American Psychoanalytic Association, 33*, 117-132.

Sullivan, H. S. (1953). *The interpersonal theory of psychiatry.* New York: Norton.

Valenstein, A. F. (2000). The older patient in psychoanalysis. *Journal of the American Psychoanalytic Association, 48*, 1563-1589.

Wagner, J. W. (2005). Psychoanalytic bias against the elderly patient: Hiding our fears under developmental milestones. *Contemporary Psychoanalysis, 41*, 77-92.

Watkins, M. (2013, August 20). Scholar saw a multicolored American culture. Albert Murray, 1916–2013. *New York Times*, A15.

Weinberg, H. (1989). Clinical aspects of friendliness and friendship. *Contemporary Psychoanalysis, 25*, 357-370.

Weiss, R. S. (1973). *Loneliness: The experience of emotional and social isolation.* Boston: MIT Press.

Part 4
Psychodynamic Psychiatry and Neuroscience

César A. Alfonso, MD

Psychodynamic psychiatry, as a branch of medicine, embraces insights gained by recent advances in neuroscience. By emphasizing therapeutic practice as its goal, as in clinical medicine, psychodynamic psychiatry avoids polarities of biological reductionism and antiscientific dogmatism and seeks paradigmatic biopsychosocial integration. This section provides a glimpse of how advances in neuroscience may inform clinical practice by crystallizing our understanding of human behavior, gene-environment interactions, and the impact of adversity, trauma and disruptions in attachments on neuroendocrine systems, adaptation and pathogenesis.

Glucksman, from New York Medical College, points out that Freud, a neurologist by training with experience in basic sciences research, was interested in explaining mental processes in neurobiological ways. Given the limited advances in neuroscience at the beginning of the twentieth century, Freud gravitated instead towards development of metapsychological theories that correlated with his clinical observations. Glucksman proceeds to summarize advances in neurosciences to update Freud's *Project for a Scientific Psychology*.

Consider for instance, how familiarity with the neural pathways involved in learning and re-experiencing, and modifiability of neural networks and neuroplasticity, corroborate the clinical utility of the theoretical construct of countertransference awareness. Learning occurs largely through repetition (neural synaptic weight) and association (neural pattern matching). Implicit, long-term procedural memory networks are in-

volved in automatic activities and behaviors. Explicit, declarative, conscious recall allows for rewiring of neural networks in reparative psychotherapeutic experiences via cognitive restructuring and interpretative insights. A concordant countertransference could be understood as neural pattern matching, akin to artificial intelligence algorithms that allow discriminating and generalizing responses from regularities of data. In a concordant countertransference a predictable generalized empathic response takes place regardless of the therapist's diverse past life experiences. A complementary countertransference occurs when the clinician's unconscious emotional memories are activated in a clinical interaction. Procedural memories may trigger a response in the therapist that is based on his or her weighted neural networks. Personal past experiences and memories from other treatments are activated in complementary countertransferences and may lead to untoward avoidance, shaming, excessive curiosity or dissociation, dampening the patient's fluid expression of affect and deflecting appropriate exploration of themes and conflicts.

Expression of affect and improvements in reflective functioning are recognized as transtheoretical and transdiagnostic psychotherapeutic curative factors. Glucksman points out how mirror neuron networks are involved in the mediation of empathy and mechanisms of introjection and identification. He also connects Freud's hypothesis of the existence the omega neural network (associated qualitatively with different affective states) mentioned in the *Project for a Scientific Psychology* and recent findings of discreet affective states being mediated by specific neuropeptides, such as oxytocin and vasopressin. Freud conceptualized the ego in the *Project* as a collective of neural networks aiming to balance pleasure with unpleasure. A contemporary elaboration of Freud's proposal is the circumplex dimensional model of emotions described by Gerber and colleagues. In this model emotional valence ranging from pleasure to unpleasure is placed on the horizontal axis and emotional activation on the vertical axis. Functional MRI studies show that the classic reward neural circuits are associated with positively valenced emotions and negative emotions engage the executive and attentional neural systems.

Chambers, from Indiana University, points out that epigenetics, the alteration of gene activity without changes in DNA sequences, is the underlying mechanism for all neuroscience and behavior. Epigenetic processes occur mainly through DNA methylation and acetylation triggered by toxins, pollutants, bacteria, viruses, radiation exposure, nutritional changes, hormonal exposure and changes *in utero* and postpartum environments. Chambers indicates that epigenetic processes may be permanent or reversible, and heritable by offspring. The interactions between acute trauma, enduring stressors, emotions, hormonal and peptide surges, up and down regulation of receptors and neurotransmission cause epigenetic changes in the brain with associated changes in endocrine and immune systems and inflammatory response. Although epigenetic changes may remain stable through life, they can be altered and reversible trough targeted drug therapies and psychotherapy, and with psychosocial and environmental interventions. Understood in this context, the neurobiology of attachment theory becomes relevant as one realizes that psychotherapy provides an opportunity for earned secure attachments.

The relationship with caregivers affects the neurobiology of the infant. Chambers points out that although the *critical period of attachment* spans the first 6 months of life,

the actual time range of the *sensitive period of development* where measurable changes occur begins during pregnancy and continues through the pre-school age years. Low levels of cortisol during the antepartum induce neuronal development and growth in the hypothalamus of the developing brain. Oxytocin levels and social interaction during the sensitive period of development also positively correlate with neuroplasticity. The hippocampus, involved in spatial and emotional memory and possessing a large number of glucocorticoid receptors, develops during the first three months of life. Neglect and abuse during at this stage results in smaller size of this brain region with long-term difficulty consolidating memories and attaining secure attachments. Abuse and neglect during the first three months of life also inhibits the progression from ventral striatal pathway activity (involved in novelty seeking) to dorsal striatal pathway activity (involved in satiety, familiarity and comfort). A developmental arrest caused by infant abuse and neglect during this phase with failure of activation of dorsal striatal circuits has been correlated with development of addictions in adulthood.

Chambers describes the amygdala (which matures by six months of age) as an emotional compass, protecting against depression and anxiety. A fully developed amygdala allows for appropriate experiences of fear and salience (discrimination between a caregiver and a stranger). Antepartum cortisol spikes and postpartum abuse and neglect correlate with a decrease in size of the amygdala. The prefrontal cortex, with an important role modulating anxiety and depression and adult attachments, develops from infancy through the third decade of life. Its precise role in development of early attachments remains unclear.

In summary, in the absence of secure attachments, stress increases amygdala activity, cortisol levels, and sympathetic nervous system response. Additionally, diminished prefrontal cortex inhibition and a hyperactive inflammatory response cause further erosion and allostatic overload resulting in poor health outcomes. Understanding the neurobiological correlates of attachment not only validates psychological theory but stresses the importance of optimizing care during the sensitive period of development of antepartum, postpartum and preschool years.

Carter, from the Kinsey Institute and Indiana University, explains in detail how developmentally appropriate social experiences and exposure to oxytocin and vasopressin neuropeptides set thresholds for sociality, affective regulation and aggression. The fact that vasopressin influences osmoregulation and vasoconstriction and oxytocin influences lactation and uterine contractions during labor has been known in medicine for years. Sexologists also found that oxytocin levels increase during orgasm and vasopressin during arousal when measured in the human sexual response cycle. In many species oxytocin mediates sexual receptivity and vasopressin courtship behaviors.

The work of Insel and colleagues at the National Institute of Mental Health and Carter and colleagues over the last three decades identified the role of neuropeptides in facilitating affiliative and prosocial behaviors and security of attachments.

Oxytocin and vasopressin neuropeptides also modulate autonomic, immune and metabolic systems when a person is challenged or faced with adversity. Early life experiences, in particular, through epigenetic mechanisms, affect receptor binding capacity and levels of these peptides. Higher oxytocin levels and receptor activation are associated with positive social behaviors, attachment security and safety. Vasopressin is associated with anxiety and aggression when faced with adversity. Both peptides are integral to attachment processes and affective bonding throughout the lifespan.

Carter discusses our evolving understanding of sex differences in the regulation and effects of oxytocin and vasopressin. Steroid-peptide interactions are complex and poorly understood and additional research is needed to clarify these time-dependent and complex interactions. However, there is sufficient evidence of distinct differences in the biology of social behavior in males and females.

The attachment system is modulated by early experiences, levels of estrogen, progesterone and androgens, circulating oxytocin and vasopressin peptides and the distribution and density of neuropeptide receptors in the brain. The neurobiology of attachment behaviors, pair and social bonding is complex and interrelated. In the same way that affective regulation with containment of aggression is dependent on a harmonious internal and external environment during the sensitive period of development, the neuroplasticity and expression of secure attachments, prosocial and affiliative behaviors are also in part mediated by situation dependent changes in neuropeptide and hormonal levels, level of activation of brain receptors and malleability of gene expression.

Freud's "Project": The Mind-Brain Connection Revisited

Myron L. Glucksman

Abstract: Freud's "Project for a Scientific Psychology" (1895) reflected his attempt to explain psychic phenomena in neurobiological terms. The recent discovery of the neuron motivated him to embark on this endeavor. His basic hypothesis was that neurons were vehicles for the conduction of "currents" or "excitations," and that they were connected to one another. Using this model, Freud attempted to describe a number of mental phenomena, including: consciousness, perception, affect, self, cognition, dreaming, memory, and symptom formation. However, he was unable to complete his exploration of these mental processes because he lacked the information and technology that became available over the following century. Subsequent discoveries, including fMRIs, PET scans, EEGs, synapses, neural networks, genetic factors, neurotransmitters, and discrete brain circuits facilitated a significant expansion of our knowledge of mind-brain phenomena. As a result, effective pharmacological treatments have been developed for schizophrenia, mood and anxiety disorders. Moreover, changes in brain function can be measured that reflect successful pharmacologic and psychotherapeutic treatment. Despite these advances, there remain limitations in our understanding of the relationship between mind and brain functions. More than a century after Freud began the "Project," the neurobiology underlying the phenomena of consciousness, unconsciousness, qualities of subjective feelings, thoughts, and memories is still not fully understood. Can we expect to reach a more comprehensive integration of mind and its neurobiological substrate a century from now? The purpose of this article is to update our knowledge of the neurobiology associated with the specific mental functions that Freud examined in the "Project," and to pose questions concerning mind-brain phenomena that will hopefully be answered in the future.

Over the span of a few weeks, Sigmund Freud (1895) wrote his "Project for a Scientific Psychology" in order to explain both normal and pathological psychic processes in neurobiological terms. He explored the following normal mental phenomena: memory, perception, consciousness, affect, cognition, self, sleep, and dreams. In addition, he examined the psychopathological

processes involved in compulsions, obsessions, conversion reactions, and phobias. It was no coincidence that the neuron had already been described in 1888 by Santiago Ramon y Cajal (1899), and that Freud was most likely well aware of its anatomical structure (cell body, axis, and dendrites). However, he was still unaware of how impulses were transmitted from one neuron to the other by means of synapses. That process remained to be described by the English neurophysiologist, Charles Sherrington (1906). Nevertheless, Freud (1895) hypothesized that neurons conducted excitations from one to the other via "contact-barriers" (p. 298) that either resisted or facilitated excitations between neurons. According to Freud (1895), there were three types of neurons: "pi," "psi," and "omega" neurons. "Pi" neurons were permeable, offered no resistance, and subserved perception; "psi" neurons were impermeable, offered resistance, and subserved memory; "omega" neurons transmitted the qualitative, subjective experiences of perception, memory, consciousness, and feelings. Affects were classified as either pleasurable or unpleasurable, and mediated through "psi" and "omega" neurons. Freud (1895) defined the ego as a network of neurons that maintained a balance between pleasure and unpleasure. It defended against psychic primary processes, and facilitated secondary processes, as well as a sense of reality. Cognition was subserved by "psi" neurons, while "omega" neurons provided the quality of thought. Anticipating his later theory of dreaming, he hypothesized that it was characterized by primary process thought in the form of "psi" neuronal activation during sleep. He also noted that dreams were wish-fulfillments, hallucinatory, and that motor activity was inhibited during dreaming. In regard to psychopathology, Freud (1895) believed that symptoms were the result of the repression of disturbing affects and thoughts, although he was unable to describe their neuronal mediation. In his attempt to explain mental mechanisms using a neuronal paradigm, Freud basically laid the foundation for his theory of psychic function: conscious, unconscious, primary process, secondary process, ego, pleasure, unpleasure, affect, defenses, repression, and symptom formation. In the absence of neurobiological discoveries that were to come later, Freud was unable to pursue his "Project"; instead, he developed a metapsychology for personality structure, development, psychodynam-

ics, and psychopathology. However, his emphasis on instincts, including libido and the death instinct, was biologically influenced (Sulloway, 1992). In fact, he continued to believe that mental functions would someday be explained by neurophysiology when he stated: "The deficiencies in our description would probably vanish if we were already in a position to replace the psychological terms by physiological or chemical ones" (Freud, 1920, p. 60). Serendipitously, he later predicted the central role of neurotransmitters when he stated, "It is here, indeed, that the hope for the future lies: the possibility that our knowledge of the operations of the hormones may give us the means of successfully combating the quantitative factors of the illnesses" (Freud, 1932, p. 154).

In this article, I intend to review some of the salient neurobiological discoveries that have been made in the succeeding 120 years since the "Project" (1895) was written. In particular, I shall focus on the neurobiology of those mental functions that Freud examined; namely, consciousness, memory, phobias, obsessions, compulsions, conversion disorders, affect, and cognition. Furthermore, I shall comment on the relevance of these discoveries in connection with our understanding of the mind, and speculate on how they might inform the psychodynamically oriented clinician.

Freud's (1932) prescience regarding the role of "hormones" in the brain was validated in the mid-20th century when Julius Axelrod (1957) discovered the neuronal-synaptic function of neurotransmitters, namely norepinephrine, epinephrine, and dopamine. The role of additional neurotransmitters soon followed, including acetylcholine, serotonin, GABA, glutamate, orexin, and other neuropeptides. Indeed, our understanding of the neuronal and neurochemical functioning of the brain has significantly expanded over the past half century (Kandel, Schwartz, Jessell, Siegelbaum, & Hudspeth, 2012). If Freud were to update the Project, he might include the following information that was unavailable when he attempted his synthesis of neuro-biology and the mind.

CONSCIOUSNESS

As far as consciousness is concerned, it is generally accepted that there is no specific location in the brain mediating conscious awareness (Farthing, 1992). Activation of the entire thalamo-cortical neuronal circuit occurs during the conscious state (Pally, 1998). A number of investigators (Baars, 2005; Crick & Koch, 1990, 2000; Pally, 1998) theorize that there is synchronized cortical neuronal oscillation in the gamma range between 30–70 Hz in the resting, conscious state. Humans, in contrast to other primates, are not only conscious of incoming sensory stimuli, but also have the capacity for self-reflection or introspection. Edelman (1989, 1992) makes the distinction between primary consciousness and self-reflective consciousness. According to him, primary consciousness is the awareness of current perceptions in the environment. Self-reflective consciousness involves the prefrontal cortex, and is concerned with internal experience. Neuroimaging studies demonstrate that during ongoing attention to external stimuli there is activation of the sensory cortex, while during introspection or self-reflective consciousness, there is activation of the prefrontal cortex (Tononi & Koch, 2008). Olds (1992) refers to a "self-awareness system" (p. 430) that involves inputs from cortical and inferior parietal areas. Panksepp (2005) speculates that an entity corresponding to self-awareness involves "the periaqueductal gray and surrounding collicular and tegmental zones... through many direct and indirect influences such as the strong two-way connections with frontal executive areas of the brain and... sensory cortices through the extended reticular and thalamic activating systems" (p. 21). Notwithstanding these descriptions of neuronal activity during consciousness and self-awareness, the qualities of self-experience, including the entire spectrum of emotions that Freud attributed to "omega" neurons, remain to be understood.

MEMORY

In regard to memory, Freud (1895) postulated that it was mediated by "differences in the facilitations between the 'psi' neurons" (p. 300). Our current understanding of memory is far more complex and continues to evolve. In brief, memory is categorized as short-term, long-term, declarative (explicit), and procedural (implicit). Memory appears to be mediated by a hippocampal-cortical neuronal network; the hippocampus regulates recent memory and the cortex stores long-term memory (Pan & Tsukada, 2006). Explicit memory, or memory for people, places, facts, and events is mediated via the hippocampus and medial temporal lobe. On the other hand, implicit memory for automatic motor and perceptual skills is mediated through the amygdala, cerebellum, and cortex (Kandel, 2012). Both explicit and implicit memory are important components of interpersonal communication, including psychotherapy. Freud's (1900) concepts of "day residue" and "free association" involve short-term and long-term memory. Dreams juxtapose long-term and short-term memory; in essence, the unconscious does not distinguish between past and present. Brockman (2001) emphasizes the roles of explicit and implicit memory in the unconscious. Kandel (1999) points out that procedural or implicit memory is operative in both the unconscious and transference phenomena. However, elements of the preconscious unconscious are mediated by the prefrontal cortex and hippocampus. The latter facilitate the transfer of procedural or implicit memories into consciousness. Reiser (2001) theorizes that memories are stored and organized via nodal memory networks, according to their affective potential. Emotions that are either experienced or symbolized in dream manifest content may lead the dreamer to recall significant events in the recent or distant past. Moreover, feelings and percepts evoked in the therapeutic relationship may resonate with unconscious memories that can influence transference. Freud (1912) recognized the importance of unconscious memory when he first described transference: "unconscious impulses…reproduce themselves in accordance with the timelessness of the unconscious" (p. 108). Psychoanalytically oriented clinicians routinely question their patients about past experiences, relationships, and feelings in connection with manifestations of transference.

A cascade of neurotransmitter, molecular, genetic, and morphological changes are involved in memory processing. These include serotonin, GABA, glutamate, norepinephrine, dopamine, protein kinases, intracellular signaling events, and structural modifications of the synapse (Johansen, Cain, Ostroff, & LeDoux, 2011; Kandel, 2012). Memory and learning are interconnected, and are essential components of adaptive or maladaptive behavior. Perhaps, the most studied phenomenon of learning and memory is fear conditioning (Kandel, 1983; Kim et al., 2011; LeDoux, 1994). Kandel (1983) demonstrated that learning (habituation and sensitization) in Aplysia (sea snail) involves both neurotransmitter release and morphological changes in the synapse. He hypothesized that psychotherapy may bring about similar neuro-synaptic and neurotransmitter changes in the human brain. LeDoux (1994, 1996) notes that fear conditioning (learning to respond to a threat) is comprised of two major pathways; thalamic-amygdala and amygdala-prefrontal cortical. The former is activated when a rapid response to an immediate threat is required; the latter becomes involved when there is time for a cognitive appraisal of the threat (Kim et al., 2011). Recent evidence reveals reciprocal functional connections between the amygdala and medial prefrontal cortex that regulate the fear response (Kim et al., 2011). Increased prefrontal cortical

activity and simultaneous decreased amygdala activity occurs during successful fear regulation. The treatment of anxiety disorders, whether psychopharmacological or psychotherapeutic, is based on the suppression of thalamic-amygdala hyperactivity. Both cognitive-behavioral and psychodynamic therapies attempt to improve cognitive (prefrontal cortex) control by means of conditioning and insight.

Of interest, is that a group of individuals has been identified in childhood who have a genetically predisposed "anxious temperament" or AT (Shackman et al., 2013). They demonstrate increased amygdala and anterior hippocampal reactivity to threat-relevant cues, as well as weaker functional connections between the amygdala and medial-frontal cortex. This observation has important implications for the treatment of anxiety, social, phobic, and posttraumatic stress disorders. For example, a child with anxious temperament (AT) who is physically or emotionally abused might be more likely to develop generalized anxiety or posttraumatic stress disorder. Similarly, a child with AT who has overprotective, distrustful parents might become socially anxious and withdrawn. One of my patients developed a food phobia as an adult because her mother believed she had childhood allergies, and warned her that she could die from an anaphylactic reaction. Another patient developed free-floating anxiety in adulthood as a consequence of being traumatized by an alcoholic, violent father. Identification of children with AT is important so that early therapeutic interventions can be instituted if they are exposed to parental or environmental stress and trauma.

HYSTERIA

Freud (1895) tentatively explored the mental mechanisms of "hysteria" in the Project. For him, hysteria included compulsions, obsessions, phobias, and conversion reactions. He attempted to correlate neuronal activity with such phenomena as repression, symbol formation, and displacement. During this period, he also published papers devoted to the psychogenesis of conversion, obsessions, and phobias (Freud, 1894a, b). According to him, conversion symptoms result when the affect associated with an unacceptable idea or event is displaced and converted to a somatic symptom (e.g., paralysis). Phobias are displaced ideas associated with anxiety, while obsessions are displaced ideas associated with various emotional states, including anxiety, guilt, shame, anger, etc. According to Freud (1895), the original idea or experience is usually connected to a sexual fantasy or activity. Although the exclusive sexual etiology of these disorders is no longer accepted, the role of repression, displacement, and symbol formation are still considered to be psychodynamically relevant in the genesis of phobias and obsessions. Recent evidence reveals that patients with OCD manifest hyperactivity of the caudate nucleus-orbitofrontal cortex neuronal circuit (Baxter et al., 1992; Saxena & Rauch, 2000; Whiteside, Port, & Abramowitz, 2004). Gillan et al. (2015) demonstrated that excessive habit formation in OCD is associated with caudate nucleus hyperactivity. Baxter et al. (1992) suggest that caudate nucleus dysfunction is associated with inadequate filtering of "worry" inputs from the orbitofrontal cortex. In view of the fact that OCD appears to have a genetic component, similar to those individuals with AT, early identification and therapeutic intervention may be helpful (Browne, Gair, Scharf, & Grice, 2014; Mataix-Cols et al., 2013). Glucksman (1995) speculates that significant intrapsychic or interpersonal threats may not be adequately modulated or neutralized in patients with OCD; instead, threats are continuously reinforced by this self-perpetuating excitatory circuit, resulting in repetitive behaviors and obsessive ideation. Displacement, symbol-formation, isolation, and undoing appear to be the psychodynamic manifestations of this dysfunctional neuronal pathway. However, treatment with either SS-RIs or cognitive-behavioral therapy can normalize or interrupt this self-sustaining circuit (Baxter et al., 1992).

CONVERSION DISORDERS

Conversion disorders remain a fascinating, yet puzzling clinical phenomenon. In *DSM-5* (American Psychiatric Association, 2013), conversion disorder is termed "functional neurological symptom disorder," and involves the voluntary motor or sensory nervous systems. It is differentiated from "somatic symptom disorder"; the latter is mediated via the voluntary or involuntary nervous systems. According to Kaplan (2014), conversion disorders are precipitated when current life stressors resonate with childhood trauma. Patients with conversion symptoms are typically unable to verbally articulate their feelings and intrapsychic conflicts. They do not have the capacity to express their internal mental state through symbolic thought and language. The neurophysiological process of "conversion" is still poorly understood. A recent study (Vuilleumier, 2014) of functional motor paralysis reveals hyperactivation of the ventromedial prefrontal cortex, precuneus, and other limbic structures, simultaneous with decreased activation of motor pathways at the cortical and subcortical level. Similar dysfunction of neuronal pathways occurs with somatosensory, visual, and memory conversion symptoms. These findings suggest that Freud's (1894a) hypothesis regarding the conversion of disturbing affect to sensory-motor pathways may have some validity. In my practice, I continue to see conversion symptoms, including atypical pain, hypesthesia, and functional seizures. Conversion reactions are common in the context of traumatic events, including combat. As a military psychiatrist, I treated a helicopter pilot who developed conversion blindness after he realized that he had accidentally attacked and killed his own soldiers. His feelings of guilt and remorse were repressed, displaced, and converted to his visual pathways and occipital cortex. Another patient was an army platoon leader who presented with bilateral upper extremity paralysis. His symptoms developed in the context of his repressed rage and murderous fantasies toward his commanding officer, whom he believed placed his men in mortal danger. His motor paralysis dramatically disappeared when he became consciously aware of his wish to strangle his superior. Recently, one of my patients presented with hypesthesia of his pubic and genital region during intercourse. In addition, he experienced either delayed or failed ejaculation. A neurological workup revealed no obvious organic cause for his symptoms. During psychotherapy, he revealed suppressed rage at his wife in connection with her manipulative, controlling behavior. As he became consciously aware of his feelings, sensation in his genitalia gradually normalized. Although current evidence demonstrates neuronal dysfunction in motor and sensory pathways associated with conversion symptoms (Black, Seritan, Taber, & Hurley, 2004; Bryant & Das, 2012; Vuilleumier, 2014), the interface between intrapsychic conflict, displaced affect, and neuronal activity remains a mystery.

PHOBIAS

Freud (1895) did not offer an explanation regarding neuronal activity associated with phobias in the Project, although he pointed out that phobias are always accompanied by anxiety (Freud, 1894b). However, his subsequent papers explored the etiology and psychodynamics of phobias and anxiety neurosis (Freud, 1909, 1917, 1926). In "The Introductory Lectures on Psychoanalysis" (Freud, 1917), he refers to his earlier research on the medulla oblongata, but then remarks, "I know nothing that could be of less interest to me for the psychological understanding of anxiety than a knowledge of the path of the nerves along which excitations pass" (Freud,

1917, p. 393). Ironically, almost a century since this statement, there is a growing body of data specifically concerned with the neuronal pathways and anatomic structures associated with anxiety, panic, phobias, and PTSD. As previously cited, certain anxiety-prone children and adults exhibit increased activation of the amygdala, hippocampus, insula, and orbitofrontal cortex (Blackford et al., 2014; Fox & Kalin, 2014; Shackman et al., 2013). These individuals, identified as having a genetic predisposition for an anxious temperament (AT), are at higher risk for developing panic disorder and social anxiety. On the other hand, cognitive-behavioral and psychodynamic therapy can normalize their dysfunctional neuronal circuits (Kim et al., 2011; Lueken et al., 2013). Etkin and Wager (2007) note that social anxiety, specific phobias, and PTSD all have increased activation of the fear pathway that includes the amygdala and insula. In a PET scan study, Furmark et al. (2002) examined cerebral blood flow (CBF) in patients with social phobia before and after cognitive-behavior therapy or medication (citalopram). There were significant decreases in CBF of the amygdala, hippocampus, and adjacent cortical areas following successful treatment using both modalities.

Paquette et al. (2003) studied the effect of cognitive-behavioral therapy (CBT) on patients with spider phobia. Prior to CBT, he observed increased activation of the right inferior frontal gyrus, parahippocampal gyrus, and visual cortex. Following successful CBT, there was decreased activation of the right inferior frontal gyrus, parahippocampal gyrus, and prefrontal cortex. Almost 100 years after Freud dismissed the importance of understanding the neuronal and anatomic pathways of anxiety, there is clear evidence of dysfunctional circuits associated with anxiety, panic disorder, and phobias. Moreover, a specific population can be identified in early childhood that exhibits increased anxiety or anxious temperament (AT) and is more likely to develop anxiety disorders. Effective treatment, including

CBT, psychodynamic psychotherapy, or medication can now be monitored and documented using fMRIs and PET scans.

COGNITION

In his exploration of cognition, Freud (1895) was more concerned with primary process than secondary process thought. Primary process refers to unconscious mentation which is illogical, symbolic, and timeless. Secondary process is conscious mentation characterized by logical thought and a linear sense of time. Freud (1895) hypothesized that both types of cognition were mediated via "psi" neurons, although they differed according to the quantity of excitation. Prior to the publication of "The Interpretation of Dreams" (1900), he observed that there was a motor paralysis during dreaming, and that cognition in dreams was "non-sensical, partly feeble-minded, or even meaningless or strangely crazy" (Freud, 1895, p. 338). He attributed the hallucinatory experience and primary process thought in dreams to another neuronal excitation that he termed "Q" (Freud, 1895, p. 339). However, he did not pursue the nature of "Q" when he developed his later theory of dreaming; namely, that it is a form of censorship over instinctually driven wishes. Nor could he envision future discoveries about dreaming; first, that it is a biologically determined rhythmic activation of neuronal projections from the midbrain to the cortex during rapid eye movement (REM) sleep (although neuronal activation may also originate in the cortex); second, that its major function is not primarily to censor instinctual impulses, but rather to facilitate memory storage, learning, problem solving, and mood regulation; third, that primary process mentation in dreams often has metaphorical meaning and can be deciphered from the manifest content (Aserinsky & Kleitman, 1953; Dement & Kleitman, 1957; Glucksman, 2001; Greenberg & Pearlman, 1993; Hobson, 1999; Kramer, 1993). Al-

though Freud never developed an integrated theory of cognition, cognitive concepts are ubiquitous in psychoanalytic theories (Baars, 2005; Basch, 1997; Semenza, 2001). Included are such phenomena as mental representations, symbol formation, ideation, beliefs, rationalization, intellectualization, splitting, and insight. Indeed, an entire field of cognitive neuropsychology has developed that is concerned with the neurobiology of cognitive processes.

AFFECT

Similar to his observations on cognition, Freud never developed a comprehensive, systematic theory of affect. In "The Project" (1895), he described two categories of affect: satisfaction and pain (p. 321). While he viewed both as forms of psychic energy, pain or unpleasure required inhibition. In his signal theory of anxiety, Freud (1926) recognized affect (namely, anxiety) as a signal with cognitive meaning. In this model, an affect (anxiety) signals the ego to take evasive action and defend against it. Anxiety and fear are considered to be synonymous by neurobiologists, and mediated via the thalamo-amygdala-cortical neuronal axis (LeDoux, 1994, 1996; Panksepp, 1999, 2005). Other affects (joy, sadness, guilt, etc.) are regulated through the amygdala, anterior cingulate, insular, and orbito-frontal cortex (Pally, 2010; Panksepp, 2005). According to Panksepp (2005), all emotions involve neurotransmitters, including norepinephrine, serotonin, acetylcholine, and glutamate. However, focal or discreet affects are thought to be mediated by specific neuropeptides; positive affects involve beta-endorphins and oxytocin, while negative affects involve CRF and cholecystokinin. Perhaps, the neurochemical, qualitative distinctions between feelings is analogous to Freud's (1895) "omega" neurons, but much more remains to be discovered in this area. Lane and coworkers (Lane & Garfield, 2005; Lane & Schwartz, 1987) describe five levels of emotional awareness: level one involves physiological arousal; level two involves action or motor tendencies; level three involves single emotions; level four involves blends of emotions; level five involves blends of blends of emotional experience. Levels one and two are implicit, and often out of conscious awareness. They are mediated via the thalamus, hypothalamus, amygdala, and basal ganglia. Levels three, four, and five are mediated by the anterior cingulate, insula, orbito-frontal cortex, and right parietal lobe. MacLean (1990) and Panksepp (1998) propose that activation of limbic and sub-cortical structures alone is sufficient for the conscious experience of emotion. However, others believe that cortical participation is necessary for emotional experience (Lane & Garfield, 2005; Mayberg, 2003). Focal awareness or immediate attention to feelings can be differentiated from reflective awareness of feelings (Farthing, 1992; Fonagy, Gergely, Jurist, & Target, 2002; Lane, Fink, Chua, & Dolan, 1997). Reflective awareness of feelings or mentalization, requires activation of the anterior cingulate and medial prefrontal cortex (Lane & Garfield, 2005). Mentalization refers to the process of explicit and implicit awareness of the feelings, thoughts, and behavior of self and others (Fonagy et al., 2002). Analogous to psychological-mindedness, it is necessary for participation in psychoanalytic or psychodynamic therapy. There is recent evidence that mentalizing corresponds to neuronal activation in the mesial frontal cortex and right temporo-parietal junction (Rizzolatti & Craighero, 2004; Rizolatti & Fogassi, 2014).

Mirror neurons appear to be a key mechanism for processing and re-creating in one's mind the intentions, actions, and feelings of another person. Mentalization most likely involves mirror neuron activation, and is necessary for normal interpersonal communication. Mirror neurons were first discovered in macaque monkeys who viewed and simulated the motor acts of other monkeys (Rizzolatti, 2001; Rizzolatti, Fadiga, Gallese, & Fogassi, 1996). During this activity, mirror neurons are activated in the ventral premotor cortex and inferior parietal lobe of macaque monkeys. In humans, mirror neurons consist of two major networks: (1) parietal lobe and premotor cortex; (2) insula and anterior-mesial frontal cortex or limbic mirror system (Cattaneo & Rizolatti, 2009). The mirror neuron system is involved with both visualized and auditory aspects of behavior (Keysers & Gazzola, 2006). A number of investigators hypothesize that mirror neurons are involved in the mediation of emotional and cognitive empathy (Bernhardt & Singer, 2012; Cattaneo & Rizolatti, 2009; Corradino & Antonietti, 2013; DeVignemont & Singer, 2006; Gallese, 2001, 2003; Gallese, Eagle, & Migone, 2007; Pally, 2010; Singer & Lamm, 2009; Singer et al., 2004). Using fMRIs, Broadbart, deGrauw, Perrett, Waiter, and Williams (2014) observed that empathy and facial imitation accuracy correspond with neuronal simulation of others' intentions in the insula, premotor, and somatosensory cortex. Specific emotions, including pain, disgust, anxiety, joy, pleasure, and distress evoke neuronal activation in the insular, cingulate, and medial prefrontal cortex (Morelli, Rameson, & Lieberman, 2014; Perry, Bentin, Bartal, Lamm, & Decety, 2010; Singer et al., 2004). The neurochemical correlates of mirror neurons are not well understood, and remain to be delineated. Moreover, evidence that mirror neurons contribute to a specific and high level of interpersonal emotional understanding remains problematic (Lamm & Majdanzic, 2015). At the present time, evidence suggests that mirror neurons are associated with cognitive and emotional empathy, but further confirmation is necessary. Nevertheless, the more we learn about mirror neurons, the more we might understand the neurobiology of empathy, introjection, identification, projective identification, and transference. From a broader perspective, Whitehead (2009) optimistically points out that mirror neurons may facilitate two cardinal features of human evolution: empathy and interdependence.

CLINICAL ILLUSTRATION

Robert* is the only child of parents who were overprotective and strict. He attended private schools, but found himself unpopular and teased because of his awkwardness. As a result, he tended to be a loner and felt self-conscious in social situations. Following graduation from law school, he found a position with a prestigious firm and specialized in an arcane area of the law. He holds himself to extremely high standards at work, and expects others to do likewise. Married, without children, he is highly critical of his wife and others. Moreover, he is excessively self-critical at his job and in social situations. Despite years of therapy and psychotropic medication, he continues to feel dissatisfied with himself, professionally inadequate, and socially awkward. During therapy sessions, Robert avoids talking about his feelings and often brings up political or topical issues in order to avoid emotionally charged ones. He is very deliberate in his choice of words and syntax. Preoccupied with potential criticism from others, he frequently misses social cues and is unable to react spontaneously. When I am with Robert, I often feel emotionally constricted, wary, and careful with my interventions. Periodically, I am the target of his anger or criticism, both of which can be withering.

What is transpiring psychodynamically between Robert and me? I know that he has an ambivalent transference that is connected to his father, who was emotionally aloof and critical. Furthermore, his mother was alcoholic, alternately seductive and volatile. Robert learned as a child to be obedient and emotionally controlled, in order to protect himself from his father's criticism and mother's manipulation. I transiently introject and identify with his frightened, emotionally inhibited, perfectionist self. Sometimes, I also feel inadequate, tentative, and reserved when I interact with him. At other times, I feel smoldering anger within myself and the potential for an eruption of rage (as Robert often feels toward others). Do these intrapsychic and interpersonal phenomena correspond to what is occurring neurobiologically within, as well as, between us? Are my mirror neurons resonating with Robert's inner cognitive-affective state? Is it reasonable to hypothesize that the projective identification and countertransference phenomena I have described are the psychodynamic correlates of mirror neuronal activation within and between us? Robert is intellectually well aware of the psychodynamic determinants for his need to be emotionally controlled and perfect. He realizes that I am neither his critical, distant father nor his unpredictably volatile mother. Multiple interpretive interventions on my part have helped him to cognitively appreciate the irrationality of his reflexive fear of criticism and rejection. Nevertheless, his amygdala-cingulate neuronal activation in the context of threatening interpersonal situations often negates his prefrontal cortical inhibition of an automatic fear response. When this occurs, he becomes symptomatic. At the beginning of treatment, Robert denied his feelings and placed paramount importance on his rational thought processes. Over time, he has developed the capacity to recognize and experience different emotional states without immediately shutting them off. Moreover, he is able to cognitively process his feelings and connect them to meaningful past and current experiences. Neurobiologically, he appears to have improved regulation of his limbic-prefrontal cortical system, as well as his mirror neuronal functioning. Anxiolytic and antidepressant medications have also helped with this regulatory process.

Does my knowledge of the neurobiological substrate of Robert's behavior facilitate his treatment? It definitely increases my awareness of the anatomical and physiological correlates of his thoughts, perceptions,

---

*Name and details have been changed to protect patient privacy.

and feelings. It also plays a role in whether or not I initiate specific psychotherapeutic interventions. For example, when I feel emotionally constricted, frightened, or angry, I suspect that my mirror neurons are simultaneously resonating with Robert's inner experience. Using that information, I can empathically suggest to him what I sense he might be feeling. If he concurs, we can jointly explore the proximate cause, as well as historical reasons for his emotional response. Repetitive interactions similar to this not only help Robert to identify his feelings, but also to understand their origin. His mirror neuronal response to me may also facilitate his ability to be more self-exploratory and self-aware. As a consequence, he is more likely able to identify with and internalize my capacity to access my feelings and express them appropriately. Hopefully, this pattern of therapeutic interaction can help him become less self-critical and fearful of the disapproval of others. Neurobiologically, one might say that Robert and I are engaged in a process of mutual mentalization involving our mirror neurons, enabling him to better modulate his cingulate-prefrontal-right temporo-parietal cortex. In turn, he is sometimes, but not always, able to feel less threatened by others and more spontaneous in expressing his feelings.

Using this clinical vignette, I have speculatively synthesized mental processes and neurobiological phenomena based on our current knowledge. Freud (1895) attempted to do so in the Project, but lacked the information and technology that is now available. As a result, he developed a metapsychology in order to explain mental phenomena. The latter constitute what is commonly referred to as "mind" or "psyche." Brookes (2004) defines mind as a phenomenological entity that refers to the "totality of subjective experience." The substratum of mind is the brain, where the objective physical events that correspond to subjective experience occur. Mind and brain are at the same time separate, but indivisible, integrated entities. Freud's abandonment of the Proj-

ect contributed to a century of dualism in psychiatry, one emphasizing subjective mental phenomena (mind), and the other concerned with objective, neurobiological processes (brain). In the recent past, there have been attempts to bridge the two entities (Beutel, Stern, & Silbersweig, 2003; Cooper, 1985; Gabbard, 2000, 2005; Glucksman, 1995; Kandel, 1998, 1999; Mundo, 2006; Pardes, 1986; Schore, 1997). Nevertheless, research into mental disorders still tends to be either mind-centered or neurobiologically focused. However, our current understanding of brain mechanisms associated with the mental phenomena addressed by Freud (1895) in the Project (consciousness, cognition, dreaming, memory, affect, anxiety, conversion, obsessions, and phobias) might pleasantly surprise him if he were alive today. Indeed, Freud (1913, p. 182) stated that "…after we have completed our psychoanalytic work we shall have to find a point of contact with biology; and we may rightly feel glad if that contact is already assured at one important point or another."

I wish to emphasize that the "point of contact" to which Freud (1913) referred, has been evolving, if not accelerating, over the past several decades. Kandel (1999) observes that there are significant areas where psychoanalysis and neurobiology converge, and can inform each other in terms of future research. First, the functions of unconscious mental processes can be further delineated utilizing information about the biology of procedural and declarative memory. Second, the neurobiology of learning and conditioning can help clarify the linkage between early experience, stress, threat, anxiety, and symptom formation. Third, the role of genetics needs to be further understood in the etiology of sexual orientation, anxiety, mood, and personality disorders. Fourth, psychotherapy outcomes need to be objectively measured in terms of structural and neurochemical changes in the brain. Schore (1997, 2003) emphasizes the importance of further exploration regarding the relationship between the orbitofrontal cortex-limbic system and affective regulation, mental representations, fantasy, and other cognitive functions. He points out that the orbitofrontal cortex undergoes critical growth during the first and second year of infancy. According to him, affective misattunement and disruptive attachment with the primary caregiver inhibits growth of the cortico-limbic system, and may result in autism, depression, and borderline personality disorder. Recent evidence suggests that parental maltreatment in early childhood may result in decreased serum oxytosin levels and the development of borderline personality disorder (Herpertz & Bertsch, 2015). They demonstrated in a placebo-controlled double-blind group design that oxytocin diminishes threat hypersensitivity in patients with borderline personality disorder. Gabbard (2000, 2005) describes a multiplicity of factors in the etiology of borderline personality disorder, including genes, environment, and interpersonal experience. He emphasizes the interplay between epigenetics and environmental influences in the etiology of borderline and other personality disorders. In addition, he points out that because neurobiology and psychodynamic phenomena utilize two separate languages, it is necessary to translate one to the other in order to more fully understand mental disorders. For example, there is accumulating evidence that major depression involves a complex interaction between genes, neurotransmitters, and experience. Caspi et al. (2003) report an alteration of the 5-HTT gene in those individuals vulnerable to depression. Beck (2008) speculates that genetic vulnerability as well as dysfunction of the amygdala-limbic-prefrontal cortex promotes cognitive distortions; namely, a focus on the negative aspects of experience and self that is characteristic of depression. Environmental factors and epigenetic mechanisms may also reduce or exacerbate the genetic expression of schizophrenia and bipolar disorder (Fass, Schroeder, Perlis, & Haggarty, 2014; Khare, Pal, & Petronis, 2011;

Rivollier, Lotersztajn, Chaumette, Krebs, & Kebir, 2014; Shorter & Miller, 2015).

Beutel et al. (2003) review the role of neuro-imaging techniques in evaluating the effects of both psychotherapy and medication on brain function associated with various disorders. A number of conditions, including OCD, panic disorder, social phobia, depression, and borderline personality have been studied pre- and post-treatment (Baxter et al., 1992; Furmark et al., 2002; Goldapple et al., 2004; Martin, Martin, Rai, Richardson, & Royall, 2001; Viinamaki, Kuikka, & Tiihonen, 1998). Mayberg (2006) observed that both antidepressants and cognitive-behavioral therapy normalize prefrontal-cortical-cingulate dysfunction in depressed patients. Beutel, Stark, Pan, Silbersweig, and Dietrich (2010) examined brain function in patients with panic disorder before and after psychodynamic therapy; dysfunctional prefrontal-cortical-limbic activity normalized following treatment. Changes in brain function of these disorders before and after psychotherapeutic intervention appears to validate recent studies on the efficacy of psychotherapy (Leichsenring, Abbass, Luyten, Hilsenroth, & Rabung, 2013; Levy, Ehrenthal, Yeomans, & Caligor, 2014). Our knowledge of brain dysfunction in the disorders that Freud (1895) included under the rubric of hysteria is rapidly expanding. Moreover, there is accumulating evidence of normalization of brain function following successful treatment of these disorders. Paradoxically, more than a century after Freud abandoned the Project (1895), knowledge of the neurobiological substrate of mind is rapidly growing. The complex interaction of neuronal activity, neurotransmitter function, genetics, epigenetics, intrapsychic, and interpersonal experience is becoming increasingly apparent. It is clearly evident that mental and neurobiological processes are integrated phenomena that reflect our human experience. Nevertheless, certain phenomena remain to be more fully explained: for example, how do thoughts, feelings, or perceptions translate into neuronal activity and neurotransmitter secretion? How do neuronal-synaptic and neurochemical changes account for the different qualities of subjective emotional experience? How do unconscious memories neuronal-chemically influence conscious cognition and feelings? What are the neuronal-chemical substrates of defense mechanisms? These and other mental functions need to be further understood in terms of mind-brain interactivity. However, in doing so, it is important to respect the different languages used in describing subjective mental experiences and their corresponding neurobiological processes. Each provides valuable information connected to different facets of the same phenomena. Keeping in mind the unique nature of each, learning from one can provide us with knowledge about the other. Although Freud's (1895) Project may have been premature, it nevertheless addressed the central issue concerning human behavior: the relationship between mind and brain. In this article, I have attempted to highlight some of the significant advances made toward understanding the neurobiology of mind, with particular emphasis on those disorders Freud (1895) examined in the Project. Hopefully, the next 120 years will further enlighten us regarding the interrelated phenomena of mental experience and neurobiological function.

REFERENCES

American Psychiatric Association. (2013). *American Psychiatric Association Desk Reference to the Diagnostic Criteria from DSM-5.* Arlington, VA: American Psychiatric Association.

Aserinsky, E., & Kleitman, N. (1953). Regularly occurring periods of eye motility and concomitant phenomena during sleep. *Science, 118,* 273-274.

Axelrod, J. (1957). O-methylation of epinephrine and other catechols in vitro and in vivo. *Science, 126,* 400-401.

Baars, B. J. (2005). Global workspace theory of consciousness. *Progress in Brain Research, 150,* 45-53.

Basch, M. F. (1997). Developmental psychology and explanatory theory in psychoanalysis. *Annals of Psychoanalysis, 5,* 229-263.

Baxter, L. R., Schwartz, J. M., Bergman, K. S., Szuba, M. P., Guze, B. H., Mazziotta, J. C., Alazraki, A., Selin, C. E., Ferng, H. K., Munford, P., & Phelps, M. E. (1992). Caudate glucose metabolic rate changes with both drug and behavior therapy for obsessive-compulsive disorder. *Archives of General Psychiatry, 49,* 681-689.

Beck, A. T. (2008). The evolution of the cognitive model of depression and its neurobiological correlates. *American Journal of Psychiatry, 165,* 969-977.

Bernhardt, B. C., & Singer, T. (2012). The neural basis of empathy. *Annual Review of Neuroscience, 35,* 1-23.

Beutel, M. E., Stark, R., Pan, H., Silbersweig, D., & Dietrich, S. (2010). Changes of brain activation pre-post short-term psychodynamic inpatient psychotherapy: An fMRI study of panic disorder patients. *Psychiatry Research, 184,* 96-104.

Beutel, M. E., Stern, E., & Silbersweig, D. A. (2003). The emerging dialogue between psychoanalysis and neuroscience: Neuroimaging perspectives. *Journal of the American Psychoanalytic Association, 51,* 773-801.

Black, D. N., Seritan, A. L., Taber, K. H., & Hurley, R. A. (2004). Conversion hysteria: Lessons from functional imaging. *Journal of Neuropsychiatry, 16,* 245-251.

Blackford, J. U., Clauss, J. A., Avery, S. N., Cowan, R. L., Benningfield, M. M., & VanDerKlok, R. M. (2014). Amygdala-cingulate intrinsic connectivity is associated with degree of social inhibition. *Biological Psychology, 99,* 15-25.

Broadbart, L., deGrauw, H., Perrett, D. I., Waiter, G. D., & Williams, J. H. G. (2014). The shared neural basis of empathy and facial imitation accuracy. *Neuroimage, 84,* 367-375.

Brockman, R. (2001). Toward a neurobiology of the unconscious. *Journal of the American Academy of Psychoanalysis, 29*(4), 601-615.

Brooks, C. E. (2004). Some comments on the nature and use of the concept of psyche in psychoanalysis and psychodynamic psychotherapy. *Journal of the American Academy of Psychoanalysis and Dynamic Psychiatry, 32*(2), 259-266.

Browne, H.A., Gair, S.L., Scharf, J.M., & Grice, D.E. (2014). Genetics of obsessive-compulsive disorder and related disorders, *Psychiatric Clinics of North America, 3*, 319-335.

Bryant, R. A., & Das, P. (2012). The neural circuitry of conversion disorder and its recovery. *Journal of Abnormal Psychology, 121*, 289-296.

Cajal, S. R. (1899). Textura del sistema nervioso del hombre y de los vertebrados. *Imprenta y Libreria de Nicolas Moya, 1*, 80-95, 106-110.

Caspi, A., Sugden, K., Moffitt, T. E., Taylor, A., Craig, I. W., & Harrington, H. L. (2003). Influence of life stress on depression moderation by a polymorphism in the 5-HTT gene. *Science, 301*, 386-389.

Cattaneo, L., & Rizzolatti, G. (2009). The mirror neuron system. *Archives of Neurology, 66*(5), 557-560.

Cooper, A. M. (1985). Will neurobiology influence psychoanalysis? *American Journal of Psychiatry, 142*(12), 1395-1402.

Corradini, A., & Antonietti, A. (2013). Mirror neurons and their function in cognitively understood empathy. *Conscious Cognition, 22*(3), 1152-1161.

Crick, F., & Koch, C. (1990). Towards a neurobiological theory of consciousness. *Sem. Neuroscientifica, 2*, 263-275.

Crick, F., & Koch, C. (2000). The unconscious homunculus. *Neuro-Psychoanalysis, 2*(1), 3-11.

Dement, W., & Kleitman, N. (1957). The relation if eye movements during sleep to dream activity: An objective method for the study of dreaming. *Journal of Experimental Psychology, 53*, 89-97.

DeVignemont, F., & Singer, T. (2006). The empathic brain: How, when and why. *Trends in Cognitive Sciences, 10*, 435-441.

Edelman, G. (1989). *The remembered present.* New York: Basic Books.

Edelman, G. (1992). *Bright air, brilliant fire.* New York: Basic Books.

Etkin, A., & Wager, T. D. (2007). Functional neuroimaging of anxiety: A meta-analysis of emotional processing in PTSD, social anxiety disorder, and specific phobia. *American Journal of Psychiatry, 164*, 1476-1488.

Farthing, G. W. (1992). *The psychology of consciousness.* Englewood Cliffs, NJ: Prentice-Hall.

Fass, D. M., Schroeder, F. A., Perlis, R. H., & Haggarty, S. J. (2014). Epigenetic mechanisms in

mood disorders: Targeting neuroplasticity. *Neuroscience, 264*, 112-130.

Fonagy, P., Gergely, G., Jurist, E. L., & Target, M. (2002). *Affect regulation, mentalization and the development of the self.* New York: Other Press.

Fox, A. S., & Kalin, N. H. (2014). A translational neuroscience approach to understanding the development of social anxiety disorder and its pathophysiology. *American Journal of Psychiatry, 171*(11), 1162-1173.

Freud, S. (1894a). The neuro-psychoses of defence. In J. Strachey (Ed. & Trans.), *The standard edition of the complete psychological works of Sigmund Freud* (Vol. 3, pp. 45-61). London: Hogarth Press.

Freud, S. (1894b). Obsessions and phobias. In J. Strachey (Ed. and Trans.), *The standard edition of the complete psychological works of Sigmund Freud* (Vol. 3, pp. 71-84). London: Hogarth Press.

Freud, S. (1895). Project for a scientific psychology. In J. Strachey (Ed. & Trans.), *The standard edition of the complete psychological works of Sigmund Freud* (Vol. 1, pp. 283-397). London: Hogarth Press.

Freud, S. (1900). The interpretation of dreams. In J. Strachey (Ed. & Trans.), *The standard edition of the complete psychological works of Sigmund Freud* (Vols. 4 and 5). London: Hogarth Press.

Freud, S. (1909). Analysis of a phobia in a five year old boy. In J. Strachey (Ed. & Trans.), *The standard edition of the complete psychological works of Sigmund Freud* (Vol. 10, pp. 5-147). London: Hogarth Press.

Freud, S. (1912). The dynamics of transference. In J. Strachey (Ed. & Trans.), *The standard edition of the complete psychological works of Sigmund Freud* (Vol. 12, p. 108). London: Hogarth Press.

Freud, S. (1913). The claims of psychoanalysis to scientific interest. In J. Strachey (Ed. & Trans.), *The standard edition of the complete psychological works of Sigmund Freud* (Vol. 13, p. 182). London: Hogarth Press.

Freud, S. (1917). Introductory lectures on psychoanalysis. In J. Strachey (Ed. & Trans.), *The standard edition of the complete psychological works of Sigmund Freud* (Vol. 16, p. 393). London: Hogarth Press.

Freud, S. (1920). Beyond the pleasure principal. In J. Strachey (Ed. & Trans.), *The standard edition of the complete psychological works of Sigmund Freud* (Vol. 18). London: Hogarth Press.

Freud, S. (1926). Inhibitions, symptoms and anxiety. In J. Strachey (Ed. & Trans.), *The standard edition of the complete psychological works of Sigmund Freud* (Vol. 20, pp. 87-174). London: Hogarth Press.

Freud, S. (1932). New introductory lectures on psychoanalysis. In J. Strachey (Ed. & Trans.), *The standard edition of the complete psychological works of Sigmund Freud* (Vol. 22, p. 154). London: Hogarth Press.

Furmark, T., Tillfors, M., Marteinsdottir, I., Fischer, H., Pissiota, A., Langstrom, B., & Frederickson, M. (2002). Common changes in cerebral blood flow in patients with social phobia treated with citalopram or cognitive-behavioral therapy. *Archives of Human Development, 3*, 30-61.

Gabbard, G. (2000). A neurobiologically informed perspective on psychotherapy. *British Journal of Psychiatry, 177*, 117-122.

Gabbard, G. (2005). Mind, brain, and personality disorders. *American Journal of Psychiatry, 162*, 648-655.

Gallese, V. (2001). The shared manifold hypothesis: From mirror neurons to empathy. *Journal of Consciousness Studies, 8*, 33-50.

Gallese, V. (2003). The roots of empathy: The shared manifold hypothesis and the neural basis of intersubjectivity. *Psychopathology, 36*, 171-180.

Gallese, V., Eagle, M. N., & Migone, P. (2007). Intentional attunement: Mirror neurons and the neural underpinnings of interpersonal relations. *Journal of the American Psychoanalytic Association, 55*(1), 131-176.

Gillan, C. M., Apergis-Schoute, A. M., Morein-Zamir, S., Urcelay, G. P., Sule, A., Fineberg, N. A., Sahakian, B. J., & Robbins, T. W. (2015). Functional neuroimaging of avoidance habits in obsessive-compulsive disorder. *American Journal of Psychiatry, 172*, 284-293.

Glucksman, M. L. (1995). Psychodynamics and neurobiology: An integrated approach. *Journal of the American Academy of Psychoanalysis, 23*(2), 179-195.

Glucksman, M. L. (2001). The dream, a psychodynamically informative instrument. *Journal of Psychotherapy Practice and Research, 10*(4), 223-230.

Goldapple, K., Zindel, S., Garson, C., Lau, M., Bieling, P., Kenney, S., & Mayberg, H. (2004). Modulation of cortical-limbic pathways in major depression. *Archives of General Psychiatry, 61*, 34-41.

Greenberg, R., & Pearlman, C. (1993). An integrated approach to dream theory: Contributions from sleep research and clinical practice. In A. Moffit, M. Kramer, & R. Hoffman (Eds.), *The functions of dreaming* (pp. 363-380). Albany, NY: State University of New York Press.

Herpertz, S. C., & Bertsch, K. (2015). A new perspective on the pathophysiology of borderline personality disorder: A model of the role of oxytocin. *American Journal of Psychiatry, 172*(9), 840-851.

Hobson, J. A. (1999). The new neuropsychology of sleep. *Neuro-Psychoanalysis, 1*, 157-183.

Johansen, J. P., Cain, C. K., Ostroff, L. E., & LeDoux, J. E. (2011). Molecular mechanisms of fear, learning, and memory. *Cell, 147*(3), 509-524.

Kandel, E. R. (1983). From metapsychology to molecular biology: Explorations into the nature of anxiety. *American Journal of Psychiatry, 140*, 1277-1293.

Kandel, E. R. (1998). A new intellectual framework for psychiatry. *American Journal of Psychiatry, 155*, 457-469.

Kandel, E. R. (1999). Biology and the future of psychoanalysis: A new intellectual framework for psychiatry revisited. *American Journal of Psychiatry, 156*(4), 505-524.

Kandel, E. R. (2012). The molecular biology of memory: cAMP, PKA, CRE, CREB-1, CREB-2, and CPEB. *Molecular Brain, 5*(14), 1-12.

Kandel, E. R., Schwartz, J. H., Jessell, T. M., Siegelbaum, S. A., & Hudspeth, A. J. (2012). *Principles of neural science.* New York: McGraw-Hill.

Kaplan, M. J. (2014). A psychodynamic perspective on treatment of patients with conversion and other somatoform disorders. *Psychodynamic Psychiatry, 42*(4), 593-615.

Keysers, C., & Gazzola, V. (2006). Towards a unifying neural theory of social cognition. *Progress in Brain Research, 156*, 379-401.

Khare, T., Pal, M., & Petronis, A. (2011). Understanding bipolar disorder: The epigenetic perspective. *Current Topics in Behavioral Neurosciences, 5*, 31-49.

Kim, M. J., Loucks, R. A., Palmer, A. L., Brown, A. C., Solomon, K. M., Marchante, A. N., & Whalen, P. J. (2011). The structural and functional connectivity of the amygdala: From normal emotion to pathological anxiety. *Behavior and Brain Research, 223*(2), 403-410.

Kramer, M. (1993). The selective mood regulatory function of dreaming: An update and revision. In A. Moffit, M. Kramer, & R. Hoffman (Eds.), *The functions of dreaming* (pp. 139-195). Albany, NY: State University of New York Press.

Lamm, C., & Majdandzic, J. (2015). The role of shared neural activations, mirror neurons, and morality in empathy—A critical comment. *Neuroscience Research, 90*, 15-24.

Lane, R. D., Fink, G. R., Chua, P. M. L., & Dolan, R. J. (1997). Neural activation during selective attention to subjective emotional responses. *Neuroreport, 8*(18), 3969-3972.

Lane, R. D., & Garfield, D. A. S. (2005). Becoming aware of feelings: Integration of cognitive-developmental, neuroscientific, and psychoanalytic perspectives. *Neuro-Psychoanalysis, 7*(1), 5-30.

Lane, R. D., & Schwartz, G. E. (1987). Levels of emotional awareness: A cognitive-developmental theory and its application to psychopathology. *American Journal of Psychiatry, 144*, 133-143.

LeDoux, J. E. (1994). Emotion, memory and the brain. *Scientific American, 270*(6), 50-57.

LeDoux, J. E. (1996). *The emotional brain: The mysterious underpinnings of emotional life.* New York: Simon and Schuster.

Leichsenring, F., Abbass, A., Luyten, P., Hilsenroth, M., & Rabung, S. (2013). The emerging evidence for long-term psychodynamic therapy. *Psychodynamic Psychiatry, 41*(3), 361-384.

Levy, K. N., Ehrenthal, J. C., Yeomans, F. E., & Caligor, E. (2014). The efficacy of psychotherapy: Focus on psychodynamic psychotherapy as an example. *Psychodynamic Psychiatry, 42*(3), 377-421.

Lueken, U., Straube, B., Konrad, C., Wittchen, H.-U., Strohle, A., Wittmann, A., Pfleiderer, B., Uhlmann, C., Arolt, V., Jansen, A., & Kircher, T. (2013). Neural substrates of treatment response to cognitive-behavioral therapy in panic disorder with agoraphobia. *American Journal of Psychiatry, 170*, 1345-1355.

MacLean, P. D. (1990). *The triune brain in evolution: Role in paleocerebral functions.* New York: Plenum.

Martin, S. D., Martin, E., Rai, S. S., Richardson, M. A., & Royall, R. (2001). Brain blood flow changes in depressed patients treated with interpersonal psychotherapy or ven-lafaxine hydrochloride: Preliminary findings. *Archives of General Psychiatry, 58*, 641-648.

Mataix-Cols, D., Boman, M., Monzani, B., Ruck, C., Serlachius, E., Langstrom, N., & Lichtenstein, P. (2013). Population-based multigenerational family clustering study of obsessive-compulsive disorder. *JAMA Psychiatry, 70*(7), 709-717.

Mayberg, H. S. (2003). Modulating dysfunctional limbic-cortical circuits in depression: Towards development of brain-based algorithms for diagnosis and optimized treatment. *British Medical Bulletin, 65*, 193-207.

Mayberg, H. S. (2006). Defining neurocircuits in depression: Insights from functional neuroimaging studies of diverse treatments. *Psychiatric Annals, 4*, 258-267.

Morelli, S. A., Rameson, L. T., & Lieberman, M. D. (2014). The neural components of empathy: Predicting daily prosocial behavior. *Cognitive, Affective, and Behavioral Neuroscience, 4*, 270-278.

Mundo, E. (2006). Neurobiology of dynamic psychotherapy: An integration possible? *Journal of the American Academy of Psychoanalysis and Dynamic Psychiatry, 34*(4), 679-691.

Olds, D. D. (1992). Consciousness: A brain-centered, informational approach. *Psychoanalytic Inquiry, 12*, 419-444.

Pally, R. (1998). Consciousness: A neuroscience perspective. *International Journal of Psychoanalysis, 79*, 971-989.

Pally, R. (2010). The brain's shared circuits of interpersonal understanding: Implications for psychoanalysis and psychodynamic psychotherapy. *Journal of the American Academy of Psychoanalysis and Dynamic Psychiatry, 38*(3), 381-411.

Pan, X., & Tsukada, M. (2006). A model of the hippocampal-cortical memory system. *Biological Cybernetics, 95*, 159-167.

Panksepp, J. (1998). *Affective neuroscience: The foundation of human and animal emotions.* New York: Oxford University Press.

Panksepp, J. (1999). Emotions as viewed by psychoanalysis and neuroscience: An exercise in consilience. *Neuropsychoanalysis, 1*, 15-38.

Panksepp, J. (2005). Commentary on becoming aware of feelings. *Neuropsychoanalysis, 7*, 40-55.

Paquette, V., Levesque, J., Mensour, B., Leroux, J. M., Beau-doin, G., Bourgouin, P., & Beauregard, M. (2003). Change the mind and you change the brain: Effects of cognitive-behavioral therapy on the neural correlates of spider phobia. *NeuroImage, 18*, 401-419.

Pardes, H. (1986). Neuroscience and psychiatry: Marriage or coexistence? *American Journal of Psychiatry, 143*, 1205-1212.

Perry, A., Bentin, S., Bartal, I. B., Lamm, C., & Decety, J. (2010). Feeling the pain of those who are different from us: Modulation of EEG in the mu/alpha range. *Cognitive, Affective, and Behavioral Neuroscience, 10*(4), 493-504.

Reiser, M. F. (2001). The dream in contemporary psychiatry. *American Journal of Psychiatry, 158*, 351-359.

Rivollier, F., Lotersztajn, L., Chaumette, B., Krebs, M. O., & Kebir, O. (2014). Epigenetics of schizophrenia: A review. *L'Encéphale, 40*(5), 380-386.

Rizzolatti, G. (2001). Reafferent copies of initiated actions in the right superior temporal cortex. *Proceedings of the National Academy of Sciences, 98*, 13995-13999.

Rizzolatti, G., & Craighero, L. (2004). The mirror neuron system. *Annual Review of Neuroscience, 27*, 169-192.

Rizzolatti, G., Fadiga, L., Gallese, V., Fogassi, L. (1996). Premotor cortex and the recognition of motor actions. *Cognitive Brain Research, 3*, 131-141.

Rizzolatti, G., & Fogassi, L. (2014). The mirror mechanism: Recent findings and perspectives. *Philosophical Transactions of the Royal Society B: Biological, 369*(1644), 20130420.

Saxena, S., & Rauch, S. L. (2000). Functional neuroimaging and the neuroanatomy of obsessive-compulsive disorder. *Psychiatric Clinics of North America, 23*, 563-586.

Schore, A. N. (1997). A century after Freud's project: Is a rapprochement between psychoanalysis and neurobiology at hand? *Journal of the American Psychoanalytic Association, 45*(3), 807-840.

Schore, A. N. (2003). *Affective dysregulation and disorders of the self*. New York: Erlbaum.

Semenza, C. (2001). Psychoanalysis and cognitive neuropsychology: Theoretical and methodological affinities. *Neuropsychoanalysis, 3*, 3-10.

Shackman, A. J., Fox, A. S., Oler, J. A., Shelton, S. E., Davidson, R. J., & Kalin, N. H. (2013). Neural mechanisms underlying heterogeneity in the presentation of anxious temperament. *Proceedings of the National Academy of Sciences, 110*, 6145-6150.

Sherrington, C. S. (1906). *The integrative action of the nervous system*. New Haven, CT: Yale University Press.

Shorter, K. R., & Miller, B. H. (2015). Epigenetic mechanisms in schizophrenia. *Progress in Biophysics and Molecular Biology, 118*(1-2), 1-7.

Singer, T., & Lamm, C. (2009). The social neuroscience of empathy. *Annals of the New York Academy of Sciences, 1150*, 81-96.

Singer, T., Seymour, B., O'Doherty, J., Kaube, H., Dolan, R. J., & Frith, C. D. (2004). Empathy for pain involves the affective but not the sensory components of pain. *Science, 303*, 1157-1161.

Sulloway, F. J. (1992). *Freud, biologist of the mind*. Cambridge: Harvard University Press.

Tononi, G., & Koch, C. (2008). The neural correlates of consciousness: An update. *Annals of the New York Academy of Sciences, 1124*, 239-261.

Viinamaki, H., Kuikka, J., & Tiihonen, J. (1998). Change in monoamine transporter density related to clinical recovery: A case-control study. *Nordic Journal of Psychiatry, 52*, 39-44.

Vuilleumier, P. (2014). Brain circuits implicated in psychogenic paralysis, in conversion disorders and hypnosis. *Clinical Neurophysiology, 44*, 323-337.

Whitehead, C. C. (2009). Brief communication-mirror neurons, the self, and culture: An essay in neopsychoanalysis. *Journal of the American Academy of Psychoanalysis and Dynamic Psychiatry, 37*, 701-712.

Whiteside, S. P., Port, J. D., & Abramowitz, J. S. (2004). A meta-analysis of functional neuroimaging in obsessive-compulsive disorder. *Psychiatry Research, 132*, 69-79.

The Neurobiology of Attachment: From Infancy to Clinical Outcomes

Joanna Chambers

Abstract: Attachment theory was developed by John Bowlby in the 1950s. He defined attachment as a specific neurobiological system that resulted in the infant connecting to the primary caretaker in such a way to create an inner working model of relationships that continues throughout life and affects the future mental health and physical health of the infant. Given the significance of this inner working model, there has been a tremendous amount of research done in animals as well as humans to better understand the neurobiology. In this article the neurobiology of early development will be outlined with respect to the formation of attachment. This article will review what we have begun to understand as the neurobiology of attachment and will describe how the relationship with the primary caretaker affects the infant in a way leading to neurobiological changes that later in life affect emotional responses, reward, and perception difficulties that we recognize as psychiatric illness and medical morbidity.

ATTACHMENT THEORY: A BRIEF HISTORY

The parent–infant bond has arguably been the most important process for human survival. While the importance of the mother–infant attachment has been understood for centuries, it was not studied until John Bowlby developed attachment theory in the 1950s. In order to put attachment theory in proper context, one must begin with a reminder of Sigmund Freud's drive theory. According to drive theory, we attached to our mothers because they fed us and gratified our oral yearnings (Freud, 1923). In other words, our attachments were derived from our libidinal drives and did not exist independently. Drive theory was largely a one-person psychology focusing on the drives and conflicts of the individual; our mother was simply an instigator who either gratified or displeased our internal drives and wishes.

Melanie Klein led us to a two-person psychology where the other person was more than an instigator of drives and wishes. The mother, in particular, shaped the psychology of the infant through representations of the good and the bad breast, the merger of the two, and the hope for reparation that allows us to stay attached to our mothers. Klein introduced the idea that we need to feel hope for reparation to stay connected to our loved ones in spite of our own aggressive drives (Kristeva, 2001). For the first time, the object had relevance in our psychology, though Klein believed that the emotional problems of children still came largely from the fantasies generated by internal conflict related to the object.

John Bowlby was a supervisee of Melanie Klein and was influenced by her, however he argued that children's emotional problems do not stem from their own internal conflicts based on a fantasy of the caretaker, but rather their emotional problems stem from *actual experiences* with their caretakers (Bretherton, 1992). Furthermore, Bowlby suggested that the need for social bonds is independent of feeding and sexual needs but equal in significance (Bowlby, 1977). Attachment theory suggests that through the earliest relationship with one's parents, one develops an internal working model of relationships, which affects the capacity for relationships later in life. These difficulties in the earliest relationships can lead to marital difficulties, difficulties relating to one's children, neuroses, and personality disorders (Bowlby, 1977). Since then, insecure attachment has also been shown to lead to difficulties with other psychiatric illnesses, including depression, anxiety disorders, substance abuse disorders, and several medical illnesses (Davies, Macfarlane, McBeth, Morriss, & Dickens, 2009; McWilliams & Bailey, 2010; Puig, Englund, Simpson, & Collins, 2013).

THE IMPORTANCE OF ATTACHMENT

Since Bowlby developed attachment theory in the 1950s, significant work has been done to investigate the importance of maternal attachment in mammals, including humans. Harry Harlow, a psychologist at the University of Wisconsin, was intrigued by John Bowlby's work on attachment theory and carried out the first scientific study of attachment theory. In an effort to better understand the implications of mother–infant attachment, Harlow isolated neonatal monkeys from their mothers shortly after birth (Suomi, Harlow, & McKinney, 1972). These monkeys developed severe psychopathology with locomotive, exploratory, and social

problems later on, demonstrating the neuro-vegetative and social effects that occur when infants are removed from their mothers. As adults, these "motherless monkeys" were unable to appropriately mother their young, demonstrating neglectful and abusive behaviors toward their young (Rupenthal, Arling, Harlow, Sackett, & Suomi, 1976). While this seems intuitive to us in the 21st century, in the 1970s when these experiments were carried out, this was revolutionary and validating of Bowlby's attachment theory.

The origins of attachment were still in question: was attachment dependent on libidinal drives or was it a separate process? To evaluate this question, Harlow's isolated monkeys were given two surrogate "mothers" to choose from: one surrogate mother was covered in terry cloth with large eyes and the other surrogate mother was made of wire with no soft covering, with small eyes, and held a bottle of food for the monkeys. If attachment was indeed derived from libidinal drives, the monkeys would show attachment behaviors toward the wire mother with food. The monkeys showed a significant preference for the soft mother while they would only go to the wire mother to eat. This demonstrated that attachment was indeed its own process, independent of libidinal drives (Suomi, Harlow, & McKinney, 1972).

Attachment to early childhood caretakers provided an inner working model for all relationships later in life. In an effort to better understand these inner working models, Mary Ainsworth, John Bowlby's collaborator, went on to define three distinct and measurable levels of attachment: secure attachment, anxious attachment, and avoidant attachment (Ainsworth & Bell, 1970). Mary Main added a fourth level, namely disorganized attachment (Main & Solomon, 1990). Anxious, avoidant, and disorganized attachment were all classified as insecure attachments. These attachment patterns could be evaluated at 12 months of age and remain consistent over the time. Secure attachment was defined as the ability to carry a representational model of attachment figures as being available, responsive, and helpful. Insecure attachment was defined as not seeking out the attachment figure when distressed or having difficulty moving away from the attachment figure, likely due to having an unresponsive, rejecting, inconsistent, or insensitive caretaker (Ainsworth & Bell, 1970).

THE DEVELOPMENT OF ATTACHMENT

In humans, similar to Harlow's "motherless monkeys," attachment security is mostly intergenerational. In fact, the mother's attachment security can predict the security of attachment of the infant with up to 75% certainty (Fonagy, Steele, & Steele, 1991). We understand this intergenerational process to be at least in part a psychological phenomenon through the interaction between the mother and her infant (Fonagy, Steele, & Steele, 1991). Watching a mother interact with her infant can be compared to a very sensitive and nuanced dance where each partner responds to the other in a complex and sometimes subtle way. This dance involves touch, eye contact, facial expression, and verbal expression in both partners. When these interactions happen synchronously, all goes well and the infant becomes securely attached. When these interactions are disjointed and cues are misunderstood, the infant's attachment to his mother becomes conflicted and he later develops insecure attachment as a result. The attunement of the mother to her infant's cues is often an unconscious process and is a significant predictor of her ability to exist in synchrony with her infant. Through this process, the infant internalizes the experiences with his mother.

During the early process of attachment, as the mother responds to her infant's needs in a sensitive way, she is teaching the infant about empathy. Through her empathy, she can essentially predict what needs the infant is conveying, be it the need for soothing, feeding, diaper changing, etc. As the mother meets the needs of the infant, he feels understood by her in a unique way. As the mother soothes her infant, he learns that his emotions can be regulated. As the mother takes pleasure in her infant, he is instilled with a sense of power as he realizes his capability to create pleasure in another person. These experiences by the infant involve significant neurobiological events that have implications for mental and medical health later in life. These experiences by the infant are also integral in forming the psychological internal working model (his mother) that is projected on to all future relationships.

There are several risk factors that can lead to interference in the mother–infant relationship and the attachment process. These include mental illness including prenatal depression and postpartum depression, insecure attachment in the mother, parental insensitivity, disrupted affective communication between parent and infant, child abuse, and child neglect (Hayes, Goodman, & Carlson, 2013). Fortunately, there is evidence to suggest that the attachment process is malleable through preschool-aged children, especially if the mother undergoes attachment-focused treatment (Hoffman, Marvin, Cooper, & Powell, 2006). Hence, there seems to be a window of opportunity for intervention and treatment for insecurely attached infants.

As we better understand the neurodevelopmental process involved in attachment, there has been a shift in increased importance of the prenatal period to be included in the sensitive period of development. This is particularly interesting as the psychological interaction between mother and infant has not yet developed at this time, yet it is clear that the infant is born with a preference for his mother's smell, his mother's milk, and his mother's voice (Vaglio, 2009). Furthermore, there is a significant correlation between mothers with antenatal depression and infants with disorganized attachment styles at 12 months (Hayes, Goodman, & Carlson, 2013). Fortunately, it has been shown that higher quality parenting in the first three months can ameliorate the risk of disorganized attachment due to antenatal depression (Hayes, Goodman, & Carlson, 2013). This leads to the conclusion that there is an interplay between the fetal period and the first three months of life that is critical for the attachment process. Understanding the neurobiology of attachment can help us uncover this interaction and possible ways to intervene.

In addition to the interpersonal and relationship problems that Bowlby identified as resulting from insecure attachment, there has been a significant link of insecure attachment to psychiatric illnesses such as depression, anxiety, and substance abuse (Heim & Nemeroff, 2001). The developing knowledge of the neurobiology of attachment allows for a greater understanding of how attachment insecurity may lead to these afflictions. The hypothalamic-pituitary-adrenal (HPA) axis and the reward neurocircuitry are likely to have very significant roles in the attachment process as well as in psychiatric illnesses and medical morbidity later in life. In order to understand these connections better, we must first explore the neurobiology of attachment.

THE NEUROBIOLOGICAL DEVELOPMENT OF THE INFANT

The Hypothalamus at Birth

The hypothalamus is developing in the fetus and is affected by the maternal HPA axis (Giesbrecht et al., 2017), and at birth, the hypothalamus is already fully developed. The hypothalamus functions through the HPA axis to produce cortisol by the adrenal glands. Cortisol has a bipartite effect on the rest of the developing brain, where in high doses, cortisol is largely neurotoxic and inhibits neuronal connections, while

lower levels of cortisol induces neuronal development and growth through neuroplasticity (Vela, 2014). Therefore, modulation of cortisol during this sensitive period of neural development is imperative for future function. Oxytocin and social interaction have been shown to decrease cortisol levels, demonstrating that even at this early stage, physical connection between a mother and her infant has an important effect on brain development and neuroplasticity (Heinrichs, Baumgartner, Kirschbaum, & Ehlert, 2003). Furthermore, adults with insecure attachment show a hyper-reactive HPA axis and cortisol response to acute stress, demonstrating that these effects are long lasting (Quirin, Pruessner, & Kuhl, 2008).

In very young rat pups, it has been shown that the HPA axis is non-functional during postnatal days 4–14 (Rincon-Cortes et al., 2015). This lack of cortisol inhibits any fear response, allowing the rat pups to attach to their mothers during this developmental phase. In a study to better understand how child abuse affects the attachment process, rat pups at days 4–14 were repeatedly exposed to an odor paired with a foot shock in the presence of the mother. Later, when the abused rats became adults, the odor actually had a positive and antidepressant effect on the rats during stress. While the study was done in rats, it has significant clinical implications in humans. This study demonstrates the very powerful and non-discriminatory attachment process. This remarkable repetitive response in the rat explains, from a neurobiological perspective, how other mammals, including humans, who are abused in their youth still attach to their abusive parents with the same vigor as the non-abused child. If a child is exposed to a sensory experience, even a traumatic one, during this sensitive time period when the neurobiology is primed for attachment, they will seek out those traumatic experiences time and again. Hence, they repeatedly seek out abusive relationships because abuse was part of the attachment process in early childhood and the abuse became rewarding. This also explains, in part, why humans with histories of abuse in childhood will seek out and attach to abusive partners as adults. In this way, we begin to see that the early attachment process is interconnected with the reward system.

The Hippocampus Develops

It is clear from the previous section that the first three months of life are important with respect to the attachment process through modulation of the HPA axis. This is also the time when the hippocampus fully matures. The hippocampus is a part of the limbic system and is involved in spatial and emotional memory. It is instrumental in consolidating declarative or explicit memories, which are facts or events, and it provides the ability to consciously recall events or facts from long-term memory (Campbell & MacQueen, 2004). As the hippocampus develops, the infant is able to recognize and remember his mother, smile at her, begin to feel a sense of pleasure with her, and begin to actively engage with her. This is an extremely crucial time with respect to the development of the mother–infant bond and by four months of age, the relationship patterns between a mother and her infant can predict the attachment security of the infant at 12 months (Beebe et al., 2012; Koulomzin et al., 2002).

The hippocampus has a large number of glucocorticoid receptors, causing significant sensitivity to stress and cortisol production through the HPA axis. When the infant is stressed, high doses of cortisol are produced, causing neurotoxicity to the hippocampus. Furthermore, the hippocampus is known to provide negative feedback to the HPA axis, decreasing cortisol production (Sapolsky, Krey, & McEwen, 1986). Hence, when the hippocampus suffers from neurotoxicity, cortisol production is further enhanced. Therefore, neglect or abuse at this stage can significantly impair the development of the hippocampus. Rat pups who were separated from their mothers during early development (a model of neglect) have been shown to have smaller hippocampi (Huot, Plotsky, Lenox, & McNamara, 2002). In humans, hippocampal glucocorticoid receptors have been shown to be affected by child abuse as well (McGowan et al., 2009). These first few months of life are vital in terms of the future relationship between attachment, stress, and object relations of the infant.

The Reward System

The young infant clearly experiences pleasure in her interactions with her mother. The social smile, which usually begins between six to eight weeks of age, is evidence for this. It is also evidence for the presence of the reward neurocircuitry. The reward system is a complex neurocircuitry which has been described as a dichotomy of two systems: the novelty seeking system and the familiarity system (Tops, Koole, IJzerman, & Buisman-Pijlman, 2014). The ventral striatal pathway is involved in novelty seeking as a reward. The dorsal striatal pathway is involved in reward related to familiarity, comfort, and satiety. Early in development, the novelty-seeking ventral striatal system is thought to be more active. During the first three months, the mother's face is novel and the infant is driven in part by the reward circuitry to look at her. As the infant is able to respond to her by smiling, body language, and eye contact, and if the mother is responsive, there is a shift to dorsal striatal activity where the familiarity of mother and the connection with her becomes rewarding. If there is neglect or abuse during this developmental phase, the development of the ventral novelty seeking system relative to the dorsal familiarity system is affected. This process has significant potential for the interaction of poor attachment with later substance abuse problems, as the reward of familiarity and comfort in relationships may not protect against the reward of substances and impulsivity (novelty). Indeed, there is evidence that both animal models and humans with poor attachments are more likely to develop substance abuse problems (Moffett et al., 2007). Furthermore, attachment style has been found to directly impact the recovery of patients hospitalized for the treatment of addictions, where insecure (avoidant) attachment leads to poor treatment outcomes (Caspers, Yucuis, Troutman, & Spinks, 2006; Fowler, Groat, & Ulanday, 2013). If the dorsal striatal reward network is not fully developed during the sensitive attachment period, one cannot develop a preference for familiarity, comfort, and satiety over the rewarding sensation of novelty brought on by substances of abuse. Strathearn (2011) found that there is an increase in activation in the ventral striatum when securely attached mothers see their infant's happy face, while there is a decrease in activation in the ventral striatum when insecurely attached mothers see their infants. Interestingly, the ventral striatum has been shown to mount a diminished response to reward in neuroimaging of individuals with a history of early childhood abuse (Teicher, Samson, Anderson, & Ohashi, 2016). This is a particularly interesting finding as it demonstrates an altered reward system in insecurely attached mothers, while also helping us better understand how insecure attachment or a history of child abuse in the mother can lead to psychiatric illnesses such as postpartum depression, where interactions with the infant is not inherently rewarding.

The Amygdala

Even before birth, the fetal amygdala is affected by his mother's affect (Qiu et al., 2015). Specifically, both depression and cortisol spikes in the mother during pregnancy have been shown to decrease the size of the amygdala later in the infant (Qiu et al., 2015). The amygdala matures at six to seven months of age (Vela, 2014). With this development, we also see the beginnings of fear and salience, two important functions

of the amygdala. The infant at this age will show stranger anxiety and protest separation from his mother. Youths who have been institutionalized and suffer emotional deprivation, who are later adopted by families in the U.S., show a difference in amygdala response when compared to youths who had been raised by their biological parents without emotional deprivation. The youths, who were 4–17 years of age at the time of the imaging study, were shown pictures of their mothers (biological or adopted mothers in the case of the adopted youths; Olavsky et al., 2013). The youths who were raised by their mothers from birth showed significant amygdala responses to their mothers but not to strangers. The youths who had been institutionalized prior to adoption demonstrated a significant amygdala response to both their mothers and the strangers. The lack of differentiation became more significant with increased age of the youth at the time of adoption. In other words, the older the child's age at adoption, the less likely their amygdala was to discriminate between the mother and the stranger. This study demonstrates that while the amygdala is important for a fear response, it is also important for the determination of salience. The study also validates the notion that there is a sensitive period of attachment development that has life-long consequences.

This leads to the question: "What happens if we remove the amygdala?" Bauman, Lavener, Mason, Capitanio, and Amaral (2004) answered that exact question in a study with macaque monkeys. The macaques' amygdalae were lesioned at two weeks of age and some interesting results were found. The monkeys without their amygdala spent more time with their mothers in the first six months. They were separated from their mothers at six months of age and placed in a holding box with equal proximity to their mothers and to a familiar female who was not their mother. In this box, the control (non-lesioned) monkeys spent all their time in proximity to their mother. The lesioned monkeys spent an equal amount of time in proximity to the familiar female as to their mother. Furthermore, the control monkeys screamed in protest at not being able to be held by their mother, while the amygdala-lesioned monkeys showed no distress at having limited proximity to their mother. So while the lesioned monkeys were content with their mothers in the first six months of life, they had no ability to understand the salience of their mother when compared to a familiar female without their amygdala.

In humans, amygdala lesions have been described in Urbach–Wiethe syndrome, an autosomal recessively inherited syndrome that causes bilateral calcifications of the amygdala in 50% of patients. In an interesting report, the psychoanalytic findings in a 38-year-old male patient with bilateral amygdala calcifications due to Urbach–Wiethe syndrome was described (Wiest & Brainin, 2010). This patient had sought treatment due to new onset panic attacks and depressive symptoms. While the patient was easily able to remember facts, he had more trouble with emotionally salient memory as he could not remember what he did while together with his friends. While he could remember if he liked a certain book or movie, he had trouble remembering what happened in the stories of the books or movies. He could only remember if a place was familiar or not, but could not recall how to get there. He was notably unable to free associate in the analytic sessions. The analyst described each session as feeling like a repetition without any connection to the previous session. He had a wide range of emotions and was able to recognize negative emotions such as anger and sadness. He was seemingly able to attach as he had a fulfilling relationship for nine years with the same woman and was able to develop a transference to his analyst. While this study is interesting, the implications for the neurobiological function of the amygdala in attachment are unclear since we do not know at what age the amygdala calcifications occurred. Given the sensitive period

of development, there is likely a difference between having a functional amygdala in the first year of life which is impaired later on and being born without an amygdala. The report does validate the function of the amygdala in the appreciation for emotional salience however. The report also suggests that the amygdala may serve as an emotional compass, without which we feel lost, causing anxiety and depression over time.

More studies have been done in the amygdala of parents in an effort to understand the role of the amygdala in parental attachment. First-time mothers, imaged with fMRI in the first postpartum month while listening to recordings of babies crying, including their own baby, demonstrate an activated neurocircuitry when hearing their own baby cry already in the first two weeks postpartum (Swain, 2008). When compared to brain responses to the control babies cries, the mothers' activated neurocircuitry included the anterior cingulate gyrus and the amygdala. The fathers, who were also imaged, did not show activation in the amygdala, but instead showed other areas of activation including the anterior cingulate, the visual cortex, and the parahippocampal gyrus. This might be the result of mothers' attachment neurocircuitry being "primed" earlier than that of fathers. This could be partially due to the effects of oxytocin elevations during the process of parturition and nursing.

Oxytocin: Attachment and Synchronicity

In pregnant mothers, there is evidence that an increase in maternal oxytocin levels during the first and second trimester of pregnancy predict mothering behavior in the postpartum (Levine, Zagoory-Sharon, Feldman, & Weller, 2007). In securely attached individuals, oxytocin levels are generally higher and increase during periods of stress, increase with play, and oxytocin and reward activation synchronize during interaction with one's infant (Pierrehumbert, Torrisi, Ansermet, Borghini, & Halfon, 2012). Women with a history of child abuse have lower oxytocin levels in general as well as during pregnancy and the postpartum period (Heim et al., 2009). This is significant for the infant because in the postpartum period, there appears to be a synchronous relationship between oxytocin in the parents and oxytocin in the infant (Levine, Zagoory-Sharon, Feldman, & Weller, 2007). When the parent and child interact with each other, the oxytocin levels increase in both the parent and the infant.

Oxytocin plays an important role in the attachment process of parents. An imaging study looking at mothers interacting with their 4–6-month-old infants showed a clear distinction in neurocircuitry between mothers described as either synchronous or intrusive with their infants (Atzil, Hendler, & Feldman, 2011). In the synchronous mothers, the right nucleus accumbens (ventral striatum) was active and showed an organized response with the prefrontal cortex (PFC). In addition, the oxytocin levels seem to increase and correlate with the neurocircuitry response. In the intrusive mothers, the left amygdala was active and showed a disorganized response with the PFC while the oxytocin levels did not correlate with the neurocircuitry response. In a separate study by Gordon, Zagoory-Sharon, Leckman, and Feldman (2010), plasma oxytocin levels in mothers correlated with the amount of time the mother spent in affectionate behavior with her infant. Furthermore, salivary oxytocin levels in both mothers and fathers increase when playing with their infants and correlate directly to infant oxytocin levels (Feldman, 2010). When fathers were given intranasal oxytocin and then interacted with their infants, the infants showed a similar increase in oxytocin during the interaction (Naber, van IJzendoorn, Deschamps, van Engeland, & Bakermans-Kranenburg, 2010; Weisman, Zagoory-Sharon, & Feldman, 2012). Securely attached mothers have an increase in oxytocin when playing

with their infants while insecurely attached mothers' oxytocin levels actually decrease with play (Strathearn, Fonagy, Amico, & Montague, 2009). Furthermore, secure attachment was correlated with higher oxytocin levels and decreased subjective stress during an acutely stressful situation (Pierrehumbert, Torrisi, Ansermet, Borghini, & Halfon, 2012). Hence, it appears that oxytocin and secure attachment may regulate the stress system.

The Maturing PreFrontal Cortex (PFC)

The prefrontal cortex (PFC) begins development in the early neonatal stage and continues to evolve through pruning until the middle of the third decade of life (Kolb et al., 2012). While the role of the immature PFC in infants and children is unclear, the mature PFC has been shown to be important in the process of attachment in adults. In a rat model of social interaction, two adult rats who are introduced under stressful conditions lessen each other's anxiety levels during a stressful challenge. If the rats are first introduced in a non-stressful situation, they will not have the same ability to modulate each others' anxiety levels: they must be introduced during a stressful event to have an anxiolytic effect on each other. This effect is directly modulated by the medial PFC (Lungwitz et al., 2014). Of course, we see this on a regular basis in human situations. For example, military veterans will tell us that their closest attachments are the other veterans who served with them. There may be a similar effect in psychotherapy, where therapists engage their patients in some of their most stressful memories, cognitions, and affects, which may, in part, contribute to the patient's attachment to the therapist. It is clear that the PFC plays an important role in the attachment process, especially later in development. In rat pups exposed to an abusive caretaker early in development, brain-derived neurotrophic factor (BDNF) gene expression has been shown to be decreased in the PFC as adults (Roth, Lubin, Funk, & Sweatt, 2009). This may have implications for later developments of depression as BDNF has been shown to be decreased in depression and increases with treatment (Duman, 2004) It is also likely that the proper development of the PFC depends on the functionality of earlier neurobiological developments. However, while the exact role of the PFC in the attachment process early in development remains unclear, it is clear that the PFC has an important role in modulating anxiety and depression, which may rely on a healthy neurobiological environment during early development.

Summary of the Neurobiology

The attachment neurobiology develops early, beginning in utero and continues through preschool age. It appears to be partially set by pruning around 24 months (Vela, 2014). This is a complex process that involves the development of HPA axis and reward system early on, followed by the development of the amygdala, followed by PFC development into adulthood. As we have a better understanding of the attachment neurocircuitry, we can see how this sensitive period of development leads to neurobiological changes later in life affecting emotional response, reward, and perception difficulties. Our understanding of neurobiology is finally catching up and validating what psychoanalytic theory has always assumed: the importance of early development and the necessary process of each stage of development, building on earlier stages and experiences.

Clinical Implications of Insecure Attachment

In a 30-year prospective study by Fan et al. (2014), infants who experienced poor attachment behaviors from their mothers at eight months of age were at higher risk for mental illness 30 years later. Depression, anxiety, and substance use disorders have all been linked to insecure attachment (Heim & Nemeroff, 2001). Medical morbidities, such as chronic pain, cardiovascular disease, and inflammation-based illnesses have also been linked to poor attachment (Davies, Macfarlane, McBeth, Morriss, & Dickens, 2009; McWilliams & Bailey, 2010; Puig, Englung, Simpson, & Collins, 2013). Adverse childhood events (ACE) have also been shown to correlate to physical illness in adulthood (Felitti et al., 1998). Epidemiological studies have shown that a lack of social relationships has similar consequences on physical health as smoking, obesity, and inactivity (Puig, Englung, Simpson, & Collins, 2013). The quality of close relationships, especially marriage partners, had a significant effect on the immune system, the neuroendocrine system, and resiliency to stress (Puig, Englung, Simpson, & Collins, 2013). Perhaps, this could be in part mediated through early attachment developments.

Avoidant attachment has been correlated to chronic back pain and neck problems, frequent and severe headaches, chronic pain, and ulcers (McWilliams & Bailey, 2010). Anxious attachment has been correlated to chronic back and neck problems, frequent and severe headaches, chronic pain, as well as strokes, myocardial infarction, hypertension, and ulcers (McWilliams & Bailey, 2010). Insecurely attached individuals perceived pain as more threatening, had a negative perception of social support, demonstrated decreased support seeking, experienced increased depression, anxiety, stress, were more inclined to catastrophize, and showed decreased adaptive coping (Meredith, Ownsworth, & Strong, 2008). Insecure attachment correlated to increased number of pain sites in people with chronic widespread pain (CWP), had twice the prevalence of CWP, and demonstrated an increase in pain-related disability (Davies, Macfarlane, McBeth, Morriss, & Dickens, 2009). Insecurely attached individuals also had four times greater chance of physical illness, four times greater chance of inflammatory related illness, and were three times more likely to have nonspecific physical symptoms (Puig, Englund, Simpson, & Collins, 2013).

It is clear from these studies that attachment security affects medical and psychological wellbeing later in life. Understanding the neurobiological underpinnings of the attachment process allows us to better identify how these morbidities may be linked to insecure attachment. Attachment insecurity may lead to these psychiatric and medical changes later in life through several neurobiological mechanisms, including stress response, inflammatory responses, neurocircuitry changes, and epigenetics. These mechanisms are also likely to interact causing a cumulative effect.

THE STRESS RESPONSE

The role of the HPA axis and cortisol is complicated and likely of great importance in the relationship between attachment security and medical and psychiatric comorbidity. Individuals with insecure attachment show a greater perception of stress when compared to securely attached individuals (Kidd, Hamer, & Steptoe, 2011). In general, cortisol levels are known to be altered in patients with depression, anxiety, posttraumatic stress disorder, as well as in insecure attachment (Kidd, Hamer, & Steptoe, 2010; Quirin, Pruessner, & Kuhl, 2008). It is therefore reasonable to assume that modulation of the hypothalamus early in development has significant effects on the individual later in life.

Interpersonal stress is increased in insecurely attached individuals and this has several neurobiological causes. In interpersonal stress, the prefrontal cortex is downregulated and its inhibitory control of the amygdala decreases (Gold, 2015). In addition, the HPA axis is activated during interpersonal stress through increased activation of the amygdala, as well as through the

lack of inhibition by the PFC, leading to increased cortisol production. Cortisol further increases amygdala activation. In addition, corticotropin releasing hormone (CRH) is increased by interpersonal stress, further increasing fear and anxiety through its effect on the sympathetic nervous system and the amygdala (Gold, 2015). While the hippocampus generally has an inhibitory effect the HPA stress response (Radley & Sawchenko, 2011), if the hippocampus has been negatively affected by elevated cortisol in infancy, the inhibitory effect of the hippocampus on the HPA axis is also likely to be compromised. One quickly begins to see that there is little inhibition in this process once it gets started and the system behaves largely in a feed forward manner, where stress increases amygdala activity, HPA activity, cortisol, CRH, and the sympathetic nervous system with minimal inhibition.

Oxytocin has many functions, including lowering HPA activity and cortisol. Cortisol increases plasma oxytocin levels, hence this serves as a negative feedback system where stress increases cortisol, which then increases oxytocin, which then decreases cortisol. In individuals who are securely attached, oxytocin levels increase in response to stress (Pierrehumbert, Torrisi, Ansermet, Borghini, & Halfon, 2012). Given that women with a history of child abuse have lower oxytocin levels in general (Heim et al., 2009), it is possible that insecurely attached individuals do not have this inhibitory process in place, allowing the stress response to escalate to higher levels. Furthermore, insecurely attached individuals are less likely to reach out to their loved ones in times of stress, may have a lower oxytocin response to interaction with loved ones, both which contribute to lower oxytocin levels (Pierrehumbert, Torrisi, Ansermet, Borghini, & Halfon, 2012; Strathearn, Fonagy, Amico, & Montague, 2009).

THE INFLAMMATORY RESPONSE

Inflammatory responses may also be a culprit in the connection between insecure attachment and psychiatric and medical morbidity. During stress, an increase in CRH causes acute stage inflammatory responses, including interleukin-6 and cytokines (Gold, 2015). While acute increases in cortisol deactivate the inflammatory system, both chronic elevations and chronic hypoactivity in cortisol levels lead to a hyperactive inflammatory system. Insulin, which also increases in response to acute stress, increases the inflammatory response and contributes to activating the sympathetic nervous system (Gold, 2015). These inflammatory responses are noteworthy as they contribute to a variety of medical complications, including: auto immune disorders; cardiovascular disease, such as hypertension, myocardial infarctions, and stroke; pain; gastric and duodenal ulcers; and cancer (Puig, Englund, Simpson, & Collins, 2013). An increase in cytokines has been shown to lead to depression, as cytokines in the brain have an effect on the production, release, and metabolism of neurotransmitters. Therefore, it may be that insecure attachment leads to early changes in CRH/HPA axis, which then leads to increases in cytokines, which contribute to the development of depression later in life. Insecure attachment may also lead to cardiovascular events through inflammatory changes (Gold, 2015).

NEUROCIRCUITRY

The effects that abuse and neglect have on the developing brain as described in this article are significant. Understanding how poor attachment leads to changes in neurocircuitry later in life is still in progress. For instance, in individuals with a history of child abuse, the amygdala is hyper-responsive to angry faces (Teicher, Samson, Anderson, & Ohashi, 2016). This hyper-responsivity may be due partly to a failure to develop appropriate inhibitory mechanisms during the first year of life. If the amygdala is faced with an aggressive, abusive, or unpredictable attachment figure in the first year of life, without appropriate modulation through oxytocin and other neural connections, hyperactivity may be the result. The reward neurocircuitry also appears to be affected by attachment, which may have implications for psychopathology later in life. For example, in depression the nucleus accumbens is less active which is largely responsible for the sense of anhedonia in depression (Satterthwaite et al., 2015). It is possible that the altered function of the nucleus accumbens developed in the early stages of life as a response to poor attachment increases the risk for anhedonia and depression. An altered reward neurocircuitry may also lead to a vulnerability to addictions. Decreased function in the PFC, which may be caused by attachment insecurity, also has a negative effect on the reward process by decreasing activity in the nucleus accumbens (Gold 2015). Given that the striatum and PFC are both involved in the development of attachment, it seems possible that insecure attachment may lead to a dysfunction in these neurocircuits, leading to later development of psychopathology.

EPIGENETICS

Gene expression is the underlying mechanism for all neuroscience and behavior. It has become increasingly clear that early environment affects gene expression. This is done through a process of methylation to various sections of the DNA, causing a difference in the expression pattern of the DNA. These methylation changes can be reversible or permanent and can be heritable by offspring (Monk, Spicer, & Champagne, 2012). More recently, in utero and postpartum environments are thought to have a significant effect on the genetic expression of the offspring, which are evident early in the infant's life and are sustained throughout their lives (Fish et al., 2004). These alterations in genetic expression seem to be affected significantly by the mother's affective state in pregnancy (Monk, Spicer, & Champagne, 2012), as well as the mother's behaviors toward the offspring in the postpartum (Fish et al., 2004). These genetic changes are implicated in many important neuropsychiatric processes, including but not limited to BDNF synthesis, neurotransmitter receptor levels and responsivity, and synaptogenesis in the offspring (Fish et al., 2004).

Epigenetics have been studied in humans as well as in other mammals. For example, rat pups exposed to various levels of licking and grooming and nursing postures showed different levels of glucocorticoid receptor gene promotors in the hippocampus, which has implications for cortisol effects on the hippocampus. These genetic alterations were found as early as the first week of life and the changes were reversible when cross-fostered (Weaver et al. 2004). In humans, McGowan et al. (2009) found that adult suicide victims with a history of child abuse had altered hippocampal glucocorticoid receptor genes, demonstrating that an abusive environment in childhood had a sustained epigenetic effect on cortisol receptors in the hippocampus. Rat pups exposed to a stressed and hence neglectful or abusive caretaker in the first week of life demonstrated altered BDNF gene expression, which lasted into adulthood (Roth et al., 2009). While these epigenetic changes appear to be relatively stable throughout life, there is some evidence that they are potentially reversible in adulthood (Weaver, Meaney, & Szyf, 2006). The suggestion that these epigenetic changes are both heritable and reversible may have significant implications for treatment in mothers who are pregnant and postpartum. If a mother has already passed epigenetic changes to her child, it may be that secure attachment behaviors may reverse these changes in the infant early on, giving the infant the opportunity to change the intergenerational pattern.

SUMMARY

While much work has been done to increase the understanding of the neurobiology of attachment, we are left with many unanswered questions that require more research. For instance, can we affect attachment style later in life? Can insecure attachment be treated? If so, how? In addition, can psychotherapy be enhanced with direct neurobiological modification, such as oxytocin or cortisol modulation? It might be interesting to check both cortisol and oxytocin levels in patients who are undergoing psychoanalysis or psychodynamic psychotherapy. Would attachment treatment be a part of the overall treatment to improve other psychiatric and medical morbidities? Given that we already have evidence that attachment treatment to postpartum mothers improves postpartum depression (Hoffman, Marvin, Cooper, & Powell, 2006), it may be worth considering for other illnesses as well.

Given what we know about the role of oxytocin and cortisol specifically, are pregnancy and the postpartum periods a natural time to intervene in mothers with poor attachment? Knowing the importance of mother's attachment process for the success of secure attachment in the infant, it may be that nature has provided us with an additional sensitive period in the attachment neurocircuitry. This would necessarily lead to significant changes in how we approach women in the obstetricians' offices as we would want to check all pregnant mothers for insecure attachments, oxytocin levels, early childhood trauma, in addition to the current monitoring of fetal heart rates, etc. Furthermore, our understanding of insecure attachment in psychiatric and medical diagnoses may change how we understand and treat these illnesses.

REFERENCES

Ainsworth, M. D. S., & Bell, S. M. (1970). Attachment, exploration, and separation: Illustrated by the behavior of one-year-olds in a strange situation. *Child Development, 41*, 49-67.

Alim, T. N., Lawson, W. B., Feder, A., Iacoviello, B. M., Saxena, S., Bailey, C. R., Greene, A. M., & Neumeister, A. (2012). Resilience to meet the challenge of addiction: Psychobiology and clinical considerations. *Alcohol Research: Current Reviews, 34*(4), 506-515.

Atzil, S., Hendler, T., & Feldman, R. (2011). Specifying the neurobiological basis of human attachment: Brain, hormones, and behavior in synchronous and intrusive mothers. *Neuropsychopharmacology, 36*, 2603-2615.

Bauman, M. D., Lavener, P., Mason, W. A., Capitanio, J. P., & Amaral, D. G. (2004). The development of mother-infant interactions after neonatal amygdala lesions in rhesus monkeys. *Journal of Neuroscience, 24*(3), 711-721.

Beebe, B., Lachmann, F., Markese, S., Buck, K. A., Bahrick, L. E., Chen, H., Cohen, P., Andrews, H., Feldstein, S., & Jaffe, J. (2012). On the origins of disorganized attachment and internal working models: Paper II. An empirical microanalysis of 4-month mother-infant interaction. *Psychoanalytic Dialogues, 22*(3), 352-374.

Bowlby, J. (1977). The making and breaking of affectional bonds. I. Aetiology and psychopathology in the light of attachment theory. An expanded version of the fiftieth Maudsley lecture, delivered before the Royal College of Psychiatrists, 19 November 1976. *British Journal of Psychiatry, 130*, 201-209.

Bretherton, I. (1992). The origins of attachment theory: John Bowlby and Mary Ainsworth. *Developmental Psychology, 28*, 759-775.

Campbell, S., & MacQueen, G. (2004). The role of the hippocampus in the pathophysiology of depression. *Journal of Psychiatry and Neuroscience, 29*(6), 417-426.

Caspers, K. M., Yucuis, R., Troutman, B., & Spinks, R. (2006). Attachment as an organizier of behavior: Implications for substance abuse problems and willingness to seek treatment. *Substance Abuse Treatment, Prevention, and Policy, 1*, 32-41.

Davies, K. A., Macfarlane, G. J., McBeth, J., Morriss, R., & Dickens, C. (2009). Insecure attachment style is associated with chronic widespread pain. *Pain, 143*(3), 200-205.

Debiec, J., & Sullivan, R. M. (2014). Intergenerational transmission of emotional trauma through amygdala-dependent mother-to-infant transfer of specific fear. *Proceedings of National Academy of Sciences, 111*(33), 12222-12227.

DeWall, C. N., Masten, C. L., Powell, C., Combs, D., Schurtz, D. R., & Eisenberger, N. I. (2012). Do neural responses to rejection depend on attachment style? An fMRI study. *Social Cognitive and Affective Neuroscience, 7*(2), 184-192.

Duman, R. (2004). Role of neurotrophic factors in the etiology and treatment of mood disorders. *Neuromolecular Medicine, 5*(1), 11-25.

Fan, A. P., Buka, S. L., Kosik, R. O., Chen, Y., Wang, S., Su, T., & Eaton, W. W. (2014). Association between maternal behavior in infancy and adult mental health: A 30-year prospective study. *Comprehensive Psychiatry, 55*, 283-289.

Feldman, R. (2010). The relational basis of adolescent adjustment: Trajectories of mother-child interactive behaviors from infancy to adolescence shape adolescents' adaptation. *Attachment and Human Development, 12*(1-2), 173-192.

Felitti, V. J., Anda, R. F., Nordenberg, D., Williamson, D. F., Spitz, A. M., Edwards, V., Koss, M. P., & Marks, J. S. (1998). Relationship of childhood abuse and household dysfunction to many of the leading causes of death in adults. The Adverse Childhood Experiences (ACE) study. *American Journal of Preventive Medicine, 14*(4), 245-258.

Fish, E. W., Shahrokh, D., Bagot, R., Caldji, C., Bredy, T., Szyf, M., & Meaney, M. J. (2004). Epigenetic programming of stress responses through variations in maternal care. *Annals of the New York Academy of Science, 1036*, 167-180.

Fonagy, P., Steele, H., & Steele, M. (1991). Maternal representations of attachment during pregnancy predict the organization of infant-mother attachment at one year of age. *Child Development, 62*, 891-905.

Fowler, J. C., Groat, M., & Ulanday, M. (2013). Attachment style and treatment completion among psychiatric inpatients with substance use disorders. *American Journal on Addictions, 22*, 14-17.

Freud, S. (1923). *The ego and the id.* New York; London: Norton.

Giesbricht, G. F., Letourneau, H., Campbell, T. S., & the Alberta Pregnancy Outcomes and Nutrition Study Team. (2017). Sexually dimorphic and interactive effects of prenatal maternal cortisol and psychological distress on infant cortisol reactivity. *Development and Psychopathology, 29*(3), 805-818.

Gold, P. W. (2015). The organization of the stress system and its dysregulation in depressive illness. *Molecular Psychiatry, 20*, 32-47.

Gordon, I., Zagoory-Sharon, O., Leckman, J. F., & Feldman, R. (2010). Oxytocin and the development of parenting in humans. *Biological Psychiatry, 68*, 377-382.

Hayes, L. J., Goodman, S. H., & Carlson, E. (2013). Maternal antenatal depression and infant disorganized attachment at 12 months. *Attachment and Human Development, 15*(2), 133-153.

Heim, C., & Nemeroff, C. B. (2001). The role of childhood trauma in the neurobiology of mood and anxiety disorders: Preclinical and clinical studies. *Biological Psychiatry, 49*(12), 1023-1039.

Heim, C., Young, L. J., Newport, D. J., Mletzko, T., Miller, A. H., & Nemeroff, C. B. (2009). Lower CSF oxytocin concentrations in women with a history of childhood abuse. *Molecular Biology, 14*, 954-958.

Heinrichs, M., Baumgartner, T., Kirschbaum, C., & Ehlert, U. (2003). Social support and oxytocin interact to suppress cortisol and subjective responses to psychosocial stress. *Biological Psychiatry, 54*(12), 1389-1398.

Hoffman, K. T., Marvin, R. S., Cooper, G., & Powell, B. (2006). Changing toddlers' and preschoolers' attachment classifications: The Circle of Security intervention. *Journal of Consulting and Clinical Psychology, 74*(6), 1017-1026.

Huot, R. L., Plotsky, P. M., Lenox, R. H., & McNamara, R. K. (2002). Neonatal maternal separation reduces hippocampal mossy fiber density in adult Long Evans rats. *Brain Research, 950,* 52-63.

Kidd, T., Hamer, M., & Steptoe, A. (2011). Examining the association between adult attachment style and cortisol responses to acute stress. *Psychoneuroendocrinology, 36*, 771-779.

Kolb, B., Mychasiuk, R., Muhammad, A., Li, Y., Frost, D. O., & Gibb, R. (2012). Experience and the developing prefrontal cortex. *Proceedings of the National Academy of Sciences, 109*(Suppl 2), 17186-17193.

Koulomzin, M., Beebe, B., Anderson, S., Jaffe, J., Feldstein, S., & Crown, C. (2002). Infant gaze, head, face, and self-touch at 4 months differentiate secure vs. avoidant attachment at 1 year: A microanalytic approach. *Attachment and Human Development, 4*(1), 3-24.

Kristeva, J. (2001). *Melanie Klein.* New York: Columbia University Press.

Levine A., Zagoory-Sharon, O., Feldman, R., & Weller, A. (2007). Oxytocin during pregnancy and early postpartum: Individual patterns and maternal-fetal attachment. *Peptides, 28*, 1162-1169.

Lungwitz, E. A., Stuber, G. D., Johnson, P. L., Dietrich, A. D., Schartz, N., Hanrahan, B., Shekhar, A., & Truitt, W. A. (2014). The role of the medial prefrontal cortex in regulating social familiarity-induced anxiolysis. *Neuropsychopharmacology, 39*, 1009-1019.

Main, M., & Solomon, J. (1990). Procedures for identifying infants as disorganzied/disoriented during the Ainsworth Strange Situation. In M. T. Greenberg, D. Cicchetti, & E. M. Cummings (Eds.), *Attachment in the preschool years: Theory, research and intervention* (pp. 121-160). Chicago: University of Chicago Press.

McGowan, P. O., Sasaki, A., D'Alessio, A. C., Dymov, S., Labonte, B., Szyf, M., Turecki, G., & Meaney, M. J. (2009). Epigenetic regulation of the glucocorticoid receptor in human brain associates with childhood abuse. *Nature Neuroscience, 1*(3), 342-348.

McWilliams, L. A., & Bailey S. J. (2010). Associations between adult attachment ratings and health conditions: Evidence from the National Comorbidity Survey Replication. *Health Psychology, 29*(4), 446-453.

Meredith, P., Ownsworth, T., & Strong, J. (2008). A review of the evidence linking adult attachment theory and chronic pain: Presenting a conceptual model. *Clinical Psychology Review, 28*, 407-429.

Moffett, M. C., Vicentic, A., Kozel, M., Plotsky, P., Francis, D. D., & Kuhar, M. J. (2007). Maternal separation alters drug intake patterns in adulthood in rats. *Biochemical Pharmacology, 73*, 321-330.

Monk, C., Spicer, J., & Champagne, F. A. (2012). Linking prenatal maternal adversity to developmental outcomes in infants: The role of epigenetic pathways. *Developmental Psychopathology, 24*(2), 1361-1376.

Morgan, J. K., Shaw, D. S., & Forbes, E. E. (2014). Maternal depression and warmth during childhood predict age 20 neural response to reward. *Journal of the American Academy of Child ans Adolescent Psychiatry, 53*(1), 108-117.

Murgatroyd, C. A., Pena, C. J., Podda, G., Nestler, E. J., & Nephew, B. C. (2016). Early life social stress induced changes in depression and anxiety associated neural pathways which are correlated with impaired maternal care. *Neuropeptides, 52*, 103-111.

Naber, F., van IJzendoorn, M. H., Deschamps, P., van Engeland H., & Bakermans-Kranenburg, M. J. (2010). Intranasal oxytocin increases fathers' observed responsiveness during play with their children: A double-blind within-subject experiment. *Psychoneuroendocrinology, 35*, 1583-1586.

Olavsky, A. K., Telzer, E. H., Shapiro, M., Humphreys, K. L., Flannery, J., Goff, B., & Tottenham, N. (2013). Indiscriminate amygdala response to mothers and strangers after early maternal deprivation. *Biological Psychiatry, 74*, 853-860.

Pierrehumbert, B., Torrisi, R., Ansermet, F., Borghini, A., & Halfon, O. (2012). Adult attachment representations predict cortisol and oxytocin responses to stress. *Attachment and Human Development, 14*(5), 453-476.

Plant, D. T., Pawlby, S., Sharp, D., Zunszain, P. A., & Pariante, C. M. (2016). Prenatal maternal depression is associated with offspring inflammation at 25 years: A prospective longitudinal cohort study. *Translational Psychiatry, 6*(11), e936, 1-8.

Puig, J., Englund, M. M., Simpson, J. A., & Collins, W. A. (2013). Predicting adult physical illness from infant attachment: A prospective longitudinal study. *Health Psychology, 32*(4), 400-417.

Qiu, A., Anh, T. T., Li, Y., Chen, H., Rifkin-Grabol, A., Broekman, B. F. P., Kwek, K., Saw, S.-M., Chong, Y.-S., Gluckman, P. D., Fortier, M. V., & Meaney, M. J. (2015). Prenatal maternal depression alters amygdala functional connectivity in 6-month old infants. *Translational Psychiatry, 5*, e508, 1-7.

Quirin, M., Pruessner, J., & Kuhl, J. (2008). HPA system regulation and adult attachment anxiety: Individual differences in reactive and awakening cortisol. *Psychoneuroendocrinology, 33*, 581-590.

Radley, J. J., & Sawchenko, P. E. (2011). A common substrate for prefrontal and hippocampal inhibition of the neuroendocrine stress response. *Journal of Neuroscience, 31*(26), 9683-9695.

Rincon-Cortes, M., Barr, G. A., Mouly, A. M., Shionoya, K., Nunez, B. S., & Sullivan, R. M. (2015). Enduring good memories of infant trauma: Rescue of adult neurobehavioral deficits via amygdala serotonin and corticosterone interaction. *Proceedings of the National Academy of Sciences, 112*(3), 881-886.

Roth, T. L., Lubin, F. D., Funk, A. J., & Sweatt, J. D. (2009). Lasting epigenetic influence of early-life adversity on the BDNF gene. *Biological Psychiatry, 65*, 760-769.

Ruppenthal, G. C., Arling, G. L., Harlow, H. F., Sackett, G. P., & Suomi, S. J. (1976). A 10-year perspective of motherless monkey behavior. *Journal of Abnormal Psychology, 85*(4), 341-349.

Sapolsky, R. Krey, L. C., & McEwen, B. S. (1986). The neuroendocrinology of stress and aging: The glucocorticoid cascade hypothesis. *Endocrine Reviews, 7*(3), 284-301.

Satterthwaite, T. D., Kable, J. W., Vandekar, L, Katchmar, N., Bassett, D. S., Baldassano, C. F., . . .Wolf, D. H. (2015). Common and dissciable dysfunction of the reward system in bipolar and unipolar depression. *Neuropsychopharmacology, 40*, 2258-2268.

Strathearn, L. (2011). Maternal neglect: Oxytocin, dopamine and the neurobiology of attachment. *Journal of Neuroendocrinology, 23*(11), 1054-1065.

Strathearn, L., Fonagy, P., Amico, J., & Montague, P. R. (2009). Adult attachment predicts maternal brain and oxytocin response to infant cues. *Neuropsychopharmacology, 34*, 2655-2666.

Suomi, S. J., Harlow, H. F., & McKinney, W. T. (1972). Monkey psychiatrists. *American Journal of Psychiatry, 128*(8), 927-932.

Swain, J. (2008). Baby stimuli and the parent brain: Functional neuroimaging of the neural substrates of parent-infant attachment. *Psychiatry, 5*(8), 28-36.

Teicher, M. H., Samson, J. A., Anderson, C. M., & Ohashi, K. (2016). The effects of childhood maltreatment on brain structure, function, and connectivity. *Nature Reviews, Neuroscience, 17*, 652-666.

Tops, M., Koole, S., IJzerman, H. I., & Buisman-Pijlman, F. T. A. (2014). Why social attachment and oxytocin protect against addiction and stress: Insights from the dynamics between ventral and dorsal corticostriatal systems. *Pharmacology, Biochemistry and Behavior, 119*, 39-48.

Vaglio, S. (2009). Chemical communication and mother-infant recognition. *Communicative and Integrative Biology, 2*(3), 279-281.

Vela, R. (2014). The effect of severe stress on early brain development, attachment, and emotions: A psychoanatomical formulation. *Psychiatric Clinics of North America, 37*, 519-534.

Weaver, I. C. G., Cervoni, N., Champagne, F. A., D'Alessio, A. C., Sharma, S., Seckl, J. R., Dymov, S., Szyf, M., . . . Meaney, M. J. (2004). Epigenitic programming by maternal behavior. *Nature Neuroscience, 7*(8), 847-854.

Weaver, I. C. G., Meaney, M. J., & Szyf, M. (2006). Maternal care effects on the hippocampal transcriptome and anxiety-mediated behaviors in the offspring that are reversible in adulthood. *Proccedings of the National Academy of Sciences of the United States of America, 103*(9), 3480-3485.

Weisman, O., Zagoory-Sharon, O., & Feldman, R. (2012). Oxytocin administration to parent enhances infant physiological and behavioral readiness for social engagement. *Biological Psychiatry, 72*, 982-989.

Wiest, G., & Brainin, E. (2010). Neuropsychoanalytic findings in a patient with bilateral lesions of the amygdala. *Neuropsychoanalysis, 12*(2), 193-200.

The Role of Oxytocin and Vasopressin in Attachment

C. Sue Carter

Abstract: Selective relationships and attachments are central to human health and well-being, both in current societies and during the course of evolution. The presence or absence of social bonds has consequences across the lifespan. The neurobiology of attachment is grounded in neuroendocrine substrates that are shared with reproduction and survival. Experimental studies of species, such as sheep or prairie voles, capable of showing selective social behaviors toward offspring or partners, have provided empirical evidence for the role of oxytocin and vasopressin in the formation of selective attachments. Developmental exposure to social experiences and to peptides, including oxytocin and vasopressin, also can "retune" the nervous system, altering thresholds for sociality, emotion regulation, and aggression. Without oxytocin and without the ability to form attachments the human brain as we know it could not exist. Knowledge of the neurobiology of attachment, and especially the role of oxytocin, also has implications for understanding both healthy behavior and treating mental disorders.

WHAT IS ATTACHMENT?

Humans are highly social mammals, immersed in networks of connections with others including the collaborative creation of families, cultures, and civilizations. Social behaviors range from the tendency to be generally gregarious to selective forms of sociality. Embedded in these complex interactions are selective social behaviors and lasting relationships, here termed social bonds or attachments.

Social bonds and attachments are hypothetical constructs. No one has ever directly measured a social bond. Attachments are not easily described or defined. The scientific use of "attachment" and "bonding" has varied across disciplines, creating additional confusion (Carter et al., 2006). Biologists working with animal models have tended to use the terms attachment and bonding interchangeably. However, in psychology strict definitions of attachment arose focused on the relationship of infants and their mothers (Bowlby, 1969).

Definitions of attachment and bonding are inferred indirectly from behavioral and physiological changes (Table 1). In general, social bonds in both human and animal research are defined by selective patterns of response to others (Carter & Keverne, 2017). Social bonds and attachments are often characterized by physical contact or cognitive attraction toward a preferred partner, and in some cases by distress or vocaliza-

The article is strongly influenced by the ideas of Stephen Porges, to whom I am grateful. Our studies on pair bonding in prairie voles were sponsored by grants from the United States National Institutes of Health (NIMH and NICHD P01 075750) and National Science Foundation. The author declares no conflicts of interest.

Table 1. Common Methods for Assessing Attachment

Partner preferences: Selective proximity, physical contact, eye contact

Aggression in defense of the partner

Autonomic, immune, or endocrine responses specific to the presence or absence of the partner

Behavioral distress (crying, agitation, anxiety) in the absence of the partner, usually resolving in the presence of the partner

Brain-region specific changes in function indexed by

    Intermediate early genes (c-fos expression)

    Functional imaging (fMRI - BOLD changes or DTI)

    Gene expression, specific to putative peptides or related neurotransmitters

    Receptor-specific changes in gene expression

tion in the absence of the partner. Changes in physiological measures, including autonomic, endocrine, or immune changes, also may be used to indirectly index selective social relationships.

THE CONSEQUENCES OF ATTACHMENT

Attachments are most often described in terms of their consequences, which may extend to all aspects of behavior and across the lifespan. Like other mammals, humans rely on positive social interactions for both safety and reproduction. The presence or absence of social relationships has profound effects on a sense of safety, as well as individual survival, reproduction, and eventually genetic survival.

Positive attachments have documented health benefits, and the absence of social bonds can be associated with both physical and mental illness (Cacioppo, Hughes, Waite, Hawkley, & Thisted, 2006). Understanding the mechanisms for the formation of attachment and the benefits of attachments, and other forms of social support, provides important insights into processes that are protective for mental and physical health.

It has been argued that social behavior is a driving force in the evolution of human nature. The biological systems that are necessary for attachments predate human cog-

nition. Attachments, often with multiple caretakers, facilitate the extended periods of nurture necessary for the emergence and optimization of human intellectual development and social development (Hrdy, 2009). The tendency to form selective pair bonds, or other kinds of social attachments, is a universal human characteristic (Fisher, 2016).

THE HORMONAL BASIS OF ATTACHMENT

At least some of the benefits of attachments may be attributed to physiological processes supported by specific chemical pathways including those that involve two neuropeptides, oxytocin and vasopressin. Oxytocin and vasopressin are genetically and structurally related with only two amino acids distinguishing the two molecules. Both evolved from a common ancestral molecule, presumed to be vasotocin (Goodson & Kingsbury, 2013).

Neither oxytocin nor vasopressin is a classical neurotransmitter, limited to local action across a synapse. Rather, these molecules appear to be released from the neuronal soma, axons, and dendrites, acting broadly in the nervous system as neuromodulators. The cells that synthesize oxytocin are most concentrated in the hypothalamus, in particular the paraventicular nucleus (PVN) and supraoptic nuclei (SON); in

Table 2. Oxytocin and Vasopressin May Influence Social Bonding via Peptide Variations

Relative abundance in brain (or measured in bodily fluids)

Differential molecular forms (e.g., mature 9 amino acid forms vs. precursors)

Selective release (in presence of a preferred partner)

Selective localization (brain-region or cell-type specific)

Co-localization with other molecules (tissue and cell-type specific; e.g., oxytocin and dopamine, or oxytocin and CRH)

Peptide receptors (region-specific variation or sensitivity)

Abundance in specific brain areas (e.g., nucleus accumbens)

Proxy tissues for noninvasive measurement (e.g., white blood cells)

Behaviorally relevant differences in sensitivity or changes in Peptides or Receptors

Species (genetic variation)

Gender (genetic and epigenetic variation)

Individual differences in genetics or epigenetics (including sensitivity)

    (e.g., single-nucleotide polymorphisms; SNPs)

    (e.g., methylation based silencing of genes regulating function)

    (e.g., intergeneration changes)

Differential experiences and adaptive changes, especially during periods of sensitivity including:

    Prenatal (e.g., stress, disease, maternal diet, drugs, etc.)

    Birth (e.g., naturally occurring variation and/or birth interventions)

    Postnatal (e.g., maternal care, stress, disease, diet, drugs, etc.)

    Adolescence (e.g., forming new relationships, disease, diet, drugs, etc.)

    Aging (e.g., loss of long-term partners, disease, diet, drugs, etc.)

these nuclei separate cells generally express oxytocin and vasopressin.

There is evidence that oxytocin from the PVN can reach the central amygdala via neuronal pathways and possibly also "expressways" allowing this molecule to quickly modulate emotional functions of the amygdala and brain stem (Stoop, Hegoburu, & van den Burg, 2015). Oxytocin can thus be released in a coordinated fashion within the brain and at the posterior pituitary and then into the general circulation (Grinevich, Knobloch-Bollmann, Eliava, Burnelli, & Chini, 2016). It is likely that the ability of oxytocin to have exceptionally broad and synchronized behavioral and physiological consequences is related to this capacity for movement throughout the brain and body, as well as the location of receptors throughout the body (Gobrogge, Jia, Liu, Wang, 2017).

Oxytocin is thus part of a dynamic system that, in a context of safety, allows the optimal expression of positive social behaviors including the selective "sociality" that characterizes social bonds. There are several mechanisms through which oxytocin may affect behavior (Table 2). Oxytocin has been implicated in social engagement and eye gaze (Quintana, Alvares, Hickie, & Guastella, 2015), which are critical in early stages of social engagement and relationship formation.

In healthy people, oxytocin seems to serve as a biological and emotional indicator of safety. Oxytocin supports emotional and autonomic processes allowing for what Porges described as "immobility without fear" (2011). In one sense this has to do with oxytocin's action on brainstem receptors, which can increase parasympathetic influences via vagal pathways and oxytocin's capacity to dampen the mobilization and defensive circuits supported by the sympathetic nervous system. "Immobility without fear" in this context is an important biobehavioral enabler providing opportunities to express attachment—it represents a "neural choice" to stay in one place. "Staying in one place" may have been an evolutionary precursor to "falling in love"—another form of attachment that is influenced by oxytocin (Carter, 1998).

In a variety of experiments oxytocin has been implicated in both the causes and consequences of attachment (Bernaets et al., 2017). Oxytocin, administered as an intranasal spray, has been shown to enhance the processing of social information and can facilitate a sense of trust or empathy (Feldman, 2017; Quintana, Alvares, Hickie, & Guastella, 2015). Oxytocin may mediate the buffering effects of social support, and modulate anxiety and over-reactivity to stressful experiences (Carter, 1998; Neumann & Slattery, 2016).

In general, oxytocin tends to support a sense of safety and social behaviors. These and other findings suggest that oxytocin has effects on the regulation of emotion, the mammalian autonomic nervous system, homeostasis, coping, and healing; functioning together these help to explain the important consequences of the presence or absence of social engagement and attachment. These adaptive properties of oxytocin further help to explain the capacity of loving relationships and psychological safety to protect and heal in the face of stress and adversity.

VASOPRESSIN AND OXYTOCIN: BOTH COMPONENTS OF AN INTEGRATED SYSTEM REGULATING SOCIAL BEHAVIOR

Oxytocin does not act alone and many of its effects are regulated by interactions with vasopressin. Vasopressin and oxytocin are functionally part of, and thus may be considered, one pathway. Both hormones are responsive to environmental and social demands, although in somewhat different ways (Carter, 1998, 2014; Neumann & Slattery, 2016). Oxytocin acting alone appears to be a component of a more social or passive coping strategy, whereas vasopressin may permit active and mobilized coping strategies (Carter, 1998, 2007).

Both oxytocin and vasopressin are necessary for the expression of selective social behaviors (Cho, DeVries, Williams, & Carter, 1999; Tabbaa, Paedae, Liu, & Wang, 2016), sexual behavior (Albers, 2015; Carter, 1992), and protection of offspring, whether that be maternal or paternal (Bosch & Neumann, 2012; Kenkel, Perkeybile, & Carter, 2017). Acting together oxytocin and vasopressin appear to support autonomic and emotional peak experiences such as falling in love, orgasm, and dealing with an initial exposure to a baby (Carter, 1992; Kenkel et al., 2012, 2013). The early stages in various passionate relationships, as well as the experience of sexual arousal and orgasm, could draw upon the capacity of oxytocin and vasopressin to permit increased sympathetic arousal without parasympathetic retraction (Carter, 1992; Kenkel et al., 2013; Norman et al., 2011).

The functions of oxytocin and vasopressin depend on their capacity to bind to a set of specific receptors. Receptors for both oxytocin and vasopressin are abundant in areas of the nervous system that regulate social, emotional, and adaptive behaviors including the amygdala, the HPA axis, and the autonomic nervous system (Gobrogge, Jia, Liu, & Wang, 2017; Stoop, Hegoburu, & van den Burg, 2015).

At the core of attachment are neurobiological systems that regulate fear and threats and those that regulate a sense of security. While oxytocin may activate the more "passive" aspects of attachment, vasopressin activates the more possessive, and in some cases more aggressive side of attachment. Activation of vasopressin receptors is essential for the more protective

Table 3. Animal Models for Studying the Biological Bases of Pair Bonding

Maternal–infant bonding:

Selective: Mothers show exclusive care for their offspring, e.g., sheep.

Maternal behavior:

Not selective, but may share physiological substrates with pair bonding, e.g., rats and voles.

Adult pair bonding:

Selective: Socially monogamous mammals showing a partner preference, e.g., prairie voles and titi monkey.

behaviors, often associated with pair bonds, especially—but not exclusively—in males (Winslow, Hastings, Carter, Harbaugh, & Insel, 1993). Animal research using receptor-specific blocking agents suggests that activation or blocking of vasopressin receptors helps to explain the complex behavioral consequences of oxytocin and vasopressin (Albers, 2015). For example, in hamsters exogenous oxytocin can increase measures of aggression, but these effects were no longer apparent if the vasopressin receptor was blocked. In contrast, in this same species effects of oxytocin on social reward required access to the oxytocin receptor (Song, Borland, Larkin, O'Malley, & Albers, 2016).

Interactions between vasopressin and oxytocin help to explain the importance of social behavior in the regulation of anxiety and responses to threats, which in some cases are promoted by vasopressin (Neumann & Slattery, 2016). Thus, together oxytocin and vasopressin, and their receptors, create a biological and genetic pathway that regulates attachment and bonding (Carter, 1998, 2014). Both peptides also are capable of modulating the autonomic, immune, and metabolic systems acting to coordinate increases or decreases in the responses in these systems in the face of challenge.

OXYTOCIN AND VASOPRESSIN SYSTEMS ARE AFFECTED BY EARLY LIFE EXPERIENCE

Oxytocin and vasopressin help to regulate social behavior across the lifespan. The plasticity of these systems provides mechanisms through which experience adapts to and prepares the body and behavior for future challenges. This assumption is supported by research evidence from humans (Feldman, 2017; Toepfer et al., 2017) and other animals (Carter, Boone, Pournajafi-Nazarloo, & Bales, 2009; Hammock, 2015) indicating that the effects of oxytocin are moderated by early life experiences. Research in prairie voles (Table 3) revealed that effects of oxytocin and vasopressin on later social bond formation could be detected as early as the first week of life, and are likely influenced by prenatal exposure to these peptides as well (Bales, Boone, Epperson, Hoffman, & Carter, 2011; Carter, Boone, Pournajafi-Nazarloo, & Bales, 2009). These effects occur, in part, because the expressions of receptors for oxytocin and vasopressin can be modulated by both genetic and epigenetic processes.

In humans it is likely that social attachments formed around the time of puberty reflect the interactions of vasopressin and oxytocin. Vasopressin is sexually dimorphic and increased in the brain by androgens, both during early development and in adulthood (De Vries & Forger, 2015). At optimal levels both oxytocin and vasopressin may contribute to the dampening of social anxiety, which would permit the approach to unfamiliar others. Following the establishment of a social bond, optimal levels of the same peptides may be involved in initiating the processes required to defend a partner against intruders or other suitors, including an experience that humans term "jealousy."

THE ABSENCE OF OR DISRUPTIONS OF ATTACHMENTS

Nurture in early life is protective across the life cycle (Welch & Ludgwig, 2017). However, most of the evidence for the effects of early experience comes from maternal separation or other disruptions of the maternal–infant relationship (Bowlby, 1969). In primate infants the absence of adequate maternal care and opportunities to form attachments has been associated with growth retardation, social withdrawal, and atypical social behaviors (Harlow, 1971). In humans, data come primarily from epidemiology and correlational studies. In the face of maternal deprivation or broken social bonds—especially after extreme traumas including sexual abuse, episodes of recurring distress—physical disorders and vulnerability to illness are increasingly obvious (see Fox, Nelson, & Zeanah, 2017; Toepfer et al., 2017).

The consequences of disrupted attachment may emerge as psychopathologies, including personality disorders (MacDonald, Berlow, & Thomas, 2013), vulnerability to drug abuse, and addictions (Buisman-Pijlman et al., 2014; Chambers & Wallingford, 2017; Zou, Song, Zhang, & Zhang, 2016). There is increasing evidence for genetic and epigenetic differences that may contribute to the capacity of individuals to cope with early life adversity (Bradley, Wingo, Davis, Mercer, & Ressler, 2013; Feldman, Monakhov, Pratt, & Ebstein, 2016; Myers et al., 2014; Rijlaarsdam et al., 2017; Smearman et

al., 2016; Toepfer et al., 2017). From this field of study is emerging strong evidence for the importance of oxytocin pathways, including oxytocin and vasopressin and their receptors, in the adaptive consequences and benefits of human attachment.

The behaviors and physiological changes associated with loss of an attachment figure, including bereavement or grief, are similar to those used to define depression. Animal research suggests that forced social separations or the absence of social attachments can trigger stress, anxiety, fear, and shutdown behaviors (Porges, 2011; Sun, Smith, Lei, Liu, & Wang, 2014). Some, but not all, of the effects of social isolation (Grippo, Trahanas, Zimmerman, Porges, & Carter, 2009; Grippo et al., 2012) or trauma (Frijlilng, 2017) can be prevented or reversed with exogenous oxytocin. Understanding the nature of physiological processes that regulate both the formation and dissolution of social attachment is essential in developing biologically informed treatments for disorders such as depression or trauma.

The effects of oxytocin and vasopressin on brain-body connections help to explain the profound health-related effects of relationships or their absence. Oxytocin and vasopressin interact to regulate the autonomic nervous system, especially in the face of stress (Porges, 2011; Yee, Kenkel, & Frijling, 2016). Autonomic actions of oxytocin and vasopressin play a role in the capacity for and expression of social bonds that arise in the face of challenge or adversity. It is likely that the capacity of these peptides to integrate the activity of different branches of the autonomic nervous system helps to explain the importance of attachment in different forms of emotion and emotion regulation. These same peptides also have effects on the immune and metabolic systems across the lifespan, helping to explain the lasting effects of emotional experiences on physical health and well-being (Amini-Khoei et al., 2017; Hammock, 2015; Welch & Ludwig, 2017).

SOCIAL BEHAVIOR HAS A DIFFERENT BIOLOGY IN MALES AND FEMALES

In the mammalian brain vasopressin synthesis is sexually dimorphic (De Vries & Forger, 2015). There is emerging evidence that responses to exogenous vasopressin are different in males and females (Carter et al., 2009; Stribley & Carter, 1999; Thompson, George, Walton, Orr, & Benson, 2006). These responses may be supported by steroids including estrogen, progesterone, and androgens. However, steroid-peptide interactions in behavior are time-dependent, complex, and poorly understood.

Vasopressin, and associated increases in the sympathetic nervous system, would allow more active or mobilized responses to challenge, including the capacity for aggression and physical violence. At the same time, it is possible that a male-biased dependency on vasopressin might explain the tendency of males to form social bonds in the face of extreme challenges such as war. Dependence on vasopressin would leave males more vulnerable to disorders characterized by reductions in social behavior and leading to increases in aggression and risk taking (Carter, 1998, 2007; Taylor, Saphire-Bernstein, & Seeman, 2010). Concurrently, males may be protected, via vasopressin and associated increases in alertness or arousal, against shut-down responses including those that characterize some forms of depression, trauma, and PTSD.

Females also produce and rely on the physiological effects of vasopressin. However, social behaviors in females may be more dependent on estrogen and estrogen-oxytocin interactions. Females are more vulnerable to disorders associated with these same shut-down responses including depression and PTSD. Females in turn may

be especially dependent on oxytocin. In the presence of deficiencies in either oxytocin or its receptor, females may be more vulnerable to disorders characterized by passive responses.

Sex differences in the biology of attachment are in general adaptive, especially in the context of sex differences in the demands of reproduction. Both vulnerabilities and resilience are sexually dimorphic. Sex differences are generally most apparent in the face of stressful experiences, including social and hormonal experiences in early life (Carter et al., 2009). Moreover, sexual dimorphism in systems related to attachment and social behavior also help to explain sex differences in the vulnerability to disorders such as depression or autism (Carter, 2007), which often involve disturbances in social behavior. Knowledge of sex differences in the functions of oxytocin and vasopressin are needed in the development of treatments for a variety of mental and physical disorders including substance abuse, schizophrenia, and trauma (Carter, 2007; MacDonald, Berlow, & Thomas, 2013; Rubin et al., 2014).

EARLY LIFE EXPERIENCES INFLUENCE THE CAPACITY FOR SUBSEQUENT ATTACHMENT

Behavioral flexibility, possibly mediated in part by oxytocin and vasopressin interactions during development, allows individuals to adapt their social systems to accommodate early experiences and environmental demands. Animal research suggests that at least some of the effects of early experience are epigenetic, modifying DNA and creating the potential for transgenerational transmission of the tendency to form social bonds (Perkeybile & Bales, 2015).

Vasopressin expression may increase following neglect or other negative social experiences in early life (Hernandez et al., 2016; Murgatroyd et al., 2009). We hypothesize that early adversity could also upregulate the vasopressin receptor, especially in brain regions necessary to allow mobilized responses in later life and possibly affecting the capacity to form attachments.

Research in voles indicates that vasopressin can be developmentally regulated by oxytocin, contributing to the capacity to form pair bonds (Bales, Lewis-Reese, Pfeifer, Kramer, & Carter, 2007). In male voles a single oxytocin exposure in early life increased the expression of the vasopressin receptor in brain areas associated with pair bonding; while in both sexes exposure to exogenous oxytocin reduced the expression of the vasopressin (V1a) receptor in other brain areas (Bales, Plotsky, Young et al., 2007). In another experiment in prairie voles dose-dependent increases in vasopressin in the first week of life were followed by increases in aggression in adulthood; these effects also were most apparent in males. The effects of early vasopressin on female aggression were weak and in females high doses appeared to inhibit later aggression (Stribley & Carter, 1999). The mechanisms underlying sex differences in the behavioral response to exogenous vasopressin remain to be understood. It is useful to recall that vasopressin is sensitive to stressors and also diet; for example salt releases oxytocin. In addition, nicotine is a potent regulator of vasopressin, so smoking, including prenatal exposure of the fetus, holds the potential to adjust this system with effects that likely differ between males and females.

Evidence from rodents also has revealed that levels of perinatal stress and varying amounts of parent–young stimulation contribute to the development of species-typical patterns of defensive aggression (Perkeybile & Bales, 2015). As one example from prairie voles, either reductions in early stimulation or excessive handling during the first week of life, both probably mediated by reduced parental care, were associated with a reduced capacity later in life to form social bonds (Carter et al., 2009). Differential early experience also was associated in adulthood with changes in central oxytocin and vasopressin and in the expression of vasopressin receptors (Bales, Boone, Epperson, Hoffman, & Carter, 2011; Bales, Lewis-Reese, Pfeifer, Kramer, & Carter, 2007).

In humans and other mammals, adaptive changes in the oxytocin and vasopressin systems, especially in early life, may alter brain receptors and their functions, possibly unregulating the oxytocin peptide or its receptor. These in turn could facilitate the capacity for attachment and also the development of adaptive resiliency across the lifespan. There is increasing evidence, including research in humans, that the response to exogenous oxytocin is moderated by early life experiences, including perceived attachment security or its absence. The release of endogenous oxytocin also has been related to early childhood abuse, with lower levels in individuals who have experienced greater emotional adversity in early life (Heim et al., 2009; Toepfer et al., 2017). Moreover, the release of oxytocin differs according to the adult attachment style of the individual. For example, a lower level of increase in oxytocin in response to a stressor was seen in individuals with a "dismissive" attachment style, compared to more securely attached individuals (Pierrehumbert, Torrisi, Ansermet, Borghini, & Halfon, 2012).

Early social history seems to be of particular importance to the capacity of oxytocin or the oxytocin receptor to buffer against various disorders. As one clinical example, neglect or abuse, especially in early life is associated with risk for the symptoms of borderline personality disorders (BPD), defined by hypervigilance toward perceived threats and atypical expressions of attachment. In some cases of BPD, oxytocin treatments administered in adulthood may be helpful (Brune, 2016). However, in other cases, treatment of individuals with BPD with oxytocin was associated with increased symptomology, including distrust (Bartz et al., 2011). Animal models and human studies of responses to intranasal oxytocin suggest that the actions of exogenous oxytocin are dose-dependent and affected by early experiences. We specifically hypothesize that oxytocin may act through effects on vasopressin receptors. These effects are likely to differ according to the gender and social history of the individual. Thus, apparently "paradoxical" actions of oxytocin might be explained in part by the capacity of oxytocin to either stimulate or depress activity in the vasopressin system. In the face of a severe challenge, oxytocin could initially support an increase and activation of the sympathetic nervous system and other components of the HPA system. A large pulse of oxytocin also might acutely activate vasopressin receptors, further supporting mobilization and potentially defensive or aggressive responses.

In summary, the interactive effects of vasopressin and oxytocin during development are only gradually being recognized. The effects of oxytocin and vasopressin are different in males and females, especially in the face of stressful experiences or trauma in early life. Our research with prairie voles has revealed lasting effects of a single perinatal exposure to oxytocin (Carter et al., 2009) or a single handling experience on the first day of life. Positive parenting (versus neglect) has lasting behavioral consequences, possibly also through tuning of the oxytocin/vasopressin pathways (Perkeybile & Bales, 2015; Welch & Ludwig, 2017).

SOURCES OF INDIVIDUAL DIFFERENCES

Individual differences in the genetics/epigenetics of the oxytocin pathways are associated with differences in social behavior and in the response to stressors. Changes in exogenous peptides, especially in early life, are components of an adjustable system that helps the mammalian body predict and manage social behaviors and other challenges.

The ability to form or express social bonds also can be disrupted by events that alter the oxytocin and vasopressin systems. Data from animal models and human epidemiology suggest that routine medical interventions (for example, oxytocin [Pitocin] use to induce labor, opioid medications that block the oxytocin system, or caesarean sections that alter exposure to endogenous oxytocin) have lasting consequences for the offspring and/or mother (Hayes, Balaban, Smith, Perry-Jenkins, & Powers, 2010; Kroll-Desrosiers et al., 2017; Song et al., 2017). Our ongoing animal research suggests that such exposures could have epigenetic efects on the oxytocin systems, including changes in DNA methylation. Such changes in turn might produce reductions in the expression of receptors for oxytocin, leaving individuals less able to respond to oxytocin, and possibly more vulnerable to the defensive effects of vasopressin.

Based on this emerging literature, we specifically hypothesize that individual differences in responses to oxytocin could reflect individual differences in the sensitivity of the oxytocin and vasopressin receptors. A reduction or upregulation in the availability of the oxytocin or vasopressin receptors may be due to genetic variation and/or epigenetic tuning of this system (Bradley, Wingo, Davis, Mercer, & Ressler, 2013; Feldman, Monakhov, Pratt, & Ebstein, 2016; Myers et al., 2014; Rijlaarsdam et al., 2017; Rubin et al., 2014; Smearman et al., 2016; Toepfer et al., 2017). Particularly intriguing is the possibility that the capacity to release peptides or to respond to these could be affected by the attachment experience and trauma history of the individual.

Building on basic research, peptide-based interventions are being developed for the treatment of an array of human disorders (Feldman, 2017; Frijling, 2017; MacDonald, Berlow, & Thomas, 2013). Data from acute or short-term studies of therapeutic effects of oxytocin are encouraging. However, under some conditions, including chronic use or exceptionally high doses, exogenous oxytocin may downregulate its own receptor. Furthermore, in individuals sensitized by a trauma history, even acute oxytocin may activate defensive responses. Because of the broad and epigenetic actions throughout the body of the hormones that regulate attachment, experiences or manipulations that involve attachment and the hormones associated with these deserve careful study.

SUMMARY

Research in humans and other mammals indicate that oxytocin, vasopressin, and their receptors, are involved in the development of the capacity to form new attachments (Carter & Keverne, 2017). These systems provide neural substrates for positive social responses toward partners and in some cases selective aggression toward strangers. In general oxytocin and activation of the oxytocin receptor permit positive social behaviors and act as signals for psychological safety. In response to a challenge, increases in the activity of the oxytocin system allow passive coping, immobilization without fear, and positive social behaviors. However, interactions between oxytocin and vasopressin and their receptors are complex and not well understood.

The vasopressin system is more often associated with anxiety and mobilization in response to stressor or traumatic events, especially in males. Together these peptides serve to permit optimal parental and sexual responses. Individual differences in the expression of the oxytocin receptor, as well as differential sensitivity of the vasopressin receptor(s) may help to explain individual differences in the vulnerability to disorders, such as postpartum depression (Bell et al., 2015), characterized by anxiety and atypical social behaviors. These relationships, with consequences for both parents and children, need further empirical study.

The mechanisms remain poorly identified through which healthy social attach-ments increase resilience and the absence of social bonds increase vulnerability. The literature supports the notion that this system is sexual dimorphic, especially in its response to stress and adversity. Both oxytocin and vasopressin and their receptors, are regulated by steroid hormones and early experiences. Birth interventions, lactation, and patterns of parenting are capable of altering these systems, with effects that have been largely ignored and which should be studied (Harris & Carter, 2013).

We propose here that oxytocin/vasopressin pathways including peptides and receptors are essential to normal attachment. These also play an important role in all aspects of behavior that are directly or indirectly dependent on relationships and attachment. Behavioral experiences associated with attachment are likely to play a direct role in the capacity of individuals to respond to oxytocin and vasopressin. Based on their evolution and the broad consequences of oxytocin and vasopressin for behavior and physiology it is not surprising that early life experiences, as well as social bonds and attachments profoundly influence mental and physical health across the lifespan.

REFERENCES

Albers, H. E. (2015). Species, sex and individual differences in the vasotocin/vasopressin system: Relationship to neurochemical signaling in the social behavior neural network. *Frontiers in Neuroendocrinology, 36,* 49-71.

Amini-Khoei, H., Mohammadj-Asl, A., Amiri, S., Hosseini, M. J., Momeny, M., Hassanipour, M. et al. (2017). Oxytocin mitigated the depressive-like behaviors of maternal separation stress through modulating mitochondrial function and neuroinflammation. *Progress in Neuro-psychopharmacology and Biobehavioral Psychiatry, 76,* 169-178.

Bales, K. L., Boone, E., Epperson, P., Hoffman, G., & Carter, C. S. (2011). Are behavioral effects of early experience mediated by oxytocin? *Frontiers in Child and Neurodevelopmental Psychiatry, 2,* 24.

Bales, K. L., Lewis-Reese, A. D., Pfeifer, L. A., Kramer, K. M., & Carter, C. S. (2007). Early experience affects the traits of monogamy in a sexually dimorphic manner. *Developmental Psychobiology, 49*, 335-342.

Bales, K. L., Plotsky, P. M., Young, L. J., Lim, M. M., Grotte, N., Ferrer, E., & Carter, C. S. (2007). Neonatal oxytocin manipulations have long-lasting, sexually dimorphic effects on vasopressin receptors. *Neuroscience, 144*, 38-45.

Bartz, J., Simeon, D., Hamilton, H., Kim, S., Crystal, S., Braun, A., Vicens, V., & Hollander, E. (2011). Oxytocin can hinder trust and cooperation in borderline personality disorder. *Social Cognition and Affective Neuroscience, 6*, 556-563.

Bell, A. F., Carter, C. S., Steer, C. D., Golding, J., Davis, J. M., Steffen, A.D., Rubin, L. H., Lillard, T. S., Gregory, S. P., Harris, J. C., & Connelly, J. J. (2015). Interaction between oxytocin receptor DNA methylation and genotype is associated with risk of postpartum depression in women without depression in pregnancy. *Frontiers in Genetics, 6*, 243. https://doi.org/10.3389/fgene.2015.00234

Bernaerts, S., Prinsen, J., Berra, E., Bosmans, G., Steyaert, J., & Alaerts, K. (2017). Long-term oxytocin administration enhances the experience of attachment. *Psychoneuroendocrinology, 78*, 1-9.

Bosch, O. J., & Neumann, I. D. (2012). Both oxytocin and vasopressin are mediators of maternal care and aggression in rodents: From central release to sites of action. *Hormones and Behavior, 61*, 293-303.

Bowlby, J. (1969). *Attachment and loss. Vol. 1, attachment.* London: Hogarth Press.

Bradley, B., Wingo, A. P., Davis, T. A., Mercer, K. B., & Ressler, K. J. (2013). Family environment and adult resilience: Contributions of positive parenting and the oxytocin receptor gene. *European Journal of Psychotraumatology, 4*. https://doi.org/10.3402/ejpt.v4i0.21659

Brune, M. (2016). On the role of oxytocin in borderline personality disorder. *British Journal of Clinical Psychology, 55*, 287-304.

Buisman-Pijlman, F., Sumracki, N. M., Gordon, J. J. Hyull, P. R., Carter, C. S., & Tops, M. (2014). Individual differences underlying susceptibility to addiction: Role for the endogenous oxytocin system. *Pharmacology, Biochemistry and Behavior, 119*, 22-28.

Cacioppo, J. T., Hughes, M. E., Waite, L. J., Hawkley, L. C., & Thisted, R. A. (2006). Loneliness as a specific risk factor for depressive symptoms: Cross-sectional and longitudinal analysis. *Psychology of Aging, 21*, 140-151.

Carter, C. S. (1992). Oxytocin and sexual behavior. *Neuroscience and Biobehavioral Reviews, 16*, 131-144.

Carter, C. S. (1998). Neuroendocrine perspectives on social attachment and love. *Psychoneuroendocrinology, 23*, 779-818.

Carter, C. S. (2007). Sex differences in oxytocin and vasopressin: Implications for autism spectrum disorders? *Behavioral Brain Research, 176*, 170-186.

Carter, C. S. (2014). Oxytocin pathways and the evolution of human behavior. *Annual Review of Psychology, 65*, 17-39.

Carter, C. S., Ahnert, L., Grossmann, K., Hrdy, S. B., Lamb, M. E., Porges, S. W., & Sachser, N. (Eds.). (2006). *Attachment and bonding: A new synthesis.* Cambridge, MA: MIT Press.

Carter, C. S., Boone, E. M., Pournajafi-Nazarloo, H., & Bales, K. L. (2009). The consequences of early experiences and exposure to oxytocin and vasopressin are sexually-dimorphic. *Developmental Neuroscience, 31*, 332-341.

Carter, C. S., & Keverne, E. B. (2017). The neurobiology of social affiliation and pair bonding. In D. W. Pfaff & M. Joels (Eds.), *Hormones, brain and behavior* (3rd ed., pp. 117-143). Oxford: Academic Press.

Chambers, R. A., & Wallingford, S. C. (2017). On mourning and recovery: Integrating stages of grief and change toward a neuroscience-based model of attachment adaptation in addiction treatment. *Psychodynamic Psychiatry, 45*(4), 451-473.

Cho, M. M., DeVries, A. C., Williams, J. R., & Carter, C. S. (1999). The effects of oxytocin and vasopressin on partner preferences in male and female prairie voles (*Microtus ochrogaster*). *Behavioral Neuroscience, 5*, 1071-1080.

De Vries, G. J., & Forger, N. G. (2015). Sex differences in the brain: A whole body perspective. *Biology of Sex Differences, 6*, 15. https://doi.org/10.1186/s13293-015-0032-z

Feldman, R. (2017). The neurobiology of human attachments. *Trends in Cognitive Science, 21*, 80-99.

Feldman, R., Monakhov, M., Pratt, M., & Ebstein, R. P. (2016). Oxytocin pathway genes: Evolutionary ancient system impacting on human alliliation, sociality, and psychopathology. *Biological Psychiatry, 79*, 174-184.

Fisher, H. (2016). *Anatomy of Love.* New York: Norton.

Fox, N. A., Nelson, C. A., & Zeanah, C. H. (2017). The effects of psychosocial deprivation on attachment: Lessons from the Bucharest Early

Intervention Project. *Psychodynamic Psychiatry, 45*(4), 441-450.

Frijling, J. L. (2017). Preventing PTSD with oxytocin: Effects of oxytocin administration on fear neurocircuitry and PTSD symptom development in recently trauma-exposed individuals. *European Journal of Psychotraumatology, 8*, 1302652. https://doi.org/10.1080.20008198.2017.1302652

Gobrogge, K., Jia, X., Liu, Y., & Wang, Z. (2017). Neurochemical mediation of affiliation and aggression associated with pair bonding. *Biological Psychiatry, 81*, 231-242.

Goodson, J. L., & Kingsbury, M. A. (2013). What's in a name? Considerations of homologies and nomenclature for vertebrate social behavior networks. *Hormones and Behavior, 64*, 103-112.

Grippo, A. J., Pournajafi-Nazarloo, H., Sanzenbacher, L., Trahanas, D. M., McNeal, N., Clarke, D. A., Porges, S. W., & Carter, C. S. (2012). Peripheral oxytocin administration buffers autonomic but not behavioral responses to environmental stressors in isolated prairie voles. *Stress, 15*, 149-61.

Grippo, A. J., Trahanas, D. M., Zimmerman, R. R., II, Porges, S. W., & Carter, C. S. (2009). Oxytocin protects against negative behavioral and autonomic consequences of long-term social isolation. *Psychoneuroendocrinology, 34*, 1542-1553.

Grinevich, V., Knobloch-Bollmann, H. S., Eliava, M., Burnelli, M., & Chini, B. (2016). Assembling the puzzle: Pathways of oxytocin signaling in the brain. *Biological Psychiatry, 79*, 155-164.

Hammock, E. A. (2015). Developmental perspectives on oxytocin and vasopressin. *Neuropsychopharmacology, 40*, 24-42.

Harlow, H. F. (1971). *Learning to love*. San Francisco, CA: Albion Publishing.

Harris, J. C., & Carter, C. S. (2013). Therapeutic interventions with oxytocin: Current status and concerns. *Journal of the Academy of Child and Adolescent Psychiatry, 52*, 998-1000.

Hayes, U. L., Balaban, S., Smith, J. Z., Perry-Jenkins, M., & Powers, S. L. (2010). Role of pelvic sensory signaling during delivery in postpartum mental health. *Journal of Reproductive and Infant Psychology, 28*, 307-323.

Heim, C., Young, L. J., Newport, D. J., Mletzko, T., Miller, A. H., & Nemeroff, C. B. (2009). Lower CSF oxytocin concentrations in women with a history of childhood abuse. *Molecular Psychiatry, 14*, 954-958.

Hernandez, V. S., Hernandez, O. R., Perez de la Mora, M., Gomora, M. J., Fuxe, K., Eiden, L. E. & Zhang, L. (2016). Hypothalamic vasopressinergic projections innervate central amygdala

GABAergic neurons: Implications for anxiety and stress coping. *Frontiers in Neural Circuits, 10*, 92.

Hrdy, S. B. (2009). *Mothers and others: The evolutionary origins of mutual understanding*. Cambridge, MA: Belknap Press.

Kenkel, W., Paredes, J., Yee, J. R., Pournajafi-Nazarloo, H., Bales, K. L., & Carter, C. S. (2012). Exposure to an infant releases oxytocin and facilitates pair-bonding in male prairie voles. *Journal of Neuroendocrinology, 24*, 874-886.

Kenkel, W. M., Paredes, J., Lewis, G. F., Yee, J. R., Pournajafi-Nazarloo, H., Grippo, A. J., Porges, S. W., & Carter, C. S. (2013). Autonomic substrates of the response to pups in male prairie voles. *PlosOne, 8*(8), e69965. https://doi.org/10.1371/journal.pone.0069965

Kenkel, W. M., Perkeybile, A. M., & Carter, C. S. (2017). The neurobiological causes and effects of alloparenting. *Developmental Neurobiology, 77*, 214-232.

Klaus, M. H., Kennel, J. H., & Klaus, P. H. (1995). *Bonding*. Reading, MA: Addison Wesley.

Kroll-Desrosiers, A. R., Nephew, B. C., Babb, J. A., Guilarte-Walker, Y., Moore Simas, T. A., & Deligiannidis, K. M. (2017). Association of peripartum synthetic oxytocin administration and depressive and anxiety disorders with the first postpartum year. *Depression and Anxiety, 34*, 137-146.

MacDonald, K., Berlow, R., & Thomas, M. L. (2013). Attachment, affective temperament, and personality disorders: A study of their relationships in psychiatric outpatients. *Journal of Affective Disorders, 151*, 932-941.

Murgatroyd, C., Patchev, A. V., Wu, Y., Micale, V., Bockmuhl, Y., Fischer, D., Holsboer, F., Wotjak, C. T., Almeida, O. F., & Spengler, D. (2009). Dynamic DNA methylation programs persistent adverse effects of early-life stress. *Nature Neuroscience, 12*, 1559-1566.

Myers, A. J., Williams, L., Gatt, J. M., McAuley-Clark, E. Z., Dobson-Stone, C., Schofield, P. R., & Nemeroff, C. B. (2014). Variation in the oxytocin receptor gene is associated with increased risk for anxiety, stress and depression in individuals with a history of exposure to early life stress. *Journal of Psychiatric Research, 59*, 93-100.

Neumann, I. D., & Slattery, D. A. (2016). Oxytocin in general anxiety and social fear: A translational approach. *Biological Psychiatry, 79*, 213-221.

Norman, G. J., Cacioppo, J. T., Morris, J. S., Malarkey, W. B., Bernston, G. G., & DeVries, A. C. (2011). Oxytocin increases autonomic cardiac control: Moderation by loneliness. *Biological Psychology, 86*, 174-180.

Perkeybile, A. M., & Bales, K. L. (2015). Early rearing experience is related to altered aggression and vasopressin production following chronic social isolation in the prairie vole. *Behavioral Brain Research, 283*, 37-46.

Pierrehumbert, B., Torrisi, R., Ansermet, F., Borghini, A., & Halfon, O. (2012). Adult attachment representations predict cortisol and oxytocin responses to stress. *Attachment and Human Development, 14*, 453-476.

Porges, S. W. (2011). *The polyvagal theory: Neurophysiological foundations of emotions, attachment, communication and self-regulation.* New York: Norton.

Quintana, D. S., Alvares, G. A., Hickie, I. B., & Guastella, A. J. (2015). Do delivery routes of intranasally administered oxytocin account for observed effects on social cognition and behavior? A two-level model. *Neuroscience and Behavioral Reviews, 49*, 182-192.

Rijlaarsdam, J., van IJzendoorn, M. H., Verhulst, F. C., Jaddoe, V. W., Feliz, J. F., Tiemeier, H., & Bakersman-Kranenburg, M. J. (2017). Prenatal stress exposure, oxytocin receptor gene (OXTR) methylation and child autistic traits: The moderating role of OXTR rs53576. *Autism Research, 10*(3), 430-438. https://doi.org/10.1002/aur.1661.

Rubin, L. H., Carter, C. S., Bishop, J. R., Pournajafi-Nazarloo, H., Drogos, L. L., Hill, S.K. et al. (2014). Reduced levels of vasopressin and reduced behavioral modulation of oxytocin in psychotic disorders. *Schizophrenia Bulletin, 40*, 1374-1384.

Smearman, E. L., Almli, L. M., Conneely, K. N., Brody, G. H., Sales, J. M., Bradley, B., Ressler, K.J., & Smith, A. K. (2016). Oxytocin receptor genetic and epigenetic variations: Association with child abuse and adult psychiatric symptoms. *Child Development, 87*, 122-134.

Song, M., Ishii, H., Toda, M., Tomimatsu, T., Katsuyama, H., Nakai, Y., & Simoya, K. (2017). Maternal depression and mother-to-infant bonding: The association of delivery mode, general health and stress markers. *Open Journal of Obstetrics and Gynecology, 7*, 155-166.

Song, Z., Borland, J. M., Larkin, T. E., O'Malley, M., & Albers, H. E. (2016). Activation of oxytocin receptors, but not arginine-vasopressin V1a receptors, in the ventral tegmental area of male Syrian hamsters is essential for the reward-like properties of social interactions. *Psychoneuroendocrinology, 74*, 164-172.

Stoop, R., Hegoburu, C., & van den Burg, E. (2015). New opportunities in vasopressin and oxytocin research: A perspective from the amygdala. *Annual Review of Neuroscience, 38*, 369-388.

Stribley, J. M., & Carter, C. S. (1999). Developmental exposure to vasopressin increases aggression in adult prairie voles. *Proceedings of the National Academy of Sciences USA, 96*, 12601-12604.

Sun, P., Smith, A. S., Lei, K., Liu, Y., & Wang, Z. (2014). Breaking bonds in male prairie voles: Long-term effects on emotional and social behavior, physiology, and neurochemistry. *Behavioral Brain Research, 265*, 22-31.

Tabbaa, M., Paedae, B., Liu, Y., & Wang, Z. (2016). Neuropeptide regulation of social attachment: The prairie vole model. *Comprehensive Physiology, 7*, 81-104.

Taylor, S. E., Saphire-Bernstein, S., & Seeman, T. E. (2010). Are plasma oxytocin in women and plasma vasopressin men biomarkers of distressed pair-bond relationships? *Psychological Science, 21*, 3-7.

Toepfer, P., Heim, C., Entringer, S., Binder, E., Wadhwa, P., & Buss, C. (2017). Oxytocin pathways in the intergenerational transmission of maternal early life stress. *Neuroscience and Biobehavioral Reviews, 73*, 293-308.

Thompson, R. R., George, K., Walton, J. C., Orr, S. P., & Benson, J. (2006). Sex-specific influences of vasopressin on human social communication. *Proceedings of the National Academy of Sciences USA, 103*, 7889-7894.

Welsh, M. G., & Ludwig, R. J. (2017). Calming Cycle Theory and the co-regulation of oxytocin. *Psychodynamic Psychiatry, 45*(4), 519-540.

Williams, J. R., Insel, T. R., Harbaugh, C. R., & Carter, C. S. (1994). Oxytocin administered centrally facilitates formation of a partner preference in female prairie voles. *Journal of Neuroendocrinology, 6*, 247-250.

Winslow, J. T., Hastings, N., Carter, C. S., Harbaugh, C. R., & Insel, T. R. (1993). A role for central vasopressin in pair bonding in monogamous prairie voles. *Nature, 365*, 545-548.

Yee, J. R., Kenkel, W. M., Frijling, J. L., Dodhia, S., Onishi, K. G., Tovar, S., et al. (2016). Oxytocin promotes functional coupling between paraventricular nucleus and both sympathetic and parasympathetic cardioregulatory nuclei. *Hormones and Behavior, 80*, 82-91.

Zou, Z., Song, H., Zhang, Y., & Zhang, X. (2016). Romantic love vs. drug addiction may inspire a new treatment for addiction. *Frontiers in Psychology, 7*, 1436.

INDEX